THE
AMERICAN
COURTS

THE
AMERICAN
COURTS

A PROCEDURAL APPROACH

JEFFREY A. JENKINS

Associate Professor and Director of Graduate Studies

School of Justice Studies

Roger Williams University

Bristol, Rhode Island

JONES AND BARTLETT PUBLISHERS

Sudbury, Massachusetts

BOSTON   TORONTO   LONDON   SINGAPORE

World Headquarters

Jones and Bartlett Publishers
40 Tall Pine Drive
Sudbury, MA 01776
978-443-5000
info@jbpub.com
www.jbpub.com

Jones and Bartlett Publishers
Canada
6339 Ormindale Way
Mississauga, Ontario L5V 1J2
Canada

Jones and Bartlett Publishers
International
Barb House, Barb Mews
London W6 7PA
United Kingdom

Jones and Bartlett's books and products are available through most bookstores and online booksellers. To contact Jones and Bartlett Publishers directly, call 800-832-0034, fax 978-443-8000, or visit our website, www.jbpub.com.

Substantial discounts on bulk quantities of Jones and Bartlett's publications are available to corporations, professional associations, and other qualified organizations. For details and specific discount information, contact the special sales department at Jones and Bartlett via the above contact information or send an email to specialsales@jbpub.com.

This publication is designed to provide accurate and authoritative information in regard to the Subject Matter covered. It is sold with the understanding that the publisher is not engaged in rendering legal, accounting, or other professional service. If legal advice or other expert assistance is required, the service of a competent professional person should be sought.

Additional illustration and photographic credits appear on page 338, which constitutes a continuation of the copyright page.

Production Credits
Publisher, Higher Education: Cathleen Sether
Acquisitions Editor: Sean Connelly
Associate Editor: Megan R. Turner
Associate Production Editor: Sarah Bayle
Associate Marketing Manager: Jessica Cormier
Manufacturing and Inventory Control Supervisor: Amy Bacus
Composition: Cape Cod Compositors, Inc.
Cover and Title Page Design: Scott Moden
Assistant Photo Researcher: Emily Howard
Cover Image: © Ken Cole/Dreamstime.com (front cover); © Matt Tromer/Shutterstock, Inc. (spine)
Printing and Binding: Courier Corporation, Westford
Cover Printing: Courier Corporation, Westford

Library of Congress Cataloging-in-Publication Data
Jenkins, Jeffrey A.
    The American courts : a procedural approach / Jeffrey A. Jenkins. — 1st ed.
        p.   cm.
    Includes bibliographical references and index.
    ISBN-13: 978-0-7637-5528-7
    ISBN-10: 0-7637-5528-1
    1. Courts—United States.   2. Procedure (Law)—United States.   I. Title.
KF8720.J46 2009
347.73'1—dc22
                                                    2009028274

6048

Printed in the United States of America
13 12 11 10 09   10 9 8 7 6 5 4 3 2 1

Contents

Preface

This book represents a plan for studying the work of the American courts. It examines the approach courts take to resolve matters that come before them. This approach, which involves examining the facts and determining how the law was meant to apply to them, is procedural. Legal procedure, or the process of applying the law, is the job of the courts in America. This book therefore examines what courts do and how they do it by considering the types of cases that courts decide and the procedures used in deciding them.

This text takes a comprehensive view of the courts. Although the criminal justice and the civil justice "systems" are often thought of as separate and unique, there is but one institution—the American "system" of courts. It has a single, central goal, which is to do justice. Therefore, this book incorporates discussions of both criminal and civil matters that come before the courts by providing a context in which the various functions of courts are examined. This is done by examining the law. Interpreting, explaining, extending, and applying the law is the work of the courts, both criminal and civil. Because of this, it is impossible to understand the work of the courts without having some understanding of law—what it is, what it does, why it matters, and perhaps most importantly, how the courts use it. A procedural approach is a process-oriented approach, and the process used by courts to give meaning to the law is the central theme of this book.

Topics Covered

This text is divided into five sections, with an introductory discussion for each:

    Section I: Courts in America
    Section II: Courts at Work
    Section III: Civil Law and Procedure in the Courts
    Section IV: Criminal Law and Procedure in the Courts
    Section V: The Changing American Courts

The first section is composed of three chapters that lay a foundation for understanding the context in which courts operate. These chapters discuss the meaning of justice, the purposes of law, and the ways in which courts operate to accomplish justice and give meaning to the law.

The second section includes five chapters that explore the work courts do by examining the various types of courts in the United States, their functions, and their relationship to each other. In particular, the distinction between federal and state courts and the nature of their authority is explored, as well as the types of cases that courts resolve and the jobs of those who work to resolve them.

The third section provides an overview of the civil law. Courts devote a considerable portion of their resources to civil cases, or those involving disputes between private parties. Section III provides a summary of the topics in civil law and the types of legal matters the law allows individuals to pursue or accomplish. Furthermore, this section devotes a chapter to civil procedure, which examines the process through which users of the courts must present their civil legal matters.

Section IV summarizes the criminal law and its application by the courts. Separate chapters discuss the substantive criminal law and criminal procedure, with the goal of helping students understand the prohibited behaviors that society has determined are worthy of punishment, as well as the procedural protections and rules employed by courts to prevent the government from violating the rights of individuals as it enforces the criminal law.

Finally, Section V considers current topics affecting the courts and the adaptive nature of courts as society changes. The final chapter in this section reconsiders the role and needs of courts as they function as an institution of society, with an eye toward the future.

This organization allows the text to be used in a variety of ways. For example, instructors teaching aspects of the criminal justice system may not wish to use or emphasize material in Chapters 9 or 10, which focus on the civil law, and instructors teaching about the civil law and operation of the courts may wish to omit the detailed discussion of criminal law and procedure found in Chapters 11 and 12. Regardless of the specific purpose in using this text, it is intended to offer a comprehensive discussion of the courts that allows flexibility in its study.

Organization of Each Chapter

Each chapter of the text starts with a brief explanation of what the chapter is about and sets out the learning objectives for the chapter. In discussing each of the chapter topics, the book incorporates case decisions, which illustrate principles of law but, more importantly, show how courts resolve disputes and apply the law. The case decisions are excerpts from actual court decisions, edited and shortened for ease of reading and to focus on the issues discussed in the text. In addition, explanatory figures and tables are used throughout to illustrate or summarize topics discussed. Each chapter also contains sidebars, which are brief and more focused discussions of topics of interest related to the chapter content. Finally, each chapter ends with key terms, discussion questions, a list of cases, Internet resources, and references, for use in review and further study.

Studying Cases

As noted previously here, each chapter contains case decisions, which are excerpts from decisions issued by actual courts. These cases are central to understanding the topics of each chapter; however, they have been liberally edited by removing many of the other case citations relied upon by the court in its written decision. This was done to make the decision easier to read for students encountering case decisions for the first time. Furthermore, instances in which a court's opinion quotes a prior decision of the same court have been removed to improve readability, and in many cases, not all of the rationale of a court is presented in order to focus the reading on the legal issues raised in the chapter in which the case decision appears. Finally, many of the case decisions also contain excerpts from some, but not all, of the concurring or dissenting opinions of other judges or justices on a court. These are included because of their particular relevance and because they help shed light on aspects of the textual topics and should be read along with the opinion of the court.

Ancillary Materials

A comprehensive set of instructor's materials, including PowerPoint presentations, lecture outlines, and a TestBank, is available on the Web site: http://criminaljustice.jpub.com/AmericanCourts.

Acknowledgments

I owe a debt of gratitude to many people for their assistance of various sorts in preparing this text. I thank the editorial team at Jones and Bartlett, especially Cathy Sether, Megan Turner, and Sarah Bayle, who have been professional and helpful in seeing the text through its final stages to publication. I am also grateful to many people who have had a hand in reviewing or assisting with preparation of the text. Several hundred of my students at Roger Williams University were instrumental in helping me think in new ways about the law and the court system, as well as reading and commenting on various drafts of the text. Mike McClallen and Ben Jenkins provided invaluable assistance in research, review of case law, and other tasks necessary to the book's completion. I very much appreciate their help. I am also grateful to my colleagues in the School of Justice Studies at Roger Williams University for their interest and support, especially Professor Tucker Wright, who provided feedback on the text and a willingness to discuss the courts and the law with me regularly. In addition, I acknowledge the Roger Williams University Foundation to Promote Scholarship and Teaching for its support. I also have appreciated the research assistance of Dr. Hillary Jenkins and the encouragement of Dr. Cheryl Jenkins, as well as the interest of many family members and friends. I also thank the Burgundy Group for its consultation and resources. I am also thankful for the many insightful and helpful comments of several reviewers of the manuscript; the text is much improved by their appraisals and suggestions:

Jimmy J. Williams
The University of Alabama

Christina L. Spudeas
Florida Atlantic University

Julie Raines
Marist College

Andrew A. Mickle
Georgia State University

Victoria Simpson Beck
University of Wisconsin, Oshkosh

Courts in America

In many ways, the American courts reflect American society. From its founding, American society has had a shared belief that the best society is a just society and that individual citizens are entitled to have their grievances heard and resolved in a fair manner. As the country has grown and developed, so too has the institution to which citizens ultimately turn for the protection and accomplishment of justice in society—the American courts.

This section, consisting of the first three chapters of the book, examines the foundations on which all courts in America are built: justice, law, and government. These concepts are interrelated by their function and importance in society. The three chapters in this section separately address these foundations by exploring the basis for the operation of American courts.

The first chapter introduces the meaning of justice in the United States and the justice "system" that has developed to achieve it. As a concept, the word justice has many meanings that vary depending on the perspective of the person using it. For example, when a crime is committed, the victim's view of bringing a perpetrator to justice will depend on the extent of the victim's loss. A central purpose of American courts is to determine what justice requires in the myriad cases that come before them. These issues are the focus of Chapter 1.

In Chapter 2, the question of what constitutes law is examined. Law is the primary tool, subject matter, and mechanism used by courts to achieve justice. Law is central to American society; without it, there would be no need for courts and no principled way of achieving justice for individuals or the larger society. Thus, Chapter 2 discusses law as a necessary concept for achieving justice and producing a just society. A lawless society is not a society at all, and only when people choose to live and govern themselves "under law" can people's perceptions of justice be realized.

American society has developed comprehensive and often complex laws that are sometimes bewildering to citizens. Chapter 2 begins to examine the structure of this legal system and the ways in which it is interpreted and applied by the courts. The distinction between criminal law and civil is discussed. Although each of these forms the basis for the criminal justice system and the civil justice system, these seemingly distinct "systems" of justice are parts of a single justice system that the courts administer.

Chapter 3 discusses the American courts and the manner in which they operate as a unified system of justice. This occurs as a result of the place that courts occupy within the American "dual" system of government, in which federal authority and state authority operate within distinct spheres. Thus, the chapter focuses on the distinction between state and federal courts and examines the concept of jurisdiction as an organizing principle. In addition, the chapter considers the goals shared by courts in the administration of justice and the need for legal procedures used to achieve fairness in the operation of courts.

Section I provides a foundation for understanding the need for courts in America, their role in society, and the manner in which they operate. In subsequent sections, this foundation is used to examine the work of specific types of courts in specific types of cases. In particular, the organization, processes, and procedures of the various courts found in America are examined, but the context for these aspects of court functioning has as its basis individual justice and its relationship to law. Section I explores that context.

American Justice 1

What Is This Chapter About?

This chapter introduces concepts relating to the justice system in the United States. For our purposes, the "justice system" means the institutions and procedures used in this country to settle disputes, whether those disputes are between individuals or between the government and one or more of its citizens. Apart from informal settlement of such disputes, the primary institution for resolving them is the courts. Thus, this chapter begins our discussion of the topic that is the focus of this book: the courts in America and the ways in which they operate.

We first consider the meaning of "justice," its role in society, and its relationship to the law. Next, we explore the nature of disputes in America and the ways in which they may be resolved. Finally, we will begin to consider the courts as an American institution, their role in society, and our need for them. This chapter concludes with an orientation to judge-made law and the structure of written court decisions.

Learning Objectives

After reading this chapter, you should be able to

1. Understand what is meant by "justice" and the different forms it may take.
2. Distinguish between formal and informal ways of resolving disputes.
3. Understand the need for a justice system and what it accomplishes.
4. Describe the role of the courts within the justice system.
5. Understand the primary characteristics of courts.

Justice in the United States

In 2006, socialite and celebrity Paris Hilton was charged with reckless driving and driving under the influence of drugs and alcohol. She pleaded no contest to the charges and was sentenced to 3 years of probation, fined $1,500, and ordered to attend an alcohol education program. She later violated the terms of her probation by failing to enroll in the alcohol education program, by being charged with two more traffic offenses (including driving her new Bentley 70 mph in a 35-mph zone at night without headlights on a suspended license), and failing to obey the court's original orders. As a result, the judge revoked her probation and ordered her to serve 45 days in jail (Johnson & Parker, 2007).

After 3 days of imprisonment, the county sheriff in charge of the jail allowed her to leave and serve the remainder of her sentence confined in her mansion home "for health reasons" (Waxman, 2007). Hearing of this, the judge who sentenced her ordered that she immediately appear before him to explain why his order (that she be imprisoned for violating her probation) was not being carried out. He then made it clear that she was to be imprisoned in jail, not at her palatial home. When Hilton was led from the courtroom, she hysterically called for her mother crying, "It isn't fair!" To what was she referring? That she was returning to jail? That the judge had treated her differently than other offenders? That "justice" for celebrities like her should be something different than it is for others? That she did not deserve to be imprisoned to begin with?

Duke lacrosse players David Evans, Colin Finnerty, and Reade Seligmann were indicted on sexual assault, and false imprisonment charges were brought by District Attorney Mike Nifong in Durham, North Carolina. Despite evidence of the students' innocence, Nifong refused to dismiss the case, lied to the court about the exonerating evidence, and was found in contempt of court (Wilson, 2007). The state's Attorney General Roy Cooper ultimately took over the case, found the students to be innocent of the charges, and dismissed the case, calling it a "tragic rush to accuse." Nifong was later disbarred as a result of his actions in the wrongful prosecution and served 24 hours in jail for contempt of court. The students subsequently sued Nifong and the District Attorney's office, claiming harm to their reputations, lost opportunities, attorneys' fees, and expenses required in defending against the false charges (Aldridge, 2008). Was this a case of justice "gone wild," or did justice ultimately prevail, despite the harm caused along the way?

Although the Paris Hilton and Duke cases, even though prominent, may not represent either justice or the justice system at its best, they do represent society's response to perceived wrongdoing and the attempt of the courts to "do justice." They also show that different individuals, whether parties to a case, participants in the justice system, or the public looking on, have varied responses and perceptions about what justice requires, but the idea of justice in American society is not just a matter involving the perspective of who is getting or giving it. Justice depends to a great extent on the system that has developed for making decisions about what constitutes justice. It also depends on the perspectives of members of society to determine what a "just" society requires of its citizens and how the procedures for achieving it should operate. This book is about that system of justice. More specifically, it is about the processes and framework through which American society seeks to achieve justice.

What Is Justice?

"Justice" is a commonly used term that defies easy definition (Arrigo, 1999; Robinson, 2002). It is a concept that relates to our ideas about what is right and wrong, what is moral, what is fair, how people should treat each other, how government should treat citizens, or the ideal for which humans should strive. One dictionary broadly defines justice as "upholding what is just, especially fair treatment and due reward in accordance with honor, standards, or law" (Pickett et al., 2000). Consistent with this definition, most Americans associate justice with words such as *fairness*, *equality*, and *goodness* and believe that they and others are entitled to and should be treated with justice.

How is justice achieved, however? When we speak of justice in America, we may be referring to formal or informal ways of accomplishing it, including, for example, our personal notions of fairness and equality, treatment of ourselves and others, and methods for resolving disputes. We expect justice in our private lives, in our relationships with others, and in the society in which we live. Social policies are used by their advocates to achieve particular conceptions of justice. Political parties have as their foundation notions of what makes a just society. Government itself expands or contracts based on the views of elected or appointed leaders about justice.

The law itself reflects society's beliefs about how justice ought to be accomplished. Justice may therefore also be defined in terms of law: "A moral ideal that the law seeks to uphold in the protection of rights and punishment of wrongs" (Martin & Law, 2009). As a "moral ideal," justice may be difficult or impossible to achieve in every case, but it is nonetheless a foundation of American society and a concept in which those in society share a belief, even if they disagree about its meaning or application.

The Preamble to the United States Constitution refers to the importance of justice in America: "We the People of the United States, in Order to form a more perfect Union, establish Justice, insure domestic Tranquility, provide for the common defence, promote the general Welfare, and secure the Blessings of Liberty to ourselves and our Posterity, do ordain and establish this Constitution for the United States of America." Thus, one of the goals of our form of constitutional government and laws made under it is to "establish justice." The law operates in the interests of justice; it is designed to help people as they govern themselves, interact with each other in their business and personal affairs, and resolve their disputes.

Justice, to a large extent, however, is subjective; what rights should be protected and what wrongs should be punished may differ from person to person. The thoughts, feelings, background, and experiences of a person affect their understanding of justice, and individual views of justice may therefore vary considerably. This is problematic. Can justice have a consistent meaning and application when its definition varies from person to person? It is through the law that justice becomes meaningful. Thus, justice and law are necessarily intertwined—the law seeks to accomplish justice, and justice is defined in terms of law.

As a result, the primary method in American society for achieving justice is through reliance on the court system to make decisions that apply to individuals and society as a whole. Those who seek justice in America rely to a great extent on the courts to implement the law and see that justice is done in a wide range of cases and disputes. An understanding of the court system, its influences, and the context in which it operates is therefore essential to considering the meaning of justice.

Courts are imperfect institutions, however. Take the case of Paris Hilton, discussed previously here. The sentence given her, although similar to sentences given to others committing the same offenses, must have seemed insignificant to her because she essentially ignored it. Because, for example, a $1,500 fine is insignificant to a wealthy person, would a larger fine have achieved justice? Conversely, was she treated too harshly when the court demanded that she be jailed after having been released by the sheriff? It is common practice for jailers to release low-level offenders for a variety of reasons, yet the court demanded she be returned to jail. Did Hilton's celebrity work against her?

Also consider the Duke lacrosse case. Clearly, the wrongful conduct of the prosecutor shows how some "bad apples" can become part of the criminal justice system, but some would argue that it was the wealth of the defendants' families who could afford private attorneys and investigative expenses that saved them from what initially seemed to be a lost cause. If the defendants had been poor or minorities or not attending a well-known private university, would the outcome be the same? Would the case have been pursued with the same vigor, even with an honest prosecutor?

Despite the best efforts of those who administer justice, questions of what is fair and what is just remain subjective. That is, justice is not a "one-size-fits-all" concept. It depends on the behavior of the individual being judged. It depends on the person doing the judging. It depends on the facts and the evidence. It depends on society's views, and it depends on the law. It is not surprising, therefore, that the concept of justice is best thought of as multifaceted, where its definition ultimately depends on the circumstances or problems to which its applies.

The case of Humberto Fidel Regalado Cuellar represents problems with which the courts are often confronted. At first blush, the case appears to be straightforward. Cuellar was driving his Volkswagen Beetle through Texas toward Mexico. He was stopped for driving erratically. Cuellar spoke no English and thus was questioned by a Spanish-speaking officer. He avoided eye contact, appeared nervous, gave varying accounts of where he had been and where he was going, had no luggage, had a wad of cash that smelled of marijuana in his shirt pocket, and made the sign of the cross while officers searched his Volkswagen. While searching the car, officers did not find any drugs, but did find $85,000 wrapped in plastic and duct tape under the rear floorboard, as well as quantities of animal hair in the rear seating area, which Cuellar claimed to be from transporting goats. Based on these facts, what would you conclude? Is Cuellar a criminal? If so, what crime was committed? Were any of Cuellar's actions illegal?

Cuellar was charged with the federal crime of money laundering, by attempting to transport money from unlawful activity outside the United States. The money laundering statute required the prosecutor to show that the transportation was designed "to conceal or disguise the nature, the location, the source, the ownership, or the control" of the money (*Cuellar v. U.S.*, 128 S.Ct. 1994, 1998 (2008)). A jury found Cuellar guilty, and he was sentenced to 78 months in prison.

After trial, Cuellar appealed to the federal court of appeals, which first overturned the conviction, then reheard the case, changed its mind, and upheld the trial court and the conviction. Read the case excerpt found in **Case Decision 1.1**, which explains why. The case was

then appealed to the United States Supreme Court, which upheld the court of appeals, dismissing Cuellar's conviction. Why did the Supreme Court overturn the conviction? Was this a just result?

The Cuellar case is unusual because it went "all the way to the Supreme Court," but otherwise, it represents the normal workings of the American court system and the processes in place to achieve justice. It also shows very clearly what courts do; they interpret the law. The case required each of the courts involved to determine what the requirements of the federal money laundering statute were and whether they were supported by the facts. Each of the cases discussed in this book involves that same process. Courts take a procedural approach to the law, and the administration of justice depends on such an approach.

Types of Justice

Given the difficulty in reaching a single definition of justice, it is not surprising that different ways of categorizing or thinking about justice have arisen. Justice is perhaps best considered, not as a single concept capable of definition, but as a collection of differing viewpoints on fairness in society. Although each of these is concerned with the concept of fairness, each examines the meaning of justice from a different societal perspective.

A primary distinction that may be drawn is between forms of "corrective justice" and forms of "distributive justice." Corrective justice relates to the manner in which individuals who violate the law should be punished. It defines justice in terms of who should be punished, how punishments should be imposed, and whether punishments bear a proper relationship to the violation of law

---

Case Decision 1.1 *Cuellar v. U.S.*, 128 S. Ct. 1994 (2008)

Opinion of the Court by Justice Thomas:

This case involves the provision of the federal money laundering statute that prohibits international transportation of the proceeds of unlawful activity. Petitioner argues that his conviction cannot stand because, while the evidence demonstrates that he took steps to hide illicit funds *en route* to Mexico, it does not show that the cross-border transport of those funds was designed to create the appearance of legitimate wealth. Although we agree with the Government that the statute does not require proof that the defendant attempted to "legitimize" tainted funds, we agree with petitioner that the Government must demonstrate that the defendant did more than merely hide the money during its transport. We therefore reverse the judgment of the Fifth Circuit.

I

On July 14, 2004, petitioner Humberto Fidel Regalado Cuellar was stopped in southern Texas for driving erratically. Driving south toward the Mexican border, about 114 miles away, petitioner had just passed the town of Eldorado. In response to the officer's questions, petitioner, who spoke no English, handed the officer a stack of papers. Included were bus tickets showing travel from a Texas border town to San Antonio on July 13 and, in the other direction, from San Antonio to Big Spring, Texas, on July 14. A Spanish-speaking officer, Trooper Danny Nuñez, was called to the scene and began questioning petitioner. Trooper Nuñez soon became suspicious because petitioner was avoiding eye contact and seemed very nervous. Petitioner claimed to be on a 3-day business trip, but he had no

(Continues)

luggage or extra clothing with him, and he gave conflicting accounts of his itinerary. When Trooper Nuñez asked petitioner about a bulge in his shirt pocket, petitioner produced a wad of cash that smelled of marijuana.

Petitioner consented to a search of the Volkswagen Beetle that he was driving. While the officers were searching the vehicle, Trooper Nuñez observed petitioner standing on the side of the road making the sign of the cross, which he interpreted to mean that petitioner knew he was in trouble. A drug detection dog alerted on the cash from petitioner's shirt pocket and on the rear area of the car. Further scrutiny uncovered a secret compartment under the rear floorboard, and inside the compartment the officers found approximately $81,000 in cash. The money was bundled in plastic bags and duct tape, and animal hair was spread in the rear of the vehicle. Petitioner claimed that he had previously transported goats in the vehicle, but Trooper Nuñez doubted that goats could fit in such a small space and suspected that the hair had been spread in an attempt to mask the smell of marijuana.

There were signs that the compartment had been recently created and that someone had attempted to cover up the bodywork: The Beetle's carpeting appeared newer than the rest of the interior, and the exterior of the vehicle appeared to have been purposely splashed with mud to cover up toolmarks, fresh paint, or other work. In the backseat, officers found a fast-food restaurant receipt dated the same day from a city farther north than petitioner claimed to have traveled. After a check of petitioner's last border crossing also proved inconsistent with his story, petitioner was arrested and interrogated. He continued to tell conflicting stories about his travels. At one point, before he knew that the officers had found the cash, he remarked to Trooper Nuñez that he had to have the car in Mexico by midnight or else his family would be "floating down the river." App. 50.

Petitioner was charged with attempting to transport the proceeds of unlawful activity across the border, knowing that the transportation was designed "to conceal or disguise the nature, the location, the source, the ownership, or the control" of the money. 18 U.S.C. § 1956(a)(2)(B)(i). After a 2-day trial, the jury found petitioner guilty. The District Court denied petitioner's motion for judgment of acquittal based on insufficient evidence and sentenced petitioner to 78 months in prison, followed by three years of supervised release.

On appeal, a divided panel of the Fifth Circuit reversed and rendered a judgment of acquittal, [holding] that, although the evidence showed that petitioner concealed the money for the purpose of transporting it, the statute requires that the purpose of the transportation itself must be to conceal or disguise the unlawful proceeds. Analogizing from cases interpreting another provision of the money laundering statute, the court held that the transportation must be undertaken in an attempt to create the appearance of legitimate wealth. Although the evidence showed intent to avoid detection while driving the funds to Mexico, it did not show that petitioner intended to create the appearance of legitimate wealth, and accordingly no rational trier of fact could have found petitioner guilty.

The Fifth Circuit granted rehearing en banc and affirmed petitioner's conviction. The court rejected as inconsistent with the statutory text petitioner's argument that the Government must prove that he attempted to create the appearance of legitimate wealth. But it held that petitioner's extensive efforts to prevent detection of the funds during transportation showed that petitioner sought to conceal or disguise the nature, location, and source, ownership, or control of the funds.

We granted certiorari.

II

The federal money laundering statute, 18 U.S.C. § 1956, prohibits specified transfers of money derived from unlawful activities. Subsection (a)(1) makes it unlawful to engage in certain financial transactions, while subsection (a)(2) criminalizes certain kinds of transportation. Petitioner was charged under the transportation provision: The indictment alleged that he attempted to transport illicit proceeds across the Mexican border "knowing that such transportation was designed in whole or in part to conceal and disguise the nature, location, source, ownership, and control" of the funds.

A

We first consider the "designed . . . to conceal" element. Petitioner argues that to satisfy this element, the Government must prove that the defendant attempted to create the appearance of legitimate wealth. Petitioner would replace "designed . . . to conceal or disguise the nature, the location, the source, the ownership, or the control of the proceeds" with "designed to create the appearance of legitimate wealth." This is consistent with the plain meaning of "money laundering," petitioner argues, because that term is commonly understood to mean disguising illegally obtained money in order to make it appear legitimate. In petitioner's view, this common understanding of "money laundering" is implicit in both the transaction and transportation provisions of the statute because concealing or disguising any of the listed attributes would necessarily have the effect of making the funds appear legitimate, and, conversely, revealing any such attribute would necessarily reveal the funds as illicit. The Government disagrees, contending that making funds appear legitimate is merely one way to accomplish money laundering, and that revealing a listed attribute would not necessarily reveal the funds' illicit nature. In any event, the Government argues, the statute should not be cabined to target only classic money laundering because Congress intended to reach any conduct that impairs the ability of law enforcement to find and recover the unlawful proceeds.

We agree with petitioner that taking steps to make funds appear legitimate is the common meaning of the term "money laundering." See American Heritage Dictionary 992 (4th ed. 2000) (hereinafter Am. Hert.) (defining "launder" as "[t]o disguise the source or nature of (illegal funds, for example) by channeling through an intermediate agent"); Black's Law Dictionary 1027 (8th ed. 2004) (hereinafter Black's) (defining "money-laundering" to mean "[t]he act of transferring illegally obtained money through legitimate people or accounts so that its original source cannot be traced"). But to the extent they are inconsistent, we must be guided by the words of the operative statutory provision, and not by the common meaning of the statute's title. Here, Congress used broad language that captures more than classic money laundering: In addition to concealing or disguising the nature or source of illegal funds, Congress also sought to reach transportation designed to conceal or disguise the location, ownership, or control of the funds. For example, a defendant who smuggles cash into Mexico with the intent of hiding it from authorities by burying it in the desert may have engaged in transportation designed to conceal the location of those funds, but his conduct would not necessarily have the effect of making the funds appear legitimate.

Nor do we find persuasive petitioner's attempt to infuse a "classic money laundering" requirement into the listed attributes. Contrary to petitioner's argument, revealing those attributes—nature, location, source, ownership, or control—would not necessarily expose the illegitimacy of the funds. Digging up the cash buried in the Mexican desert, for example, would not necessarily reveal that it was derived from unlawful activity. Indeed, of all the listed attributes, only "nature" is coextensive with the funds' illegitimate character: Exposing the nature of illicit funds would, by definition, reveal them as unlawful proceeds. But nature is only one attribute in the statute; that it may be coextensive with the creation of the appearance of legitimate wealth does not mean that Congress intended that requirement to swallow the other listed attributes.

We likewise are skeptical of petitioner's argument that violating the elements of the statute would necessarily have the effect of making the funds appear more legitimate than they did before. It is true that concealing or disguising any one of the listed attributes may have the effect of making the funds appear more legitimate—largely because concealing or disguising those attributes might impede law enforcement's ability to identify illegitimate funds—but we are not convinced that this is necessarily so. It might be possible for a defendant to conceal or disguise a listed attribute without also creating the appearance of legitimate wealth. Petitioner's "appearance of legitimate wealth" requirement simply has no basis in the operative provision's text.

B

Having concluded that the statute contains no "appearance of legitimate wealth" requirement, we next consider whether the evidence that petitioner concealed the money during transportation is sufficient to sustain his conviction. As noted, petitioner was convicted under § 1956(a)(2)(B)(i), which, in relevant part, makes it a crime to attempt to transport "funds from a place in the United States to . . . a place outside the United States . . . knowing that the . . . funds involved in the transportation . . . represent the proceeds of some form of unlawful activity and knowing that such transportation . . . is designed in whole or in part . . . to conceal or disguise the nature, the location, the source, the ownership, or the control of the proceeds of specified unlawful activity." Accordingly, the Government was required in this case to prove that petitioner (1) attempted to transport funds from the United States to Mexico, (2) knew that these funds "represent[ed] the proceeds of some form of unlawful activity,"

(*Continues*)

(*Continued*)

e.g., drug trafficking, and (3) knew that "such transportation" was designed to "conceal or disguise the nature, the location, the source, the ownership, or the control" of the funds.

It is the last of these that is at issue before us, viz., whether petitioner knew that "such transportation" was designed to conceal or disguise the specified attributes of the illegally obtained funds. In this connection, it is important to keep in mind that the critical transportation was not the transportation of the funds within this country on the way to the border. Instead, the term "such transportation" means transportation "from a place in the United States to . . . a place outside the United States"—here, from the United States to Mexico. Therefore, what the Government had to prove was that petitioner knew that taking the funds to Mexico was "designed," at least in part, to conceal or disguise their "nature," "location," "source," "ownership," or "control."

Petitioner argues that the evidence is not sufficient to sustain his conviction because concealing or disguising a listed attribute of the funds during transportation cannot satisfy the "designed . . . to conceal" element. Citing cases that interpret the identical phrase in the transaction provision to exclude "mere spending," petitioner argues that the transportation provision must exclude "mere hiding." Otherwise, petitioner contends, all cross-border transport of illicit funds would fall under the statute because people regularly make minimal efforts to conceal money, such as placing it inside a wallet or other receptacle, in order to secure it during travel. The Government responds that concealment during transportation is sufficient to satisfy this element because it is circumstantial evidence that the ultimate purpose of the transportation—*i.e.*, its "design"—is to conceal or disguise a listed attribute of the funds. This standard would not criminalize all cross-border transport of illicit funds, the Government argues, because, just as in the transaction cases, the statute encompasses only *substantial* efforts at concealment. As a result, the Government agrees with the Court of Appeals that a violation of courts the transportation provision cannot be established solely by evidence that the defendant carried money in a wallet or concealed it in some other conventional or incidental way.

We agree with petitioner that merely hiding funds during transportation is not sufficient to violate the statute, even if substantial efforts have been expended to conceal the money. Our conclusion turns on the text of § 1956(a)(2)(B)(i), and particularly on the term "design." In this context, "design" means purpose or plan; *i.e.*, the intended aim of the transportation. See Am. Hert. 491 ("To formulate a plan for; devise"; "[t]o create or contrive for a particular purpose or effect"); Black's 478 ("A plan or scheme"; "[p]urpose or intention combined with a plan"); see also Brief for United States 14 (" 'to conceive and plan out in the mind' " (quoting Webster's Third New International Dictionary 611 (1993))). Congress wrote "knowing that such transportation is designed . . . to conceal or disguise" a listed attribute of the funds, § 1956(a)(2)(B)(i), and when an act is "designed to" do something, the most natural reading is that it has that something as its purpose. The Fifth Circuit employed this meaning of design when it referred to the "transportation design or plan to get the funds out of this country."

But the Fifth Circuit went on to discuss the "design" of the transportation in a different sense. It described the packaging of the money, its placement in the hidden compartment, and the use of animal hair to mask its scent as *aspects* of the transportation" that "were designed to conceal or disguise" the nature and location of the cash. Because the Fifth Circuit used "design" to refer not to the purpose of the transportation but to the manner in which it was carried out, its use of the term in this context was consistent with the alternate meaning of "design" as structure or arrangement. See Am. Hert. 491, 492 ("To plan out in systematic, usually graphic form"; "[t]he purposeful or inventive arrangement of parts or details"); Black's 478 ("The pattern or configuration of elements in something, such as a work of art"). If the statutory term had this meaning, it would apply whenever a person transported illicit funds in a secretive manner. Judge Smith [of the court of appeals] supplied an example of this construction: A petty thief who hides money in his shoe and then walks across the border to spend the money in local bars has engaged in transportation designed to conceal the location of the money because he has hidden it in an unlikely place.

We think it implausible, however, that Congress intended this meaning of "design." If it had, it could have expressed its intention simply by writing "knowing that such transportation conceals or disguises," rather than the more complex formulation "knowing that such transportation . . . is designed . . . to conceal or disguise." § 1956(a)(2)(B)(i). It seems far more likely that Congress intended courts to apply the familiar criminal law concepts of purpose and intent than to focus exclusively on how a defendant "structured" the transportation. In addition, the structural meaning of "design" is both overinclusive and underinclusive: It would capture individuals who structured transportation in a secretive way but lacked any criminal intent (such as a person who hid illicit funds *en route* to turn them over to law enforcement); yet it would exclude individuals who fully intended to move the funds in order to impede detection by law enforcement but failed to hide them during the transportation.

To be sure, purpose and structure are often related. One may employ structure to achieve a purpose: For example, the petty thief may hide money in his shoe to prevent it from being detected as he crosses the border with the intent to hide the money in Mexico. Although transporting money in a conventional manner may suggest no particular purpose other than simply to move it from one place to another, secretively transporting it suggests, at least, that the defendant did not want the money to be detected during transport. In this case, evidence of the methods petitioner used to transport the nearly $81,000 in cash—bundled in plastic bags and hidden in a secret compartment covered with animal hair—was plainly probative of an underlying goal to prevent the funds from being detected while he drove them from the United States to Mexico. The same secretive aspects of the transportation also may be circumstantial evidence that the transportation itself was intended to avoid detection of the funds, because, for example, they may suggest that the transportation is only one step in a larger plan to facilitate the cross-border transport of the funds. But its probative force, in that context, is weak. [T]hat is, *how* one moves the money is distinct from *why* one moves the money. Evidence of the former, standing alone, is not sufficient to prove the latter.

This case illustrates why: Even with abundant evidence that petitioner had concealed the money in order to transport it, the Government's own expert witness—ICE Agent Richard Nuckles—testified that the purpose of the transportation was to compensate the leaders of the operation. ("[T]he bulk of [the money] generally goes back to Mexico, because the smuggler is the one who originated this entire process. He's going to get a large cut of the profit, and that money has to be moved back to him in Mexico"). The evidence suggested that the secretive aspects of the transportation were employed to *facilitate* the transportation, but not necessarily that secrecy was the *purpose* of the transportation. Agent Nuckles testified that the secretive manner of transportation was consistent with drug smuggling, but the Government failed to introduce any evidence that the reason drug smugglers move money to Mexico is to conceal or disguise a listed attribute of the funds.

Agent Nuckles also testified that Acuna, the Mexican border town to which petitioner was headed, has a cash economy and that U.S. currency is widely accepted there. The Fifth Circuit apparently viewed this as evidence that petitioner transported the money in order to conceal or disguise it: "[G]iven Mexico's largely cash economy, if [petitioner] had successfully transported the funds to Mexico without detection, the jury was entitled to find that the funds would have been better concealed or concealable after the transportation than before." The statutory text makes clear, however, that a conviction under this provision requires proof that the purpose—not merely effect—of the transportation was to conceal or disguise a listed attribute. Although the evidence suggested that petitioner's transportation would have had the effect of concealing the funds, the evidence did not demonstrate that such concealment was the purpose of the transportation because, for instance, there was no evidence that petitioner knew about or intended the effect.

In sum, we conclude that the evidence introduced by the Government was not sufficient to permit a reasonable jury to conclude beyond a reasonable doubt that petitioner's transportation was "designed in whole or in part . . . to conceal or disguise the nature, the location, the source, the ownership, or the control of the proceeds." § 1956(a)(2)(B)(i).

III

The provision of the money laundering statute under which petitioner was convicted requires proof that the transportation was "designed in whole or in part to conceal or disguise the nature, the location, the source, the ownership, or the control" of the funds. § 1956(a)(2)(B)(i). Although this element does not require proof that the defendant attempted to create the appearance of legitimate wealth, neither can it be satisfied solely by evidence that a defendant concealed the funds during their transport. In this case, the only evidence introduced to prove this element showed that petitioner engaged in extensive efforts to conceal the funds *en route* to Mexico, and thus his conviction cannot stand. We reverse the judgment of the Fifth Circuit.

It is so ordered.

they seek to address (Tomasi, 2002). The focus of the criminal justice system is largely on implementing corrective justice (Feinberg, 1987). Distributive justice refers to the manner in which rights, liberties, and benefits of membership in a society are allocated among its members. Distributive justice defines justice in terms of whether the parties to a dispute get what they "deserve" (Rawls, 1971, 2001). Some of the specific conceptualizations of both corrective and distributive justice are discussed later here.

Social Justice

Social justice is a broad term that encompasses notions of equality and fairness to all individuals and groups within society (Wendorf et al., 2002; Tyler & Smith, 1997). In this respect, the concepts of distributive justice and social justice are closely aligned; however, social justice may be distinguished from justice for individuals. Whereas distributive justice involves questions of whether another individual, the government, or society itself has treated a person in a manner consistent with the treatment of others or in an otherwise equitable manner, social justice examines broader influences and outcomes within society that may affect an individual, a group, or the larger society in which they exist (Douglass, 1978). It adheres to the idea that individual justice cannot be said to exist when social forces prevent subgroups within society from achieving the opportunities that others may have (Buchanan & Mathieu, 1986). This includes the idea of economic justice that addresses concerns about the distribution of economic resources among people, helping the poor, as well as job availability and advancement, and opportunities for producing wealth. Social justice also includes race, gender, or age discrimination, as well as concerns about the status of the mentally disabled in society. It highlights the need for society to adopt policies that create equal opportunities for individuals within these groups, whether through affirmative action, legislation, court action, or civic activism.

Thus, social justice is a matter that depends on the concerns of the individual or group asserting it, but always has the betterment of society as a goal. That is, proponents of social justice are typically proponents of social welfare, where the welfare of society is said to improve only to the extent that subgroups within society stand on an equal footing (Hegtvedt & Markovsky, 1995). This contrasts with the view that individual rights supersede societal interests and that social justice, to the extent that it is a goal, can only be achieved by the fair adjudication of individual cases. In other words, justice for one is justice for all.

Retributive Justice

The focus of retributive justice is the view that justice demands a penalty from those who act in a way that is harmful to others or is harmful to society. Retributive justice accomplishes the punishment goal of retribution, which is the "just deserts" philosophy that views offenders as deserving of punishment in accordance with the seriousness of their offense. Retributive justice is also said to be unilateral; that is, it seeks to "repair" justice by unilaterally imposing punishment on offenders (Wenzel et al.,

2008). To a large extent, the criminal justice system in America is based on retributive justice policies. Indeed, retributive justice may be viewed as a justification for the criminal law itself (Moore, 1997). Those who commit crimes are considered deserving of punishment and the system focuses on imposing a penalty on the offender that exacts retribution and satisfies the demands of society (Husak, 2000). These demands include safety for members of the community, punishment that deters future offenses, and to some extent victims' desire for revenge.

One basis for retributive justice as a social theory is that victims are entitled to see that those who harm them are punished, in order for the victim to find "closure" and in order for the wrongdoer to have any chance of redemption and acceptance by society (Fletcher, 1999; Moore, 1999). Retributive justice is therefore sometimes viewed as consistent with the "victims' rights" movement in criminal justice, which seeks greater input from victims in determining the liability and punishment of criminal offenders. Despite this affinity between retributive justice and victim rights, retributive justice does not depend on or provide any role for victims as necessary to accomplish justice in the punishment of offenders (Moore, 1999).

Restorative Justice

Restorative justice reflects a focus on the victim of crime. Traditionally, the criminal justice system has viewed violations of criminal law as offenses against the state, where the government's role in "bringing an offender to justice" solely involved criminal prosecution and punitive sanctions. Restorative justice attempts to shift the perspective of the system by considering the effect of criminal offenses on specific individual victims, rather than the more generalized harm inflicted on society (Strickland, 2004). It seeks to "restore" the victim to his or her precrime state by having the perpetrator make amends for the harm caused. It also has as a goal the "restoration" of the offender as a member of the community or, more generally, society. In this respect it may be viewed as bilateral, where society and the offender together seek to restore justice to the community (Wenzel et al., 2008). Thus, restorative justice has a rehabilitative emphasis where the offender benefits from his attempt to "fix" the harm caused the victim (Murphy, 1990).

This may take various forms. Offenders may be required to pay financial or other forms of restitution, such as fixing a broken window or a door lock or replacing slashed tires on a car. They may be ordered to engage in victim-offender mediation, where the offender must meet with the victim to discuss the harm and its effects. It may also include participating in community service programs focused on assistance to other victims of crimes similar to the one committed by the offender and allow the offender to see more the clearly the personal effect that his or her behavior has on others.

Procedural Justice

The idea of procedural justice is one in which the process through which disputes are resolved is paramount. The reason for this is that people will perceive outcomes as fair only to the extent that the procedures used to reach them are fair (Skitka & Crosby, 2003; Tyler, 1990). Because the emphasis is on procedure, what is considered to be just is an outcome that results from a clearly established process that is followed in the same way in each case. Thus, procedural justice defines justice not in terms of a judicial decision's effect on a person, but rather in terms of whether the individual had the opportunity to present his or her case in the same manner as other litigants. Much of our system of justice administered by courts of law is guided by principles of procedural justice.

Two aspects of procedural justice exist: fairness as it relates to the actual decision-making process used by a court and fairness involving the type of treatment people believe they have received in court (Tyler & Blader, 2000). Both of these aspects affect the confidence people have in the justice system as well as having an effect on their behavior and their perceptions of whether the system is "fair."

Questions of procedural justice have been raised about the detention without trial of suspected terrorists at a U.S. military base in Guantanamo Bay, Cuba. In *Boumediene v. Bush*, 128 S. Ct. 2229 (2008), the U.S. Supreme Court held that prisoners of the American "war on terror" being held at Guantanamo have a right to habeas corpus, which is the right of a prisoner to a hearing before a court of law in which the government must justify holding the prisoner. The case required interpretation of Article I, Section 9 of the U.S. Constitution, referred to as the "suspension clause," which provides that "the Privilege of the Writ of Habeas Corpus shall not be suspended, unless when in the Case of Rebellion or Invasion the public safety may require it." The government argued that the war on terror was a circumstance in which public safety required that the detainees be held and that the suspension clause (and Congress' approval) authorized the President to suspend habeas corpus for the Guantanamo prisoners. The government further argued that because the detainees were not on U.S. soil, they were not entitled to the benefit of constitutional rights in any case. Throughout its lengthy opinion, the Court noted that neither Congress nor the President could justify the lengthy detention (6 years) of prisoners or deny them access to the courts. The Court found that

> petitioners may invoke the fundamental procedural protections of habeas corpus. The laws and Constitution are designed to survive, and remain in force, in extraordinary times. Liberty and security can be reconciled; and in our system they are reconciled within the framework of the law. The Framers decided that habeas corpus, a right of first importance, must be a part of that framework, a part of that law (128 S. Ct. at 2277).

By finding a right to habeas corpus for non-Americans being held outside of U.S. soil, the Court was basing its conclusions on the need for procedural justice.

And Justice for All

Regardless of one's perspective on what constitutes justice or the type of justice employed, it is clear that the concept of justice relates to the treatment of people and is an important concept only to the extent that it benefits people. In the American democracy, justice involves relationships among people and the relationship of people to their government, and the law seeks to clarify those relationships. For example, in the case of *Lochner v. New York*, 198 U.S. 45, 25 S. Ct. 539, 49 L.Ed. 937 (1905), the labor movement and its unions in the state of New York sought to achieve shorter working hours for workers in many businesses, including bakeries, where workers chronically worked over 12 hours a day for 6 or 7 days a week, in unsafe working conditions for low pay. As a result, the legislature passed a law limiting the number of hours bakers could work to 10 hours per day, or no more than 60 hours per week. Many employers ignored the law, however. When one bakery owner, Joseph Lochner, did so, he was fined. He appealed the fine to the U.S. Supreme Court, claiming that he had a constitutional right to conduct his business in a manner he saw fit and that the state cannot limit his business activities by regulating working hours. The Court overturned the fine, stating that the government may not infringe Lochner's freedom to contract with his employees, unless the government could prove that an actual threat to public health existed. In a famous dissent, Justice Oliver Wendell Holmes argued that the Court could not substitute its opinion about economic matters for that of the legislature. Although the reasoning in the case was overruled nearly 30 years later, it raised important questions (that remain today) about what justice requires, the relationship between people and government, and the role of the courts.

There is little question that the working conditions of many industries in 1905 in New York were horrendous and that, as a matter of justice, the legislature's role was to address these problems. Yet, the highest Court in the country perceived justice to require the legislature to have a "hands off" attitude in economic matters, one that has been termed "laissez-faire." The Court's decision, however, was one that had far-reaching effects on workers and employers; the decision replaced the conclusions of the New York legislature regarding what was in the best interests of the people of the state. The question of judicial activism and the extent to which judges can or should replace legislative rules with their own decisions about what justice requires is a continuing debate, one which is reflected in many of the cases discussed in this book.

Our democracy provides for the institutions—legislative, executive, and judicial—that specify the ways in which rules for society will be created, enforced, and interpreted. In addition, it creates rights to which American citizens (and, to some extent, non-Americans) are entitled. These are discussed in detail in later chapters. For now, we briefly consider the boundaries of justice in the relationship between government and individual citizens.

Among many other important provisions, the Fifth Amendment to the U.S. Constitution provides that the private property of citizens shall not "be taken for public use, without just compensation." Referred to as the "Takings Clause," this constitutional right is intended to protect people from the unwarranted and uncompensated seizure of their property by the government, local, state, or federal, but the Takings Clause also anticipates that, in some circumstances, the government may have the need for property held privately; in those circumstances, the Fifth Amendment allows the government to exercise eminent domain power to seize the property for public use, as long as just compensation is paid to the owner. Normally, these circumstances involve a clear public benefit, such as taking property to build a road through the property or to erect a school building for the families of the community. The circumstances in which this government power may be exercised has been a continuing source of litigation for years, and the meaning of the Takings Clause has been an area of controversy nearly since the beginning of the country, including very recently.

Throughout the 1990s, the city of New London, Connecticut, located on Long Island Sound, was in economic decay, losing businesses, jobs, and revenue for government services. With the loss of jobs came the loss of residents. Even the state considered the city to be a "distressed municipality." In order to revitalize the city, in 2000, the city created a redevelopment plan designed to

use property along the waterfront to develop business facilities, office buildings, retail space, and condominiums in an attempt to bring jobs to the area and improve the economic future of the city. With the assistance of state funding, the city was able to purchase much of the necessary property from private landowners, but some were unwilling to sell their homes to the city. Using its power of eminent domain, the city took the property of these individuals, leaving it to the state court to decide on just compensation. It was the intention of the city to offer a long-term lease of the property to private developers so that they could rebuild the area in accordance with the redevelopment plan.

The homeowners sued the city, arguing that the city exceeded its eminent domain powers because it wanted their property solely for economic reasons, not for any public benefit. The question, of course, is whether the Fifth Amendment protects these property owners from the taking of their property by the city government, who intended to immediately transfer the property to private developers solely for economic reasons. The case made its way to the U.S. Supreme Court, which issued the opinion excerpted in **Case Decision 1.2**.

Case Decision 1.2 *Susette Kelo et al. v. City of New London, Connecticut, et al.*, 545 U.S. 469, 125 S. Ct. 2655, 162 L.Ed.2d 439 (2005)

Opinion of the court by Justice Stevens:

In 2000, the city of New London approved a development plan that, in the words of the Supreme Court of Connecticut, was "projected to create in excess of 1,000 jobs, to increase tax and other revenues, and to revitalize an economically distressed city, including its downtown and waterfront areas." In assembling the land needed for this project, the city's development agent has purchased property from willing sellers and proposes to use the power of eminent domain to acquire the remainder of the property from unwilling owners in exchange for just compensation. The question presented is whether the city's proposed disposition of this property qualifies as a "public use" within the meaning of the Takings Clause of the Fifth Amendment to the Constitution.

The city of New London (hereinafter City) sits at the junction of the Thames River and the Long Island Sound in southeastern Connecticut. Decades of economic decline led a state agency in 1990 to designate the City a "distressed municipality." These conditions prompted state and local officials to target New London, and particularly its Fort Trumbull area, for economic revitalization. To this end, respondent New London Development Corporation (NLDC), a private nonprofit entity established some years earlier to assist the City in planning economic development, was reactivated. In January 1998, the State authorized a $5.35 million bond issue to support the NLDC's planning activities and a $10 million bond issue toward the creation of a Fort Trumbull State Park. In February, the pharmaceutical company Pfizer Inc. announced that it would build a $300 million research facility on a site immediately adjacent to Fort Trumbull; local planners hoped that Pfizer would draw new business to the area, thereby serving as a catalyst to the area's rejuvenation. Upon obtaining state-level approval, the NLDC finalized an integrated development plan focused on 90 acres of the Fort Trumbull area.

The Fort Trumbull area is situated on a peninsula that juts into the Thames River. The area comprises approximately 115 privately owned properties, as well as the 32 acres of land formerly occupied by the naval facility (Trumbull State Park now occupies 18 of those 32 acres). The development plan encompasses seven parcels. Parcel 1 is designated for a waterfront conference hotel at the center of a "small urban village" that will include restaurants and shopping. Parcel 2 will be the site of approximately 80 new residences organized into an urban neighborhood and linked by public walkway to the remainder of the development, including the state park. Parcel 3, which is located immediately north of the Pfizer facility, will contain at least 90,000 square feet of research and development office space.

Parcel 4A is a 2.4-acre site that will be used either to support the adjacent state park, by providing parking or retail services for visitors, or to support the nearby marina. Parcel 4B will include a renovated marina, as well as the final stretch of the riverwalk. Parcels 5, 6, and 7 will provide land for office and retail space, parking, and water-dependent commercial uses.

The NLDC intended the development plan to capitalize on the arrival of the Pfizer facility and the new commerce it was expected to attract. In addition to creating jobs, generating tax revenue, and helping to "build momentum for the revitalization of downtown New London," the plan was also designed to make the City more attractive and to create leisure and recreational opportunities on the waterfront and in the park.

The NLDC successfully negotiated the purchase of most of the real estate in the 90-acre area, but its negotiations with petitioners failed. As a consequence, in November 2000, the NLDC initiated the condemnation proceedings that gave rise to this case.

II

Petitioner Susette Kelo has lived in the Fort Trumbull area since 1997. She has made extensive improvements to her house, which she prizes for its water view. Petitioner Wilhelmina Dery was born in her Fort Trumbull house in 1918 and has lived there her entire life. Her husband Charles (also a petitioner) has lived in the house since they married some 60 years ago. In all, the nine petitioners own 15 properties in Fort Trumbull—4 in parcel 3 of the development plan and 11 in parcel 4A. Ten of the parcels are occupied by the owner or a family member; the other five are held as investment properties. There is no allegation that any of these properties is blighted or otherwise in poor condition; rather, they were condemned only because they happen to be located in the development area.

In December 2000, petitioners brought this action in the New London Superior Court. They claimed, among other things, that the taking of their properties would violate the "public use" restriction in the Fifth Amendment. After a 7-day bench trial, the Superior Court granted a permanent restraining order prohibiting the taking of the properties located in parcel 4A (park or marina support). It, however, denied petitioners relief as to the properties located in parcel 3 (office space).

After the Superior Court ruled, both sides took appeals to the Supreme Court of Connecticut. That court held, over a dissent, that all of the City's proposed takings were valid. We granted certiorari to determine whether a city's decision to take property for the purpose of economic development satisfies the "public use" requirement of the Fifth Amendment.

III

Two polar propositions are perfectly clear. On the one hand, it has long been accepted that the sovereign may not take the property of *A* for the sole purpose of transferring it to another private party *B*, even though *A* is paid just compensation. On the other hand, it is equally clear that a State may transfer property from one private party to another if future "use by the public" is the purpose of the taking; the condemnation of land for a railroad with common-carrier duties is a familiar example. Neither of these propositions, however, determines the disposition of this case.

As for the first proposition, the City would no doubt be forbidden from taking petitioners' land for the purpose of conferring a private benefit on a particular private party. Nor would the City be allowed to take property under the mere pretext of a public purpose, when its actual purpose was to bestow a private benefit. The takings before us, however, would be executed pursuant to a "carefully considered" development plan. [T]he City's development plan was not adopted "to benefit a particular class of identifiable individuals."

On the other hand, this is not a case in which the City is planning to open the condemned land—at least not in its entirety—to use by the general public. Nor will the private lessees of the land in any sense be required to operate like common carriers, making their services available to all comers. But although such a projected use would be sufficient to satisfy the public use requirement, this "Court long ago rejected any literal requirement that condemned property be put into use for the general public." Indeed, while many state courts in the mid-19th century endorsed "use by the public" as the proper definition of public use, that narrow view steadily eroded over time. Not only was the "use by the public" test difficult to administer (*e.g.*, what proportion of the public need have access to the property? at what price?), but it proved to be impractical given the diverse and always evolving needs of society. Accordingly, when this Court began applying the Fifth Amendment to the States at the close

(Continues)

of the 19th century, it embraced the broader and more natural interpretation of public use as "public purpose." Thus, in a case upholding a mining company's use of an aerial bucket line to transport ore over property it did not own, Justice Holmes' opinion for the Court stressed "the inadequacy of use by the general public as a universal test." We have repeatedly and consistently rejected that narrow test ever since.

The disposition of this case therefore turns on the question whether the City's development plan serves a "public purpose." Without exception, our cases have defined that concept broadly, reflecting our longstanding policy of deference to legislative judgments in this field.

Viewed as a whole, our jurisprudence has recognized that the needs of society have varied between different parts of the Nation, just as they have evolved over time in response to changed circumstances. Our earliest cases in particular embodied a strong theme of federalism, emphasizing the "great respect" that we owe to state legislatures and state courts in discerning local public needs. For more than a century, our public use jurisprudence has wisely eschewed rigid formulas and intrusive scrutiny in favor of affording legislatures broad latitude in determining what public needs justify the use of the takings power.

IV

Those who govern the City were not confronted with the need to remove blight in the Fort Trumbull area, but their determination that the area was sufficiently distressed to justify a program of economic rejuvenation is entitled to our deference. The City has carefully formulated an economic development plan that it believes will provide appreciable benefits to the community, including—but by no means limited to—new jobs and increased tax revenue. As with other exercises in urban planning and development, the City is endeavoring to coordinate a variety of commercial, residential, and recreational uses of land, with the hope that they will form a whole greater than the sum of its parts. To effectuate this plan, the City has invoked a state statute that specifically authorizes the use of eminent domain to promote economic development. Given the comprehensive character of the plan, the thorough deliberation that preceded its adoption, and the limited scope of our review, it is appropriate for us, as it was in *Berman*, to resolve the challenges of the individual owners, not on a piecemeal basis, but rather in light of the entire plan. Because that plan unquestionably serves a public purpose, the takings challenged here satisfy the public use requirement of the Fifth Amendment.

To avoid this result, petitioners urge us to adopt a new bright-line rule that economic development does not qualify as a public use. Putting aside the unpersuasive suggestion that the City's plan will provide only purely economic benefits, neither precedent nor logic supports petitioners' proposal. Promoting economic development is a traditional and long accepted function of government. There is, moreover, no principled way of distinguishing economic development from the other public purposes that we have recognized. It would be incongruous to hold that the City's interest in the economic benefits to be derived from the development of the Fort Trumbull area has less of a public character than any of those other interests. Clearly, there is no basis for exempting economic development from our traditionally broad understanding of public purpose.

Petitioners contend that using eminent domain for economic development impermissibly blurs the boundary between public and private takings. Again, our cases foreclose this objection. Quite simply, the government's pursuit of a public purpose will often benefit individual private parties.

It is further argued that without a bright-line rule nothing would stop a city from transferring citizen *A*'s property to citizen *B* for the sole reason that citizen *B* will put the property to a more productive use and thus pay more taxes. Such a one-to-one transfer of property, executed outside the confines of an integrated development plan, is not presented in this case.

Alternatively, petitioners maintain that for takings of this kind we should require a "reasonable certainty" that the expected public benefits will actually accrue. Such a rule, however, would represent an even greater departure from our precedent.

Just as we decline to second-guess the City's considered judgments about the efficacy of its development plan, we also decline to second-guess the City's determinations as to what lands it needs to acquire in order to effectuate the project.

In affirming the City's authority to take petitioners' properties, we do not minimize the hardship that condemnations may entail, notwithstanding the payment of just compensation. We emphasize that nothing in our opinion precludes any State from placing further restrictions on its exercise of the takings power. Indeed, many States already impose "public use" requirements that are stricter than the federal baseline. Some of these requirements have been established as a matter of state constitutional law, while others are expressed in state eminent domain statutes that carefully limit the grounds upon which takings may be exercised. [T]he necessity and wisdom of using eminent domain to promote economic development are certainly matters of legitimate public debate. This Court's authority, however, extends only to determining whether the City's proposed condemnations are for a "public use" within the meaning of the Fifth Amendment to the Federal Constitution. Because over a century of our case law interpreting that provision dictates an affirmative answer to that question, we may not grant petitioners the relief that they seek.

The judgment of the Supreme Court of Connecticut is affirmed.

Justice O'Connor, with whom The Chief Justice, Justice Scalia, and Justice Thomas join, dissenting.

Over two centuries ago, just after the Bill of Rights was ratified, Justice Chase wrote: "An ACT of the Legislature (for I cannot call it a law) contrary to the great first principles of the social compact, cannot be considered a rightful exercise of legislative authority. A few instances will suffice to explain what I mean. [A] law that takes property from A. and gives it to B: It is against all reason and justice, for a people to entrust a Legislature with SUCH powers; and, therefore, it cannot be presumed that they have done it." *Calder v. Bull*, 3 Dall. 386, 388, 1 L.Ed. 648 (1798) (emphasis deleted).

Today the Court abandons this long-held, basic limitation on government power. Under the banner of economic development, all private property is now vulnerable to being taken and transferred to another private owner, so long as it might be upgraded—*i.e.*, given to an owner who will use it in a way that the legislature deems more beneficial to the public—in the process. To reason, as the Court does, that the incidental public benefits resulting from the subsequent ordinary use of private property render economic development takings "for public use" is to wash out any distinction between private and public use of property—and thereby effectively to delete the words "for public use" from the Takings Clause of the Fifth Amendment. Accordingly I respectfully dissent.

II

The Fifth Amendment to the Constitution, made applicable to the States by the Fourteenth Amendment, provides that "private property [shall not] be taken for public use, without just compensation." When interpreting the Constitution, we begin with the unremarkable presumption that every word in the document has independent meaning, "that no word was unnecessarily used, or needlessly added." In keeping with that presumption, we have read the Fifth Amendment's language to impose two distinct conditions on the exercise of eminent domain: "[T]he taking must be for a 'public use' and 'just compensation' must be paid to the owner."

These two limitations serve to protect "the security of Property," which Alexander Hamilton described to the Philadelphia Convention as one of the "great obj[ects] of Gov[ernment]." 1 Records of the Federal Convention of 1787, p. 302 (M. Farrand ed. 1911). Together they ensure stable property ownership by providing safeguards against excessive, unpredictable, or unfair use of the government's eminent domain power—particularly against those owners who, for whatever reasons, may be unable to protect themselves in the political process against the majority's will.

While the Takings Clause presupposes that government can take private property without the owner's consent, the just compensation requirement spreads the cost of condemnations and thus "prevents the public from loading upon one individual more than his just share of the burdens of government." The public use requirement, in turn, imposes a more basic limitation, circumscribing the very scope of the eminent domain power: Government may compel an individual to forfeit her property for the *public's* use, but not for the benefit of another private person. This requirement promotes fairness as well as security.

Where is the line between "public" and "private" property use? We give considerable deference to legislatures' determinations about what governmental activities will advantage the public. But were the political branches the sole arbiters of the public-private distinction, the Public Use Clause would amount to little more than hortatory fluff. An external, judicial check on how the public use requirement is interpreted, however limited, is necessary if this constraint on government power is to retain any meaning.

Our cases have generally identified three categories of takings that comply with the public use requirement, though it is in the nature of things that the boundaries between these categories are not

(Continues)

always firm. Two are relatively straightforward and uncontroversial. First, the sovereign may transfer private property to public ownership—such as for a road, a hospital, or a military base. Second, the sovereign may transfer private property to private parties, often common carriers, who make the property available for the public's use—such as with a railroad, a public utility, or a stadium. But "public ownership" and "use-by-the-public" are sometimes too constricting and impractical ways to define the scope of the Public Use Clause. Thus we have allowed that, in certain circumstances and to meet certain exigencies, takings that serve a public purpose also satisfy the Constitution even if the property is destined for subsequent private use.

This case returns us for the first time in over 20 years to the hard question of when a purportedly "public purpose" taking meets the public use requirement. It presents an issue of first impression: Are economic development takings constitutional? I would hold that they are not.

Because courts are ill equipped to evaluate the efficacy of proposed legislative initiatives, we rejected as unworkable the idea of courts' "deciding on what is and is not a governmental function and invalidating legislation on the basis of their view on that question at the moment of decision, a practice which has proved impracticable in other fields." Likewise, we recognized our inability to evaluate whether, in a given case, eminent domain is a necessary means by which to pursue the legislature's ends.

In moving away from our decisions sanctioning the condemnation of harmful property use, the Court today significantly expands the meaning of public use. It holds that the sovereign may take private property currently put to ordinary private use, and give it over for new, ordinary private use, so long as the new use is predicted to generate some secondary benefit for the public—such as increased tax revenue, more jobs, maybe even esthetic pleasure. But nearly any lawful use of real private property can be said to generate some incidental benefit to the public. Thus, if predicted (or even guaranteed) positive side-effects are enough to render transfer from one private party to another constitutional, then the words "for public use" do not realistically exclude *any* takings, and thus do not exert any constraint on the eminent domain power.

The Court protests that it does not sanction the bare transfer from A to B for B's benefit. It suggests two limitations on what can be taken after today's decision. First, it maintains a role for courts in ferreting out takings whose sole purpose is to bestow a benefit on the private transferee—without detailing how courts are to conduct that complicated inquiry. The trouble with economic development takings is that private benefit and incidental public benefit are, by definition, merged and mutually reinforcing. In this case, for example, any boon for Pfizer or the plan's developer is difficult to disaggregate from the promised public gains in taxes and jobs.

Even if there were a practical way to isolate the motives behind a given taking, the gesture toward a purpose test is theoretically flawed. If it is true that incidental public benefits from new private use are enough to ensure the "public purpose" in a taking, why should it matter, as far as the Fifth Amendment is concerned, what inspired the taking in the first place? How much the government does or does not desire to benefit a favored private party has no bearing on whether an economic development taking will or will not generate secondary benefit for the public. And whatever the reason for a given condemnation, the effect is the same from the constitutional perspective—private property is forcibly relinquished to new private ownership.

A second proposed limitation is implicit in the Court's opinion. The logic of today's decision is that eminent domain may only be used to upgrade—not downgrade—property. For who among us can say she already makes the most productive or attractive possible use of her property? The specter of condemnation hangs over all property. Nothing is to prevent the State from replacing any Motel 6 with a Ritz-Carlton, any home with a shopping mall, or any farm with a factory.

Finally, in a coda, the Court suggests that property owners should turn to the States, who may or may not choose to impose appropriate limits on economic development takings. This is an abdication of our responsibility. States play many important functions in our system of dual sovereignty, but compensating for our refusal to enforce properly the Federal Constitution (and a provision meant to curtail state action, no less) is not among them.

Any property may now be taken for the benefit of another private party, but the fallout from this decision will not be random. The beneficiaries are likely to be those citizens with disproportionate influence and power in the political process, including large corporations and development firms. As for the victims, the government now has license to transfer property from those with fewer resources to those with more. The Founders cannot have intended this perverse result. "[T]hat alone is a *just* government," wrote James Madison, "which *impartially* secures to every man, whatever is his *own*." For the National Gazette, Property, (Mar. 27, 1792), reprinted in 14 Papers of James Madison 266 (R. Rutland et al. eds. 1983).

I would hold that the takings in both Parcel 3 and Parcel 4A are unconstitutional, reverse the judgment of the Supreme Court of Connecticut, and remand for further proceedings.

Justice Thomas, dissenting.

Long ago, William Blackstone wrote that "the law of the land . . . postpone[s] even public necessity to the sacred and inviolable rights of private property." 1 Commentaries on the Laws of England 134-135 (1765) (hereinafter Blackstone). The Framers embodied that principle in the Constitution, allowing the government to take property not for "public necessity," but instead for "public use." Defying this understanding, the Court replaces the Public Use Clause with a "'[P]ublic [P]urpose'" Clause (or perhaps the "Diverse and Always Evolving Needs of Society" Clause [capitalization added]), a restriction that is satisfied, the Court instructs, so long as the purpose is "legitimate" and the means "not irrational" (internal quotation marks omitted). This deferential shift in phraseology enables the Court to hold, against all common sense, that a costly urban-renewal project whose stated purpose is a vague promise of new jobs and increased tax revenue, but which is also suspiciously agreeable to the Pfizer Corporation, is for a "public use."

I cannot agree. If such "economic development" takings are for a "public use," any taking is, and the Court has erased the Public Use Clause from our Constitution, as Justice O'Connor powerfully argues in dissent. I do not believe that this Court can eliminate liberties expressly enumerated in the Constitution and therefore join her dissenting opinion. Regrettably, however, the Court's error runs deeper than this. Today's decision is simply the latest in a string of our cases construing the Public Use Clause to be a virtual nullity, without the slightest nod to its original meaning. In my view, the Public Use Clause, originally understood, is a meaningful limit on the government's eminent domain power.

Was the U.S. Supreme Court's decision in the Kelo case just? Who did the Fifth Amendment protect in the case? Did it accomplish its intent? The constitutional law applied in the Kelo case arguably was intended to protect the government as it seeks to benefit the public, as much as it was intended to preserve individual rights. Moreover, the rights and protections involved are not absolute; the Fifth Amendment limits the manner in which private property may be taken and it limits the right of individuals to keep their property. Justice is thus a matter of perspective and not always absolute—what is justice for society may not seem just to individuals, and what is just for a single person may not be in the best interests of the larger society (if the Kelo plaintiffs had kept their property, would the potentially resulting economic loss to the community have been just?). Much of the law is like this, balancing the needs of society against the rights of the individual. As a result, decisions made in accordance with the law frequently involve consideration of both of these perspectives.

The Purpose of Courts

As noted previously here, the primary purpose of the courts is to achieve justice, but this does not occur in the abstract or in ways in which a particular judge deems most consistent with his or her views of a just society. It occurs in the context of disputes that require a decision to be made so that order is maintained in society and, win or lose, people believe that they have been treated fairly.

Characteristics of Courts

At their most basic, all courts have four characteristics (Murphy et al., 2006). First, they have an independent, unbiased judge. As is discussed throughout this book, the judge serves many functions. Central to these is to instill confidence in the courts through the formal and orderly resolution of disputes.

Second, courts apply preexisting norms in determining a just outcome. These norms, which include laws and rules of procedure, are applied in a uniform way to facts asserted to be true by the parties. They have various sources, which are discussed in Chapter 2.

Third, courts operate by using an adversarial process in which the parties have opposing positions. By relying on adversarial proceedings to administer justice, the issues for decision become clearly drawn, the individuals who argue them are given a full opportunity to present their version of the truth, and the proceeding itself necessarily produces an outcome presumed to accomplish justice.

Finally, all courts render a decision in which one party wins and another party loses. In complex cases, many such decisions may need to be made, and at times, different parties may be on the winning end of a decision. Regardless, however, each decision made results in a "winner" and a "loser."

In order to achieve its purpose, a court relies on formal rules of procedure. In civil cases, the rules of civil procedure govern who may bring a case to court, how cases must be presented to the court, what documents are allowed, how evidence may be presented, and the scope of the judge's discretion to make decisions. In criminal cases, the rules of criminal procedure govern similar aspects of a case as it proceeds through the court, but the rules also serve to protect the individual rights of criminal defendants.

Thus, courts can operate only in the context of the cases brought by litigants and can operate only in accordance with the specific rules of procedure affecting the type of case heard.

Disputes and Their Resolution

The history of humans has been a history of disagreement. For centuries, humans would fight over the right to possess things such as food or land, or they would fight to defend themselves or their honor. As English law developed in the 11th and 12th centuries, the king and his representatives served as judges to conduct "trials" in which disputes between parties were resolved in accordance with conceptions of justice at the time. These included *trial by battle*, in which the parties to the dispute were required to fight using swords or other weapons (later, duels using pistols were seen as more "civilized"); the victor was seen as having justice on his side and declared the winner of the dispute. In *trial by ordeal*, one or both parties were required to submit to a specified ordeal in order to show the truth of his position in the dispute. The ordeal might involve walking barefoot across hot metal or coals (trial by fire) or submersion in a tub of water (trial by water). If, after the ordeal, there were no signs of harm to the person, he was declared to be the winner of the dispute. Regardless of the dispute resolution method, the view was that God would protect the disputant whose position was just. Of course, sometimes both parties suffered horribly or died, effectively ending the matter.

The resolution of disputes evolved as humans became more "civilized." In England, the king appointed others to judge matters of dispute throughout the kingdom. These courts relied on rules and forms of procedure that made dispensing justice more predictable and based on rules of reason, in accordance with the will of the king, rather than chance.

In colonial America, courts were created under English law and government, although they functioned in ways to meet the needs of the new and growing country. There were few, if any, colonists trained as lawyers, and resolution of disputes was left to religious leaders or the colonial governor and his assistants. The law dispensed during this period was based on what was commonly known of the law by nonlegally trained citizens, and this largely stemmed from their knowledge of the Bible and religious precepts. This is not surprising when we consider that most of the early colonists were Puritans who had left England because of religious persecution and sought to create a new society based on their religious views.

Sidebar 1.1 *Colonial Punishment: Cruel and Unusual?*

Punishment in the American colonies before the Revolutionary War was harsh. Offenses against society were local and personal and were generally dealt with in a swift and public way. Thus, it was not uncommon for a colonist whose words were blasphemous to have his tongue bored with a hot iron or those found guilty of theft to be whipped at a post. Colonists were also subjected to such penalties as hanging, branding, being placed in stocks, and subjected to ducking stools, as well as fines, imprisonment, or banishment. Many of these forms of punishment were brought from the colonists' native land of England, and from these, the colonists adopted or devised painful, degrading, or embarrassing punishments in order to bring wrongdoers' behavior in line with expectations of colonial society, including both criminal violations and nonconformance with the religious practices and beliefs of the time.

Colonial leaders did not always succeed in making a punishment "fit" the crime. Not unlike today, monetary fines were common, used in an attempt to make a wrongdoer "compensate" for his improper behavior. Although forcing the guilty colonist to pay a certain sum in order to rectify their misdeeds was used, colonists were also allowed to use monetary payments in order to avoid physical punishment. This practice cannot be viewed as fair, nor was it impartial because wealthy males especially could avoid physical punishment, whereas a poor female or a child could be made to suffer lasting physical pain and scars for the same behavior. For example, the crime of slander, false statements that damage one's reputation, would often result in a fine. In one such occurrence, a minister and a colonist had a verbal altercation at a town meeting. The minister questioned the man's religious sincerity, and the man claimed the minister was a "stoned priest, and a Perjured man, guilty of simony and bribery . . . who spoke false latten and taught false doctrines" (Chapin, 1983, p. 133). The town council found both parties guilty and made each pay a fine, but not all colonists were so fortunate as to pay a fine for voicing their opinions.

Given the many forms of potential misconduct, few colonists could escape some form of physical punishment. In a religious-based society with established religious rules and practices, punishments were not lacking when one misspoke or behaved untowardly. In one incident in 1684, a colonist stated that there was "no God, no devil and no hell" (Merrill, 1945, p. 769). He was immediately found guilty, sentenced to pay a fine, and had his tongue bored with a hot iron. Many other colonists endured pain and suffered for violations of social norms that would now be considered minor or not even criminal. For example, Roger Scott of Salem, Massachusetts, in 1634 was charged of violating the Sabbath by "common sleeping at the public exercise upon the Lord's day, and for striking him that waked him" (Merrill, 1945, p. 772). The penalty for sleeping in church was to be whipped. Another man in Massachusetts was also whipped for hunting on the Sabbath, and yet another case demonstrating the strictness of colonial courts occurred in 1656 when Captain Kimble of Boston was "put into the stocks for two hours for his lewd and unseemly behavior . . . for publiquely kissing his wife on the doorstep of his home upon his return, on the Sabbath day, from a three-years' sea voyage" (Merrill, 1945, p. 772).

Public humiliation was a common form of punishment in colonial America. Those accused and convicted of public drunkenness, adultery, and theft, along with many other crimes, could expect to be punished in the village center for passing colonists to see. There were three popular methods of public shaming in this time: the stocks, the pillory, and the ducking post. The stocks consisted of a wooden framework in which the ankles of the unfortunate colonist would be restrained in the wooden stocks, requiring the guilty to sit immobile until the sentence time was up. Like the stocks, the pillory also was a wooden frame, but the guilty was forced to stand with his or her hands and neck restrained in the wooden frame. The ducking post was a chair to which the guilty was tied and repeatedly submerged in water. All of these forms of punishment were physically and emotionally harsh and humiliating. The colonist would have to suffer the rain, cold, or hot sun, and hunger and very commonly were pelted with rocks or rotten vegetables by passersby.

As painful and embarrassing as public shaming may have been, it was a relatively mild form of punishment imposed during colonial times. Torture and hanging were used to punish what were considered to be the most serious offenses. For example, the infamous Salem witch trials resulted in the execution by hanging of 19 colonists (mostly women) on being found guilty of practicing witchcraft. One woman accused was Bridget Bishop. In 1692, she was tried based on the accusations of several neighbors who claimed that on several occasions she summoned "demons" to haunt them. The judge found her guilty, and she was executed by hanging at Gallows Hill (Hawke, 1966, pp. 243–245).

By today's standards, punishment in colonial America was unusual and almost always cruel. The constitutional protections we enjoy today did not exist, and local leaders were allowed to devise such punishments as they saw fit to maintain conformity in colonial society. By adopting procedural protections for the accused, separating religious offenses from societal ones, punishing behavior and not beliefs, and focusing on the harm that results from one's act, the American courts have placed punishment of offenders within a system in which the goal is not punishment itself, but justice for victims, offenders, and society itself.

The colonial period in America saw an increase in the number of courts as the colonists settled on land, established trade and commerce, and formed communities with their attendant institutions for maintaining order such as churches, schools, and local governing bodies. Such activities and interactions among colonists led to disagreements that required resolution to keep the peace. These may have involved criminal wrongdoing such as theft, vagrancy, or failure to attend church services; land disputes about the ownership or right to farm sections of land; or "contract" disputes regarding the delivery or quality of goods bartered or sold. The governor served as judge to resolve such disputes, holding "court" a few times a year to hear cases. The governor thus served many functions, usually as religious leader, chief executive, legislator, and judge. As obvious as the separation of powers seems to us today, in colonial times in America, it was accepted that governmental functions would be handled by a small number of community leaders; that, after all, was the way it had been in England. Only after the American Revolution and the adoption of our Constitutional form of government did this begin to change.

As the country grew and moved toward independence from England, cities developed, and the number of cases involving antisocial activity or private disputes rose, requiring governors to appoint judges to travel around the countryside ("ride the circuit") to hear the variety of cases that arose. In rural communities, justices of the peace were appointed to serve the interests of the community and decide lesser matters. Although the justice of the peace has traditionally been seen as a minor judicial role, it was a dispute regarding a justice of the peace that led to the case having the greatest impact on the court system in America, *Marbury v. Madison*, 1 Cranch 137, 5 U.S. 137, 2 L.Ed. 60 (1803).

Marbury v. Madison

In 1800, national politics was as acrimonious as it is today. John Adams was the second President of the United States and sought re-election to a second term in that year. His opponent was Thomas Jefferson. (The two men were contemptuous of each other at the time, although they reconciled in later years and became fast friends.) In the election, Adams was soundly defeated, as were his Federalist colleagues in Congress; however, Adams and his Federalist Congress remained in office as "lame ducks" until March 1, 1801, giving them time to take a number of end-of-term actions impacting the future government. Among these was passage of the Organic Act, authorizing the President to appoint a large number of additional federal judges, as well as 42 additional justices of the peace for the District of Columbia.

In addition, President Adams himself made a number of decisions. First among these was appointment of his Secretary of State, John Marshall, as Chief Justice of the U.S. Supreme Court; however, Marshall would remain as Secretary of State and not begin his service as Chief Justice until the end of Adams's term.

In addition, President Adams was busy appointing new judges. After appointing a judge to office, the President would deliver a commission to his Secretary of State, John Marshall, for delivery to the new appointee. Although most of these were delivered, in the concluding days of the Adams administration and John Marshall's time as Secretary of State, a few commissions were left on the Secretary of State's desk and remained undelivered. Among these was one for an appointee to a justice of the peace position, William Marbury.

After taking office in March of 1801, President Jefferson discovered these commissions and ordered his new Secretary of State, James Madison, to not deliver them, effectively preventing Adams's appointments. Not receiving his appointment, Marbury sued, petitioning the U.S. Supreme Court to issue a writ of mandamus directing Secretary of State Madison to give him his commission. A writ of mandamus is a court order that requires a public official to perform some act which the official's public office requires be performed. Although the Court could have dismissed the petition for want of jurisdiction, it did not, giving Marshall the opportunity to craft what has become one of the most important judicial opinions in history (**Case Decision 1.3**).

Case Decision 1.3   *Marbury v. Madison*, 1 Cranch 137, 5 U.S. 137, 1803 WL 893 (D.C.), 2 L.Ed. 60 (1803)

Opinion of the Court by Chief Justice Marshall:

At the last term on the affidavits then read and filed with the clerk, a rule was granted in this case, requiring the secretary of state to shew cause why a mandamus should not issue, directing him to deliver to William Marbury his commission as a justice of the peace for the county of Washington, in the District of Columbia.

His right originates in an act of congress passed in February 1801, concerning the district of Columbia. After dividing the district into two counties, the 11th section of this law, enacts, "that there shall be appointed in and for each of the said counties, such number of discreet persons to be justices of the peace as the president of the United States shall, from time to time, think expedient, to continue in office for five years."

It appears, from the affidavits, that in compliance with this law, a commission for William Marbury as a justice of peace for the county of Washington, was signed by John Adams, then president of the United States; after which the seal of the United States was affixed to it; but the commission has never reached the person for whom it was made out. In order to determine whether he is entitled to this commission, it becomes necessary to inquire whether he has been appointed to the office. For if he has been appointed, the law continues him in office for five years, and he is entitled to the possession of those evidences of office, which, being completed, became his property.

The 2d section of the 2d article of the constitution declares, that, "the president shall nominate, and, by and with the advice and consent of the senate, shall appoint ambassadors, other public ministers and consuls, and all other officers of the United States, whose appointments are not otherwise provided for." The third section declares, that "he shall commission all the officers of the United States."

An act of congress directs the secretary of state to keep the seal of the United States, "to make out and record, and affix the said seal to all civil commissions to officers of the United States, to be appointed by the President, by and with the consent of the senate, or by the President alone; provided that the said seal shall not be affixed to any commission before the same shall have been signed by the President of the United States."

It is therefore decidedly the opinion of the court, that when a commission has been signed by the President, the appointment is made; and that the commission is complete, when the seal of the United States has been affixed to it by the secretary of state.

Mr. Marbury, then, since his commission was signed by the President, and sealed by the secretary of state, was appointed; and as the law creating the office, gave the officer a right to hold for five years, independent of the executive, the appointment was not revocable; but vested in the officer legal rights, which are protected by the laws of this country. To withhold his commission, therefore, is an act deemed by the court not warranted by law, but violative of a vested legal right.

The government of the United States has been emphatically termed a government of laws, and not of men. It will certainly cease to deserve this high appellation, if the laws furnish no remedy for the violation of a vested legal right. If this obloquy is to be cast on the jurisprudence of our country, it must arise from the peculiar character of the case.

The act to establish the judicial courts of the United States authorizes the Supreme Court "to issue writs of mandamus, in cases warranted by the principles and usages of law, to any courts appointed, or persons holding office, under the authority of the United States." The secretary of state, being a person holding an office under the authority of the United States, is precisely within the letter of the description; and if this court is not authorized to issue a writ of mandamus to such an officer, it must be because the law is unconstitutional, and therefore absolutely incapable of conferring the authority, and assigning the duties which its words purport to confer and assign.

The constitution vests the whole judicial power of the United States in one Supreme Court, and such inferior courts as congress shall, from time to time, ordain and establish. This power is expressly extended to all cases arising under the laws of the United States; and consequently, in some form, may be exercised over the present case; because the right claimed is given by a law of the United States. In the distribution of this power it is declared that "the supreme court shall have original jurisdiction in all cases affecting ambassadors, other public ministers and consuls, and those in which a state shall be a party. In all other cases, the supreme court shall have appellate jurisdiction."

It has been insisted, at the bar, that as the original grant of jurisdiction, to the supreme and inferior courts, is general, and the clause, assigning original jurisdiction to the supreme court, contains no negative or restrictive words; the power remains to the legislature, to assign original jurisdiction to that court in other cases than those specified in the article which has been recited; provided those cases belong to the judicial power of the United States. If it had been intended to leave it in the discretion of the legislature to apportion the judicial power between the supreme and inferior courts according to the will of that body, it would certainly have been useless to have proceeded further than to have defined the judicial power, and the tribunals in which it should be vested. The subsequent part of the section is mere surplusage, is entirely without meaning, if such is to be the construction. If congress remains at liberty to give this court appellate jurisdiction, where the constitution has declared their jurisdiction shall be original; and original jurisdiction where the constitution has declared it shall be appellate; the distribution of jurisdiction, made in the constitution, is form without substance.

Affirmative words are often, in their operation, negative of other objects than those affirmed; and in this case, a negative or exclusive sense must be given to them or they have no operation at all. It cannot be presumed that any clause in the constitution is intended to be without effect; and therefore such a construction is inadmissible, unless the words require it.

When an instrument organizing fundamentally a judicial system, divides it into one supreme, and so many inferior courts as the legislature may ordain and establish; then enumerates its powers, and proceeds so far to distribute them, as to define the jurisdiction of the supreme court by declaring the cases in which it shall take original jurisdiction, and that in others it shall take appellate jurisdiction; the plain import of the words seems to be, that in one class of cases its jurisdiction is original, and not appellate; in the other it is appellate, and not original. If any other construction would render the clause inoperative, that is an additional reason for rejecting such other construction, and for adhering to their obvious meaning.

To enable this court then to issue a mandamus, it must be shewn to be an exercise of appellate jurisdiction, or to be necessary to enable them to exercise appellate jurisdiction. It has been stated at the bar that the appellate jurisdiction may be exercised in a variety of forms, and that if it be the will of the legislature that a mandamus should be used for that purpose, that will must be obeyed. This is true, yet the jurisdiction must be appellate, not original. It is the essential criterion of appellate jurisdiction, that it revises and corrects the proceedings in a cause already instituted, and does not create that cause. Although, therefore, a mandamus may be directed to courts, yet to issue such a writ to an officer for the delivery of a paper, is in effect the same as to sustain an original action for that paper, and therefore seems not to belong to appellate, but to original jurisdiction. Neither is it necessary in such a case as this to enable the court to exercise its appellate jurisdiction. The authority, therefore, given to the supreme court, by the act establishing the judicial courts of the United States, to issue writs of mandamus to public officers, appears not to be warranted by the constitution; and it becomes necessary to inquire whether a jurisdiction, so conferred, can be exercised.

The question, whether an act, repugnant to the constitution, can become the law of the land, is a question deeply interesting to the United States; but, happily, not of an intricacy proportioned to its interest. It seems only necessary to recognize certain principles, supposed to have been long and well established, to decide it.

That the people have an original right to establish, for their future government, such principles as, in their opinion, shall most conduce to their own happiness, is the basis, on which the whole American fabric has been erected. The exercise of this original right is a very great exertion; nor can it, nor ought it to be frequently repeated. The principles, therefore, so established, are deemed fundamental. And as the authority, from which they proceed, is supreme, and can seldom act, they are designed to be permanent. This original and supreme will organizes the government, and assigns, to

(Continues)

different departments, their respective powers. It may either stop here; or establish certain limits not to be transcended by those departments.

The government of the United States is of the latter description. The powers of the legislature are defined, and limited; and that those limits may not be mistaken, or forgotten, the constitution is written. To what purpose are powers limited, and to what purpose is that limitation committed to writing, if these limits may, at any time, be passed by those intended to be restrained? The distinction, between a government with limited and unlimited powers, is abolished, if those limits do not confine the persons on whom they are imposed, and if acts prohibited and acts allowed, are of equal obligation. It is a proposition too plain to be contested, that the constitution controls any legislative act repugnant to it; or, that the legislature may alter the constitution by an ordinary act.

Between these alternatives there is no middle ground. The constitution is either a superior, paramount law, unchangeable by ordinary means, or it is on a level with ordinary legislative acts, and like other acts, is alterable when the legislature shall please to alter it. If the former part of the alternative be true, then a legislative act contrary to the constitution is not law: if the latter part be true, then written constitutions are absurd attempts, on the part of the people, to limit a power, in its own nature illimitable.

Certainly all those who have framed written constitutions contemplate them as forming the fundamental and paramount law of the nation, and consequently the theory of every such government must be, that an act of the legislature, repugnant to the constitution, is void. This theory is essentially attached to a written constitution, and is consequently to be considered, by this court, as one of the fundamental principles of our society. It is not therefore to be lost sight of in the further consideration of this subject.

If an act of the legislature, repugnant to the constitution, is void, does it, notwithstanding its invalidity, bind the courts, and oblige them to give it effect? Or, in other words, though it be not law, does it constitute a rule as operative as if it was a law? This would be to overthrow in fact what was established in theory; and would seem, at first view, an absurdity too gross to be insisted on. It shall, however, receive a more attentive consideration.

It is emphatically the province and duty of the judicial department to say what the law is. Those who apply the rule to particular cases must of necessity expound and interpret that rule. If two laws conflict with each other, the courts must decide on the operation of each. So if a law be in opposition to the constitution; if both the law and the constitution apply to a particular case, so that the court must either decide that case conformably to the law, disregarding the constitution; or conformably to the constitution, disregarding the law; the court must determine which of these conflicting rules governs the case. This is of the very essence of judicial duty.

If then the courts are to regard the constitution; and the constitution is superior to any ordinary act of the legislature; the constitution, and not such ordinary act, must govern the case to which they both apply. Those then who controvert the principle that the constitution is to be considered, in court, as a paramount law, are reduced to the necessity of maintaining that courts must close their eyes on the constitution, and see only the law.

This doctrine would subvert the very foundation of all written constitutions. It would declare that an act, which, according to the principles and theory of our government, is entirely void; is yet, in practice, completely obligatory. It would declare, that if the legislature shall do what is expressly forbidden, such act, notwithstanding the express prohibition, is in reality effectual. It would be giving to the legislature a practical and real omnipotence, with the same breath which professes to restrict their powers within narrow limits. It is prescribing limits, and declaring that those limits may be passed as pleasure.

That it thus reduces to nothing what we have deemed the greatest improvement on political institutions—a written constitution—would of itself be sufficient, in America, where written constitutions have been viewed with so much reverence, for rejecting the construction. But the peculiar expressions of the constitution of the United States furnish additional arguments in favour of its rejection.

The judicial power of the United States is extended to all cases arising under the constitution. Could it be the intention of those who gave this power, to say that, in using it, the constitution should not be looked into? That a case arising under the constitution should be decided without examining the instrument under which it arises? This is too extravagant to be maintained. In some cases then, the constitution must be looked into by the judges. And if they can open it at all, what part of it are they forbidden to read, or to obey?

There are many other parts of the constitution which serve to illustrate this subject. It is declared that "no tax or duty shall be laid on articles exported from any state." Suppose a duty on the export of cotton, of tobacco, or of flour; and a suit instituted to recover it. Ought judgment to be rendered in such a case? Ought the judges to close their eyes on the constitution, and only see the law.

The constitution declares that "no bill of attainder or *ex post facto* law shall be passed." If, however, such a bill should be passed and a person should be prosecuted under it; must the court condemn to death those victims whom the constitution endeavors to preserve? "No person," says the constitution, "shall be convicted of treason unless on the testimony of two witnesses to the same overt act, or on confession in open court." Here the language of the constitution is addressed especially to the courts. It prescribes, directly for them, a rule of evidence not to be departed from. If the legislature should change that rule, and declare *one* witness, or a confession *out of* court, sufficient for conviction, must the constitutional principle yield to the legislative act?

From these, and many other selections which might be made, it is apparent, that the framers of the constitution contemplated that instrument, as a rule for the government of *courts*, as well as of the legislature. Why otherwise does it direct the judges to take an oath to support it? This oath certainly applies, in an especial manner, to their conduct in their official character. How immoral to impose it on them, if they were to be used as the instruments, and the knowing instruments, for violating what they swear to support? The oath of office, too, imposed by the legislature, is completely demonstrative of the legislative opinion on this subject. It is in these words, "I do solemnly swear that I will administer justice without respect to persons, and do equal right to the poor and to the rich; and that I will faithfully and impartially discharge all the duties incumbent on me as according to the best of my abilities and understanding, agreeably to *the constitution*, and laws of the United States."

Why does a judge swear to discharge his duties agreeably to the constitution of the United States, if that constitution forms no rule for his government? If it is closed upon him, and cannot be inspected by him? If such be the real state of things, this is worse than solemn mockery. To prescribe, or to take this oath, becomes equally a crime.

It is also not entirely unworthy of observation, that in declaring what shall be the *supreme* law of the land, the *constitution* itself is first mentioned; and not the laws of the United States generally, but those only which shall be made in *pursuance* of the constitution, have that rank. Thus, the particular phraseology of the constitution of the United States confirms and strengthens the principle, supposed to be essential to all written constitutions, that a law repugnant to the constitution is void; and that *courts*, as well as other departments, are bound by that instrument.

The rule must be discharged.

Apart from the political undertones and historical backdrop of the opinion, *Marbury v. Madison* teaches a number of important lessons. First, *Marbury* created the rule that it is the job of the courts to "say what the law is." This is the heart of the principle of *judicial review*. Judicial review means that the judicial branch of government has the power to examine and determine whether acts taken by the legislative and executive branches comply with the Constitution. Furthermore, this principle therefore necessarily precludes the other branches of government from exercising this power.

Second, the decision reaffirmed that the Constitution was the Supreme law of the land and that neither the executive nor the judicial branch could act outside of or in contrast to its provisions.

Third, *Marbury* announced that the authority of the Supreme Court, like that of the other two branches of government, is found in the Constitution itself. Therefore, the Supreme Court's original jurisdiction cannot be restricted by act of Congress or Executive decree (however, it is worth noting that the Constitution authorizes Congress to determine the Court's *appellate* jurisdiction; this distinction is discussed further in Chapter 3).

A Note on Reading Cases

Courts make decisions that, in most appellate cases and some trials, are written and published. This book discusses numerous case decisions and, as noted in the preface, has included many excerpts from actual case decisions written by judges. These are found in the "Case Decision" boxes throughout the book. The first three such excerpts, *Cuellar v. U.S.*, *Kelo v. City of New London*, and *Marbury v. Madison*, were discussed earlier in this chapter. As you read the cases excerpts, however, it will be helpful to do so with a particular structure or outline of the case in your mind. Understanding this structure will be of great assistance in understanding the decisions themselves and the principles of law and legal procedure they represent. Nearly every written court decision follows this structure, and grasping the court's reasoning will be easier if you understand the way in which case decisions are drafted.

Legal "cases" are real-life stories; like all good stories, they have a beginning, a middle, and an end. They involve people who did something, and their actions created some conflict between the parties. The court process involved hearing what happened, sorting out what was important and what was not, and reaching a decision in order to resolve the conflict. The written decision reflects this process, although it is not always a chronological rendering, but reading the story and learning how a resolution about the conflict was reached are necessary to understanding the point of law a case represents. Reading cases in this way may assist you in retelling them and importantly in learning what the legal point of the story was.

The "opinion of the court" means that a majority of the judges sitting on the court hearing the case agreed as to what the conclusion should be. Normally, one of these is assigned to write the court's opinion, but it represents the opinions of all of those judges who voted in the majority for the outcome reached. At times, less than a majority of the judges will agree as to the outcome. In such cases, a written decision will still be produced by one judge, but it will represent the views of a *plurality*, rather than a majority of the court members. In such cases, a majority of the judges do not agree on the holding, the rationale, or both, and opinions by more than a single judge will be written.

Case decisions can be divided into six parts. The first two are the beginning. The second two are the middle, and the last two are the end of the story. First, every case will have a caption that is a heading that states who the parties are and the court making the decision. Second, the case decision will set out the facts that form the basis of the decision. This includes both the substantive facts regarding the dispute between the parties as well as the procedural facts regarding how the parties proceeded in attempting to resolve the dispute. Third, the legal issue or issues that the court has been called on to decide will be stated, including the sources of law that the court relies on in reaching its decision. Fourth, the court's rationale or reasons for its decision are explained. This is a detailed explanation of how the court reached its conclusion, including consideration of the facts and the requirements of the law applicable to each legal issue the case presents. Fifth, the written opinion will reach a conclusion on the legal issues and if it is an appellate decision either affirm or reverse the decision of the prior court, sometimes with instructions regarding how the case should next proceed. Finally, some cases will include additional opinions drafted by other judges on a panel of judges considering a case. These are known as concurring opinions and dissenting opinions and represent additional reasoning to support the agreement or disagreement of one or more of the judges with the majority opinion.

Caption

As the title of the case, the caption names the parties involved in the dispute. The titles in the edited case decision boxes are usually abbreviated; therefore, not all par-ties will be named in the caption in every case. By using the case citation to the law reporter in which the case is found, it is possible to view the complete caption, listing all of the parties. The caption will also show the court from which the decision was issued and the year in which it was decided. It is important to note this information in order to understand the scope of influence the court's decision may have (e.g., a U.S. Supreme Court decision will have broader applicability than a state supreme court's decision) and to understand the historical context in which the dispute arose and the decision was made.

Facts

There are two categories of facts: those that describe the actions of the parties leading to the dispute and those reflecting the procedures followed in attempting to resolve the dispute. Not all facts about the actions of the parties are important; some are relevant to the court's decision, and some are irrelevant. For example, in a contract case, knowing the ages of the parties is likely irrelevant, but in an age discrimination case, it is clearly relevant. In reading the case, therefore, it is necessary to determine which of the reported facts form the necessary basis for the court's conclusions about the law. That is, which facts, if omitted, would change the court's conclusions or are those without which the court could not reach a conclusion?

The procedural facts describe how the case proceeded to and through the courts, leading to the decision being read. Thus, this portion of the case should explain who initially filed the court action (and perhaps steps taken to resolve the matter before going to court), the court in which it was filed, the lower court's decision and the basis for it, who brought the appeal, and the grounds for appeal.

Issue

The issue in a case is the question of law that one or both parties have brought to the court to be answered. Although the issue is a question of law, it always relates to the facts, which is why it is necessary to know which facts are relevant. Courts do not answer questions in the abstract; it is only in the context of the facts of the case that the issue will be addressed. Thus, a legal issue in the Kelo case may be posed, "Does the Takings Clause allow the City of New London to transfer homeowners' property to a private entity for economic development purposes?" Some cases have only one issue; others have several. How the legal issues are stated by the court will indicate how narrowly or broadly the court's statement of the law will apply in other similar cases.

Holding

The holding is the court's *ratio decidendi*, which from the Latin means the "reason for deciding" (Garner, 2004). It is not a full explanation of the basis for the court's decision (see rationale, later here). Rather, it encapsulates the legal principle on which the case was decided and reflects the essence of the court's interpretation of the law. Thus, the holding answers the legal issue presented by the case, based on the court's application of the governing principles of law to the facts. For example, the primary holding in the Kelo case can be stated: The taking of property by a city to be used by private businesses for economic development constitutes a "public use" under the Takings Clause of the U.S. Constitution. Because the holding relates to the legal issue, each case will have as many holdings as there are issues.

Rationale

The rationale is the court's reasoning in support of its decision. This is the section of the case decision in which the court explains itself, giving the reasons why it decided the case in the way that it did. Because, in each case, a court is called on by the parties to resolve a dispute about the facts, the law, or both, the rationale will typically include a discussion of these for each of the legal issues presented. Although the issue and the holding will identify each specific provision of law at issue, whether a statute, regulation, constitutional section, or matter of common law, the rationale will examine each provision of law and explain what it means and how it leads to the holding in the case. The court's interpretation and discussion of the law may involve consideration of the history of the law being interpreted, other cases in which it was at issue, the opinions of expert commentators on a topic, the views of special interests, or other laws that may have some bearing on the case. Thus, the court's rationale is an elaboration of its *ratio decidendi*. At times, a judge who drafts a case decision will also discuss some tangential matter not necessary to the holding, referred to as *orbiter dicta*, which from Latin means "a remark by the way" (Garner, 2004). *Orbiter dicta*, or "dicta" for short, may be difficult to separate from the discussion of the court that is necessary for the holding. A good example of this is Chief Justice Marshall's opinion in *Marbury v. Madison*, even in the excerpted form found in Case Decision 1.3. Recall that the parties asked the Court to decide whether Marbury was entitled to his commission as justice of the peace but that Marshall discussed much that was not necessary to decide this issue. Indeed, *Marbury v. Madison* has become best known for the legal propositions found in Marshall's dicta, rather than in his rationale in the case (Abraham, 1998). For most of the case decisions excerpted in this book, however, the dictum is excluded in order to focus on the *ratio decidendi* and its basis.

Other Opinions

Written case decisions from appellate courts, especially the U.S. Supreme Court, may also include other opinions written by another judge sitting on the panel of judges hearing the case. A *concurring opinion* is one in which one or more judges agree with the holding of the majority, but for different or additional reasons. Although a concurring opinion is in agreement with the holding of the case, it does not represent the opinion of a majority of the court, only those judges who join in it. A *dissenting* opinion is one written by a judge who does not agree with either the holding or the rationale of the majority. The dissent is written to express the opinion of the judge writing it, as well as any other judges who agree. It is quite possible, therefore, that a court opinion may have several concurring and dissenting opinions, in addition to the opinion of the court.

Key Terms

Corrective Justice	Judicial Activism
Distributive Justice	Dispute Resolution
Social Justice	Judicial Review
Economic Justice	Court Characteristics
Retributive Justice	Rules of Procedure
Restorative Justice	*Ratio Decidendi*
Procedural Justice	*Orbiter Dicta*

Discussion Questions

1. American courts are given the task of achieving justice for citizens. What are the primary ways in which they seek to accomplish this?
2. How does the distinction between corrective and distributive justice affect the criminal and civil law?
3. In what ways do various types of justice, such as social, retributive, restorative, and procedural, affect society's approach to resolving disputes?
4. What are the four characteristics all courts share? Explain why they are important.
5. Courts rely on formal rules of procedure to achieve their goals, but why are those rules important for the parties in both criminal and civil cases?
6. Discuss the procedures used in two of the earliest forms of dispute resolution: trial by battle and trial by ordeal.
7. Written case decisions issued by courts typically include facts, issue, holding, and rationale. Explain the purpose of each of these and why they are necessary to a court's decision.

Cases

Boumediene v. Bush, 128 S. Ct. 2229 (2008).
Cuellar v. U.S., 128 S. Ct. 1994, 1998 (2008).
Kelo v. City of New London, 545 U.S. 469, 125 S. Ct. 2655, 162 L.Ed.2d 439 (2005).
Lochner v. New York, 198 U.S. 45, 25 S. Ct. 539, 49 L.Ed. 937 (1905).
Marbury v. Madison, 1 Cranch 137, 5 U.S. 137, 2 L.Ed. 60 (1803).

Criminal Justice on the Web

 For an up-to-date list of Web links, go to *The American Courts: A Procedural Approach* online companion site at http://criminaljustice.jbpub.com/AmericanCourts. The online companion site will introduce you to some of the most important sites for finding American courts information on the Internet.

References

Abraham, H. J. (1998). *The Judicial Process* (7th ed.). New York: Oxford University Press.
Aldridge, M. (2008, March 4). Duke lacrosse: After the rape scandal. *The Philadelphia Inquirer*, A1.

Arrigo, B. (Ed.). (1999). *Social Justice/Criminal Justice: The Maturation of Critical Theory in Law, Crime, and Deviance.* Belmont, CA: Wadsworth.

Buchanan, A., & Mathieu, D. (1986). Philosophy and justice. In R. L. Cohen (Ed.). *Justice: Views from the Social Sciences.* New York: Plenum.

Chapin, B. (1983). *Criminal Justice in Colonial America, 1606–1660.* Athens, GA: University of Georgia Press.

Douglass, R. B. (1978). Is distributive justice the new name for peace? *World Affairs, 141*(2), 153.

Feinberg, J. (1987). *The Moral Limits of the Criminal Law.* New York: Oxford University Press.

Fletcher, G. (1999). The place of the victim in the theory of retribution. *Buffalo Criminal Law Review, 3,* 51–64.

Garner, B. A. (Ed.). (2004). *Black's Law Dictionary* (8th ed.). St. Paul, MN: West Group.

Hawke, D. (1966). *U.S. Colonial History: Readings and Documents.* Indianapolis, IN: Bobbs-Merrill.

Hegtvedt, K. A., & Markovsky, B. (1995). Justice and injustice. In K. Cook, G. Fine, & J. House (Eds.). *Sociological Perspectives on Social Psychology.* Boston: Allyn & Bacon.

Husak, D. N. (2000). Retribution in criminal theory. *San Diego Law Review, 37,* 959–986.

Johnson, K., & Parker, L. (2007, June 8). Hilton revolving door: Out of jail, into court. *USA Today, News,* p. 2a.

Martin, E. A., & Law, J. (Eds.). (2009). *Oxford Dictionary of Law.* New York: Oxford University Press. Retrieved September 15, 2009, from http://www.oxfordreference.com.

Merrill, L. T. (1945). The Puritan policeman. *American Sociological Review, 10*(6), 766–776.

Moore, M. S. (1997). *Placing Blame: A General Theory of the Criminal Law.* Oxford: Clarendon Press.

Moore, M. S. (1999). Victims and retribution. *Buffalo Criminal Law Review, 3,* 101–125.

Murphy, J. (1990). Getting even: The role of the victim. *Social Philosophy and Policy, 7,* 209–225.

Murphy, W. F., Pritchett, C. H., Epstein, L., & Knight, J. (2006). *Courts, Judges, & Politics: An Introduction to the Judicial Process* (6th ed.). New York: McGraw-Hill.

Pickett, J. P., et al. (Eds.). (2000). *American Heritage Dictionary of the English Language* (4th ed.). Boston: Houghton Mifflin.

Rawls, J. (1971). *A Theory of Justice.* Cambridge, MA: Harvard University Press.

Rawls, J. (2001). *Justice as Fairness.* Cambridge, MA: Harvard University Press.

Robinson, M. B. (2002). *Justice Blind? Ideals and Realities of American Criminal Justice.* Upper Saddle River, NJ: Prentice Hall/Pearson.

Skitka, L. J., & Crosby, F. J. (2003). Trends in the social psychological study of justice. *Personality and Social Psychology Review, 7,* 282–285.

Strickland, R. A. (2004). *Restorative Justice.* New York: Peter Lang Publishers.

Tomasi, J. O. (2002). Justice. In K. L. Hall (Ed.), *The Oxford Companion to American Law.* New York: Oxford University Press.

Tyler, T. R. (1990). *Why People Obey the Law.* New Haven, CT: Yale University Press.

Tyler, T. R., & Blader, S. L. (2000). *Cooperation in Groups.* Philadelphia: Psychology Press.

Tyler, T. R., & Smith, H. J. (1997). Social justice and social movements. In D. Gilbert, S. Fiske, & G. Lindzey (Eds.), *Handbook of Social Psychology* (4th ed.). New York: Addison-Wesley.

Waxman, S. (2007, June 8). Paris Hilton out of jail, into a gilded cage. *The New York Times, Arts Briefly,* p. 5.

Wendorf, C. A., Alexander, S., & Firestone, I. J. (2002). Social justice and moral reasoning: An empirical integration of two paradigms in psychological research. *Social Justice Research, 15*(1), 19–39.

Wenzel, M., Okimoto, T. G., Feather, N. T., & Platow, M. J. (2008). Retributive and restorative justice. *Law and Human Behavior, 32,* 375–389.

Wilson, D. (2007, June 16). Facing sanction, Duke prosecutor says he'll resign. *The New York Times,* A1.

The Law in Society 2

What Is This Chapter About?

This chapter discusses the concept of law and the role it plays in American society. We first consider what it means to be governed by the rule of law, which creates an expectation that citizens and institutions in a society choose to live and function "under law." That is, they accept the law as governing agent and agree to act in accordance with it. From this discussion, the need for the rule of law in a democratic society will become evident.

Next, we explore the distinction between criminal and civil law and the purpose of each. As the two primary branches of the law, each serves a common goal of bringing order to society. Criminal law does this by defining antisocial behavior and prescribing punishment for it. Civil law maintains order by governing relationships and resolving disputes among individuals in the various spheres of life (and death), such as ownership of property, business matters, family concerns, and other interactions between individuals.

Finally, in this chapter, we study the sources of American law. The law takes a variety of forms, including case law, statutes, constitutions, and regulations. We examine each of these in detail and discuss where and how they are used. We also place these in the historical context of the "common law," which is the body of written and unwritten judge-made law that permeates and lends its weight to the criminal and civil law today.

Learning Objectives

After reading this chapter, you should be able to

1. Understand the concept of law and its relationship to justice.
2. Understand what is meant by the "rule of law" and its role in democracy.
3. Distinguish between criminal and civil law.
4. Identify the sources of American law and the function of each.
5. Describe the common law tradition and its effect on decision making by the courts.

The Concept of Law

Law in America is pervasive. People in this country are more aware of law, its operation, and its effects than at any other time and possibly any other place (Sarat, 1990; Sherwin, 2004). The proliferation and influence of news media, movies, and "reality" television have certainly contributed to people's understanding (and misunderstanding) of the role, function, and meaning of law. The law has become visual, dramatic, sensational, and public. In the minds of people, it represents power, money, intervention, safety, relief, happiness, sorrow—the range of human emotions, travails, and resolutions that make for good stories. As Richard Sherwin has said, "There is a two-way traffic between law and popular culture" (Sherwin, 2004, p. 95). For all its raised profile, seeming ubiquitous nature, and entertainment value, what does the concept of law mean to those for whom it seems so real?

What is law? Philosophers and legal scholars have debated the meaning of law for centuries, but its definition is elusive (Zane, 1998). Saint Thomas Aquinas defined law as "a rational standard for conduct" (Murphy, 2005). The U.S. Supreme Court has stated that law, generally speaking, is "the rules of action or conduct duly prescribed by controlling authority, and having binding legal force" (*U.S. Fidelity and Guaranty Co. v. Guenther*, 281 U.S. 34, 50 S. Ct. 165, 74 L.Ed. 683 (1930)) or "a statement of the circumstances in which the public force will be brought to bear upon men through the courts" (*American Banana Co. v. United Fruit Co.*, 213 U.S. 347 (1909)). David Kairys has claimed "law is politics" (Kairys, 1982). Part of the difficulty may be the changing nature of law; as a society in which law operates changes, so too does its laws (Raz, 2005). American society has changed significantly since its founding in 1776 and before; it has changed, developed, and evolved in terms of its government, politics, morals, religion, economics, education, social and personal relationships, population, resources, technologies, and many other ways. All of these have contributed to a definition of law that has grown and changed over time. A central implication of understanding the meaning of law is that it affects the way in which judges and policy makers interpret the law, the discretion they have in applying it, and the decisions they make using it (Finnis, 2003).

Law is commonly equated with rules, but to define "law" as "the rules" is not particularly helpful either. Indeed, it may be that to ask the meaning of "law" is itself not particularly helpful (Posner, 1987). This is because law and its meaning are important only insofar as they serve human functions; it is in the service of these many functions that the law is defined. Regardless of its specific definition, law exists and operates only within the society which creates it (Zane, 1998). Law has meaning because it helps to define relationships between and among people; the hermit living alone in the woods has no need of law. It is when people gather together, live in communities, and interact with each other that law becomes an important concept and tool that assists the community and its members in their dealings with each other and helps it continue to exist.

Law is not the only mechanism for assisting people living together in societies, however. For much of human history, reliance on law stemming from a governing authority was not paramount as a method of dispute resolution (Glenn, 2003). Custom, or norms, and religious doctrine played a greater role in the ways in which people conducted themselves and their affairs and resolved their disputes. Religious beliefs and social norms also serve to assist people in defining and governing their relationships. Both of these informal ways of governing behavior in society have a moral basis. That is, they help to define a society's view of what is right and what is wrong.

Like law, one of the functions of religion is to help people live fulfilling lives, including acceptable ways of dealing with others. Religious teachings and practices serve an important function in any society, helping people to think about themselves, their roles, and their relationship to others; however, although various religions have "laws" that become central to religious doctrine (e.g., think of the importance of the Ten Commandments in the Catholic, Protestant, and Jewish faiths), religions largely operate according to principles of voluntariness and belief. They are mostly noncoercive in practice. In American society, where religion and government are kept separate and where virtually all religious beliefs are tolerated, religion has an important place as an informal method of defining social relations.

Apart from religious influence, social "norms" also provide a means of creating an orderly society. Social norms are shared beliefs about how people should think and act in all facets of life, held in common by members of society. Although they may be related to or stem from religious views, they operate independent of them. Norms represent an informal agreement among people in a community about what behavior is acceptable or unacceptable. They may be relatively simple, such as how one should conduct oneself at the dinner table, or somewhat more complex, such as the expectations one should have when dating. Thus, norms reflect the views of most members of society regarding what is in the best interests of most members of that society. Norms may, but need not, come to be revealed in the laws adopted by a social community.

Conceptually, then, the law is distinguishable from other methods used by society to define how people should think or act. Although the law may be related to or have its basis in religious beliefs or social norms, it differs from those other governance mechanisms in at least two important ways. The first is its focus on human behavior. The law is behavior driven. Regardless of the type or function of law, it defines action, not thought, and seeks to maintain relationships among people by specifying the "what" and "how" of behaviors by humans in their societal groups.

Second, it operates in fairly formal ways. It is the level of formality that the law assumes that differentiates it from other principles in society affecting social relations. Formality is defined by specificity, comprehensiveness, and applicability. Specificity in the law is necessary to give notice of its requirements. Law cannot be vague, and its terms must be known in order to have authority and legitimacy. Formality in the law also requires comprehensiveness. It must fully address the topics to which it applies so that situations that come within its purview may find resolution under its terms. The application of the law is also an aspect of its formality. It operates in such a way as to apply to each individual in a community in accordance with the sense of justice found within the community. Thus, formality becomes evident in the form that the law takes, the procedures for implementing and enforcing it, and the institutions used to realize its goals.

Law and Justice

How does law relate to justice? Recall from Chapter 1 that, similar to law, justice has many meanings. We can relate law to justice by considering that law is a primary mechanism in society for achieving justice, although some would debate this point (Abraham, 1998). Nonetheless, it might be argued that law is the sole mechanism for achieving justice because it is through the force of law, its application, interpretation, and enforcement that people seeking justice in their lives can find recourse. When the prisoners at Guantanamo Bay (discussed in the *Boumediene* case in Chapter 1) were held without being charged and sought relief through habeas corpus, it was through the courts that they received justice by having their petition heard and granted. Furthermore, although the law has broad application throughout most of the facets of human life, it is through the courts that the law attempts to realize its goal of achieving justice. The courts have frequently relied on their "sense of justice" in deciding cases. At times, justice has itself been relied on as a legal test, as when a party's action "shocks" a court's sense of justice (Dubber, 2006). At other times, justice is viewed as central to the law and its requirements, or nearly so (*State v. Maldonado*, 137 N.J. 536, 645 A.2d 1165 (1994)) (justice favors a statute imposing strict liability on defendant who distributes a controlled substance to a person who dies from it). Thus, law is intended as the instrument of justice, the mechanism through which justice is accomplished.

We can also relate law to justice by considering justice as striving to provide equality in society. Law exists for the benefit of all who comprise society, and individuals may access the law to seek justice in their lives. This is not to say that the law operates perfectly, but it allows those seeking justice to do so without recourse to weapons and harm to others, attacks on societal institutions, or destruction of society itself. The law attempts to operate in an unbiased fashion with equal application to all who are subject to it, and this notion of fairness connects most peoples' perceptions of justice to the law under which they live.

The Rule of Law

American society depends on the *rule of law* to provide order and justice to citizens. The rule of law refers to the concept that all people and the institutions that govern them will abide by the laws determined by the majority to be best for society. When a person suggests that "no one is above the law," he or she is referring, intentionally or not, to their belief that society operates under the rule of law. In particular, democracy depends on the responsibility of its citizens to be accountable to the larger society. This happens as a result of adherence to the law. When the British philosopher David Hume referred to a "government of laws and not of men," he was speaking of the rule of law and its central role in the functioning of an orderly society, as opposed to reliance on the whims of human rulers. This very phrase came to be repeated and relied on in the early years of American law, finding its way into such documents as the Massachusetts Constitution and the famous case decision written by Chief Justice John Marshall, *Marbury v. Madison*, discussed in Chapter 1.

Thus, although the rule of law is not a uniquely American concept, it has become a cornerstone of the American democratic government and way of life. The law governing society therefore plays a central role in the way in which people in the United States conduct themselves, whether their conduct involves personal behavior, business activities, or other areas of their lives. By virtue of choosing to be a part of and participating in society, individuals become subject to the rule of law and must abide by its rules; by doing so, they benefit from the rights and freedoms found in the law.

Theories of Law

One way of understanding the concept of law is by considering different theories of law that seek to explain the basis for law and how it operates. Some theories of law have their roots in philosophy, whereas others stem from sociological or political concerns (Edmundson, 2005). Some have had long lives, whereas others are of a more recent vintage. Regardless, the goal of each of these schools of thought is to explain the meaning and purpose of law as well as a justification and need for its existence. Moreover, theories of law become important because they specify certain ways of thinking about and using the law to achieve various ends. Thus, a judge's perspective on the role of law will affect his or her approach to interpreting

the law, and a politician's theoretical views on the law will impact policy decisions made.

Although there are many theories of law with advocates in jurisprudence, legal practice, academia, and politics, there are at least five competing viewpoints that have currency. These are natural law theory, positive law theory, critical legal theory, legal realism, and the economic analysis of the law. Each of these represents a fairly comprehensive approach to law and its role. In addition, other theories have also developed to explain and justify specific areas or aspects of the law, such as theories of human rights, criminal law, and torts. **Table 2.1** summarizes the five comprehensive theories, and each is discussed in the following paragraphs.

Natural Law

Natural law is law that has a moral basis. It is said to derive from "nature" or God, but human understanding of what morality requires gives it meaning. That is, natural law requires that one should act in accordance with the law because morality demands it; it is moral reasoning that outlines the scope of the law and provides limits to its operation (George, 1999; Smith, 1997). Thus, natural law specifies that the law, in order to be considered just, must comply with our understanding of what is moral and only those laws that are consistent with moral reason carry the weight of authority and should be obeyed. Natural law stems from what society understands to be moral; although natural law and morality are not equivalent, they are so interrelated that what is moral must necessarily also comprise the law.

The idea that law has a "natural" source is believed to stem from the thinking of the Greek philosophers Plato and Aristotle and the Roman orator Cicero (Friedrichs, 2006; Morrison, 1997), who thought that notions of right and wrong must guide society and that laws and morality are therefore inextricably linked. Thus, when Thomas Jefferson stated in the Declaration of Independence that man was "endowed with certain unalienable rights" and that "among these are life, liberty and the pursuit of happiness," he was referring to natural law as the basis on which the American colonies were entitled to declare their independence from England. More recently, U.S. Supreme Court justices have relied on natural law as the basis for their decisions. For example, in *Griswold v. Connecticut*, 381 U.S. 479 (1965), the Court struck down

Table 2.1		
Theories of Law		
Theory	**Founded**	**Primary Basis for Law**
Natural Law	1300s	Morality
Positive Law	1800s	Reason
Legal Realism	1920s	Socialism
Critical Legal Theory	1970s	Politics
Economic Analysis of Law	1980s	Economics

a state statute that criminalized the use of "any drug, medicinal article or instrument for the purpose of preventing conception." Using natural law principles, the Court found that a right of privacy exists, despite the fact that no such right is specifically stated in the Constitution (see **Case Decision 2.1**).

As pointed out by Justice Black in his dissent, the Griswold case was decided in accordance with "funda- mental principles of liberty and justice," as well as "the traditions and conscience of our people." What bothered Justice Black about this application of natural law was that he found it to be "mysterious and uncertain" and therefore an inadequate basis for deciding cases.

This is the conundrum of natural law theory: how does the moral nature of law translate into legal principles of general applicability?

Case Decision 2.1 *Griswold et al. v. Connecticut*, 381 U.S. 479, 85 S. Ct. 1678, 14 L.Ed.2d 510 (1965)

Opinion of the Court by Justice Douglas:

Appellant Griswold is Executive Director of the Planned Parenthood League of Connecticut. Appellant Buxton is a licensed physician and a professor at the Yale Medical School who served as Medical Director for the League at its Center in New Haven—a center open and operating from November 1 to November 10, 1961, when appellants were arrested.

They gave information, instruction, and medical advice to married persons as to the means of preventing conception. They examined the wife and prescribed the best contraceptive device or material for her use. Fees were usually charged, although some couples were serviced free.

The statutes whose constitutionality is involved in this appeal are ss 53-32 and 54-196 of the General Statutes of Connecticut (1958 rev.). The former provides:

Any person who uses any drug, medicinal article or instrument for the purpose of preventing conception shall be fined not less than fifty dollars or imprisoned not less than sixty days nor more than one year or be both fined and imprisoned.

Section 54-196 provides:

Any person who assists, abets, counsels, causes, hires or commands another to commit any offense may be prosecuted and punished as if he were the principal offender.

The appellants were found guilty as accessories and fined $100 each, against the claim that the accessory statute as so applied violated the Fourteenth Amendment. The Appellate Division of the Circuit Court affirmed. The Supreme Court of Errors affirmed that judgment.

Coming to the merits, we are met with a wide range of questions that implicate the Due Process Clause of the Fourteenth Amendment. Overtones of some arguments suggest that *Lochner v. State of New York* (198 U.S. 45, 25 S. Ct. 539, 49 L.Ed. 937) should be our guide. But we decline that invitation. We do not sit as a super-legislature to determine the wisdom, need, and propriety of laws that touch economic problems, business affairs, or social conditions. This law, however, operates directly on an intimate relation of husband and wife and their physician's role in one aspect of that relation.

The association of people is not mentioned in the Constitution nor in the Bill of Rights. The right to educate a child in a school of the parents' choice—whether public or private or parochial—is also not mentioned. Nor is the right to study any particular subject or any foreign language. Yet the First Amendment has been construed to include certain of those rights.

[S]pecific guarantees in the Bill of Rights have penumbras, formed by emanations from those guarantees that help give them life and substance. Various guarantees create zones of privacy. The right of association contained in the penumbra of the First Amendment is one, as we have seen. The Third Amendment in its prohibition against the quartering of soldiers "in any house" in time of peace without the consent of the owner is another facet of that privacy. The Fourth Amendment explicitly affirms the "right of the people to be secure in their persons, houses, papers, and effects, against unreasonable searches and seizures." The Fifth Amendment in its Self-Incrimination Clause enables the citizen to create a zone of privacy which government may not force him to surrender to his detriment. The Ninth Amendment provides: "The enumeration in the Constitution, of certain rights, shall not be construed to deny or disparage others retained by the people."

The present case, then, concerns a relationship lying within the zone of privacy created by several fundamental constitutional guarantees. And it concerns a law which, in forbidding the use of contraceptives rather than regulating their manufacture or sale, seeks to achieve its goals by means having a maximum destructive impact upon that relationship. Such a law cannot stand in light of the familiar principle, so often applied by this Court, that a "governmental purpose to control or prevent activities constitutionally subject to state regulation may not be achieved by means which sweep unnecessarily broadly and thereby invade the area of protected freedoms." Would we allow the police to search the sacred precincts of marital bedrooms for telltale signs of the use of contraceptives? The very idea is repulsive to the notions of privacy surrounding the marriage relationship.

We deal with a right of privacy older than the Bill of Rights—older than our political parties, older than our school system. Marriage is a coming together for better or for worse, hopefully enduring, and intimate to the degree of being sacred. It is an association that promotes a way of life, not causes; a harmony in living, not political faiths; a bilateral loyalty, not commercial or social projects. Yet it is an association for as noble a purpose as any involved in our prior decisions.

Reversed.

Mr. Justice Goldberg, whom The Chief Justice and Mr. Justice Brennan join, concurring:

I agree with the Court that Connecticut's birth-control law unconstitutionally intrudes upon the right of marital privacy, and I join in its opinion and judgment. I do agree that the concept of liberty protects those personal rights that are fundamental, and is not confined to the specific terms of the Bill of Rights. My conclusion that the concept of liberty is not so restricted and that it embraces the right of marital privacy though that right is not mentioned explicitly in the Constitution is supported both by numerous decisions of this Court, referred to in the Court's opinion, and by the language and history of the Ninth Amendment. In reaching the conclusion that the right of marital privacy is protected, as being within the protected penumbra of specific guarantees of the Bill of Rights, the Court refers to the Ninth Amendment. I add these words to emphasize the relevance of that Amendment to the Court's holding.

The Ninth Amendment reads, "The enumeration in the Constitution, of certain rights, shall not be construed to deny or disparage others retained by the people." The Amendment is almost entirely the work of James Madison. It was introduced in Congress by him and passed the House and Senate with little or no debate and virtually no change in language. It was proffered to quiet expressed fears that a bill of specifically enumerated rights could not be sufficiently broad to cover all essential rights and that the specific mention of certain rights would be interpreted as a denial that others were protected. [T]he Framers did not intend that the first eight amendments be construed to exhaust the basic and fundamental rights which the Constitution guaranteed to the people.

While this Court has had little occasion to interpret the Ninth Amendment, "(i)t cannot be presumed that any clause in the constitution is intended to be without effect." In interpreting the Constitution, "real effect should be given to all the words it uses." The Ninth Amendment to the Constitution may be regarded by some as a recent discovery and may be forgotten by others, but since 1791 it has been a basic part of the Constitution which we are sworn to uphold. To hold that a right so basic and fundamental and so deep rooted in our society as the right of privacy in marriage may be infringed because that right is not guaranteed in so many words by the first eight amendments to the Constitution is to ignore the Ninth Amendment and to give it no effect whatsoever. Moreover, a judicial construction that this fundamental right is not protected by the Constitution because it is not mentioned in explicit terms by one of the first eight amendments or elsewhere in the Constitution would violate the Ninth Amendment, which specifically states that "(t)he enumeration in the Constitution, of certain rights shall not be construed to deny or disparage others retained by the people."

[T]he Ninth Amendment shows a belief of the Constitution's authors that fundamental rights exist that are not expressly enumerated in the first eight amendments and an intent that the list of rights included there not be deemed exhaustive. As any student of this Court's opinions knows, this Court has held, often unanimously, that the Fifth and Fourteenth Amendments protect certain fundamental personal liberties from abridgment by the Federal Government or the States. The Ninth Amendment simply shows the intent of the Constitution's authors that other fundamental personal rights should not be denied such protection or disparaged in any other way simply because they are not specifically listed in the first eight constitutional amendments. I do not see how this broadens the authority of the Court; rather it serves to support what this Court has been doing in protecting fundamental rights.

(Continues)

In determining which rights are fundamental, judges are not left at large to decide cases in light of their personal and private notions. Rather, they must look to the "traditions and (collective) conscience of our people" to determine whether a principle is "so rooted (there) as to be ranked as fundamental." The inquiry is whether a right involved "is of such a character that it cannot be denied without violating those 'fundamental principles of liberty and justice which lie at the base of all our civil and political institutions'." "Liberty" also "gains content from the emanations of specific (constitutional) guarantees" and "from experience with the requirements of a free society."

In sum, I believe that the right of privacy in the marital relation is fundamental and basic—a personal right "retained by the people" within the meaning of the Ninth Amendment. Connecticut cannot constitutionally abridge this fundamental right, which is protected by the Fourteenth Amendment from infringement by the States. I agree with the Court that petitioners' convictions must therefore be reversed.

Mr. Justice Black, with whom Mr. Justice Stewart joins, dissenting.

I feel constrained to add that the law is every bit as offensive to me as it is my Brethren of the majority and my Brothers Harlan, White and Goldberg who, reciting reasons why it is offensive to them, hold it unconstitutional. There is no single one of the graphic and eloquent strictures and criticisms fired at the policy of this Connecticut law either by the Court's opinion or by those of my concurring Brethren to which I cannot subscribe—except their conclusion that the evil qualities they see in the law make it unconstitutional.

The Court talks about a constitutional "right of privacy" as though there is some constitutional provision or provisions forbidding any law ever to be passed which might abridge the "privacy" of individuals. But there is not. There are, of course, guarantees in certain specific constitutional provisions which are designed in part to protect privacy at certain times and places with respect to certain activities. Such, for example, is the Fourth Amendment's guarantee against "unreasonable searches and seizures." But I think it belittles that Amendment to talk about it as though it protects nothing but "privacy." To treat it that way is to give it a niggardly interpretation, not the kind of liberal reading I think any Bill of Rights provision should be given. The average man would very likely not have his feelings soothed any more by having his property seized openly than by having it seized privately and by stealth. He simply wants his property left alone. And a person can be just as much, if not more, irritated, annoyed and injured by an unceremonious public arrest by a policeman as he is by a seizure in the privacy of his office or home.

One of the most effective ways of diluting or expanding a constitutionally guaranteed right is to substitute for the crucial word or words of a constitutional guarantee another word or words, more or less flexible and more or less restricted in meaning. This fact is well illustrated by the use of the term "right of privacy" as a comprehensive substitute for the Fourth Amendment's guarantee against "unreasonable searches and seizures." "Privacy" is a broad, abstract and ambiguous concept which can easily be shrunken in meaning but which can also, on the other hand, easily be interpreted as a constitutional ban against many things other than searches and seizures. I have expressed the view many times that First Amendment freedoms, for example, have suffered from a failure of the courts to stick to the simple language of the First Amendment in construing it, instead of invoking multitudes of words substituted for those the Framers used. For these reasons I get nowhere in this case by talking about a constitutional "right of privacy" as an emanation from one or more constitutional provisions. I like my privacy as well as the next one, but I am nevertheless compelled to admit that government has a right to invade it unless prohibited by some specific constitutional provision. For these reasons I cannot agree with the Court's judgment and the reasons it gives for holding this Connecticut law unconstitutional.

My Brother Goldberg has adopted the recent discovery that the Ninth Amendment as well as the Due Process Clause can be used by this Court as authority to strike down all state legislation which this Court thinks violates "fundamental principles of liberty and justice," or is contrary to the "traditions and (collective) conscience of our people." He also states, without proof satisfactory to me, that in making decisions on this basis judges will not consider "their personal and private notions." One may ask how they can avoid considering them. Our Court certainly has no machinery with which to take a Gallup Poll. And the scientific miracles of this age have not yet produced a gadget which the Court can use to determine what traditions are rooted in the "(collective) conscience of our people." Moreover, one would certainly have to look far beyond the language of the Ninth Amendment to find that the Framers vested in this Court any such awesome veto powers over lawmaking, either by the States or by the Congress. Nor does anything in the history of the Amendment offer any support for such a shocking doctrine. The whole history of the adoption of the Constitution and Bill of Rights points the other way. That Amendment was passed, not to broaden the powers of this Court or any other department of "the General Government," but, as every student of history knows, to assure the people that the Constitution in all its provisions was intended to limit the Federal Government to the powers granted expressly or by necessary implication. If any broad, unlimited power to hold laws unconstitutional because they offend what this Court conceives to be the "(collective) conscience of our people" is vested in this Court by the Ninth Amendment, the Fourteenth Amendment, or any other provision of the Constitution, it was not given by the Framers, but rather has been bestowed on the Court by the Court. This fact is perhaps responsible for the peculiar phenomenon that for a period of a century and a half no serious suggestion was ever made that the Ninth Amendment, enacted to protect state powers against federal invasion, could be used as a weapon of federal power to prevent state legislatures from passing laws they consider appropriate to govern local affairs. Use of any such broad, unbounded judicial authority would make of this Court's members a day-to-day constitutional convention.

I realize that many good and able men have eloquently spoken and written, sometimes in rhapsodical strains, about the duty of this Court to keep the Constitution in tune with the times. The idea is that the Constitution must be changed from time to time and that this Court is charged with a duty to make those changes. For myself, I must with all deference reject that philosophy. The Constitution makers knew the need for change and provided for it. Amendments suggested by the people's elected representatives can be submitted to the people or their selected agents for ratification. That method of change was good for our Fathers, and being somewhat old fashioned I must add it is good enough for me. And so, I cannot rely on the Due Process Clause or the Ninth Amendment or any mysterious and uncertain natural law concept as a reason for striking down this state law. The Due Process Clause with an "arbitrary and capricious" or "shocking to the conscience" formula was liberally used by this Court to strike down economic legislation in the early decades of this century, threatening, many people thought, the tranquility and stability of the Nation. That formula, based on subjective considerations of "natural justice," is no less dangerous when used to enforce this Court's views about personal rights than those about economic rights. I had thought that we had laid that formula, as a means for striking down state legislation, to rest once and for all.

So far as I am concerned, Connecticut's law as applied here is not forbidden by any provision of the Federal Constitution as that Constitution was written, and I would therefore affirm.

Mr. Justice Stewart, whom Mr. Justice Black joins, dissenting.

Since 1879 Connecticut has had on its books a law which forbids the use of contraceptives by anyone. I think this is an uncommonly silly law. As a practical matter, the law is obviously unenforceable, except in the oblique context of the present case. As a philosophical matter, I believe the use of contraceptives in the relationship of marriage should be left to personal and private choice, based upon each individual's moral, ethical, and religious beliefs. As a matter of social policy, I think professional counsel about methods of birth control should be available to all, so that each individual's choice can be meaningfully made. But we are not asked in this case to say whether we think this law is unwise, or even asinine. We are asked to hold that it violates the United States Constitution. And that I cannot do.

In the course of its opinion the Court refers to no less than six Amendments to the Constitution: the First, the Third, the Fourth, the Fifth, the Ninth, and the Fourteenth. But the Court does not say which of these Amendments, if any, it thinks is infringed by this Connecticut law.

We are told that the Due Process Clause of the Fourteenth Amendment is not, as such, the "guide" in this case. With that much I agree. There is no claim that this law, duly enacted by the Connecticut Legislature, is unconstitutionally vague. There is no claim that the appellants were denied any of the elements of procedural due process at their trial, so as to make their convictions constitutionally invalid. And, as the Court says, the day has long passed since the Due Process Clause was regarded as a proper instrument for determining "the wisdom, need, and propriety" of state laws.

As to the First, Third, Fourth, and Fifth Amendments, I can find nothing in any of them to invalidate this Connecticut law, even assuming that all those Amendments are fully applicable against the States. It has not even been argued that this is a law "respecting an establishment of

(Continues)

religion, or prohibiting the free exercise thereof." And surely, unless the solemn process of constitutional adjudication is to descend to the level of a play on words, there is not involved here any abridgment of "the freedom of speech, or of the press; or the right of the people peaceably to assemble, and to petition the Government for a redress of grievances." No soldier has been quartered in any house. There has been no search, and no seizure. Nobody has been compelled to be a witness against himself.

The Court also quotes the Ninth Amendment, and my Brother Goldberg's concurring opinion relies heavily upon it. But to say that the Ninth Amendment has anything to do with this case is to turn somersaults with history. The Ninth Amendment, like its companion the Tenth, which this Court held "states but a truism that all is retained which has not been surrendered," was framed by James Madison and adopted by the States simply to make clear that the adoption of the Bill of Rights did not alter the plan that the Federal Government was to be a government of express and limited powers, and that all rights and powers not delegated to it were retained by the people and the individual States. Until today no member of this Court has ever suggested that the Ninth Amendment meant anything else, and the idea that a federal court could ever use the Ninth Amendment to annul a law passed by the elected representatives of the people of the State of Connecticut would have caused James Madison no little wonder.

What provision of the Constitution, then, does make this state law invalid? The Court says it is the right of privacy "created by several fundamental constitutional guarantees." With all deference, I can find no such general right of privacy in the Bill of Rights, in any other part of the Constitution, or in any case ever before decided by this Court.

At the oral argument in this case we were told that the Connecticut law does not "conform to current community standards." But it is not the function of this Court to decide cases on the basis of community standards. We are here to decide cases "agreeably to the Constitution and laws of the United States." It is the essence of judicial duty to subordinate our own personal views, our own ideas of what legislation is wise and what is not. If, as I should surely hope, the law before us does not reflect the standards of the people of Connecticut, the people of Connecticut can freely exercise their true Ninth and Tenth Amendment rights to persuade their elected representatives to repeal it. That is the constitutional way to take this law off the books.

Positive Law

Positive law (sometimes referred to as *legal positivisim*) refers to law that is man made; that is, it does not depend on morality or a "higher order" for its authority, but on the rules that citizens adopt and accept as necessary to govern themselves (Friedrichs, 2006). It may be seen as attempting to create a "science" of law that is not dependent on why certain laws should be passed or how the law should operate procedurally (Bix, 2005). It seeks to explain the essence of law apart from any particular sociological or political viewpoint. This does not imply that, for a positivist, law operates in a vacuum devoid of morals or human conceptions of right and wrong. Rather, although moral principles may influence the creation and operation of law, after a law exists, it stands apart from such principles (Bix, 2000). The positivist perspective on the law is one in which law consists of definite rules and sanctions adopted by those whom society authorizes to enact such rules, and the enactment of laws does not depend on conceptions of morality (Hart, 1994). After adopted, these legal rules are intended to apply to all persons and institutions that make up society. In this view, law does not result from morality, but from what citizens believe to be in their own best interests; therefore, positive law, broadly defined, is the body of formal rules, doctrines, principles and procedures used by society to accomplish its goals. As discussed later here, these goals include maintaining order and protecting citizens in a variety of ways.

Critical Legal Theory

Critical legal theory stems from dissatisfaction in the 1970s with the ability of the law to properly address liberal social issues such as war, race, inequality, and the distribution of wealth (Tushnet, 2005). It may therefore be viewed as a collection of theories related to each other by their political and social emphasis encompassing the view that law is and should be an agent for social change, although not in the way that the law has traditionally operated. Critical legal theory emphasizes that (1) legal reasoning and political argument are the same; (2) law is not governed solely by rules of reason, but by political dealing characterized by principles that allow for the dominance of one person, institution, perspective, or interest over another; and (3) legal decisions are not authoritative, in the sense that they do not represent the final say on a matter (Tushnet, 2005).

The first point is based on the view that legal rules are nothing more than tools of advocacy. These tools can be used convincingly to produce a certain outcome in court or to support a particular public policy in order to achieve the proponent's social goals. The second point is one in which the law is viewed as classist; the legal system is controlled by the powerful for the benefit of the powerful. The legal rules developed by those in power ultimately weigh in favor of those with power, to the exclusion of those situated differently in society. The third point led to a central thesis of critical legal theory, the indeterminacy thesis, which states that all legal questions are indeterminate. This is because, from a critical legal theory perspective, any social or political position may be supported by legal principles and forms of argument (Tushnet, 1996). Because the law does not require any particular outcome in any case, judges are free to make choices about how the law should apply and what they believe an outcome should be.

Legal Realism

As a theory of law, legal realism was based in the practice of law and the outcomes achievable through it. As the name implies, legal realism was a reaction to the views of positivists or natural law proponents that application of legal rules to disputes or problems leads to clear and consistent results in each case. Rather, legal realists viewed the role of judges as applying their notions of fairness to legal cases based primarily on the facts of the case, rather than legal rules (Fisher et al., 1993; Leiter, 2005). As a result, legal rules serve only as after-the-fact rationalizations of what a judge has already decided on the basis of his or her notions of fairness (Leiter, 2005).

The idea that judges primarily based their decisions on the facts of a particular case, and not primarily on the law, has several implications. First, it means that judicial decision making is a much more personal affair because it involves a judge's reaction to a factual situation confronting the parties (Llewellyn, 1950); therefore, judicial discretion plays a much more prominent role in decision making for legal realists. Second, judicial power is more expansive than otherwise would be the case in a rule-bound system of justice. Third, the precedential effect of prior cases is important only to the extent that those cases are factually similar to the case before a judge (Leiter, 2005). To the extent that such a case represents a rule of law to be applied, the rule is applicable only to the extent the facts in the two cases are the same. Finally, the focus on the facts raises a question about what that means: How do judges weigh the facts of a case in making a decision, and what should the proper approach be? The answer to this question is as varied as judges themselves because the effect of a particular set of facts on a particular judge cannot be known. Moreover, to presume to specify what a judge's response to a particular set of facts should be is inconsistent with the idea that judging is a personal affair to begin with because it mostly involves nothing more than the judge's perceptions of what justice requires.

Economic Analysis of Law

As a theory of law, the application of economic principles to legal questions has grown in recent years. Specifically, microeconomic theory is applied to the way in which legal

rules influence individual behavior and how legal rules may be structured to affect behavior (Kornhauser, 2005). The concept of microeconomics that affects legal rules is that of "preference." Peoples' preferences are driven by self-interest. In terms of legal analysis, this means that people will prefer to act in ways that are in their own best interests, such as not engaging in behaviors prohibited by the criminal law because they will benefit from doing so or not engaging in reckless behavior because of the potential costs and losses from such action (Kornhauser, 2003).

A preference, however, is not the only force affecting individual behavior and decision making. In the law, preferences operate in the context of obligations that the law (or society) imposes. For example, people are obligated to pay their taxes and judges are obligated to follow the rulings of higher courts. These obligations at times pull against the desire to act in accordance with one's preferences (Posner, 1999). When this occurs, the way in which legal rules will be followed becomes less predictable. The economic analysis of law involves applying mathematical models to assist in this prediction.

The Criminal/Civil Distinction

Regardless of whether one adopts a "natural law" or a "positive law" perspective, the definition of "law" may also depend on the use to which it is put. These uses relate to the functions described previously here, including a whole range of actions and behaviors that members of a society may engage in. They provide a framework for orderliness within society.

In the United States, social norms are embodied in the two main branches of law reflecting the manner in which it is used: criminal and civil. It is public views regarding what constitutes an orderly society that determines what the law should be in each of these areas.

Criminal law is the branch of law used to enforce compliance with social norms. That is, it is law that specifies which personal behaviors will not be tolerated by society and demands penalties when people fail to comply with its demands. Criminal law represents the judgment of members of society (most often through their elected representatives) regarding what actions are considered to be antisocial and what should be done with individuals who engage in those actions. Whether the behavior is relatively trivial, such as "improperly" crossing a street, or more serious, such as physically harming another, it is antisocial because it is behavior determined by society to be harmful, either to the individual, society as a whole, or both. Criminal law thus reflects society's sense of "right and wrong" behavior and sets forth both the behaviors that are proscribed and the penalties that will follow from engaging in those behaviors. It is also the domain of law that defines and explains the relationship between an individual and society itself (i.e., the government, or the state), as well as the conditions in which the state may declare that a person must be punished. Criminal law consists of both the "substantive" criminal law, which involves specification of prohibited behaviors and punishments for them, and criminal procedure, which specifies the process through which enforcement of the substantive criminal law occurs, including protection of individual rights of criminal defendants. Chapters 11 and 12 discuss these two aspects of criminal law.

Civil law is law that largely governs the private affairs of individuals (including businesses) and relationships among people. Although it does reflect social norms regarding how private affairs should be conducted, it generally does not involve rules about the relationships between individuals and government, nor does it generally specify prohibited behaviors. Rather, it involves rules governing how people may carry out the affairs of life in the most orderly and beneficial way, both for the individual and for society itself.

Laws, both criminal and civil, are thus rules of applicability that are characterized by their formality; that is, they are clearly stated in writing, address only a limited and specific topic, and are enforceable by the courts. Although laws may be related to and stem from social norms, they differ from informal norms by carrying the weight of enforceability authorized by the society in which they are used. Do not confuse formality with inflexibility, however. The best laws are flexible in that they applied to a wide variety of factual situations while providing consistent results over time. In short, it is law that allows society to function. Arguably, without laws, there would be no social order.

The Purpose of Law

The law has many functions. Most basically, it is a mechanism for resolving disputes. These disputes may be between individuals (including businesses), as when a person sues another for personal injury or breach of a contract, or between the government and an individual, as when the government takes the property of another for public use under the Takings Clause of the Constitution, or between society and an individual, as when a person is prosecuted for commission of a crime. The law sometimes serves as a tool for social change, either as a direct result of particular cases brought by interested parties before the courts, or as an indirect result of a court interpretation of the law and the decision that follows from it. Other times the law functions as a reflection of society, where court decisions are informed by and are consistent with the wishes of the majority. Regardless of the particular function the law may serve, the law is meant to deal with specific factual situations that may arise in society. These situations and the way in which the law addresses them are the work of the courts.

Although the law has many functions, it serves two broad purposes: to maintain order in society and to provide protection for citizens and others who come within the nation's borders. These purposes are accomplished by the court system and other agencies that function under it.

Maintain Order

Order is maintained in society by compliance with rules, both formal and informal. Informal rules are found in many aspects of life such as home, church, and school. As discussed earlier, social norms create expectations in individuals regarding how they should act. For example, when students attend class, they typically enter the classroom, find a seat (which is usually arranged to face the instructor), wait for the instructor to arrive, and remain quiet (unless called upon) while the instructor speaks. This classroom "script" consists of informal rules, learned over years of school attendance, which educational institutions use to maintain order in the social setting of the classroom.

The law represents formal rules that also create expectations for an ordered society. These rules, consisting of laws from a variety of sources, maintain order in numerous ways. The civil law may operate to create order in the private affairs of individuals and business organizations. For example, the law of contracts provides rules for establishing mutually beneficial business relationships that create reliable expectations between the parties, as well as remedies in court for when those expectations fail. Similarly, family law governing marriage and divorce allows women and men to enter into personal relationships or sever those relationships in an orderly fashion that allows for the enforceable division of property and some assurance that the interests of children will be addressed.

The law also creates order in society by specifying prohibited behavior and the punishment that will follow. It seeks to deter people from engaging in certain types of behavior deemed to be unacceptable to society. This deterrent goal of the law is an order-maintenance one, whereby individuals must conduct themselves in accordance with societal norms or "pay the price" for their failure to do so.

Provide Protection

Society also looks to the law to provide protection to individuals as well as protection for society itself. In particular, the law offers protection of public interests and private interests. The personal safety of people is a public interest protected by defining crimes involving behavior by an individual that results in harm to another, as well as specifying the punishment for such actions. Similarly, protection of property is a public interest protected by punishment of those who violate the property rights of another by stealing or destroying their property. The criminal law also seeks to protect public institutions, both governmental and social, through the creation of crimes against public order and morality (e.g., prostitution, inciting riots) and actions targeted at the government (e.g., treason, obstruction of justice).

The law also protects the private interests that individuals may have, such as obtaining compensation from one whose negligent action caused personal injury to another person. Similarly, the law provides a mechanism for protection of the private financial interests of individuals or businesses who, for example, may enter into contracts, or desire to transfer property after death (probate law), or to divide assets and care for children in the event of divorce. All of these serve a protective function by allowing people to have reasonable expectation about the effect of their private conduct on their lives (see **Table 2.2**).

Table 2.2

The Purposes of Law

Purpose	Type of Law	Examples
Maintaining order	Criminal	Laws prohibiting disorderly conduct
Providing protection	Criminal	Laws requiring prison for assaults
Governing relationships	Civil	Laws enforcing contracts
Resolving disputes	Criminal	Laws penalizing domestic violence
	Civil	Laws governing real estate transfers
Social change	Civil	Laws requiring racial integration of schools

Sources of Law

We may also define the law in terms of its source or where the law comes from. The law has many different sources; it may be found in many places. These are a function of the historical development of the courts in the United States as well as our democratic system of government. The primary sources of law on which the court system and the public rely are common law, constitutions, statutes, and regulations.

The Common Law (Case Law)

The "common law" refers to the decisions made by judges in past cases that together comprise a body of law. It is therefore considered to be judge-made law and is not found in a single written book of law but consists of decisions previously made that may be used to inform judges' decision making in this day. The American common law tradition derives from English common law. In England, judges came to rely on certain principles of law that allowed them to decide similar factual situations that arose in cases before them. These principles came to be widely recognized as governing such facts. Later, as judges began to issue written decisions, these decisions recited the legal principles applicable to the case and had precedential value in future cases.

As the colonies were first settled in the early 17th century, the courts and legal processes of England were not well developed, even as the common law was emerging. Furthermore, there were few (if any) settlers who were trained in the formalities of English law, and strict formalities were of little use to colonists seeking to survive on foreign soil; however, as focus in the colonies shifted from day-to-day survival to the development of systems of commerce, trade, and business affairs, however rudimentary, the need for legal rules to resolve disputes arose. Nonlawyers empowered with authority from the Crown to rule the colonies (e.g., colonial governors and their designees) applied English common law as they understood it. Their

understanding of law came from their own life experiences, English custom, English cases with which they were familiar, and the Bible or Ecclesiastical law. In the 18th century and as more colonists came to America from England, some brought with them training in the law as well as a widely distributed compendium on the common law of England, Sir William Blackstone's *Commentaries on the Law of England*. Even after American independence, the body of law relied on by lawyers and judges involved cases decided under English law.

The common law then consists of the recognized principles of law that have been reflected in the written decisions of judges. Under the common law, the way in which we can understand the law on a particular topic is to read case decisions on that topic. Although today the primary source of common law is written decisions made in the United States, not England, it remains true that the most authoritative support for a legal position is found in prior judicial decisions, or case law.

Thus, case law becomes an important source of law for courts because of the weight of authority it confers. Although not all cases have equal weight as law, they all have a similar structure when announcing a decision. That is, case law stems from a factual dispute presented to a court for resolution, in which the court must determine what law governs the dispute, which facts are central to its resolution, how the law applies to the facts, and what decision is most just given the facts and the law. This process is reflected in the written decisions that issue from courts and comprise case law.

Reliance on prior case decisions to determine pending cases involves the doctrine of *stare decisis*, which means "let the decision stand." The doctrine is the basis for reliance by judges on precedent, where legal principles in prior cases are applied to present cases to reach a conclusion. *Stare decisis* and the use of prior cases as precedent thus assist judicial decision making by providing authority and legal rules in each case a judge is called on to consider. The common law develops as cases restate, interpret, and apply legal principles in new cases involving different factual situations; these new cases gain precedential value and become part of the common law.

Not all prior cases retain their precedential validity, however. There are circumstances in which a court may modify, limit, or overrule prior decisions. One example is found in **Case Decision 2.2.**

In *Arizona v. Gant*, 129 S. Ct. 1710 (2009), the U.S. Supreme Court addressed the warrantless search of a motor vehicle under the "search incident to an arrest" exception to the warrant requirement (this exception, the use of warrants, and the law of search and seizure are discussed in detail in Chapter 12). This rule stemmed from a prior case, *New York v. Belton*, 453 U.S. 454 (1981), in which the Court had allowed police to search vehicles without a warrant in cases where an occupant of the vehicle was placed under arrest. This was based on the possibility that the individual arrested may be able to reach inside the vehicle to destroy evidence or retrieve a weapon; however, the defendant in *Gant* was arrested, handcuffed, and placed in the back of a patrol car, not

Case Decision 2.2 *Arizona v. Gant*, 129 S. Ct. 1710 (2009)

Opinion of the Court by Justice Stevens:

After Rodney Gant was arrested for driving with a suspended license, handcuffed, and locked in the back of a patrol car, police officers searched his car and discovered cocaine in the pocket of a jacket on the backseat. Because Gant could not have accessed his car to retrieve weapons or evidence at the time of the search, the Arizona Supreme Court held that the search-incident-to-arrest exception to the Fourth Amendment's warrant requirement, as defined in *Chimel v. California*, 395 U.S. 752, 89 S. Ct. 2034, 23 L.Ed.2d 685 (1969), and applied to vehicle searches in *New York v. Belton*, 453 U.S. 454, 101 S. Ct. 2860, 69 L.Ed.2d 768 (1981), did not justify the search in this case. We agree with that conclusion.

Under Chimel, police may search incident to arrest only the space within an arrestee's "'immediate control,'" meaning "the area from within which he might gain possession of a weapon or destructible evidence." The safety and evidentiary justifications underlying Chimel's reaching-distance rule determine Belton's scope. Accordingly, we hold that Belton does not authorize a vehicle search incident to a recent occupant's arrest after the arrestee has been secured and cannot access the interior of the vehicle. Consistent with the holding in *Thornton v. United States*, 541 U.S. 615, 124 S. Ct. 2127, 158 L.Ed.2d 905 (2004), we also conclude that circumstances unique to the automobile context justify a search incident to arrest when it is reasonable to believe that evidence of the offense of arrest might be found in the vehicle.

I

On August 25, 1999, acting on an anonymous tip that the residence at 2524 North Walnut Avenue was being used to sell drugs, Tucson police officers Griffith and Reed knocked on the front door and asked to speak to the owner. Gant answered the door and, after identifying himself, stated that he expected the owner to return later. The officers left the residence and conducted a records check, which revealed that Gant's driver's license had been suspended and there was an outstanding warrant for his arrest for driving with a suspended license.

When the officers returned to the house that evening, they found a man near the back of the house and a woman in a car parked in front of it. After a third officer arrived, they arrested the man for providing a false name and the woman for possessing drug paraphernalia. Both arrestees were handcuffed and secured in separate patrol cars when Gant arrived. The officers recognized his car as it entered the driveway, and Officer Griffith confirmed that Gant was the driver by shining a flashlight into the car as it drove by him. Gant parked at the end of the driveway, got out of his car, and shut the door. Griffith, who was about 30 feet away, called to Gant, and they approached each other, meeting 10- to 12-feet from Gant's car. Griffith immediately arrested Gant and handcuffed him.

Because the other arrestees were secured in the only patrol cars at the scene, Griffith called for backup. When two more officers arrived, they locked Gant in the backseat of their vehicle. After Gant had been handcuffed and placed in the back of a patrol car, two officers searched his car: One of them found a gun, and the other discovered a bag of cocaine in the pocket of a jacket on the backseat.

Gant was charged with two offenses—possession of a narcotic drug for sale and possession of drug paraphernalia (i.e., the plastic bag in which the cocaine was found). He moved to suppress the evidence seized from his car on the ground that the warrantless search violated the Fourth Amendment. Among other things, Gant argued that Belton did not authorize the search of his vehicle because he posed no threat to the officers after he was handcuffed in the patrol car and because he was arrested for a traffic offense for which no evidence could be found in his vehicle. When asked at the suppression hearing why the search was conducted, Officer Griffith responded: "Because the law says we can do it."

The trial court rejected the State's contention that the officers had probable cause to search Gant's car for contraband when the search began, but it denied the motion to suppress. Relying on the fact that the police saw Gant commit the crime of driving without a license and apprehended him only shortly after he exited his car, the court held that the search was permissible as a search incident to arrest. A jury found Gant guilty on both drug counts, and he was sentenced to a 3-year term of imprisonment.

After protracted state-court proceedings, the Arizona Supreme Court concluded that the search of Gant's car was unreasonable within the meaning of the Fourth Amendment. Relying on our earlier decision in Chimel, the court observed that the search-incident-to-arrest exception to the warrant requirement is justified by interests in officer safety and evidence preservation. When "the justifications underlying Chimel no longer exist because the scene is secure and the arrestee is handcuffed, secured in the back of a patrol car, and under the supervision of an officer," the court concluded, a "warrantless search of the arrestee's car cannot be justified as necessary to protect the officers at the scene or prevent the destruction of evidence." Accordingly, the court held that the search of Gant's car was unreasonable.

The chorus that has called for us to revisit Belton includes courts, scholars, and Members of this Court who have questioned that decision's clarity and its fidelity to Fourth Amendment principles. We therefore granted the State's petition for certiorari.

II

Consistent with our precedent, our analysis begins, as it should in every case addressing the reasonableness of a warrantless search, with the basic rule that "searches conducted outside the judicial process, without prior approval by judge or magistrate, are per se unreasonable under the Fourth Amendment—subject only to a few specifically established and well-delineated exceptions." Among the exceptions to the warrant requirement is a search incident to a lawful arrest. The exception derives from interests in officer safety and evidence preservation that are typically implicated in arrest situations.

In Chimel, we held that a search incident to arrest may only include "the arrestee's person and the area 'within his immediate control'—construing that phrase to mean the area from within which he might gain possession of a weapon or destructible evidence." That limitation, which continues to define the boundaries of the exception, ensures that the scope of a search incident to arrest is commensurate with its purposes of protecting arresting officers and safeguarding any evidence of the offense of arrest that an arrestee might conceal or destroy. If there is no possibility that an arrestee could reach into the area that law enforcement officers seek to search, both justifications for the search-incident-to-arrest exception are absent and the rule does not apply.

In Belton, we considered Chimel's application to the automobile context. A lone police officer in that case stopped a speeding car in which Belton was one of four occupants. While asking for the driver's license and registration, the officer smelled burnt marijuana and observed an envelope on the car floor marked "Supergold"—a name he associated with marijuana. Thus having probable cause to believe the occupants had committed a drug offense, the officer ordered them out of the vehicle, placed them under arrest, and patted them down. Without handcuffing the arrestees, the officer "'split them up into four separate areas of the Thruway . . . so they would not be in physical touching area of each other'" and searched the vehicle, including the pocket of a jacket on the backseat, in which he found cocaine.

[W]e held that when an officer lawfully arrests "the occupant of an automobile, he may, as a contemporaneous incident of that arrest, search the passenger compartment of the automobile" and any containers therein. That holding was based in large part on our assumption "that articles inside the relatively narrow compass of the passenger compartment of an automobile are in fact generally, even if not inevitably, within 'the area into which an arrestee might reach.'"

III

Under this broad reading of Belton, a vehicle search would be authorized incident to every arrest of a recent occupant notwithstanding that in most cases the vehicle's passenger compartment will not be within the arrestee's reach at the time of the search. To read Belton as authorizing a vehicle search incident to every recent occupant's arrest would thus untether the rule from the justifications underlying the Chimel exception—a result clearly incompatible with our statement in Belton that it "in no way alters the fundamental principles established in the Chimel case regarding the basic scope of searches incident to lawful custodial arrests." Accordingly, we reject this reading of Belton and hold that the Chimel rationale authorizes police to search a vehicle incident to a recent occupant's arrest only when the arrestee is unsecured and within reaching distance of the passenger compartment at the time of the search.

[W]e also conclude that circumstances unique to the vehicle context justify a search incident to a lawful arrest when it is "reasonable to believe evidence relevant to the crime of arrest might be found in the vehicle." In many cases, as when a recent occupant is arrested for a traffic violation, there will

(Continues)

(Continued)

be no reasonable basis to believe the vehicle contains relevant evidence. But in others, the offense of arrest will supply a basis for searching the passenger compartment of an arrestee's vehicle and any containers therein.

IV

It is particularly significant that Belton searches authorize police officers to search not just the passenger compartment but every purse, briefcase, or other container within that space. A rule that gives police the power to conduct such a search whenever an individual is caught committing a traffic offense, when there is no basis for believing evidence of the offense might be found in the vehicle, creates a serious and recurring threat to the privacy of countless individuals. Indeed, the character of that threat implicates the central concern underlying the Fourth Amendment—the concern about giving police officers unbridled discretion to rummage at will among a person's private effects.

[O]fficers may search a vehicle when genuine safety or evidentiary concerns encountered during the arrest of a vehicle's recent occupant justify a search. Construing Belton broadly to allow vehicle searches incident to any arrest would serve no purpose except to provide a police entitlement, and it is anathema to the Fourth Amendment to permit a warrantless search on that basis. For these reasons, we are unpersuaded by the State's arguments that a broad reading of Belton would meaningfully further law enforcement interests and justify a substantial intrusion on individuals' privacy.

V

Our dissenting colleagues argue that the doctrine of *stare decisis* requires adherence to a broad reading of Belton even though the justifications for searching a vehicle incident to arrest are in most cases absent. The doctrine of *stare decisis* is of course "essential to the respect accorded to the judgments of the Court and to the stability of the law," but it does not compel us to follow a past decision when its rationale no longer withstands "careful analysis."

We have never relied on *stare decisis* to justify the continuance of an unconstitutional police practice. And we would be particularly loath to uphold an unconstitutional result in a case that is so easily distinguished from the decisions that arguably compel it.

The experience of the 28 years since we decided Belton has shown that the generalization underpinning the broad reading of that decision is unfounded. We now know that articles inside the passenger compartment are rarely "within 'the area into which an arrestee might reach,' " and blind adherence to Belton's faulty assumption would authorize myriad unconstitutional searches. The doctrine of *stare decisis* does not require us to approve routine constitutional violations.

VI

Police may search a vehicle incident to a recent occupant's arrest only if the arrestee is within reaching distance of the passenger compartment at the time of the search or it is reasonable to believe the vehicle contains evidence of the offense of arrest. When these justifications are absent, a search of an arrestee's vehicle will be unreasonable unless police obtain a warrant or show that another exception to the warrant requirement applies. The Arizona Supreme Court correctly held that this case involved an unreasonable search. Accordingly, the judgment of the State Supreme Court is affirmed.

It is so ordered.

accessible to his car which the police searched and in which they found cocaine. Thus, the question for the Court was whether the search was legal, but more specifically, whether the rule in *Belton* must be applied as precedent?

Although the Court in *Gant* relied on its search and seizure precedents in other cases, it refused to apply the Belton holding and found that the Belton case should be limited, although the dissenting Justices in the case argued that the majority had overruled *Belton*. Regardless, if *stare decisis* had been strictly applied, a warrantless vehicle search by police after Gant had been arrested would have been justified under *Belton*. The Court's discussion of *stare*

decisis and its justifications for changes in the law of vehicle searches make it plain that the rule of precedent is not so inflexible that prior case law must always apply: "We have never relied on stare decisis to justify the continuance of an unconstitutional police practice" (129 S. Ct. at 1722).

Constitutional Law

The U.S. Constitution and the laws passed in accordance with its provisions constitute the "supreme law of the land" (U.S. Cont., Art. VI, Sec. 2). This means that all laws in the United States are subservient to provisions of the U.S. Constitution. A state's laws may grant greater rights to its citizens than the Constitution confers, but it may not confer less. Stated differently, states may adopt whatever laws they wish, provided that they do not conflict with the U.S. Constitution. As the supreme law of the land, all provisions of the U.S. Constitution represent sources of law relied on by American courts.

The U.S. Constitution provides the organizing scheme for American government, with Articles I, II, and III creating and specifying the powers of the Legislative, Executive, and Judiciary branches of government. Article III, addressing the federal judiciary branch, is discussed in detail in Chapter 4. As most students have already learned, the function of the Legislative branch is to make the law. The function of the Executive branch is to enforce the law, and the judiciary function is to interpret the law. By separating these functions into distinct branches of government, the founders of the country created a new structure for central governance that represented a significant departure from the original Articles of Confederation used to join the states together (see **Sidebar 2.1**).

Sidebar 2.1 *The Articles of Confederation: Beginnings of the Constitution*

In June of 1776, the Second Continental Congress met in Philadelphia and formed a committee to draft what became the Declaration of Independence, adopted on July 4, 1776, but also in June of that year, the Second Continental Congress formed a committee to draft what became the Articles of Confederation and Perpetual Union Between the States (the "Articles"), a document intended to govern the shared interests of the colonies. The Articles, however, were not adopted until November of 1777 and were not effective until ratified by the states in 1781.

The Revolutionary War and the separation of the colonies from the Crown spurred the creation of a unified government, but one in which, as stated in Article 2 of the Articles, "Each State retains its sovereignty, freedom, and independence." The intent was "to enter into a firm league of friendship with each other for their common defence, the security of their liberties, and their mutual and general welfare" (Articles, Art. 3). The Articles thus created the first government framework for the fledgling nation, calling itself for the first time "The United States of America."

It also created a framework of legal protections for states' interests. One of the central complaints of the colonies against the King of England was that colonists had been deprived of representation in Parliament, and the states who made up the Second Continental Congress were each concerned about the dangers of centralized power in a national government. They were not about to fight a revolution against England only to find a new American government continuing to deprive them of their ability to operate as they saw fit. Therefore, Article IV of the Articles provided:

The better to secure and perpetuate mutual friendship and intercourse among the people of the different States in this Union, the free inhabitants of each of these States, paupers,

vagabonds, and fugitives from justice excepted, shall be entitled to all privileges and immunities of free citizens in the several States; and the people of each State shall have free ingress and regress to and from any other State, and shall enjoy therein all the privileges of trade and commerce, subject to the same duties, impositions, and restrictions as the inhabitants thereof respectively, provided that such restrictions shall not extend so far as to prevent the removal of property imported into any State, to any other State, of which the owner is an inhabitant; provided also that no imposition, duties or restriction shall be laid by any State, on the property of the United States, or either of them.

If any person guilty of, or charged with, treason, felony, or other high misdemeanor in any State, shall flee from justice, and be found in any of the United States, he shall, upon demand of the Governor or executive power of the State from which he fled, be delivered up and removed to the State having jurisdiction of his offense.

Full faith and credit shall be given in each of these States to the records, acts, and judicial proceedings of the courts and magistrates of every other State.

Thus, the Articles recognized the rights to commerce and property enjoyed by the individual states, as well as their right to criminal justice within their borders, protected by extradition. It further protected state justice systems by recognizing the states' right to "full faith and credit" of their court proceedings.

As important as the Articles were in giving the states the unifying structure of a national government, however, it became apparent that they did not sufficiently address many problems if the states were to become an independent nation. First among these was the problem of representation; the Articles gave each state one equal vote in Congress, despite the widely varying population of each. In addition, the only mechanism for resolving disputes between the states was Congress itself. Because each state operated its own system of courts, an independent tribunal for hearing cases involving citizens of different states did not exist, and it became evident that Congress could not hear every dispute that might arise between the states. Furthermore, trade between the states and between the states and foreign governments was a matter of state sovereignty under the Articles; there was no regulation of the manner in which such trade could or should occur.

As a result of these problems, almost immediately after the adoption of the Articles, the Continental Congress began to draft and debate a new Constitution. The resulting document, ratified in 1788, replaced the Articles and became, by its own terms, "the supreme law of the land." The Articles of Confederation served the nation for 7 years at the outset of the country and in many ways made the adoption of the U.S. Constitution possible. The now familiar provisions of the Constitution, including the creation of three branches of government, a bicameral legislature, and retaining protection for states' rights, resolved many of the deficiencies in the Articles. The Constitution, with the Articles as its forerunner, provided an enduring structure that, in the words of Chief Justice Marshall, was "intended to endure for ages to come, and consequently, to be adapted to the various crises of human affairs" (*McCulloch v. Maryland*, 17 U.S. 316, 1819).

The legislative branch, Congress, makes law by adopting federal statutes, discussed further later here. The executive branch, responsible for the "enforcement" of the law, does this through a variety of executive agencies, each of which is also responsible for the creation of regulations, which give effect to statutes drafted by Congress. These are also discussed later here.

It is the Amendments to the Constitution in which constitutional law having the greatest effect on judicial decision making is found. In particular, the first ten amendments, the "Bill of Rights," serve as the cornerstone of individual rights for American citizens. In both civil and criminal cases, these Amendments are responsible for generating considerable activity in the courts. In particular, the rights contained in the following Amendments are a frequent source of law in criminal or civil cases.

Amendment I: "Congress shall make no law respecting an establishment of religion, or prohibiting the free exercise thereof; or abridging the freedom of speech, or of the press; or the right of the people peaceably to assemble, and to petition the Government for a redress of grievances."

The First Amendment contains several well-known, if not well-understood, rights. First, it prevents the government from passing laws that "establish" a particular religion, or laws that prevent one from the free practice of his or her religion. It has been said that the Constitution creates a "wall of separation" between church and state (*Everson v. Board of Education*, 330 U.S. 1, 16 (1947)). This has been interpreted to mean that the government may do nothing to support or favor one religion over another, nor can it act in any way that prevents persons from worshiping in any way that they choose.

Protection for freedom of speech reflects the Framers' concern about governmental censorship of citizens. Although not every form of expression is protected by the First Amendment (e.g., threats to safety, some forms of obscenity), "speech" extends beyond verbal expression to include symbolic acts such as wearing armbands or political buttons, holding signs, or burning the flag.

Freedom of the press involves the writing or publication of ideas for distribution to others. Individuals may not be punished by the government for the written expression of their ideas, nor may the government, with limited exceptions, forbid their publication. This protection generally applies to radio and television broadcasts as well as newspapers and magazines and extends to most expression over the Internet as well.

The freedom of assembly protects citizens from government intrusion on meetings with others for lawful purposes. Although the government may restrict such meetings for health or safety reasons, it may not do so unreasonably, or punish participation. The First Amendment also prevents the government from limiting a citizen's ability to communicate with, or "petition," the government about matters of public or private concern.

Amendment II: "A well regulated militia, being necessary for the security of a free State, the right of the people to keep and bear arms, shall not be infringed."

This controversial Amendment, protecting the "right of the people to keep and bear arms," has become a source of debate in discussions of gun control. Although its original purpose in allowing citizens to protect themselves and take up arms against foreign invaders is relatively clear, its applicability in the current day is less clear. Some argue that the right is not an individual right to own and use guns, but is a collective right granted to states to establish and arm militias. Others argue that the right is granted to every individual to own guns for his or her protection. Regardless, the right has been interpreted as preventing the federal government from overzealous restriction of gun rights, not state governments.

Amendment III: "No soldier shall, in time of peace be quartered in any house, without the consent of the Owner, nor in time of war, but in a manner to be prescribed by law."

The Third Amendment appears to have limited applicability in the United States today. It stems from the practice of British soldiers before and during the American Revolution taking the homes of citizens for housing.

Amendment IV: "The right of the people to be secure in their persons, houses, papers, and effects, against unreasonable searches and seizures, shall not be violated, and no Warrants shall issue, but upon probable cause, supported by Oath or affirmation, and particularly describing the place to be searched, and the persons or things to be seized."

The government or its agents (usually police officers) cannot unreasonably enter into or take a citizen's property without two things: a court order, called a "warrant," and "probable cause," which means a reasonable likelihood that a person has been involved in a crime or that evidence of crime may be found in a particular place. This requirement extends to the arrest of suspects as well. Although numerous exceptions to these rules exist, the purpose of these protections is to prevent the government from taking unjustifiable action against a people or their property.

Amendment V: "No person shall be held to answer for a capital, or otherwise infamous crime, unless on a presentment or indictment of a Grand Jury, except in cases arising in the land or naval forces, or in the militia, when in actual service in time of War or public danger; nor shall any person be subject for the same offence to be twice put in jeopardy of life or limb; nor shall be compelled in any criminal case to be a witness against himself, nor be deprived of life, liberty, or property, without due process of law; nor shall private property be taken for public use, without just compensation."

In federal felony cases (except military matters), a grand jury must return an indictment, or statement of charges, before a criminal defendant may be prosecuted. A grand jury consists of a group of citizens who must determine whether probable cause exists to charge the defendant.

This is intended to allow a defendant's fellow citizens to provide a "second look" at whether there is sufficient basis for a prosecution, rather than leaving it entirely up to the government with the possibility of abuse by charging political rivals.

The well-known prohibition on double jeopardy prohibits the government from prosecuting a defendant again for the same offense and prevents multiple punishments after conviction for an offense. The scope and application of double jeopardy has grown to involve many exceptions.

The privilege against self-incrimination allows a criminal defendant to not testify at trial as well as not provide any information to the government in anticipation of prosecution. The protection is limited to testimony, however, and does not extend to such things as fingerprints, blood alcohol tests, or lineup appearances.

The "due process" clause of the Fifth Amendment provides important fundamental rights in criminal cases, including notice of the charges, the presumption of innocence, and the right to an impartial decision maker. It recognizes the three categories of punishment for offenders: deprivation of life, liberty, or property.

Finally, the Fifth Amendment requires just compensation be paid when property is taken for "public use." As discussed in Chapter 1, the meaning of public use has changed over time and broadened the circumstances in which private property may be taken by the government.

Amendment VI: "In all criminal prosecutions, the accused shall enjoy the right to a speedy and public trial, by an impartial jury of the State and district wherein the crime shall have been committed, which district shall have been previously ascertained by law, and to be informed of the nature and cause of the accusation; to be confronted with the witnesses against him; to have compulsory process for obtaining witnesses in his favor, and to have the assistance of counsel for his defence."

The speedy trial requirement of this amendment demands that the government not delay prosecution of the defendant unnecessarily. The length of time before trial, the reason for any delay, and whether the defendant is prejudiced by the delay are factors courts consider in determining whether this right has been violated. State and federal statutes specify the time within which a trial must be held, which may vary in different jurisdictions.

A public trial is also required. This right protects the defendant from secret proceedings by the government with the potential for improper government or judicial action and unfairness to the accused. It also serves to foster confidence in the court system.

The right to an impartial jury in criminal cases also offers protection against improper judicial behavior and attempts to ensure fairness in proceedings in which a defendant's life, liberty, or property may be at stake. Many rules and procedures have developed to protect this right; these are discussed in detail in Chapter 3.

The right to notice of the charges is consistent with and more specific than the due process protection found in the Fifth Amendment. In order to defend against the government's accusations, a defendant must know with specificity what those charges are, both in terms of his or her behavior and the law that is alleged to have been violated.

Criminal defendants also have a right to confront witnesses against them and to compel witnesses to appear at trial to testify. The confrontation clause is designed to allow cross-examination of witnesses to test the truthfulness of their testimony as well as the extent of the witnesses' knowledge. This contributes to the defendant's ability to present a defense by offering other evidence to rebut the adverse witnesses' claims.

The Sixth Amendment also guarantees the right to effective assistance of counsel in criminal cases where the defendant's liberty is at stake. This right exists at each stage of proceedings in which the defendant's rights may be affected, not just at trial. If a defendant lacks the ability to pay an attorney, the state must provide one free of charge. Although a defendant may waive the right to counsel, this can only occur intentionally and knowingly.

Amendment VII: "In suits at common law, where the value in controversy shall exceed twenty dollars, the right of trial by jury shall be preserved, and no fact tried by a jury shall be otherwise re-examined in any court of the United States, than according to the rules of the common law."

This amendment preserves the right to a jury trial in federal civil cases involving more than 20 dollars; however, federal courts rules of civil procedure generally do not authorize cases where the amount in controversy is only 20 dollars.

Amendment VIII: "Excessive bail shall not be required, nor excessive fines imposed, nor cruel and unusual punishments inflicted."

Bail is money deposited with the Court in order to guarantee a defendant's return to face trial at a future date. Although the Eighth Amendment does not create a right to bail, it is presumed to exist provided the defendant is not a flight risk or danger to the public. Bail is "excessive" when it is more than is reasonably necessary to ensure that the defendant return for trial.

This amendment also prohibits "cruel and unusual" punishments. The meaning of this phrase has been frequently litigated, perhaps most often in the context of capital punishment. It has been interpreted to require "proportionality," where the punishment must be proportional to the seriousness of the crime, and it must relate to the goals of punishment for that crime.

Amendment IX: "The enumeration in the Constitution, of certain rights, shall not be construed to deny or disparage others retained by the people."

Although somewhat vague on its face, this Constitutional provision appears to have been intended to preserve for the people rights not specifically mentioned in the Constitution, rather than allowing the government to deny the existence of such rights. What rights these are has been a source of debate, and as the *Griswold* case demonstrates, the Supreme Court has interpreted the Ninth Amendment to expand on the rights specifically mentioned in the Constitution.

> *Amendment X*: "The powers not delegated to the United States by the Constitution, nor prohibited by it to the States, are reserved to the States respectively, or to the people."

The Tenth Amendment seeks to ensure that all powers not specifically given to the federal government remain with the states or the people themselves. This reflects the principles of "federalism," discussed in Chapter 4, which formulate the distinction between federal and state power and rights of citizens within each.

Additional amendments added after the Bill of Rights have particular importance as sources of law and for the operation of the courts. Among these is the Fourteenth Amendment, which clarifies the effect of certain rights found in the first 10 amendments on the states.

> *Amendment XIV*: "Section 1. All persons born or naturalized in the United States, and subject to the jurisdiction thereof, are citizens of the United States and of the State wherein they reside. No State shall make or enforce any law which shall abridge the privileges or immunities of citizens of the United States, nor shall any State deprive any person of life, liberty, or property, without due process of law; nor deny to any person within its jurisdiction the equal protection of the laws. . . ."

The Fourteenth Amendment, adopted in 1868, explicitly recognizes the "dual" citizenship of people within the United States, preserving their rights as citizens of their home states and, importantly, making some of their federal rights applicable to the states. It also prevents the states from passing laws that "abridge" the federal rights of citizens. Specifically, it takes the due process clause of the Fifth Amendment and makes it applicable to the states, preventing states from denying individuals the right to due process. It also prevents states from denying citizens "equal protection" of the laws, which means that states may not unreasonably create classifications of people to whom their laws may be applied differently.

Although some of these rights and protections are familiar to most people (like the freedom of speech and religion), others are less well recognized and understood. The meaning of these provisions of law is the domain of the courts. In relying on them as sources of law and interpreting their meaning, courts have expanded the scope of citizens' rights.

In addition to the U.S. Constitution, each state has its own constitution that serves as an important source of law in that state. State constitutions frequently adopt the rights and protections found in the U.S. Constitution, and in some states, those rights are broader than those found in the federal constitution. Although states are free to provide greater rights and protections than the U.S. Constitution provides, they may not restrict the rights found in the U.S. Constitution.

Statutory Law

Statutes are the result of legislative lawmaking. When Congress passes a law, it becomes a statute found in the United States Code, the collection of such laws. Federal statutes continually address a variety of civil and criminal concerns, as well as matters relating to the operation of government. Although the political process affects what becomes statutory law and the specific content included in statutes, once adopted, it is the role of the courts to clarify what the laws require. Conversely, some legislation is intended specifically to reverse or modify decisions by the courts.

Similarly, each state's legislature works to adopt laws applicable within that state. These state statutes address matters of concern to the citizens of that state. Both civil and criminal matters are the subject of state statutes, and the primary focus of state court decision making is the application and interpretation of state statutes.

Regulatory Law

Regulations are rules promulgated by administrative agencies in the Executive branch of government. Both federal and state agencies adopt regulations. Their purpose is to implement the statutory law by specifying the details of what a statute requires and the way in which it will operate. Regulations must therefore be consistent with the provisions of a statute and not "go beyond" what a statute says. For example, if a statute were to state "no person under the age of 16 shall be issued a driver's license unless such person is a resident of a farming community," the motor vehicle division, an executive agency, might adopt a regulation specifying what constitutes a "farming community" as well as when a person under 16 years old is a resident. Regulatory law is important because it has a direct impact on the persons to whom it applies.

Key Terms

Law	Rule of Law
Social Norms	Judicial Discretion
Religion and Law	Substantive Law
Natural Law	Procedural Law
Legal Positivism	Common Law
Critical Legal Theory	*Stare Decisis*
Legal Realism	Branches of Government
Economic Analysis of Law	Bill of Rights

Discussion Questions

1. How does law differ from religious beliefs and social norms?
2. How are law and justice related? In what ways does one affect the other?
3. What is the common goal each theory of law shares, and how does this affect the application of law?

4. What are the five primary theories of law? How do they differ in their approach to achieving justice?

5. Why is the "rule of law" important in a democratic society?

6. Discuss the central purpose of law, and explain how it is accomplished by both the criminal and civil law.

7. U.S. law is found in four primary sources. What are they? Which branch of government is responsible for creation of each?

8. What is "common law," and what effect does it have on decision making by American courts?

Cases

American Banana Co. v. United Fruit Co., 213 U.S. 347 (1909).

Arizona v. Gant, 129 S. Ct. 1710 (2009).

Everson v. Board of Education, 330 U.S. 1, 16, 50 S. Ct. 165, (1947).

Griswold v. Connecticut, 381 U.S. 479 (1965).

Marbury v. Madison, 1 Cranch 137, 5 U.S. 137, 2 L.Ed. 60 (1803).

McCulloch v. Maryland, 17 U.S. 316 (1819).

New York v. Belton, 453 U.S. 454 (1981).

State v. Maldonado, 137 N.J. 536, 645 A.2d 1165 (1994).

U.S. Fidelity and Guaranty Co. v. Guenther, 281 U.S. 34, 50 S. Ct. 165, 74 L.Ed. 683 (1930).

Criminal Justice on the Web

 For an up-to-date list of Web links, go to *The American Courts: A Procedural Approach* online companion site at http://criminal justice.jbpub.com/AmericanCourts. The online companion site will introduce you to some of the most important sites for finding American courts information on the Internet.

References

Abraham, H. J. (1998). *The Judicial Process* (7th ed.). New York: Oxford University Press.

Bix, B. H. (2000). On the dividing line between natural law theory and legal positivism. *Notre Dame Law Review*, 75, 1613–1624.

Bix, B. H. (2005). Legal positivism. In M. P. Golding & W. A. Edmundson (Eds.), *The Blackwell Guide to the Philosophy of Law and Legal Theory*. Malden, MA: Blackwell Publishing.

Dubber, M. D. (2006). *The Sense of Justice: Empathy in Law and Punishment*. New York: New York University Press.

Edmundson, W. A. (2005). Introduction. In M. P. Golding & W. A. Edmundson (Eds.), *The Blackwell Guide to the Philosophy of Law and Legal Theory*. Malden, MA: Blackwell Publishing.

Finnis, J. (2003). Law and what I truly should decide. *American Journal of Jurisprudence*, 48, 107–130.

Fisher, W. W., Horwitz, M. J., & Reed, T. A. (Eds.). (1993). *American Legal Realism*. New York: Oxford University Press.

Friedrichs, D. O. (2006). *Law in Our Lives: An Introduction* (2nd ed.). Los Angeles: Roxbury.

George, R. P. (1999). *In Defense of Natural Law*. New York: Oxford University Press.

Glenn, H. P. (2003). A transnational concept of law. In P. Cane & M. Tushnet (Eds.), *The Oxford Handbook of Legal Studies*. New York: Oxford University Press.

Hart, H. L. A. (1994). *The Concept of Law* (2nd ed.). Oxford: Oxford University Press.

Kairys, D. (1982). *The Politics of Law*. New York: Pantheon Books.

Kornhauser, L. A. (2003). Preference, well-being and morality in social decision. *Journal of Legal Studies*, 33(1), 303–330.

Kornhauser, L. A. (2005). Economic rationality in the analysis of legal rules and institutions. In M. P. Golding & W. A. Edmundson (Eds.), *The Blackwell Guide to the Philosophy of Law and Legal Theory*. Malden, MA: Blackwell Publishing.

Leiter, B. (2005). American legal realism. In M. P. Golding & W. A. Edmundson (Eds.), *The Blackwell Guide to the Philosophy of Law and Legal Theory*. Malden, MA: Blackwell Publishing.

Llewellyn, K. (1950). Remarks on the theory of appellate decision and the rules and canons about how statutes are to be construed. *Vanderbilt Law Review*, 3, 395–406.

Morrison, W. (1997). *Jurisprudence: From the Greeks to Post-Moderism*. London: Cavendish.

Murphy, M. C. (2005). Natural law theory. In M. P. Golding & W. A. Edmundson (Eds.), *The Blackwell Guide to the Philosophy of Law and Legal Theory*. Malden, MA: Blackwell Publishing.

Posner, R. A. (1987). The decline of law as an autonomous discipline: 1962–1987. *Harvard Law Review*, 100, 761–780.

Posner, R. A. (1999). *The Problematics of Moral and Legal Theory*. Cambridge, MA: Harvard University Press.

Raz, J. (2005). Can there be a theory of law? In M. P. Golding & W. A. Edmundson (Eds.), *The Blackwell Guide to the Philosophy of Law and Legal Theory*. Malden, MA: Blackwell Publishing.

Sarat, A. (1990). "The law is all over:" Power, resistance, and the legal consciousness of the welfare poor. *Yale Journal of Law and the Humanities*, 2, 343–379.

Sherwin, R. K. (2004). Law in popular culture. In A. Sarat (Ed.), *The Blackwell Companion to Law and Society*. Malden, MA: Blackwell Publishing.

Smith, S. D. (1997). Natural law and contemporary moral thought: A guide for the perplexed. *American Journal of Jurisprudence*, 42, 299–330.

Tushnet, M. V. (1996). Defending the indeterminacy thesis. *Quinnipiac Law Review*, 16, 339–356.

Tushnet, M. V. (2005). Critical legal theory. In M. P. Golding & W. A. Edmundson (Eds.), *The Blackwell Guide to the Philosophy of Law and Legal Theory*. Malden, MA: Blackwell Publishing.

Zane, J. M. (1998). *The Story of Law* (2nd ed.). Indianapolis, IN: Liberty Fund.

The Courts and Their Operation

3

What Is This Chapter About?

This chapter discusses the American court system. In the United States, a dual system of courts exists as a result of our dual system of government, federal and state. We examine the distinction between the state and federal courts and consider the operational aspects that they share. Of particular importance is the legal concept of jurisdiction, or the authority to decide cases, which we examine in detail. The types of jurisdiction that exist, along with the function they have in the operation of a court, is a useful starting place for understanding how courts decide cases.

We next consider the goals that courts share. All courts seek to do what justice requires in rendering decisions; the ways in which this is achieved are examined. These include maintaining objectivity in all stages of the legal proceeding, making decisions based on the established facts and the law. Courts also must provide an orderly forum for a fair and equitable hearing of each case. In addition, courts strive to adhere to rules of procedure, both to ensure fairness and regulate the proceeding. Rules of procedure are intended to accomplish these purposes. Furthermore, the goal of all courts is to provide litigants with a clear outcome at the conclusion of the case. The lack of a decision or uncertainty regarding a decision would undercut a central role in dispensing justice.

This chapter also examines the way in which American courts operate in accordance with an adversarial system, rather than an inquisitorial system, which is found in other countries. The characteristics of the adversarial system serve to satisfy the demands of justice. Some of these characteristics include the opposing positions of the parties, equal access to information, designated burdens and standards of proof, and an emphasis on procedure over outcome. In criminal cases, the presumption of innocence is also an important and necessary aspect of the adversarial system.

Finally, this chapter outlines the functions of trial courts and appellate courts. As courts of original jurisdiction, trial courts determine the facts in each case and apply the law to the facts found. The distinction between a bench trial and a jury trial is discussed, and the steps of

the trial process are presented, including jury selection, discovery and other pretrial matters, activities at trial, and postjudgment matters. The review function of appellate courts is also examined in terms of the limitations on appellate courts, the nature of judicial review, and the types of decisions that they can issue.

Learning Objectives

After reading this chapter, you should be able to

1. Distinguish between federal and state courts.
2. Understand the meaning and limits of a court's jurisdiction.
3. Describe the types of jurisdiction that may limit a court's authority.
4. Identify the goals that all courts share.
5. Distinguish the adversarial system from the inquisitorial system.
6. Describe the characteristics of the adversarial system.
7. Understand the different functions of trial and appellate courts.
8. Explain each step in the trial process.
9. Explain the appellate process.

The American Courts and Systems of Government

The courts in the justice system of the United States are as numerous as they are varied. These courts accomplish a broad array of tasks relating to the functioning of society, including the processing, trial, and sentencing of offenders in serious and less-serious criminal cases, resolving disputes involving large and small amounts of money, handling complex multistate lawsuits, deciding constitutional issues affecting citizens' rights, certifying marriages and divorces, passing property on death, and a multitude of other matters involving everyday life in America. It is therefore not surprising that there are a large number of courts needed to perform functions such as these and that these courts are found in large cities, small towns, and everywhere in between.

We can begin to understand the operation of the courts by classifying them in terms of their functioning and the areas in which they are granted authority to make decisions. One such classification involves whether a court operated as a branch of the federal government or the state government. These parallel systems of courts, although somewhat similar in their operation, handle different types of disputes and look to different sources for their authority. *Federal courts* are those that handle matters of federal concern and operate under the authority of the U.S. government. *State courts* operate solely within and under the authority of the states in which they are located.

As separate systems of justice, the state and federal courts act independently, and with limited exceptions, one system has no direct authority or influence over the other. Although it is true that, as discussed in Chapter 2, the U.S. Constitution is the "law of the land" and is therefore enforceable against actions by state and local governments, states are nonetheless sovereign entities of government and are the sole source of authority for matters occurring within their borders. It is each state, therefore, that has responsibility for the operation of its own courts. Chapter 4 closely examines the structure of the federal courts, and Chapter 5 considers state court systems in detail. In this chapter, we address considerations involving the operation of the U.S. courts in general, regardless of their state or federal authority.

Court Jurisdiction

A key to understanding the operation of the courts is the concept of *jurisdiction*. Jurisdiction refers to the scope of a court's authority to make decisions. If a court lacks jurisdiction, it is without any power whatsoever to hear or make any decisions in a case, except the decision about whether it has jurisdiction. Generally, jurisdiction serves to limit the scope of a court's authority and help to define the function of a court. Many different classifications are used to consider the scope of a court's power. The various types of jurisdiction and the ways in which they restrict or allow court decision making are discussed later here. There are, however, three types of jurisdiction that always must be present before a court has the power to make any decision. They involve what a case is about, who a case involves, and where the facts relating to a case occurred. These are known as *subject matter jurisdiction*, *personal jurisdiction*, and *geographic jurisdiction*.

Jurisdiction over the Subject Matter

Courts may also be distinguished by the subject matter of cases that come before them (*Arbaugh v. Y & H Corp.*, 546 U.S. 500 (2006)). Broadly, we may classify courts as handling criminal cases or civil cases, but some courts may hear both criminal and civil cases, depending on their statutory authorization. Subject matter jurisdiction may also refer to the specific issues that a court may be called on to decide. For instance, a court's subject matter jurisdiction may be limited to misdemeanor criminal cases, or

civil cases involving less than $10,000. All federal courts except for the U.S. Supreme Court have limited subject matter jurisdiction because their authority comes from Congress who determined what the function of each federal court should be (*Da Silva v. Kinsho International Corp.*, 229 F.3d 358 (2d Cir. 2000)). Along with a grant of subject matter jurisdiction, a court may inherently exercise *ancillary jurisdiction*, which allows a court to make all decisions and assert all powers necessary to exercise subject matter jurisdiction (*Chambers v. Nasco*, 501 U.S. 32 (1991)).

Personal Jurisdiction

The reach of a court's power is limited to certain definable persons or things. This distinction stems from the king's courts of equity in England, where disputes between persons were decided, and the later courts of "law," in which decisions regarding various types of property disputes were resolved. American courts may hear either type of matter, whether relating to persons or things (*Kunkel v. U.S.*, 140 F. Supp. 591 (S.D.Cal. 1956)); however, the nature of the power relates to distinct types of jurisdiction, referred to as *in personam jurisdiction* (relating to persons) and *in rem jurisdiction* (relating to things). A court need have only one of these forms of personal jurisdiction, along with subject matter jurisdiction, in order to hear and decide a case. *In personam jurisdiction* gives a court authority to decide matters relating to persons who are physically present within the borders of the state in which the court is located. In criminal cases, jurisdiction over an accused in another state may be obtained through a process called *extradition*, allowing a court of the state where the defendant is physically located to order that the accused be delivered to the authorities of another state. Unless the accused can be brought within the borders of the state seeking to charge him, that state's courts will have no jurisdiction over that person. In civil cases, a state's *long-arm statute* may allow a court to have authority over a nonresident, where that person has had some contact with the state that relates to the matter before the court. A long-arm statute thus provides a court with jurisdiction over a nonresident in a civil case, but generally only if the nonresident is alleged to have done something that is specified in the statute and has had "minimum contacts" with the state (see, e.g., *Buckingham, Doolittle & Burroughs, LLP v. Kar Kare Automotive Group, Inc.*, 987 So. 2d 818 (Fla. App. 4th Dist. 2008)).

In rem (Latin, "about or relating to a thing") jurisdiction allows a court to make decisions relating to some property, whether real, personal, tangible, or intangible, regardless of the person who owns or possesses it. The property that is the subject of the court action is referred to as the *res* (Latin, "thing"). *In rem* jurisdiction is based on the location of the *res*. That is, if the property is located where the court is located, the court is likely to have authority over it. Most legal proceedings involving real estate are *in rem* actions because the court in the district where the property is located has authority over it; however, the same may said of personal property such as automobiles, jewelry, money, or anything else that may be moved from place to place.

Geographic (Territorial) Jurisdiction

Courts generally are granted authority within the area in which they are located. Thus, "geographic" jurisdiction refers to a court's authority to decide matters only within certain geographic boundaries. Most commonly, state borders are the boundaries for the operation of state courts, but other geographic boundaries, such as county lines or statutorily defined districts, may also limit a court's power. In federal courts, geographic jurisdiction exists only within the United States and its territories. For federal trial courts, jurisdiction resides within federal "districts," which are defined as state borders or areas within a state (for states with more than one federal trial court). Federal court jurisdiction for appeals is defined by "circuits," which are multistate areas within the country and its territories. Although there are exceptions, geographic jurisdiction allows courts to make decisions affecting people that reside or are physically present within the applicable geographic boundaries, property that is located within those boundaries, or events that occur within those boundaries. Case Decision 3.1 involves a dispute about the personal and subject matter jurisdiction of a court to decide where a dead body should be interred.

Case Decision 3.1 *Attal v. Taylor*, 2008 WL 2861654 (Cal. App. 4 Dist. 2008)

Decision of the court by Judge McIntyre:

Sharon Taylor Attal petitioned the superior court to disinter the body of her mother, Joan Taylor, so that it could be re-interred with Sharon's deceased brother, Mark Taylor. John Taylor, another of Sharon's brothers, filed a cross-petition requesting that Mark's body be disinterred so that it could be reinterred with Joan's. Sharon appeals the superior court order denying her petition and conditionally granting John's cross-petition. She contends that (1) she was not required to obtain court approval before having Joan's body exhumed and reinterred; (2) the superior court abused its discretion in denying her petition; (3) the court lacked subject matter jurisdiction over John's cross-petition, which she contends required the resolution of religious disputes; (4) the court lacked personal jurisdiction over her as to John's petition; (5) John lacked standing to bring his cross-petition. . . . We find her arguments unavailing and affirm the order.

Factual and Procedural Background

Joan was born in March 1918 as Sadie Rabinowitz, to Jewish parents. When she became emancipated, she changed her name to Joan Robbins. As a result of marriage, Joan took on the surname Taylor; during the marriage, she and her husband had four children: Sharon, Dennis, John and Mark. Joan was a practicing Presbyterian and raised her children in accordance with that faith. After Joan's husband abandoned the family in 1957, their marriage was dissolved in 1962.

In September 1985, after Joan was hospitalized with a serious illness, Mark purchased two crypt spaces at El Camino Park and Cemetery (the Cemetery), specifying that he and Joan would each be buried there and naming Sharon as a joint tenant owner of the crypt spaces. Joan, who by Sharon's own admission was not "religiously observant" of the Jewish faith, agreed to Mark's plan and was happy with it.

Joan passed away in November 1988 and a Presbyterian minister officiated over her funeral service. Contrary to Judaic principles specifying that a Jewish person's body should be buried in the ground, Joan's body was placed in the crypt in accordance with her expectations, Mark's written directive and the wishes of all four children.

In 1989, Sharon began practicing Judaism as her religious faith. That same year, Mark set up a pre-needs trust with the Cemetery, identifying his faith as Presbyterian, documenting his intent to be entombed rather than buried and specifying that Sharon was to provide instructions about the poems and other materials to be read at his funeral. In 2002, Mark executed a will in which he directed that his body be interred with Joan's in the crypt after he died.

When Mark died in April 2003 in Mexico, however, Sharon disregarded his written directive and attempted to have his body interred at A.M. Israel Mortuary, a Jewish cemetery there. A.M. Israel Mortuary declined Sharon's request because Mark had not practiced Judaism during his life.

After Mark's body was returned to the United States, Sharon discussed Mark's interment with the Cemetery and proposed having his body buried in the Jewish (Mount Sinai) section of the Cemetery. Both Dennis and John were upset by Sharon's proposal, although Sharon insisted on it, particularly after the Cemetery indicated that Mark would have to be placed on his side to fit into a standard sized coffin, as necessary to fit in the crypt. Sharon also insisted on having a Jewish service for Mark, but

(Continues)

(Continued)

Dennis and John declined to participate in that service, instead holding a separate, Christian service for the remainder of the family and Mark's friends.

In March 2005, Dennis's wife, Patricia, was diagnosed with Stage IV lung cancer and, after Patricia became seriously ill, Sharon offered to give Dennis the crypt spaces Mark had purchased for himself and Joan if Dennis purchased the burial plot next to Mark's, transferred the plot to her and paid the costs of moving Joan's remains to the new plot. Because he and Patricia liked the location of the crypt where Joan's body was compared to other spaces that were available, Dennis agreed to Sharon's proposal and purchased the plot next to where Mark was buried.

Dennis and Sharon executed written documents providing for the transfer of ownership of the new plot from Dennis to Sharon and the crypt space to Dennis and for the disinterment and reinterment of Joan's remains. Sharon planned to have Joan's body removed from the crypt, disrobed, shrouded, placed in a new casket (a Jewish liner) and reinterred, pursuant to an Orthodox Jewish ceremony, next to Mark's grave in the Mount Sinai section of the Cemetery in November 2006.

The evidence is conflicting on whether John was aware of his siblings' agreement before late October 2006; however, it is undisputed that in early November 2006, John contacted the Cemetery to object to the planned removal of his mother's remains and retained an attorney. John's attorney demanded that Sharon explain why she had disregarded Mark's directions that he was to be interred in the crypt and provide the legal basis for her actions.

Shortly after John's contact with the Cemetery, it notified Sharon that it would proceed with Joan's reinterment only if she obtained a court order. Sharon sent the Cemetery e-mails indicating that she and Dennis were legally entitled to disinter and reinter Joan's remains without any input from John and that John would never take any action, other than making verbal threats, to stop that process because he was "too cheap" to put up any of his own money for a legal fight.

After Sharon's efforts to get the Cemetery to proceed without a court order failed, she filed a disinterment petition in the superior court on March 28, 2007, naming John and the Cemetery as respondents. (All further dates are in 2007 except as otherwise noted.) Shortly thereafter Patricia lost her fight with cancer and Dennis filed a petition similar to Sharon's. Both petitions relied in part on Sharon's declaration, which provided in part that she was unable to carry out Mark's wishes for his remains to be placed in the crypt because doing so was a "physical impossibility." At some point not evident from the record, the court set Sharon's petition for hearing on May 3.

After service of the petitions, John's attorney noticed an ex parte appearance in Dennis's case, seeking to clarify how the court intended to handle the matter procedurally and specifically requesting that the court continue the hearing date on Sharon's petition so that he could conduct discovery before having to respond. Dennis's counsel, who represented to the court that he was specially appearing on Sharon's behalf as well, requested that the court consolidate the proceedings on the two petitions and expedite the hearing date. The court granted Dennis's consolidation request and denied both the petitioners' request for an expedited hearing date and John's request for deferment of the hearing. Without objection, the court ordered that further briefing be filed and served five days before the hearing date. John filed and served his written opposition and a cross-petition to disinter Mark's remains so that they could be placed in the crypt in accordance with the directions in Mark's will. Sharon addressed both the original petitions and John's cross-petition in her reply.

The superior court denied the petitions by Sharon and Dennis and granted John's cross-petition, subject to modification if Mark's remains were not able to fit in the crypt "in any manner." Sharon appeals.

Discussion

The rights and obligations concerning disposition of dead bodies are governed by certain provisions of the Health and Safety Code. . . . Once a body is interred, the law imposes substantial restrictions on its movement. Thus, a deceased person's remains cannot be removed from a cemetery without a written order of the health department or the superior court. Further, a party may also be required to obtain either the consent of the deceased's family members (here, "the [deceased's] surviving children") or the permission of the superior court.

Pursuant to well-established law, disinterment is recognized as an extraordinary remedy, one that will be granted only under very unusual circumstances. Only some rare emergency could move a court of equity to take a body from its grave in consecrated ground. . . . The dead are to rest where they have been laid unless reason of substance is brought forward for disturbing their repose.

A petition to exhume and reinter a body is an equitable proceeding that is addressed to the sound discretion of the superior court. . . . Although not necessarily determinative, the decedent's wishes are of particular importance in balancing the equities involved. . . .

A. Subject Matter Jurisdiction

Sharon contends that the superior court lacked subject matter jurisdiction to consider John's opposition to her petition or John's cross-petition because those pleadings required the court to resolve religious disputes between the two siblings. The establishment clause of the First Amendment to the United States Constitution and its California counterpart preclude civil courts from adjudicating property disputes based on religious doctrine.

A court may, however, apply neutral principles of law to resolve such disputes, so long as the court stays free from "entanglement in questions of religious doctrine, polity, and practice." Civil courts do not inhibit free exercise of religion, or establish religion, by merely opening their doors to disputes between people of differing religious beliefs; rather, First Amendment concerns are implicated only where the courts undertake to resolve controversies over religious doctrine and practice, matters of "purely ecclesiastical concern."

Here, John's pleadings did not seek to resolve issues of religious doctrine or practice, nor did the court attempt to resolve those types of issues in ruling on the matters before it. Rather, John's petition and opposition to Sharon's petition merely disputed the proper disposition of Joan's and Mark's remains and the court applied the neutral principles of law set forth in the Health and Safety Code and the common law in determining how to rule on the parties' petitions. Although, as Sharon correctly points out, the court inquired about whether Joan and Mark had been practicing the Jewish faith during their lives, its questions properly sought to elicit evidence relevant to an important issue in this matter, that is, the decedents' wishes as to the disposition of their remains after death. The court's inquiry in this regard was thus not improper, nor did it render the court without subject matter jurisdiction over the matters pending before it.

B. Personal Jurisdiction over Sharon

Sharon contends that the superior court lacked personal jurisdiction over her as it related to John's petition. However, when a nonresident plaintiff commences an action, she submits to the court's personal jurisdiction on any cross-complaint (in this case, cross-petition) filed against her by a defendant. Such a plaintiff is deemed to have consented to the court's jurisdiction "for all purposes for which justice to [the] defendant requir[es] his presence." This "is the price . . . the state may exact as the condition of opening its courts to the plaintiff."

In accordance with these principles, Sharon consented to the superior court's personal jurisdiction over her by filing her petition to disinter Joan's remains and thus John was not required to serve her. . . . Sharon's contention that the court lacked personal jurisdiction over her as relating to John's petition is without merit.

C. John's Standing

Sharon also suggests that John lacked standing to bring a petition to disinter Mark's remains because he did not suffer any injury in connection with Mark's interment, because he lacked any legal right to have his views on that matter considered or honored and because, as a resident of Florida, he lacked the minimum contacts with California necessary to establish the court's personal jurisdiction over him. These arguments are not well taken.

John clearly consented to the California courts' exercise of personal jurisdiction over him when he filed his cross-petition here. Further, pursuant to section 7525, subdivision (c), the consent of Mark's "surviving brothers or sisters" was required to exhume and reinter his body and, in accordance with our analysis of subsection (b) of that statute above, the statute required the consent of all such siblings. (Although the statutory language is written in the disjunctive, its use of the word "or," when considered in the context of the remainder of the statute, appears to be in error.) As such, the statute accords John standing to assert Mark's rights under sections 7100 and 7100.1.

For these reasons, Sharon's contention that John lacked standing to bring the cross-petition is without merit. . . .

The order is affirmed.

Other Aspects of Jurisdiction

General Jurisdiction

A court of general jurisdiction is one that has authority to decide any type of matter brought before it. This may include criminal matters such as felonies or misdemeanors, or civil matters of any type, whether complex or simple, involving either large or small amounts of money. By state or local rule, a court of general jurisdiction may be assigned to hear only certain types of cases. For example, a criminal division or a civil division of a state's courts may be created where judges are assigned to one of the divisions, but such divisions are usually for the sake of efficiency in the operation of the courts and do not take away the court's general jurisdiction. Unless a court's power has been limited in some way, it is presumed to be a court of general jurisdiction.

Limited Jurisdiction

A court of limited jurisdiction finds its authority in a specific legislative grant to hear particular types of cases. Although there are many limitations on a court's authority, the term *limited* with respect to the jurisdiction of the court refers only to the subject matter of a case. Probate courts, which hear matters relating to the transfer of property after death, and family courts, which address issues relating to marriage, divorce, and children, are examples of courts of limited jurisdiction.

Original Jurisdiction

Original jurisdiction is the authority of a court to decide the facts and render a judgment in the first instance. The court's power is thus "original" in the sense that it is the first court to hear a matter. Courts with original jurisdiction are trial courts, whose function is to determine the facts in each case it hears, apply the applicable law to the facts, and decide what outcome is consistent with the law and the facts.

Appellate Jurisdiction

An appellate court usually has no authority to decide facts and therefore generally lacks original jurisdiction. Its power is the power to review a decision by a lower court, to determine whether the law was properly applied to the facts (i.e., whether mistakes of law were made by the trial

court). The appellate court also examines whether procedural mistakes were made during a trial that prevented a just outcome.

Exclusive Jurisdiction

Exclusive jurisdiction in a court exists when the court is the only one authorized, by statute or constitution, to hear certain kinds of cases. There normally must be a specific provision of law from one of these sources that grants authority to the particular court alone. For example, a family or juvenile court usually has exclusive jurisdiction to hear matters relating to minors.

Concurrent Jurisdiction

Jurisdiction is said to be "concurrent" when different courts have the authority to hear a particular type of case. For example, a state trial court may have authority to hear disputes involving wills and estates, or such a case may be brought in a specialized probate court.

Diversity Jurisdiction

When the parties in civil cases are from different states, the issue of diversity jurisdiction applies. The question is whether the matter should be heard in state court or federal court. Under Article III, Section 2 of the U.S. Constitution, a plaintiff is entitled to file a lawsuit in either the state or federal court in the district where the plaintiff resides or the events giving rise to the complaint occurred. If the plaintiff chooses state court, the defendant may "remove" the case to the federal court to be tried there; however, if the plaintiff chooses federal court, or the defendant removes the case to federal court, the "amount in controversy" must be $75,000 or greater.

Venue

Venue refers to the place in which a case is tried. It is therefore related to geographic jurisdiction in that it involves the proper location of a court to decide a matter, but it does not in itself confer any power to decide. Based on the case that comes before a court, venue is determined to exist in the court where events occurred or the parties reside. A related legal concept is that of forum *non conveniens*, which allows transfer of a case to another court holding jurisdiction and in which venue is proper, in the interests of justice. The choice of venue and its relationship to jurisdiction is discussed in **Case Decision 3.2**.

Case Decision 3.2   *Sigurdsson v. Nodeen*, 180 Md. App. 326, 950 A.2d 848 (2008)

Decision of the Court by Judge Eyler:

This is an appeal from an order transferring a "complaint for modification of custody" of Wade Hampton Price, IV ("Wade") from the Circuit Court for Calvert County to the Circuit Court for Anne Arundel County. Wade was born in Anne Arundel County on June 1, 2004. Before his birth, his father, Wade Hampton Price, III ("Father"), died in a drowning accident. When Wade was born, his mother, Anja Sigurdsson ("Mother") was addicted to illegal drugs, and indeed tested positive for cocaine while at the hospital.

Wade was in Mother's custody in Anne Arundel County from his birth until December 2004. Beginning then, he was in the custody of Kealy Roderer, one of Wade's Father's sisters (i.e., a paternal aunt). Until May 2005, Roderer lived at various addresses in North Carolina and northern Virginia. From May 2005 forward, she was living in northern Virginia with her sister, Janey P. Nodeen, and Janey's husband, Thomas W. Nodeen. The Nodeens also are Wade's paternal aunt and uncle.

On December 1, 2004, Mother executed a document agreeing to Roderer's having custody of Wade. The document was not submitted to a court for approval. On December 13, 2004, in the Circuit Court for Anne Arundel County, Roderer obtained an emergency *ex parte* custody order for Wade. In the same court, she sought legal and physical custody of Wade, against Mother. Eventually, for reasons not clear from the record, the Nodeens became Wade's custodians and intervened as plaintiffs in the custody case, and Roderer dropped her custody claim.

Mother's mother, Marianne Sigurdsson ("Grandmother"), also intervened in the custody case, as a defendant. Beginning in August 2005, Grandmother was given visitation with Wade. During her visits, she supervised visitation between Mother and Wade.

The custody case was tried in the Circuit Court for Anne Arundel County for five days in June of 2006. Mother was present for the trial. The primary adversaries for custody of Wade were the Nodeens and Grandmother. Recognizing that she did not have a sufficient track record of sobriety to keep custody of Wade, Mother did not assert her custody rights and stipulated to the need for Wade to be in the custody of a third party. Thus, the real issue before the court was whether Wade should be in the custody of the Nodeens or Grandmother.

On July 11, 2006, the court awarded sole legal and physical custody of Wade to the Nodeens. It established a visitation schedule by which Mother and Grandmother would have Wade every other weekend; two non-consecutive weeks during the summer; and certain holidays. All visitation between Mother and Wade was to be supervised by Grandmother. Mother noted an appeal of the decision, but voluntarily dismissed the appeal before her brief was due.

As mentioned above, from Wade's birth through December 2004, when Roderer filed for custody, Mother was living in Anne Arundel County. In December 2004, she was living in Annapolis. In January 2005 and February 2005, she was living in Edgewater; and from June 2005 until February 2006, she was living in Glen Burnie. The record is unclear as to whether Mother still was living in Anne Arundel County when the case was tried in June 2006.

On June 6, 2007, eleven months after the Circuit Court for Anne Arundel County granted custody to the Nodeens, Mother filed, in the Circuit Court for Calvert County, a "Complaint for Modification of Child Custody Order." The complaint named the Nodeens as defendants and listed Mother's address as 3913 14th Street, Chesapeake Beach, a town in Calvert County. On October 15, 2007, Mother changed her address in the court's file to a Post Office Box in Owings, Maryland, which also is in Calvert County.

The Nodeens filed a preliminary motion to dismiss or to transfer, for improper venue, asserting that the modification complaint properly, or more conveniently, should be handled in the Circuit Court for Anne Arundel County. They alleged that Wade's primary residence for most of his life had been Anne Arundel County or northern Virginia, never Calvert County; that, although their primary residence is in northern Virginia, they have a second home, which in fact is a yacht, that is harbored in Anne Arundel County, and where they and Wade spend many weekends; that, since Wade's birth, Mother has lived at numerous locations, most of which are in Anne Arundel County; that the Anne Arundel County Child Protective Services Unit and the County Custody Evaluation Unit of the Circuit Court for Anne Arundel County had conducted investigations about Wade at the end of 2004 and in 2005; that Mother has another child with whom she has significant contact who lives with his

(Continues)

(Continued)

father, Dana Winter, in Anne Arundel County, and Mr. Winter was a witness at trial in June 2006; and that Mother's father (from whom Grandmother is divorced) lives in Anne Arundel County.

In opposition to the motion to dismiss or transfer, Mother argued that Wade's connections to Anne Arundel County are tenuous; that he was not currently living there, but in northern Virginia; and that only her current residence, in Calvert County, not her prior residences elsewhere, was relevant to the issue of venue. She further argued that Md. Code (1957, 2006 Repl. Vol., 2007 Cum. Supp.), section 6-202(5) of the Courts and Judicial Proceedings Article ("CJ"), controls venue in this case, and the only proper venue under that statute is Calvert County, where she lives. Moreover, under CJ section 6-202(5), Anne Arundel County is not a proper venue, as neither she nor Wade nor the Nodeens live there; and a circuit court is not authorized to transfer a case to a jurisdiction that is an improper venue. Alternatively, Mother argued that, even if there is venue in Anne Arundel County, the balance of convenience weighed in favor of the case remaining in Calvert County.

On September 20, 2007, the court granted the Nodeens' motion and ordered the case transferred to the Circuit Court for Anne Arundel County. Mother filed a notice of appeal from that order. In this Court, Mother is the appellant and the Nodeens are the appellees.

We shall include more facts as pertinent to our discussion.

Discussion

(A)

The general venue statute in Maryland, CJ section 6-201, states:

> (a) *Civil actions.*—Subject to the provisions of §§ 6-202 and 6-203 of this subtitle and unless otherwise provided by law, a civil action shall be brought in a county where the defendant resides, carries on a regular business, is employed, or habitually engages in a vocation. . . .
>
> (b) *Multiple defendants.*—If there is more than one defendant, and there is no single venue applicable to all defendants, under subsection (a), all may be sued in a county in which any one of them could be sued, or in the county where the cause of action arose.

CJ section 6-202, entitled "Additional venue permitted," states in relevant part that, in addition to venue as provided in CJ sections 6-201 and 6-203, "the following actions may be brought in the indicated county: . . . (5) Action relating to custody, guardianship, maintenance, or support of a child—Where the father, alleged father, or mother of the child resides, or where the child resides." (None of the provisions of CJ section 6-203 apply to the case at bar.)

The venues in CJ sections 6-201 and 6-202 are alternative, in that neither one has a priority over the other. Also, the residency of a child is the same as that of the person to whom custody of the child has been granted. Here, Wade's residency is the residency of the Nodeens.

The defense of improper venue must be raised by preliminary motion, filed before an answer is filed. If the defense of improper venue is not so raised, and an answer is filed, the defense is waived. Rule 2-327 governs the transfer of a civil action from one circuit court to another for a number of purposes, including improper venue, convenience of the parties and witnesses, and "[a]ctions involving common questions of law and fact." Subsection (b), "Improper venue," states that, "[i]f a court sustains a defense of improper venue but determines that in the interest of justice the action should not be dismissed, it may transfer the action to any county in which it could have been brought." Thus, a meritorious motion to dismiss for improper venue may be disposed of by the court's granting the motion and dismissing the case or by its issuing an order transferring the action to a court having venue.

The civil *forum non conveniens* doctrine is set forth in subsection (c) of Rule 2-327, "Convenience of the parties and witnesses," which states:

> On motion of any party, the court may transfer any action to any other circuit court where the action might have been brought if the transfer is for the convenience of the parties and witnesses and serves the interests of justice.

Finally, subsection (d) allows, in certain circumstances, the transfer of a civil case when "civil actions involving one or more common questions of law or fact are pending in the same judicial circuit." In that situation, "the actions or any claims or issues in the actions may be transferred in accordance with this section for consolidated pretrial proceedings or trial to a circuit court in which (A) the actions to be transferred might have been brought, **and** (B) similar actions are pending." Rule 2-327(d)(1) (emphasis added). Thus, even when venue is proper, a circuit court may transfer the action to another circuit court, for *forum non conveniens* purposes, or to another circuit court in the same judicial circuit, when there are actions involving common questions. In either situation, however, the circuit court to which the transfer is made must be a court having proper venue, *i.e.*, a court in which the action being transferred "might have been filed."

(B)

Mother contends that the Circuit Court for Calvert County erred in transferring her "Complaint for Modification of Child Custody Order" to the Circuit Court for Anne Arundel County because, when she filed the complaint in Calvert County, the Circuit Court for Anne Arundel County was not a court in which the complaint might have been filed. In other words, venue did not exist in Anne Arundel County when the complaint was filed and, therefore, transfer to the Circuit Court for Anne Arundel County was in error. Specifically, Mother maintains that, when she filed her complaint, the Nodeens were residing in northern Virginia, and hence neither they nor Wade were residents of Anne Arundel County or occupied any status that would make venue proper in Anne Arundel County for any of them, under CJ section 6-201(a); and that, under CJ section 6-202(5), Wade's residence was northern Virginia, Wade's Father was dead, and Mother was residing in Calvert County. Thus, not only was venue proper in Calvert County, it was the only county in which venue was proper when the complaint was filed. In the alternative, Mother contends that, if there was venue in Anne Arundel County, the Circuit Court for Calvert County abused its discretion by transferring the case there.

The Nodeens do not respond to Mother's first contention, that transfer to Anne Arundel County was in error because, when her "Complaint for Modification of Child Custody Order" was filed, venue was not proper in that county. They do not argue, generally, that venue was proper in Anne Arundel County when the complaint was filed on June 6, 2007; specifically, they do not argue that the presence of their yacht in a harbor in Anne Arundel County waters gave them, or Wade, residency in Anne Arundel County.

In response to Mother's second contention, respecting *forum non conveniens*, the Nodeens argue that a circuit court has broad discretion in deciding whether to transfer an action to another circuit court, and must do so by applying a balancing test. The balancing test requires the court to "weigh in the balance of the convenience of the witnesses and those public interest factors of systemic integrity and fairness that, in addition to private concerns, come under the heading of the interest of justice." They maintain that, here, the numerous contacts that Wade has had and continues to have with Anne Arundel County in his short life, the presence of some witnesses in that county, and the involvement of the Circuit Court for Anne Arundel County in this case—in terms of custody investigations having been performed through that court, that court actually having tried the custody case and rendered a decision on it less than a year before, and, even more important, the presiding judge at trial having the most information necessary to decide the "complaint for modification"—all militate in favor of the court's exercise of discretion to transfer the case to the Circuit Court for Anne Arundel County. . . .

Maryland law is clear that it is error, and therefore an abuse of discretion, for a circuit court to transfer a case to another circuit court that does not have venue. As the rules make plain, a transfer for improper venue or based on forum *non conveniens* or to consolidate with another related case in the same judicial circuit must be made to a court in which the action being transferred "could have been brought," in the case of improper venue, or "might have been brought," in the case of convenience or consolidation. It is therefore a threshold question whether the Circuit Court for Anne Arundel County had venue in this case when the "Complaint for Modification of Child Custody Order" was filed in the Circuit Court for Calvert County.

A brief discussion of the differences between venue and jurisdiction is in order, given the procedural history and status of the custody dispute in the case at bar. "Jurisdiction" refers to the fundamental power of a court to decide a dispute, by virtue of the nature of the dispute (subject matter jurisdiction) and the connection between the defendant and the state (personal jurisdiction). [J]urisdiction refers to two quite distinct concepts: (i) the *power* of a court to render a valid decree, and (ii) the *propriety* of granting the relief sought. To ascertain whether a court has power, it is necessary to consult the Constitution of the State and the applicable statutes. These usually concern two aspects: (a) jurisdiction over the person—obtained by proper service of process—and (b) jurisdiction over the subject matter—the cause of action and the relief sought. . . .

(Continues)

(Continued)

Here, the transferor and transferee circuit courts both have jurisdiction over the issue of custody of Wade. Both courts are general equity courts that have the power to decide custody issues, under Md. Code (1957, 2006 Repl. Vol.), section 1-201(a)(5) of the Family Law Article ("FL"). Neither side has asserted at any time in the proceedings that Virginia should, does, or may have jurisdiction. The Circuit Court for Anne Arundel County actually exercised its jurisdiction in this respect when it decided the issue of custody, after a trial on the merits, by order of July 11, 2006. Having done so, it has "continuing jurisdiction," as a court issuing a custody decision retains the power to modify it. Venue does not concern the power of a court to decide an issue. It concerns the place, among courts having jurisdiction, that an action will be litigated.

As CJ sections 6-201 and 6-202 make clear by their plain language, the proper venue for an action is to be determined as of the time the action is filed. In December 2004, when Roderer (later replaced by the Nodeens) filed suit for custody of Wade, Mother, the original defendant, was living in Anne Arundel County. Therefore, under either CJ section 6-201 or 6-202, the Circuit Court for Anne Arundel County was a proper venue for the custody case. Indeed, Anne Arundel County was the only proper venue at that time. Mother was the only defendant, as Father had died, and she lived in Anne Arundel County. Roderer and the Nodeens lived out of state. Apparently, Grandmother was living in Calvert County at that time, but her residence was not a factor because grandparent status is not covered by CJ section 6-202 and Grandmother was not a defendant in the action, so as to be covered by CJ section 6-201. Rather, Grandmother intervened in the action, which Roderer and the Nodeens already had filed, and was pending in Anne Arundel County. [The] plaintiff has broad discretion to choose forum and transfer should only be granted when the balance weighs strongly in favor of the moving party.

When Mother filed her modification complaint in June 2007, the residential status of the parties had changed. Mother no longer was living in Anne Arundel County. Rather, she was residing in Calvert County. Wade was in the custody of the Nodeens, by court order, and therefore was residing in northern Virginia. Thus, none of the parties were residing in Anne Arundel County when Mother filed her complaint; and there is nothing in the record or the arguments made to suggest that any other basis for venue in Anne Arundel County existed under CJ section 6-201. If the filing of the modification complaint marked the bringing of an "action," within the meaning of CJ sections 6-201 and 6-202, then, even though the Circuit Court for Anne Arundel County had continuing jurisdiction over its custody order of July 11, 2006, it did not have venue.

. . . Without question, Mother, as a party to the custody case in the Circuit Court for Anne Arundel County, could have filed a motion in that court seeking modification of the June 11, 2006 custody order in favor of the Nodeens; and that court would have had jurisdiction to decide the material change in circumstances and best interest issues. Mother chose, however, to file in the Circuit Court for Calvert County a "Complaint for Modification of Child Custody Order" of the Circuit Court for Anne Arundel County. Upon consideration of the relevant case law, we conclude that either vehicle—a motion filed in the Circuit Court for Anne Arundel County or a complaint filed to modify custody, thus commencing an action in another circuit court—was available to Mother.

[O]nce a final custody order has been issued by a court, an application to modify custody may be made in that same court, by motion, or in another court having jurisdiction and venue, by bringing a new custody action. In either situation, the decision whether to modify is governed by the material change in circumstances and best interest standards. Thus, in the case at bar, the fact that the Circuit Court for Anne Arundel County already had exercised jurisdiction over the issue of custody of Wade, and that it had continuing jurisdiction over its custody order for Wade, did not preclude Mother from filing a new action, in another circuit court, to modify custody.

That is what Mother did, by means of filing her "Complaint for Modification of Child Custody Order" in the Circuit Court for Calvert County. Venue was proper in that court and . . . venue no longer was proper in the original court that had issued the custody order now sought to be modified. It was legal error, therefore, for the court to transfer the case to the Circuit Court for Anne Arundel County, either on the basis of improper venue, or *forum inconveniens*. Although the Nodeens are correct that a circuit court has broad discretion in deciding whether to transfer a case to another circuit court, on venue grounds, that discretion must be exercised in accordance with established legal principles. In this case, it was not. Therefore, we shall vacate the order of the Circuit Court for Calvert County transferring Mother's action to modify custody to the Circuit Court for Anne Arundel County.

Order vacated. Costs to be paid by the appellees.

Standing

The existence of jurisdiction by a court is a necessary prerequisite to the operation of the court in any particular matter, but it is not the only prerequisite. In addition, a party who seeks to use the court system must have *standing* to do so. Although jurisdiction involves the power of a court to hear and decide a case, standing relates to the right of a plaintiff to ask a court to hear a matter.

In order to have standing, the party invoking the jurisdiction of the court must have a personal interest in the case. This means that "a claimant must present an injury that is concrete, particularized, and actual or imminent; fairly traceable to the defendant's challenged behavior; and likely to be redressed by a favorable ruling" (*Davis v. Federal Election Commission*, 128 S. Ct. 2759, 2768 (2008)). A concrete and particularized injury is one that affects the person bringing suit in a personal way. The harm cannot be speculative or hypothetical; the plaintiff must have actually suffered harm or be about to suffer individual harm. In addition, the harm must have resulted from the defendant's actions, not from some other causes. Finally, the plaintiff's injury must be one that is capable of being resolved by the court (*Lujan v. National Wildlife Federation*, 497 U.S. 871 (1990)). When any of these aspects of standing is lacking, the case will be dismissed.

Court Goals

In accordance with its jurisdiction, a court has the power to make decisions that allow it to administer justice under the law. This power is inherent in the operation of a court; that is, it is assumed that a court may take all actions necessary to administer justice, provided its actions do not conflict with the law. Stated in terms of the court's jurisdiction, a court has all powers necessary to exercise its jurisdiction and decide cases properly brought before it.

Thus, the primary goal of a court is to decide cases brought before it by a party who has standing to do so. If the court is a trial court, this means that the court decides the facts in a given case and applies the law to those facts. Thus, trial courts make decisions about whether the facts asserted by the plaintiff are true. If the facts are found to be true, the trial court then decides how the law affects those facts and what the law requires to be done. Of course, if the facts are found not to be true, the case will be dismissed or a verdict for the defendant will be entered. A central function of the court, therefore, is to serve as an objective tribunal in which the respective claims of the parties may be heard. Objectivity requires unbiased decision making based on facts, without influence by the opinions and views of the decision maker. Thus, litigants turn to the courts as an independent agency with the expectation that their positions will be considered and a decision rendered in an objective manner.

If the court is an appellate court, it also serves as an objective tribunal, but with a different goal. An appellate court does not decide facts; its appellate jurisdiction generally prevents it from doing so. Rather, it examines the record made in the trial court and determines whether errors of law were made in any of the trial court's decisions.

These may relate to preliminary matters and motions to dismiss, discovery disputes, evidentiary rulings, and judgments about the meaning and application of the law.

Courts also must provide a forum for a fair and equitable hearing on the merits of the case. This requires that the parties, whether in a civil or criminal proceeding, be given the opportunity to present all facts and legal arguments in favor of their positions and that the case be decided on the basis of the facts and law. Furthermore, fairness requires that no bias be shown to one side or the other and that the case not be prejudged in favor of or against either party.

Adherence to rules of procedure is also part of the court's functioning. The court must determine and regulate the rules so that the development of the case for each side is orderly. Rules of procedure are intended to provide for both order in the proceeding and fairness. As noted earlier, justice is achieved by adhering to the process, not attempting to achieve a particular outcome.

Courts must also provide litigants with a clear outcome after hearing or trial. That is, courts are called on to make decisions, and those decisions must provide parties with a clear result that provides certainty to the parties. Indeed, given that the central purpose of the court system is to dispense justice, the lack of a decision or uncertainty regarding a decision would undercut the reasons for presenting matters to an independent tribunal.

Courts bear considerable responsibility toward the parties, particularly in criminal cases; therefore, the court will seek to encourage, if not ensure, competent legal representation of the parties. Especially in modern times and with the growing complexity of the legal system, it becomes increasing difficult for parties to represent themselves in a manner that provides justice.

The Adversary System

The operation of the court system in the United States is based on an *adversary* system. An adversary system is one in which the positions of the parties are in opposition to each other (Feeley, 1987). The clearly drawn contrast between the viewpoints of the parties is presumed to result in a fair outcome. In the adversary system, the parties, through their attorneys, control the manner in which the case proceeds by determining what evidence will be presented to the court, the "truth" that such evidence is intended to support, and the order of such presentation of evidence (Frank, 1963). The judge serves as an unbiased "referee" who ensures that the rules of procedure are followed. An adversarial system of justice has several procedural characteristics, or hallmarks, unique to its operation.

Hallmarks of the Adversarial System
Clash of Viewpoints

The adversarial system requires that there be a conflict between two opposing parties. As a result of this clash of opposing positions, it is presumed that the truth of the matter will emerge. Our system of justice is therefore designed to allow for the parties to present their positions as arguments that both make assertions on their own behalf and attack the evidence and arguments of their "opponent." This procedural approach is reflected in the nearly universal use of attorneys to represent parties (attorneys often advertise themselves as "hard-hitting" or "killer dogs"), in the pleadings (e.g., from the outset, there is a "complaint" and "answer"), in the discovery process (where each side attempts to ferret out the "weaknesses" in the other side), in the trial process (cross-examination is often viewed as an attempt to "demolish" the credibility of witnesses), and in the outcome (parties nearly always characterize the outcome as a "win," even when they have "lost!"). The clash of opposing views is thus designed to allow for all relevant facts in a case to have the opportunity to emerge and be "tested" for their veracity. Because our system is one in which decisions should be based on facts, not assumptions or conjecture, this "combat" style of determining the truth has become a central tenant of our system of justice.

No Trial by "Ambush"

The corollary of the clash of opposing views is the need for cases to be tried even-handedly. As a result, one basis for the adversarial system is that the parties will stand on an equal footing procedurally in the presentation of their cases, with access to all information relevant to the case.

> In general, the public has a right to every person's evidence at trial. At its core, the adversary system is based upon the proposition that an examination of all of the persons possessing relevant information, which will lead to the discovery of all of the relevant facts, will produce a just result. (*Glenn v. Plante*, 269 Wis.2d 575, 676 N.W.2d 413 (2004))

The role of the judge, therefore, is to make certain that the parties have access to the court to resolve disputes in the course of the litigation, that both sides will be heard on disputes that arise, and that evidence will be made available in a timely fashion. A party may not "ambush" its opponent by presenting evidence at trial that has not been made available to the other side, and each side is presumed to have equal access to and knowledge of the facts before trial.

Burden of Proof

The "burden of proof" refers to the party in litigation that has the responsibility to present evidence to prove a point. Burdens of proof may fall on either party in a civil case, on either the prosecution or defense in a criminal case, and may shift from one party to another throughout a case. Most well known, perhaps, is that the burden of proof falls on the prosecution in a criminal case. What is the burden that the prosecution shoulders? It is to prove the elements of the crime charged in order to establish the defendant's guilt. Similarly, a criminal defendant has the burden of proving the requirements of the defenses that he or she may assert. Thus, the burden of proof simply establishes *who* is required to come forward with evidence at various points as a case develops.

Standard of Proof

The "standard of proof" refers to the amount of evidence that must be brought forward, regardless of who has the burden of proof. The courts have developed and applied three standards of proof to be used in different circumstances. These are proof *beyond a reasonable doubt*, proof by *clear and convincing evidence*, and proof by a *preponderance of the evidence*.

The "beyond a reasonable doubt" standard is used in criminal cases and is the level of proof that must be brought forward by the prosecution before conviction of the defendant can occur. How much proof is "beyond a reasonable doubt?" Judges have explained the standard in different ways to juries, but a typical jury instruction states that jurors must be "convinced to a moral certainty" of the truth of the evidence brought forward before they can convict in a criminal case. It therefore relates to the degree of confidence that a juror must have in his or her own decision. Although this amount of confidence need not be absolute certainty, it requires the highest degree of confidence. The need for this high standard of proof stems from the consequences to the defendant and to society of an erroneous decision.

The importance of a beyond a reasonable doubt standard in criminal cases was discussed by the United States Supreme Court in *In re Winship* (397 U.S. 358 (1970). In that case, the Court held that the beyond a reasonable doubt standard must be applied before a juvenile may be adjudicated to be delinquent. Although a case involving the juvenile courts (see Chapter 8), they made it clear why the highest standard of proof must apply in criminal cases:

> Lest there remain any doubt about the constitutional stature of the reasonable-doubt standard, we explicitly hold that the Due Process Clause protects the accused against conviction except upon proof beyond a reasonable doubt of every fact necessary to constitute the crime with which he is charged. (*In re Winship*, 397 U.S. at 364)

The Court noted that this requirement serves several important goals: It reduces the risk of wrongful conviction; it gives substance and meaning to the presumption of innocence, and it instills public confidence in the criminal justice system. The opinion is found in **Case Decision 3.3.**

Case Decision 3.3   *In re Winship*, 397 U.S. 358 (1970)

Opinion of the Court by Justice Brennan:

Constitutional questions decided by this Court concerning the juvenile process have centered on the adjudicatory stage at "which a determination is made as to whether a juvenile is a 'delinquent' as a result of alleged misconduct on his part, with the consequence that he may be committed to a state institution." This case presents the single, narrow question whether proof beyond a reasonable doubt is among the "essentials of due process and fair treatment" required during the adjudicatory stage when a juvenile is charged with an act which would constitute a crime if committed by an adult.

Section 712 of the New York Family Court Act defines a juvenile delinquent as "a person over seven and less than sixteen years of age who does any act which, if done by an adult, would constitute a crime." During a 1967 adjudicatory hearing, conducted pursuant to the Act, a judge in New York Family Court found that appellant, then a 12-year-old boy, had entered a locker and stolen $112 from a woman's pocketbook. The petition which charged appellant with delinquency alleged that his act, "if done by an adult, would constitute the crime or crimes of Larceny." The judge acknowledged that the proof might not establish guilt beyond a reasonable doubt, but rejected appellant's contention that such proof was required by the Fourteenth Amendment. The judge relied instead on section 744(b) of the New York Family Court Act which provides that "(a)ny determination at the conclusion of (an adjudicatory) hearing that a (juvenile) did an act or acts must be based on a preponderance of the evidence." During a subsequent dispositional hearing, appellant was ordered placed in a training school for an initial period of 18 months, subject to annual extensions of his commitment until his 18th birthday—six years in appellant's case. The Appellate Division of the New York Supreme Court, First Judicial Department, affirmed without opinion. The New York Court of Appeals then affirmed by a four-to-three vote, expressly sustaining the constitutionality of section 744(b). We noted probable jurisdiction. We reverse.

I

The requirement that guilt of a criminal charge be established by proof beyond a reasonable doubt dates at least from our early years as a Nation. The "demand for a higher degree of persuasion in criminal cases was recurrently expressed from ancient times, (though) its crystallization into the formula 'beyond a reasonable doubt' seems to have occurred as late as 1798. It is now accepted in common law jurisdictions as the measure of persuasion by which the prosecution must convince the trier of all the essential elements of guilt." C. McCormick, Evidence 321, pp. 681–682 (1954); see also 9 J. Wigmore, Evidence, 2497 (3d ed. 1940). Although virtually unanimous adherence to the reasonable-doubt standard in common-law jurisdictions may not conclusively establish it as a requirement of due process, such adherence does "reflect a profound judgment about the way in which law should be enforced and justice administered."

Expressions in many opinions of this Court indicate that it has long been assumed that proof of a criminal charge beyond a reasonable doubt is constitutionally required. Mr. Justice Frankfurter stated that "(i)t is the duty of the Government to establish guilt beyond a reasonable doubt. This notion—basic in our law and rightly one of the boasts of a free society—is a requirement and a safeguard of due process of law in the historic, procedural content of 'due process.'" In a similar vein, the Court [has] said that "(g)uilt in a criminal case must be proved beyond a reasonable doubt and by evidence confined to that which long experience in the common-law tradition, to some extent embodied in the Constitution, has crystallized into rules of evidence consistent with that standard. These rules are historically grounded rights of our system, developed to safeguard men from dubious and unjust convictions, with resulting forfeitures of life, liberty and property." [T]he requirement is implicit in "constitutions (which) recognize the fundamental principles that are deemed essential for the protection of life and liberty." "No man should be deprived of his life under the forms of law unless the jurors who try him are able, upon their consciences, to say that the evidence before them is sufficient to show beyond a reasonable doubt the existence of every fact necessary to constitute the crime charged."

The reasonable-doubt standard plays a vital role in the American scheme of criminal procedure. It is a prime instrument for reducing the risk of convictions resting on factual error. The standard provides concrete substance for the presumption of innocence—that bedrock "axiomatic and elementary" principle whose "enforcement lies at the foundation of the administration of our criminal law."

The requirement of proof beyond a reasonable doubt has this vital role in our criminal procedure for cogent reasons. The accused during a criminal prosecution has at stake interest of immense importance, both because of the possibility that he may lose his liberty upon conviction

(Continues)

and because of the certainty that he would be stigmatized by the conviction. Accordingly, a society that values the good name and freedom of every individual should not condemn a man for commission of a crime when there is reasonable doubt about his guilt. As we [have] said: "There is always in litigation a margin of error, representing error in fact finding, which both parties must take into account. Where one party has at stake an interest of transcending value—as a criminal defendant his liberty—this margin of error is reduced as to him by the process of placing on the other party the burden of persuading the fact finder at the conclusion of the trial of his guilt beyond a reasonable doubt. Due process commands that no man shall lose his liberty unless the Government has borne the burden of convincing the fact finder of his guilt." To this end, the reasonable-doubt standard is indispensable.

Moreover, use of the reasonable-doubt standard is indispensable to command the respect and confidence of the community in applications of the criminal law. It is critical that the moral force of the criminal law not be diluted by a standard of proof that leaves people in doubt whether innocent men are being condemned. It is also important in our free society that every individual going about his ordinary affairs have confidence that his government cannot adjudge him guilty of a criminal offense without convincing a proper fact finder of his guilt with utmost certainty.

Lest there remain any doubt about the constitutional stature of the reasonable-doubt standard, we explicitly hold that the Due Process Clause protects the accused against conviction except upon proof beyond a reasonable doubt of every fact necessary to constitute the crime with which he is charged.

II

We turn to the question whether juveniles, like adults, are constitutionally entitled to proof beyond a reasonable doubt when they are charged with violation of a criminal law. The same considerations that demand extreme caution in fact finding to protect the innocent adult apply as well to the innocent child.

Nor do we perceive any merit in the argument that to afford juveniles the protection of proof beyond a reasonable doubt would risk destruction of beneficial aspects of the juvenile process. Use of the reasonable-doubt standard during the adjudicatory hearing will not disturb New York's policies that a finding that a child has violated a criminal law does not constitute a criminal conviction, that such a finding does not deprive the child of his civil rights, and that juvenile proceedings are confidential. Nor will there be any effect on the informality, flexibility, or speed of the hearing at which the fact finding takes place. And the opportunity during the post-adjudicatory or dispositional hearing for a wide-ranging review of the child's social history and for his individualized treatment will remain unimpaired. Similarly, there will be no effect on the procedures distinctive to juvenile proceedings that are employed prior to the adjudicatory hearing.

It is true, of course, that the juvenile may be engaging in a general course of conduct inimical to his welfare that calls for judicial intervention. But that intervention cannot take the form of subjecting the child to the stigma of a finding that he violated a criminal law and to the possibility of institutional confinement on proof insufficient to convict him were he an adult.

III

In sum, the constitutional safeguard of proof beyond a reasonable doubt is as much required during the adjudicatory stage of a delinquency proceeding as are those constitutional safeguards of notice of charges, right to counsel, the rights of confrontation and examination, and the privilege against self-incrimination. We therefore hold, in agreement with Chief Judge Fuld in dissent in the Court of Appeals, "that, where a 12-year-old child is charged with an act of stealing which renders him liable to confinement for as long as six years, then, as a matter of due process the case against him must be proved beyond a reasonable doubt."

Reversed.

Concurring Opinion by Justice Harlan:

No one, I daresay, would contend that state juvenile court trials are subject to no federal constitutional limitations. Differences have existed, however, among the members of this Court as to what constitutional protections do apply.

The present case draws in question the validity of a New York statute that permits a determination of juvenile delinquency, founded on a charge of criminal conduct, to be made on a standard of proof that is less rigorous than that which would obtain had the accused been tried for the same conduct in an ordinary criminal case. While I am in full agreement that this statutory provision offends the requirement of fundamental fairness embodied in the Due Process Clause of the Fourteenth Amendment, I am constrained to add something to what my Brother Brennan has written for the Court, lest the true nature of the constitutional problem presented become obscured or the impact on state juvenile court systems of what the Court holds today be exaggerated.

I

Professor Wigmore, in discussing the various attempts by courts to define how convinced one must be to be convinced beyond a reasonable doubt, wryly observed: "The truth is that no one has yet invented or discovered a mode of measurement for the intensity of human belief. Hence there can be yet no successful method of communicating intelligibly a sound method of self-analysis for one's belief," 9 J. Wigmore, Evidence 325 (3d ed. 1940).

Notwithstanding Professor Wigmore's skepticism, we have before us a case where the choice of the standard of proof has made a difference: the juvenile court judge below forthrightly acknowledged that he believed by a preponderance of the evidence, but was not convinced beyond a reasonable doubt, that appellant stole $112 from the complainant's pocketbook. Moreover, even though the labels used for alternative standards of proof are vague and not a very sure guide to decision making, the choice of the standard for a particular variety of adjudication does, I think, reflect a very fundamental assessment of the comparative social costs of erroneous factual determinations.

To explain why I think this so, I begin by stating two propositions, neither of which I believe can be fairly disputed. First, in a judicial proceeding in which there is a dispute about the facts of some earlier event, the fact finder cannot acquire unassailably accurate knowledge of what happened. Instead, all the fact finder can acquire is a belief of what probably happened. The intensity of this belief—the degree to which a fact finder is convinced that a given act actually occurred—can, of course, vary. In this regard, a standard of proof represents an attempt to instruct the fact finder concerning the degree of confidence our society thinks he should have in the correctness of factual conclusions for a particular type of adjudication. Although the phrases "preponderance of the evidence" and "proof beyond a reasonable doubt" are quantitatively imprecise, they do communicate to the finder of fact different notions concerning the degree of confidence he is expected to have in the correctness of his factual conclusions.

A second proposition, which is really nothing more than a corollary of the first, is that the trier of fact will sometimes, despite his best efforts, be wrong in his factual conclusions. In a lawsuit between two parties, a factual error can make a difference in one of two ways. First, it can result in a judgment in favor of the plaintiff when the true facts warrant a judgment for the defendant. The analogue in a criminal case would be the conviction of an innocent man. On the other hand, an erroneous factual determination can result in a judgment for the defendant when the true facts justify a judgment in plaintiff's favor. The criminal analogue would be the acquittal of a guilty man.

The standard of proof influences the relative frequency of these two types of erroneous outcomes. If, for example, the standard of proof for a criminal trial were a preponderance of the evidence rather than proof beyond a reasonable doubt, there would be a smaller risk of factual errors that result in freeing guilty persons, but a far greater risk of factual errors that result in convicting the innocent. Because the standard of proof affects the comparative frequency of these two types of erroneous outcomes, the choice of the standard to be applied in a particular kind of litigation should, in a rational world, reflect an assessment of the comparative social disutility of each.

When one makes such an assessment, the reason for different standards of proof in civil as opposed to criminal litigation becomes apparent. In a civil suit between two private parties for money damages, for example, we view it as no more serious in general for there to be an erroneous verdict in the defendant's favor than for there to be an erroneous verdict in the plaintiff's favor. A preponderance of the evidence standard therefore seems peculiarly appropriate for, as explained most sensibly, it simply requires the trier of fact "to believe that the existence of a fact is more probable than its nonexistence before (he) may find in favor of the party who has the burden to persuade the (judge) of the fact's existence." F. James, Civil Procedure 250–251 (1965).

(Continues)

(Continued)

In a criminal case, on the other hand, we do not view the social disutility of convicting an innocent man as equivalent to the disutility of acquitting someone who is guilty. As Mr. Justice Brennan wrote for the Court in *Speiser v. Randall*, 357 U.S. 513, 525–526 (1958):

> There is always in litigation a margin of error, representing error in fact finding, which both parties must take into account. Where one party has at stake an interest of transcending value—as a criminal defendant his liberty—this margin of error is reduced as to him by the process of placing on the other party the burden of persuading the fact-finder at the conclusion of the trial of his guilt beyond a reasonable doubt.

In this context, I view the requirement of proof beyond a reasonable doubt in a criminal case as bottomed on a fundamental value determination of our society that it is far worse to convict an innocent man than to let a guilty man go free. It is only because of the nearly complete and long-standing acceptance of the reasonable-doubt standard by the States in criminal trials that the Court has not before today had to hold explicitly that due process, as an expression of fundamental procedural fairness, requires a more stringent standard for criminal trials than for ordinary civil litigation.

II

When one assesses the consequences of an erroneous factual determination in a juvenile delinquency proceeding in which a youth is accused of a crime, I think it must be concluded that, while the consequences are not identical to those in a criminal case, the differences will not support a distinction in the standard of proof. First, and of paramount importance, a factual error here, as in a criminal case, exposes the accused to a complete loss of his personal liberty through a state-imposed confinement away from his home, family, and friends. And, second, a delinquency determination, to some extent at least, stigmatizes a youth in that it is by definition bottomed on a finding that the accused committed a crime. Although there are no doubt costs to society (and possibly even to the youth himself) in letting a guilty youth go free, I think here, as in a criminal case, it is far worse to declare an innocent youth a delinquent. I therefore agree that a juvenile court judge should be no less convinced of the factual conclusion that the accused committed the criminal act with which he is charged than would be required in a criminal trial.

III

I wish to emphasize that there is no automatic congruence between the procedural requirements imposed by due process in a criminal case, and those imposed by due process in juvenile cases. It is of great importance, in my view, that procedural strictures not be constitutionally imposed that jeopardize the essential elements of the State's purpose in creating juvenile courts. In this regard, I think it worth emphasizing that the requirement of proof beyond a reasonable doubt that a juvenile committed a criminal act before he is found to be a delinquent does not (1) interfere with the worthy goal of rehabilitating the juvenile, (2) make any significant difference in the extent to which a youth is stigmatized as a "criminal" because he has been found to be a delinquent, or (3) burden the juvenile courts with a procedural requirement that will make juvenile adjudications significantly more time consuming, or rigid. Today's decision simply requires a juvenile court judge to be more confident in his belief that the youth did the act with which he has been charged.

Justice Harlan's concurrence in Winship is particularly informative on the significance of the beyond a reasonable doubt standard in criminal justice. He noted that

> even though the labels used for alternative standards of proof are vague and not a very sure guide to decision making, the choice of the standard for a particular variety of adjudication does, I think, reflect a very fundamental assessment of the comparative social costs of erroneous factual determinations. (*Winship*, 397 U.S. at 370)

It was these social costs—lack of confidence in the criminal law, fear of the government, potential loss of individual liberty—that led him to conclude that the high standard of proof was necessary because "it is far worse to convict an innocent man than to let a guilty man go free" (Id. at 372).

A "preponderance of the evidence" has been characterized as the "greater weight" of evidence to prove a point. If a juror (or a judge) finds it to be more probable than not that something occurred, the preponderance of the evidence standard is being applied. Thus, when the trier of fact believes there is sufficient evidence to "tip the scales" in favor of establishing a fact, it must take it to be true. It is generally used in civil cases and is the standard required of the defendant in criminal cases.

Clear and convincing evidence is that amount of evidence that is more than a preponderance of the evidence but less than "beyond a reasonable doubt." It must therefore be sufficient evidence to do more than "tip the scales" in favor of one side or the other. This standard of proof is employed in civil cases, usually involving constitutional matters.

Presumption of Innocence

In criminal cases, the defendant is presumed innocent until proven guilty by the prosecution. This presumption is given meaning by the requirement that the prosecution carries a heavy burden of proving the defendant's guilt, employing the beyond a reasonable doubt standard. Along with placing the burden of proving guilt on the prosecution in criminal cases, the presumption of innocence reflects the adversarial system's desire to "even the playing field" when the power of the state is brought against an individual. Were it otherwise, every defendant charged would likely be convicted because a presumption of guilt at the outset would require little additional evidence by the prosecution to prove and considerable evidence on the part of the defendant to overcome.

The importance of the presumption of innocence as part of the adversary system in criminal cases has long been held central to concepts of justice and fairness under the law:

> The principle that there is a presumption of innocence in favor of the accused is the undoubted law, axiomatic and elementary, and its enforcement lies at the foundation of the administration of our criminal law. (*Coffin v. U.S.*, 156 U.S. 432 (1895)).

Emphasis on Procedure

The adversarial system is a procedural system. That is, the emphasis in the system is the process of adjudication. Our system of justice is one in which procedural aspects of the law are of central importance; by following the proper procedures, our system assumes that the correct outcome will result.

By its emphasis on procedure, the adversarial system has as its focus the constitutional requirements of due process. The Due Process Clause of the Fifth and Fourteenth Amendments requires the protection of certain fundamental rights of defendants in criminal cases, including notice of the charges, a right to counsel at nearly all stages of the criminal proceedings, the right to an impartial decision maker, the rights of confrontation and examination, and the privilege against self-incrimination. Under the adversary system, adherence to these procedural protections gives society confidence that justice will be served by the outcome of a case.

The Inquisitorial System

The adversarial system is not the only system of justice, although it is the most common. Another approach to conflict resolution in some countries is known as the inquisitorial system.

The inquisitorial system is employed in some European countries and is prevalent in Latin American countries. It involves an investigative process whereby the parties in a dispute (either criminal or civil) provide evidence collectively to the court, who conduct proceedings to determine the truth of the allegations or the merit of the plaintiff's claims (Strier, 1992). These proceedings are conducted by judges, with attorneys playing an investigative and ancillary role. The judge questions the parties and the witnesses and reviews documentary and physical evidence and on this basis makes a decision. Thus, the "trial" is quite different than in an adversarial proceeding and amounts to an investigation of the facts. Indeed, the role of attorneys for the parties in the process is more cooperative than adversarial. Although there are variations on this process, it is one that is designed to provide independent consideration of the positions of the parties, where the function of the judge is paramount, and the emphasis is on obtaining the correct outcome, rather than focusing on technical procedures.

Court Functions

The function of a court is determined in large part by the jurisdiction of the court. That is, the nature of a court's authority determines what the court actually does. In accomplishing its goals, courts with similar jurisdiction operate in similar ways. Thus, courts with original jurisdiction, trial courts, must conduct hearings required by our adversary system, the state and federal constitutions, and American views of justice. Trial courts, whether handling civil matters or criminal cases, must also proceed in ways that achieve fairness for both parties, and the job of appellate courts to review the trial court's actions involves certain activities. We now discuss the functions of each of these types of courts.

Trial Courts

Trial courts function by following an orderly process involving stages through which cases proceed. These stages make up the *trial process*, the steps of which are similar, although not the same, in both civil and criminal cases. The trial process reflects the functions that trial courts fulfill and the activities they must accomplish before a final decision may be reached. When a case "moves" through the trial process, specific activities undertaken by the parties or by the court are accomplished in each of the steps discussed later here. At any stage of the trial process, however, a case may be settled, precluding the need for further action.

Pretrial Matters

Pretrial matters are intended to lay the groundwork for further proceedings in a case, dispose of some or all aspects of a case, or ensure that all interests in a case are fairly represented. These matters are somewhat different in criminal and civil cases, although each of the following procedural matters serves to move the case toward a conclusion.

The Complaint

Whether civil or criminal, a defendant's formal involvement with the court system begins with the filing of a pleading known as a *complaint*. A civil complaint is filed by a plaintiff, who invokes the jurisdiction of the court to resolve a dispute the plaintiff has with the defendant. A civil complaint must set forth the factual basis for the claims being made by the plaintiff, why the plaintiff believes he or she is entitled to relief, and what relief the court is being asked to order. The defendant submits an *answer* to the complaint, stating why the relief sought should not be granted. These initial pleadings are discussed in more detail in Chapter 10.

A criminal complaint is a document filed by the prosecutor that specifies the charges being brought against the defendant: the statute that has been violated and the facts alleged to show that the statute was violated. It may be filed either before or after the defendant is taken into custody (arrested). The document cites the specific statutes violated and states what specific actions the defendant took that violated the statutes. It is also signed by the prosecutor and sworn to under oath. The criminal complaint is the document used by the judge at the preliminary hearing (discussed later here) to decide whether the defendant should be in custody or remain in the custody of the state; therefore, by stating the specific facts alleged to have occurred, the complaint serves two important functions: to formally notify the defendant of the charges and to attempt to convince the judge that there is probable cause to believe that the defendant committed the offense.

Initial Appearance/Preliminary Hearing

When a person has been arrested, he or she must be brought before a judge or magistrate without delay or within a certain number of days specified by statute. There are several purposes for the initial appearance. These include formally notifying defendants of the charges, advising them of their rights, setting bail, protecting them from extensive interrogation by the police, and making the process public to avoid secret prosecution where defendants' rights may be violated (*Gerstein v. Pugh*, 420 U.S. 103, 95 S. Ct. 854 (1975)). For lesser offenses, the initial appearance may be the only appearance, where a guilty plea may be accepted and a sentence imposed. For serious offenses, however, a plea typically is not made until arraignment. In some jurisdictions, and depending on the charges, the initial appearance may be conducted at the same time as the preliminary hearing.

A preliminary hearing is conducted by the judge to determine whether there is probable cause for the charges against the defendant. Probable cause is sufficient evidence to believe that the defendant committed the offense charged. It is an important initial test of the state's evidence at this early stage to allow an independent decision maker (the judge) to determine whether the defendant should continue to be held for trial on the charges.

Arraignment

In criminal cases, the defendant is *arraigned* at a hearing in which the charges against him or her are read and the defendant's plea is entered. There are three pleas that a defendant may make: not guilty, guilty, and *nolo contendere* (no contest). If a defendant refuses to enter a plea, or

"stands mute," before the court, a plea of not guilty will be entered.

To plead not guilty means that the defendant wishes to contest all of the allegations made against him and to exercise his right to a trial on the charges. The pleas of guilty and *nolo contendere* mean that the defendant does not contest the allegations and will submit to sentencing by the court. These two pleas differ in that a guilty plea is an admission of guilt, whereas a *nolo contendere* plea is not an admission of guilt but an admission that the prosecution has sufficient evidence to convict the defendant should the case proceed to trial.

Because there is not an admission of guilt with a *nolo contendere* plea, it generally cannot be used as evidence against the defendant in any subsequent civil trial. Either of these two pleas may only be entered with the court's permission, after the court is satisfied that the plea is entered voluntarily, knowingly, and on the advice of counsel. This is required by Rule 11(e) of the Federal Rules of Criminal Procedure, on which most states have modeled their own rules or statutes governing the trial process.

Although most defendants at the arraignment plead not guilty, the smaller number who enter pleas of guilty or *nolo contendere* will preclude the need for a trial and typically proceed directly to sentencing. For lesser offenses, this may occur at the time of the arraignment; for more serious offenses, a sentencing hearing will be scheduled.

Pretrial Motions

Pretrial motions in both civil and criminal cases serve a number of functions: to clarify the allegations, to begin to gauge the strength of the parties' positions, to help the parties weigh the merits of settlement, and to plan for the course of the litigation. Most common among these is a motion to dismiss, in both civil and criminal cases, and a motion for failure to state a case on which relief may be granted (also known as a 12b-6 motion) in civil cases. Both of these motions set forth grounds on which the complaint is deficient and ask the court to dismiss the case. Further discussion of these and other motions is found in Chapters 10 and 12.

Other Pretrial Matters

In many jurisdictions, there is an initial conference between the parties and the judge to set a schedule for activities in the litigation and setting a date for trial. In some courts, mandatory settlement conferences between the parties are required before trial. In addition, the court may conduct hearings on evidentiary, discovery, or other matters presented by motion from the parties.

Discovery

The term *discovery* refers to a process of obtaining evidence from an adverse party and developing facts that may be used at trial. Recall that the adversary system requires that both parties have access to the facts and that there be no "ambush" at trial. The discovery process is a mechanism that helps to satisfy this requirement. By allowing each side to obtain evidence in the possession or knowledge of the other before trial, discovery also allows the parties to examine the weight, credibility, and accuracy of the evidence likely to be introduced at trial. This is important as the parties assess the strengths and weaknesses of their case, and consider the possibility of settlement or plea bargain.

The process of discovery in civil cases is one that requires parties, on request, to disclose relevant information to each other. It allows each party to obtain documents, video or tape recordings, physical evidence, and sometimes testimony before trial. In civil cases, this may take the form of interrogatories (written questioning of the party), depositions (in-person questioning of witnesses before trial), and requests for production of documents. In civil cases, however, disclosure by one party is not generally required if not requested by the other party. Although the judge is usually not actively involved in the discovery process itself, he or she may be called on to resolve disputes relating to discovery matters.

In some jurisdictions, discovery is limited in civil cases to avoid the potential undue burden of discovery requests on one or both parties. Despite the important role that the process of discovery plays in preparation for trial, abuse of the process is common. This chiefly occurs when a party attempts to overwhelm their opponent with discovery requests that are costly or time consuming to respond to. This often leads to disputes between the parties, motions, and hearings to compel disclosure of information or to prevent disclosure of information as too burdensome.

The discovery process differs in criminal cases. Traditionally, there was no discovery in criminal trials, based on the theory that if prosecution witnesses were known before trial they would be subjected to possible intimidation or harm. This has changed considerably, and the modern approach is to allow the defendant any information in the possession of the prosecution that will allow defense against the charges, particularly where that evidence is exculpatory. Indeed, the U.S. Supreme Court has made it clear that the government is required to disclose to the defendant any evidence that is favorable to the defense (*Brady v. Maryland*, 373 U.S. 83 (1963)). When this rule is violated, a conviction against the defendant must be overturned. **Case Decision 3.4** demonstrates the importance of this rule as it applies to criminal cases.

Case Decision 3.4 *Youngblood v. West Virginia*, 547 U.S. 867 (2006)

Per Curiam Opinion.

In April 2001, the State of West Virginia indicted petitioner Denver A. Youngblood, Jr., on charges including abduction of three young women, Katara, Kimberly, and Wendy, and two instances of sexual assault upon Katara. The cases went to trial in 2003 in the Circuit Court of Morgan County, where a jury convicted Youngblood of two counts of sexual assault, two counts of brandishing a firearm, and one count of indecent exposure. The conviction rested principally on the testimony of the three women that they were held captive by Youngblood and a friend of his, statements by Katara that she was forced at gunpoint to perform oral sex on Youngblood, and evidence consistent with a claim by Katara about disposal of certain physical evidence of their sexual encounter. Youngblood was sentenced to a combined term of 26 to 60 years' imprisonment, with 25 to 60 of those years directly attributable to the sexual-assault convictions.

Several months after being sentenced, Youngblood moved to set aside the verdict. He claimed that an investigator working on his case had uncovered new and exculpatory evidence, in the form of a graphically explicit note that both squarely contradicted the State's account of the incidents and directly supported Youngblood's consensual-sex defense. The note, apparently written by Kimberly and Wendy, taunted Youngblood and his friend for having been "played" for fools, warned them that the girls had vandalized the house where Youngblood brought them, and mockingly thanked Youngblood for performing oral sex on Katara. The note was said to have been shown to a state trooper investigating the sexual-assault allegations against Youngblood; the trooper allegedly read the note but declined to take possession of it, and told the person who produced it to destroy it. Youngblood argued that the suppression of this evidence violated the State's federal constitutional obligation to disclose evidence favorable to the defense, and in support of his argument he referred to cases citing and applying *Brady v. Maryland*, 373 U.S. 83, 83 S. Ct. 1194, 10 L.Ed.2d 215 (1963).

The trial court denied Youngblood a new trial, saying that the note provided only impeachment, but not exculpatory, evidence. The trial court did not discuss Brady or its scope, but expressed the view that the investigating trooper had attached no importance to the note, and because he had failed to give it to the prosecutor the State could not now be faulted for failing to share it with Youngblood's counsel.

A bare majority of the Supreme Court of Appeals of West Virginia affirmed, finding no abuse of discretion on the part of the trial court, but without examining the specific constitutional claims

(Continues)

(Continued)

associated with the alleged suppression of favorable evidence. Justice Davis, dissenting in an opinion that Justice Starcher joined, unambiguously characterized the trooper's instruction to discard the new evidence as a Brady violation. The dissenters concluded that the note indicating that Youngblood engaged in consensual sex with Katara had been suppressed and was material, both because it was at odds with the testimony provided by the State's three chief witnesses (Katara, Kimberly, and Wendy) and also because it was entirely consistent with Youngblood's defense at trial that his sexual encounters with Katara were consensual. Youngblood then filed this petition for a writ of certiorari.

A Brady violation occurs when the government fails to disclose evidence materially favorable to the accused. This Court has held that the Brady duty extends to impeachment evidence as well as exculpatory evidence, and Brady suppression occurs when the government fails to turn over even evidence that is "known only to police investigators and not to the prosecutor," *Kyles v. Whitley*, 514 U.S. 419, 437–38 (1995) ("[T]he individual prosecutor has a duty to learn of any favorable evidence known to the others acting on the government's behalf in the case, including the police"). The reversal of a conviction is required upon a "showing that the favorable evidence could reasonably be taken to put the whole case in such a different light as to undermine confidence in the verdict." Id., at 435.

Youngblood clearly presented a federal constitutional Brady claim to the State Supreme Court, as he had to the trial court. And, as noted, the dissenting justices discerned the significance of the issue raised. If this Court is to reach the merits of this case, it would be better to have the benefit of the views of the full Supreme Court of Appeals of West Virginia on the Brady issue. We, therefore, grant the petition for certiorari, vacate the judgment of the State Supreme Court, and remand the case for further proceedings not inconsistent with this opinion.

It is so ordered.

Trial

The adversary system is perhaps most evident in the trial, the "battle" through which a just outcome is intended to be revealed. A judge must oversee several phases of a trial. Trials are intended to be organized and orderly, and the judge plays a central role in maintaining order during a trial and the opportunity for a fair presentation of the case by each party. The trial process involves a series of activities designed to allow a full and fair hearing of the facts and issues presented by the parties in a case. In general, the steps in a trial, whether civil or criminal, involve selection of a jury, opening statements, examination and cross-examination of witnesses, closing arguments, jury instructions, and rendering a verdict.

Trials may take place in less than an hour or require months (or even years!) of work before a resolution can be reached. In some trials, the judge alone determines what facts can be established after hearing and weighing the evidence and rules on the basis of his or her factual findings. In other cases, a jury hears the evidence and determines, in criminal cases, whether the defendant is guilty or, in civil cases, whether the plaintiff's allegations are supported. Thus, the first distinction affecting the trial process is whether a case will be decided by a judge or a jury.

Bench Trials

A bench trial is a trial conducted before a judge without a jury. During a bench trial, the judge functions as the "fact finder," which in a jury trial is the function of the jury.

Thus, in addition to controlling the trial process and ruling on trial objections, the judge must consider the evidence presented, weigh the credibility of witnesses, determine which "version" of the facts is true, and reach a decision about the guilt of the defendant.

Jury Trials

As the "trier of fact," the task of the jury is to determine what facts the evidence presented by the parties supports. After being instructed on the applicable law, the jury then reaches a decision in the case. Thus, jury trials represent American justice in its most basic form: a group of fellow citizens deciding what justice demands.

Although we may speak of a "jury of one's peers," there is no right to such a jury, even if it could be determined who "one's peers" are. The process for selection of a jury is to identify those individuals who can reach an impartial decision about the defendant's guilt. Jury selection involves choosing a jury that can impartially hear the evidence, the arguments of the parties, and decide whether the defendant is guilty as alleged in the criminal complaint or indictment. The judge takes considerable care to remove individuals from the jury who have the potential for prejudice for or against either party.

The process of jury selection begins with a group of prospective jurors usually compiled according to statute from voting registration lists, driver's license information, tax rolls, or other sources. This group is referred to as the *venire*. By identifying individuals from a variety of sources relating to their citizenship within the communities in which they live, the court seeks to assemble a *venire* that is representative of the district in which the case will be tried and one that satisfies minimum qualifications for jury service, such as residence, age, and literacy.

From the venire, jurors are selected for a particular case through a process known as *voir dire*. *Voir dire*, which means "to speak the truth," refers to the questioning of prospective jurors about their ability to hear evidence and render an unbiased verdict. This questioning is done by the judge and the attorneys for the parties. The questions usually relate to the prospective jurors' knowledge of the case or similar cases, feelings about the issues raised by the case, involvement in past cases, opinions about punishment, and so forth. Based on jurors' answers to these questions, the attorneys or the judge choose individuals for the jury or exclude individuals from sitting on the jury. If the attorney for either party wishes to exclude a prospective juror, he or she may *challenge* the prospective juror, which means a request that the judge dismiss a juror from hearing the case. There are two types of challenges: challenge for cause and peremptory challenge. A challenge for cause may be used when the attorney for one party feels that a prospective juror may be prejudiced toward a party in some way by having some relationship to one of the parties, by expressing bias in some way, or by indicating that he or she lacks the ability to be open minded about the case. Attorneys may use a challenge for cause as often as necessary when they believe a prospective juror, by answers during *voir dire*, has exhibited prejudice or an inability to fairly consider the evidence. A peremptory challenge is one that may be used to dismiss a prospective juror without stating a reason for the dismissal. Thus, a peremptory challenge may be used to remove a person from the jury for nearly any reason; however, this reason cannot be because of the race or gender of the prospective juror.

Attorneys use jury selection as their first opportunity to "connect" with the jurors in the case, as it is from the *venire* that the jury ultimately will be chosen. It is often said that first impressions are lasting, and it is during jury selection that jurors will get a first impression of the parties and their attorneys. Although the judge usually explains what the case is about in general terms and although no evidence is presented or discussed, jury selection allows the attorneys to begin to "get to know" the jurors who will hear the case. Thus, in addition to selecting jurors whom they believe will be most favorable to their client, jury selection does begin the trial process in the real and important sense that it is the first opportunity for the attorneys to sway the jury—by making a good impression.

Opening Statements

After the jury has been selected, the trial may begin with opening statements. An opening statement gives each party the opportunity to preview the case for the jury or judge. This means that each party can explain to the jury what facts they believe the evidence will show and why a decision in their favor is warranted. Although there are many theories about what makes the best opening, at a minimum it is an opportunity for the attorneys to present their version of the facts, that is, their "story" of the case, in order to influence the jurors to find in favor of their client.

In civil cases, the plaintiff's attorney begins by explaining how the evidence supports a verdict in favor of the plaintiff. In criminal cases, the prosecutor outlines the state's case against the defendant with an explanation of what evidence will be presented and what it will show. Counsel for the defendant then explains how the evidence justifies a verdict for the defendant. In some jurisdictions the defendant's opening statement may be reserved until the completion of the prosecution's introduction of evidence. Opening statements are not intended to be argumentative; that is, attorneys cannot argue about evidence that has not yet been admitted. Nonetheless, attorneys for the parties attempt to persuade the jury or the judge that the evidence to come should lead to a conclusion in their favor.

Evidence

Evidence in a trial may take many forms. With some exceptions, the test for whether evidence may be admitted at trial is whether it is *relevant* to some issue the case presents. As long as some evidence, whether a statement by a witness, a document, or a physical object, reasonably relates to the determination of some fact, it is admissible at trial.

Testimonial evidence involves statements made by witnesses at trial or before. Such evidence may be presented in court by *fact witnesses* who testify about what they know about some aspect of the case (e.g., "The defendant was hitchhiking in his blood-stained shirt when I was driving down Route 1 at 1 am and picked him up"). There are different types of fact witnesses. One is a *character witness*, who testifies about the character of someone he or she knows (e.g., "I have known the defendant since he was a child and know that he is an honest person"). Another type of fact witness is an *eyewitness*, who, as the name implies, actually observed something occur that is relevant to the case (e.g., "I saw the defendant point a gun at the bank teller"). Testimonial evidence may also be offered by an *expert witness*, who gives an opinion about some aspect of the case (e.g., "in my opinion, only someone who has training in the installation of alarm systems could have disabled the alarm in the bank"). Only witnesses who are qualified by the court as experts in some field may offer their opinion; all other witnesses must limit their testimony to the facts that they know to be true.

Testimonial evidence may be elicited either by *direct examination* or by *cross-examination*. Direct examination involves the questioning of a witness favorable to a party in order to introduce facts in support of a party's position. Adverse witnesses, or witnesses that will testify counter to a party's interests, may be cross-examined to determine the accuracy or truth of their assertions.

A second type of evidence is *physical evidence*. Physical evidence consists of tangible objects, such as a firearm, a broken automobile part, a briefcase full of money, or the impression of a footprint, that are relevant to the case.

Physical evidence requires establishment of a "chain of custody" to show the source of the physical evidence and who had contact with it before reaching the courtroom. This helps to show that the evidence is relevant to the case and has not been tampered with or otherwise affected before trial.

Another type of evidence is *documentary evidence*. As the names implies, documentary evidence is written documents, papers, notes, and so forth that relate to the case. Thus, a bank statement showing the defendant made a cash deposit in the same amount stolen from a convenience store would constitute documentary evidence. Similarly, a written contract showing the agreement of parties is a central piece of documentary evidence in a breach of contract case.

The introduction of evidence in a trial begins with the plaintiff's or the prosecution's witnesses. Because it is the plaintiff or the prosecution who must present evidence sufficient to convince the jury, it is that party who must present a *prima facie case*. That is, the plaintiff or the prosecution carries the burden of proving that the defendant violated the law or is civilly liable. If the plaintiff or prosecution fails to do so, the defendant may file a motion to dismiss the case. If this motion is denied, the defense proceeds to introduce evidence to support its case. The defendant in a civil case presents his or her version of the facts, attempting to show that the plaintiff's version cannot be true or that the law does not create liability on the defendant's part. Although the defendant in a criminal case is not required to testify or, indeed, to present any evidence at all, normally the defendant will offer evidence to rebut allegations by the prosecution and demonstrate that the defendant should not be held criminally liable.

Closing Arguments

After each party has "rested," that is, presented all of their evidence, closing arguments are made. The purpose of a closing argument is to summarize the evidence, highlight weaknesses in the other side's case, and specifically argue that the only conclusion to be reached is a verdict for the party making the argument. Although closing arguments may sometimes be imaginative or even theatrical, they may not stray beyond the evidence presented in the case (**Sidebar 3.1**).

Sidebar 3.1 *Great Trials in History*

The mechanism through which courts resolve disputes is the trial. Although trials have taken many forms and followed different procedures over time and in different places, all trials share the characteristic of being a forum in which the disputants receive a hearing. The hearing provides the opportunity for presenting evidence and argument in an attempt to convince opponents, listeners, and most importantly decision makers of the merits of one's position.

Sometimes the evidence, the testimony, and the argument are spellbinding. Sometimes the outcome has broader significance beyond the effects on the parties.

Here are three famous and historical trials in which both were true.

399 B.C.: **The Trial of Socrates**

In 399 B.C., Socrates was tried for impiety and corrupting the youth of Athens with antidemocratic ideas. At the age of 70 years, Socrates' life was well examined during his 10-hour trial because a jury of 500 Athenian men and many public citizens witnessed the event. Prosecutors Meletus, Lycon, and Antyon detailed the case against Socrates, which was based on his exhortations to followers that ordinary people, behaving like a herd of sheep, cannot acquire the intelligence necessary to form a good society and are therefore incapable of governing themselves. Although these transgressions sound like mere words, rather than a crime, Socrates' teachings led two of his pupils to revolt against the Athenian democracy in bloody coups, the second of which, led by Critius in the year 404 B.C., resulted in a bloody battle in which over 1,500 of Athens' most prominent democrats were executed. Socrates' religious views were also challenged at trial as prosecutors claimed that he had failed to observe rites, prayers, and offerings of sacrifices to the Athenian gods. After arguments by both the prosecution and defense, the 500 jurors found Socrates guilty of corrupting Athenian youth, of refusing to recognize the Athenian gods, and of introducing new gods to society. He was sentenced to death by drinking a cup of hemlock. Perhaps one of the first martyrs for free speech, Socrates became the father of apologetics (the theological defense of Christianity by proof) and the Socratic method of questioning to develop knowledge. Believing in his cause to his death, he used his final statements to the jury to provoke rather than plead with them, stating "The unexamined life is not worth living."

1692: **The Salem Witch Trials**

In the early months of 1692, the sleepy town of Salem, Massachusetts, watched in horror as several young girls appeared to lose their minds in a series of epileptic-like fits. This behavior seemed so unnatural to the townspeople that three women were subsequently arrested and accused of causing these fits using forms of witchcraft. These arrests, based on little more than suspicion and fear, became the first in a series of accusations that snowballed into more than 150 arrests in the counties of Essex, Suffolk, and Middlesex over the next 15 months. The admission of *spectral evidence*, or evidence based on events that occur in a dream or vision, was particularly crucial in generating arrests, as witnesses came forward to accuse a suspect of attacking them in their dreams, which would be taken as evidence of guilt. Many voiced skepticism as to the validity of this type of evidence, but they were also accused of witchcraft and thrown into jail.

In the summer of 1692, Massachusetts Governor William Phips created a special court to try the accused. Grand juries endorsed numerous indictments, and many suspects went to trial. The use of spectral evidence made it difficult for any suspect to escape conviction, and every person who went to trial in this court was sentenced to death. During the summer of 1692, 19 people were hanged. One person was crushed to death by stones, and five people died in prison. It was not until the winter of that year that calls for the exclusion of spectral evidence in court were issued and Governor Phips finally ordered the court to require proof of guilt using tangible evidence. After this decision, 28 accused witches were acquitted, and by May of 1693, all who remained imprisoned on suspicion of witchcraft were released. Although these trials remain as a stain on Massachusetts history and its justice system, they became a turning point in which colonial courts reinforced the need for a presumption of innocence.

1925: John Scopes "Monkey" Trial

The Scopes "Monkey" Trial is the most well-known debate concerning the teaching of evolution in American classrooms. In the summer of 1925, the small town of Dayton, Tennessee, exploded in a media frenzy as high school biology teacher John Scopes was accused of illegally teaching Darwin's theory of evolution in his classroom. The prosecutor, famed attorney William Jennings Bryan Jr., mounted the case against Scopes, arguing that "if evolution wins, Christianity goes. . . ." Lead attorney for the defense, Clarence Darrow, did not refute these charges, but rather embraced Scopes' actions and argued that denying the teaching of evolution in schools was unconstitutional.

During the 8-day trial, both the prosecution and defense abandoned the details and actions of Scopes and rather debated issues of evolution versus the literal interpretation of the Bible. Darrow, in fact, implored the jury to return a guilty verdict, in the hopes that he could further his cause by appealing the decision to the Tennessee Supreme Court. The 12-man jury upheld the so-called Monkey law, which forbade the teaching of evolution in the classroom. It found Scopes guilty of illegally teaching that "man descended from monkeys." Judge John T. Raulston fined Scopes $100. On appeal, the Tennessee Supreme Court dismissed the case on the grounds that the jury, not Judge Raulston, should have determined the fine. Although Scopes (and his advocate Darrow) had no further recourse in the courts, public opinion appeared to favor the defense, and in 1925, 13 of the 15 states considering antievolution legislation voted against restricting the teaching of evolution. It was not until 1968, however, in *Epperson v. Arkansas*, that the U.S. Supreme Court ruled that laws prohibiting the teaching of evolution are unconstitutional.

Jury Deliberation

After closing arguments, the judge gives final instructions to the jury to guide their deliberations. The set of jury instructions is a written document that explains the duty of the jury and the law to be applied in the case. This may include the requirements of the applicable civil law or the elements of the offense charged and any defenses available to the defendant and the way in which deliberations should

be conducted. Jury instructions may also include a summary of the evidence, an explanation of the burden and standards of proof, and the effect of evidentiary rulings that were made. In addition, the jury is typically instructed not to discuss the case with anyone outside of the jury room and, at times, is instructed to not read newspapers, magazines, or watch television. This is to keep the jury members from being influenced by information they may receive outside of the courtroom because their decision should be based on evidence and arguments heard in court. The judge has considerable discretion regarding what to include in the instructions, but may not comment on the evidence or offer an opinion about what it may show. Attorneys for the parties commonly request that certain instructions be included, but the judge need not include them.

After receiving the judge's instructions, the jury enters the jury room to reach a verdict. At times, the jury may be *sequestered*, or kept together in a single location outside of courtroom hours so that they will not be influenced by media they may see or read or people to whom they may have contact. Normally, however, the jury will go home at night and remain together in the jury room during business hours and discuss the case in order to reach a verdict.

If the jury cannot reach a verdict, the judge will admonish jury members to try to reach an agreement; however, if the judge becomes convinced that there is a *hung jury*, where the members of the jury cannot reach an agreement regardless of how much time they deliberate, the judge will declare a *mistrial* and dismiss the jury. After a mistrial, the case may be retried by the plaintiff or prosecutor.

Despite hundreds of years of jury deliberations, relatively little is known about the ways in which juries reach verdicts, in part due to the secrecy of the proceedings and in part due to the variety of cases considered and the personalities, backgrounds, and perceptions of jury members. Although the jury is instructed to evaluate the evidence and reach a decision based on the evidence, the jury is free to consider what it wishes in reaching a verdict. In criminal cases this means that, at times, the jury will disregard the evidence and reach a verdict favorable to the defendant. When this occurs, the case is considered to be one of *jury nullification*. Although our adversary system does not encourage or condone jury nullification, neither does it prohibit jury nullification, in recognition of and respect for the authority of juries to reach just verdicts.

Sentencing

When a defendant is convicted, the judge enters a judgment of guilt and conducts a hearing in which the defendant is sentenced. The judge has considerable discretion in sentencing. At the sentencing hearing, the judge may hear testimony and consider documentation about the defendant from a variety of sources, including the defendant himself, his family or friends, the victim, other community members affected, prior criminal acts of the defendant, and any other information about the defendant that may be helpful in determining a just sentence.

Although the judge has discretion to determine a proper sentence, this discretion is not limitless. State and federal criminal statutes typically specify a range of punishment for an offense, often specified as a minimum and maximum term of incarceration. Some statutes require a mandatory sentence. In addition, sentencing guidelines assist the judge in determining sentences. For example, the Sentencing Reform Act of 1984 required the use of sentencing guidelines. The guidelines specified sentences for numerous offenses and categories of a defendant's criminal history. Federal judges are required to sentence in accordance with guidelines and can only vary from the guidelines in a limited range of cases. Some states have also adopted sentencing guidelines. A further discussion of the sentencing process is found in Chapter 12.

Posttrial Matters

As with pretrial matters, the parties may file motions after trial addressing some aspect of the trial. Unlike an appeal (as discussed later here), a posttrial motion seeks a reconsideration of some issue at trial, asks for clarification of a decision, or seeks to have a verdict dismissed altogether.

Appellate Courts

An appellate court consists of a panel of judges that hear appeals. That is, after a trial verdict or a decision by a judge has been made, a party may file an appeal in order to correct errors that he or she believes were made in the trial court. Generally, appeals do not give parties a "second bite at the apple." Nonetheless, in some instances, the errors made in the trial court are so severe that the only way to correct them is to conduct another trial. The judges (as few as three and as many as nine) review transcripts of the trial and other documents to reach a decision by consensus about what occurred in the trial court and what "corrective" measures, if any, should be taken.

In exercising its appellate jurisdiction, an appellate court serves the important function of review; that is, it allows parties the opportunity for an independent examination of potential errors affecting the result at trial. This function, although important in itself, also serves to help build confidence in the judicial system by ensuring that litigants will have a group of judges examine what occurred in the court below and correct injustices that may have resulted.

In addition, appellate courts issue written opinions to explain the basis for their decisions. These written opinions, or case law, serve as precedent in future cases. The doctrine of *stare decisis* serves as both the tool and the restraint on court decision making. This means that courts within the same geographic jurisdiction are bound by these prior decisions and must apply the legal rules they represent in subsequent cases.

This rule of precedent serves several important purposes. First, it provides consistency in the law by requiring that cases involving similar legal principles be decided in similar ways. Consistency may be viewed as one of the meanings of justice and therefore provides courts with a

mechanism for achieving justice. Furthermore, if members of society are to conform their conduct in accordance with the law, consistent rulings allow them to understand the legal consequences of their actions. Moreover, when people understand the basis for a court decision and see that similar rulings will be made in similar cases, they are more likely to have confidence in our justice system (Murphy et al., 2006).

Second, rulings based on precedent allow for greater efficiency in the court system. That is, judges need not "reinvent the wheel" in every case that comes before them. Although nearly every case is unique in some respect, the ability to apply a previously devised and reasoned legal principle allows judges to make decisions more quickly.

Third, the rule of precedent allows for growth and development of the law (Abraham, 1998). The common law grows as judges write opinions that find their place in the body of cases that precede them. As judges apply the law to new cases involving factual situations not previously decided, new interpretations of law join the common law and expand the precedents available in future cases. Thus, although the rule of precedent may be restrictive in its effect on individual cases, it is expansive in its effect on the common law.

Key Terms

Jurisdiction	Standard of Proof
Federal Courts	Presumption of Innocence
State Courts	Discovery
In rem	Trier of Fact
In personam	Procedure
Venue	*Voir Dire*
Standing	Peremptory Challenge
Objectivity	Due Process
The Adversarial System	Witnesses
Burden of Proof	Evidence

Discussion Questions

1. Why is the legal concept of jurisdiction important for the operation of American courts?
2. What types of jurisdiction must exist in order for a court to hear a case? How does each one differ?
3. A plaintiff in a civil case must have "standing" in order for his or her case to be heard. Why?
4. What are some common goals that all courts share?
5. What are the hallmarks of an adversarial system of justice and why are American courts based on such a system?
6. What are the different standards of proof used in evaluating evidence and when is each applied?
7. What purposes do trial courts and appellate courts serve, and in what ways do they differ?
8. What are the steps in the trial process? How do they differ for criminal and civil cases?
9. The rule of *stare decisis* requires courts to adhere to the prior rulings of higher courts. What purposes does this rule serve?

Cases

Arbaugh v. Y & H Corp., 546 U.S. 500 (2006).

Attal v. Taylor.

Brady v. Maryland, 373 U.S. 83 (1963).

Buckingham, Doolittle & Burroughs, LLP v. Kar Kare Automotive Group, Inc., 987 So. 2d 818 (Fla. App. 4th Dist. 2008).

Chambers v. Nasco, 501 U.S. 32 (1991).

Coffin v. U.S., 156 U.S. 432 (1895).

Da Silva v. Kinsho International Corp., 229 F.3d 358 (2d Cir. 2000).

Davis v. Federal Election Commission, 128 S. Ct. 2759, 2768 (2008).

Gerstein v. Pugh, 420 U.S. 103, 95 S. Ct. 854 (1975).

Glenn v. Plante, 269 Wis.2d 575, 676 N.W.2d 413 (2004).

In re Winship, 397 U.S. 358 (1970).

Kunkel v. U.S., 140 F. Supp 591 (S.D.Cal. 1956).

Lujan v. National Wildlife Federation, 497 U.S. 871 (1990).

Sigurdsson v. Nedeen, 180 Md. App. 326, 950 A.2d 848 (2008).

Youngblood v. West Virginia, 547 U.S. 867 (2006).

Criminal Justice on the Web

 For an up-to-date list of Web links, go to *The American Courts: A Procedural Approach* online companion site at http://criminaljustice.jbpub.com/AmericanCourts. The online companion site will introduce you to some of the most important sites for finding American courts information on the Internet.

References

Abraham, H. J. (1998). *The Judicial Process* (7th ed.). New York: Oxford University Press.

Feeley, M. (1987). The adversary system. In R. J. Janoski (Ed.), *Encyclopedia of the American Judicial System*. New York: Scribners.

Frank, J. (1963). *Courts on Trial: Myth and Reality in American Justice*. New York: Athenaeum.

Murphy, W. F., Pritchett, C. H., Epstein, L., & Knight, J. (2006). *Courts, Judges, & Politics: An Introduction to the Judicial Process* (6th ed.). New York: McGraw-Hill.

Strier, F. (1992). What can the American adversary system learn from an inquisitorial system of justice? *Judicature*, 76, 109–132.

Courts at Work

The work of the courts is to resolve disputes. The dispute may be a criminal matter, in which the dispute is between the government and an individual to determine whether the criminal laws were violated, or it may be a civil dispute, in which an individual claims that he or she has suffered harm because of the actions of another. The subject matter of these disputes is as varied as life itself, ranging from disputes about custody of children, kidnapping, juvenile involvement in gangs, or ownership of property. This section explores the types of courts that resolve various types of disputes.

Chapter 4 considers the federal courts. Beginning with the constitutional basis for these courts, their role in deciding federal questions is discussed. In addition, the organizational structure of the federal courts is presented in terms of their geographical distribution across the country and their hierarchical authority. As one of the three branches of federal government, the federal courts operate alongside courts of the states in which they are located, yet limit their jurisdiction to cases involving questions of federal concern. The relationship of the federal government to the states is examined in terms of the division of powers between them and the effects of this division on the courts. The concept of federalism, which helps to define the respective authority of federal and state courts, is introduced. This chapter also addresses the types and functions of different federal courts. Particular attention is paid to the U.S. Supreme Court, the appointment of its Justices, and process of Supreme Court decision making.

In Chapter 5, the state courts are contrasted with courts within the federal system. This includes an overview of the wide array of state and local courts in the United States, along with a discussion of the types of cases they handle. Although state court systems share some similarities with federal courts, they work independently of the federal courts. And work they do! Courts that operate under state authority handle over 10 times as many criminal and civil cases as do federal courts, ranging from murder to petty theft and from wrongful death to will disputes. As Chapter 5 makes plain, the variety and number of state courts and the cases that they decide give the

states considerable responsibility for the administration of justice in America.

Chapter 6 also considers the work of those who labor in the courtrooms of America. The central participants in the justice system include the parties who bring cases to court. In criminal cases, these are the government and the criminal defendant. In civil cases, the parties are the plaintiff, who alleges some form of harm, and the defendant, whose actions are alleged to have caused the harm. Although the parties are the ones who seek to obtain justice, they are most often represented by attorneys whose job it is to present the case in court and accomplish their client's goals, consistent with the law. In criminal cases, the prosecutor is an attorney who represents the government and seeks to prove that the defendant violated the law. A criminal defense attorney has the goal of dismissing or reducing the charges and the potential sentence if the defendant is convicted. In civil cases, attorneys for each party zealously advocate for their clients by seeking to obtain a judgment from the court in their client's favor. Chapter 6 also explores the respective roles of judges and juries and the decisions that they are called on to make. The parties, the attorneys, the judge, and the jury are core participants involved in allowing the courts to dispense justice.

The work of the courts also includes cases handled by two courts of limited jurisdiction found in nearly every state. These are family courts and juvenile courts. Family courts, as the name suggests, are those that decide cases involving family-related matters. These include such disputes as those relating to divorce and the division of property it entails, as well as resolving child custody disputes. In addition, the termination of parental rights is an area in which a parent is alleged by the state to be unfit, requiring intervention by a family court to resolve the matter. The adoption of children is also a subject for the family courts. These are all discussed in Chapter 7.

The juvenile courts are the subject of Chapter 8. These are courts in which jurisdiction, in most states, is limited to decisions involving those who are under the age of 18 years. This typically involves minors who are alleged to have violated the criminal law or committed offenses that exist for only those below a certain age or "status" offenses. Such courts may also handle cases involving children who are "wayward" or "incorrigible," such as children in need of supervision, truants, or runaways. The juvenile courts therefore play a central role in the juvenile justice system, which is often viewed as "parallel" to the adult criminal justice system.

Taken together, the chapters that make up Section II provide an overview of the various courts in the United States, their functions, and the people that make them work. It will become apparent that the American courts are marked by the allocation of decision-making authority in various places, but together they work toward the goal of achieving justice for all members of society.

Federal Courts | 4

What Is This Chapter About?

This chapter focuses on the court system operated by the federal government. We begin by examining the concept of federalism, the idea that some powers have been entrusted by our constitution to the federal government, whereas other powers remain with the states as sovereign governments under their individual state constitutions. The concept of federalism therefore has implications for the operation of the courts and the division of powers among them to hear certain types of cases. Understanding this division will assist us in understanding the structure and function of the federal courts.

Next this chapter considers the jurisdiction and structure of the federal courts, stemming from an analysis of Article Three, Section One of the United States Constitution, which provides the legal basis for the existence of the federal court system. This involves a discussion of the distinction among the trial courts, appellate courts, and specialized courts. The operation of the U.S. Supreme Court, the cases that it chooses to hear, and its relationship to state supreme courts are also examined.

The chapter ends with an examination of potential conflicts between state and federal courts. To the extent that jurisdiction of the two systems overlaps, we examine who decides how such conflicts may be resolved.

Learning Objectives

After reading this chapter, you should be able to

1. Understand the concept of federalism and its effect on state and federal courts.
2. Understand the constitutional basis for the federal courts.
3. Explain the structure of the federal court system.
4. Describe the way in which cases come before the U.S. Supreme Court.
5. Identify potential conflicts between state and federal courts.

The Federal Courts and American Government

The United States of America, as the name implies, embodies a dual system of government—each state functions as a sovereign entity governed by its own laws, but also operates as a part of the unified federation represented by the federal government. This was the vision of the founders at the beginning of our democracy and that of the Framers in establishing the constitution on which the federation would rely: *E pluribus unum*, as found in the original motto of the country, "one out of many." (The official motto was later changed to "In God We Trust," but the original motto remains part of the Great Seal of the United States.) This dual system of government has given rise to a dual system of courts (as noted in the previous chapter): state courts and federal courts. These separate systems of justice have led to considerable complexity in the way in which cases may be decided and the law necessary to decide them. As discussed in the next chapter, each state has created courts of various types to handle matters of state concern. The federal courts, whose functions and structure are determined by the Constitution and by Congress, address matters of federal concern. What is a matter of federal concern, however? Should the prosecution of a kidnapper occur in state court or federal? Do state banking laws apply to the failure of a locally owned and operated bank, and where can a depositor seek recourse? In short, which matters are the province of the federal courts, and which are to be resolved in state courts? These questions are questions of federalism, which is the concept of shared authority reflected in our dual system of government and the courts.

Federalism

The federal courts were born out of a struggle to define the relationship between the states and the new national government as the Framers attempted to create a new governmental structure. That governmental structure, after much debate, ultimately became one in which a national government with legislative, executive, and judicial branches was created. This national government was not envisioned as usurping the power of the states, but to work for the common interests of the newly formed federation of states. Federalism is a political concept that involves the relative effects of distinct powers held by state governments to decide matters of law, in relationship to the powers granted to the federal government. Given the dual system of courts in the United States, federalism therefore has significant effects on the way in which these court systems are structured and operate and has influenced the role that federal courts have come to play in American society (Abraham, 1998).

Federalism embodies the idea that people may look to two distinct sources of governance, federal and state, and that each source of government will have separate spheres of influence.

These spheres of influence, although at times not altogether clear, were anticipated in the U.S. Constitution, which discusses the relationship between the state and federal governments. The Supremacy Clause, Article VI, Section 2 of the U.S. Constitution, states that the "Constitution, and the Laws of the United States . . . shall be the supreme law of the land; and the judges in every State shall be bound thereby, anything in the Constitution or laws of any State to the contrary notwithstanding." Thus, the federal Constitution makes it clear that state laws cannot contradict any constitutional provision of federal law; because federal law is "supreme," it takes precedence over state enactments that are in contrast to the Constitution and valid federal laws.

In addition, state court judges (as well as federal judges) who interpret state law are "bound" to follow the Constitution and other federal laws in their decision making. This means that they must find state laws invalid when they conflict with federal law, including the Constitution. Thus, both state and federal judges are unified by their allegiance to interpretation of laws that are consistent with the federal Constitution, yet they operate in separate and distinct spheres of influence, with state concerns of a local character, and federal concerns that cross state boundaries.

The Tenth Amendment to the Constitution also addresses the relationship of the states and the national government with respect to legal rights of citizens: "The powers not delegated to the United States by the Constitution, nor prohibited by it to the States, are reserved to the States respectively, or to the people." This provision, although not specifically stating what powers were "reserved" to the states, does make clear that the Framers contemplated that some matters were to be left up to the states to decide for themselves.

Perhaps the most authoritative and clearest statement of the meaning of federalism comes from the U.S. Supreme Court:

[Our federalism] is a proper respect for state functions, a recognition of the fact that the entire country is made up of a Union of separate state governments, and a continuance of the belief that the National Government will fare best if the States and their institutions are left free to perform their separate functions in their separate ways. . . . The concept does not mean blind deference to "States' Rights" any more than it means centralization of control over every important issue in our National Government and its courts. The Framers rejected both of these courses. What the concept does represent is a system in which there is sensitivity to the legitimate interests of both State and National Governments, and in which the National Government, anxious though it may be to vindicate and protect federal rights and federal interests, always endeavors to do so in ways that will not unduly interfere with the legitimate activities of the States. It should never be forgotten that this slogan, "Our Federalism," born in the early struggling days of our Union of States, occupies a highly important place in our Nation's history and its future. (*Younger v. Harris*, 410 U.S. 37, 44-45, 401 S. Ct. 746, 750-751, 27 L.Ed.2d 669, 673-74 (1971))

Thus, federalism is a historic principle of government and law that balances the rights and powers of the states with those of the federal government, and the possibility of tension between the two becomes evident in the operation of the federal courts. In *Younger* and other cases, therefore, the Supreme Court has cautioned against the exercise of jurisdiction by the federal courts when there is no overriding federal interest in the matter being decided.

In creating a federal judicial branch of the national government, the Framers specified in Article III, Section 2, that the judicial power "shall extend to all Cases, in Law and Equity, arising under this Constitution, the Laws of the United States, and Treaties made, or which shall be made under their Authority." Thus, it is clear from the plain language of the Constitution that the federal courts have no power except in "cases" that are brought to the federal courts. This requirement that a conflict must first exist is, as discussed earlier, the basis for our adversary system. This prevents the federal courts from being "advisory" bodies to the other branches of government or their officials. Similarly, it is not the role of the federal courts to interfere, by issuing rulings, in the operation of the governments of the individual states, except to the extent that an actual controversy exists involving some aspect of federal law.

In addition, federal courts may decline to exercise their jurisdiction in some cases in which the legal issues involved in the case are best left for decision to a state. Referred to as the *abstention* doctrine, the prohibition against a federal court hearing a matter that would otherwise be within its jurisdiction is a recognition that the sphere of authority held by the federal courts may overlap with the state courts, and in the interests of federalism, the state court should be allowed to decide the matter (Anderson, 2007). The purpose of the abstention doctrine is thus "to preserve the balance between state and federal sovereignty" (Wright & Kane, 2002). Under the abstention doctrine, federal courts will "abstain" from hearing a case when the interests of a state in some matter are much greater than the interests of the federal government. In particular, this occurs when a state court case has already been filed. It implicates important state interests, and it gives the plaintiff an opportunity to litigate issues that could have been litigated in federal court if the state case was not ongoing. For example, in the *Younger* case quoted previously, the defendant Harris was a proponent of communism and a member of the Progressive Labor Party. As a result of his activities, he was charged in state court under a California statute that criminalized the actions of one who advocates criminal means or the use of violence to bring about political or industrial change. Claiming that the statute was unconstitutional, Harris brought suit in federal district court to stop the state court criminal proceeding against him. The court found that the statute was unconstitutional and issued an injunction against the State of California from continuing with the prosecution against Harris. The U.S. Supreme Court reversed, finding that national policy—federalism—prevents federal courts from enjoining the actions of state courts, except in rare circumstances (*Younger*, 410 U.S. at 42, 401 S. Ct. at 750, 27 L.Ed.2d at 673). Thus, the rule has become clear that, even in cases where a federal court would normally have jurisdiction, such as claims regarding the constitutionality of a statute, the federal court should not interfere with a state's right to enforce its own laws.

In addition to the broad abstention doctrine, there are specific areas of state law that have been carved out, creating exceptions to the exercise of federal jurisdiction. Two of these, the divorce exception and the probate exception, address areas of law that have traditionally been local matters and in which local laws and practices have governed. In *Marshall v. Marshall*, 547 U.S. 293, 126 S. Ct. 1735, 164 L.Ed.2d 480 (2006), the U.S. Supreme Court discussed these exceptions and their basis in concepts of federalism. The case involved a dispute over the distribution of an estate between the widow of the decedent and the decedent's son. Normally, the probate of an estate after death is settled in state courts under state law, and any disputes about how property should be distributed after death are resolved in the state probate court. In the *Marshall* case, claims were filed in Texas probate court to determine who was entitled to the estate's assets; however, although the probate case was proceeding, the widow, Vickie Lynn Marshall, more famously known as Anna Nicole Smith, claiming mounting debt and a lack of assets after her 90-year-old husband's death, filed for bankruptcy in the federal Bankruptcy Court in California. The decedent's son, Pierce, intervened in the bankruptcy case, claiming that Vickie Lynn defamed him by alleging that he had engaged in forgery and fraud to try to get his father to leave the estate to him instead of to her. Vickie Lynn filed a counterclaim asserting that Pierce interfered with her right to an inheritance, and the bankruptcy court found in Vickie Lynn's favor, awarding her $449 million. The case was then reconsidered in the Federal District Court, who agreed with the Bankruptcy Court's award of $449 million and awarded Vickie Lynn an additional $88 million. On appeal, the federal court of appeals overturned the judgment and the award, finding that the district court should not have heard the case because of the "probate exception" to federal jurisdiction. This decision was appealed to the U.S. Supreme Court, which reversed the court of appeals, finding that the exercise of federal jurisdiction by the district court was appropriate (see **Case Decision 4.1**).

Case Decision 4.1 *Marshall v. Marshall*, 547 U.S. 293, 126 S. Ct. 1735, 164 L.Ed.2d 480 (2006)

Opinion of the Court by Justice Ginsburg:

In *Cohens v. Virginia*, Chief Justice Marshall famously cautioned: "It is most true that this Court will not take jurisdiction if it should not: but it is equally true, that it must take jurisdiction, if it should. . . . We have no more right to decline the exercise of jurisdiction which is given, than to usurp that which is not given." 6 Wheat. 264, 404, 5 L.Ed. 257 (1821). Among longstanding limitations on federal jurisdiction otherwise properly exercised are the so-called "domestic relations" and "probate" exceptions. Neither is compelled by the text of the Constitution or federal statute. Both are judicially created doctrines stemming in large measure from misty understandings of English legal history. In the years following Marshall's 1821 pronouncement, courts have sometimes lost sight of his admonition and have rendered decisions expansively interpreting the two exceptions.

Nevertheless, the Ninth Circuit in the instant case read the probate exception broadly to exclude from the federal courts' adjudicatory authority "not only direct challenges to a will or trust, but also questions which would ordinarily be decided by a probate court in determining the validity of the decedent's estate planning instrument." The Court of Appeals further held that a State's vesting of exclusive jurisdiction over probate matters in a special court strips federal courts of jurisdiction to entertain any "probate related matter," including claims respecting "tax liability, debt, gift, [or] tort." We hold that the Ninth Circuit had no warrant from Congress, or from decisions of this Court, for its sweeping extension of the probate exception.

I. Petitioner, Vickie Lynn Marshall (Vickie), also known as Anna Nicole Smith, is the surviving widow of J. Howard Marshall II (J. Howard). Vickie and J. Howard met in October 1991. After a

(Continues)

courtship lasting more than two years, they were married on June 27, 1994. J. Howard died on August 4, 1995. Although he lavished gifts and significant sums of money on Vickie during their courtship and marriage, J. Howard did not include anything for Vickie in his will. According to Vickie, J. Howard intended to provide for her financial security through a gift in the form of a "catch-all" trust.

Respondent, E. Pierce Marshall (Pierce), one of J. Howard's sons, was the ultimate beneficiary of J. Howard's estate plan, which consisted of a living trust and a "pourover" will. Under the terms of the will, all of J. Howard's assets not already included in the trust were to be transferred to the trust upon his death.

Competing claims regarding J. Howard's fortune ignited proceedings in both state and federal courts. In January 1996, while J. Howard's estate was subject to ongoing proceedings in Probate Court in Harris County, Texas, Vickie filed for bankruptcy under Chapter 11 of the Bankruptcy Code, in the United States Bankruptcy Court for the Central District of California. In June 1996, Pierce filed a proof of claim in the federal bankruptcy proceeding, alleging that Vickie had defamed him when, shortly after J. Howard's death, lawyers representing Vickie told members of the press that Pierce had engaged in forgery, fraud, and overreaching to gain control of his father's assets. Pierce sought a declaration that the debt he asserted in that claim was not dischargeable in bankruptcy. Vickie answered, asserting truth as a defense. She also filed counterclaims, among them a claim that Pierce had tortiously interfered with a gift she expected. Vickie alleged that Pierce prevented the transfer of his father's intended gift to her by, among other things: effectively imprisoning J. Howard against his wishes; surrounding him with hired guards for the purpose of preventing personal contact between him and Vickie; making misrepresentations to J. Howard; and transferring property against J. Howard's expressed wishes.

Vickie's tortious interference counterclaim turned her objection to Pierce's claim into an adversary proceeding. In that proceeding, the Bankruptcy Court granted summary judgment in favor of Vickie on Pierce's claim and, after a trial on the merits, entered judgment for Vickie on her tortious interference counterclaim. The Bankruptcy Court also held that both Vickie's objection to Pierce's claim and Vickie's counterclaim qualified as "core proceedings," which meant that the court had authority to enter a final judgment disposing of those claims. The court awarded Vickie compensatory damages of more than $449 million—less whatever she recovered in the ongoing probate action in Texas—as well as $25 million in punitive damages.

Pierce filed a post-trial motion to dismiss for lack of subject-matter jurisdiction, asserting that Vickie's tortious interference claim could be tried only in the Texas probate proceedings. The Bankruptcy Court held that "the 'probate exception' argument was waived" because it was not timely raised. [T]he court observed that a federal court has jurisdiction to "adjudicate rights in probate property, so long as its final judgment does not undertake to interfere with the state court's possession of the property."

Meanwhile, in the Texas Probate Court, Pierce sought a declaration that the living trust and his father's will were valid. Vickie, in turn, challenged the validity of the will and filed a tortious interference claim against Pierce, but voluntarily dismissed both claims once the Bankruptcy Court entered its judgment. Following a jury trial, the Probate Court declared the living trust and J. Howard's will valid.

Back in the federal forum, Pierce sought district-court review of the Bankruptcy Court's judgment. While rejecting the Bankruptcy Court's determination that Pierce had forfeited any argument based on the probate exception, the District Court held that the exception did not reach Vickie's claim. The Bankruptcy Court "did not assert jurisdiction generally over the probate proceedings . . . or take control over [the] estate's assets," the District Court observed, "[t]hus, the probate exception would bar federal jurisdiction over Vickie's counterclaim only if such jurisdiction would 'interfere' with the probate proceedings," Federal jurisdiction would not "interfere" with the probate proceedings, the District Court concluded, because: (1) success on Vickie's counterclaim did not necessitate any declaration that J. Howard's will was invalid; and (2) under Texas law, probate courts do not have exclusive jurisdiction to entertain claims of the kind asserted in Vickie's counterclaim.

The District Court also held that Vickie's claim did not qualify as a "core proceedin[g]." A bankruptcy court may exercise plenary power only over "core proceedings." In non-core matters, a bankruptcy court may not enter final judgment; it has authority to issue only proposed findings of fact and conclusions of law, which are reviewed *de novo* by the district court. Accordingly, the District Court treated the Bankruptcy Court's judgment as "proposed[,] rather than final," and undertook a "comprehensive, complete, and independent review of" the Bankruptcy Court's determinations.

Adopting and supplementing the Bankruptcy Court's findings, the District Court determined that Pierce had tortiously interfered with Vickie's expectancy. Specifically, the District Court found that J. Howard directed his lawyers to prepare an *inter vivos* trust for Vickie consisting of half the appreciation of his assets from the date of their marriage. It further found that Pierce conspired to suppress or destroy the trust instrument and to strip J. Howard of his assets by backdating, altering, and otherwise falsifying documents, arranging for surveillance of J. Howard and Vickie, and presenting documents to J. Howard under false pretenses. Based on these findings, the District Court awarded Vickie some $44.3 million in compensatory damages. In addition, finding "overwhelming" evidence of Pierce's "willfulness, maliciousness, and fraud," the District Court awarded an equal amount in punitive damages.

The Court of Appeals for the Ninth Circuit reversed. The appeals court recognized that Vickie's claim "does not involve the administration of an estate, the probate of a will, or any other purely probate matter." Nevertheless, the court held that the probate exception bars federal jurisdiction in this case. In the Ninth Circuit's view, a claim falls within the probate exception if it raises "questions which would ordinarily be decided by a probate court in determining the validity of the decedent's estate planning instrument," whether those questions involve "fraud, undue influence [or,] tortious interference with the testator's intent."

The Ninth Circuit was also of the view that state-court delineation of a probate court's exclusive adjudicatory authority could control federal subject-matter jurisdiction. In this regard, the Court of Appeals stated: "Where a state has relegated jurisdiction over probate matters to a special court and [the] state's trial courts of general jurisdiction do not have jurisdiction to hear probate matters, then federal courts also lack jurisdiction over probate matters." Noting that "[t]he [P]robate [C]ourt ruled it had exclusive jurisdiction over all of Vickie['s] claims," the Ninth Circuit held that "ruling . . . binding on the United States [D]istrict [C]ourt."

We granted certiorari to resolve the apparent confusion among federal courts concerning the scope of the probate exception. Satisfied that the instant case does not fall within the ambit of the narrow exception recognized by our decisions, we reverse the Ninth Circuit's judgment.

II. In *Ankenbrandt v. Richards*, 504 U.S. 689, 112 S. Ct. 2206, 119 L.Ed.2d 468 (1992), we addressed both the derivation and the limits of the "domestic relations exception" to the exercise of federal jurisdiction. Carol Ankenbrandt, a citizen of Missouri, brought suit in Federal District Court on behalf of her daughters, naming as defendants their father (Ankenbrandt's former husband) and his female companion, both citizens of Louisiana. Ankenbrandt's complaint sought damages for the defendants' alleged sexual and physical abuse of the children. Federal jurisdiction was predicated on diversity of citizenship. The District Court dismissed the case for lack of subject-matter jurisdiction, holding that Ankenbrandt's suit fell within "the 'domestic relations' exception to diversity jurisdiction." The Court of Appeals agreed and affirmed. We reversed the Court of Appeals' judgment.

Holding that the District Court improperly refrained from exercising jurisdiction over Ankenbrandt's tort claim, we traced explanation of the current domestic relations exception to *Barber v. Barber*, 21 How. 582, 16 L.Ed. 226 (1859). In *Barber*, the Court upheld federal-court authority, in a diversity case, to enforce an alimony award decreed by a state court. In dicta, however, the *Barber* Court announced—without citation or discussion—that federal courts lack jurisdiction over suits for divorce or the allowance of alimony.

Finding no Article III impediment to federal-court jurisdiction in domestic relations cases, the Court in *Ankenbrandt* anchored the exception in Congress' original provision for diversity jurisdiction. Beginning at the beginning, the Court recalled:

"The Judiciary Act of 1789 provided that 'the circuit courts shall have original cognizance, concurrent with the courts of the several States, of *all suits of a civil nature at common law or in equity, where the matter in dispute exceeds*, exclusive of costs, the sum or value of *five hundred dollars*, and . . . an alien is a party, or the suit is *between a citizen of the State where the suit is brought, and a citizen of another State*.'" (quoting Act of Sept. 24, 1789, § 11, 1 Stat. 78; emphasis added in *Ankenbrandt*).

The defining phrase, "all suits of a civil nature at common law or in equity," the Court stressed, remained in successive statutory provisions for diversity jurisdiction until 1948, when Congress adopted the more economical phrase, "all civil actions." 1948 Judicial Code and Judiciary Act, 62 Stat. 930, 28 U.S.C. 1332.

(Continues)

(Continued)

The *Barber* majority, we acknowledged in *Ankenbrandt*, did not expressly tie its announcement of a domestic relations exception to the text of the diversity statute. But the dissenters in that case made the connection. They stated that English courts of chancery lacked authority to issue divorce and alimony decrees. Because "the jurisdiction of the courts of the United States in chancery is bounded by that of the chancery in England," the dissenters reasoned, our federal courts similarly lack authority to decree divorces or award alimony. Such relief, in other words, would not fall within the diversity statute's original grant of jurisdiction over "all suits of a civil nature at common law or in equity." We concluded in *Ankenbrandt* that "it may be inferred fairly that the jurisdictional limitation recognized by the [*Barber*] Court rested on th[e] statutory basis" indicated by the dissenters in that case.

We were "content" in *Ankenbrandt* "to rest our conclusion that a domestic relations exception exists as a matter of statutory construction not on the accuracy of the historical justifications on which [the exception] was seemingly based." "[R]ather," we relied on "Congress' apparent acceptance of this construction of the diversity jurisdiction provisions in the years prior to 1948, when the statute limited jurisdiction to 'suits of a civil nature at common law or in equity.'" We further determined that Congress did not intend to terminate the exception in 1948 when it "replace[d] the law/equity distinction with the phrase 'all civil actions.'" Absent contrary indications, we presumed that Congress meant to leave undisturbed "the Court's nearly century-long interpretation" of the diversity statute "to contain an exception for certain domestic relations matters."

We nevertheless emphasized in *Ankenbrandt* that the exception covers only "a narrow range of domestic relations issues." The *Barber* Court itself, we reminded, "sanctioned the exercise of federal jurisdiction over the enforcement of an alimony decree that had been properly obtained in a state court of competent jurisdiction." Noting that some lower federal courts had applied the domestic relations exception "well beyond the circumscribed situations posed by *Barber* and its progeny," we clarified that only "divorce, alimony, and child custody decrees" remain outside federal jurisdictional bounds. While recognizing the "special proficiency developed by state tribunals . . . in handling issues that arise in the granting of [divorce, alimony, and child custody] decrees," we viewed federal courts as equally equipped to deal with complaints alleging the commission of torts.

III. Federal jurisdiction in this case is premised on 28 U.S.C. § 1334, the statute vesting in federal district courts jurisdiction in bankruptcy cases and related proceedings. Decisions of this Court have recognized a "probate exception," kin to the domestic relations exception, to otherwise proper federal jurisdiction. Like the domestic relations exception, the probate exception has been linked to language contained in the Judiciary Act of 1789.

Markham, the Court's most recent and pathmarking pronouncement on the probate exception, stated that "the equity jurisdiction conferred by the Judiciary Act of 1789 . . . , which is that of the English Court of Chancery in 1789, did not extend to probate matters." As in *Ankenbrandt* so in this case, "[w]e have no occasion . . . to join the historical debate" over the scope of English chancery jurisdiction in 1789, for Vickie Marshall's claim falls far outside the bounds of the probate exception described in *Markham*. We therefore need not consider in this case whether there exists any uncodified probate exception to federal bankruptcy jurisdiction under § 1334.

In *Markham*, the plaintiff Alien Property Custodian commenced suit in Federal District Court against an executor and resident heirs to determine the Custodian's asserted rights regarding a decedent's estate. Jurisdiction was predicated on § 24(1) of the Judicial Code, now 28 U.S.C. § 1345, which provides for federal jurisdiction over suits brought by an officer of the United States. At the time the federal suit commenced, the estate was undergoing probate administration in a state court. The Custodian had issued an order vesting in himself all right, title, and interest of German legatees. He sought and gained in the District Court a judgment determining that the resident heirs had no interest in the estate, and that the Custodian, substituting himself for the German legatees, was entitled to the entire net estate, including specified real estate passing under the will.

Reversing the Ninth Circuit, which had ordered the case dismissed for want of federal subject-matter jurisdiction, this Court held that federal jurisdiction was properly invoked. The Court first stated:

"It is true that a federal court has no jurisdiction to probate a will or administer an estate. . . . But it has been established by a long series of decisions of this Court that federal courts of equity have jurisdiction to entertain suits 'in favor of creditors, legatees and heirs' and other claimants against a decedent's estate 'to establish their claims' so long as the federal court does not interfere with the probate proceedings or assume general jurisdiction of the probate or control of the property in the custody of the state court."

Next, the Court described a probate exception of distinctly limited scope:

> "[W]hile a federal court may not exercise its jurisdiction to disturb or affect the possession of property in the custody of a state court, . . . it may exercise its jurisdiction to adjudicate rights in such property where the final judgment does not undertake to interfere with the state court's possession save to the extent that the state court is bound by the judgment to recognize the right adjudicated by the federal court."

The first of the above-quoted passages from *Markham* is not a model of clear statement. The Court observed that federal courts have jurisdiction to entertain suits to determine the rights of creditors, legatees, heirs, and other claimants against a decedent's estate, "so long as the federal court does not *interfere with the probate proceedings.*" Lower federal courts have puzzled over the meaning of the words "interfere with the probate proceedings," and some have read those words to block federal jurisdiction over a range of matters well beyond probate of a will or administration of a decedent's estate.

We read *Markham's* enigmatic words, in sync with the second above-quoted passage, to proscribe "disturb[ing] or affect[ing] the possession of property in the custody of a state court." True, that reading renders the first-quoted passage in part redundant, but redundancy in this context, we do not doubt, is preferable to incoherence. In short, we comprehend the "interference" language in *Markham* as essentially a reiteration of the general principle that, when one court is exercising *in rem* jurisdiction over a *res*, a second court will not assume *in rem* jurisdiction over the same *res*. Thus, the probate exception reserves to state probate courts the probate or annulment of a will and the administration of a decedent's estate; it also precludes federal courts from endeavoring to dispose of property that is in the custody of a state probate court. But it does not bar federal courts from adjudicating matters outside those confines and otherwise within federal jurisdiction.

A. As the Court of Appeals correctly observed, Vickie's claim does not "involve the administration of an estate, the probate of a will, or any other purely probate matter." Provoked by Pierce's claim in the bankruptcy proceedings, Vickie's claim, like Carol Ankenbrandt's, alleges a widely recognized tort. ("One who by fraud, duress or other tortious means intentionally prevents another from receiving from a third person an inheritance or gift that [s]he would otherwise have received is subject to liability to the other for loss of the inheritance or gift."). Vickie seeks an *in personam* judgment against Pierce, not the probate or annulment of a will. Nor does she seek to reach a *res* in the custody of a state court.

Furthermore, no "sound policy considerations" militate in favor of extending the probate exception to cover the case at hand. Trial courts, both federal and state, often address conduct of the kind Vickie alleges. State probate courts possess no "special proficiency . . . in handling [such] issues."

B. The Court of Appeals advanced an alternate basis for its conclusion that the federal courts lack jurisdiction over Vickie's claim. Noting that the Texas Probate Court "ruled it had exclusive jurisdiction over all of Vickie Lynn Marshall's claims against E. Pierce Marshall," the Ninth Circuit held that "ruling . . . binding on the United States [D]istrict [C]ourt." We reject that determination.

Texas courts have recognized a state-law tort action for interference with an expected inheritance or gift, modeled on the Restatement formulation. It is clear that Texas law governs the substantive elements of Vickie's tortious interference claim. It is also clear, however, that Texas may not reserve to its probate courts the exclusive right to adjudicate a transitory tort. We have long recognized that "a State cannot create a transitory cause of action and at the same time destroy the right to sue on that transitory cause of action in any court having jurisdiction." Jurisdiction is determined " by the law of the court's creation and cannot be defeated by the extraterritorial operation of a [state] statute . . . , even though it created the right of action." Directly on point, we have held that the jurisdiction of the federal courts, "having existed from the beginning of the Federal government, [can] not be impaired by subsequent state legislation creating courts of probate."

Our decision in *Durfee v. Duke,* 375 U.S. 106, 84 S. Ct. 242, 11 L.Ed.2d 186 (1963), relied upon by the Ninth Circuit, is not to the contrary. *Durfee* stands only for the proposition that a state court's final judgment determining *its own* jurisdiction ordinarily qualifies for full faith and credit, so long as the jurisdictional issue was fully and fairly litigated in the court that rendered the judgment. At issue here, however, is not the Texas Probate Court's jurisdiction, but the federal courts' jurisdiction to entertain Vickie's tortious interference claim. Under our federal system, Texas cannot render its probate courts

(Continues)

exclusively competent to entertain a claim of that genre. We therefore hold that the District Court properly asserted jurisdiction over Vickie's counterclaim against Pierce.

IV. After determining that Vickie's claim was not a "core proceeding," the District Court reviewed the case *de novo* and entered its final judgment on March 7, 2002. The Texas Probate Court's judgment became final on February 11, 2002, nearly one month earlier. The Court of Appeals considered only the issue of federal subject-matter jurisdiction. It did not address the question whether Vickie's claim was "core"; nor did it address Pierce's arguments concerning claim and issue preclusion. These issues remain open for consideration on remand.

For the reasons stated, the judgment of the Court of Appeals for the Ninth Circuit is reversed, and the case is remanded for further proceedings consistent with this opinion.

It is so ordered.

The Court's decision in *Marshall* was based on its finding that Vickie Lynn's claim against Pierce did not involve a probate matter, but was a tort claim for interference with her inheritance. As such, the Supreme Court held that the federal district court was not treading on the jurisdiction of the state probate court, which was not the sole forum in which such claims could be resolved. It found that the state probate court could not assert that it had exclusive jurisdiction in all matters that may relate in any way to disputes about an estate because some legal issues (such as fraud, forgery, and interference with the expectation of an inheritance) fall within a federal court's subject matter jurisdiction.

One may view the *Marshall* decision as the usurpation of state power by the federal courts. After all, the case began as a probate matter that, as the "probate exception" itself recognizes, is an area traditionally reserved for state courts. Also, the Texas probate court awarded the estate to Pierce, after finding that he had not engaged in any improper behavior. The federal courts effectively vacated this decision, granting to Vickie Lynn the value of the estate and more. Alternatively, one may also view this case as one in which the federal courts (bankruptcy, district, and Supreme) were doing the job they are intended to do: resolve cases that come before them, provided such cases fall within their jurisdiction. The *Marshall* case thus represents the tension that at times arises as a result of our dual system of courts.

Federal Court Authority

The Constitutional Basis for the Federal Courts

Article III of the U.S. Constitution creates the U.S. Supreme Court and authorizes Congress to create "inferior" federal courts, as specified in Section 1: "The judicial Power of the United States shall be vested in one Supreme Court, and in such inferior courts as the Congress may from time to time ordain and establish."

Article III thus anticipates that the Supreme Court, as the highest federal court, is to be at the head of the judicial branch of government. It was a source of debate at the time the Constitution was drafted whether Article III should also specify what other courts should make up the judicial branch and what their powers should be. Furthermore, it was unclear what the relationship between these new federal courts and the existing state courts would be. Some of the Framers were concerned that these federal courts would usurp the power of state courts and that a federal Supreme Court was sufficient for deciding matters of federal law that the state courts could not agree on or otherwise incorrectly interpreted. Other Framers felt that the Constitution should completely set out the structure of the courts and the powers necessary to decide matters of both national and state concern. The compromise reached is the one we have today—lower federal courts throughout the country created by Congress and overseen by the Supreme Court.

This compromise is reflected in Section 2 of Article III, which lists the subject matter jurisdiction of the federal courts as well as specifying the types of original and appellate jurisdiction of the Supreme Court. By granting Congress the power to create the lower federal courts, the Framers allowed the states, through their representatives in Congress, to have influence over the federal judiciary. This exercise of federalism allowed a new federal court system to develop side by side with the state court systems already in place.

There is also a second Constitutional basis for the creation of federal courts. It is found in Article I, which creates the legislative branch of government and specifies its powers. One of these powers is the power to create courts inferior to the Supreme Court. These are discussed later here.

The Statutory Basis for the Federal Courts

The Constitution authorized Congress to create whatever courts it deemed necessary for the operation of the judicial branch, provided that they are "inferior" to, or subject to, the powers of the Supreme Court. Congress first did this in the Judiciary Act of 1789. The first Judiciary Act was crucial in setting up a national system of courts for interpreting federal law. It was this Act that first envisioned a three-tier system of federal courts—district courts, circuit courts, and the Supreme Court—a structure that largely remains in place today.

Thirteen district courts were created by the Act, 11 for each of the states ratifying the Constitution and one each for Maine (then part of Massachusetts) and Kentucky (then part of Virginia). These courts were intended to serve as trial courts in matters of federal concern and were given original jurisdiction in cases of admiralty, minor civil cases, and lesser criminal matters.

The Judiciary Act of 1789 also created circuit courts made up of a district judge and two supreme court justices who "rode the circuit"; that is, the judges traveled from place to place within the area served by the court. Three circuits were created: eastern, middle, and southern, each made up of states within those regions. The Act granted the circuit courts original jurisdiction to hear more serious criminal and civil cases, as well as appellate jurisdiction to hear appeals in some cases from the district courts. As a result of subsequent modifications of the Act changing the jurisdiction of the circuit courts, today they are primarily courts of appeal. Moreover, as the nation expanded, so too did the number of circuits, with 13 circuits in existence today, as shown in **Figure 4.1**, and discussed in more detail later here.

In addition, the Act specified the jurisdiction of the Supreme Court. It granted to the Supreme Court appellate jurisdiction in cases decided in the circuit courts, as well as authority to hear appeals from state courts in federal matters, including matters of state law claimed to be in violation of the Constitution. It also authorized the Supreme Court to issues writs of mandamus "to any courts appointed, or persons holding office, under the authority of the United States." Recall from Chapter 1 that it was this provision of the Act that was found to violate Article III of the Constitution in *Marbury v. Madison*.

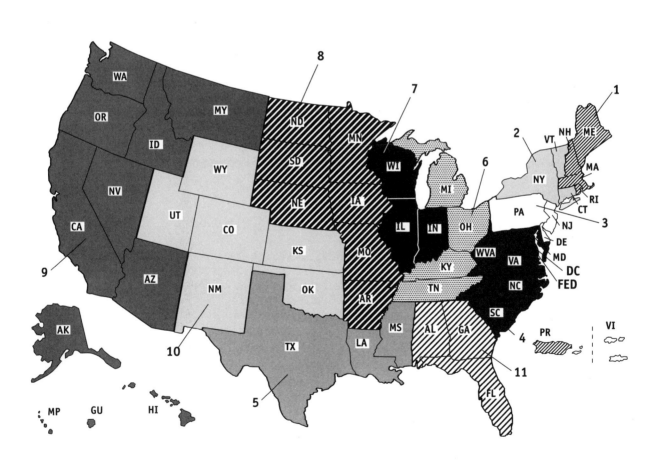

Figure 4.1

Federal District Courts and Circuit Courts of Appeals in the United States.

Source: Administrative Office of the U.S. Courts, http://www.uscourts.gov.

Structure of the Federal Court System

Courts that were created under Article III of the Constitution, referred to as "Constitutional courts," or "Article III courts," comprise a three-tier system of trial courts, appellate courts, and the U.S. Supreme Court. Courts created by Congress using its authorization found in Article I, Section 8, of the U.S. Constitution, referred to as "Legislative Courts," or "Article I courts," are specialized courts of limited jurisdiction and are included as part of the federal court system to handle specific types of cases relating to matters arising as a result of federal legislation. Other courts, more specialized still, have been created by Congress over time to address specific legal needs or areas of the country. **Table 4.1** shows the structure of the federal court system and the function of the courts within it. Despite the terms "constitutional" and "legislative," all of these courts exist as a direct result of authorization found in the U.S. Constitution. Also, with the exception of the U.S. Supreme Court, all of the federal courts were created by Congress pursuant to its explicit power to do so. Thus, the terms "constitutional" and "legislative" do not refer to the source of the court's existence, but to its jurisdiction and functioning.

A "structure" to the American court system implies a hierarchy of power with respect to the application and interpretation of law. This means, for example, that a trial court, in deciding the facts and applying the law, is not free to craft whatever legal rules it wishes in reaching a conclusion. Its interpretation of the law and the applicability of that law are limited to interpretations previously made by "higher" courts, such as a court of appeals. Thus, the U.S. District Courts must follow interpretations of law made by the U.S. Courts of Appeals for the circuit in which the district court is located. The Court of Appeals, likewise, may not interpret the law in ways that are contrary to decisions of the U.S. Supreme Court.

The relationship between the rulings of appellate courts and trial courts has been the subject of many court decisions (e.g., *Ute Indian Tribe v. State of Utah*, 935 F. Supp. 1473 (D.Utah, 1996); *Jaffree v. Bd of School Commissioners*, 459 U.S. 1314, 103 S. Ct. 842, 74 L.Ed.2d 924 (1983). One such case, *Litman v. Massachusetts Mut. Life Ins. Co.*, 825 F.2d 1506 (11th Cir. 1987), examined the organization of the federal court system and the responsibilities of the courts within it. In that case, a U.S. District Court dismissed a case on the motion of one of the parties, after it had been remanded (sent back to the lower court) for a new trial by a three-judge panel of the Eleventh Circuit Court of Appeals. The nonmoving party then appealed to the Eleventh Court of Appeals, which, sitting en banc, found that the District court had improperly ignored the Court of Appeal's prior order for a new trial by ignoring its obligation to follow any mandate (order) issued by the higher court. The Eleventh Circuit's opinion on the purpose of the court structure, found in **Case Decision 4.2**, is instructive.

Table 4.1

Structure and Function of the Federal Courts

Court Classifications	Function
Constitutional Courts	
United States Supreme Court	Appeals from Courts of Appeals, State Supreme Courts
United States Courts of Appeals	Appeals from lower federal courts
United States District Courts	Civil and criminal trials within district
United States Bankruptcy Courts	Bankruptcy cases
United States Court of International Trade	Imports, exports, and other trade matters involving federal laws
Legislative Courts	
United States Court of Federal Claims	Contract and other money claims against the federal government
United States Court of Appeals for the Armed Forces	Appeals in military criminal cases
United States Court of Appeals for Veteran Claims	Appeals from Veterans Administration
United States Tax Court	Trials involving taxes owed to IRS
Other Federal Courts	
Territorial Courts	Trials in U.S. Territories
District of Columbia Courts	Trials and appeals in Washington, DC
Judicial Panel on Multidistrict Litigation	Consolidate civil cases in a single district
Foreign Intelligence Surveillance Court	Issue warrants in national security cases

Case Decision 4.2 *Litman v. Massachusetts Mut. Life Ins. Co.*, 825 F.2d 1506 (11th Cir. 1987)

Decision of the Court by Judge Fay:

The case was taken in banc to consider whether the mandate in *Litman v. Massachusetts Mutual Life Insurance Co.*, 739 F.2d 1549 (11th Cir. 1984) ("*Litman I*") was properly executed. The mandate included an order for a new trial on punitive damages. The district court did not conduct a new trial, however, because it was of the opinion that the "Waiver of a Right to New Trial and Consent to Entry of Judgment" presented by Massachusetts Mutual ("Mass Mutual") was an acceptable alternative disposition of the case. We REVERSE and REMAND for a new trial on punitive damages. Because this case involves the structural relationship between the appellate court and district court within the judicial hierarchy, we examine the creation of the federal court system, the tools that emerged to enforce the three-tier structure and the institutional values the tools are designed to perpetuate.

I. Historical Perspective of the Organization of the Federal Court System

Judicial power is created by the Constitution and Congress. Art. III of the Constitution provides: "[t]he judicial Power of the United States, shall be vested in one Supreme Court, and in such inferior Courts as the Congress may from time to time ordain and establish." U.S. Const., art. III, § 1. As early as 1789, Congress created district courts and circuits courts. Judiciary Act of 1789, ch. 20, 1 Stat. 73. In 1891, Congress passed the Evarts Act, Act of Mar. 3, 1891, 26 Stat. 826, which established the circuit court of appeals as a separate intermediate level court. The primary objective of the Evarts Act was to relieve the Supreme Court of the excessive burden imposed upon it arising from the rapid growth of the country, and the steady increase in litigation, by transferring a considerable part of its appellate jurisdiction to the Circuit Court of Appeals, and making the judgments of that Court final, absent compelling circumstances. Today's judicial structure emerged when Congress passed the Judicial Code of 1911, Mar. 3, 1911, ch. 231, 36 Stat. 1131, which aligned the circuit courts as those handling most appeals and assigned the district court as the general trial court of original jurisdiction. In so doing, Congress established the three tier system as well as the chain of command within the judiciary hierarchy.

The Constitution confers jurisdictional powers on the Supreme Court. See U.S. Const., art. III, § 2. The Court has limited original jurisdiction and exercises appellate jurisdiction, either by direct appeal or by the discretionary writ of certiorari, over the district courts, the courts of appeals, and the highest courts of the states. The Supreme Court has the power to make determinations as to the law of the land that binds all courts. By statute Congress has assigned jurisdictional powers to both district and circuit courts. The district courts are courts of original jurisdiction. The circuit courts have appellate jurisdiction over district courts, administrative agencies and exercise power to issue original writs in appropriate cases. Appellate courts have the power to issue mandates which are commands that cannot be ignored. Absent a Supreme Court decision to the contrary, district courts are compelled to follow mandates of appellate courts.

The three tier system evolved purposefully and deliberately and operates to define the proper allocation of authority and responsibility within the judicial system. Experience has demonstrated that the system works. Throughout history courts at all three levels have recognized that careful observation of this allocation of authority is necessary for a properly functioning judiciary. When district courts err, appellate courts do not hesitate to correct mistakes and confine the court to its authorized boundaries. When an appellate court errs, the Supreme Court does likewise.

II. Institutional Tools, Values and Illustrations

There are several methods used to ensure order is maintained within the judicial hierarchy. Pursuant to statutory provisions, appellate courts have the authority to issue writs of mandamus. The historic use of the writ of mandamus issued by an appellate court has been to exert its revisory appellate power over the district court. The writ affords an "effective means of confining the inferior court to a lawful exercise of its prescribed jurisdiction, or of compelling it to exercise its authority when it is its duty to do so." The writ of mandamus, while an extreme remedy, is still used when a district court

(Continues)

usurps power or abuses its discretion. The writ is a tool used to keep the courts functioning within the constitutional and congressional design.

The Supreme Court, by accepting cases through the discretionary writ of certiorari, has kept order within the courts. The notion that the federal district courts and circuit courts of appeal must adhere to controlling Supreme Court decisions is reinforced whenever necessary. The Court emphasized the need to adhere to the hierarc[hic]al structure of the federal court system created by the Constitution and Congress. "[U]nless we wish anarchy to prevail within the federal judicial system, a precedent of this Court must be followed by the lower federal courts no matter how misguided the judges of those courts may think it to be."

A recent case serves as a compelling illustration. In *Jaffree v. Board of School Comm'rs*, 554 F. Supp. 1104 (S.D.Ala.1983), the district court held that the fourteenth amendment did not incorporate the establishment clause of the first amendment against the States. The district court ruled that the United States Supreme Court had erred. Justice Powell, in his capacity of Circuit Justice for the Eleventh Circuit, entered an interlocutory emergency stay of the judgment of the district court and stated that, "[u]nless and until this Court reconsiders the following decisions, they appear to control this case. In my view, the District Court was obligated to follow them. Similarly, my own authority as Circuit Justice is limited by controlling decisions of the full Court."

Thereafter, the Court of Appeals for the Eleventh Circuit reversed the district court's order dismissing the complaint. The Court emphasized the district court's obligation to adhere to Supreme Court precedent. The Supreme Court had considered the historical implications and concluded that its present interpretation of the first and fourteenth amendments is consistent with the historical evidence. Even though the district court concluded that the Supreme Court erred it was required to follow the controlling decision. The Supreme Court affirmed the judgment of the court of appeals. *Wallace v. Jaffree*, 472 U.S. 38, 105 S. Ct. 2479, 86 L.Ed.2d 29 (1985) (this appeal dealt with the narrow question of whether a period of silence for "meditation or voluntary prayer" established religion within the meaning of the first amendment). The message sent to the district court from both the Supreme Court and the court of appeals was clear—it had an obligation to follow precedent.

Many devices have been created to ensure that authority, jurisdiction and responsibility remain properly allocated among the three levels of courts within the federal judiciary. The discussion above merely serves to illustrate the point. The courts within the system have differing responsibilities and standards and values must be formulated and communicated in order to ensure that the process functions.

Institutional tools perpetuate the value of stability and predictability—essential factors in the proper operation of the judiciary. Predictability is essential not only to lawyers who must advise their clients about the law, but also to the notion of judicial review in creating a stable body of law. It is generally thought that appellate courts are in a better position than trial courts to accommodate the need for stability. Reviewing courts are better able to maintain the necessary continuity of doctrine over time. The uniformity achieved is not necessarily rigid; the appellate court "can change, or can react to advocacy or external reality to alter the direction of its commands." P. Carrington, D. Meador & M. Rosenberg, Justice on Appeal p. 148 (1976). But the primary mission of the courts recognizes this particular feature.

"Judicial precedence serves as the foundation of our federal judicial system. Adherence to it results in stability and predictability." In *Moragne v. States Marine Lines*, 398 U.S. 375, 90 S. Ct. 1772, 26 L.Ed.2d 339 (1970) the Supreme Court discussed the reasons for adhering to precedent:

> Among these are the desirability that the law furnish a clear guide for the conduct of individuals, to enable them to plan their affairs with assurance against untoward surprise; the importance of furthering fair and expeditious adjudication by eliminating the need to relitigate every relevant proposition in every case; and the necessity of maintaining public faith in the judiciary as a source of impersonal and reasoned judgments. The confidence of people in their ability to predict the legal consequences of their actions is vitally necessary to facilitate the planning of primary activity.

Each tier in the judicial hierarchy has its responsibility once a mandate is issued. A mandate may be vague or precise resulting from the disposition of those issues presented which vary widely from the rather simple to the most complex. Determining the scope of a mandate can present problems with interpretation. The case law is replete with examples of disputes arising from interpretations of mandates. The disputes focus on the relationship between the appellate courts and district courts and center on the proper allocation of authority and responsibility.

When an appellate court issues a specific mandate it is not subject to interpretation; the district court has an obligation to carry out the order. A different result would encourage and invite district courts to engage in *ad hoc* analysis of the propriety of appellate court rulings. Post mandate maneuvering in the district courts would undermine the authority of appellate courts and create a great deal of uncertainty in the judicial process. It would also eliminate any hope of finality.

III. *Litman v. Mass Mutual*

With the foregoing principles in mind, we focus on the dispute before us which raises the issue of whether the opinion in *Litman v. Massachusetts Mutual Life Insurance Co.*, 739 F.2d 1549 (11th Cir. 1984) ("*Litman I*"), when viewed in its totality, allows for the district court's order on remand.

This was an action for breach of general agency contract and two counts of slander brought by Bernard Litman ("Litman") against Massachusetts Mutual Life Insurance Company ("Mass Mutual"). The trial resulted in a jury verdict for Litman on all three counts and judgment was entered in the amount of $2,500,234. The jury's verdict included separate compensatory damage awards for the breach of contract claim and each of the two claims of slander. The punitive damage award for the slander was undifferentiated. It was assessed in response to a single question on the special verdict form.

Mass Mutual appealed on several grounds and challenged the punitive damage award asserting alternative theories. Mass Mutual argued that it was entitled to judgment on the issue of punitive damages and in the alternative, that the amount of punitive damages awarded was excessive entitling it to a new trial. Our court affirmed the judgment of the district court with one exception. Finding that the statement made by a Mass Mutual spokesman to a prospective employer of Litman, could not be slander as a matter of law, the court reversed the $100,000 slander award which necessarily resulted in a reversal of the entire punitive damage award. The case was remanded to the district court for a new trial solely on the issue of punitive damages. Mass Mutual made no motions to modify the ruling or to withdraw its challenge to the award of punitive damages.

On remand, Mass Mutual filed a written "Waiver of Right to New Trial and Consent to Entry of Judgment." Mass Mutual stated that it was now content to accept the original jury verdict on the punitive damage issue in the interest of terminating the suit. The district court accepted Mass Mutual's argument that if a *prima facie* case for the award of punitive damages against Mass Mutual were shown at all, under our opinion a jury would consider only a portion of the original $250,000 award for the remaining claim which was based on the statements made by two Mass Mutual employees to Litman's former salesmen. Memorandum in Support of Mass Mutual's Waiver at 3, *Litman* (No. 78-3314 Civ-EBD). Accepting this argument the district court concluded that a new trial on punitive damages would be inappropriate, and was not required by the mandate. The district court acknowledged that the *Litman I* opinion did not hold that the punitive damage award was excessive as a matter of law, but interpreted the holding to indicate that the award was improperly inflated. The district court framed the issue presented by Mass Mutual as a new one. Specifically, the issue as stated by the district court was whether "a [d]efendant, whose right to a new trial has been recognized by the Court of Appeals, [can] waive that right by offering to accept the original judgment, in the situation where the infirmity at the first trial necessarily inflated [p]laintiff's recovery [?]." *Litman v. Massachusetts Mutual Life Insurance Co.*, No. 78-3314 Civ-EBD p. 5 (S.D.Fla. August 20, 1985). The district court answered the question in the affirmative. Final judgment was entered in favor of Litman in the amount of $250,000, with interest from the date of entry of the original final judgment, plus taxable costs of the litigation. *Id.*

The mandate was clear and specific—the district court was to conduct a new trial solely on the issue of punitive damages. Mass Mutual argues that under Florida law and the facts of this case, a right to a new trial on punitive damages belonged to it alone. We disagree. Our opinion in *Litman I* governs the rights and obligations of both parties. Once the appellate ruling became final, the right to a new trial belonged to neither party individually but rather to both. The law of the case prescribed the outcome and could not be altered. Although Litman had no right under Florida law to seek a new trial on punitive damages, the first appeal left Litman in a position where the original judgment was set aside yet the basis for the punitive damage award was affirmed. The law of the case

(*Continues*)

established that Litman was entitled to punitive damages. Both parties had a right for a jury to set the amount. But the original judgment as to the amount of punitive damages was null and void. It no longer existed.

It is uncontroverted that money is the center of this dispute. This is the reality of many lawsuits. Litman concedes a desire to maximize his recovery by insisting that Mass Mutual submit to a new trial which it obtained at his expense. Mass Mutual, on the other hand, suggests that its sole interest is terminating the litigation. Although understandable such a decision is not possible after one has taken full advantage of its appellate rights and "lost." It is rather the type of decision required prior to an appeal. Perhaps justifiably fearful of the consequences, Mass Mutual "waived" its right to a new trial and consented to reinstate the original verdict and judgment. Mass Mutual has no right to waive the trial ordered by the law of the case nor can the district court reinstate a verdict which has been vacated by this court. District courts lack the authority to resurrect that which the court of appeals has voided.

That the result may be fair is not the issue we address. Mass Mutual's "waiver" effectively modified the mandate by unilateral action. We hold today that a successful appellant cannot change its mind and take unilateral action in a trial court to modify a mandate of this court. Such post-decision maneuvering undermines the process creating confusion, uncertainty and potential abuse.

We feel confident the district court thought it was doing justice in this case by issuing the order reinstating the jury verdict. Trial judges are more directly and immediately confronted by the demands of doing justice, case by case, than are we; indeed, this is their primary office and duty. Yet it is the considered judgment of our policy that in the long run—if not perhaps in the given case—justice is better served by adherence to general rules. The consequences of *ad hoc* examinations of the propriety of unambiguous mandates are too grave to be allowed.

IV. Conclusion

The mandate is a tool used to ensure that institutional values are maintained and that the allocation of authority and responsibility remains consistent with the design established under the law of our form of government. When an appellate court issues a clear and precise mandate, namely an order for a new trial on punitive damages, the district court is obligated to follow the instruction. Accordingly, we REVERSE and REMAND the case to the district court with instructions to conduct a trial on the issue of punitive damages as originally ordered.

As the appellate court in *Litman* discussed, the justice system would be unable to function without a "chain of command within the judicial hierarchy" (825 F.2d at 1508). The three-tier structure of the federal courts was designed to specify the sources of authority within the court system and the responsibilities of the courts. The justice is therefore self-correcting in the sense that appellate courts exercise a supervisory function over lower courts by correcting mistakes they may make and ensuring that lines of jurisdictional authority are maintained. Thus, the structure of the court system is designed not only for affording individual litigants the right of appeal, but it serves the more important function of creating order and confidence in our system of justice.

Constitutional (Article III) Courts

Because Constitutional courts are those federal courts whose authority stems from Article III of the Constitution, these courts fall in the category of courts contemplated by the Framers as constituting the judicial branch of government. These courts are the U.S. Supreme Court, the U.S. Circuit Courts of Appeal, and the U.S. District Courts, as well as several other courts within the purview of the judicial branch, as discussed later here.

The types of cases that the constitutional courts may handle fall into two categories. These relate to the specific grants of jurisdiction found in Article III. First are those cases relating to certain subjects: the Constitution, federal law, treaties, admiralty, and maritime laws. The second category involves the parties to a case over which the federal courts may have jurisdiction. These are the federal government, including any of its branches, agencies, or divisions, a state (unless suit was brought by a citizen of another state or foreign country), citizens of different states, ambassadors or representatives of foreign countries, and citizens of the same state claiming title to land in two or more states.

Although the entire scope of federal court jurisdiction falls into the previously mentioned categories, the federal courts are not required to exercise their jurisdiction in all of these areas. For example, The U.S. Supreme Court chooses only those cases that it believes to be most significant, and Congress has placed limits on the amount in controversy (currently $75,000) as a threshold before one may have access to the federal courts. Furthermore, from time to time, Congress has granted exclusive jurisdiction for one or more of the above types of cases to various federal courts, in the interests of efficiency and justice.

United States Supreme Court

The U.S. Supreme Court is the only court specifically mentioned and created in the U.S. Constitution. This is more than an interesting historical note, given the balance of power the Framers sought to achieve in the first three articles of the Constitution because it reflects the important fact that it is this court that forms the foundation of the judicial branch of the national government. Much has been written about the U.S. Supreme Court, and it is perhaps the most discussed court in the news media. This is not surprising, given the significance of the decisions made by the court and their effects (or potential effects) on American society.

Appointment of Justices

The U.S Supreme Court has nine members—a Chief Justice and eight Associate Justices. This has not always been the case; originally, there were five members of the Court, and the makeup of the court has ranged from 5 to 10 members throughout American history. Although the U.S. Constitution specified that there be a Supreme Court, it did not specify its size, and Congress has created or removed justices from time to time, largely based on political maneuvering (Abraham, 1998). Since 1869, however, the number of justices has remained at nine and is likely to stay that way for the foreseeable future (see **Table 4.2**).

The process of appointment to a seat on the U.S. Supreme Court is political (Segal et al., 2005; Murphy et al., 2006). Under Article II of the Constitution, the President alone is authorized to nominate and appoint Supreme Court Justices "by and with the advice and consent of the Senate." This has come to mean that any candidate for the high court chosen by the President must receive approval from the Senate before taking office. Despite the language in the Constitution, in practice, the President does not seek the "advice" of the Senate (except perhaps from Senators in his own party), nor does the Senate give it. Before consenting to a Supreme Court candidate, however, the Senate investigates and conducts hearings where the views of Senators regarding the nominee become known and, to some extent, the views of the nominee himself or herself become known. It is the political, social, and legal views of the nominee that may ultimately determine whether the consent of the Senate is forthcoming.

Historically, it was not always clear what the "advice and consent" language of Article II was intended to accomplish. It was discussed by the Framers and was the subject of several of the Federalist Papers, which were essentially newspaper columns written to inform the public and gain support for the new Constitution, among other topics. Although written under the pseudonym "Publius," it was later determined by scholars that the Federalist Papers had several authors, including James Madison, Alexander Hamilton, and John Jay, the first Chief Justice of the Supreme Court. In The Federalist Number 76, written in 1788, Hamilton argued that nomination and appointment of public officials, including Supreme Court Justices, should be with the advice and consent of a legislative body (see **Sidebar 4.1**). This would, he suggested, minimize political influences and potential patronage that would likely exist if either the President alone or the Congress alone were allowed to appoint public officials.

Table 4.2

Number of U.S. Supreme Court Justices Over Time

Year	Number of Justices	Legislation	Purpose
1789	6	Judiciary Act of 1789	Organized Supreme Court pursuant to U.S. Constitution, Art III
1801	5	Judiciary Act of 1801	Created separate circuit judgeships, removed requirement that justices "ride the circuit," and reduced number of justices
1802	6	Judiciary Act of 1802, 2 Stat. 132	Repealed Judiciary Act of 1801
1807	7	Judiciary Act of 1807, 2 Stat. 420	Expanded number of circuits and corresponding number of justices
1837	9	Judiciary Act of 1837, 5 Stat. 176	Expanded number of circuits and corresponding number of justices
1863	10	Judiciary Act of 1863, 12 Stat. 794	Expanded number of circuits and corresponding number of justices
1866	7	Judiciary Act of 1866, 14 Stat. 209	Reorganized and reduced number of circuits and justices
1869	9	Judiciary Act of 1869, 16 Stat. 44	Increased number of justices to correspond to number of circuits, reduced "circuit riding" of justices

Adapted from: Federal Judicial Center, *The Supreme Court of the United States and the Federal Judiciary*. Retrieved September 11, 2009, from http://www.fjc.gov/public/home.nsf/hisc.

Sidebar 4.1 *The Federalist Papers, No. 76 by Alexander Hamilton (1788)*

To the People of the State of New York:

THE President is "to NOMINATE, and, by and with the advice and consent of the Senate, to appoint ambassadors, other public ministers and consuls, judges of the Supreme Court, and all other officers of the United States whose appointments are not otherwise provided for in the Constitution."

It has been observed in a former paper, that "the true test of a good government is its aptitude and tendency to produce a good administration." If the justness of this observation be admitted, the mode of appointing the officers of the United States contained in the foregoing clauses, must, when examined, be allowed to be entitled to particular commendation. It is not easy to conceive a plan better calculated than this to promote a judicious choice of men for filling the offices of the Union; and it will not need proof, that on this point must essentially depend the character of its administration.

It will be agreed on all hands, that the power of appointment, in ordinary cases, ought to be modified in one of three ways. It ought either to be vested in a single man, or in a SELECT assembly of a moderate number; or in a single man, with the concurrence of such an assembly. Those who have themselves reflected upon the subject, or who have attended to the observations made in other parts of these papers, in relation to the appointment of the President, will, I presume, agree to the position, that there would always be great probability of having the place supplied by a man of abilities, at least respectable. Premising this, I proceed to lay it down as a rule, that one man of discernment is better fitted to analyze and estimate the peculiar qualities adapted to particular offices, than a body of men of equal or perhaps even of superior discernment.

The sole and undivided responsibility of one man will naturally beget a livelier sense of duty and a more exact regard to reputation. He will, on this account, feel himself under stronger obligations, and more interested to investigate with care the qualities requisite to the stations to be filled, and to prefer with impartiality the persons who may have the fairest pretensions to them. He will have FEWER personal attachments to gratify, than a body of men who may each be supposed to have an equal number, and will be so much the less liable to be misled by the sentiments of friendship and of affection. A single well-directed man, by a single understanding, cannot be distracted and warped by that diversity of views, feelings, and interests, which frequently distract and warp the resolutions of a collective body.

The truth of the principles here advanced seems to have been felt by the most intelligent of those who have found fault with the provision made, in this respect, by the convention. They contend that the President ought solely to have been authorized to make the appointments under the federal government. But it is easy to show, that every advantage to be expected from such an arrangement would, in substance, be derived from the power of NOMINATION, which is proposed to be conferred upon him; while several disadvantages which might attend the absolute power of appointment in the hands of that officer would be avoided. In the act of nomination, his judgment alone would be exercised; and as it would be his sole duty to point out the man who, with the approbation of the Senate, should fill an office, his responsibility would be as complete as if he were to make the final appointment. There can, in this view, be no difference between nominating and appointing. The same motives which would influence a proper discharge of his duty in one case, would exist in the other. And as no man could be appointed but on his previous nomination, every man who might be appointed would be, in fact, his choice.

But might not his nomination be overruled? I grant it might, yet this could only be to make place for another nomination by himself. The person ultimately appointed must be the object of his preference, though perhaps not in the first degree. It is also not very probable that his nomination would often be overruled. The Senate could not be tempted, by the preference they might feel to another, to reject the one proposed; because they could not assure themselves, that the person they might wish would be brought forward by a second or by any subsequent nomination. They could not even be certain that a future nomination would present a candidate in any degree more acceptable to them; and as their dissent might cast a kind of stigma upon the individual rejected, and might have the appearance of a reflection upon the judgment of the chief magistrate, it is not likely that their sanction would often be refused, where there were not special and strong reasons for the refusal.

To what purpose then require the co-operation of the Senate? I answer, that the necessity of their concurrence would have a powerful, though, in general, a silent operation. It would be an excellent check upon a spirit of favoritism in the President, and would tend greatly to prevent the appointment of unfit characters from State prejudice, from family connection, from personal attachment, or from a view to popularity. In addition to this, it would be an efficacious source of stability in the administration.

It will readily be comprehended, that a man who had himself the sole disposition of offices, would be governed much more by his private inclinations and interests, than when he was bound to submit the propriety of his choice to the discussion and determination of a different and independent body, and that body an entire branch of the legislature. The possibility of rejection would be a strong motive to care in proposing. The danger to his own reputation, and, in the case of an elective magistrate, to his political existence, from betraying a spirit of favoritism, or an unbecoming pur-

Despite Hamilton's concern about minimizing the potential effects of politics in the appointment of Supreme Court Justices, the process remains political even with the "checks and balances" of the "advice and consent" provision. The social and political ideology of candidates certainly plays a role in the selection and nomination process today. It is expected that a nominee put forward by the President will be a member of his own political party, but it is the particular views of that nominee on the social and economic issues of the day, which may range from abortion and first amendment rights to corporate governance and responsibility, that may require a President to accept a candidate whose views do not align with his own in order to garner the approval of the Senate.

Other factors also affect who will be nominated and appointed to the Supreme Court. These include the judicial experience and legal background of the candidate, the area of the country in which the candidate resides, the relationship of the candidate to the President, and the race, gender, or religion of the candidate. The job of the President in selecting a nominee is to choose an individual according to the characteristics that are most important to him while being cognizant of the fact that these characteristics will matter to members of the Senate, who must ultimately consent.

Jurisdiction of the Court

The U.S. Supreme Court has both original and appellate jurisdiction. In nearly every case, however, it exercises only its appellate jurisdiction. Nonetheless, Article III grants the Court original jurisdiction in cases involving the federal government and a state; two or more states; foreign ambassadors, ministers, or consuls; and a citizen of one state against another state. The latter source of original jurisdiction was later abolished by the Eleventh Amendment. Of the remaining, the Court would exercise its original jurisdiction in an appropriate case involving a dispute between states (a rarity), but has concurrent jurisdiction with the District Courts in the remaining two areas, alleviating the need for it to hear such cases in the first instance.

Given the foregoing, the U.S. Supreme Court first and foremost is an appellate court. Two primary sources of exclusive appellate jurisdiction exist: cases from the highest court of a state and cases from a U.S. Court of Appeals.

An aggrieved party from one of these courts may appeal to the U.S. Supreme Court by petitioning for *certiorari* ("make more certain"). Only if the case presents a "substantial" federal question, under the U.S. Constitution or a federal statute, will the Court agree to hear a case. In recent years, the Court has agreed to hear fewer than 5% of the cases presented. Although it is sometimes not altogether clear why the Court chooses to hear a particular case, the cases it does hear are nearly always cases of *first impression*, which are cases involving a point of law that the Court has not previously decided.

Work of the Court

There are three ways a case may come before the United States Supreme Court: (1) writ of appeal, (2) certification, and (3) writ of certiorari. A writ of appeal is a right to an appeal created by federal statute; however, few such rights to appeal are found in the federal statutes because these were severely limited by Congressional Act in 1988. Even the few that could be considered reviewable, such as certain claims relating to civil rights or the election laws, are very unlikely to be granted because the "right" still must, in the view of the Supreme Court, involve a federal question that is substantial. In effect, this makes writs of appeal discretionary with the court and not a normal means of obtaining Supreme Court review as a practical matter.

Certification may be used when a federal court of appeal seeks a clarification from the U.S. Supreme Court on some important question of law that the appellate court is unable to decide. Certification is essentially never used because it is the job of the federal appellate courts to decide such questions before they reach the high court. It is inherent in the structure of the federal court system that lower courts do not shift their responsibilities to higher courts. Thus, it would be a very rare thing indeed for a question to reach the Supreme Court by certification.

Almost without exception, the Court hears cases by writ of *certiorari*. It is not altogether clear what criteria the Court uses before accepting a case. What is known is that each Justice considers the merits of every petition for certiorari, which includes briefs of the legal issues by the parties, and decides whether the case should be heard. A case will be accepted if any four of the Justices agree that it should be heard. This is known as the "Rule of Four," and although it has been commented on by Justices from time to time, the basis on which the four make their decisions is not revealed. Cases that are accepted are those that have some importance to the interpretation of the law that is not limited to the factual dispute between the parties. Not only must it involve some federal question—a question that involves federal law—but the legal question raised must be one of "substance" that has broader implications for U.S. law than just resolving the dispute between the parties.

Supreme Court Rule 10 provides some guidance in understanding the types of cases that may be accepted. The rule is found in **Sidebar 4.2**. It indicates some important considerations used by the Court in deciding which cases will be heard. These include cases in which (1) the reasons for the appeal are "compelling," (2) there is a conflict between U.S. Courts of Appeals in different circuits,

(3) there is a conflict between a U.S. Court of Appeals and a state supreme court, (4) a U.S. Court of Appeals has departed from the "accepted and usual course of judicial proceedings," (5) there is a conflict regarding an interpretation of federal law by a state supreme court and either another state supreme court or a U.S. Court of Appeals, (6) there is a conflict regarding an interpretation of federal law by a state or federal court and a prior interpretation of that law by the U.S. Supreme Court, or (7) the case raises an important question of federal law that has not been previously decided by the U.S. Supreme Court. As Rule 10 also indicates, these categories are not exclusive in that they are "neither controlling nor fully measuring the Court's discretion." Although Rule 10 itself does not reveal the specific issues that may lead a justice to vote in favor of acceptance on a case, it seems clear that cases that fall outside of the previously mentioned categories are extremely unlikely to be heard.

Sidebar 4.2   U.S. Supreme Court Rule 10, Considerations Governing Review on Certiorari

Review on a writ of certiorari is not a matter of right, but of judicial discretion. A petition for a writ of certiorari will be granted only for compelling reasons. The following, although neither controlling nor fully measuring the Court's discretion, indicate the character of the reasons the Court considers:

(a) a United States court of appeals has entered a decision in conflict with the decision of another United States court of appeals on the same important matter; has decided an important federal question in a way that conflicts with a decision by a state court of last resort; or has so far departed from the accepted and usual course of judicial proceedings, or sanctioned such a departure by a lower court, as to call for an exercise of this Court's supervisory power;

(b) a state court of last resort has decided an important federal question in a way that conflicts with the decision of another state court of last resort or of a United States court of appeals;

(c) a state court or a United States court of appeals has decided an important question of federal law that has not been, but should be, settled by this Court, or has decided an important federal question in a way that conflicts with relevant decisions of this Court.

A petition for a writ of certiorari is rarely granted when the asserted error consists of erroneous factual findings or the misapplication of a properly stated rule of law.

After a case has been accepted for hearing by the Supreme Court, several things happen. The parties prepare briefs of the legal issues in the case, arguing the merits of their respective positions. Additional briefs may also be prepared by nonparties who have a particular interest in the case, sometimes at the request of the Court, more commonly on their own request. These *amicus curiae*

("friend of the court") briefs are filed by civic or professional organizations, state governments, or the federal government in order to "inform" the Court of issues of wider applicability related to the case that may not be raised by the parties.

After briefing, oral arguments are held in which the lawyers for the parties argue their side of the case and in which the justices ask questions in order to clarify aspects of the case or examine issues not adequately addressed in the briefs. The parties are strictly limited to 30 minutes each and may be stopped midsentence after that time limit is reached. While the Court is in session, oral arguments are held during 3 days of the week, twice a month. These sessions are open to the public and offer the most visible means of observing the work of the court, which is otherwise conducted behind closed doors.

After oral arguments, during the remaining 2 days of the weeks in which oral arguments are held, the Court holds a "conference" of the justices during which decisions are reached on each case. The conference is a private meeting among the justices in which each expresses his or her views of the case, and a vote is held. According to justices who have spoken about what occurs during the conference, there is no discussion or argument about a case where one justice tries to convince another. Rather, each justice is simply given an opportunity to express his or her views on the case, and the votes for affirmance or reversal are tallied. After this vote, the chief justice (if his or her vote was part of the majority) assigns the case to one of the justices for drafting the majority opinion. If the chief justice was not in the majority, the most senior member of the majority will assign the drafting of the case. After it has been written, the majority opinion is circulated among the justices, giving them the opportunity to join in the opinion, write a concurring opinion, or write a dissenting opinion. Occasionally, a majority opinion will be prepared *per curiam* ("for the Court"), and the author remains unidentified.

United States Courts of Appeals

The U.S. Courts of Appeals have appellate jurisdiction to hear cases originating in the U.S. District Courts and the legislative courts, as well as decisions made by some federal executive agencies. There are 13 U.S. Courts of Appeals. Twelve of the 13 Circuit Courts of Appeal are distributed geographically throughout the country (see Figure 4.1). The thirteenth, created in 1982, is the U.S. Court of Appeals for the Federal Circuit. It does not have specific geographic jurisdiction, but operates nationally to hear appeals in specialized cases involving patents, tax claims, and decisions made by various executive agencies, boards, and commissions.

Like all other judges of "Article III" courts, judges of the U.S. Courts of Appeals are appointed by the President with the "advice and consent" of the Senate and serve "during Good Behavior," which is to say, for life. There are 179 judges on the U.S. Courts of Appeals, with some circuits with a greater number of judgeships than others, depending on the number of appeals filed. Appeals are usually heard by three judge panels, although for some particularly significant cases, the court will hear an appeal *en banc*, which means that all judges in the circuit will hear arguments and participate in the decision of the case.

All appeals in the U.S. Court of Appeals are begun by filing a "Notice of Appeal" within the time required by the appellate rules and submit a copy of the trial record, which includes a transcript of the trial and other related documents. An appellate court does not retry the facts of a case but relies on the trial record to determine whether mistakes were made at trial. The parties then file briefs with the Court of Appeals in which they argue why the decision of the lower court should be reversed or affirmed. The court may then schedule oral arguments in which each party has a limited amount of time to argue further the points presented in the appellate brief and answer questions that the judges may have. Finally, in nearly all cases, a written decision of the court is published.

In the vast majority of cases, a decision by the U.S. Court of Appeals is final. That is, because it is extremely unlikely an appeal will be accepted by the U.S. Supreme Court, a litigant or criminal defendant will have no further recourse from a decision of the court of appeals (Segal et al., 1995). Given this fact, the U.S. Courts of Appeals hold a place of considerable influence in the federal court system because their interpretation of federal becomes binding in the case decided and in future cases.

United States District Courts

The U.S. District Courts are courts of general jurisdiction, handling both criminal and civil cases involving some aspect of federal law. There is a total of 94 U.S. District Courts, with at least one U.S. District Court in each state and U.S. territory, and some more heavily populated states having as many as four. As the primary trial courts of the federal system, these courts share an increasing burden of cases, civil and criminal, pertaining to federal law. Often described as the "workhorses" of the federal system, presently there are nearly 280,000 civil cases and nearly 70,000 criminal cases that these trial courts are handling. The workload of these courts will likely continue to rise because the number of civil cases filed has seen growth of over 8% in the past 5 years, despite a decline in federal criminal cases of about 5% during that period (Duff, 2009).

U.S. District Court judges, like all federal judges appointed under Article III, are nominated by the President and confirmed on the "advice and consent" of the Senate. These judges serve lifetime appointments (Article III states that they "shall hold their Offices during good Behavior"), and as also provided in Article III, their compensation may not be "diminished" for as long as they hold their office. Depending on their caseloads, some district courts have many judges (e.g., there are 44 judges in the U.S. District Court for the Southern District of New York), whereas others have few (e.g., there are just two judges in the U.S. District Court for the District of North Dakota).

Although there is considerable variety in the types of criminal cases heard in state courts (see Chapter 5), federal courts handle a predominance of one type of criminal case—drug violations, involving the possession, manufacture, and sale or distribution of controlled substances. In addition to these cases, however, the federal district courts conduct trials involving other types of criminal activity. These include violent crimes such as bank robbery or racketeering and property crimes such as theft of U.S. property by federal employees or theft of property through the U.S. postal service. Furthermore, the U.S. District Courts have jurisdiction in cases of fraud involving taxes, social security, or other federal payment programs, as well as fraudulent trading in stocks and other securities. Other areas in which large numbers of cases are handled by the federal district courts involve firearms offenses and immigration matters.

The U.S. District Courts also hear a variety of civil cases. Provided the jurisdictional prerequisites are met (generally, $75,000 minimum, diversity of citizenship, and/or presentation of a federal question), the courts will address a wide range of civil matters. These may include contract cases, such as insurance claims, breach of lease agreements to which the government is a party, or defaulted student loans. They may involve tort claims, such as injuries from defective products, motor vehicle injuries involving federally owned vehicles, or medical malpractice in federal facilities. Other cases involve real property, such as actions for condemnation or foreclosure. The federal courts are also responsible for hearing cases involving the violation of civil rights, such as employment discrimination cases, as well as violations of other rights protected by statute, such as antitrust, copyrights and trademark infringement, and claims under the labor laws. Finally, the federal district courts also hear large numbers of petitions from prisoners that, after a prisoner has been sentenced, become civil matters. These include petitions for habeas corpus, conditions of detention, or civil rights violations.

District Court judges are assisted in the handling of this wide variety of cases by other judicial officers. Beginning in 1968, the U.S. District Courts were authorized by Congress to appoint federal magistrates to handle some of the day-to-day ministerial tasks required by the federal trial courts. These officers, now called *Magistrate Judges*, have broad judicial powers to act in the capacity of a judge while handling aspects of the court's work. Magistrate judges, both full and part time, are appointed for a term of 8-year terms (or 4 years for part-time appointees) by the Chief Judge of each district. Magistrate judges were created by Congress in 1968 to assist district court judges with their growing workload. Because these judicial officers are appointed from within the judiciary branch (and not by the President) and do not serve life terms, they lack the full powers of Article III judges. Nonetheless, they serve several very important roles in the operation of the federal courts.

Magistrate judges assist district court judges in both criminal and civil cases by handling hearings at various stages of the trial process. Criminal matters may include pleas or trials in misdemeanor cases, or handling the initial appearance, conducting the preliminary hearing, or setting bail in a felony case. In civil cases magistrate judges perform a variety of tasks throughout the proceeding, including holding pretrial hearings, conducting settlement conferences, resolving discovery disputes, and even conducting trials in some matters where the parties agree to be heard by the magistrate. Together with that of the district court judges, the work of the magistrate judges allows the district courts to operate efficiently and carry out their necessary and vital functions.

United States Bankruptcy Courts

There are also other judicial officers that assist the U.S. District Court. These are bankruptcy judges, appointed by the Chief Judge of the district court for 14-year terms. The U.S. Bankruptcy Court operates as an arm of the District Courts, with original and exclusive jurisdiction in cases involving the federal bankruptcy code. These cases range from small matters involving individuals who are no longer able to keep up with house, car, or other payments on their debt to complex cases involving the dissolution or restructuring of large companies. As a result of changes in the bankruptcy laws by Congress in 2005, the caseload of these judges has declined by about half since that time. Although this reduction is significant, the bankruptcy court still accounts for nearly 700,000 case filings each year (Duff, 2009).

United States Court of International Trade

As the name implies, the U.S. Court of International Trade addresses cases involving trade, that is, the import and export for goods for sale and distribution. These cases generally are contract disputes relating to trade as well as disputes about tariffs, or taxes imposed on imports or exports, by the government. The court was created by the Customs Court Act of 1980. Before that time, international trade cases were handled by the U.S. Customs Court, which was first created in 1926 as a legislative court, but was designated a constitutional court by Congress in 1956. The Customs Court was reorganized into the Court of International Trade in 1980 to clarify its procedures and broaden its powers in order to address better problems of international trade, which it has been able to do as this area has grown tremendously with the global economy. Although the court has the same powers as the U.S. District Courts today, it exercises them in a much narrower range of jurisdiction, as indicated previously here. Individual judges hear most cases, although some complex cases or those with greater implications for international trade are heard by three-judge panels. Some of the powers granted to the court include ordering parties to pay money damages and issuing injunctions and writs of mandamus.

The court consists of nine members. By statute, no more than five members of the court may be from the same political party. This makes the court unique in that it is the only federal court that has a restriction as to the political views of the members who make up the court. As with all constitutional courts, judges are appointed by the President, with the advice and consent of the Senate.

Legislative (Article I) Courts

Congress has also created other courts using authorization found in Article I, Section 8, of the U.S. Constitution, which states, "The Congress shall have the power . . . [t]o constitute Tribunals inferior to the supreme Court." These courts, referred to as Article I courts or "legislative" courts, are specialized courts of limited jurisdiction and include are part of the federal court system. These include the U.S. Court of Federal Claims, the U.S. Court of Appeals for the Armed Forces, the U.S. Court of Appeals for Veteran Claims, and the U.S. Tax Court.

United States Court of Federal Claims

Cases that come before the U.S. Court of Federal Claims are those involving disputes with the federal government over amounts of money owed by the government to a business or to a person, or money owed to the government. Given the large volume of cases handled by the court, it has 16 judges. These are appointed by the President with the advice and consent of the Senate for 15 year terms.

The federal government conducts billions of dollars worth of business each year with private contractors and has millions of employees. As a result, the need for courts to hear disputes over money involving the government is significant. These cases may arise under a contract (such as when the government orders goods or services from a company and fails to pay) or claims over federal employees' wages. They may also involve a statute or regulation (such as a tax dispute) or even the U.S. Constitution (such as the exercise of eminent domain power under the Takings Clause). In addition to cases such as these, the court is also authorized to handle cases of personal injury resulting from the use of vaccines, which are federally regulated. Because the court is the place in which citizens may seek recovery of money against the federal government, it has been called the "People's Court."

United States Court of Appeals for the Armed Forces

The U.S. Court of Appeals for the Armed Forces is a court created by Congress to provide an avenue of appellate review for military personnel who are governed by the Uniform Code of Military Justice and the court martials that are conducted under it. Because court martials are conducted outside of the civilian justice system, those who are adjudicated under the military system of justice cannot avail themselves of traditional routes of appeal through either state or federal courts of appeal. Thus, the interests of justice for military personnel required that independent oversight of decisions made in the military courts be available, and this appellate court was created in

1951. It consists of five civilian judges appointed by the President for 15-year terms.

United States Court of Appeals for Veteran Claims

As indicated in the name of this court, veterans of the U.S. Armed Forces who have been denied benefits or otherwise adversely affected by a decision of the Department of Veteran Affairs may now appeal to this court, which was not created until 1988. It is therefore the newest of the federal courts. Before its creation, veterans had no recourse from decisions made by that executive agency because there was no statutory right (or route) for appeals.

The United States Tax Court

The U.S. Tax Court was created to resolve disputes between individuals or companies and the Internal Revenue Service involving payment of federal taxes. The court consists of 19 judges appointed by the President who serve for 15-year terms. Cases that come before the Tax Court may range from a few thousand dollars to millions of dollars, and given the specialized nature of the issues that come before the court, all judges are experts in the field of taxation.

Other Federal Courts

Judicial Panel on Multidistrict Litigation

Although the Judicial Panel on Multidistrict Litigation (JPML) was established by Congress as a federal court, it is unlike any other federal court in its makeup and function. It consists of seven judges from either the U.S. District Courts or the U.S. Courts of Appeals who are appointed by the Chief Justice of the U.S. Supreme Court. No two judges are from the same district, ensuring some degree of geographic representativeness on the panel. The work of the court is to decide whether civil cases involving common fact questions and issues should be transferred to a single district court for pretrial proceedings. Examples of such cases include personal injuries from defective products such as breast implants or automobile tires, train or airplane crashes, asbestos claims, patent infringement, or stockholder lawsuits. These are cases that have been filed in federal courts throughout the country, and the court consolidates them in order to handle more efficiently matters that may relate to each case before trial. After consolidated, all cases are transferred to a single U.S. District Court until trial, when each lawsuit is returned to the district court in the state in which it was filed. Typical pretrial matters include hearings on proper parties, motions to dismiss or for summary judgment, and discovery disputes. The JPML also selects the judge who will be responsible for the pretrial hearings.

Thus, the JPML does not decide the merits of any case; it decides only whether consolidating a case with other similar cases and transferring the case to a single district court would be in the interests of justice; however, the JPML serves an important function in streamlining litigation as it moves through the federal courts. The consolidation of cases thus saves the courts and the parties case time and money by providing a single forum through which discovery is accomplished and provides greater certainty in ruling in a consistent fashion on all pretrial motions.

Territorial Courts

Territorial Courts are the federal courts that sit in the territories of the United States: Guam, the Northern Mariana Islands, and the Virgin Islands. Until 1966, the District Court of Puerto Rico was a territorial court, when Congress made it a constitutional court just like all U.S. District Courts. Territorial courts have the same jurisdiction as the U.S. District Courts, but are also responsible for hearing local (nonfederal) matters as well. For many of the states in the country, before statehood was granted, a territorial court was established to handle civil and criminal matters occurring within territorial borders relating to federal law. Judges in the territorial courts are appointed by the President for terms of 10 years.

District of Columbia Courts

Because of the unique place that Washington, DC, occupies in the country, neither a state nor a territory, Congress has provided specially for its courts since 1801. There is one U.S. District Court for the District of Columbia, which is a constitutional court with the same jurisdiction as those in the states. In addition, to handling local matters, Congress created District of Columbia Superior Court and the District of Columbia Court of Appeals, which operate in a similar fashion to state trial and appellate courts.

Foreign Intelligence Surveillance Court

The Foreign Intelligence Surveillance Court (FISC) was created in 1978 by Congress's passage of the Foreign Intelligence Surveillance Act (FISA). FISA's purpose was to guard against warrantless searches, including wiretaps, conducted by the federal government in the name of national security. The FISC was created to review applications and issue warrants in cases relating to national security, in a similar fashion to the way in which warrants are issued by judges in state criminal cases. Unlike in criminal cases, however, where the purpose is generally to obtain evidence of criminal activity, a warrant application to the FISC is designed for gathering intelligence relating to terrorist activity. Although evidence of crime may result from the intelligence gathered, obtaining evidence is not the main goal.

The warrants relate to the surveillance of known or suspected terrorists within the United States or those who are in some way connected to terrorist organizations. Although the court's role was important before the terrorist attacks of September 11, 2001, its activities assumed even greater importance after that date with the passage of the USA Patriot Act of 2001. That act increased the number of members of the FISC from 7 to 1 and expanded the powers of the executive branch to gather information of terrorist activity under FISA, including the use of warrantless searches within the United States in some circumstances.

Key Terms

Dual System of Government
Federalism
Supremacy Clause
Three-Tier Court System
Constitutional Courts
Legislative Courts

U.S. Supreme Court
Judicial Appointment
Advise and Consent
Federalist Papers
Certiorari
Federal Question

Discussion Questions

1. What is Federalism, and how does it affect the relationship between federal and state courts?
2. In what ways is the jurisdiction of the federal courts limited?
3. Which Articles of the U.S. Constitution establish the federal court system, and what courts are created in them?
4. Describe the function of (1) the U.S. District Courts, (2) the U.S. Courts of Appeals, and (3) the U.S. Supreme Court.
5. How many U.S. Supreme Court justices presently sit on the Court? What is the process through which justices obtain seats on the Supreme Court?
6. What is the process by which cases reach the Supreme Court?

Cases

Jaffree v. Bd of School Commissioners, 459 U.S. 1314, 103 S. Ct. 842, 74 L.Ed.2d 924 (1983).

Litman v. Massachusetts Mut. Life Ins. Co., 825 F.2d 1506 (11th Cir. 1987).

Marbury v. Madison, 1 Cranch 137, 5 U.S. 137, 2 L.Ed. 60 (1803).

Marshall v. Marshall, 547 U.S. 293, 126 S. Ct. 1735, 164 L.Ed.2d 480 (2006).

Ute Indian Tribe v. State of Utah, 935 F.Supp. 1473 (D.Utah, 1996).

Younger v. Harris, 410 U.S. 37, 44-45, 401 S.Ct. 746, 750-751, 27 L.Ed.2d 669, 673-74 (1971).

Criminal Justice on the Web

 For an up-to-date list of Web links, go to *The American Courts: A Procedural Approach* online companion site at http://criminaljustice.jbpub.com/AmericanCourts. The online companion site will introduce you to some of the most important sites for finding American courts information on the Internet.

References

Abraham, H. J. (1998). *The Judicial Process* (7th ed.). New York: Oxford University Press.

Anderson, B. S. (2007). "Our federalism:" The Younger abstention doctrine and its companions. *Florida Bar Journal, 81*, 9–19.

Duff, J. C. (2009). Administrative Office of the United States Courts, 2008 Annual Report of the Director: Judicial Business of the United States Courts. Washington, DC: U.S. Government Printing Office.

Murphy, W. F., Pritchett, C. H., Epstein, L., & Knight, J. (2006). *Courts, Judges, & Politics: An Introduction to the Judicial Process* (6th ed.). New York: McGraw-Hill.

Segal, J. A., Songer, D. R., & Cameron, C. M. (1995). Decision making on the U.S. Court of Appeals. In L. Epstein (Ed.), *Contemplating Courts*. Washington, DC: CQ Press.

Segal, J. A., Spaeth, H. J., & Benesh, S. C. (2005). *The Supreme Court in the American Legal System*. New York: Cambridge University Press.

Wright, C. A., & Kane, M. K. (2002). *Law of Federal Courts* (6th ed.). St. Paul, MN: West Group.

State Courts 5

What Is This Chapter About?

This chapter examines the structure and operation of state court systems across the United States. We begin with a historical overview of the courts, briefly tracing their development from colonial times to the present. Although the courts have changed in many significant respects, the operation of today's courts continues to reflect aspects of their past.

We then turn to the structure of state court systems. Structure refers to the different types of courts that operate within the states, differences in their jurisdiction, and the hierarchical relationships among them. Although the 50 different state court systems are best characterized by the variety of their organization, they each have courts of original jurisdiction that handle such criminal matters as misdemeanors or felonies and such civil matters as small claims, or divorce cases, or commercial litigation, as well as courts that hear appeals. We study examples from different states to see how different court structures accomplish similar goals. Finally, we examine the ways in which judges are appointed to the bench and the processes they use to make decisions.

Learning Objectives

After reading this chapter, you should be able to

1. Distinguish state courts from federal courts.
2. Understand the ways in which state court systems have changed over time.
3. Identify traditional aspects of state courts that continue to influence the operation of the courts.
4. Explain the general structure of state court systems and variations that exist.
5. Understand the way in which different types of courts within a state may operate.
6. Describe the types of cases that state courts decide.
7. Understand the methods used for judicial appointments.
8. Explain the processes of judicial decision making.

Court Systems in the States

Compared with the federal court system in the United States, the system of state courts is massive in size, organization, and productivity. Although there are about 108 federal courts, there are some 16,000 state courts (LaFountain et al., 2006). Although there are about 1,700 full-time federal judges, there are approximately 10,000 full-time state judges and over twice that many part-time ones. Although the federal courts handle about 400,000 cases each year (excluding bankruptcy cases), the state courts across the country dispose of nearly 50 million civil and criminal cases, excluding traffic and other minor violations (Strickland et al., 2008). Based on these statistics alone, there is little question that state courts have significant responsibility for carrying out justice in the United States. As important as the federal courts are, the reach of the state courts, their role in resolving disputes, and their influence in everyday life are enormous.

Although the structure of state governments is very similar to that of the federal government (with a legislative, executive, and judicial branch), the organization of state court systems varies considerably. Although only one federal court system exists in the United States, there are 50 state court systems; therefore, it is difficult to generalize and summarize the operation of state courts in a way that applies to all of them. States differ in the way they appoint judges, in the number of courts they believe necessary to accomplish justice, in the authority they give to those courts, and in the names they give to judges and to the courts over which they preside. Despite these variations in their sources of authority and their operations, at their most basic, all state court systems have trial and appellate courts. Trial courts in the states are either courts of general jurisdiction or courts of limited jurisdiction. At the appellate level, all states have a court of last resort (usually called a supreme court), and many have an intermediate appellate court, as in the federal system. These structural distinctions are discussed in detail later here.

It is what occurs inside these courts, however, that makes the state courts different from the federal courts. First, the vast majority of both criminal and civil cases are handled by state courts. Most of the criminal law is state law, either statutory or common law. The prosecution of crime has therefore traditionally been the domain of state courts. Moreover, the impact of crime, whether involving property or violence, falls almost exclusively on local communities. Consequently, the interests of states and localities in dealing with crime are significant.

Second, the vast majority of civil disputes are handled by state courts. As was true of criminal matters, civil disputes are most often matters of local concern, such as cases involving medical malpractice, auto accidents, or contract disputes. Even in cases involving federal questions, such as claims involving first amendment rights, securities law, or civil rights, litigation normally begins and ends in state courts.

Third, the variety of cases adjudicated in state courts is considerable. Not only do state courts resolve both criminal and civil disputes, but these cases may be very serious or relatively minor, may involve large sums of money or little money, or may impact many people or only a few. In addition, cases in state courts touch essentially every area of law. State courts resolve cases involving traffic violations, juvenile delinquency, drunk driving, shoplifting, domestic disputes, simple or aggravated assaults, weapons violations, and homicide cases, among myriad others. It is also not unusual for those same state courts to hear cases involving divorce and child custody arrangements, arguments between neighbors over a property line, disputes about insurance coverage, allegations of defective workmanship in the construction of a home, failure to pay a bill, or claims of wrongful firing from a job in the course of any week. Cases such as these are about life itself, and state courts are intimately involved in peoples' lives.

Finally, citizens' understanding of the courts comes largely from activities of the state courts—the local flavor of state courts is reflected in the keen interest of the public in their activities. Although television shows and movies also contribute to peoples' understanding (and misunderstanding) of legal processes and the operation of the courts, the media frequently reports on actual cases that are decided by state courts, much more frequently than activities of the federal courts. This allows the public to see and form opinions about what goes on in the judicial branch of government (see **Sidebar 5.1**).

Sidebar 5.1   *Courts on Television*

Most people's knowledge of the court system is limited, and most of what they know (or think they know) about courts is based on what they have seen on television. Throughout the history of television programming, there regularly have been shows about crime and those who investigate it, prosecute it, and commit it. Civil disputes, too, have become popular avenues of interest for the 1-hour television show. The setting for such shows centers on the court as the place where it all happens. The drama

of the courtroom has come to be seen as a rich source of entertainment, and the participants in this drama—the judges, the lawyers, the witnesses, and the parties—become an ever-changing cast of characters on which the show is built; however, although this programming can be entertaining and attract many viewers, it does not portray the criminal justice system and the courts with complete accuracy. Americans watch television to be entertained; producers and writers therefore create fictitious plots and characters that will be pleasing to the audience and fit within a half-hour or 1-hour time slot. Representing reality in the courtroom is not the goal. As a result, crime shows use aspects of courtroom reality to support the fictitious plot.

"Perry Mason" was one of the first dramas on television dealing with the criminal law. In this series, the main character was a talented defense attorney who kept his clients from being convicted. The star of this was nearly always the "smoking gun"—that piece of evidence or testimony that sealed the case shut, exonerating Perry's accused client.

A more modern version of the crime drama, *Law and Order* (including its manifestations as "Criminal Intent" and "Special Victims Unit"), offers one of the more realistic portrayals of criminal law on television. It shows the investigation of crimes, collection of evidence, and discovery of witnesses, as well as the arrest and prosecution of criminals.

Although the criminal law and its application in court are usually depicted realistically, law enforcement and prosecutors are typically depicted as the good guys seeking justice and fairness for all involved.

Examples such as these of the criminal courts in action, even if not completely accurate, help viewers watching the shows to be entertained, but also to give them a sense of the workings of the justice system. Shows of this type must necessarily be created in a manner that allows the lay person to enjoy the shows without extensive previous knowledge of laws and criminal procedure. Producers are to be similarly forgiven for the time constraints within which they must bring criminal cases (as well as subplots) to a satisfying conclusion.

Fictitious crime shows are not the only portrayal of courts on television. Reality television shows that open the lives of interesting (and not so interesting) individuals have also grown popular, and the televising and dramatizing of real criminal trials now capture the public's attention. High-profile cases such as the trials of OJ Simpson were mesmerizing to many, and Tru-TV (formerly Court TV) regularly features the twists and turns of actual criminal cases from courtrooms across the country. Many stay glued to their televisions for daily reports of the latest trial and its outcome.

Taken a step further, reality television now offers the ability to create the drama of the courtroom with shows featuring a "real" judge who resolves relatively minor disputes between parties who agree to appear on the show and abide by the judge's ruling. Sometimes referred to as "syndi-courts" because of their wide distribution due to the selling of broadcast rights, the "judges" who star in them have become household names: Judge Judy, Judge Joe Brown, Judge Mathis, and the one who began this genre of show in the 1980s, Judge Wapner. Although many of these are retired or former judges, on their shows they are arbitrators—private individuals whom the disputants agree to have decide their case. The judge's robe and gavel is a costume, and the television set is arranged to look like a courtroom, but they have no jurisdiction; their only authority to decide comes from the agreement signed by the parties. The contract specifies the procedural and evidentiary rules under which the case will be heard, and these rules are not the same as formal court rules. Neither is the judge bound by the requirements of substantive law or the ethical principles governing judges. Furthermore, although the parties have a real dispute to resolve, they have little stake in the outcome because the show's producers agree to pay any judgment against the losing party. As a result of these differences and the goal of entertainment rather than adjudication, the syndi-courts present a very misleading view of the court system to the viewing public.

Development of State Courts

Unlike the American federal courts, whose beginnings can be traced to the Constitution and the Judiciary Act of 1798, the state courts in the United States find their historical roots in English law and the practical needs of colonists trying to function as a society in the new world. The English courts, with their formal methods of pleading cases, organizing structure, and methods of argument, in a rudimentary sense served as a model for courts in the colonies. Because the colonies operated under royal charters or the direct authority of the English Crown, they were subject to English law during the 17th and 18th centuries. As a result, it was English law and the English court system that was most familiar and understood by those needing to resolve disputes, including the royally appointed governors.

This is not to say there were not many informal methods of justice in the colonies, including religious proscriptions and punishments, but for the most severe violations of public order, both civil and criminal, formal hearings were necessary both to make decisions in individual cases and to instill confidence in citizens that fairness would prevail within their newly formed societies.

As the colonies grew, however, these courts began to be shaped by the economic and social growth of the country and the development of its cities and towns. Specific needs requiring legal decision making included handling a broad range of matters relating to the governance of a town or county, such as controlling the appointment of local officials and the fledgling electoral process, protection of property interests, support for and enforcement of local religious observances, enforcement of contracts, and punishment of offenders. In form, however, the colonial courts continued to operate in similar fashion to the English courts, with the use of specialized forms of pleading and reliance on formal procedural requirements for

implementing the common law in matters that came before them.

After the adoption of the U.S. Constitution and the creation of the tripartite government and the federal judiciary, the role and operation of the state courts began to change somewhat. In the 1800s, courts became more limited and well defined in their operations. The constitutional notion of separation of powers, whereby branches of government acted autonomously within their constitutional authority, served to limit the courts' authority by clarifying the relationship between the courts, the laws, and the governance of local affairs, but courts remained largely in the control of localities. Funding was mostly the responsibility of cities, towns, or counties. This allowed for great disparities both within states and in different states in the qualifications and training of court personnel, especially judges, and the salaries they received. It also allowed people within local jurisdictions to control the actions of judges by withholding funding or removing judges from office for making unpopular decisions. As the population of states grew, numerous trial courts within cities and towns were created, leading to haphazard and overlapping jurisdiction without centralized authority.

In the 20th century, courts across the United States began to examine their practices and processes more closely. This was due to the increasing caseloads of many courts and the desire for greater consistency in decision making. Over time, this new emphasis sought to accomplish two things. First, it sought to bring greater professionalism to the judiciary. Many states began to require that judges hold law degrees or to have other formal training in the law. Although most judicial offices today require such qualifications, there are still municipal or other local courts that do not require judges to be trained as lawyers. Professionalism among judges accomplishes many things. Most prominently, it provides consistency in legal decision making because of a shared approach to and understanding of the law. It also serves to increase public confidence in the court system by helping ensure that decisions will be based on the rule of law and not on political and popular influences or personal biases.

The second change brought about by states' focus on the court system in the 20th century was restructuring of the court system. Although remnants of the earlier days of duplicative and fragmented court administration remain today, most state court systems have become just that—courts that are part of larger state system in which the judicial branch of government provides oversight for all or most courts operating within the state. These changes in the structure and operation of courts continue to evolve but have resulted in two models of court organization, unified and nonunified courts. The distinction between these court structures and the courts found within them are discussed later here.

Jurisdiction of State Courts

An understanding of the structure of courts within a state returns us to the topic of jurisdiction. Jurisdiction is the authority of a court to decide particular types of cases. At its most basic, a state court system provides for courts with jurisdiction to hold trials in criminal and civil cases, as well as independent courts to hear appeals from decisions made in the trial courts. Thus, the distinction between original jurisdiction and appellate jurisdiction is an important one that forms the basis for the relationship between courts in a state court system. That is, most court systems are structured such that courts with original jurisdiction operate independently of courts with appellate jurisdiction. As summarized in **Figure 5.1**, all state court systems have a court of last resort and numerous trial courts that operate with different geographic jurisdiction throughout the state. In addition, many states have intermediate appellate courts that help relieve the court of last resort from being overburdened by caseloads.

Court of Last Resort

The court of last resort in a state is the highest appellate court, whose function it is to decide appeals on matters of law, either state or federal, from the lower state courts (Segal et al., 2005). As the name suggests, a court of last resort is the last court in which a party may receive a hearing on their case, unless the case involves issues of federal law. The final hearing is normally limited to issues of law and is usually discretionary with the court. A state court of last resort is most commonly called a supreme court, although some states use other names such as supreme judicial court or simply court of appeals. Every state has at least one court of

last resort, but two states, Texas and Oklahoma, have two such courts, one each for criminal and civil cases.

Courts of last resort in the states consist of a panel of justices, all of whom consider each case that the court agrees to hear. This panel may have varying numbers of justices, determined by the state constitution or legislation of the state in which the court sits. The most common number of justices is seven, although some states have five and others have nine. Regardless, all states have an odd number of justices hearing all cases on this highest court so that in most cases an even split among the justices will not occur, resulting in uncertainty on a question of law.

Most of the appeals heard by the court of last resort involve review of decisions by the intermediate appellate court in the states that have them; therefore, the court of last resort for the most part serves to correct interpretations of law made by the lower appellate court. In this respect, decisions from the court are final on all matters of state (but not federal) law (see Hall, 2001; Solimine & Walker, 1999).

Intermediate Appellate Court

Intermediate courts of appeal are courts within the states that hear initial appeals from the trial courts. As caseloads have increased over time, these courts were established to preserve the right of appeal and relieve the courts of last resort from hearing every appeal, which became an increasingly difficult or impossible task, especially in

Court Level	Jurisdiction
1. Court of Last Resort (COLR) • Usually referred to as the Supreme Court • "Highest" court within a state • May have original jurisdiction in limited cases • Appellate review may be mandatory for some types of cases	Appellate jurisdiction
2. Intermediate Appellate Courts (IAC) • First route of appeal in most cases • Appeals from general and limited jurisdiction trial courts • Appeals usually mandatory, but may be discretionary for some types of cases	Appellate jurisdiction
3. General Jurisdiction Courts • Serious criminal cases (felonies) • Civil cases exceed certain amount (e.g., $5,000)	Original jurisdiction
4. Limited Jurisdiction Courts • Less serious criminal cases (misdemeanors, traffic violations) • May handle preliminary hearings, bail in felony cases • Civil cases of lesser amounts (small claims)	Original jurisdiction

Figure 5.1

Organization of State Courts

states with fast-growing populations; therefore, of the two types of appellate courts, intermediate appellate courts issue more opinions, in part because many of the cases they hear involve mandatory jurisdiction—cases in which the parties have a right to an appeal in the intermediate appellate court. Nonetheless, 11 states remain without intermediate courts of appeal; in these, the first appeal of right is to the court of last resort. The organization of the intermediate court of appeals varies, with some states creating separate courts for different geographical districts, whereas other states have one court for the entire state. Some states have many judges on the court (California, the largest, has 130), and other states have few (Alaska has only three).

Cases that come before an intermediate court of appeals are usually heard by three judge panels, although occasionally cases are considered *en banc*. Practice among the states for disposing of cases in these courts varies, however. Some states employ a combination of assigning cases to either a "summary" or "full" calendar. A summary calendar is one in which the court makes a decision on the basis of briefs alone, without oral argument, whereas a full calendar involves consideration of briefs and oral arguments before a decision is reached. The latter usually results in a signed or *per curiam* opinion, whereas the former typically results in a memorandum opinion. A summary calendar allows an intermediate appellate court to dispose efficiently of large numbers of cases in which complex legal questions are not presented or the applicable law is relatively clear, despite the parties' dispute. In more complex cases or those involving legal questions of first impression or novel legal theories, a signed opinion is most likely to be issued. This more detailed explanation of the rationale for the way in which the law was interpreted allows the case to serve as precedent or give the court of last resort, should there be a further appeal, the opportunity to understand the basis for the intermediate appellate court's conclusions.

Trial Court

State trial courts are courts of original jurisdiction; that is, they are the courts in which a case must initially be filed. Courts of original jurisdiction are where cases are heard "in the first instance" and where most cases are resolved. As the name denotes, trial courts hold trials in the cases that are filed, but to think of courts as only conducting trials is mistaken. In fact, most cases that are filed, both civil and criminal, do not result in a trial because they are disposed of by settlement or dismissal before trial. Furthermore, the majority of cases that are resolved by trial courts do not end in an appeal. Thus, state trial courts are responsible for beginning and ending the process of dispensing justice, and most cases therefore find resolution in these courts.

In most states, trial courts are of two types: courts of general jurisdiction and courts of limited jurisdiction. The primary distinction between these types of courts is the nature of the cases that they have jurisdiction to hear. Limited jurisdiction trial courts are those that are author-

ized to handle civil cases involving small claims and criminal cases involving lesser charges. All other cases fall under the authority of general jurisdiction courts. Together, these courts account for virtually every type of case that is filed.

Courts of General Jurisdiction

Courts of general jurisdiction are trial courts responsible for hearing both criminal and civil cases that, in most states, are not within the jurisdiction of the courts of limited jurisdiction (discussed later here). Specifically, these are the trial courts that handle more serious criminal cases (felonies) as well as civil cases involving larger sums of money, more complex disputes, or other matters specified by statute (such as writs of mandamus or election disputes). Courts of general jurisdiction are therefore the primary trial courts in the state court system in which most cases are filed and from which most appeals are taken to the intermediate appellate court.

A general jurisdiction court is a *court of record*, which means that all proceedings before the court are recorded and a transcript is produced. One judge (as opposed to a panel of judges) usually presides over these courts, and cases may be tried and decided by the judge alone or with a jury. States use different names when referring to their general jurisdiction courts, including circuit courts, superior courts, district courts, and courts of common pleas. The state of New York calls its general jurisdiction courts supreme courts, which leads to considerable confusion for legal practitioners in states for whom "supreme court" is reserved for the court of last resort; therefore, the name of a court does not always indicate what jurisdiction it has.

Courts of Limited Jurisdiction

Sometimes referred to as "lower" state courts, the courts of limited jurisdiction typically involve those courts that decide criminal cases of lesser seriousness (misdemeanors), civil cases involving lesser amounts of money, or cases involving specific categories of cases. Thus, the term "limited jurisdiction" specifies that only certain types of cases may be heard in these courts, unlike the "general jurisdiction" courts, which are authorized to hear nearly any type of case. Limited jurisdiction courts may be referred to as small claims courts, district courts, municipal courts, metropolitan courts, among other names. These courts are presided over by one judge who hears cases with or without a jury. It is estimated that there are over 14,000 courts of limited jurisdiction in which nearly 30 million cases are filed each year. Given the number and variety of cases heard, these courts are truly "people's courts."

In addition to the small claims civil matters and less serious criminal matters decided in these courts, many limited jurisdiction state courts are authorized to handle only special types of cases. These "specialized" courts have limited subject matter jurisdiction in matters such as traffic cases, drug cases, or cases in which a gun was used. Some of the more common of the specialized courts are juvenile courts, in which violations of law by minors are adjudicated; family courts, in which divorce cases, adoptions, and guardianship of children or incompetent older persons is determined; and probate courts, in which property is distributed after death. The operation and function of family courts are discussed in more detail in Chapter 7.

Unified Court Systems

In an attempt to conserve resources and streamline the operations of their courts, some states have created what is known as a *unified* court system. A unified court system is one that has two primary characteristics. First, a unified court system operates under the centralized authority of the state government, looking to the state for funding and administrative control. Second, a unified court system is characterized by the filing of cases in one court, rather than spreading jurisdiction among courts of general and limited jurisdiction. Thus, a unified system will have a court of last resort, usually an intermediate appellate court, and a general jurisdiction trial court in which all cases are initially filed. Unlike in a nonunified court system, the place of filing does not depend on the seriousness of a crime, the monetary value of a case, or the specialized subject matter involved. For example, in a nonunified court system, it is possible for a criminal felony case to be filed in

a court of limited jurisdiction for arraignment or a preliminary hearing and later filed again in the general jurisdiction court. Similarly, a civil case may be filed as a "small claim" in the limited jurisdiction court but later be found to involve the possibility of higher monetary damages, justifying transfer to the court of general jurisdiction. Unified court systems are more operationally efficient because the potential for multiple filing of cases is eliminated.

Although many state court systems refer to themselves as unified and may be to some extent, only 10 states have restructured their courts in a way that satisfies the previous definition. These are California, Connecticut, Illinois, Iowa, Kansas, Minnesota, Missouri, North Dakota, South Dakota, and Wisconsin. Examples of unified (California) and nonunified (New York) court structures are found in **Figures 5.2** and **5.3** respectively.

Selection and Appointment of State Court Judges

The time in office for state court judges varies substantially from that of federal judges. Although federal judges serve lifetime appointments (at least those in "constitutional" courts), judges in all states but Rhode Island serve

---

Supreme Court (Court of Last Resort)

- Seven justices sit en banc
- Mandatory jurisdiction in capital criminal, disciplinary cases
- Discretionary jurisdiction in civil, noncapital criminal, administrative, juvenile, original proceeding, interlocutory decision cases

Courts of Appeal (Intermediate Appellate Court)

- Six judicial districts
- One-hundred five justices sit in panels
- Mandatory jurisdiction in civil, noncapital criminal, administrative, juvenile cases
- Discretionary jurisdiction in administrative agency, original proceeding, interlocutory decision case

Superior Court (General Jurisdiction Trial Courts)

- Fifty-eight courts, one for each county
- 1,548 judges
- Tort, contract, real property, miscellaneous civil, criminal, domestic relations, juvenile, traffic/other violations
- Exclusive limited jurisdiction in small claims, probate/estate, mental health cases
- Limited appellate jurisdiction in civil appeals from administrative agencies
- Jury trials (except in appeals, domestic relations, and juvenile cases)

Figure 5.2

Structure of the California courts (unified)

Source: Adapted from Court Statistics Project, National Center for State Courts, *California Court Structure Chart.* Retrieved August 17, 2009, from http://www.ncsconline.org/D_Research/Ct_Struct/state_inc.asp?STATE=CA.

Court of Appeals (Court of Last Resort)

- Seven judges sit en banc
- Mandatory or discretionary jurisdiction in civil, capital criminal, administrative, juvenile, original proceedings cases

Appellate Terms of Supreme Court (Intermediate Appellate Court)

- Fourteen justices sit in panels
- Mandatory jurisdiction in civil, criminal, juvenile cases
- Discretionary jurisdiction in criminal, juvenile cases

Appellate Divisions of Supreme Court (Intermediate Appellate Court)

- Sixty justices sit in panels
- Mandatory or discretionary jurisdiction in civil, criminal, administrative, juvenile, lawyer discipline, original proceeding

Supreme Court (General Jurisdiction Trial Court)

- Three hundred twenty-six justices plus 59 judges from the Court of Claims sit in 12 districts
- Jury trials in tort, contract, real property, other civil cases
- Exclusive jurisdiction for divorce
- Felony and misdemeanor criminal cases

County Court (General Jurisdiction Trial Court)

- One hundred twenty-nine judges (57 are also Surrogates' or Family Court judges)
- Jury trials in tort, contract, real property (up to $25,000), miscellaneous civil, criminal, civil appeals

Court of Claims (Limited Jurisdiction Trial Court)

- Eighty-six judges (59 are also Supreme Court justices)
- Bench trials only in tort, contract, or real property cases involving the state

Family Court (Limited Jurisdiction Trial Court)

- One hundred twenty-seven judges (six are also County Court judges)
- Bench trials only in guardianship, domestic relations cases
- Exclusive jurisdiction in domestic violence and juvenile cases

Civil Court of the City of New York (Limited Jurisdiction Trial Court)

- One hundred twenty judges
- Jury trials in tort, contract, real property (up to $25,000), small claims (up to $5000), other civil cases

Figure 5.3
Structure of the New York courts (nonunified)

Surrogates' Court (Limited Jurisdiction Trial Court)

- Thirty-one surrogates plus 51 County Court judges
- Jury trials in probate/estate
- Adoption cases

District Court (Limited Jurisdiction Trial Court)

- Fifty judges
- Jurisdiction in Nassau and Suffolk counties
- Jury trials in tort, contract, real property ($0 to $15,000), small claims (up to $5,000)
- Preliminary hearings in misdemeanor and felony cases
- Traffic and ordinance violations

Criminal Court of the City of New York (Limited Jurisdiction Trial Court)

- One hundred seven judges
- Jury trials for serious misdemeanors
- Misdemeanors, traffic and ordinance violations

City Court (Limited Jurisdiction Trial Court)

- One hundred fifty-eight judges
- Jury trials in serious misdemeanor cases
- Tort, contract, real property (up to $15,000), small claims (up to $5,000)
- Felony, misdemeanor, preliminary hearings
- Traffic and ordinance violations

Town and Village Justice Court (Limited Jurisdiction Trial Court)

- Locally funded
- 2,300 justices
- Jury trials in most cases
- Tort, contract, real property ($0 to $3,000), small claims (up to $3,000)
- Misdemeanor, preliminary hearings
- Traffic and ordinance violations

Figure 5.3

(Continued)

Source: Adapted from Court Statistics Project, *National Center for State Courts, New York Court Structure Chart*. Retrieved August 17, 2009, from http://www.ncsconline.org/D_Research/Ct_Struct/state_inc.asp?STATE=NY.

limited terms in office, generally ranging from 4 to 15 years, subject to re-election or reappointment. Rhode Island judges serve for life, and those in Massachusetts and New Hampshire serve until 70 years old.

The manner in which state court judges reach office differs considerably from that of federal judges. Although federal judges are appointed by the president with the "advice and consent" of the Senate, state judges are either elected by the people or appointed by the governor or the state legislature, but there are many variations on each of these methods (Segal et al., 2005; Glick & Emmert, 1987).

Most states that use the appointment method for seating judges authorize the governor to make such appointments. This may occur with input from the state legislature, similar to the "advice and consent" of the Senate in federal appointments, or it may be in the governor's sole discretion. In a few states, the legislature retains the power to appoint judges. Regardless of the method of appointment, however, the people have only indirect influence (by their election of the governor and legislators) on the judiciary.

In many states, trial and appellate judges are elective positions. The election may be either partisan or nonpartisan. Partisan elections are those in which each judicial candidate's political party appears on the ballot, and the candidates may use their party affiliation while campaigning. In nonpartisan judicial elections, the candidates may not identify themselves by political party. In some states, after the initial election of a judge, he or she must subsequently run in an uncontested election in which voters must decide whether to retain the judge. This allows voters who may become disenchanted with the performance of a judge a mechanism for removing them from office.

Campaigning by state judicial candidates, whether in partisan or nonpartisan elections, traditionally has differed from campaigns conducted by candidates for other public offices because of the "unseemly" nature of politics. That is, judges and judges-to-be have been reticent to attack other candidates for their views, engage in fundraising activities, or express their views on the variety of social issues of importance to a state or community. This is due, in large part, to the desire of candidates aspiring to judgeships to present a judicial demeanor—appearing unbiased, objective, fair, and beyond the influence of special interests or individuals, all qualities assumed to be essential for judges. The normal rough and tumble of politics has been entered only tentatively by most judicial candidates, given their desire to convince the public of their judicial comportment. As a result, it has often been the case that the public knows little about the candidates,

their backgrounds, their ideological views, or the reasons why they believe they should assume office. This has left the electorate with little or no basis for making informed decisions about the individuals who should occupy the judicial branch of government.

In addition to the desire of judge candidates to appear judicial, judicial codes and ethical rules in most states have restricted the topics that judges may address in public, including on the campaign trail. For example, the New Mexico Code of Judicial Conduct does not allow judges to "publicly endorse or publicly oppose a candidate for public office through the news media or in campaign literature." The reason for this is to preserve the state's interest and the public's confidence in the impartiality of its judges (In *Re Vincent*, 143 N.M. 56, 172 P.3d 605 (2007)). Restrictions on the speech of judges and judicial candidates and the need for impartiality were the subjects of *Republican Party of Minnesota v. White*, 536 U.S. 765, 122 S. Ct. 2528, 153 L.Ed.2d 694 (2002), a case in which the U.S. Supreme Court struck down a rule restricting the First Amendment rights of judicial candidates. In that case, the State of Minnesota had an "announce clause" in its Code of Judicial Conduct that prevented judicial candidates from announcing their views "on disputed legal or political issues." The Court's opinion, excerpted in **Case Decision 5.1**, changed the nature of campaigning for judicial candidates in state courts.

Case Decision 5.1   *Republican Party of Minnesota v. White*, 536 U.S. 765, 122 S. Ct. 2528, 153 L.Ed.2d 694 (2002)

Decision of the Court by Justice Scalia:

The question presented in this case is whether the First Amendment permits the Minnesota Supreme Court to prohibit candidates for judicial election in that State from announcing their views on disputed legal and political issues.

I

Since Minnesota's admission to the Union in 1858, the State's Constitution has provided for the selection of all state judges by popular election. Since 1912, those elections have been nonpartisan. Since 1974, they have been subject to a legal restriction which states that a "candidate for a judicial office, including an incumbent judge," shall not "announce his or her views on disputed legal or political issues." This prohibition, promulgated by the Minnesota Supreme Court and based on Canon 7(B) of the 1972 American Bar Association (ABA) Model Code of Judicial Conduct, is known as the "announce clause." Incumbent judges who violate it are subject to discipline, including removal, censure, civil penalties, and suspension without pay. Lawyers who run for judicial office also must comply with the announce clause. Those who violate it are subject to, *inter alia*, disbarment, suspension, and probation.

In 1996, one of the petitioners, Gregory Wersal, ran for associate justice of the Minnesota Supreme Court. In the course of the campaign, he distributed literature criticizing several Minnesota Supreme Court decisions on issues such as crime, welfare, and abortion. A complaint against Wersal challenging, among other things, the propriety of this literature was filed with the Office of Lawyers Professional Responsibility, the agency which, under the direction of the Minnesota Lawyers Professional Responsibility Board, investigates and prosecutes ethical violations of lawyer candidates for judicial office. The Lawyers Board dismissed the complaint; with regard to the charges that his campaign materials violated the announce clause, it expressed doubt whether the clause could constitutionally be enforced.

(Continues)

Nonetheless, fearing that further ethical complaints would jeopardize his ability to practice law, Wersal withdrew from the election. In 1998, Wersal ran again for the same office. Early in that race, he sought an advisory opinion from the Lawyers Board with regard to whether it planned to enforce the announce clause. The Lawyers Board responded equivocally, stating that, although it had significant doubts about the constitutionality of the provision, it was unable to answer his question because he had not submitted a list of the announcements he wished to make.

Shortly thereafter, Wersal filed this lawsuit in Federal District Court against respondents, seeking, *inter alia*, a declaration that the announce clause violates the First Amendment and an injunction against its enforcement. Wersal alleged that he was forced to refrain from announcing his views on disputed issues during the 1998 campaign, to the point where he declined response to questions put to him by the press and public, out of concern that he might run afoul of the announce clause. Other plaintiffs in the suit, including the Minnesota Republican Party, alleged that, because the clause kept Wersal from announcing his views, they were unable to learn those views and support or oppose his candidacy accordingly. The parties filed cross-motions for summary judgment, and the District Court found in favor of respondents, holding that the announce clause did not violate the First Amendment. Over a dissent by Judge Beam, the United States Court of Appeals for the Eighth Circuit affirmed. We granted certiorari.

II

Before considering the constitutionality of the announce clause, we must be clear about its meaning. Its text says that a candidate for judicial office shall not "announce his or her views on disputed legal or political issues." We know that "announc[ing] . . . views" on an issue covers much more than *promising* to decide an issue a particular way. The prohibition extends to the candidate's mere statement of his current position, even if he does not bind himself to maintain that position after election.

There are, however, some limitations that the Minnesota Supreme Court has placed upon the scope of the announce clause that are not (to put it politely) immediately apparent from its text. The statements that formed the basis of the complaint against Wersal in 1996 included criticism of past decisions of the Minnesota Supreme Court. One piece of campaign literature stated that "[t]he Minnesota Supreme Court has issued decisions which are marked by their disregard for the Legislature and a lack of common sense." It went on to criticize a decision excluding from evidence confessions by criminal defendants that were not tape-recorded, asking "[s]hould we conclude that because the Supreme Court does not trust police, it allows confessed criminals to go free?" It criticized a decision striking down a state law restricting welfare benefits, asserting that "[i]t's the Legislature which should set our spending policies." And it criticized a decision requiring public financing of abortions for poor women as "unprecedented" and a "pro-abortion stance." Although one would think that all of these statements touched on disputed legal or political issues, they did not (or at least do not now) fall within the scope of the announce clause. The Judicial Board issued an opinion stating that judicial candidates may criticize past decisions, and the Lawyers Board refused to discipline Wersal for the foregoing statements because, in part, it thought they did not violate the announce clause. The Eighth Circuit relied on the Judicial Board's opinion in upholding the announce clause, and the Minnesota Supreme Court recently embraced the Eighth Circuit's interpretation.

There are yet further limitations upon the apparent plain meaning of the announce clause: In light of the constitutional concerns, the District Court construed the clause to reach only disputed issues that are likely to come before the candidate if he is elected judge. The Eighth Circuit accepted this limiting interpretation by the District Court, and in addition construed the clause to allow general discussions of case law and judicial philosophy. The Supreme Court of Minnesota adopted these interpretations as well when it ordered enforcement of the announce clause in accordance with the Eighth Circuit's opinion.

It seems to us, however, that—like the text of the announce clause itself—these limitations upon the text of the announce clause are not all that they appear to be. First, respondents acknowledged at oral argument that statements critical of past judicial decisions are *not* permissible if the candidate also states that he is against *stare decisis*. Thus, candidates must choose between stating their views critical of past decisions and stating their views in opposition to *stare decisis*. Or, to look at it more concretely, they may state their view that prior decisions were erroneous only if they do not assert that they, if elected, have any power to eliminate erroneous decisions. Second, limiting the scope of the clause to issues likely to come before a court is not much of a limitation at all. One would hardly expect the "disputed legal or political issues" raised in the course of a state judicial election to include such matters as whether the Federal Government should end the embargo of Cuba. Quite obviously, they will be those legal or political disputes that are the proper (or by past decisions have been made the improper) business of the state courts. And within that relevant category, "[t]here is almost no legal or political issue that is unlikely to come before a judge of an American court, state or federal, of general jurisdiction." Third, construing the clause to allow "general" discussions of case law and judicial philosophy turns out to be of little help in an election campaign. At oral argument, respondents gave, as an example of this exception, that a candidate is free to assert that he is a 'strict constructionist.' But that, like most other philosophical generalities, has little meaningful content for the electorate unless it is exemplified by application to a particular issue of construction likely to come before a court—for example, whether a particular statute runs afoul of any provision of the Constitution. Respondents conceded that the announce clause would prohibit the candidate from exemplifying his philosophy in this fashion. Without such application to real-life issues, all candidates can claim to be "strict constructionists" with equal (and unhelpful) plausibility.

In any event, it is clear that the announce clause prohibits a judicial candidate from stating his views on any specific nonfanciful legal question within the province of the court for which he is running, except in the context of discussing past decisions—and in the latter context as well, if he expresses the view that he is not bound by *stare decisis*.

Respondents contend that this still leaves plenty of topics for discussion on the campaign trail. These include a candidate's "character," "education," "work habits," and "how [he] would handle administrative duties if elected." Indeed, the Judicial Board has printed a list of preapproved questions which judicial candidates are allowed to answer. These include how the candidate feels about cameras in the courtroom, how he would go about reducing the caseload, how the costs of judicial administration can be reduced, and how he proposes to ensure that minorities and women are treated more fairly by the court system. Whether this list of preapproved subjects, and other topics not prohibited by the announce clause, adequately fulfill the First Amendment's guarantee of freedom of speech is the question to which we now turn.

III

As the Court of Appeals recognized, the announce clause both prohibits speech on the basis of its content and burdens a category of speech that is "at the core of our First Amendment freedoms"—speech about the qualifications of candidates for public office. The Court of Appeals concluded that the proper test to be applied to determine the constitutionality of such a restriction is what our cases have called strict scrutiny; the parties do not dispute that this is correct. Under the strict-scrutiny test, respondents have the burden to prove that the announce clause is (1) narrowly tailored, to serve (2) a compelling state interest. In order for respondents to show that the announce clause is narrowly tailored, they must demonstrate that it does not "unnecessarily circumscrib[e] protected expression."

The Court of Appeals concluded that respondents had established two interests as sufficiently compelling to justify the announce clause: preserving the impartiality of the state judiciary and preserving the appearance of the impartiality of the state judiciary. Respondents reassert these two interests before us, arguing that the first is compelling because it protects the due process rights of litigants, and that the second is compelling because it preserves public confidence in the judiciary. Respondents are rather vague, however, about what they mean by "impartiality." Indeed, although the term is used throughout the Eighth Circuit's opinion, the briefs, the Minnesota Code of Judicial Conduct, and the ABA Codes of Judicial Conduct, none of these sources bothers to define it. Clarity on this point is essential before we can decide whether impartiality is indeed a compelling state interest, and, if so, whether the announce clause is narrowly tailored to achieve it.

A

One meaning of "impartiality" in the judicial context—and of course its root meaning—is the lack of bias for or against either *party* to the proceeding. Impartiality in this sense assures equal application of the law. That is, it guarantees a party that the judge who hears his case will apply the law to him in the same way he applies it to any other party. This is the traditional sense in which the term is used. We think it plain that the announce clause is not narrowly tailored to serve impartiality (or the appearance of impartiality) in this sense. Indeed, the clause is barely tailored to serve that interest *at all*, inasmuch as it does not restrict speech for or against particular *parties*, but rather speech for or against particular *issues*. To be sure, when a case arises that turns on a legal issue on which the judge (as a

(Continues)

candidate) had taken a particular stand, the party taking the opposite stand is likely to lose. But not because of any bias against that party, or favoritism toward the other party. *Any* party taking that position is just as likely to lose. The judge is applying the law (as he sees it) evenhandedly.

B

It is perhaps possible to use the term "impartiality" in the judicial context (though this is certainly not a common usage) to mean lack of preconception in favor of or against a particular *legal view*. This sort of impartiality would be concerned, not with guaranteeing litigants equal application of the law, but rather with guaranteeing them an equal chance to persuade the court on the legal points in their case. Impartiality in this sense may well be an interest served by the announce clause, but it is not a *compelling* state interest, as strict scrutiny requires. A judge's lack of predisposition regarding the relevant legal issues in a case has never been thought a necessary component of equal justice, and with good reason. For one thing, it is virtually impossible to find a judge who does not have preconceptions about the law. As then-Justice Rehnquist observed of our own Court: "Since most Justices come to this bench no earlier than their middle years, it would be unusual if they had not by that time formulated at least some tentative notions that would influence them in their interpretation of the sweeping clauses of the Constitution and their interaction with one another. It would be not merely unusual, but extraordinary, if they had not at least given opinions as to constitutional issues in their previous legal careers." Indeed, even if it were possible to select judges who did not have preconceived views on legal issues, it would hardly be desirable to do so. "Proof that a Justice's mind at the time he joined the Court was a complete *tabula rasa* in the area of constitutional adjudication would be evidence of lack of qualification, not lack of bias." The Minnesota Constitution positively forbids the selection to courts of general jurisdiction of judges who are impartial in the sense of having no views on the law. And since avoiding judicial preconceptions on legal issues is neither possible nor desirable, pretending otherwise by attempting to preserve the "appearance" of that type of impartiality can hardly be a compelling state interest either.

C

A third possible meaning of "impartiality" (again not a common one) might be described as open-mindedness. This quality in a judge demands, not that he have no preconceptions on legal issues, but that he be willing to consider views that oppose his preconceptions, and remain open to persuasion, when the issues arise in a pending case. This sort of impartiality seeks to guarantee each litigant, not an *equal* chance to win the legal points in the case, but at least *some* chance of doing so. It may well be that impartiality in this sense, and the appearance of it, are desirable in the judiciary, but we need not pursue that inquiry, since we do not believe the Minnesota Supreme Court adopted the announce clause for that purpose.

Respondents argue that the announce clause serves the interest in open-mindedness, or at least in the appearance of openmindedness, because it relieves a judge from pressure to rule a certain way in order to maintain consistency with statements the judge has previously made. The problem is, however, that statements in election campaigns are such an infinitesimal portion of the public commitments to legal positions that judges (or judges-to-be) undertake, that this object of the prohibition is implausible. Before they arrive on the bench (whether by election or otherwise) judges have often committed themselves on legal issues that they must later rule upon. More common still is a judge's confronting a legal issue on which he has expressed an opinion while on the bench. Most frequently, of course, that prior expression will have occurred in ruling on an earlier case. But judges often state their views on disputed legal issues outside the context of adjudication—in classes that they conduct, and in books and speeches. Like the ABA Codes of Judicial Conduct, the Minnesota Code not only permits but encourages this. That is quite incompatible with the notion that the need for open-mindedness (or for the appearance of open-mindedness) lies behind the prohibition at issue here.

The short of the matter is this: In Minnesota, a candidate for judicial office may not say "I think it is constitutional for the legislature to prohibit same-sex marriages." He may say the very same thing, however, up until the very day before he declares himself a candidate, and may say it repeatedly (until litigation is pending) after he is elected. As a means of pursuing the objective of open-mindedness that respondents now articulate, the announce clause is so woefully underinclusive as to render belief in that purpose a challenge to the credulous.

Moreover, the notion that the special context of electioneering justifies an *abridgment* of the right to speak out on disputed issues sets our First Amendment jurisprudence on its head. "[D]ebate on the qualifications of candidates" is "at the core of our electoral process and of the First Amendment freedoms," not at the edges. We have never allowed the government to prohibit candidates from communicating relevant information to voters during an election.

IV

To sustain the announce clause, the Eighth Circuit relied heavily on the fact that a pervasive practice of prohibiting judicial candidates from discussing disputed legal and political issues developed during the last half of the 20th century. It is true that a "universal and long-established" tradition of prohibiting certain conduct creates "a strong presumption" that the prohibition is constitutional: "Principles of liberty fundamental enough to have been embodied within constitutional guarantees are not readily erased from the Nation's consciousness." The practice of prohibiting speech by judicial candidates on disputed issues, however, is neither long nor universal.

At the time of the founding, only Vermont (before it became a State) selected any of its judges by election. Starting with Georgia in 1812, States began to provide for judicial election, a development rapidly accelerated by Jacksonian democracy. By the time of the Civil War, the great majority of States elected their judges. We know of no restrictions upon statements that could be made by judicial candidates (including judges) throughout the 19th and the first quarter of the 20th century. Indeed, judicial elections were generally partisan during this period, the movement toward nonpartisan judicial elections not even beginning until the 1870s. Thus, not only were judicial candidates (including judges) discussing disputed legal and political issues on the campaign trail, but they were touting party affiliations and angling for party nominations all the while.

There is an obvious tension between the article of Minnesota's popularly approved Constitution which provides that judges shall be elected, and the Minnesota Supreme Court's announce clause which places most subjects of interest to the voters off limits. (The candidate-speech restrictions of all the other States that have them are also the product of judicial fiat.) The disparity is perhaps unsurprising, since the ABA, which originated the announce clause, has long been an opponent of judicial elections. That opposition may be well taken (it certainly had the support of the Founders of the Federal Government), but the First Amendment does not permit it to achieve its goal by leaving the principle of elections in place while preventing candidates from discussing what the elections are about.

The Minnesota Supreme Court's canon of judicial conduct prohibiting candidates for judicial election from announcing their views on disputed legal and political issues violates the First Amendment. Accordingly, we reverse the grant of summary judgment to respondents and remand the case for proceedings consistent with this opinion.

It is so ordered.

Justice O'Connor, concurring.

I join the opinion of the Court but write separately to express my concerns about judicial elections generally. I am concerned that, even aside from what judicial candidates may say while campaigning, the very practice of electing judges undermines this interest.

We of course want judges to be impartial, in the sense of being free from any personal stake in the outcome of the cases to which they are assigned. But if judges are subject to regular elections they are likely to feel that they have at least some personal stake in the outcome of every publicized case. Elected judges cannot help being aware that if the public is not satisfied with the outcome of a particular case, it could hurt their reelection prospects. Even if judges were able to suppress their awareness of the potential electoral consequences of their decisions and refrain from acting on it, the public's confidence in the judiciary could be undermined simply by the possibility that judges would be unable to do so.

Moreover, contested elections generally entail campaigning. And campaigning for a judicial post today can require substantial funds. Unless the pool of judicial candidates is limited to those wealthy enough to independently fund their campaigns, a limitation unrelated to judicial skill, the cost of campaigning requires judicial candidates to engage in fundraising. Yet relying on campaign donations may leave judges feeling indebted to certain parties or interest groups. Even if judges

(*Continues*)

were able to refrain from favoring donors, the mere possibility that judges' decisions may be motivated by the desire to repay campaign contributors is likely to undermine the public's confidence in the judiciary.

Despite these significant problems, 39 States currently employ some form of judicial elections for their appellate courts, general jurisdiction trial courts, or both. Judicial elections were not always so prevalent. The first 29 States of the Union adopted methods for selecting judges that did not involve popular elections. As the Court explains, however, beginning with Georgia in 1812, States began adopting systems for judicial elections. From the 1830s until the 1850s, as part of the Jacksonian movement toward greater popular control of public office, this trend accelerated. By the beginning of the 20th century, however, elected judiciaries increasingly came to be viewed as incompetent and corrupt, and criticism of partisan judicial elections mounted. In 1906, Roscoe Pound gave a speech to the American Bar Association in which he claimed that "compelling judges to become politicians, in many jurisdictions has almost destroyed the traditional respect for the bench."

In response to such concerns, some States adopted a modified system of judicial selection that became known as the Missouri Plan (because Missouri was the first State to adopt it for most of its judicial posts). Under the Missouri Plan, judges are appointed by a high elected official, generally from a list of nominees put together by a nonpartisan nominating commission, and then subsequently stand for unopposed retention elections in which voters are asked whether the judges should be recalled. If a judge is recalled, the vacancy is filled through a new nomination and appointment. This system obviously reduces threats to judicial impartiality, even if it does not eliminate all popular pressure on judges. The Missouri Plan is currently used to fill at least some judicial offices in 15 States.

Thirty-one States, however, still use popular elections to select some or all of their appellate and/or general jurisdiction trial court judges, who thereafter run for reelection periodically. Of these, slightly more than half use nonpartisan elections, and the rest use partisan elections. Most of the States that do not have any form of judicial elections choose judges through executive nomination and legislative confirmation.

Minnesota has chosen to select its judges through contested popular elections instead of through an appointment system or a combined appointment and retention election system along the lines of the Missouri Plan. In doing so the State has voluntarily taken on the risks to judicial bias described above. As a result, the State's claim that it needs to significantly restrict judges' speech in order to protect judicial impartiality is particularly troubling. If the State has a problem with judicial impartiality, it is largely one the State brought upon itself by continuing the practice of popularly electing judges.

Justice Kennedy, concurring.

I agree with the Court that Minnesota's prohibition on judicial candidates' announcing their legal views is an unconstitutional abridgment of the freedom of speech. There is authority for the Court to apply strict scrutiny analysis to resolve some First Amendment cases, and the Court explains in clear and forceful terms why the Minnesota regulatory scheme fails that test. So I join its opinion.

I adhere to my view, however, that content-based speech restrictions that do not fall within any traditional exception should be invalidated without inquiry into narrow tailoring or compelling government interests. The speech at issue here does not come within any of the exceptions to the First Amendment recognized by the Court. "Here, a law is directed to speech alone where the speech in question is not obscene, not defamatory, not words tantamount to an act otherwise criminal, not an impairment of some other constitutional right, not an incitement to lawless action, and not calculated or likely to bring about imminent harm the State has the substantive power to prevent. No further inquiry is necessary to reject the State's argument that the statute should be upheld." The political speech of candidates is at the heart of the First Amendment, and direct restrictions on the content of candidate speech are simply beyond the power of government to impose.

Here, Minnesota has sought to justify its speech restriction as one necessary to maintain the integrity of its judiciary. Nothing in the Court's opinion should be read to cast doubt on the vital importance of this state interest. Courts, in our system, elaborate principles of law in the course of resolving disputes. The power and the prerogative of a court to perform this function rest, in the end, upon the respect accorded to its judgments. The citizen's respect for judgments depends in turn upon the issuing court's absolute probity. Judicial integrity is, in consequence, a state interest of the highest order.

Articulated standards of judicial conduct may advance this interest. To comprehend, then to codify, the essence of judicial integrity is a hard task, however. "The work of deciding cases goes on every day in hundreds of courts throughout the land. Any judge, one might suppose, would find it easy to describe the process which he had followed a thousand times and more. Nothing could be farther from the truth." B. Cardozo, The Nature of the Judicial Process 9 (1921). Much the same can be said of explicit standards to ensure judicial integrity. To strive for judicial integrity is the work of a lifetime. That should not dissuade the profession. The difficulty of the undertaking does not mean we should refrain from the attempt. Explicit standards of judicial conduct provide essential guidance for judges in the proper discharge of their duties and the honorable conduct of their office. The legislative bodies, judicial committees, and professional associations that promulgate those standards perform a vital public service. Yet these standards may not be used by the State to abridge the speech of aspiring judges in a judicial campaign.

Minnesota may choose to have an elected judiciary. It may strive to define those characteristics that exemplify judicial excellence. It may enshrine its definitions in a code of judicial conduct. It may adopt recusal standards more rigorous than due process requires, and censure judges who violate these standards. What Minnesota may not do, however, is censor what the people hear as they undertake to decide for themselves which candidate is most likely to be an exemplary judicial officer. Deciding the relevance of candidate speech is the right of the voters, not the State. The law in question here contradicts the principle that unabridged speech is the foundation of political freedom.

The State of Minnesota no doubt was concerned, as many citizens and thoughtful commentators are concerned, that judicial campaigns in an age of frenetic fundraising and mass media may foster disrespect for the legal system. Indeed, from the beginning there have been those who believed that the rough-and-tumble of politics would bring our governmental institutions into ill repute. And some have sought to cure this tendency with governmental restrictions on political speech. Cooler heads have always recognized, however, that these measures abridge the freedom of speech—not because the state interest is insufficiently compelling, but simply because content-based restrictions on political speech are "expressly and positively forbidden by" the First Amendment. The State cannot opt for an elected judiciary and then assert that its democracy, in order to work as desired, compels the abridgment of speech.

If Minnesota believes that certain sorts of candidate speech disclose flaws in the candidate's credentials, democracy and free speech are their own correctives. The legal profession, the legal academy, the press, voluntary groups, political and civic leaders, and all interested citizens can use their own First Amendment freedoms to protest statements inconsistent with standards of judicial neutrality and judicial excellence. Indeed, if democracy is to fulfill its promise, they must do so. They must reach voters who are uninterested or uninformed or blinded by partisanship, and they must urge upon the voters a higher and better understanding of the judicial function and a stronger commitment to preserving its finest traditions. Free elections and free speech are a powerful combination: Together they may advance our understanding of the rule of law and further a commitment to its precepts.

There is general consensus that the design of the Federal Constitution, including lifetime tenure and appointment by nomination and confirmation, has preserved the independence of the Federal Judiciary. In resolving this case, however, we should refrain from criticism of the State's choice to use open elections to select those persons most likely to achieve judicial excellence. States are free to choose this mechanism rather than, say, appointment and confirmation. By condemning judicial elections across the board, we implicitly condemn countless elected state judges and without warrant. Many of them, despite the difficulties imposed by the election system, have discovered in the law the enlightenment, instruction, and inspiration that make them independent-minded and faithful jurists of real integrity. We should not, even by inadvertence, "impute to judges a lack of firmness, wisdom, or honor."

These considerations serve but to reinforce the conclusion that Minnesota's regulatory scheme is flawed. By abridging speech based on its content, Minnesota impeaches its own system of free and open elections. The State may not regulate the content of candidate speech merely because the speakers are candidates. This case does not present the question whether a State may restrict the speech of judges because they are judges—for example, as part of a code of judicial conduct; the law at issue here regulates judges only when and because they are candidates.

Petitioner Gregory Wersal was not a sitting judge but a challenger; he had not voluntarily entered into an employment relationship with the State or surrendered any First Amendment rights. His speech may not be controlled or abridged in this manner. Even the undoubted interest of the State in the excellence of its judiciary does not allow it to restrain candidate speech by reason of its content. Minnesota's attempt to regulate campaign speech is impermissible.

As an alternative to judicial appointments or elections, some states employ modified approaches. These take various forms, but generally involve the use of a committee made up of lawyers and members of the public whose job it is to review applications from judicial candidates and make recommendations to the governor or legislature as to who should be appointed. The governor or legislature then may choose from a list of recommended candidates. Once appointed, the judge must run for office in the next election in order to retain the judgeship. Sometimes called a "merit selection committee," or referred to as the "Missouri plan" (after the state that first adopted it), the purpose of this method is to provide an independent review of the qualifications of candidates and lessen the politicization of the process (Segal et al., 2005).

State Court Decision Making

As in the federal courts, the decision making processes in state courts differ according to whether the court is a trial or an appellate court. Although the focus of appellate courts is to review the procedures and law applied in the trial courts, the focus of trial court decision making is the finding of facts and determining how the law applied to those facts. Thus, the fact-finding function encompasses a significant portion of the activities of trial courts. The differences in decision-making processes made by these two types of courts are discussed later here.

Trial Court Decision Making

Trial courts are confronted with many decision-making problems from the time a case is filed until a verdict is reached, and in some cases, additional problems requiring a judge's decision arise after a verdict. These problems can be classified as either decisions of fact or decisions of law. Decisions of fact are made by either a judge (in a bench trial) or a jury (in a jury trial). They require a decision as to what evidence is relevant to the claims to be tried, what weight should be given to the evidence, and whether that evidence is presented in accordance with rules intended to provide a fair and just determination of the facts. Thus, when a judge overrules or sustains the objection of a party during the questioning of a witness or regarding the admission of physical evidence, the judge is making a decision of fact. When a jury decides that a criminal defendant is guilty or that a contract has been breached or that a person's injuries resulted from mistakes made by a doctor, it is making decisions about the facts in a case.

Decisions of law require application of the law to the facts and the interpretation or meaning of some provision of law. The former is the province of the trier of fact, and the latter is one of the functions of the trial judge. Civil lawsuits and criminal cases are filed on the basis of legal principles; that is, they must assert a violation of legal rights or criminal law. The court's task is to determine what legal rules are applicable, how they should be interpreted, and how they apply to the case.

This is accomplished by the judge in considering, for example, motions for summary judgment, in deciding what evidence should or should not be excluded, and by instructing the jury on the requirements of the law. The judge determines what law is applicable by considering the allegations in the complaint and the source of law that is asserted there as the basis for the case. This may be statutory, regulatory, constitutional, or common law. Regardless, the trial judge is bound to interpretations of law made by the state's appellate courts. Thus, although trial judges have considerable power to adjudicate cases within the scope of procedural rules, they are constrained in their application of the law by *stare decisis* and the rule of precedent.

Appellate Court Decision Making

State appellate courts decide the meaning and application of law, but not the facts, in cases that properly come before them. The word "properly" means that the case must be one that the appellate court has jurisdiction to hear and that the legal issues to be heard were raised by at least one party and "preserved for appeal." This means that a record of the problem of law needs to have been made at trial as, for example, when a defendant's attorney in a criminal case objects to the admission of evidence that he claims was obtained as a result of an illegal search and seizure. If an objection to the evidence is not made, it is not preserved and cannot later be used as the basis for an appeal.

When legal issues are presented properly before the appellate court, it is empowered to examine the decisions made by the trial judge relating to those issues or, when the appellate court is the court of last resort, decisions regarding interpretation of the law made by an intermediate appellate court. Appellate courts do not decide facts; however, this does not mean that they do not review the decisions of trial judges for potential errors of fact. An appellate court may be called on to review factual determinations made by the trial judge regarding the evidence presented at trial. Specifically, a trial court's decision regarding whether discovery regarding certain factual inquiries should be allowed, or regarding the admissibility of certain evidence at trial, is an area often reviewed by appellate courts (see Benesh & Martinek, 2002).

In addition, some cases on appeal involve mixed questions of fact and law. For example, *State v. Mata*, 275 Neb. 1, 745 N.W.2d 229 (2008), found in **Case Decision 5.2** and discussed later here, considered whether electrocution was a constitutionally valid method of capital punishment by examining facts relating to the methods of capital punishment used in the United States. For the most part, however, the facts determined to be true by the judge or jury at trial are also assumed to be true and relied on in its examination of the law by the appellate court. The appellate court considers the requirements of the law, decides how they apply to the facts as found by the trial court, and reaches a conclusion about whether the outcome at trial was correct or incorrect.

Case Decision 5.2 *State of Nebraska v. Mata*, 275 Neb. 1, 745 N.W.2d 229 (2008)

Opinion of the Court by Justice Connolly:

Introduction

A jury convicted Raymond Mata, Jr., of first degree murder and kidnapping. A three-judge panel sentenced Mata to death for the first degree premeditated murder of 3-year-old Adam Gomez. The presiding judge sentenced him to life imprisonment for kidnapping. Between his sentencing and our decision in his first direct appeal, the U.S. Supreme Court decided *Ring v. Arizona*, 536 U.S. 584, 122 S. Ct. 2428, 153 L.Ed.2d 556 (2002) which required juries to find whether aggravating circumstances exist in death penalty cases. [W]e affirmed both of Mata's convictions, but, applying *Ring* we vacated his death sentence and remanded the cause for resentencing. After a jury found the existence of an aggravating circumstance, a three-judge panel resentenced Mata to death.

In this appeal, Mata argues that this court and the trial court erred in numerous respects regarding his resentencing. He also argues that electrocution is cruel and unusual punishment prohibited by the U.S. and Nebraska Constitutions.

Constitutionality of Electrocution

Mata contends that the district court erred in failing to find that death by electrocution unconstitutionally imposes cruel and unusual punishment. The State, however, contends that Mata has failed to carry his burden of proof that electrocution is cruel and unusual punishment. It further contends no precedent exists to support Mata's position because neither this court nor the U.S. Supreme Court has ever held that a method of inflicting death is unconstitutional.

We pause to clarify what this case is not about. Mata does not argue that the death penalty, in any form, violates the U.S. and Nebraska Constitutions, nor could he. "[T]he death penalty, when properly imposed by a state, does not violate either the eighth or [the] fourteenth amendment [to] the United States Constitution or Neb. Const. art. [I], § 9." So the issue before us is not whether Mata will be executed, but only whether the current statutory method of execution is constitutional.

We have affirmed Mata's conviction and death sentence; we have affirmed the jury's finding that his crime was exceptionally depraved; and we have determined that the imposition of the death sentence in this case is proportional to that in the same or similar circumstances. But this court's finding that Mata's crime was heinous does not negate our duty to safeguard our state Constitution.

Obviously, all capital offenses involve heinous crimes. The people of Nebraska, through the Legislature, have determined that in some circumstances, the State may impose the death penalty. And we may not interfere unless the State's procedures in executing the prisoner violate constitutional requirements.

We limit our analysis to whether the State may constitutionally execute a sentence of death by electrocution. We must decide whether electrocution is prohibited by the Nebraska Constitution's proscription against inflicting cruel and unusual punishment. That determination, however, does not affect Mata's sentence of death.

(a) Nebraska Constitution Governs the Issue

It is correct that we have held that electrocution does not constitute cruel and unusual punishment within the meaning of the U.S. or Nebraska Constitution. But we have not previously had the opportunity to review a factual record showing electrocution's physiological effects on a prisoner, nor have we relied on any case in which such evidence was reviewed. Instead, we have relied on U.S. Supreme Court decisions. As explained below, those cases contain factual assumptions that some of the Court's more recent cases have called into question.

Unlike other recent cases where we declined to revisit this issue, Mata's constitutional challenge to electrocution is not procedurally barred and the parties have presented us with a full evidentiary record. We conclude that evolving standards of decency are applicable to method-of-execution challenges. Those standards require that we now review the evidence presented in this case in the light of modern scientific knowledge.

(Continues)

At the trial level, Mata moved for a declaration that electrocution is cruel and unusual punishment under both the federal and state Constitutions. The issue was developed and tried as a challenge under both Constitutions. Although in his brief, Mata assigned that electrocution violates the U.S. Constitution, he did not specifically cite to the Nebraska Constitution's prohibition against cruel and unusual punishment. Under our court rules, this oversight could preclude us from considering the state constitutional issue. However, because of the death penalty's severity and irrevocability, we have not strictly enforced briefing rules on capital defendants.

Moreover, for reasons explained below, we conclude that the Nebraska Constitution governs this issue. We have already decided that we have a constitutional responsibility to determine whether electrocution is lawful. We stayed the execution of Carey Dean Moore, another death row inmate, pending the outcome of that determination. Also, three other cases on our docket have raised the constitutionality of electrocution under the Nebraska Constitution. We conclude that it is imperative for this court to resolve this issue. In fulfilling our responsibility and in the interest of judicial economy, we excuse the technical omission in Mata's brief.

The Nebraska Constitution, article I, § 9, mirrors the U.S. Constitution's Eighth Amendment: "Excessive bail shall not be required, nor excessive fines imposed, nor cruel and unusual punishment inflicted." Obviously, we cannot, under the U.S. Constitution, declare that electrocution violates its cruel and unusual punishment provision because the U.S. Supreme Court has held otherwise. And we have stated that the Nebraska Constitution's cruel and unusual punishment provision "does not require more than does the [Eighth Amendment to the] U.S. Constitution." But as we will explain, we now believe this issue should be resolved by this court.

Like this court, the U.S. Supreme Court has never reviewed objective evidence regarding electrocution's constitutionality. The Supreme Court based its holdings on state courts' factual assumptions, which, in turn, relied on untested science from 1890. Because we conclude that we can no longer rely on those factual assumptions and because no other state imposes electrocution as its sole method of execution, we will decide the issue under the Nebraska Constitution.

(i) Early U.S. Supreme Court Decisions on Electrocution

In 1890, in *In re Kemmler*, 136 U.S. 436, 10 S. Ct. 930, 34 L.Ed. 519 (1890) the U.S. Supreme Court decided the State of New York could proceed with the first execution by electrocution. New York had carried out death sentences by hanging until the governor recommended in 1886 that the Legislature find a less barbarous method. Commercially available electricity was new, and states had not used it for an execution. But after a legislative commission reported in 1888 that electrocution was the most humane and practical method of execution known to modern science, the state enacted electrocution as its mode of execution. William Kemmler, the first prisoner scheduled to die by electrocution, challenged the method as cruel and unusual punishment. He alleged electrocution violated his right to due process under both the state and federal Constitutions.

On appeal, the U.S. Supreme Court said that cruel and unusual punishment could not be defined with precision. It stated, however, that certain types of punishment clearly fell within the Eighth Amendment's prohibition: "Punishments are cruel when they involve torture or a lingering death; but the punishment of death is not cruel, within the meaning of that word as used in the Constitution. It implies there [is] something inhuman and barbarous, something more than the mere extinguishment of life."

Over the last 118 years, the *In re Kemmler* standard has remained the baseline criterion under the Eighth Amendment for evaluating a method of execution. Our review of these early cases illustrates that the U.S. Supreme Court's case law on electrocution relies on unexamined factual assumptions about an electric current's physiological effects on a human. This obvious omission in the Court's jurisprudence results from three factors: (1) the Court's limited knowledge about an electrocution's effect on the human body, (2) the states' desire to find a more humane method of execution than hanging, and (3) the Court's view, when electrocution was first introduced, that the Eighth Amendment was not intended as a restraint on state legislatures' determinations of punishment. But that view has changed. The Supreme Court has specifically held that the Eighth Amendment is a restraint on legislative power to impose punishment. And it has held the 8th Amendment applies to the states through the 14th Amendment.

(ii) This Court's Duty to Safeguard Constitutional Rights

It is our duty to protect the constitutional rights afforded under both the federal and state Constitutions. We conclude that we can no longer rely on the factual assumptions implicit in U.S.

Supreme Court precedent pertaining to the constitutionality of execution by electrocution. Because we are now presented with evidence of a nature and quality that the Supreme Court never considered when it held electrocution was not cruel and unusual punishment, we cannot rationally defer to federal precedent.

As discussed, we cannot determine how the U.S. Supreme Court would decide a challenge to electrocution as a method of execution under the federal Constitution if it were presented with this evidence. But we note that some of the Court's recent decisions and dissents have called attention to outdated factual assumptions in the Court's precedent. We also know that the Court is highly unlikely to accept an appeal on the issue from any other jurisdiction that has electrocution as an alternative method of execution. The Court has held that a condemned prisoner waives a constitutional challenge to a method of execution if he or she voluntarily selects that method. Only in Nebraska is electrocution the mandated method of execution; there is no alternative.

We reject the dissent's suggestion that we are bound by questionable federal precedent and should allow Mata to attempt a further appeal to the U.S. Supreme Court. It is not our function to predict whether the Supreme Court would grant a writ of certiorari in this case. But it is our duty as constitutional officers to decide the challenge presented in this automatic appeal, based on the record of the case, as tried and decided. And we will not shirk or abdicate our duty to safeguard the constitutional rights afforded by our state Constitution. We conclude that whether electrocution is cruel and unusual punishment is an issue that has fallen to this court to determine.

(b) Legal Standards Defining Cruel and Unusual Punishment

Although we conclude that the Nebraska Constitution governs this issue, because both the federal and state Constitutions prohibit cruel and unusual punishment, we look to federal precedent for guidance regarding general standards to maintain harmony between parallel constitutional provisions.

(i) Substantial Risk That Prisoner Will Suffer Unnecessary and Wanton Pain

The baseline criterion in a challenge to a punishment is whether it imposes torture or a lingering death that is unnecessary to the mere extinguishment of life. "The traditional humanity of modern Anglo-American law forbids the infliction of unnecessary pain in the execution of the death sentence" and cruelty inherent in the execution method itself. "[T]he execution shall be so instantaneous and substantially painless that the punishment shall be reduced, as nearly as possible, to no more than that of death itself." Capital punishment "must not involve the unnecessary and wanton infliction of pain."

A single accident, however, does not show that a method of execution is inherently cruel. But a pattern of prisoners suffering unnecessary pain presents a different circumstance. A method of execution violates the prohibition against cruel and unusual punishment if there is a substantial foreseeable risk, inherent in the method, that a prisoner will suffer unnecessary pain.

Prisoners are not required to show that their execution will actually result in unnecessary pain. The human body does not respond uniformly to electric current. And, obviously, there are no first-person accounts of an execution that a court can consult. So, courts must necessarily deal with probabilities. The prohibition against cruel and unusual punishment, however, protects prisoners against sufficiently imminent dangers and current infliction of unnecessary pain.

(ii) Evolving Standards of Decency

The State argues the U.S. Supreme Court applies distinct and separate constitutional standards under the Eighth Amendment. It argues that the standard depends upon whether the defendant claims that a punishment is disproportionate or that the method of inflicting the punishment is cruel. The State further argues under this disjunctive scheme that "subjective" standards of decency are not applicable to method-of-punishment claims. And so, according to the State, the only relevant inquiry is whether the method is cruel or barbarous. The State further claims the "unusual" component is the only relevant inquiry in claims that a punishment is excessive or disproportionate. We disagree with the State's analysis.

The prohibition against cruel and unusual punishment is not a static concept and "must draw its meaning from the evolving standards of decency that mark the progress of a maturing society." A court must evaluate claims that punishment is cruel and unusual "in the light of contemporary human knowledge."

(*Continues*)

(Continued)

The State incorrectly asserts that a court's evaluation of contemporary values is subjective. The U.S. Supreme Court looks to objective criteria for this inquiry, the most reliable of which is legislation enacted by this nation's legislatures. We acknowledge that the Court has stated that an excessiveness claim is judged under currently prevailing standards of decency. But it has also considered both cruelty and unusualness when dealing with disproportionality claims.

We decline to hold that under the Nebraska Constitution, evolving standards of decency apply only to claims of disproportional punishment. We conclude that evolving standards of decency must apply to claims that the State's intended method of execution inflicts unnecessary and wanton pain. To hold otherwise would not comport with the U.S. Supreme Court's consistent holdings that the death penalty is different, both in its severity and irrevocability. The constitutional prohibition against cruel and unusual punishment would be meaningless if the punishment would have to be rejected by every state before it could be cruel and unusual.

Regarding evolving standards, the evidence showed that by 1949, 26 states had changed their execution method from hanging to electrocution, but that no state had adopted electrocution since. Instead, states began adopting lethal gas as their execution method. By 1973, 12 states were using lethal gas and 20 states were using electrocution. Then, in 1977, lethal injection was introduced.

By 1999, of the 38 states that permitted capital punishment, 34 states offered lethal injection as either a choice or the exclusive method of execution and only four states authorized electrocution as their exclusive method of execution. In 2000, Georgia switched from electrocution to lethal injection as its sole method of execution for capital offenses committed on or after May 1, 2000. Florida also switched in 2000 from electrocution to lethal injection unless the person sentenced to death affirmatively elects electrocution. Finally, in 2002, Alabama followed Florida's lead. Thus, as of July 1, 2002, Nebraska is the only state in the nation to require electrocution as its sole method of execution.

Responding to horror stories of "botched" electrocutions in Florida, some states selected lethal injection. It has been stated that courts have switched to lethal injection "because it is universally recognized as the most humane method of execution, least apt to cause unnecessary pain." Faced with changing societal values, we cannot ignore Nebraska's status as the last state to retain electrocution as its sole method of execution.

(iii) Dignity of Man

"A penalty also must accord with 'the dignity of man,'" which is the basic concept underlying the prohibition against cruel and unusual punishment. The U.S. Supreme Court has implicitly condemned some punishments as barbaric, such as beheading and drawing and quartering, that inflict unnecessary physical violence. We agree that barbarous punishments include those that mutilate the prisoner's body even if they do not cause conscious pain. We conclude that such punishments do not comport with the Eighth Amendment's dignity of man standard.

In sum, we conclude that the relevant legal standards in deciding whether electrocution is cruel and unusual punishment are whether the State's chosen method of execution (1) presents a substantial risk that a prisoner will suffer unnecessary and wanton pain in an execution, (2) violates the evolving standards of decency that mark a mature society, and (3) minimizes physical violence and mutilation of the prisoner's body. Having established the relevant legal standards, we turn to our standard of review.

Conclusion: Electrocution Is Cruel and Unusual Punishment

Besides presenting a substantial risk of unnecessary pain, we conclude that electrocution is unnecessarily cruel in its purposeless infliction of physical violence and mutilation of the prisoner's body. Electrocution's proven history of burning and charring bodies is inconsistent with both the concepts of evolving standards of decency and the dignity of man. Other states have recognized that early assumptions about an instantaneous and painless death were simply incorrect and that there are more humane methods of carrying out the death penalty. Examined under modern scientific knowledge, "[electrocution] has proven itself to be a dinosaur more befitting the laboratory of Baron Frankenstein than the death chamber" of state prisons. We conclude that death by electrocution violates the prohibition against cruel and unusual punishment in Neb. Const. art. I, § 9.

Sentence affirmed, and execution stayed.

Chief Justice Heavican, concurring in part, and dissenting in part:

I respectfully dissent from the majority's conclusion that electrocution—a means of execution used in America for well over a century—is no longer constitutional. I therefore write separately to not only voice my dissent from that conclusion, but also to express sincere reservations with several aspects of the analysis used to generate it.

Early in its analysis, the majority acknowledges that the U.S. Supreme Court has indicated electrocution is not cruel and unusual. Accordingly, the majority concedes that it has no authority to hold that electrocution violates the Eighth Amendment. But as it is this court's "duty to safeguard our state Constitution," the majority purports to resolve whether "electrocution is prohibited by the Nebraska Constitution's proscription against inflicting cruel and unusual punishment." After a lengthy analysis, the majority concludes that electrocution is, in fact, a violation of the Nebraska Constitution.

The concern, of course, is that we have long held that our constitution's cruel-and-unusual-punishment provision is no more stringent than is the Eighth Amendment to the federal Constitution. Thus, if the Nebraska Constitution does not require anything more than the federal Constitution regarding cruel and unusual punishment, and the U.S. Supreme Court has indicated that electrocution is not cruel and unusual under the federal Constitution, I cannot see how electrocution violates the Nebraska Constitution.

Conceivably, the majority could have reached its result by merely overruling the cases which established the similarity between the Nebraska and federal Constitutions. However, the majority's opinion lacks any such declaration. I trust that if the majority intended such a sweeping change in our constitutional doctrine, it would have done so explicitly.

Moreover, even if the majority had held that the Nebraska Constitution requires more than the federal Constitution, such a position would be difficult to defend. As the majority acknowledges, the cruel-and-unusual-punishment provision in article I, § 9, of the Nebraska Constitution contains the exact same language as that found in the Eighth Amendment. Both provisions provide that "[e]xcessive bail shall not be required, nor excessive fines imposed, nor cruel and unusual punishment[s] inflicted." Of course, it would be exceedingly difficult—and perhaps a touch disingenuous—to insist that identical language has two different meanings.

It should be indisputable that either the Nebraska Constitution is a mirror of the Eighth Amendment, in which case U.S. Supreme Court precedent is conclusive, or that the Nebraska Constitution requires more than the Eighth Amendment, in which case this court would not be bound by U.S. Supreme Court case law. By contradicting U.S. Supreme Court precedent and yet declining to say that article I, § 9, is any different than the Eighth Amendment, the majority has left us in a sort of constitutional limbo: Our state's constitutional limit on cruel and unusual punishment is not quite like the federal Constitution, yet not quite distinct from it either.

The confusion surrounding the majority's constitutional analysis is heightened when the majority relies on "federal precedent for guidance" on this issue. The numerous subsequent cites to federal case law confirm that the majority retained federal court approaches to this Eighth Amendment question, yet jettisoned the U.S. Supreme Court's ultimate answer. In other words, the majority relied upon those aspects of federal law that supported its conclusion and ignored the remainder that did not.

[T]he majority points out that Nebraska is the only state that mandates electrocution and that the U.S. Supreme Court will almost certainly not "accept an appeal on the issue from any other jurisdiction." As such, the majority feels an ultimate determination as to the constitutionality of electrocution "has fallen to this court."

These comments suggest the majority believes that by striking down electrocution under the Nebraska Constitution, it is doing what the modern U.S. Supreme Court would do under the Eighth Amendment if it, too, were "presented with evidence of a nature and quality that the Supreme Court never considered when it held electrocution was not cruel and unusual punishment." This would explain the majority's decision to resolve this case under article I, § 9, of the Nebraska Constitution—a move that obviates the need to defer to "antiquated" U.S. Supreme Court authority—yet nonetheless rely entirely on federal Eighth Amendment precedent.

Of course, if the majority were truly confident that it is not doing anything the U.S. Supreme Court itself would not do today, it would not have been necessary to draw the Nebraska Constitution into the question. Instead, the majority could have simply emphasized *In re Kemmler's* antiquity, highlighted the uniqueness of this factual record, and then expressed that it wished it could—but was unable to—reach a different result. This would have given the U.S. Supreme Court the opportunity to

(Continues)

grant certiorari and overrule precedent the majority believes is so clearly outdated. Instead, the majority chooses to essentially retain the Eighth Amendment's proscriptions but avoids the problem of having to overrule a U.S. Supreme Court decision by purporting to reach its result under the Nebraska Constitution.

While this approach may serve the majority's purpose, I believe it does so at the expense of clarity in our constitutional doctrine. Before today's decision, lower courts could rest with confidence on the belief that our constitution requires nothing more than the Eighth Amendment with regard to methods of punishment. By reaching a conclusion that contradicts U.S. Supreme Court precedent, this decision will give lower courts reason to question that belief. At a minimum, attorneys may exploit the ambiguity in today's decision in subsequent cases.

Given the majority's reliance on the Nebraska Constitution, there may be speculation that today's decision is immune from certiorari review. If true, the majority's decision would conclusively resolve the constitutionality of electrocution because, as the last state that mandates electrocution, the U.S. Supreme Court could only address the constitutionality of execution on an appeal from this court. For reasons set forth below, I am of the belief that today's decision is not immune from certiorari review despite the majority's references to the Nebraska Constitution.

It is well settled that the U.S. Supreme Court is precluded from hearing an appeal from a state's highest court where that court's decision was the product of state law—statutory or constitutional. This rule of independent and adequate state grounds reflects the principle that state courts are the final arbiters of their own laws. In such cases, it would be superfluous, and thus a violation of Article III's proscription against advisory opinions, for the Court to resolve any remaining federal issues. The question, however, is how to identify whether a state court's decision truly rests on independent and adequate state grounds. The Court addressed this very question in *Michigan v. Long*, 463 U.S. 1032, 103 S. Ct. 3469, 77 L.Ed.2d 1201 (1983).

At issue in *Long* was whether a police officer could conduct a protective search of the passenger compartment of an automobile that had been lawfully stopped. Citing its state constitution, the Fourth Amendment, and federal case law, the Michigan Supreme Court concluded that such a search was illegal. The U.S. Supreme Court granted certiorari. Before addressing the merits of the case, the respondent argued that the U.S. Supreme Court did not have jurisdiction to hear the case because the Michigan Supreme Court's decision was based on the Michigan Constitution and thus had an independent and adequate state ground.

In response to that argument, the U.S. Supreme Court announced that when a state court decision fairly appears to rest primarily on federal law, or to be interwoven with the federal law, and when the adequacy and independence of any possible state law ground is not clear from the face of the opinion, we will accept as the most reasonable explanation that the state court decided the case the way it did because it believed that federal law required it to do so. Id., 463 U.S. at 1040-41, 103 S. Ct. 3469.

Applying its rule to the case before it, the U.S. Supreme Court in *Long* concluded that the Michigan Supreme Court's decision did *not* rest on independent and adequate state grounds. The Court noted that "[a]part from its two citations to the State Constitution, the [Michigan Supreme Court] relied *exclusively* on its understanding of . . . federal cases." Moreover, the Court observed that "[n]ot a single state case was cited to support the state court's holding that the search of the passenger compartment was unconstitutional."

The same is true of the majority's opinion in this case. Although the majority refers to the Nebraska Constitution, it fails to cite to a single Nebraska case in support of its conclusion that electrocution is unconstitutional. The entirety of the majority's analysis is based on cites to federal case law. Indeed, the majority itself conceded that it "look[ed] to federal precedent for guidance" in deciding this issue. Under *Long*, such reliance suggests that the majority's decision is without an independent state ground.

The majority's assertion that "the Nebraska Constitution governs this issue" does not at all diminish this fact. First, the majority never declares that the Nebraska Constitution is more restrictive than the Eighth Amendment. But even if it had, that alone would almost certainly not have been enough to overcome the effect of the majority's reliance on federal case law in light of *Long*: "Even if we accept that the Michigan Constitution has been interpreted to provide independent protection for certain rights also secured under the Fourth Amendment, it fairly appears in this case that the Michigan Supreme Court rested its decision primarily on federal law." As a result, the majority's "references to the State Constitution in no way indicate that the decision below rested on grounds in any way *independent* from the state court's interpretation of federal law."

Having detailed several concerns with the majority's opinion, I come now to what I believe is its most troublesome aspect: reliance on so-called evolving standards of decency. It is true that electrocution has fallen into disfavor among American jurisdictions. Nebraska is the only jurisdiction that retains the electric chair as the sole method of execution and is one of a handful of states that uses the electric chair at all. Even so, it is not necessarily true that the movement away from electrocution has been uniformly precipitated by concerns regarding decency. It may be, for example, that states widely favor lethal injection over electrocution simply because lethal injection is a more practical method of terminating a life.

There is also reason to believe that "[t]he nationwide change to lethal injection was motivated at least as much by a desire to end the litigation over the previous methods [of execution] and the attendant delays as it was by the actual desire to abandon the old methods [themselves]." For example, there is evidence that the change from cyanide gas to lethal injection in California was prompted not by humanitarian concerns, but, rather, to avoid protracted and costly legal challenges to the use of cyanide gas by death row inmates. It is tempting to speculate that Florida's legislature may have been motivated by similar concerns when it changed from electrocution to lethal injection after the U.S. Supreme Court agreed to review the Florida Supreme Court decision upholding electrocution. But even if the trend away from electrocution could be explained solely on the basis of humanitarian concerns, I would still not be convinced that such a concern should factor into our constitutional analysis.

The most significant difficulty with a concern for contemporary standards is that it inherently tempts judges to inject their own subjective values into the constitutional analysis. The danger in such subjectivity is subtle but nonetheless potent. Judges do not sit as a body of elected representatives, as do legislatures. While this distinction provides a degree of independence necessary for judges to make the unpopular decisions that a neutral reading of the law sometimes compels, it also renders courts ill suited "to respond to the will and consequently the moral values of the people."

Although some may view the Constitution as an invitation to "our judges, to expand on the . . . freedoms that are uniquely our heritage," see, e.g., Laurence H. Tribe, God Save This Honorable Court 45 (1985), this view somewhat naively assumes that judges will always seek to "expand" rather than constrict liberties. If left free to supplant their own values on the cases before them, judges may just as easily seek to limit individual rights as expand them. This, of course, is to say nothing of the fact that a true expansion of rights is a practical impossibility. It is often the case that an expansion of rights for one group results in a loss of rights for others. In this way, subjective judicial decision making paves "a two-way street that handles traffic both to and from individual rights" (Antonin Scalia, Originalism: The Lesser Evil, 57 U.Cin.L.Rev. 849, 856 (1989)) and therefore presents a danger to any and all ideologies.

The majority downplays the concern that "a court's evaluation of contemporary values is subjective" by pointing out that the U.S. Supreme Court looks only "to objective criteria for this inquiry." However, one can argue that recent Supreme Court history confirms that even courts which initially intend to keep the inquiry into evolving standards truly objective will inevitably allow subjective value judgments to creep into the analysis.

There is also the possibility that concern for contemporary standards of decency will eventually lead courts to rely on foreign law. I agree that a legislature assessing the wisdom of a law might want to consider how business is done elsewhere. But a court's role is not to speculate on how a law might be written more effectively; its role is to assess what laws are forbidden by our constitutions. And yet all pretense of state or federal constitutional interpretation is lost the moment a judge looks to foreign law. [A] concern with contemporary standards of decency will inevitably lead to reliance on foreign law. After all, although our nation has a unique experience with constitutional interpretation, we have no monopoly on humanity.

Of course, it would be naive to assume that the influence of foreign law will always result in an "expansion" of personal liberties. For example, Justice Scalia has observed that reliance on foreign law would jeopardize the Fourth Amendment's exclusionary rule, abortion rights, and our nation's adherence to the separation of church and state. Therefore, the specter that judges will rely on foreign law when interpreting our state and federal Constitutions is a broad-based concern.

The final problem with drawing inferences from legislative responses to the death penalty is that such a practice fundamentally misunderstands the intent of constitutional prohibitions on cruel and unusual punishment. In concluding that electrocution is cruel and unusual, the majority points out

(*Continues*)

(*Continued*)

that virtually every other death penalty state now uses lethal injection as their primary, if not solitary, method of execution. According to the majority, the switch to lethal injection has come "'because it is universally recognized as the most humane method of execution.'"

However, as noted previously, the Eighth Amendment only prohibits governments from using cruel methods of punishment; it does not demand that they use the most humane methods. As such, it makes no sense to interpret that provision by looking to legislative enactments prompted by the desire to minimize cruelty. A legislative consensus that lethal injection is *more* humane than electrocution does not mean that electrocution is cruel in a more absolute sense. And yet, it seems to me that a more absolute definition of cruelty is, or at least should be, the concern under our constitutions.

The majority's alternative—a preoccupation with national consensus—is at once too lax and too strict in limiting methods of punishment. It is too lax because "[i]t reduces the function of the [E]ighth [A]mendment to bringing the occasionally deviant state into line with the rest." As Professor Chemerinsky observed, such an "approach would mean that horrible torture would be permitted under the Constitution so long as most states engaged in the practice." Erwin Chemerinsky, *The Vanishing Constitution*, 103 Harv. L. Rev. 43, 88 (1989).

The skin-patch hypothetical illustrates why reliance on contemporary standards of decency is too strict. To refresh, assume that a skin patch is developed which, when applied to an inmate's arm, executes a prisoner as quickly and painlessly as lethal injection. Assume further that only one state continues to use lethal injection and every other death penalty jurisdiction switches to the skin patch. Would such a shift render lethal injection cruel and unusual punishment? It would if "cruel and unusual" is defined according to contemporary standards. But it would be a stretch to say that simply having one's arm held down while attendants search for a vein and insert a needle is unconstitutionally "cruel."

For these reasons, I believe that evolving standards of decency, even when based solely on evidence of legislative action, are best left out of the constitutional analysis. As alluded to above, I believe it far more accurate to say that the Eighth Amendment and article I, § 9, were designed solely to protect against "deliberate indifference to an unreasonable risk of severe and prolonged pain in execution."

Regardless of the precise standard we use, hopefully the above has demonstrated that there is nothing to gain and much to lose by attempting to rely on contemporary standards of decency in assessing the constitutionality of a punishment. Of course, the U.S. Supreme Court's current case law forecloses us from construing the Eighth Amendment in line with these views. It does not, however, prevent us from refusing to make such an approach part and parcel of this state's constitution.

Because I sincerely believe this precedent will have adverse consequences in future cases, I respectfully dissent from the portion of the majority opinion that finds electrocution to be unconstitutional.

Standards of Review

How appellate courts reach their conclusions depends on the "standard of review" applied to the trial court's actions. The standard of review refers to the degree of deference an appellate court will give to a trial judge's decisions. The most deferential standard is called "abuse of discretion." It is used by an appellate court to test the sufficiency of the evidence presented at trial to support the trial court's judgment or when factual issues are presented for appeal that relate to the admission of evidence should have been allowed by the trial judge. Under this standard, the appellate court presumes that the trial court's factual determinations are correct; they will be set aside only if they are arbitrary, capricious, or have no reasonable justification. Generally, a trial court's decisions about the facts need to be supported by "substantial evidence," which means that the court's decisions cannot be contrary to what most of the evidence in a case would show. For example, in a bank robbery case, if the defendant was caught with currency on his person that had serial numbers matching those of money taken from the bank robbery and three witnesses identified the defendant as having

demanded money from the teller, it would be an abuse of discretion to exclude the money found on the defendant from evidence because to do so would be clearly inconsistent with the totality of the evidence.

The second standard is one used when the appellate court considers only whether a mistake of law was made by the trial court. This standard, referred to as "independent" or "*de novo*" review, examines decisions about the law made by the trial judge, giving no deference to conclusions of law that the trial judge reached. The appellate court reviews the legal issues in the case as if no decision about the law had been previously made by the lower court. It allows the appellate court to interpret the law and apply it to the facts of the case found in the record, giving no deference to the way in which the lower court interpreted and applied the law. For example, if a state statute prevents the admission of evidence relating to a rape victim's past sexual conduct and a trial judge were to allow testimony by one of the victim's former boyfriends, the appellate court would likely reverse the trial court's decision because it violates the requirements of the state statute.

Regardless of which appellate review standard applies, the appellate court must determine whether the mistake made in the court below is one of "harmless" error or one of "reversible" error. Harmless error is a mistake that does not result in prejudice or harm to the party asserting its existence. When harmless error occurs, the appellate court concludes that the outcome of the case would not have changed even if the error had not been made. Reversible error involves a mistake made in the lower court that requires a different outcome; that is, it is not harmless. When reversible error occurs that is so severe that the trial cannot be said to have been fair, it is referred to as "plain" or "fundamental" error. This type of error will result in reversal even if the error has not been raised by a party on appeal. For example, if a trial judge denied a criminal defendant the right to have counsel present at a hearing, plain error would result, requiring reversal of a subsequent conviction.

The Rule of Precedent

In Chapter 3, the rule of precedent was discussed as a method of judicial decision making in which lower courts must follow the holdings of higher courts. This allows for efficient decision-making because courts need not reinterpret the law in every way new case. It also creates consistency and growth in the law. Based on the concept of *stare decisis*, the rule of precedent thus requires state trial courts to apply interpretations of law made by all of the state's appellate courts, and intermediate appellate courts must follow the rulings of the state's court of last resort. This decision-making rule both provides order to the judicial hierarchy and accomplishes the goals of *stare decisis*.

Consistent with the rule of precedent, the courts of one state are not bound by interpretations of law made by the courts of another state. Because each state's laws and system of government are sovereign, they operate independently from other states, and the judicial hierarchy stops at the state's borders. Furthermore, when a state appellate court's decision involves the interpretation of state law, but not federal law, federal courts will also give precedential effect to that decision under the principle of federalism (Solimine & Walker, 1999). This includes the rule that the U.S. Supreme Court will not review the decision of a state's highest court unless that decision somehow involves or implicates federal law. Moreover, a state appellate court need not follow rulings made by the U.S. Supreme Court when a case it decides involves only state law.

The issue of when a state appellate court, particularly a state's court of last resort, must adhere to decisions of the U.S. Supreme Court is more troublesome, however. When a state court case involves an issue of federal law, the decision by the state court is reviewable by the U.S. Supreme Court, but it is not always clear whether a case involves an issue of federal law requiring the state court to abide by Supreme Court precedent. The court has stated that if a state court decision rests on "adequate and independent state law grounds," the Supreme Court will decline to review it. The Court in *Michigan v. Long*, 463 U.S. 1032,

103 S. Ct. 3469, 77 L.Ed.2d 1201 (1983) discussed the purpose for this rule:

> Respect for the independence of state courts, as well as avoidance of rendering advisory opinions, have been the cornerstones of this Court's refusal to decide cases where there is an adequate and independent state ground. It is precisely because of this for state courts, and this desire to avoid advisory opinions, that we do not wish to continue to decide issues of state law that go beyond the opinion that we review, or to require state courts to reconsider cases to clarify the grounds of their decisions. Accordingly, when, as in this case, a state court decision fairly appears to rest primarily on federal law, or to be interwoven with the federal law, and then the adequacy and independence of any possible state law ground is not clear from the face of the opinion, we will accept as the most reasonable explanation that the state court decided the case the way it did because it believed that federal law required it to do so. If a state court chooses merely to rely on federal precedents as it would on the precedents of all other jurisdictions, then it need only make clear by a plain statement in its judgment or opinion that the federal cases are being used only for the purpose of guidance, and do not themselves compel the result that the court has reached. In this way, both justice and judicial administration will be greatly improved. If the state court decision indicates clearly and expressly that it is alternatively based on bona fide separate, adequate, and independent grounds, we, of course, will not undertake to review the decision. (*Id.* at 1040–41, 103 S. Ct. at 3476, 77 L.Ed.2d at 1208.)

Thus, when a state court relies on state law for its decision, it is not subject to review by the U.S. Supreme Court. This has led state courts and state court litigants to rely more heavily on their state constitutions when seeking to find legal justification for individual rights that will not be subject to Supreme Court review. Sometimes referred to as "new judicial federalism," this reliance on state, rather than federal, constitutional law allows states to adopt social policies stemming from individual rights that will apply without federal "interference" within their borders (Solimine & Walker, 1999; Friesen, 1997). An example of this is the interpretation of state constitutional provisions by state courts of last resort finding a right to marry by homosexuals (see, e.g., *Kerrigan v. Commissioner of Public Health*, 389 Conn. 135, 957 A.2d 407 (2008); *Goodridge v. Dept. of Public Health*, 440 Mass. 309, 798 N.E.2d 941 (2003)).

The reliance on a state constitution to address a social issue was also addressed in *State v. Mata*, 275 Neb. 1, 745 N.W.2d 229 (2008). In that case, the Nebraska Supreme Court found that state's constitution prevented the imposition of the death penalty by electrocution. The court, in accordance with the "adequate and independent state grounds" test articulated in *Long*, specifically stated that it was deciding the case under the Nebraska Constitution, not the federal constitution.

The *Mata* court indicated that it could not overrule precedent by the U.S. Supreme Court relating to electrocution, claiming "we will decide the issue under the Nebraska Constitution." As Chief Justice Heavican pointed out in dissent, however, it is not always easy to determine whether a state court's decision rests on adequate and independent state grounds. Despite the *Mata* court's statement that it was interpreting the Nebraska Constitution, it relied solely on federal cases in determining its meaning. Although the U.S. Supreme Court declined to review the Nebraska Supreme Court's decision, the standards to be used in determining when such review is appropriate are less than clear.

Appellate Court Outcomes

Decisions made by courts of last resort, as well as all appellate courts, result in one of four outcomes: (1) signed opinions, (2) *per curiam* opinions, (3) memorandum opinions, and (4) orders. Which of these mechanisms is used by the appellate court to dispose of a case is determined by either the significance of the legal issues presented or the procedural posture that brought the case to the court in the first place, including whether a right to appeal exists or whether it is mandatory or discretionary with the court.

Signed opinions of the court are full opinions written by one judge and with which a majority of the members of the court "join," or agree, with the conclusion. A signed opinion explains the facts on which the decision is based, the legal issues decided, and the reasoning used to reach the decision. Thus, these are decisions that are reached "on the merits," which means that the court considers the full record of proceedings with the facts found by the court below, analyzes the applicable law as it applied to the facts and proceedings of the case, and reached a decision on the basis of these. A signed decision has precedential effect, which means that the legal principles it decides govern future cases and must be adhered to by lower courts.

Per curiam ("by the court") opinions are written opinions that are anonymous decisions that reflect the view of the court regarding the appropriate disposition of a case. They are usually, but not always, shorter explanations of the law and legal conclusions reached in a case. A *per curiam* opinion does not have an identified author and therefore is unsigned. Nonetheless, it carries the weight of law in deciding a case, explains the rationale and legal basis for the decision, and has precedential effect. It is not altogether clear what reasons will lead a court to resort to a *per curiam* opinion (Ray, 2002). It may be the sensitive nature of the subject matter or the application of well-established law to a case.

A memorandum decision is an opinion that sets out the court's decision with little or no rationale. It is typically used in cases in which appeal is a matter of right, but the law and the conclusion governing the case are clear. A memorandum will therefore usually cite the legal precedents or other law on which the decision is based and succinctly state the outcome in the case.

An order is a short directive as to the outcome in a case. Sometimes referred to as a "summary" disposition, it has the effect of finality just as a signed opinion, *per curiam* decision, or memorandum, but states only the court's decision with no explanation of the basis for the decision. By a simple order such as this, the court may announce its decision to affirm or reverse the court below, but more commonly it is used to dismiss an appeal (and thereby end a case), or it may "vacate," or declare void, a prior decision made by itself or the court below. By use of an order, a court may also transfer a case to another court based on jurisdiction or venue or to remand a case for further findings.

Key Terms

State Court Structure	Abuse of Discretion
Limited Jurisdiction	Substantial Evidence
General Jurisdiction	*De Novo* Review
Court of Last Resort	Harmless Error
Intermediate Appellate Court	Reversible Error
Unified Court System	Adequate and Independent
Nonpartisan Judicial	State Grounds
Elections	Signed Opinion
Advice and Consent	*Per Curiam* Opinion
Merit Selection	Memorandum Opinion
Standard of Review	Summary Disposition

Discussion Questions

1. How does the jurisdiction of state courts differ from that of federal courts?
2. In what ways have state courts in the United States evolved since the founding of the country?
3. What types of original jurisdiction do state courts possess?
4. What kinds of cases may a state's court of last resort hear? What is the nature of the decisions it may make?
5. How are courts of general jurisdiction different from courts of limited jurisdiction?
6. What is a unified court system and what are its benefits?
7. What are the ways in which a state court judge may assume office?

Cases

Goodridge v. Dept. of Public Health, 440 Mass. 309, 798 N.E.2d 941 (2003).
In Re Vincent, 143 N.M. 56, 172 P.3d 605 (2007).
Kerrigan v. Commissioner of Public Health, 389 Conn. 135, 957 A.2d 407 (2008).
Michigan v. Long, 463 U.S. 1032, 103 S. Ct. 3469, 77 L.Ed.2d 1201 (1983).
Republican Party of Minnesota v. White, 536 U.S. 765, 122 S. Ct. 2528, 153 L.Ed.2d 694 (2002).
State v. Mata, 275 Neb. 1, 745 N.W.2d 229 (2008).

Criminal Justice on the Web

 For an up-to-date list of Web links, go to *The American Courts: A Procedural Approach* online companion site at http://criminal justice.jbpub.com/AmericanCourts. The online companion site will introduce you to some of the most important sites for finding American courts information on the Internet.

References

Benesh, S. C., & Martinek, W. L. (2002). State supreme court decision making in confession cases. *Justice System Journal, 23,* 109–129.

Friesen, J. (1997). State courts as sources of constitutional law: How to become independently wealthy. *Notre Dame Law Review, 72,* 1065–1085.

Glick, H. R., & Emmert, C. (1987). Selection systems and judicial characteristics: The recruitment of state supreme court justices. *Judicature, 70,* 228–248.

Hall, M. G. (2001). State supreme courts in American democracy: Probing the myths of judicial reform. *American Political Science Review, 95,* 315–335.

LaFountain, R. C., Schauffler, R. Y., Strickland, S. M., Raftery, W. E., & Bromage, C. G. (Eds.). (2006). *Examining the Work of State Courts, 2005.* Williamsburg, VA: National Center for State Courts.

Ray, L. K. (2002). The history of the per curiam opinion: Consensus and individual expression on the Supreme Court. *Journal of Supreme Court History, 27,* 176–193.

Segal, J. A., Spaeth, H. J., & Benesh, S. C. (2005). *The Supreme Court in the American Legal System.* New York: Cambridge University Press.

Solimine, M. E., & Walker, J. L. (1999). *Respecting State Courts: The Inevitability of Judicial Federalism.* Westport, CT: Greenwood Press.

Strickland, S. M., Bromage, C. G., Gibson, S. A., & Raftery, W. E. (2008). *State Court Caseload Statistics, 2007.* Williamsburg, VA: National Center for State Courts.

Participants at Court

6

What Is This Chapter About?

This chapter identifies the individuals who participate in the courts. This includes the parties who initiate court action and have something at stake in the proceeding, the attorneys who represent them, and the judges and juries who serve as decision makers.

In criminal cases, the parties are the state and the criminal defendant alleged to have violated the law. We consider whether the state adequately represents the interests of society in criminal cases and examine what interests the state seeks to vindicate. This chapter also addresses the importance of procedural protections for criminal defendants. The role of the prosecutor and the line between prosecutorial discretion and prosecutorial misconduct is explored, as well as the function and goals of the criminal defense attorney. In addition, the role of judges and the deliberations of juries are examined.

In civil cases, private individuals use the courts to resolve disputes. These individuals may be ordinary people, but most often they are corporations or other business entities and governmental agencies or officials. This chapter explores whether the court system, as a public institution, best serves the public by adjudicating such cases. In this chapter, we outline the various roles that attorneys play in civil cases, and we also differentiate the roles of judge and jury in civil cases from those in criminal cases.

Learning Objectives

After reading this chapter, you should be able to

1. Identify the court participants in civil and criminal cases.
2. Describe the goals and activities of each of the individuals who participate in court.
3. Explain the relationship between prosecutorial discretion and misconduct.
4. Understand the role of the jury as distinct from that of the judge.
5. Describe the importance of procedural protections for criminal defendants.
6. Identify the various roles that attorneys may play in civil cases.

Most courthouses are busy places. On weekdays, people mill around the place—lawyers and business people in suits, police officers in uniform, criminal defendants in prison garb with arm or leg restraints, others wearing the only clothes they own. Some look comfortable in the building, having been there often. Some look fearful and uncertain about what will happen next. Others look confused about where they are or why they are there, whereas others are overwhelmed with their situation, as it is explained to them by a lawyer, judge, or social worker. Most are carrying papers, folders, boxes, or briefcases full of documents. Some line the halls, talking on cell phones loudly, angrily, or in hushed tones. Some have children in tow. Some have smiles. Some look and act distraught, and others move efficiently about the place from office to office, courtroom to courtroom.

Who are all of these people? Why are they here? What business does each have in America's courts? What brings people from every economic status, social background, racial or ethnic group, or geographic area together? The courts are places where the reality of justice (and sometimes injustice) occurs. They are places where the problems of living in a modern society involving crime, property, money, relationships, agreements, and disagreements are resolved, sometimes in satisfactory ways and sometimes in less than satisfactory ways. Those who participate in the courts on a daily basis play a vital role in defining that system of justice. Beginning with the parties who seek adjudication in the court, this section explores not only who these individuals are (judges, juries, attorneys, court staff), but the procedural aspects of their roles.

The Participants in Criminal Cases

The Parties

Because criminal cases involve claims that a person has engaged in antisocial behavior, the parties in a criminal case are society (variously termed the "people," the "state," the "government") and an individual person accused of violating the criminal law. In some criminal cases, multiple defendants may have their cases consolidated and tried together for the same crime, but most often, the criminal justice system prosecutes and punishes wrongdoers one at a time. Therefore, the individual person brought to court to face criminal charges does so alone; society seeks to hold the person accountable for his or her own actions.

The government, acting on behalf of society, is a powerful opposing party in criminal cases. The full force of society's criminal laws and criminal justice system confronts the defendant. In addition, the investigative powers of the law enforcement agencies, the considerable discretion granted to prosecutors, and the judicial power to impose punishments all work to vindicate the people's interest in an orderly society. The result is that the defendant faces a formidable foe.

The defendant is not left to battle alone unaided, however. State and federal constitutional guarantees provide procedural tools to assist the defendant in leveling the playing field. The right to counsel, due process, and the exclusionary rule, among others (all discussed in Chapter 10), are designed to protect the defendant against government overreaching and ensure a fair process.

The Prosecutor

In criminal cases, society itself has an interest in preventing crime and therefore does not wish wrongdoers to go unpunished. The job of the prosecutor, as an agent of the executive branch of government, is to represent society's interest by seeking to have the defendant punished for behavior that violates society's norms as reflected in its laws. Criminal cases are therefore prosecuted on behalf of the citizens of a state (or the United States) with a designation such as "*State v.* _____" or "*People v.* _____."

Prosecutors are granted broad powers to carry out justice. As attorneys, they zealously advocate on behalf of society, yet also have a duty to the criminal justice system in which they operate to do what is fair and in the interest of justice. They play a central role in the investigation and resolution of criminal cases by working with all of those involved in the criminal justice systems: police officers, defendants and their counsel, judges, juries, victims, probation officers, social workers, corrections officials, and others. In the exercise of their powers, prosecutors have considerable discretion. Within the procedural framework of the court system, they are authorized to determine the manner in which cases will be presented to the court. Specifically, this means that prosecutors decide whether a defendant will be prosecuted and what the charges will be, how and what evidence will be presented, and what sentencing recommendations to make on conviction.

Prosecutors operate at the federal, state, or local levels. Each state has at least one federal prosecutor, called the U.S. Attorney, whose job is to prosecute violations of federal criminal law, as well as other duties such as defending lawsuits brought against the federal government in that state. U.S. Attorneys are appointed by the President with the "advice and consent" of the Senate and operate as part of the Department of Justice under its head, the Attorney General of the United States. In most states, the Attorney General of the state is the chief law enforcement

officer and, along with his or her assistants (usually called assistant attorneys general or state's attorneys), has responsibility for prosecution of crime. In addition, prosecutors at the county or local levels, usually called district attorneys, handle the majority of criminal cases in their states. State and local prosecutors may be elected or appointed, and their positions may be full-time or part-time, depending on the size of and extent of crime within a community.

Regardless of the level at which a prosecutor may function (federal, state, or local), the prosecutor's role is similar. The primary functions of a prosecutor are to investigate whether the facts support a violation of the criminal law, to decide whether to charge a person with a crime, to decide what crime to charge, and to prepare a criminal case for trial. In cities or larger metropolitan areas, the prosecutor's office may operate like a large law firm, with numerous assistant prosecutors who handle the majority of cases that come through the office. It is not unusual for such offices to have several divisions that focus on particular types of cases, such as separate divisions for misdemeanors, felonies, juvenile cases, or financial crimes. In less populated areas, a single prosecutor may be responsible for all criminal matters, operating much like a sole practitioner in private practice, but no matter the setting, the prosecutor is a public servant who seeks justice when violations of criminal law occur.

Thus, generally speaking, it is the duty of a prosecutor to enforce the criminal law. This means that he or she must see that those who violate the criminal law are punished, without regard to the characteristics or social standing of the individual charged. In doing so, however, it is also the duty of the prosecutor to proceed in a manner that is fair to both criminal defendant and the interests of society. Like all attorneys, the prosecutor is an officer of the court and is bound to work in the interests of justice. That does not mean that he or she cannot argue against the positions of a criminal defendant or forcefully advocate on behalf of the government but that this must be done in an ethical way consistent with the rules of court and principles of the adversary system. In addition, a prosecutor has a duty to the citizens he or she serves or, more generally, the society that has granted the prosecutorial power. This means that the harm caused to victims and their interests should be taken into account, and punishment should be sought that satisfies the societal goals of seeking recompense for victims and deterring future crime.

Because prosecutors are either appointed by elected leaders or are themselves elected, the position of prosecutor is clearly a political one. In an ideal world, a prosecutor would not allow his or her personal views or political ambitions to affect the "people's business" of prosecuting crime; however, given the discretion that prosecutors are allowed, it is possible for them to be swayed in their decision making as a result of public pressures or political issues. In practice, then, prosecutors are usually quite sensitive to public sentiment and sometimes pursue cases in which weak evidence exists or fail to pursue vigorously strong cases in which political pressure favoring a defendant is brought to bear. Voter constituencies and special interest groups are examples of political influences that may influence prosecutorial conduct. Thus, prosecutors are sometimes faced with an ethical dilemma—should prosecutions occur without regard to the political environment in which the prosecutor operates, or should politics be one of the factors considered in deciding to prosecute or how to prosecute alleged crime?

Given the political pressures that prosecutors sometimes face, there are times when prosecutors abuse their discretion, forgetting their duty to serve justice by following the siren call of overly zealous advocacy in the desire to "win" at all costs. An example of such a prosecutor is Mike Nifong, discussed in Chapter 1, who wrongfully prosecuted three lacrosse players at Duke University. As a result, he was disbarred from the practice of law and forced to resign as District Attorney. The order of disbarment from the disciplinary committee is excerpted in **Case Decision 6.1.**

Case Decision 6.1 *State Bar of North Carolina v. Nifong,* Disciplinary Hearing Commission Order

STATE OF NORTH CAROLINA WAKE COUNTY	BEFORE THE DISCIPLINARY HEARING COMMISSION OF THE NORTH CAROLINA STATE BAR
THE NORTH CAROLINA STATE BAR,	06 DHC 35
Plaintiff,	
v.	
MICHAEL B. NIFONG, Attorney,	AMENDED FINDINGS OF FACT, CONCLUSIONS OF LAW AND ORDER OF DISCIPLINE
Defendant.	

A hearing in this matter was conducted on June 12 through June 16, 2007, before a Hearing Committee composed of F. Lane Williamson, Chair, and members Sharon B. Alexander and R. Mitchel Tyler. Plaintiff, the North Carolina State Bar, was represented by Katherine E. Jean, Douglas 1. Brocker, and Carmen K. Hoyme. Defendant, Michael B. Nifong, was represented by attorneys David B. Freedman and Dudley A. Witt. Based upon the admissions contained in the pleadings and upon the evidence presented at the hearing, this Hearing Committee makes, by clear, cogent and convincing evidence, the following

Findings of Fact

1. Plaintiff, the North Carolina State Bar, is a body duly organized under the laws of North Carolina and is the proper party to bring this proceeding under the authority granted it in Chapter 84 of the General Statutes of North Carolina, and the Rules and Regulations of the North Carolina State Bar (Chapter 1 of Title 27 of the North Carolina Administrative Code).

2. Defendant, Michael B. Nifong (hereinafter "Nifong"), was admitted to the North Carolina State Bar on August 19, 1978, and is, and was at all times referred to herein, an attorney at law licensed to practice in North Carolina, subject to the laws of the State of North Carolina, the Rules and Regulations of the North Carolina State Bar and the Revised Rules of Professional Conduct.

3. During all times relevant to this complaint, Nifong actively engaged in the practice of law in the State of North Carolina as District Attorney for the Fourteenth Prosecutorial District in Durham County, North Carolina.

4. Nifong was appointed District Attorney in 2005. In late March 2006, Nifong was engaged in a highly contested political campaign to retain his office.

(Continues)

(Continued)

5. In the early morning hours of March 14, 2006, an exotic dancer named Crystal Mangum reported that she had been raped by three men during a party at 610 North Buchanan Boulevard in Durham. Ms. Mangum asserted that she had been vaginally, rectally, and orally penetrated with no condom used during the assault and with at least some of the alleged perpetrators ejaculating.

6. Various pieces of evidence were collected for later DNA testing, including evidence commonly referred to as a "rape kit," which contained cheek scrapings, oral, vaginal, and rectal swabs, a pubic hair combing, and a pair of Ms. Mangum's underwear.

7. The Durham Police Department (DPD) initiated an investigation in what would come to be known as "the Duke Lacrosse case" and executed a search warrant on the house at 610 North Buchanan Boulevard on March 16, 2006. The investigation revealed that the residents of 610 North Buchanan were captains of the Duke University lacrosse team, and that a majority of the other attendees at the March 13, 2006, party were members of the team.

8. On March 16, 2006, the three residents of 610 North Buchanan voluntarily assisted DPD in executing a search warrant at their residence. During the search, numerous pieces of evidence were seized for later testing. The three residents also provided voluntary statements and voluntarily submitted DNA samples for comparison testing purposes. One of the three residents was David Evans, who was later indicted for the alleged attack on Ms. Mangum.

9. On March 22, 2006, Nifong's office assisted a DPD investigator in obtaining a Nontestimonial Identification Order (NTO) to compel the suspects in the case to be photographed and to provide DNA samples.

10. On March 23, 2006, DNA samples from all 46 Caucasian members of the Duke University 2006 Men's Lacrosse Team were obtained pursuant to the NTO.

11. When Nifong learned of the case on March 24, 2006, he immediately recognized that the case would garner significant media attention and decided to handle the case himself, rather than having it handled by the assistant district attorney in his office who would ordinarily handle such cases.

12. On March 24, 2006, Nifong informed DPD that he was assuming primary responsibility for prosecuting any criminal charges resulting from the investigation and directed the DPD to go through him for direction as to the conduct of the factual investigation of those matters.

13. On March 27, 2006, the rape kit items and DNA samples from the lacrosse players were delivered to the State Bureau of Investigation (SBI) lab for testing and examination, including DNA testing.

14. On March 27, 2006, Nifong was briefed by Sergeant Gottlieb and Investigator Himan of the DPD about the status of the investigation to date. Gottlieb and Himan discussed with Nifong a number of weaknesses in the case, including that Ms. Mangum had made inconsistent statements to the police and had changed her story several times, that the other dancer who was present at the party during the alleged attack disputed Ms. Mangum's story of an alleged assault, that Ms. Mangum had already viewed two photo arrays and had not identified any alleged attackers, and that the three team captains had voluntarily cooperated with police and had denied that the alleged attack occurred.

15. During or within a few days of the initial briefing by Gottlieb and Himan, Nifong acknowledged to Gottlieb and Himan that the Duke Lacrosse case would be a very hard case to win in court and said "you know, we're fucked."

16. Beginning on March 27, within hours after he received the initial briefing from Gottlieb and Himan, Nifong made public comments and statements to representatives of the news media about the Duke Lacrosse case and participated in interviews with various newspapers and television stations and other representatives of news media.

17. Between March 27 and March 31, Nifong stated to a reporter for WRAL TV news that lacrosse team members denied the rape accusations, that team members admitted that there was underage drinking at the party, and that otherwise team members were not cooperating with authorities.

18. Between March 27 and March 31, 2006, Nifong stated to a reporter for ABC 11 TV News that he might also consider charging other players for not coming forward with information, stating "[m]y guess is that some of this stonewall of silence that we have seen may tend to crumble once charges start to come out."

19. Between March 27 and March 31, 2006, Nifong stated to a reporter for the *New York Times*, "There are three people who went into the bathroom with the young lady, and whether the other people there knew what was going on at the time, they do now and have not come forward. I'm disappointed that no one has been enough of a man to come forward. And if they would have spoken up at the time, this may never have happened."

20. Between March 27 and March 31, 2006, Nifong stated to a reporter for NBC 17 News that the lacrosse team members were standing together and refusing to talk with investigators and that he might bring aiding-and-abetting charges against some of the players who were not cooperating with the investigation.

21. Between March 27 and March 31, 2006, Nifong stated to a reporter for the *Durham Herald Sun* newspaper that lacrosse players still refused to speak with investigators.

22. Between March 27 and March 31, 2006, Nifong made the following statements to Rene Syler of CBS News: "The lacrosse team, clearly, has not been fully cooperative" in the investigation; "The university, I believe, has done pretty much everything that they can under the circumstances. They, obviously, don't have a lot of control over whether or not the lacrosse team members actually speak to the police. I think that their silence is as a result of advice with counsel"; "If it's not the way it's been reported, then why are they so unwilling to tell us what, in their words, did take place that night?"; that he believed a crime occurred; that "the guilty will stand trial"; and "There's no doubt a sexual assault took place."

23. Between March 27 and March 31, 2006, Nifong made the following statements to a reporter for NBC 17 TV News: "The information that I have does lead me to conclude that a rape did occur"; "I'm making a statement to the Durham community and, as a citizen of Durham, am making a statement for the Durham community. This is not the kind of activity we condone, and it must be dealt with quickly and harshly"; "The circumstances of the rape indicated a deep racial motivation for some of the things that were done. It makes a crime that is by its nature one of the most offensive and invasive even more so"; and "This is not a case of people drinking and it getting out of hand from that. This is something much, much beyond that."

24. Between March 27 and March 31, 2006, Nifong stated to a reporter for ESPN, "And one would wonder why one needs an attorney if one was not charged and had not done anything wrong."

25. Between March 27 and March 31, 2006, Nifong stated to a reporter for CBS News that "the investigation at that time was certainly consistent with a sexual assault having taken place, as was the victim's demeanor at the time of the examination."

26. Between March 27 and March 31, 2006, Nifong made the following statements to a reporter for MSNBC: "There is evidence of trauma in the victim's vaginal area that was noted when she was examined by a nurse at the hospital"; "her general demeanor was suggested—suggestive of the fact that she had been through a traumatic situation"; "I am convinced there was a rape, yes, sir"; and "The circumstances of the case are not suggestive of the alternate explanation that has been suggested by some of the members of the situation."

27. Between March 27 and March 31, 2006, Nifong stated to a reporter for the *Raleigh News and Observer* newspaper, "I am satisfied that she was sexually assaulted at this residence."

28. Between March 27 and March 31, 2006, Nifong stated to a reporter for the *USA Today* newspaper, "Somebody's wrong about that sexual assault. Either I'm wrong, or they're not telling the truth about it."

29. Between March 27 and March 31, 2006, Nifong made the following statements to a reporter for ABC 11 TV News: "I don't think you can classify anything about what went on as a prank that got out of hand or drinking that took place by people who are underage"; "In this case, where you have the act of rape—essentially a gang rape—is bad enough in and of itself, but when it's made with racial epithets against the victim, I mean, it's just absolutely unconscionable"; and "The contempt that was shown for the victim, based on her race was totally abhorrent. It adds another layer of reprehensibleness, to a crime that is already reprehensible."

30. Between March 27 and March 31, 2006, Nifong stated to a reporter for ABC News, "It is a case that talks about what this community stands for."

31. Between March 27 and March 31, 2006, Nifong stated to a reporter for the New York Times, "The thing that most of us found so abhorrent, and the reason I decided to take it over myself, was the combination gang-like rape activity accompanied by the racial slurs and general racial hostility."

32. Between March 27 and March 31, 2006, Nifong stated to a reporter for CBS News, "The racial slurs involved are relevant to show the mindset . . . involved in this particular attack" and "obviously, it made what is already an extremely reprehensible act even more reprehensible."

33. Between March 27 and March 31, 2006, Nifong stated to a reporter for WRAL TV News, "What happened here was one of the worst things that's happened since I have become district attorney" and

(Continues)

(*Continued*)

"[w]hen I look at what happened, I was appalled. I think that most people in this community are appalled."

34. On or after March 27, 2006, Nifong stated to a reporter for the *Charlotte Observer* newspaper, "I would not be surprised if condoms were used. Probably an exotic dancer would not be your first choice for unprotected sex."

35. On or about March 29, 2006, Nifong stated during an interview with a reporter for CNN that "[i]t just seems like a shame that they are not willing to violate this seeming sacred sense of loyalty to team for loyalty to community."

36. On March 30, 2006, the SBI notified Nifong that the SBI had examined the items from the rape kit and was unable to find any semen, blood, or saliva on any of those items.

37. On March 31, 2006, Nifong stated to a reporter for MSNBC, "Somebody had an arm around her like this, which she then had to struggle with in order to be able to breathe. . . . She was struggling just to be able to breathe" and "[i]f a condom were used, then we might expect that there would not be any DNA evidence recovered from say a vaginal swab."

38. In March or April, 2006, Nifong stated to a representative of the news media that a rape examination of Ms. Mangum done at Duke Medical Center the morning of the alleged attack revealed evidence of bruising consistent with a brutal sexual assault, "with the most likely place it happened at the lacrosse team party."

39. In April 2006, Nifong stated to a reporter for *Newsweek Magazine* that the police took Ms. Mangum to a hospital where a nurse concluded that she had suffered injuries consistent with a sexual assault.

40. In April 2006, Nifong stated to a reporter for the *Raleigh News and Observer* newspaper, "I would like to think that somebody [not involved in the attack] has the human decency to call up and say, 'What am I doing covering up for a bunch of hooligans?' "

41. In April 2006, Nifong stated to a reporter, "They don't want to admit to the enormity of what they have done."

42. In an April 2006 conversation with a representative of the *Raleigh News and Observer* newspaper, Nifong compared the alleged rape to the quadruple homicide at Alpine Road Townhouse and multiple cross burnings that outraged the city of Durham in 2005 and stated "I'm not going to let Durham's view in the minds of the world to be a bunch of lacrosse players from Duke raping a black girl in Durham."

43. On April 4, 2006, DPD conducted a photographic identification procedure in which photographs of 46 members of the Duke Lacrosse team were shown to Ms. Mangum. Ms. Mangum was told at the beginning of the procedure that DPD had reason to believe all 46 of the men depicted in the photographs she would view were present at the party at which she contended the attack had occurred. The procedure followed in this photographic identification procedure was conceived and/or approved by Nifong. During the photographic identification procedure, Ms. Mangum identified Collin Finnerty and Reade Seligman as her attackers with "100% certainty" and identified David Evans as one of her attackers with "90% certainty." Ms. Mangum had previously viewed photographic identification procedures which included photographs of Reade Seligman and David Evans and not identified either of them in the prior procedures.

44. On April 5, 2006, Nifong's office sought and obtained an Order permitting transfer of the rape kit items from the SBI to a private company called DNA Security, Inc. ("DSI") for more sensitive DNA testing than the SBI could perform. The reference DNA specimens obtained from the lacrosse players pursuant to the NTO were also transferred to DSI for testing, as were reference specimens from several other individuals with whom Ms. Mangum acknowledged having consensual sexual relations, including her boyfriend.

45. As justification for its Order permitting transfer of the evidence to DSI, the Court noted that the additional testing Nifong's office sought in its petition was "believed to be material and relevant to this investigation, and that any male cells found among the victim's swabs from the rape kit can be evidence of an assault and may lead to the identification of the perpetrator."

46. Between April 7 and April 10, 2006, DSI performed testing and analysis of DNA found on the rape kit items. Between April 7 and April 10, DSI found DNA from up to four different males on several items of evidence from the rape kit and found that the male DNA on the rape kit items was inconsistent with the profiles of the lacrosse team members.

47. During a meeting on April 10, 2006 among Nifong, two DPD officers and Dr. Brian Meehan, lab director for DSI, Dr. Meehan discussed with Nifong the results of the analyses performed by DSI to that point and explained that DSI had found DNA from up to four different males on several items of evidence from the rape kit and that the DNA on the rape kit items was inconsistent with the profiles of all lacrosse team members.

48. The evidence and information referred to above in paragraphs 46 and 47 was evidence or information which tended to negate the guilt of the lacrosse team members identified as suspects in the NTO.

49. After the April 10, 2006 meeting with Dr. Meehan, Nifong stated to a reporter for ABC 11 TV News that DNA testing other than that performed by the SBI had not yet come back and that there was other evidence, including the accuser being able to identify at least one of the alleged attackers.

50. While discussing DNA testing at a public forum at North Carolina Central University on April 11, 2006, in the presence of representatives of the news media, Nifong stated that if there was no DNA found "[i]t doesn't mean nothing happened. It just means nothing was left behind."

51. On April 17, 2006, Nifong sought and obtained indictments against Collin Finnerty and Reade Seligman for first-degree rape, first-degree sex offense, and kidnapping. (The indicted members of the Duke lacrosse team are referred to collectively herein as "the Duke Defendants").

52. Before April 17, 2006, Nifong refused offers from counsel for David Evans, who was eventually indicted, to consider evidence and information that they contended either provided an alibi or otherwise demonstrated that their client did not commit any crime.

53. On April 19, 2006, two days after being indicted, Duke Defendant Reade Seligman through counsel served Nifong with a request or motion for discovery material, including, *inter alia*, witness statements, the results of any tests, all DNA analysis, and any exculpatory information.

54. By April 20, 2006, DSI had performed additional DNA testing and analysis and found DNA from multiple males on at least one additional piece of evidence from the rape kit.

55. By April 20, 2006, from its testing and analysis, DSI had determined that all the lacrosse players, including the two who had already been indicted, were scientifically excluded as possible contributors of the DNA from multiple males found on several evidence items from the rape kit.

56. On April 21, 2006, Nifong again met with Dr. Meehan and the two DPD officers to discuss all of the results of the DNA testing and analyses performed by DSI to date. During this meeting, Dr. Meehan told Nifong that: (a) DNA from multiple males had been found on several items from the rape kit, and (b) all of the lacrosse players, including the two players against whom Nifong had already sought and obtained indictments, were excluded as possible contributors of this DNA because none of their DNA profiles matched or were consistent with any of the DNA found on the rape kit items.

57. The evidence and information referred to above in paragraphs 54 through 56 was evidence or information which tended to negate the guilt of the Duke Defendants.

58. At the April 21 meeting, Dr. Meehan told Nifong that DSI's testing had revealed DNA on two fingernail specimens that were incomplete but were consistent with the DNA profiles of two unindicted lacrosse players, including DNA on a fingernail found in David Evans' garbage can which was incomplete but which was consistent with David Evans' DNA profile, and DNA from the vaginal swab that was consistent with the DNA profile of Ms. Mangum's boyfriend.

59. During the April 21, 2006 meeting, Nifong notified Dr. Meehan that he would require a written report to be produced concerning DSI's testing that reflected the matches found between DNA on evidence items and known reference specimens. Nifong told Dr. Meehan he would let Dr. Meehan know when he needed the report.

60. Sometime between April 21 and May 12, Nifong notified Dr. Meehan that he would need for him to prepare the written report for an upcoming court proceeding. As requested by Nifong, Dr. Meehan prepared a report that reflected the matches found by DSI between DNA found on evidence items and known reference specimens. This written report did not reflect that DSI had found DNA on rape kit items from multiple males who had not provided reference specimens for comparison ("multiple unidentified males") and did not reflect that all 46 members of the lacrosse team had been scientifically excluded as possible contributors of the male DNA on the rape kit items.

61. In May, 2006, Nifong made the following statements to a reporter for WRAL TV News: "My guess is that there are many questions that many people are asking that they would not be asking if

(Continues)

they saw the results"; "They're not things that the defense releases unless they unquestionably support their positions"; and "So, the fact that they're making statements about what the reports are saying, and not actually showing the reports, should in and of itself raise some red flags."

62. On or before April 18, 2006, Nifong stated to a reporter for *Newsweek Magazine* that the victim's "impaired state was not necessarily voluntary. . . . [I]f I had a witness who saw her right before this and she was not intoxicated, and then I had a witness who said that she was given a drink at the party and after taking a few sips of that drink acted in a particular way, that could be evidence of something other than intoxication, or at least other than voluntary intoxication?"

63. On May 12, 2006, Nifong again met with Dr. Meehan and two DPD officers and discussed the results of DSI's testing to date. During that meeting, consistent with Nifong's prior request, Dr. Meehan provided Nifong a 10-page written report which set forth the results of DNA tests on only the three evidence specimens that contained DNA consistent with DNA profiles from several known reference specimens. The three items in DSI's written report concerned DNA profiles on two fingernail specimens that were incomplete but were consistent with the DNA profiles of two unindicted lacrosse players, including DNA on a fingernail found in David Evans' garbage can which was incomplete but was consistent with David Evans' DNA profile, and DNA from the vaginal swab that was consistent with the DNA profile of Ms. Mangum's boyfriend. DSI's written report did not disclose the existence of any of the multiple unidentified male DNA found on the rape kit items, although it did list the evidence items on which the unidentified DNA had been discovered.

64. Nifong personally received DSI's written report from Dr. Meehan on May 12, 2006, and later that day provided it to counsel for the two Duke Defendants who had been indicted and for David Evans, among others.

65. When he received DSI's written report and provided it to counsel for the Duke Defendants, Nifong was fully aware of the test results that were omitted from the written report, including the test results revealing the existence of DNA from multiple unidentified males on rape kit items.

66. Three days later, on May 15, 2006, Nifong sought and obtained an indictment against David Evans for first-degree rape, first-degree sex offense, and kidnapping.

67. On May 17, Duke Defendant Collin Finnerty served discovery requests on Nifong, which specifically asked that any expert witness "prepare, and furnish to the defendant, a report of the results of *any* (not only the ones about which the expert expects to testify) examinations or tests conducted by the expert."

68. On May 18, 2006, Nifong provided various discovery materials to all three Duke Defendants, including another copy of DSI's written report, in connection with a hearing in the case on that same day. The discovery materials Nifong provided on May 18 did not include any underlying data or information concerning DSI's testing and analysis. The materials Nifong provided also did not include any documentation or information indicating the presence of DNA from multiple unidentified males on the rape kit items. Nifong also did not provide in the discovery materials any written or recorded memorialization of the substance of Dr. Meehan's oral statements made during his meetings with Nifong in April and May 2006 concerning the results of all DSI's tests and examinations, including the existence of DNA from multiple unidentified males on the rape kit items ("memorializations of Dr. Meehan's oral statements").

69. DSI's tests and examinations revealing the existence of DNA from multiple unidentified males on rape kit items and Dr. Meehan's oral statements regarding the existence of that DNA were evidence that tended to negate the guilt of the accused; Collin Finnerty, Reade Seligman and David Evans.

70. Accompanying the discovery materials, Nifong served and filed with the Court written responses to the Duke Defendants' discovery requests. In these responses, Nifong stated: "The State is not aware of any additional material or information which may be exculpatory in nature with respect to the Defendant." In his written discovery responses, Nifong also identified Dr. Meehan and R. W. Scales, another person at DSI, as expert witnesses reasonably expected to testify at the trial of the underlying criminal cases pursuant to N.C. Gen. Stat. § 15A-903(a)(2). Nifong also gave notice in the written discovery responses of the State's intent to introduce scientific data accompanied by expert testimony. Nifong represented in the written discovery responses that all of the reports of those experts had been provided to the Duke Defendants.

71. At the time he made these representations to the Court and to the Duke Defendants in his written discovery responses, Nifong was aware of the existence of DNA from multiple unidentified males

on the rape kit items, was aware that DSI's written report did not reveal the existence of this evidence, and was aware that he had not provided the Duke Defendants with memorializations of Dr. Meehan's oral statements regarding the existence of this evidence.

72. The representations contained in Nifong's May 18 written discovery responses were intentional misrepresentations and intentional false statements of material fact to opposing counsel and to the Court.

73. At the May 18, 2006 hearing, the Honorable Ronald Stephens, Superior Court Judge presiding, asked Nifong if he had provided the Duke Defendants all discovery materials.

74. In response to Judge Stephens' inquiry, Nifong stated: "I've turned over everything I have."

75. Nifong's response to Judge Stephens' question was a misrepresentation and a false statement of material fact.

76. On June 19, 2006, Nifong issued a press release to representatives of the news media stating, "None of the 'facts' I know at this time, indeed, none of the evidence I have seen from any source, has changed the opinion that I expressed initially."

77. On June 19, 2006, counsel for the Duke Defendants requested various materials from Nifong, including a report or written statement of the meeting between Nifong and Dr. Meehan to discuss the DNA test results. This request was addressed at a hearing before Judge Stephens on June 22, 2006.

78. In response to the Duke Defendants' June 19 discovery request and in response to Judge Stephens' direct inquiry, Nifong stated in open court that, other than what was contained in DSI's written report, all of his communications with Dr. Meehan were privileged "work product." Nifong represented to Judge Stephens, "That's pretty much correct, your Honor. We received the reports, which [defense counsel] has received, and we talked about how we would likely use that, and that's what we did."

79. At the time Nifong made these representations to Judge Stephens on June 22, Nifong knew that he had discussed with Dr. Meehan on three occasions the existence of DNA from multiple unidentified males on the rape kit items, which evidence was not disclosed in DSI's written report, and knew that Dr. Meehan's statements to him revealing the existence of DNA from multiple unidentified males on the rape kit items were not privileged work product.

80. Nifong's representations to Judge Stephens at the June 22 hearing were intentional misrepresentations and intentional false statements of material fact to the Court and to opposing counsel.

81. During the June 22 hearing, Judge Stephens entered an Order directing Nifong to provide Collin Finnerty and later all the Duke Defendants with, among other things, "results of tests and examinations, or any other matter or evidence obtained during the investigation of the offenses alleged to have been committed by the defendant" and statements of any witnesses taken during the investigation, with oral statements to be reduced to written or recorded form.

82. Nifong did not provide the Duke Defendants with "results of tests and examinations, or any other matter or evidence obtained during the investigation of the offenses alleged to have been committed by the defendant" and did not provide the Duke Defendants with statements of any witnesses taken during the investigation, with oral statements reduced to written or recorded form.

83. Nifong did not comply with Judge Stephens' June 22 Order.

84. On August 31, 2006, the Duke Defendants collectively filed a Joint Omnibus Motion to Compel Discovery seeking, among other things, the complete file and all underlying data regarding DSI's work and the substance of any discoverable comments made by Dr. Meehan during his meetings with Nifong and two DPD officers on April 10, April 21, and May 12, 2006. The Joint Omnibus Motion was addressed by the Honorable Osmond W. Smith III, Superior Court Judge presiding, at a hearing on September 22, 2006.

85. At the September 22 hearing, counsel for the Duke Defendants specifically stated in open court that the Duke Defendants were seeking the results of any tests finding any additional DNA on Ms. Mangum even if it did not match any of the Duke Defendants or other individuals for whom the State had provided reference DNA specimens for comparison.

86. In response to a direct question from Judge Smith, Nifong represented that DSI's written report encompassed all tests performed by DSI and everything discussed at his meetings with Dr. Meehan in April and May 2006. The following exchange occurred immediately thereafter on the Duke Defendants' request for memorializations of Dr. Meehan's oral statements:

(Continues)

(Continued)

Judge Smith: "So you represent there are no other statements from Dr. Meehan?"

Mr. Nifong: "No other statements. No other statements made to me."

87. At the time Nifong made these representations to Judge Smith, he was aware that Dr. Meehan had told him in their meetings about the existence of DNA from multiple unidentified males on the rape kit items, was aware that he had not provided the Duke Defendants with a written or recorded memorialization of Dr. Meehan's statements and was aware that the existence of that DNA was not revealed in DSI's written report.

88. Nifong's statements and responses to Judge Smith at the September 22 hearing were intentional misrepresentations and intentional false statements of material fact to the Court and to opposing counsel.

89. On September 22, Judge Smith ordered Nifong to provide the Duke Defendants the complete files and underlying data from both the SBI and DSI by October 20, 2006.

90. On October 19, 2006 counsel for David Evans faxed to Nifong a proposed order reflecting Judge Smith's September 22 ruling. The proposed order stated, in paragraph 4, "Regarding the defendants' request for a report of statements made by Dr. Brian Meehan of DNA Security, Inc., during two separate meetings among Dr. Meehan, District Attorney Mike Nifong, Sgt. Mark Gottlieb, and Inv. Benjamin Himan in April 2006 . . . Mr. Nifong represented that those meetings involved the State's request for YSTR testing, Dr. Meehan's report of the results of those tests, and a discussion of how the State intended to use those results in the course of the trial of these matters. Mr. Nifong indicated that he did not discuss the facts of the case with Dr. Meehan and that Dr. Meehan said nothing during those meetings beyond what was encompassed in the final report of DNA Security, dated May 12, 2006. The Court accepted Mr. Nifong's representation about those meetings and held that there were no additional discoverable statements by Dr. Meehan for the State to produce."

91. On October 24, 2006, Nifong responded by letter to defense counsel's October 19, 2006 letter and proposed order. In his response, Nifong identified two changes he believed were appropriate to two portions of the proposed order, made no mention of any changes he believed were appropriate to paragraph 4, and said "the proposed order seems satisfactory" and "it seems to reflect with acceptable accuracy the rulings of Judge Smith on September 22."

92. On October 27, 2006, Nifong provided 1,844 pages of underlying documents and materials from DSI to the Duke Defendants pursuant to the Court's September 22, 2006 Order but did not provide the Duke Defendants a complete written report from DSI setting forth the results of all of its tests and examinations, including the existence of DNA from multiple unidentified males on the rape kit items, and did not provide the Duke Defendants with any written or recorded memorializations of Dr. Meehan's oral statements.

93. After reviewing the underlying data provided to them on October 27 for between 60 and 100 hours, counsel for the Duke Defendants determined that DSI's written report did not include the results of all DNA tests performed by DSI and determined that DSI had found DNA from multiple unidentified males on the rape kit items and that such results were not included in DSI's written report.

94. On December 13, 2006, the Duke Defendants filed a Motion to Compel Discovery: Expert DNA Analysis, detailing their discovery of the existence of DNA from multiple unidentified males on the rape kit items and explaining that this evidence had not been included in DSI's written report. The motion did not allege any attempt or agreement to conceal the potentially exculpatory DNA evidence or test results. The Motion to Compel Discovery: Expert DNA Analysis was addressed by the Honorable Osmond W. Smith III, Superior Court Judge presiding, at a hearing on December 15, 2006.

95. At the December 15 hearing, both in chambers and again in open court, Nifong stated or implied to Judge Smith that he was unaware of the existence of DNA from multiple unidentified males on the rape kit items until he received the December 13 motion and/or was unaware that the results of any DNA testing performed by DSI had been excluded from DSI's written report. Nifong stated to Judge Smith in open court: "The first I heard of this particular situation was when I was served with these reports—this motion on Wednesday of this week."

96. Nifong's representations that he was unaware of the existence of DNA from multiple unidentified males on the rape kit items and/or that he was unaware of the exclusion of such evidence from DSI's written report, were intentional misrepresentations and intentional false statements of material fact to the Court and to opposing counsel.

97. During the December 15 hearing, Dr. Meehan testified under oath to the following statements:

 a. he discussed with Nifong at the April 10, April 21, May 12 meetings the results of all tests conducted by DSI to date, including the potentially exculpatory DNA test results;

 b. he and Nifong discussed and agreed that "we would only disclose or show on our report those reference specimens that matched evidence items";

 c. DSI's report did not set forth the results of all tests and examinations DSI conducted in the case but was limited to only some results;

 d. the limited report was the result of "an intentional limitation" arrived at between him and Nifong "not to report on the results of all examinations and tests" that DSI performed;

 e. the failure to provide all test and examination results purportedly was based on privacy concerns; and

 f. he would have prepared a report setting forth the results of all DSI's tests and examinations if he had been requested to do so by Nifong or other representatives of the State of North Carolina at any time after May 12.

98. Immediately after the December 15 hearing, Nifong stated to a representative of the news media: "And we were trying to, just as Dr. Meehan said, trying to avoid dragging any names through the mud but at the same time his report made it clear that all the information was available if they wanted it and they have every word of it."

99. On January 12, 2007, Nifong recused himself from the prosecution of the Duke Defendants.

100. On January 13, 2007, the Attorney General of North Carolina took over the Duke Lacrosse case and began to review evidence and undertake further investigation.

101. After an intensive review of the evidence, the Attorney General concluded that Ms. Mangum's credibility was suspect, her various inconsistent allegations were incredible and were contradicted by other evidence in the case, and that credible and verifiable evidence demonstrated that the Duke Defendants could not have participated in an attack during the time it was alleged to have occurred.

102. Based on its finding that no credible evidence supported the allegation that the crimes occurred, the Attorney General declared Reade Seligman, Collin Finnerty, and David Evans innocent of all charges in the Duke Lacrosse case. The cases against the Duke Defendants were dismissed on April 11, 2007.

103. Nifong had in his possession, no later than April 10, 2006, an oral report from Dr. Meehan of the reports of test results showing the existence of DNA from multiple unidentified males on rape kit items.

104. From at least May 12, 2006 through January 12, 2007, Nifong never provided the Duke Defendants a complete report setting forth the results of all examinations and tests conducted by DSI and never provided the Duke Defendants with memorializations of Dr. Meehan's oral statements concerning the results of all examinations and tests conducted by DSI in written, recorded or any other form.

105. On or about December 20, 2006, Nifong received a letter of notice and substance of grievance from the Grievance Committee of the North Carolina State Bar alleging that: (a) he failed to provide the Duke Defendants with evidence regarding the existence of DNA from multiple unidentified males on the rape kit items; (b) he agreed with Dr. Meehan not to provide those results; and (c) he falsely represented to the Court that he was unaware of these results or their omission from DSI's report prior to receiving the Duke Defendants' December 13 motion to compel discovery.

106. Nifong initially responded to the Grievance Committee in a letter dated December 28, 2006, and supplemented his initial response, at the request of State Bar counsel, in a letter dated January 16, 2007.

107. In his responses to the Grievance Committee, Nifong: (a) acknowledged that he had discussed with Dr. Meehan during meetings in April and May 2006 the results of all DSI's testing, including the existence of DNA from multiple unidentified males on the rape kit items; (b) denied that he had agreed with Dr. Meehan to exclude the potentially exculpatory DNA test results from DSI's report; (c) stated that he viewed the evidence of DNA from multiple unidentified males on the rape kit items as

(Continues)

(Continued)

"noninculpatory" rather than as "specifically exculpatory"; and (d) represented that the discussion and agreement with Dr. Meehan to limit the information in DSI's report was based on privacy concerns about releasing the names and DNA profiles of the lacrosse players and others providing known reference specimens.

108. DSI's written report listed DNA profiles for Ms. Mangum, Ms. Mangum's boyfriend, and David Evans and Kevin Coleman, two lacrosse players who had not been indicted at the time the report was released, and listed the names of all 50 persons who had contributed reference DNA specimens for comparison.

109. Nifong further represented in his responses to the Grievance Committee that he did not realize that the existence of DNA from multiple unidentified males on the rape kit items was not included in DSI's report when he provided it to the Duke Defendants or thereafter, until he received defense counsel's December 13 motion to compel.

110. Nifong's representation to the Grievance Committee that he did not realize that the existence of DNA from multiple unidentified males on the rape kit items was not included in DSI's report from May 12 until he received the December 13 motion to compel was a false statement of material fact made in connection with a disciplinary matter, and was made knowingly.

111. Nifong also represented in his responses to the Grievance Committee that, by stating to the Court at the beginning of the December 15 hearing that the motion was the "first [he] heard of this particular situation," he was referring not to the existence of DNA from multiple unidentified males on the rape kit items but to the Duke Defendants' purported allegation that he had made an intentional attempt to conceal such evidence from them.

112. Counsel for the Duke Defendants did not allege any intentional attempt by Nifong to conceal the DNA evidence from them in either their December 13 motion to compel or their remarks to the Court prior to Nifong's statement.

113. Nifong's responses to the Grievance Committee set forth in paragraph 111 concerning his representations to the Court at the December 15, 2006, hearing were false statements of material fact made in connection with a disciplinary matter, and were made knowingly.

114. Nifong was required by statute and by court order to disclose to the Duke Defendants that tests had been performed which revealed the existence of DNA from multiple unidentified males on the rape kit items.

115. Nifong knew or reasonably should have known that his statements to representatives of the news media set forth in paragraphs 17–35, 37–42, 49–50, 61–62, and 76 above would be disseminated by means of public communication.

116. Nifong knew or reasonably should have known that his statements to representatives of the news media set forth in paragraphs 17–35, 37–42, 49–50, 61–62, and 76 above had a substantial likelihood of prejudicing the criminal adjudicative proceeding.

117. Nifong knew or reasonably should have known that his statements to representatives of the news media set forth in paragraphs 17–35, 37–42, 49–50, 61–62, and 76 above had a substantial likelihood of heightening public condemnation of the accused.

Based upon the preceding FINDINGS OF FACT, the Hearing Committee makes the following

Conclusions of Law

(a) By making statements to representatives of the news media including but not limited to those set forth in paragraphs 17–35, 37–42, 49–50, 61–62, and 76, Nifong made extrajudicial statements he knew or reasonably should have known would be disseminated by means of public communication and would have a substantial likelihood of materially prejudicing an adjudicative proceeding in the matter, in violation of Rule 3.6(a), and made extrajudicial statements that had a substantial likelihood of heightening public condemnation of the accused, in violation of Rule 3.8(f) of the Revised Rules of Professional Conduct.

(b) By instructing Dr. Meehan to prepare a report containing positive matches, Nifong knowingly disobeyed an obligation under the rules of a tribunal in violation of Rule 3.4(c) of the Revised Rules of Professional Conduct.

(c) By not providing to the Duke Defendants prior to November 16, 2006, a complete report setting forth the results of all tests and examinations conducted by DSI, including the existence of DNA from multiple unidentified males on the rape kit items and including written or recorded memorializations of Dr. Meehan's oral statements, Nifong:

    i. did not make timely disclosure to the defense of all evidence or information known to him that tended to negate the guilt of the accused, in violation of former Rule 3.8(d) of the Revised Rules of Professional Conduct; and

    ii. failed to make a reasonably diligent effort to comply with a legally proper discovery request, in violation of former Rule 3.4(d) of the Revised Rules of Professional Conduct;

(d) By never providing the Duke Defendants on or after November 16, 2006, and prior to his recusal on January 12, 2007, a report setting forth the results of all tests or examinations conducted by DSI, including the existence of DNA from multiple unidentified males on the rape kit items and including written or recorded memorializations of Dr. Meehan's oral statements, Nifong:

    i. did not, after a reasonably diligent inquiry, make timely disclosure to the defense of all evidence or information required to be disclosed by applicable law, rules of procedure, or court opinions, including all evidence or information known to him that tended to negate the guilt of the accused, in violation of current Rule 3.8(d) of the Revised Rules of Professional Conduct; and

    ii. failed to disclose evidence or information that he knew, or reasonably should have known, was subject to disclosure under applicable law, rules of procedure or evidence, or court opinions, in violation of current Rule 3.4(d)(3) of the Revised Rules of Professional Conduct.

(e) By falsely representing to the Court and to counsel for the Duke Defendants that he had provided all discoverable material in his possession and that the substance of all Dr. Meehan's oral statements to him concerning the results of all examinations and tests conducted by DSI were included in DSI's written report, Nifong made false statements of material fact or law to a tribunal in violation of Rule 3.3(a)(l), made false statements of material fact to a third person in the course of representing a client in violation of Rule 4.1, and engaged in conduct involving dishonesty, fraud, deceit or misrepresentation in violation of Rule 8.4(c) of the Revised Rules of Professional Conduct.

(f) By representing or implying to the Court that he was not aware of the existence on rape kit items of DNA from multiple unidentified males who were not members of the lacrosse team and/or that he was not aware of the exclusion of that evidence from DSI's written report at the beginning of the December 15, 2006, hearing, Nifong made false statements of material fact or law to a tribunal in violation of Rule 3.3(a)(I) and engaged in conduct involving dishonesty, fraud, deceit or misrepresentation in violation of Rule 8.4(c) of the Revised Rules of Professional Conduct.

(g) By falsely representing to the Grievance Committee of the State Bar that: (i) he did not realize that the test results revealing the presence of DNA from multiple unidentified males on the rape kit items were not included in DSI's report when he provided it to the Duke Defendants or thereafter, and (ii) his statements to the Court at the beginning of the December 15 hearing referred not to the existence of DNA from multiple unidentified males on the rape kit items but to the Duke Defendants' purported allegation that he had engaged in an intentional attempt to conceal such evidence, Nifong made knowingly false statements of material fact in connection with a disciplinary matter in violation of Rule 8.1(a), and engaged in conduct involving dishonesty, fraud, deceit or misrepresentation in violation of Rule 8.4(c) of the Revised Rules of Professional Conduct.

(h) Each of the violations set forth above separately, and the pattern of conduct revealed when they are viewed together, constitutes conduct prejudicial to the administration of justice in violation of Rule 8.4(d) of the Revised Rules of Professional Conduct.

Based upon the foregoing findings of fact and conclusions of law, the Hearing Committee makes by clear, cogent, and convincing evidence, the following additional

Findings of Fact Regarding Discipline

    1. Nifong's misconduct is aggravated by the following factors:
       a. dishonest or selfish motive;
       b. a pattern of misconduct;
       c. multiple offenses;
       d. refusal to acknowledge wrongful nature of conduct in connection with his handling of the DNA evidence;
       e. vulnerability of the victims, Collin Finnerty, Reade Seligman and David Evans; and
       f. substantial experience in the practice of law.

(Continues)

(Continued)

   2. Nifong's misconduct is mitigated by the following factors:
     a. absence of a prior disciplinary record; and
     b. good reputation.
   3. The aggravating factors outweigh the mitigating factors.
   4. Nifong's misconduct resulted in significant actual harm to Reade Seligman, Collin Finnerty, and David Evans and their families. Defendant's conduct was, at least, a major contributing factor in the exceptionally intense national and local media coverage the Duke Lacrosse case received and in the public condemnation heaped upon the Duke Defendants. As a result of Nifong's misconduct, these young men experienced heightened public scorn and loss of privacy while facing very serious criminal charges of which the Attorney General of North Carolina ultimately concluded they were innocent.
   5. Nifong's misconduct resulted in significant actual harm to the legal profession. Nifong's conduct has created a perception among the public within and outside North Carolina that lawyers in general and prosecutors in particular cannot be trusted and can be expected to lie to the court and to opposing counsel. Nifong's dishonesty to the court and to his opposing counsel, fellow attorneys, harmed the profession. Attorneys have a duty to communicate honestly with the court and with each other. When attorneys do not do so, they engender distrust among fellow lawyers and from the public, thereby harming the profession as a whole.
   6. Nifong's misconduct resulted in prejudice to and significant actual harm to the justice system. Nifong has caused a perception among the public within and outside North Carolina that there is a systemic problem in the North Carolina justice system and that a criminal defendant can only get justice if he or she can afford to hire an expensive lawyer with unlimited resources to figure out what is being withheld by the prosecutor.
   7. Nifong's false statements to the Grievance Committee of the North Carolina State Bar interfered with the State Bar's ability to regulate attorneys and therefore undermined the privilege of lawyers in this State to remain self-regulating.
   8. This Hearing Committee has considered all alternatives and finds that no discipline other than disbarment will adequately protect the public, the judicial system and the profession, given the clear demonstration of dishonest conduct, multiple violations, the pattern of dishonesty established by the evidence, and Nifong's failure to recognize or acknowledge the wrongfulness of his conduct with regard to withholding of the DNA evidence and making false representations to opposing counsel and to the Court. Furthermore, entry of an order imposing discipline less than disbarment would fail to acknowledge the seriousness of the offenses committed by Nifong and would send the wrong message to attorneys regarding the conduct expected of members of the Bar in this State.

Based upon the foregoing findings of fact, conclusions of law and additional findings of fact regarding discipline, the Hearing Committee hereby enters the following

Order of Discipline

   1. Michael B. Nifong is hereby DISBARRED from the practice of law.
   2. Nifong shall surrender his law license and membership card to the Secretary of the State Bar no later than 30 days from service of this order upon him.
   3. Nifong shall pay the costs of this proceeding as assessed by the Secretary of the N.C. State Bar, including DHC costs and including costs of the transcription and depositions taken in this case as follows: court reporter costs; videographer and videotaping costs; transcription costs; shipping, handling, and transmittal costs; and witness costs. Defendant must pay the costs within 90 days of service upon him of the statement of costs by the Secretary.
   4. Nifong shall comply with all provisions of 27 NCAC 1B § .0124 of the North Carolina State Bar Discipline & Disability Rules ("Discipline Rules").

Signed by the Chair with the consent of the other hearing committee members, this the 24th day of July, 2007.

As the order in Case Decision 6.1 indicates, the committee was particularly troubled by Nifong's failure to satisfy his obligations to the system that he pledged to serve. Nifong faced re-election and was under pressure to protect his political interests. The committee found that this affected his ability to put his service to the public and the interests of justice above his personal interest in re-election. It found that he significantly harmed the defendant students, who became victims as a result of his actions, harmed the legal profession, and harmed the justice system and public confidence in it. In this latter regard, the committee found that he created a public perception that "a criminal defendant can only get justice if he or she can afford to hire an expensive lawyer with unlimited resources." This is the very result that the criminal justice system is designed to avoid. Prosecutors violate society's trust in them by using their discretion to harm, rather than serve, the public.

Despite the potential for abuse of prosecutorial power, thousands of prosecutors toil in courtrooms across America, handling heavy caseloads to represent honorably the people they serve. They prosecute millions of criminal cases filed each year, in order to protect the public, realize justice for victims, and enforce the criminal law. As egregious as the Nifong case was, it is not the norm, and despite the political and other pressures prosecutors face, they are arguably the most important public servants in the criminal justice system.

The Defendant

In criminal cases, the defendant is the person charged with a violation of the criminal law. It is important to recognize that, in a criminal case, the defendant stands in a position adverse to society. As noted earlier, the government brings its considerable resources to bear on vindicating society's interest in compliance with the criminal law. Most criminal defendants are suspicious and untrusting of the prosecution and the criminal justice system, a position that is not altogether unreasonable. For this reason, among others, it is not uncommon for criminal defendants to plead guilty to some charge (usually as a result of a plea bargain) in an effort to avoid the consequences of being subjected to the criminal trial process.

The consequences to the defendant of being prosecuted are most often significant. First, in many cases, the defendant is unable to post bail, sometimes as little as $100, and remains incarcerated until trial. Incarceration before trial has considerable effects on the defendant's life, including limited access to counsel, uncertainty regarding the status of the case, the stigma of incarceration, loss of employment, and limited contact with family members, including children. In addition, incarcerated criminal defendants, although presumed innocent, are stripped of their freedom for a time and left to encounter an often-hostile prison environment. Second, the charges faced by the defendant may be severe and the trial process daunting. The defendant may not fully understand the charges filed or the factual basis for the charges. Given this lack of understanding, it may be difficult for the defendant to

provide counsel with much, if any, assistance in preparation for trial. It is therefore not surprising that most criminal defendants believe themselves to be innocent of the crime charged. Third, the consequence of losing at trial (which occurs in excess of 90% of criminal trials) and being sentenced to potentially more severe punishment leads many defendants to accept plea agreements.

It is because of the severity of the process and its consequences that the individual rights and protections of criminal defendants found in the Sixth Amendment are especially important. These are discussed in detail in Chapter 12, but include the right to a speedy and public trial, the right to a jury, the right to notice of the charges, the right to confront adverse witnesses and compel appearance of favorable ones, and the right to counsel. In addition, the high standard of proof placed on the prosecution (beyond a reasonable doubt) coupled with a lower standard of proof for the defendant's defenses (a preponderance of the evidence) is intended to protect the defendant from the fallibility of evidence and its presentation. Whether they succeed in doing this is another matter.

In addition to the effects of prosecution on a defendant, much is known about the characteristics of those who are incarcerated for crimes. As indicated in **Table 6.1**, prison and jail inmates are primarily male, under 30 years old, and from minority groups.

There has been much debate as to why prison and jails are mostly populated with young male minorities (mostly African American). Some would suggest they are subjected to profiling by police. Others have claimed that the courts unfairly punish such defendants more harshly, whereas others argue that social conditions cause such individual to engage in serious crime at greater rates. About half are incarcerated for violent crimes, and about

| **Table 6.1** |||
| **Characteristics of State Prison and Local Jail Inmates** |||
Characteristic	**State Prisons**	**Local Jails**
Gender		
Male	93.4%	88%
Female		6.6%
12%		
Ethnicity		
Minority	64%	64%
Nonminority	36%	36%
Age		
Under 35	57%	62%
35 or Older	43%	38%
Type of crime		
Violent	49%	50%
Property	20%	22%
Drug	21%	37%

Source: Data from United States Department of Justice, Bureau of Justice Statistics. Retrieved August 17, 2009, from http://www.ojp.usdoj.gov/bjs.

21% are in state prison for drug offenses. Understanding these characteristics may assist in addressing the problem of crime, but in the meantime, the prosecution of these defendants will continue.

Defense Counsel

A criminal defendant is not required to obtain a lawyer to represent him or her in court. With few exceptions, the defendant may act *pro se* ("on his own behalf"), provided that he or she has at least a rudimentary understanding of the case against him or her and the trial process, as well as the ability to present a defense. Although some are able to do this adequately, the criminal defense attorney is often the only hope a defendant has of remaining free from incarceration. In criminal cases, the defendant's liberty is often at stake, and the goal of the attorney at each stage of the proceedings is to secure the defendant's freedom, if possible; however, the realities of criminal prosecutions are such that defense attorneys often become laborers in what is known as the "courtroom work group," where the defense attorney must work together with the prosecutor, the judge, probation or correctional officers, social workers, and sometimes others to achieve as favorable an outcome as possible for his or her client. Although the popular image of the job of a criminal defense attorney, from movies, television, and the media may be to obtain an acquittal through sleuthing and dramatic courtroom advocacy, in the majority of cases, defense counsel is primarily seeking from the prosecutor either a reduction in the charges or a lesser sentencing recommendation (preferably probation) or both.

Nonetheless, the importance of defense counsel cannot be underestimated. Indeed, the Supreme Court has made it clear that criminal defendants have a right to counsel whenever their liberty is at stake in a prosecution, and the government must provide indigent defendants with an attorney to secure this right (*Gideon v. Wainwright*, 372 U.S. 335 (1963)). The right to counsel for those who cannot afford an attorney is relied on extensively; it is estimated that 82% of state court defendants and nearly two thirds of federal court defendants have counsel provided to them by the government (Harlow, 2000). This is accomplished in a variety of ways. Some states and localities staff a public defender's office, others employ attorneys on a contract basis to defend indigent defendants, and still others appoint attorneys who volunteer their time. Thus, it is clear that large proportions of criminal defendants, at least at the time that they are appointed counsel, satisfy the definition of indigence. As a result, attorneys who represent indigent clients are among the most overworked in the profession, handling very large caseloads and representing defendants facing a range of sanctions in a variety of cases.

The criminal defense attorney stands on an equal footing with the prosecutor in the eyes of the court. He or she shares the same obligation as the prosecutor to represent his or her client zealously. This includes investigating the facts by locating and identifying witnesses, representing the defendant at pretrial hearings and at trial, and arguing for a lesser sentence upon conviction, but perhaps the most important role the defense counsel plays is in counseling the defendant about the trial process and providing advice regarding the likely outcome. Along with this is the defense attorney's role in *plea bargaining*, the process through which trial is avoided. This involves the defendant's entry of a guilty plea to some charge (usually less than the initial one) with a recommendation to the court of a lesser sentence by the prosecutor.

The Participants in Civil Cases

The Parties

The parties to a civil case are the individuals, business entities, or government agencies that have a dispute or some other unsettled legal matter requiring a judge to make a decision. Most often, the parties are there for unpleasant reasons. They may be seeking compensation for permanent injuries suffered in a car accident where someone else was at fault. They may be owed money for work they performed or for goods they sold and were not paid. There may be asking a judge to decide how property should be distributed after the death of a family member. Regardless of the specific problem, however, a dispute between the parties usually exists. Generally speaking, the parties are adverse to each other. That is, consistent with the adversary system of justice, the parties have a conflict that they are unable to resolve themselves or that requires an independent application of the law. By presenting their conflicting viewpoints in court, a judge can examine the law and (peacefully) resolve the matter. This is true regardless of the specific nature of the dispute. It is evident, therefore, that without the parties, as well as their inability to reach a compromise on their problem, there would be no need for courts.

In civil cases, who may be a party to a lawsuit is governed by Rules 17-25 of the Federal Rules of Civil Procedure or their state equivalents. These rules discuss several important background concepts that assist in understanding who may rightfully present a claim in court. These include who may or must be included in a civil lawsuit and the relationship between parties. At a minimum, civil cases proceed with a plaintiff and a defendant, the primary adverse parties to the case.

The Plaintiff

A plaintiff is the party in a civil case that initiates a lawsuit. This is done by filing a civil complaint, which is a court pleading that sets out the facts from which the dispute stems and the legal basis for a judgment in the plaintiff's favor. It also requests some form of relief from the court, which may be specific or a general request for damages or other relief that the court deems to be "just and proper." If the plaintiff is successful, the judgment may therefore take several forms that either the law requires or the judge believes to be fair, but it usually consists of either a determination that the defendant is liable for money damages or that the defendant must do something or refrain from doing something (a restraining order). For example, if a person believes he or she has been harmed as a result of a doctor's treatment, he or she may file a complaint for medical malpractice, seeking money as compensation for personal injury resulting from the doctor's actions. If a person has been threatened by another, he or she may file a complaint seeking an injunction, which is a court order requiring the defendant to stay away from the plaintiff. A plaintiff is sometimes referred to as a complainant or a petitioner.

Because the plaintiff initiates the lawsuit, he or she has considerable control over the legal proceedings. This occurs because the facts asserted in the complaint are within the plaintiff's knowledge and control, and the legal basis for the relief sought is specified by the plaintiff. This is not to say that the nature of the case may not later change as a result of motions filed or defenses raised by the defendant, but the initial parameters of the lawsuit are set out by the plaintiff.

In addition to having some legal basis for presenting a claim to the court, there is an additional requirement that a plaintiff must meet. The plaintiff must have *standing*. Standing is a legal concept that refers to right of a party to invoke the jurisdiction of the court because the claims being asserted, if proven, would show that the plaintiff has suffered or will suffer some specific and concrete harm. That is, standing requires that the plaintiff have a personal interest in the outcome of the case. Without this, there can be no clash of views that the adversary system requires. The plaintiff's "interest" may not be a generalized one. There must be some actual injury to the plaintiff that is alleged to have resulted from the defendant's actions.

The Defendant

The defendant in a civil case is the party being sued; that is, the defendant is named in the civil complaint. The defendant is notified of the claims against him or her by a formal process called "service of process," which involves a certification by a person that they "served" or personally provided the defendant with a copy of the complaint. Service of process is governed by Rule 4 of the Rules of Civil Procedure, which requires the plaintiff to obtain a summons from the court directing the defendant to respond to the complaint by a certain date, usually 30 days.

The failure of a defendant to respond in some way to a civil complaint may result in a *default judgment*, which is a judgment in the plaintiff's favor without a trial. Thus, the defendant will usually submit an answer or some other pleading generally denying the truth of the allegations of the plaintiff's complaint and raise certain *affirmative defenses* to show why he or she should be liable.

Defendants in civil cases often have much at stake. Because most civil cases seek money damages, the defendant may face considerable financial loss. Where the defendant is an individual, even one who is being sued for acting in a professional capacity (such as a doctor in a malpractice case), the uncertainties of litigation may create emotional stress, and the litigation itself may be time consuming, emotionally draining, and costly; therefore, it is usually the defendant's goal to have the plaintiff's claims, in full or in part, dismissed at the earliest opportu-

nity. In seeking to accomplish this, the defendant will engage in the process of discovery to establish the basis for the plaintiff's allegations. Because the plaintiff has the burden of proving the allegations made in the Complaint, discovery will reveal the evidentiary support (or lack thereof) for each of the plaintiff's claims. The defendant uses the discovery process to determine what evidence the plaintiff may be able to bring forth at trial and where such evidence is lacking file a motion to dismiss the plaintiff's claims.

The Attorneys

Despite the public perception of lawyers as greedy "sharks" and "ambulance chasers," along with thousands of derogatory lawyer jokes (some of which actually are funny), the court system in America depends on attorneys. The complexity of the U.S. legal system requires representation by a lawyer in most cases. Most cases, civil and criminal, begin and end with representation by an attorney.

Plaintiff's Attorney

The job of a plaintiff's attorney, in most civil cases, is to obtain some form of relief for his or her client. The term "relief" refers to the mitigation of some harm suffered by the plaintiff. This may mean filing suit in court seeking contractual, compensatory, or punitive damages, an injunction ordering someone to do something or refrain from doing something, a declaration regarding the validity of an agreement (such as an insurance contract), or an order involving transfer of title to property.

The plaintiff's attorney represents the plaintiff by investigating the facts surrounding the plaintiff's claim, providing advice on the legal merits of the claim, preparing the civil complaint, discussing or negotiating settlement, and pursuing the matter through trial and possibly appeal. The plaintiff's attorney is responsible for understanding the potential significance of the facts and law that may apply to those facts and advocates on behalf of the client in order to achieve the client's objectives.

Defense Attorney

In civil cases, the defendant usually retains an attorney in private practice to represent him or her in the case. Where the defendant is a state or federal public agency, representation is handled through the state Attorney General's or U.S. Attorney's office, by government attorneys that work for a particular agency, or by private attorneys hired by the governmental agency. The defense attorney's goal is to dismiss all or part of the claims made in the lawsuit. Responses to the pleadings filed by the plaintiff are usually designed to assist in accomplishing this.

The Decision Makers

The Judge

Although the court is the place in which society's interests in justice are satisfied, the authority to accomplish American justice is found in judges. This is, perhaps, the reason why judges are esteemed, if not revered. To most people, judges represent justice, and indeed, although they are not always successful in doing what the public or the parties believe to be just, judges do attempt to provide a forum in which the parties can have some confidence in the fairness of the proceedings, whether the hearing involves a criminal or civil matter.

Just as there are courts that perform different functions, the judges who preside over those courts operate in a variety of ways. Some judges have responsibility for a broad range of cases, perhaps hearing a shoplifting case and a domestic assault matter in the morning and a contract action, auto accident case, and divorce in the afternoon. Other judges hear only certain types of cases, such as an exclusive assignment of felonies, personal injury or contract lawsuits, or antitrust litigation. The job of a majority of judges is to conduct trials, but the job of appellate judges, reviewing trial transcripts, researching legal principles, and writing decisions for publication, is quite different. Although judicial power specifically related to the functions of a particular judicial office, the scope of judicial power is affected by a number of influences, outlined later here.

The Scope and Limits of Judicial Power

The source of judicial power is found in the office held by judges. Although this appears to be a truism, it reflects an important limitation on judicial power: It is not the men or women who sit as judges who are granted considerable authority over the lives and affairs of others; it is the position they are called on to fill that requires such authority. What, however, is the nature of the authority that judges have?

Judges are granted the authority to make decisions, and they have considerable discretion in the decisions that they make. The nature of decision making is such that it involves choosing among alternative courses of action. Given the uncertainties that sometimes exist in the law and the facts of a particular case, the discretion of a judge may play a significant role in the course of litigation throughout the trial, as well as in the ultimate outcome of the case.

The decisions made by judges, however, occur in specified circumstances under certain conditions. Apart from the myriad decisions relating to scheduling and office management, judges often are called on to make a decision about some substantive aspects of a case as it proceeds toward and through the trial. Some of these occur in response to a motion made by one of the parties, whereas others are made during or after the trial. For example, if a defendant hospital in a medical malpractice case has refused to produce health records of "all persons who have been patients of Dr. Jones in the past three years" on the grounds that the request violates patient privacy rights, the plaintiff may file a motion to compel production of the documents, asking the court to order the hospital to provide the health records. Before a decision on the motion is made, however, the judge will make certain that all parties affected by a decision on the motion have been notified and have an opportunity to respond to the motion. Often, a hearing will be held before a decision is rendered, where the parties will present oral argument and address questions that the judge may have. The judge may then make a ruling on the motion from the bench, or take the matter "under advisement" and issue a written decision at a later time.

Other decisions, such as rulings on trial objections to the presentation of evidence or other matters, are made during trial. For example, if defense counsel in a criminal case objects to the prosecutor's attempt to introduce hearsay evidence elicited from a witness, the judge will make an immediate decision as to whether the witness statement is hearsay, whether it complies with an exception to the hearsay rule, and the potential harm to the defendant that may result from admission of the statement. In addition to these types of substantive rulings, the judge, in a bench trial, will have the task of reaching a decision based on the evidence of the defendant's liability, whether civil or criminal. In most criminal trials, following input from both the prosecution and defense, it is the judge who decides an appropriate sentence.

In addition to the circumstances in which a decision must be made, the judge's decision will always relate to some specific and concrete issue in the case, and the decision will be made in accordance governing law or legal principles. In the previous example regarding discovery, the issue presented by the motion would likely be whether the requested patient records are protected by law or are otherwise discoverable. This would involve a determination of what the law requires, including the review of case law or statutes relevant to the matter. Thus, the decision to be made is clearly focused by the issue, directs the judge to applicable law, and allows application of the law to the problem to be resolved. This is the process judges follow in essentially every decision made in a case.

Finally, it is apparent that a decision is just that—an outcome that is decided by the judge on some matter presented for decision. The decision made, however, must be clearly articulated in a manner that allows the parties to govern their behavior and their own decision making as the case proceeds to trial or after its conclusion. It is, after all, the point of relying on the courts—to have an independent arbiter resolve a dispute between the parties, whether a civil dispute or dispute about whether a crime has been committed. Thus, the decision reached by a judge must be one, which is consistent with the law, which has been openly after notice and a hearing by the parties, and in which the parties understand from the decision how next to govern their behavior.

Thus, judges have the power to control the proceedings over which they preside. This control extends to the conduct of courtroom trials and hearings, the behavior of the parties, and the work of attorneys. In one case, *People v. Muhammad*, 108 Cal. App. 4th 313, 133 Cal. Rptr. 2d 308 (Cal. App. 2003) (found in **Case Decision 6.2**), the judge imposed a sanction on an attorney for using peremptory challenges in a way that resulted in the discriminatory selection of a jury.

Case Decision 6.2   *People v. Muhammad,* 108 Cal. App. 4th 313, 133 Cal. Rptr. 2d 308 (Cal. App. 2003)

Decision of the Court by Judge Epstein:

It is a general rule that, outside of a contempt proceeding, trial courts lack inherent power to impose a monetary sanction against an attorney for misconduct in court. The authority to impose such a sanction must be found in a statute. This has been the declared law in California for at least the past 25 years. We apply it here in the context of a monetary fine levied against a prosecutor for exercising jury peremptory challenges.

In this case, the court found that the prosecutor had improperly exercised peremptory challenges, leading to a mistrial and dismissal of the venire panel. Acting under Code of Civil Procedure section 177.5, the court assessed a $1,500 sanction against her. The People and the prosecutor seek appellate review of the finding and the order. We find sufficient support in the record for the finding. But it is a requisite to application of the statute that a court order be violated, and we find no such court order in this case. Since the statute does not apply and the trial court lacks inherent power to impose the fine, the order imposing it must be reversed.

Procedural and Factual Summary

The defendant was charged with murder. The present appeal arises out of her third trial, the first two having ended in mistrial due to the jury's inability to reach a verdict.

Following the court's voir dire of prospective jurors, the court discussed attorney voir dire at sidebar. The court made it clear that it would only allow questions going to a challenge for cause. On that basis, it rejected defense counsel's request to ask prospective jurors how they would evaluate testimony, although the court indicated that it would allow questions as to whether they would apply the same standard to all witnesses. The prosecutor said she wanted to ask questions about employment, but acknowledged "that's not generally cause." The court agreed that it was not, and the prosecutor said she had no questions related to cause. The trial court admonished both sides to keep their voir dire tight.

The attorneys then proceeded to exercise peremptory challenges to prospective jurors and to briefly ask questions of prospective jurors seated in place of those who had been excused. When the prosecutor had excused nine prospective jurors, defense counsel argu[ed] that the prosecutor had engaged in a "systematic exclusion" of prospective jurors based on ethnicity. Addressing the prosecutor, the court stated: "Indeed, . . . there's been a—what appears to be a systematic exclusion of minorities by you." The court recounted the challenges she had made. A white male was understandably excluded because he had indicated a dislike of lawyers. The balance was made up of two Asians; three African-Americans; one Hispanic; a female Caucasian; and one person whose ethnicity was difficult to categorize. The court concluded, "I think you have some explaining to do."

The court effectively having found a prima facie showing of prohibited group bias, the prosecutor proceeded to explain her strikes. The Asians, she said, each had exhibited difficulty with the English language. The court agreed with respect to one of them ("I can accept that"). For several of the other ethnic minority prospective jurors, the explanation was that the trial would involve technical evidence, especially from the coroner, and, based on their occupations, the prosecutor did not believe the prospective jurors were up to understanding the case. One was "a janitor or a tailor," two others were "janitors" and one a custodian, which was the reason for excusing her. Another prospective juror, a Hispanic female, was a clerk with a public health agency, and the prosecutor could "only assume as a county employee she's much like our clerks, she's basically a filing individual. Based on that, again, I didn't believe she could comprehend the testimony." Still another dismissed prospective juror, a female African-American, was a customer service representative, "they're the individuals that you call when you want your phone company service . . . based on technical, but a background in whether or not they could comprehend the testimony, I just base it—based on a calculated assumption or guess as to what their level of comprehension's going to be."

The trial court found "a clear violation. None of these reasons do I find a convincing reason for excusing them." The court asked defense counsel what he wanted to do. Counsel moved for a mistrial. The court granted the motion. After dismissing the remaining members of the venire, the court

(Continues)

addressed the prosecutor: "I find what you have done [is] not only illegal, but immoral and unethical, Ms. Lopez. What sanctions should I impose? My inclination is to impose sanctions in terms of monetary sanctions in the amount of $1,500 pursuant to section 177.5. My further inclination is to deny you the right to use peremptory challenges during jury selection tomorrow." The court responded to the prosecutor's statement that defense counsel had used all of his peremptories against white prospective jurors with the observation that it was defense counsel who laid the challenge, "and I listened to your reasons and your reasons were simply unacceptable, they're not credible reasons for excusing the people that you excused." The prosecutor asked the court to note that there were prospective jurors with "clearly English comprehension difficulties." The court agreed that was the case with respect to a couple of them, "but you're kicking off a perfectly capable confident and intelligent woman in your last peremptory, Juror No. 7, your peremptory No. 9 and some of the other reasons simply don't quash [*sic:* wash]. The technicalities of your case aren't so technical that these people couldn't listen to the case and I don't buy it."

The court issued an order to show cause why the prosecutor should not be sanctioned $1,500 under and, after further colloquy, set the hearing for the following day.

On that day the prosecutor was present together with another deputy district attorney, who appeared on her behalf. That deputy argued that section 177.5 does not apply to an advocacy situation such as jury selection, that there had been no warning from the trial court that the prosecutor's conduct might be sanctionable, nor had she violated a court order. Counsel also disputed whether a violation had occurred at all. He concluded with a suggestion that the court treat the entire matter as a warning and proceed with the case. The trial court declined to do that, and ordered that the sanction stand in the amount of $1,500, which it stayed.

There was no fourth trial. On the following day, following appropriate waivers, the defendant entered a guilty plea to the amended charge of voluntary manslaughter and was sentenced to state prison. The People filed an appeal from the sanction order. The appeal shows the prosecutor both as appellant and "real party in interest." The People also sought our intervention by writ to overturn the sanction order. We denied the petition because the People had an adequate remedy at law through its pending appeal.

Discussion

I

The appeal is authorized by section 904.1, subdivision (b), which permits an appeal after final judgment from a sanction order where the amount is less than $5,000.

Technically, the respondent in the case, if there is one, is the defendant, Sarina Lenee Muhammad. Having accepted a plea bargain and having been sentenced accordingly, she obviously has no interest in the present dispute, and has not made an appearance on appeal. We are in receipt of a "Respondent's Brief" filed on behalf of the Superior Court. Since the briefing did not raise an issue about the authority of the trial court to participate as a party in the appeal, we sent a letter to counsel, inviting them to advise the court by letter brief of their position with respect to whether the Superior Court could appear, brief, and argue as "respondent" in the case and, if not, what procedure we should follow.

The Superior Court's letter in response argues that this is the unusual case in which the trial court itself has sufficient standing and interest to appear as a party on appeal. In their response, the People agree that the trial court is entitled to recognition as a party.

The Superior Court's letter cites a number of cases in which trial courts have appeared as a responding party in an appellate review of a sanction order. The observation is correct, although none of these cases discussed the propriety of the trial court's participation. One was a writ proceeding, and in another the opinion simply noted an argument of the county counsel "representing the trial court."

As a general rule, the role of a trial court is to decide cases, not to participate as a litigant in their resolution. The latter role is for the parties, not the court. Nevertheless, there are rare and limited situations in which the trial court itself may participate in the appellate process. We note that even in these rare cases, the judge is not a proper party on appeal and that there is authority that the trial court may only defend itself in a writ proceeding, rather than initiate such a proceeding.

These unusual exceptions typically occur when a question is presented involving important issues about the trial court's authority to control proceedings before it, which none of the litigating parties has an interest in pursuing.

That fits this case. As we have discussed, the defendant has no interest in whether the trial court was correct in imposing a monetary sanction against the prosecutor. And the County of Los Angeles, to which the sanction was payable, has not sought to intervene in any capacity. The trial court, as a court, has a legitimate interest in its authority to impose a monetary sanction against an attorney for courtroom misconduct. No one other than the court has any interest in defending the court's position.

Nevertheless, the trial court is not and cannot be a party in a direct appeal from a case it has tried. The few cases that have treated the question have allowed the court to participate in writ proceedings in which the court is named (albeit nominally in most cases) as the respondent. That is not our case, and we decline to convert this appeal into a writ proceeding at this point.

There is an alternative, suggested by the trial court in its letter responding to our request for briefing on this issue. It is that we treat the trial court's "Responding Brief" as a brief amicus curiae. The court's briefing has been helpful in our analysis of the issues, and we believe this to be a proper request. We shall proceed on that basis.

We granted the request of the Los Angeles County Public Defender to file a brief amicus curiae. It has done so, arguing that the sanction order should be reversed.

II

The rule is that "the use of peremptory challenges to remove prospective jurors on the sole ground of group bias violates the right to trial by a jury drawn from a representative cross-section of the community" under article I, section 6 of the California Constitution. The federal rule is the same, although based on the equal protection clause. These cases have been followed and applied by hundreds of others, and the rule they announce is among the best known principles of trial court procedure. While peremptory challenges based on group bias are unconstitutional, challenges on virtually any other bona fide ground are permissible. "[T]he law recognizes that a peremptory challenge may be predicated on a broad spectrum of evidence suggestive of juror partiality. The evidence may range from the obviously serious to the apparently trivial, from the virtually certain to the highly speculative."

If a party brings a challenge, raising the issue of whether one or more jury peremptories by another side was exercised on the basis of group bias, and the trial court explicitly or implicitly finds that the challenging party has made a prima facie showing of that impropriety, the burden shifts to the other side to justify its strikes. It is then up to the trial judge to decide whether the reason offered is truth or pretext. "[S]uch a ruling 'requires trial judges to make difficult and often close judgments. They are in a good position to make such determinations, however, on the basis of their knowledge of local conditions and of local prosecutors.' They are also well situated to bring to bear on this question their powers of observation, their understanding of trial techniques, and their broad judicial experience. We are confident of their ability to distinguish a true case of group discrimination by peremptory challenges from a spurious claim interposed simply for purposes of harassment or delay."

The trial court's judgment is entitled to considerable deference. This is especially true when the bench officer is an experienced trial judge. We take judicial notice that, when this case was tried, the trial judge had over 17 years of trial experience, and 13 years of experience before that as a prosecutor.

The trial judge listened to the prosecutor's explanations for her peremptory challenges. He agreed that two of them were justified by her explanations. (The prospective juror who had demonstrated a dislike of attorneys, and one who had particular difficulty with the English language.) But he rejected her explanations that ethnic minority prospective jurors she challenged were not up to understanding the case to be tried. As a general proposition, an honestly held belief that a prospective juror will be unable to understand the case is a legitimate basis for a peremptory challenge. And a prosecutor's peremptory challenges are presumed to be exercised in a constitutional manner. But the presumption is rebuttable; the trial judge implicitly found that it was rebutted in this case. A fair reading—indeed, the only reading—of his statements is that he found the explanations offered were intended to disguise the actual reason for peremptory challenges: group bias. As the judge put it, he did not "buy it."

Most of the reported cases involving challenges involve trial court decisions crediting a prosecutor's explanation. "So long as the trial court makes a sincere and reasoned effort to evaluate the nondiscriminatory justifications offered, its conclusions are entitled to deference on appeal." No less deference is due when the trial court finds the explanation to be pretext, as this judge emphatically did. Based on a reading of the transcript of the proceedings, we cannot say the trial judge called it wrong.

We therefore uphold the trial court's ruling that the prosecutor exercised jury peremptory challenges on the basis of group bias. Given that, and defense counsel's motion for a new trial, the court

(Continues)

(*Continued*)

had no alternative but to dismiss the remaining venire and grant the motion for mistrial. We also note that since the challenged prospective jurors already had been excused, the trial court did not have the option of simply seating them notwithstanding the challenge.

Having been forced to declare a mistrial because of the unconstitutional conduct of the prosecutor, the trial court turned to the issue of monetary sanction. So do we.

III

As we stated at the outset, it is a fundamental rule in this state that aside from a contempt proceeding, a monetary sanction can only be imposed against an attorney when authorized by a statute. In the leading case, the plaintiff's attorney improperly read jurors' notes written on copies of exhibits that had been given to them as an aid in following the trial. The trial judge felt obliged to declare a mistrial. He did so, and imposed a $700 fine on the offending attorney to compensate opposing counsel for wasted time in the aborted trial. The Supreme Court surveyed the law and policy considerations that bore on the issue, and gave a negative answer to the question whether, "absent statutory authority, a court may award attorney's fees as a sanction under its *supervisory* power."

The trial court justified the monetary sanction in this case under section 177.5. That statute authorizes a sanction of up to $1,500, payable to the county, "for any violation of a lawful court order by a person, done without good cause or substantial justification." The statute applies to criminal as well as civil cases. It does not require that the offending act be "willful," but only that it be committed without good cause or substantial justification.

The statute also requires that the order imposing sanctions "be in writing and shall recite in detail the conduct or circumstances justifying the order." Although the trial judge orally described the conduct and circumstances justifying the order, there was no written order or statement of circumstances. On appeal, the trial court concedes this deficiency and asks that we remand the case so that it may be cured. In light of our conclusion that no court order was violated, a remand would serve no purpose.

We find nothing in this discussion that prevents a trial court from imposing monetary sanctions against the attorney whose misconduct provokes a mistrial. The offending attorney may be misusing the peremptory challenge privilege precisely to provoke a mistrial. A mistrial is still mandatory unless the offended party is willing to waive the right to that remedy. It would make no sense in a case where the offended party invokes its right to mistrial, to allow the offending attorney to escape sanctions on that account. If anything, there is a stronger reason to impose monetary sanctions when a mistrial is declared than when the offended party waives its right to mistrial and the case proceeds with the remaining jury venire.

The district attorney argued at the order to show cause hearing that a warning may serve the function of an order. Certainly if a court admonishes counsel that a repetition of specific conduct will result in a monetary sanction, that statement is tantamount to an order not to repeat the conduct, and should suffice. But it did not occur in this case.

It follows that we must reverse the monetary sanction. What should a trial court do in order to preserve the option of imposing a monetary sanction should the conduct of counsel merit that option? Make an order. Yet it seems degrading to the judicial process and to the attorneys who practice before our courts for a court to have to warn counsel that, on penalty of a monetary sanction, they must not violate the Constitution. Based on our reading of cases in the literature, it appears that the issue usually is raised more than once if it is raised at all, thus giving the court an opportunity to issue an appropriate admonition. And, of course, we see only cases in which the question of a challenge is raised at trial, then raised again on appeal. We are confident that most attorneys steer well clear of a constitutional misuse of jury peremptory challenges, and that trial judges are able to "distinguish bona fide reasons from sham excuses."

Appellant's brief describes the trial court's ruling in this case as an "arbitrary, mean-spirited order, in patent derogation of the law." It was in derogation of the law because the conduct did not violate a court order, and the ruling was not stated in writing with an explanation of the justifying circumstances. Aside from that, we disagree with the characterization. A violation only occurs when an attorney deliberately misuses jury peremptory challenges to exclude a prospective juror on the basis of group bias. As the trial court concluded, that is illegal and unprofessional.

The order appealed from, imposing a monetary sanction against counsel, is reversed. No costs are awarded.

One of the interesting aspects of the *Muhammad* case is that the trial court itself was a "party in interest" in the appeal because it was the sanction order directing the prosecuting attorney to pay a fine that became the subject of the appeal. The appellate court noted that the trial court could not be a party in an appeal involving a case over which it presided, but allowed the trial court to appear as *amicus curiae*, and on that basis was able to consider the arguments of the court supporting its imposition of sanctions. Although ultimately the appellate court found that the fine was improper, it did so not because the trial court lacked the power to control court proceedings or the conduct of attorneys, but because the trial court failed to use a primary tool available to it: entry of an order. As the court stated, "What should a trial court do in order to preserve the option of imposing a monetary sanction should the conduct of counsel merit that option? Make an order."

Despite the authority granted to judges to make decisions and the discretion that they have, the power of judges is not without limits. There are many mechanisms that serve to limit the authority of judges. Perhaps most important among these is the use of self-restraint. That is, judges are able to use no more of their powers than is necessary to accomplish what justice requires. The image of the wise and benevolent judge, although perhaps fictitious, is not wholly without some truth—most judges recognize the potential for abuse that their position entails and use their discretionary powers in beneficial ways. Whether it involves matters of constitutional interpretation, the application of statutory law, considering the arguments of counsel, or personal views about the liability of criminal or civil defendants, judges mostly seek to act in accordance with trust afforded their position by society.

Apart from the judiciary's own ability to limit its powers, there are other influences on the decision making of judges. These include mandates and provisions of the law, the wishes and control of the parties themselves, public opinion, the political and governmental processes, and the court system itself. Each of these, in different ways, serves to mediate the potential harshness (or "softness") that a judge's decision making may entail.

The law and the legal process itself serve as a limitation on judicial power. Although the decisions of judges often involve interpreting the law, in many cases, prior case decisions are clearly applicable, and the principle of *stare decisis* restrains the judge's power to reach conclusions that may be inconsistent with such case law. Similarly, statutory provisions often state in plain language what the law requires, and judges are not free to depart from such law in their decision making. Statutes specifying minimum sentences for certain crimes, or "three strikes" legislation, are examples of such laws. In addition, the use of juries serves as a legal limitation on judges' power. Only in very limited circumstances (such as when a jury verdict is clearly contrary to the evidence or because of juror misconduct) are judges free to depart from the conclusions reached by jurors. Indeed, the jury process itself may be viewed as a way of distributing decision-making power away from individual judges on the theory that collective decision making is less fallible.

The parties to a case also serve to limit the power a judge may wield. As the initiator of a court case, either the plaintiff or prosecutor may decide (usually based on lack of evidence) to voluntarily dismiss a complaint. Moreover, at any time in a civil case, the parties may enter into a settlement agreement that usually disposes of all or part of a case. Similarly, in a criminal case, the defendant may accept a plea agreement that takes the case out of the judge's or jury's hands. Although a plea bargain requires the judge's approval, the vast majority of plea agreements are accepted by the judge. In addition, knowing that the parties may appeal an unfavorable outcome based on decisions made by the judge may affect the care taken by a judge in issuing rulings.

Judges may also be sensitive to publicity that a case may garner, particularly to publicity regarding rulings made by the judge. Despite the fact that many judges are appointed for life for the very reason that they should not be subjected to the potential loss of employment as a result of unpopular decisions, judges are nonetheless public servants whose judicial behavior may be scrutinized by the media or special interest groups. Such scrutiny is usually designed to have the effect of influencing judicial decision making. Although judges are not subjected to the impeachment process for decisions they make on the bench, some state and local judges, especially if appointed for a term of years, may find their tenure on the bench limited by unpopular decisions or decisions that do not comply with politicians' interpretations of law (see **Sidebar 6.1**).

Sidebar 6.1 *When Good Judges Go Bad*

Judges, whether state or federal, trial or appellate, are entrusted with a public responsibility to administer justice. Society authorizes them to make binding decisions that affect those who appear before them. The American judicial system is one that requires objectivity, impartiality, and morality by judges. When judges take the power of their position and use it to make decisions that lack these characteristics or when they act in ways that call these characteristics into question, they act in contrast to the public interest and diminish public confidence in the justice system. Like all citizens, they must be accountable for their behavior, but this is especially true when their actions affect their ability to judge.

On Memorial Day in 2004, Chief Judge John Brennan of the Second Judicial District Court in New Mexico was pulled over and arrested for driving while intoxicated. Judge Brennan was a respected judge who had been on the bench for almost 25 years. When arrested, he and his companion, a female employee with the state's Commission on Higher Education, also had cocaine in their possession. He was charged with these crimes, pled guilty, and was sentenced to 2 days of house arrest and 2 years of probation. He subsequently stepped down from the bench and gave up his license to practice law.

On March 11, 2005, Judge Robert M. Restaino, was presiding over his docket of domestic violence cases in the

(Continues)

Niagara Falls, New York, City Court. During the proceedings, a cell phone rang in the courtroom. When the judge asked whose phone it was, no one came forward. The judge then announced, "Every single person is going to jail unless I get that instrument now." When this threat did not produce the phone, the judge had each of the 46 defendants in court searched, he questioned them about it, and he imposed bail on each one (requiring that they be taken into custody), even though such defendants were normally released on personal recognizance. Fourteen of the defendants were unable to post bail and were sent to the county jail. Only defendants were searched and questioned, not court personnel, attorneys, or others in the courtroom.

As a result of this behavior, The New York Commission on Judicial Conduct removed Judge Restaino from office, stating, "In causing 46 individuals to be deprived of their liberty out of pique and frustration, respondent abandoned his role as a reasonable, fair jurist and instead became a petty tyrant, abusing his judicial power and placing himself above the law he was sworn to administer. It is tragic that in a crowded courtroom, only the individual wearing judicial robes, symbolizing his exalted status and the power it conferred, seems to have been oblivious to the enormous injustice caused by his rash and reckless behavior."

Another case involving two Pittsburgh judges shows the harmful effects that greed may have on the administration of justice. From 2003 to 2008, these two judges sat on the juvenile court and sentenced juveniles to incarceration in juvenile facilities run by a private company. Many of the juveniles were first-time offenders incarcerated for minor offenses that typically involved little or no punishment, such as petty theft, fighting, and trespassing. One 15-year-old girl who satirized the assistant principal of her high school on MySpace was sentenced to 3 months in the facility for harassment. Nearly all of the juveniles were not represented by attorneys. Although a juvenile's disposition is normally within the discretion of the court, the lack of procedural protections for the juveniles and the excessive punishments resulted from a comprehensive scheme involving kickbacks of over $2.6 million these judges received from the company that owned the juvenile facilities. They were charged with income tax fraud and wire fraud in connection with the kickbacks, accepted a plea deal, were sentenced to 87 months in federal prison, and were forced to resign and give up their law licenses. Many of the youths sentenced by the judges filed civil lawsuits against them for violation of their constitutional rights. The Pennsylvania Supreme Court expunged the records of all juveniles affected.

Cases such as these reveal the susceptibility to imperfection that exists in the justice system. Any system in which great authority over others is entrusted to humans will have some judges who are unable to overcome their temptations to commit wrongful acts, which often have dire consequences for individuals and always have significant effects on the court system. Breaches of trust lead to a lack of confidence, and public confidence in the justice system is a crucial aspect of the operation of the courts.

Judicial Decision Making

The judiciary occupies a unique position in our system of separation of powers, and that is why the job of a judge differs in a fundamental way from that of a legislator or executive. The purpose of the judiciary is not to reflect public opinion in its deliberations or to satisfy public opinion with its decisions. Rather, it is to ensure that the ordinary laws do not run contrary to the more fundamental law of the Constitution, to resolve disputes and controversies surrounding the law, and to resolve disputes among contesting parties over the meaning of the law and the Constitution (*League of United Latin American Citizens Council v. Clements*, 914 F.2d 620 (5th Cir. 1990)).

The processes through which judges make decisions vary to a considerable extent with the individual judge, but the process followed is consistent. In making decisions, judges are affected by legal factors, such as their view of the requirements and demands of the law, the potential effects of their decisions, and the influence of legal ethics. They are also affected by personal characteristics, however, such as their moral perspectives, philosophical or religious views, personal experiences, and beliefs about the proper exercise of discretion. Judgments made by judges are sometimes affected as much by these personal characteristics as by the requirements of the law.

Trial judges, in bench trials, are "finders of fact," which means that, in the absence of a jury, it falls on the judge to weigh evidence and decide which "version" of the facts is most reliable and credible. Based on this determination regarding the facts, the trial judge then considers what the law requires and, applying the law to the facts, reaches a decision in the cases. This is the legal reasoning process. In jury trials, when trial judges are not "finders of fact," the responsibility for selecting the appropriate legal rules to be applied in a case still rests with the judge, who will outline the law in the instructions to the jury, and the process of applying the law to the facts proceeds similarly after the facts have been determined by the jury.

Appellate judges, on the other hand, focus exclusively on the law and assume the existence of facts found in the record of the trial court. Thus, appellate judges limit themselves to interpreting the law and, based on their interpretation, reversing or affirming the decision reached at trial. A case may involve one or several of the primary sources of law—case law, statutes, or constitutions. The reliance on precedent and matters of constitutional or statutory interpretation, although ultimately the central province of appellate judges, is also the basis for decisions by trial court judges who are also regularly confronted with the need to use them.

The rule of *stare decisis* and the principle of precedent were introduced in Chapter 2. *Stare decisis* ("let the decision stand") is the rule that legal principles in prior cases are applied to present cases to reach a conclusion; however, the process is less mechanical than it sounds. In many prior appellate decisions, the focus and holding are very narrow, limiting the applicability of the decision. Moreover, given that most controversies that reach the courtroom present some unique aspects of fact or law, it is not always possible to find case precedent that perfectly applies. The rule of precedent has been referred to as "reasoning by example." This means that a prior case (or cases) must be found that is similar to the case to be decided. Similarity may be based on a legal issue presented by the current case, the facts, or both. After a prior case has been found, the legal rule that relates to the similarity between the cases is examined to see whether it would assist in determining the outcome of the case to be decided. If so, the precedential rule is "applied" to the current case to reach a conclusion. Although this outline of the process reflects the principle, the rule of precedent is not simply a matter of matching up prior cases with new ones. This is because new cases constantly present new facts, and legal rules in old cases must often be shaped to fit new circumstances. Thus, as new cases are decided, their holdings often serve to modify, extend, limit, or reaffirm the common law.

In addition to deciding cases by reliance on precedent, judges are frequently called on to interpret statutory law. Interpretation is not a problem when the plain meaning of the statute is evident; however, statutory interpretation sometimes presents considerable difficulty for judges. The primary source of this difficulty is ambiguity. The "plain" meaning of the words written into the statute may be subject to different meanings in different circumstances. The legislative process at times leaves the law less clear than it needs to be, and judges are left to resolve the meaning of such ambiguities. Consider the following example: A state has a law that penalizes anyone who "refuses to obey any lawful order of a police officer given in the lawful performance of his duties." The police receive a complaint about a loud party in a neighborhood, arrive at the house, and tell everyone not living there to leave. When a partygoer who does not live there refuses to leave, she is arrested and charged with violating the statute. At court, the judge is confronted with a number of questions regarding this seemingly clear statute, including whether the officer was acting in the "lawful performance of his duties" and whether the order to leave the party was "lawful." The meaning of the word lawful and how it should be applied to the facts above are less than perfectly clear, requiring interpretation on the part of the judge.

When the meaning of a statute is not clear, judges look beyond the words themselves to ascertain what the legislative branch meant in passing a law. The question is this: Where should they look? This question continues to be a source of debate because different judges take different approaches and, at times, reach different conclusions as they "apply" the law. There are three primary methods of resolving ambiguities of statutory law. These are (1) examining the intent of the legislature; (2) determining the purpose of the law; and (3) considering the meaning of the statute in modern context.

Legislative intent refers to what the legislative body that adopted the law intended to accomplish by its passage. This intent may be found in a variety of sources, most commonly legislative history recorded at the time a statute was discussed in the legislative body, written commentary on a bill by its authors or sponsors, and other contemporaneous statements about a law at the time of its passage. Judges who focus on legislative intent to resolve statutory ambiguity attempt, from the historical context in which a statute was drafted, to determine what the intent was of the legislative body, although at times multiple "intents" by different legislators may become evident. What the judge determines the intent to have been can have significant consequences for the meaning of the statute and, ultimately, for the decision reached in a particular case.

Legislative purpose refers to determining the purpose for which the law was adopted. Legislative "purpose" can be distinguished from "intent" in that purpose focuses on what was to be accomplished by passage of the legislation, whereas intent refers to why the statute needed to be passed. The purpose of a law is often stated at the beginning of a statute, although purpose itself is not always clear, but by focusing on the end result of the legislation, it is often easier for a judge to measure the facts of a particular case against the result contemplated in such situations by the statute.

Finally, judges' interpretations of the law may involve examining the text of a statute, not in terms of the historical context in which it was written, but in a modern-day context. Referred to as "dynamic statutory interpretation," it considers the language of a statute as changeable over time; thus, what a statute meant at the time it was written may differ from its current meaning. Those judges who apply this method of interpretation believe that, as society changes along with the problems confronted by the courts, statutory laws should be given meaning in the modern society in which they are to be applied.

The Jury

Juries are decision makers. As noted in Chapter 3, jury selection is central to the trial process and intended to result in a group of 6 or 12 persons who can reach an unbiased decision based on the evidence. The jury is selected from a *venire*, or pool of potential jurors, usually by the attorneys for the parties along with the judge. Based on information provided by members of the venire on juror questionnaires, as well as through questioning by the judge or attorneys (the process known as *voir dire*), attorneys for the parties attempt to identify jurors whom they believe will be favorable to their positions, or at least not biased against them. The use of peremptory challenges and challenges for cause is common, necessary, and viewed as contributing to the fairness of the process; however, as the Mohammad case (found in Case Decision 6.2) and many other cases have made clear, attorneys may not use peremptory challenges to remove potential jurors based on their race.

During trial, the jury listens to the evidence and the arguments of the parties. In most jurisdictions, jurors are not allowed to take notes or ask questions during trial. Moreover, at times the jury is asked to retire to the jury room so that matters relating to the evidence may be discussed or argued outside of their hearing. At other times, the jury is instructed by the judge to ignore arguments or statements made by witnesses or their attorneys, and not use them in their decision making. In general, however, the jury must pay attention to what occurs in the courtroom, who speaks, and what is said so that they can render a decision based on the trial presentations.

After trial but before the case is turned over to the jury for decision, the judge instructs the jury on the law of the case. Jury instructions are intended to focus the jury on the issues in the case and how the law should be applied, given the facts that the jury may find to be true. The instructions typically will discuss the elements that need to be proven by the plaintiff or the prosecution, any defenses that may preclude liability by the defendant, the burdens of proof, and how certain facts, if proven, should affect the jury's decision about the outcome of the case. In addition, the instructions usually will direct the jury to elect a foreman to be moderator of the deliberations and to communicate with the judge. Along with the instructions, the jury is provided with a verdict form on which the foreman can record the jury's decision about liability, as well as the amount of damages in a civil case. Thus, although it is up to the jury to decide which facts are true based on the evidence presented at trial, it is the judge's job to teach the jury, in the written instructions, what the applicable law is and how to report its decision.

Although jury instructions are given to the jury by the judge, each side of a case has the opportunity to present and argue for the adoption of instructions that it believes should be given to the jury. The instructions submitted by each side reflect the parties' versions of the theory and issues in the case and the conclusions they believe the law requires to be found based on the facts. The attorneys for each side therefore try to convince the judge that their version of the instructions most accurately reflects the applicable law and should be used by the jury. The judge need not accept the requested instructions from either party but may choose some instructions from each or may completely draft his or her own. Many states have standardized jury instructions for particular types of cases that summarize the legal issues for the jury.

When the jury members retire to the jury room to deliberate about the case, they are empowered to render a decision. Indeed, the jury is not typically dismissed until it has done so. Although interviews with jurors over many years have given some indication of what occurs during jury deliberations, the proceedings are private. Not even the judge is privy to juror deliberations. In most cases, a foreman is elected by the members of jury whose primary job is to moderate discussion of the case and communicate the decision of the jury to the court. Although there may be some initial discussion, usually early in the deliberations a vote will be taken to determine the views of the jurors. Before deciding, the jury will review the physical and documentary evidence, consider the testimony, review the judge's instructions, and try to reach a unanimous decision. Although unanimity is not required in either civil or criminal cases, a verdict always requires a majority of jurors to agree. When this is not possible, the judge may declare a mistrial, allowing a retrial of the case.

Key Terms

Adverse	Complaint
Plaintiff	Answer
Defendant	Service of Process
Prosecutor	Default Judgment
Judge	Affirmative Defenses
Jury	

Discussion Questions

1. Who are the participants in criminal and civil cases, and what roles do they play in the dispute resolution process?
2. How do the goals of each of these participants in court differ?
3. When does prosecutorial discretion "cross the line" and become misconduct?
4. What is the primary source of procedural protections for criminal defendants? Why are these necessary?
5. What is a civil complaint? Why is a service of process important?
6. What are the some of the various functions that an attorney—for either the prosecution, plaintiff, or defense—might play in a case?
7. What authority do judges have? What is the source of their authority?
8. How does the law and legal process serve as a limitation on judicial power?
9. What is the function of the jury in a criminal case? How does its function differ in a civil case?
10. What is the purpose of jury instructions?

Cases

Gideon v. Wainwright, 372 U.S. 335 (1963).

League of United Latin American Citizens Council v. Clements, 914 F.2d 620 (5th Cir. 1990)

People v. Muhammad, 108 Cal. App. 4th 313, 133 Cal. Rptr. 2d 308 (Cal. App. 2003).

Criminal Justice on the Web

For an up-to-date list of Web links, go to *The American Courts: A Procedural Approach* online companion site at http://criminal justice.jbpub.com/AmericanCourts. The online companion site will introduce you to some of the most important sites for finding American courts information on the Internet.

Reference

Harlow, C. W. (2000). *Defense Counsel in Criminal Cases*. Washington, DC: Bureau of Justice Statistics.

Family Courts   7

What Is This Chapter About?

This chapter is about the courts that handle family matters, other than cases involving juvenile behavior. Family courts handle a wide range of cases that affect American life, such as divorce, adoption, domestic disputes, cases of child abuse and neglect, and termination of parental rights.

The chapter examines the basis for the family courts by considering statutory authority that specifies the role of family courts within a state justice system, as well as the functions of the family courts. A large proportion of the caseload of family courts involves hearing divorce cases. The requirements of marriage are outlined, and the current controversies involving gay marriage and civil unions are discussed. Marriage and divorce as legal concepts are discussed, as well as the process of divorce. This includes the various ways in which divorce proceedings bring about the result of ending a marriage agreement. In addition, the manner in which property is divided between spouses, spousal and child support, and the economic and child custody issues faced by divorcing parents and resolved by family courts is discussed. In addition, family courts are typically responsible for adoptions; the legal issues relating to the adoption of children are addressed, as well as issues relating to the termination of parental rights.

Learning Objectives

After reading this chapter, you should be able to

1. Identify the functions of family courts.
2. Describe the legal bases for marriage and divorce.
3. Explain the function and requirements of premarital agreements.
4. Understand the issues addressed by a family court in divorce cases.
5. Explain how property may be divided in divorce cases.
6. Understand how family courts resolve child custody issues.
7. Outline the steps involved in adoption of a child.
8. Describe the process for terminating parental rights, and explain when it is necessary.

The family, in all of its various forms, is widely recognized as central to American life, and the family court therefore has a unique place in American society. This is because it addresses matters that relate in a most intimate way to the American family: marriage and relationships, building families, the support and care of children, the rights of parents, and the rights of children. Each of these areas, although central to American life and personal autonomy, is a matter of law. As such, it is necessary for the courts to address issues, problems, and disputes that arise in each of these areas and, in effect, preserve their centrality and importance.

The term "family court" refers as much or more to its function as to its physical presence within a state court system. In some states, it functions within the general jurisdiction of the state's trial courts, and in others, it operates as a division of the courts of general jurisdiction, whereas in others, it serves as an independent court of limited jurisdiction. Although the functions and organization may vary, the need for its operations is constant across the United States.

In most states, the caseload of the family court is handled separately from that of the juvenile court. As the name implies, the juvenile court is responsible for matters relating to minors—in some states, it is referred to as the children's court and exists as a division of the family court. This chapter is limited to discussion of issues facing the family courts, not those of the juvenile courts. The juvenile courts are the subject of Chapter 8.

The Functions of Family Courts

Although relatively few marriage ceremonies actually take place in family courtrooms or are conducted by family court judges, family courts frequently consider the terms under which marriage agreements come to fruition as married couples live together, acquire property, earn livings, and have children. The family court's involvement in these most private and intimate matters most often involves interpretation and application of the laws governing divorce and its corresponding topics of child custody and division of marital assets. In addition, family court judges also regularly consider family matters as they address legal procedures and issues relating to adoption of children.

These traditional areas continue to make up a large part of the workload of family courts. However, the areas of responsibility for family courts continue to expand as family law, like other areas of the law, develops and evolves as society changes. For example, the increase in couples cohabitating and parenting children without marriage and court rulings and legislation granting homosexual couples the right to marry have changed the legal landscape of family law.

Marriage

For most people (at least, most women), the word "marriage" conjures up pictures of a wedding: the bride, the dress, the flowers, the church, the reception, the cake, the honeymoon. As important as these aspects of social life are, they do not create a marriage. As much as the public may perceive marriage as a personal, social, and perhaps religious experience binding two people together, it fundamentally represents a legal act. From a legal perspective, marriage requires a contract reflecting an agreement to be together in a personal and social way. Although there are differing requirements from state to state, generally, the contract need not take any specific form and may be written, oral, or created by the actions of the parties. The other common requirements are that neither of the parties be currently married and that they are not related by blood to a certain degree (such as no closer than second cousins).

Once established, marriage continues in existence until one of the parties dies or divorce is ordered by a court. Marriage creates a legal status recognized by society that, like all contracts, produces certain benefits for the parties as well as obligations from entering into the agreement. These legal consequences of marriage affect various aspects of life, including living arrangements, financial responsibility, property ownership, inheritance, health care, children, retirement benefits, and taxes. It is evident that marriage has comprehensive effects on many aspects of life; for that reason, in addition to the many personal reasons one enters into such an agreement, marriage brings about a significant change in one's circumstances. As the U.S. Supreme Court has stated, "Marriage is one of the 'basic civil rights of man,' fundamental to our very existence and survival" (*Loving v. Virginia*, 388 U.S. 1, 12, 87 S. Ct. 1817, 1824, 18 L.Ed.2d 1010 (1967)).

Traditional Marriage

Various definitions of and perspectives on marriage can be found, but the traditional view was that marriage exists when a man and a woman entered into personal and social bonds, recognized in religion and law (Simon & Altstein, 2003). Like most of American law, marriage in America finds its roots in England, where the concept of *coverture*

applied. Blackstone discussed this concept in the 18th century:

> By marriage, the husband and wife are one person in law: that is, the very being or legal existence of the woman is suspended during the marriage, or at least is incorporated and consolidated into that of the husband; under whose wing, protection, and *cover*, she performs every thing; . . . and her condition during her marriage is called her *coverture*. Upon this principle, of a union of person in husband and wife, depend almost all the legal rights, duties, and disabilities, that either of them acquire by the marriage. (Blackstone, 1770; quoted in *Ellis v. Estate of Ellis*, 169 P.2d. 441, 2007 UT 77 (2007))

Although by today's standards this approach seems lacking in equality, even this early view of marriage contemplated the responsibilities and benefits that both the wife and husband would "acquire by the marriage." The American view of marriage largely accepted that women were in a secondary role to their husbands, at least in business affairs, but that view began to change in the 1960s. Although the causes of this paradigm shift vary, the rise of feminism, more liberal views of sexuality, and growing acceptance of cohabitation outside of marriage certainly contributed (Shumway, 2003). Marriage agreements became based to a greater degree on mutual responsibilities and benefits of husbands and wives, including in decisions regarding producing and raising children.

Common Law Marriage

Common law marriage exists when a man and woman live together and hold themselves out as husband and wife, despite not having satisfied the formalities of a marriage agreement. For example, the requirements for a common law marriage under Texas law are "(1) an agreement to be married; (2) living together in Texas as husband and wife subsequent to the agreement to be married; and (3) representing to others in Texas that they were married" (*Ayala v. Valderas*, 2008 WL 46661846 (Tx. Ct. App. 2008)). It is allowed in only 11 states, and many other states will not recognize common law marriages created in those few that do allow them.

Because common law marriages are not formalized in accordance with generally accepted legal principles, they sometimes create problems.

Nontraditional Marriage

Because marriage has traditionally been between a man and a woman, same-sex couples in most states were unable to marry. In response, some states, such as Vermont, have adopted statutes authorizing *civil unions*, which allowed same-sex couples to recognize their relationships legally. Although not redefining marriage, these laws provided a mechanism in which same-sex couples could receive some of the legal benefits of marriage, as well as public recognition of their commitment to another person (Ronfani, 2007).

In other states, however, marriage itself has undergone a significant transformation relative to traditional norms.

In *Baehr v. Lewin* 74 Haw. 530, 852 P.2d 44 (1993), the Hawaii Supreme Court decided that same-sex couples were entitled to receive marriage licenses on the same basis as males and females who wished to marry. The court held that it was discriminatory to deny same-sex couples the right to marry, despite the historical requirement that only men and women could do so. As a result, the state adopted a constitutional amendment specifying that marriage may exist only between a man and a woman.

In addition, because same-sex marriage became a national issue as a result of the Hawaii decision and a similar one in Alaska, Congress passed the Defense of Marriage Act of 1996, which simply states that

> No State, territory, or possession of the United States, or Indian tribe, shall be required to give effect to any public act, record, or judicial proceeding of any other State, territory, possession, or tribe respecting a relationship between persons of the same sex that is treated as a marriage under the laws of such other State, territory, possession, or tribe, or a right or claim arising from such relationship. (28 U.S.C. § 1738C)

Despite the federal statutory prohibition on same-sex marriages, it has little effect on the practice of marriage because marriage is almost exclusively governed by state law, and some states have seen fit to define marriage in nontraditional ways.

In *Goodridge v. Department of Public Health,* 440 Mass. 309, 798 N.E.2d 941 (2003), the Massachusetts Supreme Judicial Court, in a 4–3 decision, held that the denial of marriage licenses to same-sex couples violated the state constitution's equal protection clause. In a lengthy opinion filed over the dissents of three of the justices, the court found that the decision

> marks a change in the history of our marriage law. Many people hold deep-seated religious, moral, and ethical convictions that marriage should be limited to the union of one man and one woman, and that homosexual conduct is immoral. Many hold equally strong religious, moral, and ethical convictions that same-sex couples are entitled to be married, and that homosexual persons should be treated no differently than their heterosexual neighbors. Neither view answers the question before us. Our concern is with the Massachusetts Constitution as a charter of governance for every person properly within its reach. Our obligation is to define the liberty of all, not to mandate our own moral code. (440 Mass. at 312, 798 N.E.2d at 948)

Regardless of one's view of the issue, the court was correct in noting the change to the definition of marriage its decision brought about.

Decisions like this affecting the traditional view of marriage have been met with public outcry. After the California Supreme Court found that the denial of marriage licenses to same-sex couples violated its state constitution, a ballot initiative was begun to amend the constitution with a definition of marriage as between a man and a woman. The initiative passed in the November 2008 general election.

Along with the right to same-sex marriage created by the Massachusetts' Supreme Judicial Court's and other state supreme courts' interpretations of their state constitutions, a spillover effect of legal issues for other states has been created. Same-sex couples who wish to marry but are not residents of a same-sex marriage state now travel from their home state to marry in the same-sex marriage state, in order to benefit from the new definition of marriage; however, when they subsequently return to their home states and wish to birth children, adopt children, or divorce, those other states have been left to decide the effects of the same-sex marriage state's laws on its own citizens (see, e.g., *S.J.L.S. v. T.L.S.*, 265 S.W.3d 804 (Ky. App. 2008); *Chambers v. Ormiston*, 935 A.2d 956 (R.I. 2007); *Conaway v. Deane*, 401 Md. 219, 932 A.2d 571 (2007)).

Premarital (Prenuptial) Agreements

As the traditional view of marriage began to change in 1960s, new approaches to the financial aspects of relationships also began to change. One of these was the development of *premarital agreements* (often called prenuptial agreements and, sometimes, antenuptial agreements). Premarital agreements are made in contemplation of marriage to govern various aspects of the marital relationship. Chief among these is the distribution of assets upon divorce.

Many states have enacted statutes to govern the content and interpretation of premarital agreements. Most of these are based on the Uniform Premarital Agreement Act, which is a sample act drafted in 1983 by the National Conference of Commissioners on Uniform State Laws for use by state legislatures to make the preparation of premarital agreements consistent. For example, California's version of the Act specifies the following:

> (a) Parties to a premarital agreement may contract with respect to all of the following:
>   (1) The rights and obligations of each of the parties in any of the property of either or both of them whenever and wherever acquired or located.
>   (2) The right to buy, sell, use, transfer, exchange, abandon, lease, consume, expend, assign, create a security interest in, mortgage, encumber, dispose of, or otherwise manage and control property.
>   (3) The disposition of property upon separation, marital dissolution, death, or the occurrence or nonoccurrence of any other event.
>   (4) The making of a will, trust, or other arrangement to carry out the provisions of the agreement.
>   (5) The ownership rights in and disposition of the death benefit from a life insurance policy.
>   (6) The choice of law governing the construction of the agreement.
>   (7) Any other matter, including their personal rights and obligations, not in violation of public policy or a statute imposing a criminal penalty.
> (b) The right of a child to support may not be adversely affected by a premarital agreement.
> (c) Any provision in a premarital agreement regarding spousal support, including, but not limited to, a waiver of it, is not enforceable if the party against whom enforcement of the spousal support provision is sought was not

represented by independent counsel at the time the agreement containing the provision was signed, or if the provision regarding spousal support is unconscionable at the time of enforcement. An otherwise unenforceable provision in a premarital agreement regarding spousal support may not become enforceable solely because the party against whom enforcement is sought was represented by independent counsel. (Cal. Family Code § 1612; West, 2004)

This Act, similar to those adopted in many states, is noteworthy for both its breadth and its limitations. First, it allows couples to agree in almost any way they wish about nearly every type of property they may own, as well as "any other matter" that does not violate public policy or is a crime. Second, the agreement will have no effect on child support. Third, any provision of the agreement that limits support for a spouse when the marriage ends will be enforceable only if the spouse whose support may be limited was represented by counsel at the time the agreement was drafted. Although couples generally do not like to contemplate divorce at the same time that they are contemplating marriage, a premarital agreement drafted in accordance with state law can assist the parties in their planning as well as cause them to consider aspects of the relationship that they might not otherwise consider.

Divorce

As is well known, *divorce* is the term given to the legal dissolution of a marriage. If marriage is an agreement, divorce is the termination of that agreement, which can be accomplished only as a result of a court order. A divorce decree from a family court thus ends the marriage and sets out the terms for distributing property to the individuals involved and specifies arrangements for the care and continuing relationships with children.

Types of Divorce

There are two types of legal proceedings in which divorce may be accomplished. These are unilateral divorce and divorce by mutual consent. Unilateral divorces are contested. That is, they are initiated by one of the parties in an adversarial proceeding in which a response by the nonfiling party is required. In this context, contested does not necessarily mean a lack of agreement about termination of the marriage or even the distribution of property, although that may be the case; it simply means that only one of the parties has asserted grounds to justify a divorce. Unilateral divorces may be one of two types, fault or no fault. In fault-based divorces, the plaintiff alleges specific grounds for the divorce. Most common are adultery, cruelty or physical abuse, drug or alcohol abuse, or abandonment. In no-fault divorce, the grounds are simply "irreconcilable differences" that have led to an irretrievable breakdown of the marriage. Divorce by mutual consent is an uncontested divorce in which the parties agree that the marriage cannot continue and agree as to the distribution of property, child care, and visitation.

Consequences of Divorce

Much has been said about the growth of divorce and its effects on American society. It is often noted that 50 percent of marriages in the United States end in divorce, which means that there is family court intervention in at least half of the marriages that occur. Divorce can have significant consequences for the parties (see **Sidebar 7.1**). These may be both emotional and financial. With respect to the latter, the consequences may be particularly severe for women (Weitzman, 1985). The typical woman who experiences divorce also suffers a decline in her financial status after the divorce. The reasons for this vary, but it has been found that women are far more likely than men to become responsible for child care after divorce, which imposes limitations on their employment possibilities and earning potential (see Thompson & Amato, 1999). In addition, the adequacy of or failure to pay child support by the ex-husband contributes to a diminution in the ex-wife's economic status (Weitzman, 1985).

Sidebar 7.1 *Divorce Court*

Divorce is a growth business. About half of first marriages will end in divorce, as well as nearly two thirds of second marriages and three fourths of third marriages. Because divorce can be finalized only with a court order, some involvement with the court system occurs with every divorce. Legally, the dissolution of a marriage is no more difficult or complex than other types of disputes handled by courts, but the effects on those affected by the divorce are often much more significant. Although the word "nasty" is often used descriptively in divorce, it refers to the attitudes and behaviors of the parties, not to the legal process or a court's involvement.

The reasons why marriages fail vary, but most involve a lack of communication about problems in the marriage central to the lives of one or both parties. This often leads to marital conflicts and arguments, another frequently cited basis for divorce, or infidelity, which typically represents a party's ultimate refusal to communicate. Other less common reasons involve abusive behavior by a spouse, alcohol or drug abuse, or other personal problems. The court, or the court process, becomes a forum for forced communication and resolution, not of all problems, but of the financial and child support and custody issues facing the parties. Communication about these issues occurs, either directly between the parties, with the assistance of a mediator, or through the parties' attorneys.

The marital problems of others are of great interest to the American public. Reporting on the divorce proceedings of the rich and famous is a favorite tabloid pastime, and the mainstream press joins in. In one famous Hollywood divorce, the breakup of Lucille Ball and Desi Arnez in 1960 allegedly resulted from Arnez's drinking and womanizing. Although they remained friendly for the rest of their lives, Lucille Ball cited the time of the divorce as one of the worst of her life, a sentiment likely shared by most who experience it. Financially, the divorce proved to be beneficial for Ball because she gained control of the television production company formerly owned with her husband, Desilu, becoming the first female president of such a business.

More recently, the very intimate details of the lives of famous divorcing couples sometimes become daily news. In 2006, Britney Spears sought to divorce her husband Kevin Federline, claiming irreconcilable differences and seeking custody of her two sons, both under the age of 5 years. This became one of the most publicized divorces, with ongoing filming, photos, and reports of the events in the couple's lives, particularly Spears' apparent mental breakdown, reported drug use, subsequent loss of custody of her children, two periods of time in rehabilitation facilities, and derailed singing career. In 2007, the divorce was finalized with an undisclosed financial settlement and a shared custody arrangement for the children.

Some divorce disputes involve large sums of money. After basketball star Michael Jordan's divorce from his wife Juanita, he paid her over $150 million. The divorce of former Beatle Paul McCartney and Heather Mills cost him about $60 million, and Harrison Ford's 2004 divorce included his payment of $85 million plus a percentage of future profits from some of his films, including the *Indiana Jones* movies and *The Fugitive*. Even when the parties in such cases are cordial to each other, the amounts of money involved make resolution of the case more difficult and time consuming because the spouses generally do not agree on what is "fair"—except in the case of singer Neil Diamond. After his divorce from his wife of 25 years and payment to her of about $150 million, he stated that she was "worth every penny."

Not just the rich and famous have public divorces, however. Some people seek the limelight in order to air their divorces for the viewing public. As most people realize, divorce may be traumatic, but it can also be dramatic and therefore entertaining. That is the premise behind the popular television reality series *Divorce Court*, which is the oldest "court" television show, having first aired in 1957. A "judge" (there have been many over the years) serves as an arbitrator in divorce cases that couples have already filed in an actual court. The spouses agree to argue their claims for property, alimony, child support, and custody and explain how the often-shocking behavior of the other party has led to the divorce. The judge's decisions result in a settlement agreement between the parties.

Despite public fascination with divorce and many people's private experiences with it, for most people, divorce is a painful experience. Its causes are many, and the demands of a society that constantly seeks to reinvent itself in its pursuit of happiness suggest that this area of a family court's work will not soon diminish.

Although divorce is a personal matter that has consequences for the parties, it is also one that has societal consequences (Glendon, 1989). For example, children experience higher levels of stress and feelings of insecurity both during and after divorce, which often translate into behavior or performance problems in school (Wallerstein et al., 2000). Moreover, the absence of a father in the home, which frequently occurs because mothers are most often granted custody by the family courts, is correlated with such social problems as delinquency, violent behavior, and teenage pregnancy (Weitzman, 1985).

Separation

Although less commonly used in the United States, *separation* is usually taken by courts as definitive grounds for the termination of the marriage. Separation means that the spouses continuously live apart for a specified period of time.

Separation may be formal or informal. Formal, or legal, separation means that a court has entered an order directing the parties to live apart. It may also include terms as to living arrangements, contact between the spouses, access to marital property, debts, and children. Formal separation is sometimes used as an alternative to divorce, perhaps for religious or financial reasons. A more common basis for formal separation is where the parties are clearly contemplating divorce and the separation serves as precursor in which many issues relevant to the divorce may be resolved.

Informal separation occurs when spouses agree between themselves to live separate and apart from each other on a continuous basis, but if this is done with the intent to remain married, they may not be considered to be separated. Similarly, spouses who live apart for other reasons, such as employment, economic, or social reasons, are not considered to be separated. Thus, living apart is not sufficient, by itself, to constitute a separation affecting marital status.

Division of Property

The division of property owned during the marriage is a primary area of dispute between the parties in contested divorce cases. Indeed, most divorce litigation involves how property should be divided, and the law in this area differs considerably across the states. This property nearly always includes real estate, bank accounts, and investments but frequently also includes personal property such as cars, jewelry, furnishings, and artwork, even pets! The job of the family court is to determine a way to divide the property that is fair to parties and complies with the legal requirements of the state.

A central legal distinction affecting the distribution of property in divorce is between separate and community property. The majority of states are separate property states in which property belongs to the person who has title to it. In a separate property state, a bank account in one spouse's name is presumed to be owned by that spouse; similarly, a car or a house is owned by the spouse in whose name it is. Furthermore, income is the property of the spouse who earns it.

In community-property states, all property acquired during marriage is owned equally by both spouses, and each is presumed to have an equal share in all income earned during the marriage. A spouse may own separate property in a community-property state, but only if it was acquired prior to the marriage or received as an inheritance or gift. It must also be kept separate from the community property, such as maintaining a bank account in the individual spouse's name with the designation "as her sole and separate property." The community property states are primarily in the western part of the country: Arizona, California, Idaho, Nevada, New Mexico, Louisiana, Texas, Washington, and Wisconsin.

This distinction is important because it serves as a starting point for understanding the laws governing distribution of property in divorce cases, which do not follow any single pattern across the states. In dividing marital property during divorce, separate property states generally follow an "equitable distribution" method of dividing property between the spouses. This means that the law requires the property to be divided fairly and equitably; however, the meaning of "equitable" distribution varies considerably in the separate property states. In all states, property owned jointly by the spouses, called "marital property," will be included in the equitable distribution. In addition, in some states, all property owned separately by the parties during the marriage, with limited exceptions, is considered as part of the total available to be fairly distributed. Thus, the "separate" character of the property is essentially ignored for purposes of the divorce. In other states, property considered by the court for distribution will be limited to either jointly owned property or property acquired or used for the benefit of both spouses during the marriage. In these states, property owned by one spouse before marriage will be excluded for distribution purposes. In general, judges in separate property states are given considerable discretion in the division of assets.

In community-property states, all property acquired during the marriage that is community property is distributed at divorce. Separate property that has been separately maintained will generally belong to the spouse who owns it. Two problems that frequently arise in determining whether property is community or separate are *commingling* and *transmutation* of assets. Assets are commingled when separate property is merged with community property. This most commonly occurs when cash that is separate property is placed in a joint bank account. The effect of commingling is to change the character of the property from separate to community, or marital property, which then will be distributed to both spouses at divorce. Transmutation involves the treatment of property by both spouses as community property. For example, if a woman inherits a house and places the names of both spouses on the deed, the inheritance (which otherwise would have been separate property) is transmuted into community property.

In determining how to divide property between the spouses fairly, the court may look at a number of factors. Generally, equitable means equal, especially in community property states; however, whether marital property will be evenly divided can be affected by the nature of relationship and the behavior of the parties. The court may rely on both economic and noneconomic factors in mak-

ing this determination. Gross inequity in the contribution of economic assets, such as earning power, during the marriage may lead a court to award a greater share of marital property to a spouse who, for example, stayed home to care for children and did not earn income outside of the home. Courts may also consider the conduct of one or both spouses as relevant. For example, if the evidence establishes that one spouse had an affair, this may affect distribution of property, or if one party attempts to hide assets in anticipation of divorce, the court may grant the other spouse a greater share of those assets.

Child Support

Issues relating to children are often the source of disputes between spouses, although courts frequently use methods such as required mediation to avoid them. The family court's focus in deciding child support, custody, and visitation rights is to do what is in the best interests of the child.

Child support is money paid by a parent who does not have full-time custody of a child to the parent who does have custody. The payment is intended to be used for the living expenses and other financial requirements for the upbringing of the child. The payment usually lasts until the child is no longer a minor, but sometimes child support continues for a period of time while the child pursues higher education. Child support is not automatically granted. When parents have joint custody of a child, a court may presume that a child's needs will be met by both parents, and a payment from one to the other may not be necessary. Conversely, when one parent has sole custody of a child, child support may be warranted even if the custodial parent is capable of supporting the child alone.

Although states have historically allowed judges the discretion to decide the appropriate amount of child support, in the 1980s, Congress required states to adopt guidelines for child support amounts. This was largely due to the growing problem of child poverty and children born to unwed mothers, which Congress attributed in part to the nonpayment of child support as well as what it believed to be insufficient child support amounts awarded by family courts. Although the guidelines subsequently adopted were not originally intended to be binding on judges, they have become presumptive in most states. Because family courts have jurisdiction over matters relating to children and their welfare, whether in divorce cases or other matters, the guidelines have become useful tools for the courts and social services agencies in examining child support issues.

States generally take one of three approaches to the calculation of child support. The first of these looks only at the income of the noncustodial parent and awards a percentage of that income. The second, usually called the income shares approach, considers the incomes of both parents. It determines a total amount required for a child's support based on the total income and assigns an obligation to each parent based on his or her individual income, on a pro rata basis. The third method, known as the Melson formula, sets a basic amount for living expenses for each parent, as well as each child. A percentage of any income above these amounts is awarded in child support. The goal of this method is to allow children more than a basic support amount, allowing them to approximate the standard of living of their parents, as they would if they were living together. As noted previously here, family court judges have considerable discretion to depart from their state's guidelines in appropriate cases. This may occur when there are large differences in the incomes of the parents or if there are other financial resources available for the child's benefit.

Custody and Visitation

Custody and visitation issues are in the discretion of the family court. Traditionally, there has been a presumption that children should be in the custody of their mother, known as the "tender years doctrine." This presumption has been rejected in the majority of jurisdictions by statute, and a gender-based decision making relating to custody is no longer legally justified, having largely been replaced by the focus on the best interests of the child. Even in the many cases where the divorcing parents are able to agree on custody, the family court will consider the current living situation of the child, including school and extracurricular activities, healthcare needs, and the child's own wishes in determining what is in the child's best interests. In addition, an increasing number of courts now find that joint custody arrangements are in the child's best interests.

In a small but growing number of cases, custody becomes such a charged issue that a parent cannot accept a court's custody decision and absconds with the child. In such cases, a parent would move to another state, filing a petition for custody in the new state's family court. Once custody had been granted in the new state, the problem arose as to which family court order should govern the situation? To address this problem, in 1980, Congress passed the Parental Kidnapping Prevention Act (28 U.S.C. 1738A), which provides that

[t]he appropriate authorities of every State shall enforce according to its terms, and shall not modify except as provided in subsections (f), (g), and (h) of this section, any custody determination or visitation determination made

consistently with the provisions of this section by a court of another State.

The purpose of the act is to discourage the practice of moving from state to state to avoid custody orders and to clarify the jurisdictional rules governing which state court's custody order should take precedence.

Visitation refers to the right given a noncustodial parent by a family court to visit his or her children. This is routinely granted, except in divorces in which the noncustodial parent was found to be abusive, addicted to alcohol or drugs, or living in an unsafe environment. In some cases, a family court judge will specify in detail the days, hours, and places in which visitation may occur; in other cases, visitation may be worked out between the parents. As with custody and depending on the age of the child, his or her wishes may also be considered.

It is not uncommon for grandparents to seek visitation with their grandchildren (Jackson, 1994). States and family courts have normally allowed grandparent visitation; however, in some cases, it becomes a source of dispute between the divorcing spouses. One such case, *Troxel v. Granville*, 530 U.S. 57, 120 S. Ct. 2054, 147 L.Ed.2d 49 (2000), involved a Washington state statute that provided

[a]ny person may petition the court for visitation rights at any time including, but not limited to, custody proceedings. The court may order visitation rights for any person when visitation may serve the best interest of the child whether or not there has been any change of circumstances. (RCWA 26.10.160(3))

The case involved two girls whose mother restricted visitation by the girls' paternal grandparents after their father had died. The issue for the Court was whether the statute unconstitutionally infringed on the mother's right to determine who may visit her children. The opinion is found in **Case Decision 7.1**.

In finding that the Washington statute infringed on the mother's right to direct the upbringing of her children, including whom they may associate with through visitation, Justice O'Connor noted that the Constitution did not allow a judge to substitute his views of what was best for

---

Case Decision 7.1 *Troxel v. Granville*, 530 U.S. 57, 120 S. Ct. 2054, 147 L.Ed.2d 49 (2000)

Decision of the Court with an Opinion by Justice O'Connor:

Section 26.10.160(3) of the Revised Code of Washington permits "[a]ny person" to petition a superior court for visitation rights "at any time," and authorizes that court to grant such visitation rights whenever "visitation may serve the best interest of the child." Petitioners Jenifer and Gary Troxel petitioned a Washington Superior Court for the right to visit their grandchildren, Isabelle and Natalie Troxel. Respondent Tommie Granville, the mother of Isabelle and Natalie, opposed the petition. The case ultimately reached the Washington Supreme Court, which held that § 26.10.160(3) unconstitutionally interferes with the fundamental right of parents to rear their children.

(Continues)

I

Tommie Granville and Brad Troxel shared a relationship that ended in June 1991. The two never married, but they had two daughters, Isabelle and Natalie. Jenifer and Gary Troxel are Brad's parents, and thus the paternal grandparents of Isabelle and Natalie. After Tommie and Brad separated in 1991, Brad lived with his parents and regularly brought his daughters to his parents' home for weekend visitation. Brad committed suicide in May 1993. Although the Troxels at first continued to see Isabelle and Natalie on a regular basis after their son's death, Tommie Granville informed the Troxels in October 1993 that she wished to limit their visitation with her daughters to one short visit per month.

In December 1993, the Troxels commenced the present action by filing, in the Washington Superior Court for Skagit County, a petition to obtain visitation rights with Isabelle and Natalie. The Troxels filed their petition under Section 26.10.160(3). Section 26.10.160(3) provides: "Any person may petition the court for visitation rights at any time including, but not limited to, custody proceedings. The court may order visitation rights for any person when visitation may serve the best interest of the child whether or not there has been any change of circumstances." At trial, the Troxels requested two weekends of overnight visitation per month and two weeks of visitation each summer. Granville did not oppose visitation altogether, but instead asked the court to order one day of visitation per month with no overnight stay. In 1995, the Superior Court issued an oral ruling and entered a visitation decree ordering visitation one weekend per month, one week during the summer, and four hours on both of the petitioning grandparents' birthdays.

Granville appealed, during which time she married Kelly Wynn. Before addressing the merits of Granville's appeal, the Washington Court of Appeals remanded the case to the Superior Court for entry of written findings of fact and conclusions of law. On remand, the Superior Court found that visitation was in Isabelle's and Natalie's best interests:

> "The Petitioners [the Troxels] are part of a large, central, loving family, all located in this area, and the Petitioners can provide opportunities for the children in the areas of cousins and music. . . . The court took into consideration all factors regarding the best interest of the children and considered all the testimony before it. The children would be benefitted from spending quality time with the Petitioners, provided that that time is balanced with time with the childrens' [*sic*] nuclear family. The court finds that the childrens' [*sic*] best interests are served by spending time with their mother and stepfather's other six children."

Approximately nine months after the Superior Court entered its order on remand, Granville's husband formally adopted Isabelle and Natalie.

The Washington Court of Appeals reversed the lower court's visitation order and dismissed the Troxels' petition for visitation, holding that nonparents lack standing to seek visitation under Section 26.10.160(3) unless a custody action is pending. In the Court of Appeals' view, that limitation on nonparental visitation actions was "consistent with the constitutional restrictions on state interference with parents' fundamental liberty interest in the care, custody, and management of their children." Having resolved the case on the statutory ground, however, the Court of Appeals did not expressly pass on Granville's constitutional challenge to the visitation statute.

The Washington Supreme Court granted the Troxels' petition for review and, after consolidating their case with two other visitation cases, affirmed. The court disagreed with the Court of Appeals' decision on the statutory issue and found that the plain language of Section 26.10.160(3) gave the Troxels standing to seek visitation, irrespective of whether a custody action was pending. The Washington Supreme Court nevertheless agreed with the Court of Appeals' ultimate conclusion that the Troxels could not obtain visitation of Isabelle and Natalie pursuant to Section 26.10.160(3). The court rested its decision on the Federal Constitution, holding that Section 26.10.160(3) unconstitutionally infringes on the fundamental right of parents to rear their children. In the court's view, there were at least two problems with the nonparental visitation statute. First, according to the Washington Supreme Court, the Constitution permits a State to interfere with the right of parents to rear their children only to prevent harm or potential harm to a child. Section 26.10.160(3) fails that standard because it requires no threshold showing of harm. Second, by allowing "'any person' to petition for forced visitation of a child at 'any time' with the only requirement being that the visitation serve the best interest of the child," the Washington visitation statute sweeps too broadly. "It is not within the province of the state to make significant decisions concerning the custody of children merely because it could make a 'better' decision." The Washington Supreme Court held that "[p]arents have a right to limit visitation of their children with third persons," and that between parents and judges, "the parents should be the ones to choose whether to expose their children to certain people or ideas." Four justices dissented from the Washington Supreme Court's holding on the constitutionality of the statute.

We granted certiorari, and now affirm the judgment.

II

The demographic changes of the past century make it difficult to speak of an average American family. The composition of families varies greatly from household to household. While many children may have two married parents and grandparents who visit regularly, many other children are raised in single-parent households. In 1996, children living with only one parent accounted for 28 percent of all children under age 18 in the United States. U.S. Dept. of Commerce, Bureau of Census, Current Population Reports, 1997 Population Profile of the United States 27 (1998). Understandably, in these single-parent households, persons outside the nuclear family are called upon with increasing frequency to assist in the everyday tasks of child rearing. In many cases, grandparents play an important role. For example, in 1998, approximately 4 million children—or 5.6 percent of all children under age 18—lived in the household of their grandparents. U.S. Dept. of Commerce, Bureau of Census, Current Population Reports, Marital Status and Living Arrangements: March 1998 (Update), p. i (1998).

The nationwide enactment of nonparental visitation statutes is assuredly due, in some part, to the States' recognition of these changing realities of the American family. Because grandparents and other relatives undertake duties of a parental nature in many households, States have sought to ensure the welfare of the children therein by protecting the relationships those children form with such third parties. The States' nonparental visitation statutes are further supported by a recognition, which varies from State to State, that children should have the opportunity to benefit from relationships with statutorily specified persons—for example, their grandparents. The extension of statutory rights in this area to persons other than a child's parents, however, comes with an obvious cost. For example, the State's recognition of an independent third-party interest in a child can place a substantial burden on the traditional parent–child relationship. Contrary to Justice Stevens' accusation, our description of state nonparental visitation statutes in these terms, of course, is not meant to suggest that "children are so much chattel." Rather, our terminology is intended to highlight the fact that these statutes can present questions of constitutional import. In this case, we are presented with just such a question. Specifically, we are asked to decide whether Section 26.10.160(3), as applied to Tommie Granville and her family, violates the Federal Constitution.

The Fourteenth Amendment provides that no State shall "deprive any person of life, liberty, or property, without due process of law." We have long recognized that the Amendment's Due Process Clause, like its Fifth Amendment counterpart, "guarantees more than fair process." The Clause also includes a substantive component that "provides heightened protection against government interference with certain fundamental rights and liberty interests."

The liberty interest at issue in this case—the interest of parents in the care, custody, and control of their children—is perhaps the oldest of the fundamental liberty interests recognized by this Court. More than 75 years ago, in *Meyer v. Nebraska*, 262 U.S. 390, 399, 401, 43 S. Ct. 625, 67 L.Ed. 1042 (1923), we held that the "liberty" protected by the Due Process Clause includes the right of parents to "establish a home and bring up children" and "to control the education of their own." Two years later, in *Pierce v. Society of Sisters*, 268 U.S. 510, 534–535, 45 S. Ct. 571, 69 L.Ed. 1070 (1925), we again held that the "liberty of parents and guardians" includes the right "to direct the upbringing and education of children under their control." We explained in *Pierce* that "[t]he child is not the mere creature of the State; those who nurture him and direct his destiny have the right, coupled with the high duty, to recognize and prepare him for additional obligations." We returned to the subject in *Prince v. Massachusetts*, 321 U.S. 158, 64 S. Ct. 438, 88 L.Ed. 645 (1944), and again confirmed that there is a constitutional dimension to the right of parents to direct the upbringing of their children. "It is cardinal with us that the custody, care and nurture of the child reside first in the parents, whose primary function and freedom include preparation for obligations the state can neither supply nor hinder."

In subsequent cases also, we have recognized the fundamental right of parents to make decisions concerning the care, custody, and control of their children. In light of this extensive precedent, it cannot now be doubted that the Due Process Clause of the Fourteenth Amendment protects the fundamental right of parents to make decisions concerning the care, custody, and control of their children.

(Continues)

Section 26.10.160(3), as applied to Granville and her family in this case, unconstitutionally infringes on that fundamental parental right. The Washington nonparental visitation statute is breathtakingly broad. According to the statute's text, "*Any person* may petition the court for visitation rights *at any time*," and the court may grant such visitation rights whenever "visitation may serve *the best interest of the child*" (emphases added). That language effectively permits any third party seeking visitation to subject any decision by a parent concerning visitation of the parent's children to state-court review. Once the visitation petition has been filed in court and the matter is placed before a judge, a parent's decision that visitation would not be in the child's best interest is accorded no deference. Section 26.10.160(3) contains no requirement that a court accord the parent's decision any presumption of validity or any weight whatsoever. Instead, the Washington statute places the best-interest determination solely in the hands of the judge. Should the judge disagree with the parent's estimation of the child's best interests, the judge's view necessarily prevails. Thus, in practical effect, in the State of Washington a court can disregard and overturn any decision by a fit custodial parent concerning visitation whenever a third party affected by the decision files a visitation petition, based solely on the judge's determination of the child's best interests.

Turning to the facts of this case, the record reveals that the Superior Court's order was based on precisely the type of mere disagreement we have just described and nothing more. The Superior Court's order was not founded on any special factors that might justify the State's interference with Granville's fundamental right to make decisions concerning the rearing of her two daughters. To be sure, this case involves a visitation petition filed by grandparents soon after the death of their son—the father of Isabelle and Natalie—but the combination of several factors here compels our conclusion that Section 26.10.160(3), as applied, exceeded the bounds of the Due Process Clause.

First, the Troxels did not allege, and no court has found, that Granville was an unfit parent. That aspect of the case is important, for there is a presumption that fit parents act in the best interests of their children. Accordingly, so long as a parent adequately cares for his or her children (*i.e.*, is fit), there will normally be no reason for the State to inject itself into the private realm of the family to further question the ability of that parent to make the best decisions concerning the rearing of that parent's children. The problem here is not that the Washington Superior Court intervened, but that when it did so, it gave no special weight at all to Granville's determination of her daughters' best interests. More importantly, it appears that the Superior Court applied exactly the opposite presumption. In reciting its oral ruling after the conclusion of closing arguments, the Superior Court judge explained:

> The burden is to show that it is in the best interest of the children to have some visitation and some quality time with their grandparents. I think in most situations a commonsensical approach [is that] it is normally in the best interest of the children to spend quality time with the grandparent, unless the grandparent, [*sic*] there are some issues or problems involved wherein the grandparents, their lifestyles are going to impact adversely upon the children. That certainly isn't the case here from what I can tell.

The judge's comments suggest that he presumed the grandparents' request should be granted unless the children would be "impact[ed] adversely." In effect, the judge placed on Granville, the fit custodial parent, the burden of *disproving* that visitation would be in the best interest of her daughters. The judge reiterated moments later: "I think [visitation with the Troxels] would be in the best interest of the children and I haven't been shown it is not in [the] best interest of the children."

The decisional framework employed by the Superior Court directly contravened the traditional presumption that a fit parent will act in the best interest of his or her child. In that respect, the court's presumption failed to provide any protection for Granville's fundamental constitutional right to make decisions concerning the rearing of her own daughters. In an ideal world, parents might always seek to cultivate the bonds between grandparents and their grandchildren. Needless to say, however, our world is far from perfect, and in it the decision whether such an intergenerational relationship would be beneficial in any specific case is for the parent to make in the first instance. And, if a fit parent's decision of the kind at issue here becomes subject to judicial review, the court must accord at least some special weight to the parent's own determination.

Finally, we note that there is no allegation that Granville ever sought to cut off visitation entirely. Rather, the present dispute originated when Granville informed the Troxels that she would prefer to restrict their visitation with Isabelle and Natalie to one short visit per month and special holidays. In the Superior Court proceedings Granville did not oppose visitation but instead asked that the duration of any visitation order be shorter than that requested by the Troxels. While the Troxels requested two weekends per month and two full weeks in the summer, Granville asked the Superior Court to order only one day of visitation per month (with no overnight stay) and participation in the Granville family's holiday celebrations. The Superior Court gave no weight to Granville's having assented to visitation even before the filing of any visitation petition or subsequent court intervention. The court instead rejected Granville's proposal and settled on a middle ground, ordering one weekend of visitation per month, one week in the summer, and time on both of the petitioning grandparents' birthdays. Significantly, many other States expressly provide by statute that courts may not award visitation unless a parent has denied (or unreasonably denied) visitation to the concerned third party.

Considered together with the Superior Court's reasons for awarding visitation to the Troxels, the combination of these factors demonstrates that the visitation order in this case was an unconstitutional infringement on Granville's fundamental right to make decisions concerning the care, custody, and control of her two daughters. The Washington Superior Court failed to accord the determination of Granville, a fit custodial parent, any material weight. In fact, the Superior Court made only two formal findings in support of its visitation order. First, the Troxels "are part of a large, central, loving family, all located in this area, and the [Troxels] can provide opportunities for the children in the areas of cousins and music." Second, "[t]he children would be benefitted from spending quality time with the [Troxels], provided that that time is balanced with time with the childrens' [sic] nuclear family." These slender findings, in combination with the court's announced presumption in favor of grandparent visitation and its failure to accord significant weight to Granville's already having offered meaningful visitation to the Troxels, show that this case involves nothing more than a simple disagreement between the Washington Superior Court and Granville concerning her children's best interests. The Superior Court's announced reason for ordering one week of visitation in the summer demonstrates our conclusion well: "I look back on some personal experiences. . . . We always spen[t] as kids a week with one set of grandparents and another set of grandparents, [and] it happened to work out in our family that [it] turned out to be an enjoyable experience. Maybe that can, in this family, if that is how it works out." As we have explained, the Due Process Clause does not permit a State to infringe on the fundamental right of parents to make child rearing decisions simply because a state judge believes a "better" decision could be made. Neither the Washington nonparental visitation statute generally—which places no limits on either the persons who may petition for visitation or the circumstances in which such a petition may be granted—nor the Superior Court in this specific case required anything more. Accordingly, we hold that Section 26.10.160(3), as applied in this case, is unconstitutional.

Because we rest our decision on the sweeping breadth of Section 26.10.160(3) and the application of that broad, unlimited power in this case, we do not consider the primary constitutional question passed on by the Washington Supreme Court—whether the Due Process Clause requires all nonparental visitation statutes to include a showing of harm or potential harm to the child as a condition precedent to granting visitation. We do not, and need not, define today the precise scope of the parental due process right in the visitation context. Because much state-court adjudication in this context occurs on a case-by-case basis, we would be hesitant to hold that specific nonparental visitation statutes violate the Due Process Clause as a *per se* matter. All 50 States have statutes that provide for grandparent visitation in some form.

[T]he burden of litigating a domestic relations proceeding can itself be "so disruptive of the parent–child relationship that the constitutional right of a custodial parent to make certain basic determinations for the child's welfare becomes implicated." In this case, the litigation costs incurred by Granville on her trip through the Washington court system and to this Court are without a doubt already substantial. As we have explained, it is apparent that the entry of the visitation order in this case violated the Constitution. We should say so now, without forcing the parties into additional litigation that would further burden Granville's parental right. We therefore hold that the application of Section 26.10.160(3) to Granville and her family violated her due process right to make decisions concerning the care, custody, and control of her daughters.

Accordingly, the judgment of the Washington Supreme Court is affirmed.

Dissenting Opinion by Justice Scalia:

In my view, a right of parents to direct the upbringing of their children is among the "unalienable Rights" with which the Declaration of Independence proclaims "all men . . . are endowed by their Creator." And in my view that right is also among the "othe[r] [rights] retained by the people" which the Ninth Amendment says the Constitution's enumeration of rights "shall not be construed to deny or disparage." The Declaration of Independence, however, is not a legal prescription conferring powers

(Continues)

(Continued)

upon the courts; and the Constitution's refusal to "deny or disparage" other rights is far removed from affirming any one of them, and even further removed from authorizing judges to identify what they might be, and to enforce the judges' list against laws duly enacted by the people. Consequently, while I would think it entirely compatible with the commitment to representative democracy set forth in the founding documents to argue, in legislative chambers or in electoral campaigns, that the State has *no power* to interfere with parents' authority over the rearing of their children, I do not believe that the power which the Constitution confers upon me *as a judge* entitles me to deny legal effect to laws that (in my view) infringe upon what is (in my view) that unenumerated right.

Judicial vindication of "parental rights" under a Constitution that does not even mention them requires not only a judicially crafted definition of parents, but also—unless, as no one believes, the parental rights are to be absolute—judicially approved assessments of "harm to the child" and judicially defined gradations of other persons (grandparents, extended family, adoptive family in an adoption later found to be invalid, long-term guardians, etc.) who may have some claim against the wishes of the parents. I note that respondent is asserting only, *on her own behalf*, a substantive due process right to direct the upbringing of her own children, and is not asserting, *on behalf of her children*, their First Amendment rights of association or free exercise. I therefore do not have occasion to consider whether, and under what circumstances, the parent could assert the latter enumerated rights. If we embrace this unenumerated right, I think it obvious—whether we affirm or reverse the judgment here, or remand—that we will be ushering in a new regime of judicially prescribed, and federally prescribed, family law. I have no reason to believe that federal judges will be better at this than state legislatures; and state legislatures have the great advantages of doing harm in a more circumscribed area, of being able to correct their mistakes in a flash, and of being removable by the people.

For these reasons, I would reverse the judgment below.

the children for those of the parent, when the parent was not found to be in any way unfit to make parental decisions. Interestingly, this was similar to one reason why Justice Scalia dissented. Justice Scalia would have reversed the Washington Supreme Court's finding that the statute was unconstitutional in part because he viewed the role of judges (like himself) to be limited. Specifically, he viewed the Washington Supreme Court (and the U.S. Supreme Court) as substituting their judgment for that of the elected Washington legislature regarding the rules governing visitation. The case thus raises an interesting question: What role should family judges play in determining what is in the best interests of the child, or does the parent always know best?

Spousal Support

Spousal support consists of payment by one spouse to the other spouse for living expenses after divorce. It has traditionally been referred to as alimony and is sometimes called maintenance. Similar to child support payments, spousal support is separate from the property settlement, which divides the marital assets. It is most likely to be granted for a limited period of time and typically only in those cases in which the spouse receiving the support, usually the woman, has limited or no other means of support. Thus, the relative income of each spouse is a factor in whether spousal support will be ordered, as is the ability of the spouse needing support to earn an income. The length of time the couple was married may also affect the

decision to award spousal support; in the case of an older spouse, courts sometimes will order that payments be made for the spouse's lifetime.

Adoption

In addition to the legal issues relating to property and children in divorce matters, the domain of the family courts also relates to building families through adoption. Adoption refers to the process of terminating one parental relationship (if it exists) and creating another. From a legal (and, most often, parental) standpoint, adopted children are treated as if they were natural-born children. All adoptions are governed by state statute. These statutes set forth qualifications for adoptive parents. For example, although either single persons or married couples may become adoptive parents, extensive background information must be provided to state agencies, including motivation for adoption, approach to parenting, child care experience, other members of the household, all past marital or partnership relationships, medical and psychological reports, financial information, employment history, religion, and criminal background.

As with any issue in the courts involving children, the focus of any inquiry regarding adoption is whether the adoption will be in the best interests of the child. Generally, adoptive children must fall within the jurisdiction of the state. Any child without parents may be eligible for adoption. Thus, a child whose parents are deceased is eligible to be adopted, as well as any child whose natural parents' rights have been terminated.

A natural parent has a right to a relationship with his or her child. Unless that relationship is severed by a court, the child cannot be adopted by another parent. Thus, a child may have a natural mother and an adoptive father, a natural father and an adoptive mother, or both adoptive parents. The key is whether the parental role being assumed by the adoptive parent has been terminated in the natural parent. The termination of parental rights is therefore usually a necessary precursor to adoption.

Termination of Parental Rights

The central purpose of terminating parental rights is not to "prepare" a child for adoption; rather, it is to protect the child. There are many reasons for terminating parental rights, but each stems from a failure of a parent to act in his or her child's best interests. For example, the Rhode Island statute addressing termination of parental rights provides four primary reasons for terminating parental rights:

§ 15-7-7 Termination of parental rights.—(a) The court shall, upon a petition duly filed by a governmental child placement agency or licensed child placement agency after notice to the parent and a hearing on the petition, terminate any and all legal rights of the parent to the child, including the right to notice of any subsequent adoption proceedings involving the child, if the court finds as a fact by clear and convincing evidence that:

(1) The parent has willfully neglected to provide proper care and maintenance for the child for a period of at least one year where financially able to do so. In determining whether the parent has willfully neglected to provide proper care and maintenance for the child, the court may disregard contributions to support which are of an infrequent and insubstantial nature; or

(2) The parent is unfit by reason of conduct or conditions seriously detrimental to the child; such as, but not limited to, the following:

(i) Institutionalization of the parent, including imprisonment, for a duration as to render it improbable for the parent to care for the child for an extended period of time;

(ii) Conduct toward any child of a cruel or abusive nature;

(iii) The child has been placed in the legal custody or care of the department for children, youth, and families and the parent has a chronic substance abuse problem and the parent's prognosis indicates that the child will not be able to return to the custody of the parent within a reasonable period of time, considering the child's age and the need for a permanent home. The fact that a parent has been unable to provide care for a child for a period of twelve (12) months due to substance abuse shall constitute prima facie evidence of a chronic substance abuse problem;

(iv) The child has been placed with the department for children, youth, and families and the court has previously involuntarily terminated parental rights to another child of the parent and the parent continues to lack the ability or willingness to respond to services which would rehabilitate the parent and provided further that the court finds it is improbable that an additional period of services

would result in reunification within a reasonable period of time considering the child's age and the need for a permanent home;

(v) The parent has subjected the child to aggravated circumstances, which circumstances shall be abandonment, torture, chronic abuse and sexual abuse;

(vi) The parent has committed murder or voluntary manslaughter on another of his or her children or has committed a felony assault resulting in serious bodily injury on that child or another of his or her children or has aided or abetted, attempted, conspired or solicited to commit such a murder or voluntary manslaughter; or

(vii) The parent has exhibited behavior or conduct that is seriously detrimental to the child, for a duration as to render it improbable for the parent to care for the child for an extended period of time;

(3) The child has been placed in the legal custody or care of the department for children, youth, and families for at least twelve (12) months, and the parents were offered or received services to correct the situation which led to the child being placed; provided, that there is not a substantial probability that the child will be able to return safely to the parents' care within a reasonable period of time considering the child's age and the need for a permanent home; or

(4) The parent has abandoned or deserted the child. A lack of communication or contact with the child for at least a six (6) month period shall constitute prima facie evidence of abandonment or desertion. In the event that parents of an infant have had no contact or communication with the infant for a period of six (6) months the department shall file a petition pursuant to this section and the family court shall conduct expedited hearings on the petition. R. I. G. L. 1956, Sec. 15-7-7.

As specified in the statute, there are four reasons that may justify terminating a parent's rights in his or her child. These are (1) willful neglect of the child by the parent, (2) being an unfit parent, (3) if the child is a ward of the state and the conditions justifying it are unlikely to change, and (4) if the child has been abandoned by the parent.

Family courts generally have a much greater interest in preserving parental rights than in terminating them. Termination of parental rights involves a severe infringement of a fundamental right to have a relationship with and care for a child, and the consequences of doing so for the state are also severe because the state must take over that role until such time as adoption may occur (which, sadly, in many cases it does not).

As much as the state seeks to preserve the parent–child relationship, when it decides to act to terminate, the state interests are adverse to the parent's. State action to end a parent's relationship with his or her child is not unlike a criminal proceeding, where the bad acts of the parent justifying the termination are on trial. As the Supreme Court has said, "Few forms of state action are both so severe and so irreversible" (*Santosky v. Kramer*, 455 U.S. 745, 759, 102 S. Ct. 1388, 1399, 71 L.Ed.2d 599, 610 (1982)).

Nonetheless, where the statutory criteria are met, termination of parental rights will be deemed to be in the best interests of the child. Note, however, that the criteria under the Rhode Island statute must be satisfied by "clear and convincing" evidence, which requires a higher standard of proof than the lower "preponderance of the evidence," required in most civil proceedings. Although that has always been the standard in Rhode Island, before 1982, many states used the lower "preponderance" standard in cases involving termination of parental rights. In that year, the U.S Supreme Court decided *Santosky v. Kramer*, 455 U.S. 745, 102 S. Ct. 1388, 71 L.Ed.2d 599 (1982), requiring that the clear and convincing standard be used in any hearing in which parental rights may be terminated (**Case Decision 7.2**).

In *Santosky*, the Court was particularly concerned about the gravity of the irreversible decision to terminate a parent's relationship with her child. As the Court noted

The fundamental liberty interest of natural parents in the care, custody, and management of their child does not evaporate simply because they have not been model parents or have lost temporary custody of their child to the State. Even when blood relationships are strained, parents retain a vital interest in preventing the irretrievable

Case Decision 7.2 *Santosky v. Kramer*, 455 U.S. 745, 102 S. Ct. 1388, 71 L.Ed.2d 599 (1982)

Opinion of the Court by Justice Blackmun:

Under New York law, the State may terminate, over parental objection, the rights of parents in their natural child upon a finding that the child is "permanently neglected." The New York Family Court Act § 622 (McKinney 1975 and Supp. 1981–1982) (Fam. Ct. Act) requires that only a "fair preponderance of the evidence" support that finding. Thus, in New York, the factual certainty required to extinguish the parent–child relationship is no greater than that necessary to award money damages in an ordinary civil action.

Today we hold that the Due Process Clause of the Fourteenth Amendment demands more than this. Before a State may sever completely and irrevocably the rights of parents in their natural child, due process requires that the State support its allegations by at least clear and convincing evidence.

I

A

New York authorizes its officials to remove a child temporarily from his or her home if the child appears "neglected," within the meaning of Art. 10 of the Family Court Act. Once removed, a child under the age of 18 customarily is placed "in the care of an authorized agency," usually a state institution or a foster home. At that point, "the state's first obligation is to help the family with services to . . . reunite it. . . ." But if convinced that "positive, nurturing parent–child relationships no longer exist," the State may initiate "permanent neglect" proceedings to free the child for adoption.

The State bifurcates its permanent neglect proceeding into "fact-finding" and "dispositional" hearings. At the fact-finding stage, the State must prove that the child has been "permanently neglected," as defined by Fam. Ct. Act. The Family Court judge then determines at a subsequent dispositional hearing what placement would serve the child's best interests.

At the fact-finding hearing, the State must establish, among other things, that for more than a year after the child entered state custody, the agency "made diligent efforts to encourage and strengthen the parental relationship." The State must further prove that during that same period, the child's natural parents failed "substantially and continuously or repeatedly to maintain contact with or plan for the future of the child although physically and financially able to do so." Should the State support its allegations by "a fair preponderance of the evidence," the child may be declared permanently neglected. That declaration empowers the Family Court judge to terminate permanently the natural parents' rights in the child. Termination denies the natural parents physical custody, as well as the rights ever to visit, communicate with, or regain custody of the child.

New York's permanent neglect statute provides natural parents with certain procedural protections. Most notably, natural parents have a statutory right to the assistance of counsel and of court-appointed counsel if they are indigent. But New York permits its officials to establish "permanent neglect" with less proof than most States require. Thirty-five States, the District of Columbia, and the Virgin Islands currently specify a higher standard of proof, in parental rights termination proceedings, than a "fair preponderance of the evidence." The only analogous federal statute of which we are aware permits termination of parental rights solely upon "evidence beyond a reasonable doubt." Indian Child Welfare Act of 1978. The question here is whether New York's "fair preponderance of the evidence" standard is constitutionally sufficient.

B

Petitioners John Santosky II and Annie Santosky are the natural parents of Tina and John III. In November 1973, after incidents reflecting parental neglect, respondent Kramer, Commissioner of the Ulster County Department of Social Services, initiated a neglect proceeding and removed Tina from her natural home. About 10 months later, he removed John III and placed him with foster parents. On the day John was taken, Annie Santosky gave birth to a third child, Jed. When Jed was only three days old, respondent transferred him to a foster home on the ground that immediate removal was necessary to avoid imminent danger to his life or health.

In October 1978, respondent petitioned the Ulster County Family Court to terminate petitioners' parental rights in the three children. Petitioners challenged the constitutionality of the "fair preponderance of the evidence" standard. The Family Court Judge rejected this constitutional challenge, and weighed the evidence under the statutory standard. While acknowledging that the Santoskys had maintained contact with their children, the judge found those visits "at best superficial and devoid of any real emotional content." After deciding that the agency had made "'diligent efforts' to encourage and strengthen the parental relationship," he concluded that the Santoskys were incapable, even with public assistance, of planning for the future of their children. The judge later held a dispositional hearing and ruled that the best interests of the three children required permanent termination of the Santoskys' custody. Since respondent Kramer took custody of Tina, John III, and Jed, the Santoskys have had two other children, James and Jeremy. The State has taken no action to remove these younger children. At oral argument, counsel for respondents replied affirmatively when asked whether he was asserting that petitioners were "unfit to handle the three older ones but not unfit to handle the two younger ones."

Petitioners appealed, again contesting the constitutionality of § 622's standard of proof. The New York Supreme Court, Appellate Division, affirmed, holding application of the preponderance-of-the-evidence standard "proper and constitutional." That standard, the court reasoned, "recognizes and seeks to balance rights possessed by the child . . . with those of the natural parents. . . ."

The New York Court of Appeals then dismissed petitioners' appeal to that court "upon the ground that no substantial constitutional question is directly involved." We granted certiorari to consider petitioners' constitutional claim.

II

Last Term in *Lassiter v. Department of Social Services*, 452 U.S. 18, 101 S. Ct. 2153, 68 L.Ed.2d 640 (1981), this Court, by a 5-4 vote, held that the Fourteenth Amendment's Due Process Clause does not require the appointment of counsel for indigent parents in every parental status termination proceeding. The case casts light, however, on the two central questions here—whether process is constitutionally due a natural parent at a State's parental rights termination proceeding, and, if so, what process is due.

In *Lassiter*, it was "not disputed that state intervention to terminate the relationship between [a parent] and [the] child must be accomplished by procedures meeting the requisites of the Due Process Clause." The absence of dispute reflected this Court's historical recognition that freedom of personal choice in matters of family life is a fundamental liberty interest protected by the Fourteenth Amendment.

The fundamental liberty interest of natural parents in the care, custody, and management of their child does not evaporate simply because they have not been model parents or have lost temporary custody of their child to the State. Even when blood relationships are strained, parents retain a vital interest in preventing the irretrievable destruction of their family life. If anything, persons faced with forced dissolution of their parental rights have a more critical need for procedural protections than do those resisting state intervention into ongoing family affairs. When the State moves to destroy weakened familial bonds, it must provide the parents with fundamentally fair procedures.

In *Lassiter*, the Court and three dissenters agreed that the nature of the process due in parental rights termination proceedings turns on a balancing of "three distinct factors:" the private interests affected by the proceeding; the risk of error created by the State's chosen procedure; and the countervailing governmental interest supporting use of the challenged procedure. While the respective *Lassiter* opinions disputed whether those factors should be weighed against a presumption disfavoring appointed counsel for one not threatened with loss of physical liberty, that concern is irrelevant

(Continues)

here. Unlike the Court's right-to-counsel rulings, its decisions concerning constitutional burdens of proof have not turned on any presumption favoring any particular standard. To the contrary, the Court has engaged in a straightforward consideration of the factors to determine whether a particular standard of proof in a particular proceeding satisfies due process.

"The function of a standard of proof, as that concept is embodied in the Due Process Clause and in the realm of fact finding, is to 'instruct the fact finder concerning the degree of confidence our society thinks he should have in the correctness of factual conclusions for a particular type of adjudication.'" [I]n any given proceeding, the minimum standard of proof tolerated by the due process requirement reflects not only the weight of the private and public interests affected, but also a societal judgment about how the risk of error should be distributed between the litigants.

Thus, while private parties may be interested intensely in a civil dispute over money damages, application of a "fair preponderance of the evidence" standard indicates both society's "minimal concern with the outcome," and a conclusion that the litigants should "share the risk of error in roughly equal fashion." When the State brings a criminal action to deny a defendant liberty or life, however, "the interests of the defendant are of such magnitude that historically and without any explicit constitutional requirement they have been protected by standards of proof designed to exclude as nearly as possible the likelihood of an erroneous judgment." The stringency of the "beyond a reasonable doubt" standard bespeaks the "weight and gravity" of the private interest affected, society's interest in avoiding erroneous convictions, and a judgment that those interests together require that "society impos[e] almost the entire risk of error upon itself."

The "minimum requirements [of procedural due process] being a matter of federal law, they are not diminished by the fact that the State may have specified its own procedures that it may deem adequate for determining the preconditions to adverse official action. Moreover, the degree of proof required in a particular type of proceeding "is the kind of question which has traditionally been left to the judiciary to resolve." "In cases involving individual rights, whether criminal or civil, '[t]he standard of proof [at a minimum] reflects the value society places on individual liberty.'"

This Court has mandated an intermediate standard of proof—"clear and convincing evidence"— when the individual interests at stake in a state proceeding are both "particularly important" and "more substantial than mere loss of money." [T]he Court has deemed this level of certainty necessary to preserve fundamental fairness in a variety of government-initiated proceedings that threaten the individual involved with "a significant deprivation of liberty" or "stigma."

In *Lassiter*, to be sure, the Court held that fundamental fairness may be maintained in parental rights termination proceedings even when some procedures are mandated only on a case-by-case basis, rather than through rules of general application. But this Court never has approved case-by-case determination of the proper *standard of proof* for a given proceeding. Standards of proof, like other "procedural due process rules[,] are shaped by the risk of error inherent in the truth-finding process as applied to the *generality of cases*, not the rare exceptions." Since the litigants and the fact finder must know at the outset of a given proceeding how the risk of error will be allocated, the standard of proof necessarily must be calibrated in advance. Retrospective case-by-case review cannot preserve fundamental fairness when a class of proceedings is governed by a constitutionally defective evidentiary standard.

III

In parental rights termination proceedings, the private interest affected is commanding; the risk of error from using a preponderance standard is substantial; and the countervailing governmental interest favoring that standard is comparatively slight. Evaluation of the three factors compels the conclusion that use of a "fair preponderance of the evidence" standard in such proceedings is inconsistent with due process.

A

Lassiter declared it "plain beyond the need for multiple citation" that a natural parent's "desire for and right to 'the companionship, care, custody, and management of his or her children'" is an interest far more precious than any property right. When the State initiates a parental rights termination proceeding, it seeks not merely to infringe that fundamental liberty interest, but to end it. "If the State prevails, it will have worked a unique kind of deprivation. . . . A parent's interest in the accuracy and justice of the decision to terminate his or her parental status is, therefore, a commanding one."

In government-initiated proceedings to determine juvenile delinquency, civil commitment, deportation, and denaturalization, this Court has identified losses of individual liberty sufficiently serious to warrant imposition of an elevated burden of proof. Yet juvenile delinquency adjudications, civil commitment, deportation, and denaturalization, at least to a degree, are all *reversible* official actions. Once affirmed on appeal, a New York decision terminating parental rights is *final* and irrevocable. Few forms of state action are both so severe and so irreversible.

Thus, the first *Eldridge* factor—the private interest affected—weighs heavily against use of the preponderance standard at a state-initiated permanent neglect proceeding. We do not deny that the child and his foster parents are also deeply interested in the outcome of that contest. But at the fact-finding stage of the New York proceeding, the focus emphatically is not on them.

The fact finding does not purport—and is not intended—to balance the child's interest in a normal family home against the parents' interest in raising the child. Nor does it purport to determine whether the natural parents or the foster parents would provide the better home. Rather, the fact-finding hearing pits the State directly against the parents. The State marshals an array of public resources to prove its case and disprove the parents' case. Victory by the State not only makes termination of parental rights possible; it entails a judicial determination that the parents are unfit to raise their own children.

At the fact finding, the State cannot presume that a child and his parents are adversaries. After the State has established parental unfitness at that initial proceeding, the court may assume at the *dispositional* stage that the interests of the child and the natural parents do diverge. But until the State proves parental unfitness, the child and his parents share a vital interest in preventing erroneous termination of their natural relationship. Thus, at the fact finding, the interests of the child and his natural parents coincide to favor use of error-reducing procedures.

For the foster parents, the State's failure to prove permanent neglect may prolong the delay and uncertainty until their foster child is freed for adoption. But for the natural parents, a finding of permanent neglect can cut off forever their rights in their child. Given this disparity of consequence, we have no difficulty finding that the balance of private interests strongly favors heightened procedural protections.

B

[W]e next must consider both the risk of erroneous deprivation of private interests resulting from use of a "fair preponderance" standard and the likelihood that a higher evidentiary standard would reduce that risk. Since the fact-finding phase of a permanent neglect proceeding is an adversary contest between the State and the natural parents, the relevant question is whether a preponderance standard fairly allocates the risk of an erroneous fact finding between these two parties.

In New York, the fact-finding stage of a state-initiated permanent neglect proceeding bears many of the indicia of a criminal trial. The Commissioner of Social Services charges the parents with permanent neglect. They are served by summons. The fact-finding hearing is conducted pursuant to formal rules of evidence. The State, the parents, and the child are all represented by counsel. The State seeks to establish a series of historical facts about the intensity of its agency's efforts to reunite the family, the infrequency and insubstantiality of the parents' contacts with their child, and the parents' inability or unwillingness to formulate a plan for the child's future. The attorneys submit documentary evidence, and call witnesses who are subject to cross-examination. Based on all the evidence, the judge then determines whether the State has proved the statutory elements of permanent neglect by a fair preponderance of the evidence.

At such a proceeding, numerous factors combine to magnify the risk of erroneous fact finding. Permanent neglect proceedings employ imprecise substantive standards that leave determinations unusually open to the subjective values of the judge. In appraising the nature and quality of a complex series of encounters among the agency, the parents, and the child, the court possesses unusual discretion to underweigh probative facts that might favor the parent. Because parents subject to termination proceedings are often poor, uneducated, or members of minority groups, such proceedings are often vulnerable to judgments based on cultural or class bias.

The State's ability to assemble its case almost inevitably dwarfs the parents' ability to mount a defense. No predetermined limits restrict the sums an agency may spend in prosecuting a given termination proceeding. The State's attorney usually will be expert on the issues contested and the procedures employed at the fact-finding hearing, and enjoys full access to all public records concerning the family. The State may call on experts in family relations, psychology, and medicine to bolster its case. Furthermore, the primary witnesses at the hearing will be the agency's own professional caseworkers

(Continues)

(Continued)

whom the State has empowered both to investigate the family situation and to testify against the parents. Indeed, because the child is already in agency custody, the State even has the power to shape the historical events that form the basis for termination.

The disparity between the adversaries' litigation resources is matched by a striking asymmetry in their litigation options. Unlike criminal defendants, natural parents have no "double jeopardy" defense against repeated state termination efforts. If the State initially fails to win termination, as New York did here, it always can try once again to cut off the parents' rights after gathering more or better evidence. Yet even when the parents have attained the level of fitness required by the State, they have no similar means by which they can forestall future termination efforts.

Coupled with a "fair preponderance of the evidence" standard, these factors create a significant prospect of erroneous termination. A standard of proof that by its very terms demands consideration of the quantity, rather than the quality, of the evidence may misdirect the fact finder in the marginal case. Given the weight of the private interests at stake, the social cost of even occasional error is sizable.

The Appellate Division approved New York's preponderance standard on the ground that it properly "balanced rights possessed by the child . . . with those of the natural parents. . . ." By so saying, the court suggested that a preponderance standard properly allocates the risk of error *between* the parents and the child. That view is fundamentally mistaken.

The court's theory assumes that termination of the natural parents' rights invariably will benefit the child. Yet we have noted above that the parents and the child share an interest in avoiding erroneous termination. Even accepting the court's assumption, we cannot agree with its conclusion that a preponderance standard fairly distributes the risk of error between parent and child. Use of that standard reflects the judgment that society is nearly neutral between erroneous termination of parental rights and erroneous failure to terminate those rights. For the child, the likely consequence of an erroneous failure to terminate is preservation of an uneasy status quo. For the natural parents, however, the consequence of an erroneous termination is the unnecessary destruction of their natural family. A standard that allocates the risk of error nearly equally between those two outcomes does not reflect properly their relative severity.

C

Two state interests are at stake in parental rights termination proceedings—a *parens patriae* interest in preserving and promoting the welfare of the child and a fiscal and administrative interest in reducing the cost and burden of such proceedings. A standard of proof more strict than preponderance of the evidence is consistent with both interests.

As *parens patriae*, the State's goal is to provide the child with a permanent home. Yet while there is still reason to believe that positive, nurturing parent–child relationships exist, the *parens patriae* interest favors preservation, not severance, of natural familial bonds. Any *parens patriae* interest in terminating the natural parents' rights arises only at the dispositional phase, *after* the parents have been found unfit.

Unlike a constitutional requirement of hearings, or court-appointed counsel, a stricter standard of proof would reduce factual error without imposing substantial fiscal burdens upon the State. As we have observed, 35 States already have adopted a higher standard by statute or court decision without apparent effect on the speed, form, or cost of their fact-finding proceedings.

Nor would an elevated standard of proof create any real administrative burdens for the State's fact finders. New York Family Court judges already are familiar with a higher evidentiary standard in other parental rights termination proceedings not involving permanent neglect. New York also demands at least clear and convincing evidence in proceedings of far less moment than parental rights termination proceedings. We cannot believe that it would burden the State unduly to require that its fact finders have the same factual certainty when terminating the parent–child relationship as they must have to suspend a driver's license.

IV

The logical conclusion of this balancing process is that the "fair preponderance of the evidence" standard prescribed by Fam. Ct. Act § 622 violates the Due Process Clause of the Fourteenth Amendment. Thus, at a parental rights termination proceeding, a near-equal allocation of risk between the parents and the State is constitutionally intolerable. The next question, then, is whether a "beyond a reasonable doubt" or a "clear and convincing" standard is constitutionally mandated.

Like civil commitment hearings, termination proceedings often require the fact finder to evaluate medical and psychiatric testimony, and to decide issues difficult to prove to a level of absolute certainty, such as lack of parental motive, absence of affection between parent and child, and failure of parental foresight and progress. The substantive standards applied vary from State to State. Although Congress found a "beyond a reasonable doubt" standard proper in one type of parental rights termination case, another legislative body might well conclude that a reasonable-doubt standard would erect an unreasonable barrier to state efforts to free permanently neglected children for adoption.

A majority of the States have concluded that a "clear and convincing evidence" standard of proof strikes a fair balance between the rights of the natural parents and the State's legitimate concerns. We hold that such a standard adequately conveys to the fact finder the level of subjective certainty about his factual conclusions necessary to satisfy due process. We further hold that determination of the precise burden equal to or greater than that standard is a matter of state law properly left to state legislatures and state courts.

We, of course, express no view on the merits of petitioners' claims. At a hearing conducted under a constitutionally proper standard, they may or may not prevail. Without deciding the outcome under any of the standards we have approved, we vacate the judgment of the Appellate Division and remand the case for further proceedings not inconsistent with this opinion.

Dissent by Justice Rehnquist, joined by Chief Justice Burger, Justice White, and Justice O'Connor:

I believe that few of us would care to live in a society where every aspect of life was regulated by a single source of law, whether that source be this Court or some other organ of our complex body politic. But today's decision certainly moves us in that direction. By parsing the New York scheme and holding one narrow provision unconstitutional, the majority invites further federal-court intrusion into every facet of state family law. If ever there were an area in which federal courts should heed the admonition of Justice Holmes that "a page of history is worth a volume of logic," it is in the area of domestic relations. This area has been left to the States from time immemorial, and not without good reason.

Equally as troubling is the majority's due process analysis. The Fourteenth Amendment guarantees that a State will treat individuals with "fundamental fairness" whenever its actions infringe their protected liberty or property interests. By adoption of the procedures relevant to this case, New York has created an exhaustive program to assist parents in regaining the custody of their children and to protect parents from the unfair deprivation of their parental rights. And yet the majority's myopic scrutiny of the standard of proof blinds it to the very considerations and procedures which make the New York scheme "fundamentally fair."

I

State intervention in domestic relations has always been an unhappy but necessary feature of life in our organized society. For all of our experience in this area, we have found no fully satisfactory solutions to the painful problem of child abuse and neglect. We have found, however, that leaving the States free to experiment with various remedies has produced novel approaches and promising progress.

Throughout this experience the Court has scrupulously refrained from interfering with state answers to domestic relations questions. This is not to say that the Court should blink at clear constitutional violations in state statutes, but rather that in this area, of all areas, "substantial weight must be given to the good-faith judgments of the individuals [administering a program] . . . that the procedures they have provided assure fair consideration of the . . . claims of individuals."

This case presents a classic occasion for such solicitude. New York has enacted a comprehensive plan to aid marginal parents in regaining the custody of their child. The central purpose of the New York plan is to reunite divided families. Adoption of the preponderance-of-the-evidence standard represents New York's good-faith effort to balance the interest of parents against the legitimate interests of the child and the State. These earnest efforts by state officials should be given weight in the Court's application of due process principles.

II

As the majority opinion notes, petitioners are the parents of five children, three of whom were removed from petitioners' care on or before August 22, 1974. During the next four and one-half

(*Continues*)

(*Continued*)

years, those three children were in the custody of the State and in the care of foster homes or institutions, and the State was diligently engaged in efforts to prepare petitioners for the children's return. Those efforts were unsuccessful, however, and on April 10, 1979, the New York Family Court for Ulster County terminated petitioners' parental rights as to the three children removed in 1974 or earlier. This termination was preceded by a judicial finding that petitioners had failed to plan for the return and future of their children, a statutory category of permanent neglect. Petitioners now contend, and the Court today holds, that they were denied due process of law, not because of a general inadequacy of procedural protections, but simply because the finding of permanent neglect was made on the basis of a preponderance of the evidence adduced at the termination hearing.

In determining whether such liberty or property interests are implicated by a particular government action, "we must look not to the 'weight' but to the nature of the interest at stake." I do not disagree with the majority's conclusion that the interest of parents in their relationship with their children is sufficiently fundamental to come within the finite class of liberty interests protected by the Fourteenth Amendment. It is the majority's answer to this question with which I disagree.

A

Due process of law is a flexible constitutional principle. The requirements which it imposes upon governmental actions vary with the situations to which it applies. The adequacy of a scheme of procedural protections cannot, therefore, be determined merely by the application of general principles unrelated to the peculiarities of the case at hand.

Given this flexibility, it is obvious that a proper due process inquiry cannot be made by focusing upon one narrow provision of the challenged statutory scheme. Such a focus threatens to overlook factors which may introduce constitutionally adequate protections into a particular government action. Courts must examine *all* procedural protections offered by the State, and must assess the *cumulative* effect of such safeguards. Only through such a broad inquiry may courts determine whether a challenged governmental action satisfies the due process requirement of "fundamental fairness." In this case, it is just such a broad look at the New York scheme which reveals its fundamental fairness.

The termination of parental rights on the basis of permanent neglect can occur under New York law only by order of the Family Court. Fully understood, the New York system is a comprehensive program to *aid* parents such as petitioners. Only as a last resort, when "diligent efforts" to reunite the family have failed, does New York authorize the termination of parental rights. The procedures for termination of those relationships which cannot be aided and which threaten permanent injury to the child, administered by a judge who has supervised the case from the first temporary removal through the final termination, cannot be viewed as fundamentally unfair. The facts of this case demonstrate the fairness of the system.

In accordance with the statutory requirements set forth above, the court found that petitioners' failure to plan for the future of their children, who were then seven, five, and four years old and had been out of petitioners' custody for at least four years, rose to the level of permanent neglect. At a subsequent dispositional hearing, the court terminated petitioners' parental rights, thereby freeing the three children for adoption.

[T]he State's extraordinary 4-year effort to reunite petitioners' family was not just unsuccessful, it was altogether rebuffed by parents unwilling to improve their circumstances sufficiently to permit a return of their children. At every step of this protracted process petitioners were accorded those procedures and protections which traditionally have been required by due process of law. Moreover, from the beginning to the end of this sad story all judicial determinations were made by one Family Court Judge. After four and one-half years of involvement with petitioners, more than seven complete hearings, and additional periodic supervision of the State's rehabilitative efforts, the judge no doubt was intimately familiar with this case and the prospects for petitioners' rehabilitation.

It is inconceivable to me that these procedures were "fundamentally unfair" to petitioners. Only by its obsessive focus on the standard of proof and its almost complete disregard of the facts of this case does the majority find otherwise. As the discussion above indicates, however, such a focus does not comport with the flexible standard of fundamental fairness embodied in the Due Process Clause of the Fourteenth Amendment.

B

In addition to the basic fairness of the process afforded petitioners, the standard of proof chosen by New York clearly reflects a constitutionally permissible balance of the interests at stake in this case. The standard of proof "represents an attempt to instruct the fact finder concerning the degree of confidence our society thinks he should have in the correctness of factual conclusions for a particular type of adjudication. In this respect, the standard of proof is a crucial component of legal process, the primary function of which is "to minimize the risk of erroneous decisions."

In determining the propriety of a particular standard of proof in a given case, however, it is not enough simply to say that we are trying to minimize the risk of error. Because errors in fact finding affect more than one interest, we try to minimize error as to those interests which we consider to be most important.

When the standard of proof is understood as reflecting such an assessment, an examination of the interests at stake in a particular case becomes essential to determining the propriety of the specified standard of proof. The interests at stake in this case demonstrate that New York has selected a constitutionally permissible standard of proof. On one side is the interest of parents in a continuation of the family unit and the raising of their own children. The importance of this interest cannot easily be overstated. Few consequences of judicial action are so grave as the severance of natural family ties. Even the convict committed to prison and thereby deprived of his physical liberty often retains the love and support of family members. On the other side of the termination proceeding are the often countervailing interests of the child. A stable, loving home life is essential to a child's physical, emotional, and spiritual well-being. It requires no citation of authority to assert that children who are abused in their youth generally face extraordinary problems developing into responsible, productive citizens. The same can be said of children who, though not physically or emotionally abused, are passed from one foster home to another with no constancy of love, trust, or discipline. If the Family Court makes an incorrect factual determination resulting in a failure to terminate a parent–child relationship which rightfully should be ended, the child involved must return either to an abusive home or to the often unstable world of foster care. The reality of these risks is magnified by the fact that the only families faced with termination actions are those which have voluntarily surrendered custody of their child to the State, or, as in this case, those from which the child has been removed by judicial action because of threatened irreparable injury through abuse or neglect. Permanent neglect findings also occur only in families where the child has been in foster care for at least one year.

When, in the context of a permanent neglect termination proceeding, the interests of the child and the State in a stable, nurturing home life are balanced against the interests of the parents in the rearing of their child, it cannot be said that either set of interests is so clearly paramount as to require that the risk of error be allocated to one side or the other. Accordingly, a State constitutionally may conclude that the risk of error should be borne in roughly equal fashion by use of the preponderance-of-the-evidence standard of proof. This is precisely the balance which has been struck by the New York Legislature: "It is the intent of the legislature in enacting this section to provide procedures not only assuring that the rights of the natural parent are protected, but also, where positive, nurturing parent–child relationships no longer exist, furthering the best interests, needs, and rights of the child by terminating the parental rights and freeing the child for adoption."

III

For the reasons heretofore stated, I believe that the Court today errs in concluding that the New York standard of proof in parental-rights termination proceedings violates due process of law. The decision disregards New York's earnest efforts to *aid* parents in regaining the custody of their children and a host of procedural protections placed around parental rights and interests. The Court finds a constitutional violation only by a tunnel-vision application of due process principles that altogether loses sight of the unmistakable fairness of the New York procedure.

Even more worrisome, today's decision cavalierly rejects the considered judgment of the New York Legislature in an area traditionally entrusted to state care. The Court thereby begins, I fear, a trend of federal intervention in state family law matters which surely will stifle creative responses to vexing problems. Accordingly, I dissent.

destruction of their family life. If anything, persons faced with forced dissolution of their parental rights have a more critical need for procedural protections than do those resisting state intervention into ongoing family affairs. When the State moves to destroy weakened familial bonds, it must provide the parents with fundamentally fair procedures.

The majority in *Santosky* was centrally concerned about protecting the fundamental rights of parents to have custody of their children, a right it said was "precious," and it therefore found a higher level of proof necessary to accomplish this. Some Justices, however, were not convinced that the highest federal Court should even be involved in family affairs. As Justice Rehnquist noted in his dissent, family law "has been left to the States from time immemorial," and he and the other dissenting Justices were concerned about continued "federal-court intrusion into every facet of state family law." Thus, the question of federalism was a central concern to the dissenters in the case and potential growth of federal court intervention into everyday life. Few matters are more central to everyday life than the adoption of children, their care, and the rights of parents who bear responsibility for them.

Key Terms

Coverture	Child Support
Common Law Marriage	Tender Years Doctrine
Civil Union	Custody
Premarital Agreement	Visitation
Unilateral Divorce	Spousal Support
Marital Property	Adoption
Community Property	Termination of Parental
Commingling	Rights
Transmutation	

Discussion Questions

1. What are the functions of the family court?
2. What are the legal requirements for marriage?
3. What are the primary issues that the family court must resolve in a divorce case?
4. Why do people enter into premarital agreements?
5. What is the difference between unilateral divorce and divorce by mutual consent? What does each involve?
6. How do family courts resolve child custody issues?
7. What decisions must a family court make in order to accomplish an adoption?
8. What are four reasons for terminating parental rights?

Cases

Ayala v. Valderas, 2008 WL 46661846 (Tx. Ct. App. 2008).
Baehr v. Lewin, 74 Haw. 530, 852 P.2d 44 (1993).
Chambers v. Ormiston, 935 A.2d 956 (R.I. 2007).
Conaway v. Deane, 401 Md. 219, 932 A.2d 571 (2007).
Ellis v. Estate of Ellis, 169 P.2d. 441, 2007 UT 77 (2007).
Goodridge v. Department of Public Health, 440 Mass. 309, 798 N.E.2d 941 (2003).
Loving v. Virginia, 388 U.S. 1, 87 S. Ct. 1817, 18 L.Ed.2d 1010 (1967).
Santosky v. Kramer, 455 U.S. 745, 102 S. Ct. 1388, 71 L.Ed.2d 599 (1982).
S.J.L.S. v. T.L.S., 265 S.W.3d 804 (Ky. App. 2008).
Troxel v. Granville, 530 U.S. 57, 120 S. Ct. 2054, 147 L.Ed.2d 49 (2000).

Criminal Justice on the Web

For an up-to-date list of Web links, go to *The American Courts: A Procedural Approach* online companion site at http://criminal justice.jbpub.com/AmericanCourts. The online companion site will introduce you to some of the most important sites for finding American courts information on the Internet.

References

Glendon, M. (1989). *The Transformations of Family Law: State, Law and Family in the United States and Western Europe.* Chicago: University of Chicago Press.

Jackson, A. M. (1994). Coming of age of grandparent visitation rights. *American University Law Review, 1,* 43–65.

Ronfani, P. (2007). Marriage and informal unions. In D. S. Clark (Ed.), *Encyclopedia of Law and Society: American and Global Perspectives.* Thousand Oaks, CA: Sage Publications.

Shumway, D. R. (2003). *Modern Love: Romance, Intimacy, and the Marriage Crisis.* New York: New York University Press.

Simon, R. J., & Altstein, H. (2003). *Global Perspectives on Social Issues: Marriage and Divorce.* Lanham, MD: Lexington Books.

Thompson, R. A., & Amato, P. R. (Eds.). (1999). *The Postdivorce Family: Children, Parenting and Society.* Beverly Hills, CA: Sage Publications.

Wallerstein, J. S., Lewis, J. M., & Blakeslee, S. (2000). *The Unexpected Legacy of Divorce: A Twenty-Five Year Landmark Study.* New York: Hyperion.

Weitzman, L. J. (1985). *The Divorce Revolution: The Unexpected Social and Economic Consequences for Women and Children in America.* New York: Free Press.

Juvenile Courts | 8

What Is This Chapter About?

This chapter is about the courts that handle matters relating to minors. These include juveniles who commit criminal acts or other violations of law. They also include minors who are runaways, truants, children in need of supervision, and children who are victims of abuse and neglect.

The chapter begins with the background of the juvenile courts and the historical need for a separate court to handle cases involving juvenile behavior. The concept of *parens patriae* (the state as parent) is presented as a guiding principle in the development of the courts, and whether the concept retains vitality today is considered. The goals of the juvenile court are discussed and distinguished from those of the adult criminal court. Procedural protections afforded juveniles today as a result of Supreme Court decisions are also discussed in the context of the goals of the juvenile court.

In addition, this chapter examines the jurisdiction of the juvenile court. This includes the types of cases handled and the relationship of juvenile courts to other courts within a state's court system. Furthermore, the various ways in which juvenile courts are organized is discussed.

Finally, this chapter outlines the process of adjudication in juvenile courts. This process shares similarities with the criminal process but is distinct in the treatment of youth within the system, the steps involved in the process, and the language and labels used to describe various aspects of the process. In addition, the different disposition options for juvenile cases are discussed.

Learning Objectives

After reading this chapter, you should be able to

1. Explain the legal distinction between adults and children.
2. Understand the historical basis for the juvenile court.
3. Explain the concept of *parens patriae* and its influence on the juvenile court.
4. Recognize differences between the constitutional rights of juveniles and adults.
5. Understand the role of juvenile courts within a state court system.
6. Identify the jurisdiction of juvenile courts.
7. Describe the disposition options for juvenile courts.

The juvenile justice system is a system of justice administered through specialized courts (usually called "juvenile" or "children's" courts) to decide cases in which minors commit offenses against society. These may be criminal offenses or lesser "status" offenses, which involve behavior that is only illegal when committed by a minor. Regardless of the offense, the juvenile courts operate independently of criminal courts in the United States based on the presumption that minors are capable of rehabilitation, and the processes used for punishing adult criminals should not apply to children and adolescents.

The history of the juvenile justice system provides the backdrop for the establishment of the juvenile courts. Prior to the 20th century, children who committed criminal offenses were tried in much the same way as adults; no separate processes, courts, or methods of punishment existed. The first juvenile court was established in 1899, but before that time, reformers had taken steps to help children who violated the law or were "incorrigible" to develop into productive citizens.

Establishment of Juvenile Institutions

In the early 19th century, the United States experienced tremendous growth as a result of immigration. The population of cities such as Boston, New York, and Philadelphia grew considerably, and along with this growth, social problems such as poverty, unemployment, and crime grew as well. The popular perception of the time was that poverty and crime were inextricably linked, and the poor came to be viewed as a threat to society. The response to this was incarceration of adult criminals in the harshest conditions. The problem of poverty was not just an adult problem, however—it affected children directly and indirectly, and a growing crime problem among poor youth became evident. Although the solution for adults was incarceration, reformers held out hope for the reformation of child law breakers, and as a result, the institutionalization of "problem" children began with the establishment of "houses of refuge" (Bernard, 1992). The first of these was created in 1825 in New York, with others in Boston and Philadelphia following shortly after, and the goal of each was to teach children to become useful and productive, able to join and contribute to society as adults. The houses of refuge focused on the value of hard work and the development of minimal skills, with discipline and production emphasized. The house of refuge engaged each child in a variety of productive work, such as farming, building furniture, or sewing clothing, for which the institution was paid by enterprising businessmen who profited greatly from the labor. The money paid to the house of refuge was used in its operation for the support of the children.

Children could be committed to a house of refuge by a village leader or parent with or without a court hearing. Once confined, a child stayed for an indeterminate amount of time, up to age 21. After that, they were apprenticed to tradesmen in the cities for a period of indentured servitude. Depending on the "master," this "apprenticeship" was either formative or suffered through until the youth ran away.

These problems, along with the civil war ravaging the country by the mid 19th century, led to a rethinking of the approach to reforming children. There was also no evidence that the houses of refuge were solving the child crime problem, which continued to grow. A progressive movement to improve the living conditions of poor children and rehabilitate youthful offenders developed, called the "child savers" (Platt, 1977). Rather than the failed houses of refuge, they advocated reformatories whose specific purpose was to "reform," or inculcate moral values into children viewed as starting out on the wrong path.

The reformatories were located in rural areas outside of cities, where the corrupting influence of the city could not reach. Importantly, the reformatories were also subject to government control, which was a central goal of the child savers movement—to push for legislation allowing the state and/or local government to intervene when parents could not "control" their child. In addition to the support for reformatories, legislation also granted jurisdiction to courts for hearing matters pertaining to juveniles that were not only criminal cases, but cases involving children considered to be delinquent, incorrigible, a runaway, or vagrant were within the authority of the court.

Parens Patriae

The philosophy governing 19th century attempts to rehabilitate children was that of *parens patriae*, literally, "parent of the country." This stemmed from the English view that the king had the right to intervene in the lives of his subjects and was used to direct the care of orphans and widows in that country. Applying the principle of *parens patriae* in this country, reformers viewed society itself as having the power to support, train, and otherwise assist children who were poor or who engaged in antisocial behavior. In 1838, the doctrine was first discussed in an American court case, *Ex Parte Crouse* (4 Whart. 9, 1839 WL 3700, Pa. 1839), in which the Pennsylvania Supreme Court considered a petition for habeus corpus from the father of Mary Ann Crouse, a young girl, to release her from a house of refuge after she had been committed there by the girl's mother because of her "vicious conduct." The court's opinion is found in **Case Decision 8.1**.

Case Decision 8.1 *Ex parte Crouse*, 4 Whart. 9, 1839 WL 3700 (Pa. 1839)

Per Curiam Opinion:

HABEAS CORPUS

The provisions of the acts of 23rd of March 1826, and 10th of April, 1835, which authorize the committal of infants to the House of Refuge, under certain circumstances, and their detention there, without a previous trial by jury, are not unconstitutional.

This was a habeas corpus directed to the keeper and managers of the "House of Refuge," in the county of Philadelphia, requiring them to produce before the Court one Mary Ann Crouse, an infant, detained in that institution. The petition for the habeas corpus was in the name of her father.

By the return to the writ it appeared, that the girl had been committed to the custody of the managers by virtue of a warrant under the hand and seal of Morton M'Michael, Esq., a justice of the peace of the county of Philadelphia, which recited that complaint and due proof had been made before him by Mary Crouse, the mother of the said Mary Ann Crouse, "that the said infant by reason of vicious conduct, has rendered her control beyond the power of the said complainant, and made it manifestly requisite that from regard to the moral and future welfare of the said infant she should be placed under the guardianship of the managers of the House of Refuge"; and the said alderman certified that in his opinion the said infant was "a proper subject for the said House of Refuge." Appended to the warrant of commitment were the names and places of residence of the witnesses examined, and the substance of the testimony given by them respectively, upon which the adjudication of the magistrate was founded.

The House of Refuge was established in pursuance of an act of assembly passed on the 23rd day of March, 1826. The 6th section of that act declared that the managers should, "at their discretion, receive into the said House of Refuge, such children who shall be taken up or committed as vagrants, or upon any criminal charge, or duly convicted of criminal offences, as may be in the judgment of the Court of Oyer and Terminer, or of the Court of Quarter Sessions of the peace of the county, or of the Mayor's Court of the city of Philadelphia, or of any alderman or justice of the peace, or of the managers of the Alms-house and house of employment, be deemed proper objects." By a supplement to the act passed on the 10th day of April 1835, it was declared, that in lieu of the provisions of the act of 1826, it should be lawful for the managers of the House of Refuge "at their discretion, to receive into their care and guardianship, infants, males under the age of twenty-one years, and females under the age of eighteen years, committed to their custody in either of the following modes, viz. First: infants committed by an alderman or justice of the peace on the complaint and due proof made to him by the parent, guardian or next friend of such infant, that by reason of incorrigible or vicious conduct such infant has rendered his or her control beyond the power of such parent, guardian or next friend, and made it manifestly requisite that from regard for the morals and future welfare of such infant, he or she should be placed under the guardianship of the managers of the House of Refuge. Second: infants committed by the authority aforesaid, where complaint and due proof have been made that such infant is a proper subject for the guardianship of the managers of the House of Refuge, in consequence of vagrancy, or of incorrigible or vicious conduct, and that from the moral depravity or otherwise of the parent or next friend in whose custody such infant may be, such parent or next friend is incapable or unwilling to exercise the proper care and discipline over such incorrigible or vicious infant. Third: infants committed by the Courts of this commonwealth in the mode provided by the act to which this is a supplement."

The House of Refuge is not a prison, but a school. Where reformation, and not punishment, is the end, it may indeed be used as a prison for juvenile convicts who would else be committed to a common gaol [jail]; and in respect to these, the constitutionality of the act which incorporated it, stands clear of controversy. It is only in respect of the application of its discipline to subjects admitted on the order of a court, a magistrate, or the managers of the Alms-house, that a doubt is entertained. The object of the charity is reformation, by training its inmates to industry; by imbuing their minds with principles of morality and religion; by furnishing them with means to earn a living; and, above all, by separating them from the corrupting influence of improper associates. To this end, may not the natural parents, when unequal to the task of education, or unworthy of it, be superseded by the *parens patriae*, or common guardian of the community? It is to be remembered that the public has a paramount interest in the virtue and knowledge of its members, and that, of strict right, the business of education belongs to it. That parents are ordinarily entrusted with it, is because it can seldom be put into better hands; but where they are incompetent or corrupt, what is there to prevent the public from withdrawing their faculties, held, as they obviously are, at its sufferance? The right of parental control is a natural, but not an unalienable one. It is not excepted by the declaration of rights out of the subjects of ordinary legislation; and it consequently remains subject to the ordinary legislative power, which, if wantonly or inconveniently used, would soon be constitutionally restricted, but the competency of which, as the government is constituted, cannot be doubted. As to abridgment of indefeasible rights by confinement of the person, it is no more than what is borne, to a greater or less extent, in every school; and we know of no natural right to exemption from restraints which conduce to an infant's welfare. Nor is there a doubt of the propriety of their application in the particular instance. The infant has been snatched from a course which must have ended in confirmed depravity; and, not only is the restraint of her person lawful, but it would be an act of extreme cruelty to release her from it.

Remanded.

The court in *Crouse* noted that the *parens patriae* power of the state to educate children takes the place of that of the natural parents. It also explained the beneficial purposes of the house of refuge:

> The object of the charity is reformation, by training its inmates to industry; by imbuing their minds with principles of morality and religion; by furnishing them with means to earn a living; and, above all, by separating them from the corrupting influence of improper associates. To this end, may not the natural parents, when unequal to the task of education, or unworthy of it, be superseded by the *parens patriae*, or common guardian of the community? It is to be remembered that the public has a paramount interest in the virtue and knowledge of its members, and that, of strict right, the business of education belongs to it.

Parens patriae thus became the prevailing justification for intervening in the lives of children who committed crimes or were viewed as incorrigible. A central implication of this philosophical justification, in which the state may intervene when it is in a child's best interests to do so, is that it may run contrary to the due process rights of children, discussed further later here. Nonetheless, the *parens patriae* doctrine continued to influence juvenile justice policy throughout the 19th and 20th centuries, and its historical influence continues to be felt in the juvenile justice system today.

Adjudicating Juveniles

As noted previously here, it was not until 1899 that the first juvenile court was established in Illinois. Other states quickly followed in establishing their own juvenile courts, and by 1940, every state had a court designated to hear matters pertaining to juveniles. These courts were largely founded on the basis of the *parens patriae* philosophy, where the goal was not to harshly punish those who committed crime, but to rehabilitate. That orientation continues today, at least in philosophy, if not fully in practice.

Due Process Rights of Juveniles

Under the *parens patriae* doctrine, juvenile courts were intended to take a benevolent approach to the youthful wrongdoers who came before the court; however, as the 20th century progressed, some argued that juvenile courts, although giving lip service to this approach, in practice conducted adversarial proceedings in which minors received little beneficence while lacking procedural rights designed to protect criminal defendants from unfair processes and unjust outcomes. This began to change in 1960s as a result of attention by the U.S. Supreme Court to the due process rights of juveniles. Due process rights are those rights guaranteed by the U.S. Constitution that require specific processes to be followed by the government before it may punish an individual. As the Fourteenth Amendment states: "No state shall . . . deprive any person of life, liberty, or property, without due process of law."

In the first Supreme Court case directly addressing the due process rights of juveniles, *Kent v. U.S.*, 383 U.S. 541, 86 S. Ct. 1045, 16 L.Ed.2d 84 (1966), 16-year-old Morris Kent was accused of breaking into a house, stealing a wallet, and raping the woman who lived there. He was held for a week and interrogated by police without the presence of a parent or lawyer and then "waived," or transferred, from the juvenile court to the adult criminal court by the juvenile court judge. This occurred without a hearing or any record as to the reasons for the transfer. He was subsequently tried in adult court, found guilty of the housebreaking and theft charges and found not guilty by reason of insanity for rape. He was committed to a mental institution until he was no longer mentally ill and sentenced to 30 to 90 years for housebreaking and theft charges.

The Supreme Court overturned the convictions and determination of insanity. It held that such a "critically important" stage of the juvenile proceeding as transfer to adult court requires a hearing, representation by counsel, and notification of the reasons for the transfer. The court found that

> [t]here is much evidence that some juvenile courts, including the District of Columbia, lack the personnel, facilities, and techniques to perform adequately as representatives of the State in a *parens patriae* capacity, at least with respect to children charged with a law violation. There is evidence, in fact, that there may be grounds for concern that the child receives the worst of both worlds: that he gets neither the protections accorded to adults nor the solicitous care and regenerative treatment postulated for children.

The Court's ruling is significant because it marked a turning point in the operation of the juvenile justice system by recognizing that minors, at least those charged with serious crimes, cannot be denied the beneficence of *parens patriae* and treated as adults, while also being denied their due process rights to a hearing, counsel, and notification of the basis for the adverse decision.

A year later, the Supreme Court considered another case involving the juvenile courts and the rights of juveniles charged with violations of law. *In re Gault* (387 U.S. 1, 87 S. Ct. 1428, 18 L.Ed.2d 527 (1967)) involved a 15-year-old boy from Arizona who was charged with making "lewd" telephone calls to a neighbor, Mrs. Cook. Gerald Gault was sent to a detention facility without notifying his mother, questioned without an adult present, and after a short hearing, was found to be delinquent and sent to the state "industrial school" until he was 21. Had he been an adult who committed the same offense, the maximum penalty would have been a fine of $50 and 2 months in jail. The Court's opinion is found in **Case Decision 8.2.**

Case Decision 8.2   *In re Gault*, 387 U.S. 1, 87 S. Ct. 1428, 18 L.Ed.2d 527 (1967)

Opinion of the Court by Justice Fortas:

This is an appeal from a judgment of the Supreme Court of Arizona affirming the dismissal of a petition for a writ of habeas corpus. The petition sought the release of Gerald Francis Gault, appellants' 15-year-old son, who had been committed as a juvenile delinquent to the State Industrial School by the Juvenile Court of Gila County, Arizona. The Supreme Court of Arizona affirmed dismissal of the writ against various arguments which included an attack upon the constitutionality of the Arizona Juvenile Code because of its alleged denial of procedural due process rights to juveniles charged with being 'delinquents.' We do not agree, and we reverse.

I

On Monday, June 8, 1964, at about 10 a.m., Gerald Francis Gault and a friend, Ronald Lewis, were taken into custody by the Sheriff of Gila County. Gerald was then still subject to a six months' probation order which had been entered on February 25, 1964, as a result of his having been in the company of another boy who had stolen a wallet from a lady's purse. The police action on June 8 was taken as the result of a verbal complaint by a neighbor of the boys, Mrs. Cook, about a telephone call made to her in which the caller or callers made lewd or indecent remarks. It will suffice for purposes of this opinion to say that the remarks or questions put to her were of the irritatingly offensive, adolescent, sex variety.

At the time Gerald was picked up, his mother and father were both at work. No notice that Gerald was being taken into custody was left at the home. No other steps were taken to advise them that their son had, in effect, been arrested. Gerald was taken to the Children's Detention Home. When his mother arrived home at about 6 o'clock, Gerald was not there. Gerald's older brother was sent to look for him at the trailer home of the Lewis family. He apparently learned then that Gerald was in custody. He so informed his mother. The two of them went to the Detention Home. The deputy probation officer, Flagg, who was also superintendent of the Detention Home, told Mrs. Gault 'why Jerry was there' and said that a hearing would be held in Juvenile Court at 3 o'clock the following day, June 9.

Officer Flagg filed a petition with the court on the hearing day, June 9, 1964. It was not served on the Gaults. Indeed, none of them saw this petition until the habeas corpus hearing on August 17, 1964. The petition was entirely formal. It made no reference to any factual basis for the judicial action which it initiated. It recited only that 'said minor is under the age of eighteen years, and is in need of the protection of this Honorable Court; (and that) said minor is a delinquent minor.' It prayed for a hearing and an order regarding 'the care and custody of said minor.' Officer Flagg executed a formal affidavit in support of the petition.

On June 9, Gerald, his mother, his older brother, and Probation Officers Flagg and Henderson appeared before the Juvenile Judge in chambers. Gerald's father was not there. He was at work out of the city. Mrs. Cook, the complainant, was not there. No one was sworn at this hearing. No transcript or recording was made. No memorandum or record of the substance of the proceedings was prepared. Our information about the proceedings and the subsequent hearing on June 15, derives entirely from the testimony of the Juvenile Court Judge, Mr. and Mrs. Gault and Officer Flagg at the habeas corpus proceeding conducted two months later. From this, it appears that at the June 9 hearing Gerald was questioned by the judge about the telephone call. There was conflict as to what he said. His mother recalled that Gerald said he only dialed Mrs. Cook's number and handed the telephone to his friend, Ronald. Officer Flagg recalled that Gerald had admitted making the lewd remarks. Judge McGhee testified that Gerald 'admitted making one of these (lewd) statements.' At the conclusion of the hearing, the judge said he would 'think about it.' Gerald was taken back to the Detention Home. He was not sent to his own home with his parents. On June 11 or 12, after having been detained since June 8, Gerald was released and driven home. There is no explanation in the record as to why he was kept in the Detention Home or why he was released. At 5 p.m. on the day of Gerald's release, Mrs. Gault received a note signed by Officer Flagg. It was on plain paper, not letterhead. Its entire text was as follows:

'Mrs. Gault:
 'Judge McGHEE has set Monday June 15, 1964 at 11:00 A.M. as the date and time for further Hearings on Gerald's delinquency
 '/s/ Flagg'

(Continues)

(Continued)

At the appointed time on Monday, June 15, Gerald, his father and mother, Ronald Lewis and his father, and Officers Flagg and Henderson were present before Judge McGhee. Witnesses at the habeas corpus proceeding differed in their recollections of Gerald's testimony at the June 15 hearing. Mr. and Mrs. Gault recalled that Gerald again testified that he had only dialed the number and that the other boy had made the remarks. Officer Flagg agreed that at this hearing Gerald did not admit making the lewd remarks. But Judge McGhee recalled that 'there was some admission again of some of the lewd statements. He didn't admit any of the more serious lewd statements.' Again, the complainant, Mrs. Cook, was not present. Mrs. Gault asked that Mrs. Cook be present 'so she could see which boy that done the talking, the dirty talking over the phone.' The Juvenile Judge said 'she didn't have to be present at that hearing.' The judge did not speak to Mrs. Cook or communicate with her at any time. Probation Officer Flagg had talked to her once—over the telephone on June 9.

At this June 15 hearing a 'referral report' made by the probation officers was filed with the court, although not disclosed to Gerald or his parents. This listed the charge as 'Lewd Phone Calls.' At the conclusion of the hearing, the judge committed Gerald as a juvenile delinquent to the State Industrial School 'for the period of his minority (that is, until 21), unless sooner discharged by due process of law.' An order to that effect was entered. It recites that 'after a full hearing and due deliberation the Court finds that said minor is a delinquent child, and that said minor is of the age of 15 years.'

No appeal is permitted by Arizona law in juvenile cases. On August 3, 1964, a petition for a writ of habeas corpus was filed with the Supreme Court of Arizona and referred by it to the Superior Court for hearing.

The Superior Court dismissed the writ, and appellants sought review in the Arizona Supreme Court. The Supreme Court handed down an elaborate and wide-ranging opinion affirming dismissal of the writ and stating the court's conclusions as to the issues raised by appellants and other aspects of the juvenile process. In their jurisdictional statement and brief in this Court, appellants do not urge upon us all of the points passed upon by the Supreme Court of Arizona. They urge that we hold the Juvenile Code of Arizona invalid on its face or as applied in this case because, contrary to the Due Process Clause of the Fourteenth Amendment, the juvenile is taken from the custody of his parents and committed to a state institution pursuant to proceedings in which the Juvenile Court has virtually unlimited discretion, and in which the following basic rights are denied:

1. Notice of the charges;
2. Right to counsel;
3. Right to confrontation and cross-examination;
4. Privilege against self-incrimination;
5. Right to a transcript of the proceedings; and
6. Right to appellate review.

II

This Court has not heretofore decided the precise question. In *Kent v. United States*, 383 U.S. 541, 86 S. Ct. 1045, 16 L.Ed.2d 84 (1966), we considered the requirements for a valid waiver of the 'exclusive' jurisdiction of the Juvenile Court of the District of Columbia so that a juvenile could be tried in the adult criminal court of the District. Although our decision turned upon the language of the statute, we emphasized the necessity that 'the basic requirements of due process and fairness' be satisfied in such proceedings.

The history and theory underlying this development are well-known, but a recapitulation is necessary for purposes of this opinion. The Juvenile Court movement began in this country at the end of the last century. From the juvenile court statute adopted in Illinois in 1899, the system has spread to every State in the Union, the District of Columbia, and Puerto Rico. The constitutionality of juvenile court laws has been sustained in over 40 jurisdictions against a variety of attacks.

The early reformers were appalled by adult procedures and penalties, and by the fact that children could be given long prison sentences and mixed in jails with hardened criminals. They were profoundly convinced that society's duty to the child could not be confined by the concept of justice alone. They believed that society's role was not to ascertain whether the child was 'guilty' or 'innocent,' but 'what is he, how has he become what he is, and what had best be done in his interest and in the interest of the state to save him from a downward career.' Julian Mack, The Juvenile Court, 23 Harv. L.

Rev. 104, 119-120 (1909). The child—essentially good, as they saw it—was to be made 'to feel that he is the object of (the state's) care and solicitude,' not that he was under arrest or on trial. The rules of criminal procedure were therefore altogether inapplicable. The apparent rigidities, technicalities, and harshness which they observed in both substantive and procedural criminal law were therefore to be discarded. The idea of crime and punishment was to be abandoned. The child was to be 'treated' and 'rehabilitated' and the procedures, from apprehension through institutionalization, were to be 'clinical' rather than punitive.

These results were to be achieved, without coming to conceptual and constitutional grief, by insisting that the proceedings were not adversary, but that the state was proceeding as parens patriae. The Latin phrase proved to be a great help to those who sought to rationalize the exclusion of juveniles from the constitutional scheme; but its meaning is murky and its historic credentials are of dubious relevance. The phrase was taken from chancery practice, where, however, it was used to describe the power of the state to act in loco parentis for the purpose of protecting the property interests and the person of the child. But there is no trace of the doctrine in the history of criminal jurisprudence. At common law, children under seven were considered incapable of possessing criminal intent. Beyond that age, they were subjected to arrest, trial, and in theory to punishment like adult offenders. In these old days, the state was not deemed to have authority to accord them fewer procedural rights than adults.

The right of the state, as parens patriae, to deny to the child procedural rights available to his elders was elaborated by the assertion that a child, unlike an adult, has a right 'not to liberty but to custody.' He can be made to attorn to his parents, to go to school, etc. If his parents default in effectively performing their custodial functions—that is, if the child is 'delinquent'—the state may intervene. In doing so, it does not deprive the child of any rights, because he has none. It merely provides the 'custody' to which the child is entitled. On this basis, proceedings involving juveniles were described as 'civil' not 'criminal' and therefore not subject to the requirements which restrict the state when it seeks to deprive a person of his liberty.

Accordingly, the highest motives and most enlightened impulses led to a peculiar system for juveniles, unknown to our law in any comparable context. The constitutional and theoretical basis for this peculiar system is—to say the least—debatable. And in practice, as we remarked in the *Kent* case, the results have not been entirely satisfactory. Juvenile Court history has again demonstrated that unbridled discretion, however benevolently motivated, is frequently a poor substitute for principle and procedure.

Due process of law is the primary and indispensable foundation of individual freedom. It is the basic and essential term in the social compact which defines the rights of the individual and delimits the powers which the state may exercise. As Mr. Justice Frankfurter has said: 'The history of American freedom is, in no small measure, the history of procedure.' But, in addition, the procedural rules which have been fashioned from the generality of due process are our best instruments for the distillation and evaluation of essential facts from the conflicting welter of data that life and our adversary methods present. It is these instruments of due process which enhance the possibility that truth will emerge from the confrontation of opposing versions and conflicting data. 'Procedure is to law what 'scientific method' is to science.' Foster, Social Work, the Law, and Social Action, in Social Casework, July 1964, pp. 383, 386.

We do not mean by this to denigrate the juvenile court process or to suggest that there are not aspects of the juvenile system relating to offenders which are valuable. But the features of the juvenile system which its proponents have asserted are of unique benefit will not be impaired by constitutional domestication.

[I]t is urged that the juvenile benefits from informal proceedings in the court. The early conception of the Juvenile Court proceeding was one in which a fatherly judge touched the heart and conscience of the erring youth by talking over his problems, by paternal advice and admonition, and in which, in extreme situations, benevolent and wise institutions of the State provided guidance and help 'to save him from downward career.' Then, as now, goodwill and compassion were admirably prevalent. But recent studies have, with surprising unanimity, entered sharp dissent as to the validity of this gentle conception. They suggest that the appearance as well as the actuality of fairness, impartiality and orderliness—in short, the essentials of due process—may be a more impressive and more therapeutic attitude so far as the juvenile is concerned. Of course, it is not suggested that

(Continues)

(*Continued*)

juvenile court judges should fail appropriately to take account, in their demeanor and conduct, of the emotional and psychological attitude of the juveniles with whom they are confronted. While due process requirements will, in some instances, introduce a degree of order and regularity to Juvenile Court proceedings to determine delinquency, and in contested cases will introduce some elements of the adversary system, nothing will require that the conception of the kindly juvenile judge be replaced by its opposite, nor do we here rule upon the question whether ordinary due process requirements must be observed with respect to hearings to determine the disposition of the delinquent child.

Ultimately, however, we confront the reality of that portion of the Juvenile Court process with which we deal in this case. A boy is charged with misconduct. The boy is committed to an institution where he may be restrained of liberty for years. It is of no constitutional consequence—and of limited practical meaning—that the institution to which he is committed is called an Industrial School. The fact of the matter is that, however euphemistic the title, a 'receiving home' or an 'industrial school' for juveniles is an institution of confinement in which the child is incarcerated for a greater or lesser time. His world becomes 'a building with whitewashed walls, regimented routine and institutional hours.' Instead of mother and father and sisters and brothers and friends and classmates, his world is peopled by guards, custodians, state employees, and 'delinquents' confined with him for anything from waywardness to rape and homicide.

In view of this, it would be extraordinary if our Constitution did not require the procedural regularity and the exercise of care implied in the phrase 'due process.' Under our Constitution, the condition of being a boy does not justify a kangaroo court. The traditional ideas of Juvenile Court procedure, indeed, contemplated that time would be available and care would be used to establish precisely what the juvenile did and why he did it—was it a prank of adolescence or a brutal act threatening serious consequences to himself or society unless corrected? The essential difference between Gerald's case and a normal criminal case is that safeguards available to adults were discarded in Gerald's case. The summary procedure as well as the long commitment was possible because Gerald was 15 years of age instead of over 18.

If Gerald had been over 18, he would not have been subject to Juvenile Court proceedings. For the particular offense immediately involved, the maximum punishment would have been a fine of $5 to $50, or imprisonment in jail for not more than two months. Instead, he was committed to custody for a maximum of six years. If he had been over 18 and had committed an offense to which such a sentence might apply, he would have been entitled to substantial rights under the Constitution of the United States as well as under Arizona's laws and constitution. The United States Constitution would guarantee him rights and protections with respect to arrest, search, and seizure, and pretrial interrogation. It would assure him of specific notice of the charges and adequate time to decide his course of action and to prepare his defense. He would be entitled to clear advice that he could be represented by counsel, and, at least if a felony were involved, the State would be required to provide counsel if his parents were unable to afford it. If the court acted on the basis of his confession, careful procedures would be required to assure its voluntariness. If the case went to trial, confrontation and opportunity for cross-examination would be guaranteed. So wide a gulf between the State's treatment of the adult and of the child requires a bridge sturdier than mere verbiage, and reasons more persuasive than cliche can provide.

III

NOTICE OF CHARGES

Appellants allege that the Arizona Juvenile Code is unconstitutional or alternatively that the proceedings before the Juvenile Court were constitutionally defective because of failure to provide adequate notice of the hearings. No notice was given to Gerald's parents when he was taken into custody on Monday, June 8. On that night, when Mrs. Gault went to the Detention Home, she was orally informed that there would be a hearing the next afternoon and was told the reason why Gerald was in custody. The only written notice Gerald's parents received at any time was a note on plain paper from Officer Flagg delivered on Thursday or Friday, June 11 or 12, to the effect that the judge had set Monday, June 15, 'for further Hearings on Gerald's delinquency.'

A 'petition' was filed with the court on June 9 by Officer Flagg, reciting only that he was informed and believed that 'said minor is a delinquent minor and that it is necessary that some order be made by the Honorable Court for said minor's welfare.' The applicable Arizona statute provides for a petition to be filed in Juvenile Court, alleging in general terms that the child is 'neglected, dependent or delinquent.' The statute explicitly states that such a general allegation is sufficient, 'without alleging the facts.' There is no requirement that the petition be served and it was not served upon, given to, or shown to Gerald or his parents.

Notice, to comply with due process requirements, must be given sufficiently in advance of scheduled court proceedings so that reasonable opportunity to prepare will be afforded, and it must 'set forth the alleged misconduct with particularity.' The 'initial hearing' in the present case was a hearing on the merits. Notice at that time is not timely; and even if there were a conceivable purpose served by the deferral proposed by the court below, it would have to yield to the requirements that the child and his parents or guardian be notified, in writing, of the specific charge or factual allegations to be considered at the hearing, and that such written notice be given at the earliest practicable time, and in any event sufficiently in advance of the hearing to permit preparation. Due process of law requires notice of the sort we have described—that is, notice which would be deemed constitutionally adequate in a civil or criminal proceeding. It does not allow a hearing to be held in which a youth's freedom and his parents' right to his custody are at stake without giving them timely notice, in advance of the hearing, of the specific issues that they must meet.

IV

RIGHT TO COUNSEL

Appellants charge that the Juvenile Court proceedings were fatally defective because the court did not advise Gerald or his parents of their right to counsel, and proceeded with the hearing, the adjudication of delinquency and the order of commitment in the absence of counsel for the child and his parents or an express waiver of the right thereto. The Supreme Court of Arizona referred to a provision of the Juvenile Code which it characterized as requiring 'that the probation officer shall look after the interests of neglected, delinquent and dependent children,' including representing their interests in court. The court argued that 'The parent and the probation officer may be relied upon to protect the infant's interests.'

We do not agree. Probation officers, in the Arizona scheme, are also arresting officers. They initiate proceedings and file petitions which they verify, as here, alleging the delinquency of the child; and they testify, as here, against the child. And here the probation officer was also superintendent of the Detention Home. The probation officer cannot act as counsel for the child. His role in the adjudicatory hearing, by statute and in fact, is as arresting officer and witness against the child. Nor can the judge represent the child. A proceeding where the issue is whether the child will be found to be 'delinquent' and subjected to the loss of his liberty for years is comparable in seriousness to a felony prosecution. The juvenile needs the assistance of counsel to cope with problems of law, to make skilled inquiry into the facts, to insist upon regularity of the proceedings, and to ascertain whether he has a defense and to prepare and submit it.

V

CONFRONTATION, SELF-INCRIMINATION, CROSS-EXAMINATION

Appellants urge that the writ of habeas corpus should have been granted because of the denial of the rights of confrontation and cross-examination in the Juvenile Court hearings, and because the privilege against self-incrimination was not observed. The Juvenile Court Judge testified at the habeas corpus hearing that he had proceeded on the basis of Gerald's admissions at the two hearings. Appellants attack this on the ground that the admissions were obtained in disregard of the privilege against self-incrimination.

Our first question, then, is whether Gerald's admission was improperly obtained and relied on as the basis of decision, in conflict with the Federal Constitution. For this purpose, it is necessary briefly to recall the relevant facts.

Mrs. Cook, the complainant, and the recipient of the alleged telephone call, was not called as a witness. Gerald's mother asked the Juvenile Court Judge why Mrs. Cook was not present and the judge replied that 'she didn't have to be present.' So far as appears, Mrs. Cook was spoken to only once, by Officer Flagg, and this was by telephone. The judge did not speak with her on any occasion. Gerald had been questioned by the probation officer after having been taken into custody. The exact circumstances of this questioning do not appear but any admissions Gerald may have made at this time do

(Continues)

not appear in the record. Gerald was also questioned by the Juvenile Court Judge at each of the two hearings. The judge testified in the habeas corpus proceeding that Gerald admitted making 'some of the lewd statements (but not) any of the more serious lewd statements.' Neither Gerald nor his parents were advised that he did not have to testify or make a statement, or that an incriminating statement might result in his commitment as a 'delinquent.'

In reviewing this conclusion of Arizona's Supreme Court, we emphasize again that we are here concerned only with a proceeding to determine whether a minor is a 'delinquent' and which may result in commitment to a state institution. Specifically, the question is whether, in such a proceeding, an admission by the juvenile may be used against him in the absence of clear and unequivocal evidence that the admission was made with knowledge that he was not obliged to speak and would not be penalized for remaining silent. In light of *Miranda v. State of Arizona*, 384 U.S. 436, 86 S. Ct. 1602, 16 L.Ed.2d 694 (1966), we must also consider whether, if the privilege against self-incrimination is available, it can effectively be waived unless counsel is present or the right to counsel has been waived. It would indeed be surprising if the privilege against self-incrimination were available to hardened criminals but not to children.

It would be entirely unrealistic to carve out of the Fifth Amendment all statements by juveniles on the ground that these cannot lead to 'criminal' involvement. In the first place, juvenile proceedings to determine 'delinquency,' which may lead to commitment to a state institution, must be regarded as 'criminal' for purposes of the privilege against self-incrimination. To hold otherwise would be to disregard substance because of the feeble enticement of the 'civil' label-of-convenience which has been attached to juvenile proceedings. For this purpose, at least, commitment is a deprivation of liberty. It is incarceration against one's will, whether it is called 'criminal' or 'civil.' And our Constitution guarantees that no person shall be 'compelled' to be a witness against himself when he is threatened with deprivation of his liberty—a command which this Court has broadly applied and generously implemented in accordance with the teaching of the history of the privilege and its great office in mankind's battle for freedom.

In addition, the fact of the matter is that there is little or no assurance in Arizona, as in most if not all of the States, that a juvenile apprehended and interrogated by the police or even by the Juvenile Court itself will remain outside of the reach of adult courts as a consequence of the offense for which he has been taken into custody. In Arizona, as in other States, provision is made for Juvenile Courts to relinquish or waive jurisdiction to the ordinary criminal courts. In the present case, when Gerald Gault was interrogated concerning violation of a section of the Arizona Criminal Code, it could not be certain that the Juvenile Court Judge would decide to 'suspend' criminal prosecution in court for adults by proceeding to an adjudication in Juvenile Court.

It is also urged, as the Supreme Court of Arizona here asserted, that the juvenile and presumably his parents should not be advised of the juvenile's right to silence because confession is good for the child as the commencement of the assumed therapy of the juvenile court process, and he should be encouraged to assume an attitude of trust and confidence toward the officials of the juvenile process. This proposition has been subjected to widespread challenge on the basis of current reappraisals of the rhetoric and realities of the handling of juvenile offenders.

In fact, evidence is accumulating that confessions by juveniles do not aid in 'individualized treatment,' as the court below put it, and that compelling the child to answer questions, without warning or advice as to his right to remain silent, does not serve this or any other good purpose. [I]t seems probable that where children are induced to confess by 'paternal' urgings on the part of officials and the confession is then followed by disciplinary action, the child's reaction is likely to be hostile and adverse—the child may well feel that he has been led or tricked into confession and that despite his confession, he is being punished. Further, authoritative opinion has cast formidable doubt upon the reliability and trustworthiness of 'confessions' by children.

We conclude that the constitutional privilege against self-incrimination is applicable in the case of juveniles as it is with respect to adults. If counsel was not present for some permissible reason when an admission was obtained, the greatest care must be taken to assure that the admission was voluntary, in the sense not only that it was not coerced or suggested, but also that it was not the product of ignorance of rights or of adolescent fantasy, fright or despair.

The 'confession' of Gerald Gault was first obtained by Officer Flagg, out of the presence of Gerald's parents, without counsel and without advising him of his right to silence, as far as appears. The judgment of the Juvenile Court was stated by the judge to be based on Gerald's admissions in court.

Neither 'admission' was reduced to writing, and, to say the least, the process by which the 'admissions,' were obtained and received must be characterized as lacking the certainty and order which are required of proceedings of such formidable consequences. Apart from the 'admission,' there was nothing upon which a judgment or finding might be based. There was no sworn testimony. Mrs. Cook, the complainant, was not present. Absent a valid confession adequate to support the determination of the Juvenile Court, confrontation and sworn testimony by witnesses available for cross-examination were essential for a finding of 'delinquency' and an order committing Gerald to a state institution for a maximum of six years.

As we said in *Kent*, with respect to waiver proceedings, 'there is no place in our system of law of reaching a result of such tremendous consequences without ceremony.' We now hold that, absent a valid confession, a determination of delinquency and an order of commitment to a state institution cannot be sustained in the absence of sworn testimony subjected to the opportunity for cross-examination in accordance with our law and constitutional requirements.

For the reasons stated, the judgment of the Supreme Court of Arizona is reversed and the cause remanded for further proceedings not inconsistent with this opinion. It is so ordered.

Gault was a sweeping decision. Although it recognized the beneficial basis for the development of the juvenile courts, it found that the operation of these courts is inconsistent with the rights of those under the age of 18 found in the Constitution. During adjudicatory hearings where a determination of delinquency may be made, as the Court held, these rights include the right to notice of the charges, the right to counsel, right to confront an accuser and cross-examine witnesses, the Fifth Amendment privilege against self-incrimination, and the right to a record with factual findings in support of the decision. In addition to change in juvenile justice practice brought about by the decision, *Gault* and other Supreme Court holdings that shortly followed it also brought some degree of confusion to state juvenile justice systems. As a California appellate court explained in 1977:

> The Juvenile Court Law is, and has been, a battleground of divergent and often warring social and legal philosophies. On the one hand, we find those who believe thoroughly in the *parens patriae* philosophy of the original Juvenile Court Law. On the other hand, we find those who believe that blind obedience to that philosophy and its resulting disregard of constitutional rights of young people has, in many respects, reduced the juvenile court to little more than a kangaroo court for young people. We also have a battle to the death between those who, at the risk of oversimplification, believe in the lock-the-kids-up-and-throw-the-key-away philosophy and those who, again at the same risk of oversimplification, insist that every underage criminal, no matter how vicious, is but a misguided child and is to be treated as such. These conflicts have, from time to time, resulted in a hodge-podge of legislation.

Between 1903, when California created its first juvenile court, until the late 1950s, the juvenile court picture in this state had become a checkerboard of inconsistent practices and procedure varying from county to county and judge to judge. The law had become a jumble of amendments and amendments to amendments. In 1961, the Legislature enacted that which has become known as the 1961 Juvenile Court Law. This was indeed a legislative milestone. The 1961 law appeared to satisfactorily bridge the gap between the feuding social and legal philosophies. It was simple, workable, understandable, and relatively uncomplicated; however, the handing down of certain U.S. Supreme Court decisions (*Breed v. Jones*, 421 U.S. 519, 95 S. Ct. 1779, 44 L.Ed.2d 346 (1975); *In re Winship*, 397 U.S. 358, 90 S. Ct. 1068, 25 L.Ed.2d 368 (1970); *In re Gault*, 387 U.S. 1, 87 S. Ct. 1428, 18 L.Ed.2d 527 (1967); *Kent v. United States*, 383 U.S. 541, 86 S. Ct. 1045, 16 L.Ed.2d 84 (1966)) necessitated certain changes in the law. As a result, each legislative session since 1961 has resulted in some legislative tinkering with the basic law. Also, the 1976 offering appears to have been a major effort aimed at a reconciliation between the competing social and legal forces and theories (*In re Ronald S.*, 138 Cal. Rptr. 387, 389, 69 Cal. App. 3rd. 866, 868 (Cal. App. 1977)).

Differentiating Juvenile and Criminal Courts

Despite the increased similarity between juvenile and adult courts as a result of the Supreme Court's recognition of due process rights of children, juvenile courts retain their distinctiveness in addressing the problems of delinquent youth. Juvenile courts continue to be distinguished from adult criminal courts in several ways because of the age of those who appear in the court and the court's goal of helping the child. These include the level of formality with which they operate, the absence of criminal records, the lack of jury trials, consideration of the juvenile's social situation, and their continuing rehabilitative emphasis. Although several of these were discussed by the U.S. Supreme Court in Gault and rejected as justifications for the continued denial of juvenile due process, the court noted their value:

> While due process requirements will, in some instances, introduce a degree of order and regularity to Juvenile Court proceedings to determine delinquency, and in contested

cases will introduce some elements of the adversary system, nothing will require that the conception of the kindly juvenile judge be replaced by its opposite. [T]he observance of due process standards, intelligently and not ruthlessly administered, will not compel the States to abandon or displace any of the substantive benefits of the juvenile process.

Level of Formality

Juvenile courts have traditionally been marked by informality. This is seen in the setting in which hearings occur and the manner in which hearings are conducted. Often, hearings are held in a judge's chambers or conference rooms, rather than imposing courtrooms. Nonetheless, some juvenile hearings, especially for more serious charges, assume the characteristics of an adversarial trial and take place in a courtroom setting.

Adjudication hearings in juvenile court also are conducted with a lesser degree of formality than criminal trials. Although a prosecutor and defense attorney are both present, the rules of evidence applicable in criminal cases are not used in the juvenile courts of most jurisdictions. Thus, evidence that may not be admissible in a criminal trial may be considered by the juvenile court judge. In addition, juvenile hearings, for the most part, are private. This means that the public may not attend the hearing—only the juvenile, the judge, the parents or guardians, the attorneys, and court staff may be present. This is intended to prevent the stigmatizing effect of public disclosure as well as preserve the goal of allowing the juvenile to leave his or her past behind as part of rehabilitation.

No Right to Jury

Although, as discussed previously, the U.S. Supreme Court has granted to juveniles many of the constitutional rights applicable to adults in criminal trials, the right to a jury is not among them. In *McKeiver v. Pennsylvania*, 403 U.S. 528, 91 S. Ct. 1976, 29 L.Ed.2d 647 (1971), the Court held that a jury trial was not required in juvenile proceedings for two primary reasons. First, the Court believed that a jury would "put an effective end to what has been the idealistic prospect of an intimate, informal protective proceeding." Second, jury trials in criminal cases were not necessarily fairer to defendants and, in juvenile cases, were unlikely to lead to better decision making. Although some states have allowed juries in certain juvenile cases, most continue to follow the lead of the Supreme Court by not doing so.

Absence of Criminal Records

A juvenile adjudication does not result in a finding of "guilty" or "not guilty." This is partly due to the fact that minors are generally considered to be less culpable for their actions. It is also due, in part, to the fact that the juvenile court continues to be considered civil, rather than criminal, in nature. A juvenile may be found to be "delinquent" or to be a "status offender."

One implication of the lack of guilt in juvenile cases is that the juvenile does not have a criminal record that follows him as he matures. Indeed, in most states, there is limited disclosure of juvenile court records to the public, and most have procedures that expunge the record of many types of offenses after a juvenile reaches the age of 21 years.

Consideration of Social Background

Juvenile courts, unlike courts in most criminal cases, take into account the upbringing and social background of the minor in deciding a proper disposition of a case. Thus, the family situation of a juvenile, functioning in the school setting, mental and physical health, friends and associates, and extracurricular activities may all be factors considered.

Rehabilitative Emphasis

As has been discussed earlier, juvenile courts have as a goal the rehabilitation of juveniles. Although this may also be the goal of some judges in adult criminal cases, sentencing in the adult system is primarily punitive. In recent years, partly because of public pressure to "get tough" on juvenile offenders, juvenile courts have come to rely more on sanctions in the disposition of cases. Nonetheless, rehabilitation and treatment alternatives remain the hallmark of juvenile courts.

Juvenile Court Process

The process employed by juvenile courts to determine whether a juvenile has committed an offense and what a proper disposition of the case should be is unlike that employed by adult courts. This difference is largely due to the goals of juvenile courts, which seek to emphasize the rehabilitation of youthful offenders.

Juvenile Court Goals

The operation of the juvenile courts reflects this different orientation toward youthful offenders, where trials are not conducted, but "adjudications" held; criminal complaints are not filed, but "delinquency petitions" are used; offenders were not convicted, but found "delinquent"; and juveniles are not sentenced, but a "disposition" of the case is made. A goal of the courts is to mitigate the harshness that often accompanies the criminal justice system for adults by seeking alternative ways of addressing juvenile behavior in order to help, rather than punish, the minor. For example, New Mexico law explains the reasons for a separate court process for juveniles who commit crimes:

> Consistent with the protection of the public interest, to remove from children committing delinquent acts the adult consequences of criminal behavior, but to still hold children committing delinquent acts accountable for their actions to the extent of the child's age, education, mental and physical condition, background and all other relevant factors, and to provide a program of supervision, care and rehabilitation, including rehabilitative restitution by the child to the victims of the child's delinquent act to the extent that the child is reasonably able to do so. (Delinquency Act, 32A-2-1 NMSA 1978)

Thus, a juvenile court's primary task is to handle adjudications in the state's juvenile justice system and decide how best to help youthful offenders while protecting the interests of the public in maintaining an orderly society. In general, a juvenile court's jurisdiction extends only to those under the age of 18 years. At that magic age, teenagers are considered to be adults and are subject to the adult criminal justice system for illegal behavior.

As a result, juvenile courts generally handle three types of cases. First, delinquency cases involve adjudicating minors who have committed offenses that are also criminal offenses for adults. When a minor is found to have violated a criminal law, he or she is considered to be delinquent. The term *delinquency* is used to reflect the rehabilitative emphasis of the juvenile court and avoid the stigma that is attached to the word "criminal," although some would question whether the term "delinquent" is any less stigmatizing than the word "criminal." Second, status offenses receive the attention of the juvenile court. A *status offense* is behavior that is illegal for a minor, but would not be a crime if committed by an adult. Status offenses are violations, not considered to be crimes, that are nonetheless illegal for minors, but not adults, to commit. They address those who have the "status" of youth and are designed to protect minors from engaging in behavior that society has decided it is not in their best interest to do. Examples of status offenses include underage possession of alcohol or purchase of cigarettes or violating a curfew. The third category of cases involves those of dependent children. These are minors without supervision and include runaways and children in need of supervision.

Waiver to Adult Court

The *Kent* case, discussed previously here, involved a juvenile who, without a hearing, had been transferred for trial in an adult criminal court. The Court considered the transfer decision to be a critical step in adjudicatory process because it results in the transfer of a minor to adult criminal court and the loss of the rehabilitative focus found in the juvenile court. Given the potential for punitive sentencing that often results in criminal cases involving serious charges, the Court required a hearing, representation by counsel, and written notification of the basis for the decision at this significant stage of a juvenile proceeding.

The waiver of jurisdiction by a juvenile court has been an aspect of the juvenile justice process since the inception of juvenile courts. Although the procedure is primarily used for those who commit the most serious offenses, the consequences of waiver are severe (Redding, 2008). There are many intended and unintended effects of waiver. Most directly, the juvenile transferred to adult criminal court for trial is subject to pretrial detention in the criminal system, trial by jury in a court open to the public, and more severe punishment that usually includes incarceration, up to and including life imprisonment.

Basis for Transfer

Two criteria must be considered as the basis for a decision to transfer a juvenile to adult criminal court. These are the age of the juvenile and the crime alleged to have been committed. The age required for transfer varies considerably from state to state. Although most states do not specify a minimum age for transfer, many have statutes providing for jurisdiction in the adult criminal court at age 14 and below, depending on the offense committed (Griffin et al., 1998).

The alleged crime is also a factor in the transfer decision. Again, considerable variation exists across states in the crimes for which transfer may be allowed. Most commonly, transfer is available for murder in most states, and many designate certain serious felonies as eligible for transfer. Nearly half the states allow transfer for certain drug-related offenses. Many states also make weapons offenses transferable, as well as certain serious property offenses (Griffin et al., 1998) (see **Sidebar 8.1**).

Sidebar 8.1 *When Is a Child Not a Child?*

On May 31, 2009, Mister Saunders ("Mister" is his first name) turned 21 years old. A 21st birthday is often a momentous one, and so it was for Mister Saunders. Not because he reached the legal drinking age or because he was now fully an adult, but because he was released from the New Mexico Youth Diagnostic and Development Center (YDDC), the place where juvenile offenders are incarcerated. He had been incarcerated in YDDC since 2002 when, as a 13-year-old, he admitted that he had committed aggravated burglary, rape, and brutally murdered Melissa Albert, a University of New Mexico student. He was committed to the YDDC until he was 21, the longest period the law allowed. After reaching that age, he was released, without probation, reporting, follow-up, or supervision of any kind. Mister Saunders is now a free man.

Saunders did not act alone, however. His accomplice was 15-year-old Benny Mora, Jr. Mora allegedly held Melissa's arms while Saunders stabbed her 13 times then raped her as she died. Because New Mexico law allowed 15-year-olds to be charged as adults for murder, Mora was charged in criminal court. He pled guilty to second-degree murder, kidnapping, aggravated burglary, and conspiracy and was sentenced to 45 years in the state prison.

Which of the two, Saunders or Mora, received the fairer sentence? Should there be such a difference in outcome based on the 2-year difference between age 13 and 15? Was justice served?

Heinous crimes committed by juveniles such as Saunders and Mora or even younger children, although unusual, have become a focus of media attention in recent years. Public reaction to such reports is mixed with some calling for more adult-like sanctions against youthful wrongdoers, whereas others believe societal or family problems are at the root of such behavior, calling for a less punitive resolution. The juvenile courts, with their rehabilitative emphasis, are often ill-equipped to deal with children who commit serious offenses. How is a

(Continues)

system designed to treat youthful wrongdoers differently from adults to deal with children who have committed adult crimes? Do adults and children deserve the same, or different, treatment based on their age or the crime committed? Should age continue to be the distinguishing factor allowing the rehabilitative emphasis of the juvenile courts to apply, or should the severity of the crime determine which court has jurisdiction?

The difficulty of how to resolve cases of serious crime by youthful offenders increases as the age of the youth decreases. On February 12, 1993, 10-year-olds Jon Venables and Robert Thompson were recorded on surveillance cameras at the Bootle Strand Shopping Center in Liverpool, England, leading 2-year-old James Bulger away while his mother searched frantically for her only son. The toddler was later found dead by some railroad tracks, his small body mutilated and beaten to death. Store videos from that day showed the 10-year-olds shoplifting small items from stores before the abduction. They were also seen trying to befriend other small boys and attempted to take at least one other. Thompson and Venables were tried and convicted of James' murder (Great Britain has no juvenile courts for serious offenders, although the trial procedures for children differ) and sentenced to a minimum of 8 years in a youth facility. Shortly after serving that time, they were released by a parole board because of their good behavior. The board also determined that they were no longer a threat to society. Given the finding that the boys (now 18 years old) were no longer a threat and had been rehabilitated, was the outcome just? As with the American juvenile justice system, when the goal of rehabilitation is achieved, does society have any interest in continuing to incarcerate a youthful offender?

In November of 2008, an 8-year-old boy shot his father Vincent Romero and a friend, Timothy Romans, with a 22-caliber rifle. The killings occurred in the small town of St. Johns, Arizona, in which the boy lived with his father and his stepmother. The boy was initially considered a witness to the shootings, but after being interviewed by the police (without a family member or attorney present), he confessed to the shootings. His motivation was unclear, but he later referred to being tired of spankings from his father. In order to avoid a trial, the boy agreed to a plea deal in which he pled guilty to one count of negligent manslaughter in Romans' death. Prosecutors agreed that also requiring the boy to admit that he killed his father could be too traumatizing. The agreement required the boy to receive extensive ongoing therapy, but he was not incarcerated or otherwise required to be committed to a juvenile facility. Was this outcome proper? Can an 8-year-old knowingly plead guilty or, for that matter, knowingly kill?

Cases such as these demonstrate the difficulties with an age-based approach to determining culpability. Although the law seems to have settled on allowing increased culpability as age increases, there is considerable state-to-state variability in when a child should no longer be considered a child for purposes of prosecuting certain serious crimes such as murder. The balance of relevant factors—the act committed, the effects on the victim and society, and the potential for rehabilitation—differs according to views of people and lawmakers in a given place. What course of action is suitable in such cases may not always be predictable, but it should satisfy the need for justice confronting the people affected.

Methods of Transfer

The decision to transfer a juvenile to adult court has traditionally been for the judge to make, but as part of growing legislative movement to hold juveniles criminally responsible for a greater range of offenses, there are now three ways in which a juvenile can be transferred to adult court. Although variations on these exist from state to state, these are judicial waiver, direct file, and statutory exclusion.

Judicial Waiver

Judicial waiver is the traditional method of transferring a juvenile to adult court. It is called "waiver" because the judge waives the jurisdiction of the juvenile court, and specifies that the juveniles be tried as a criminal defendant. A majority of states allow this method of transfer. Waiver involves a decision by the juvenile judge that a case should be prosecuted as a crime in adult court. There are three types of judicial waiver: discretionary waiver, mandatory waiver, and presumptive waiver. States that use discretionary waiver allow the juvenile judge discretion to make the waiver decision. This approach contemplates case-by-case consideration of what will be best for the juvenile and what will best serve the public interest. Mandatory waiver occurs as a result of a statute that specifies that the juvenile judge must transfer cases that meet certain age and crime seriousness criteria. Thus, the judge is required to make the decision in those cases and has no discretion to do otherwise. Presumptive waiver statutes specify that waiver is appropriate for certain types of crimes and if certain criteria are met and place the burden of proving otherwise on the juvenile. If the juvenile cannot prove that the waiver criteria are satisfied, the judge must transfer the case to adult court.

Criteria to be considered in making the waiver decision vary across states. Some states indicate that transfer is proper when it is in the best interests of the child and for the protection of the public (Griffin et al., 1998). Others are more specific about the factors to be considered by the juvenile judge, such as the factors outlined by the U.S. Supreme Court in an appendix to the *Kent* decision, which include the following:

1. The seriousness of the alleged offense and whether protection of the community requires waiver
2. Whether the alleged offense was aggressive, violent, premeditated, or willful
3. Whether the alleged offense was against person or property and whether personal injury resulted
4. The merit of the complaint, that is, whether there is evidence upon which a Grand Jury may return an indictment
5. The desirability of trial and disposition of the entire offense in one court when the juvenile's associates in the alleged offense are adults

6. The sophistication and maturity of the juvenile as determined by consideration of his home, environmental situation, emotional attitude, and pattern of living
7. The record and previous history of the juvenile, including previous contacts with the juvenile justice system
8. The prospects for adequate protection of the public and the likelihood of reasonable rehabilitation of the juvenile by the use of procedures, services, and facilities currently available to the juvenile court

Not all of these criteria need be satisfied but must be considered by the court, and some must form the basis for the decision.

Direct File

The *direct file* method of transfer gives the prosecutor the discretion to file charges against a juvenile in adult court, provided that certain age and crime criteria are met. In these cases, the juvenile court and the adult criminal court have concurrent jurisdiction. This method therefore gives considerable power to the prosecutor, who already has the power to determine what charges will be filed. Most importantly, because the direct file method does not involve a hearing in the juvenile court, none of the due process protections from *Kent* or *Gault* apply. That is not to say that juveniles being considered for transfer do not have constitutional rights; rather, they have no opportunity to assert those rights until the case has already been filed in adult criminal court in the first instance, placing the juvenile defendant at a disadvantage if he or she hopes for a juvenile adjudication. Furthermore, there is no judicial oversight of the process because the jurisdiction of the court is not invoked until the charges are filed. The opportunity for the juvenile to argue in criminal court that he or she should be transferred to juvenile court must wait until charges are filed. This is known as *reverse waiver* and is allowed in only about half of the states (Griffin et al., 1998).

Statutory Exclusion

Statutory exclusion refers to a method whereby certain offenses are removed entirely from juvenile court jurisdiction and must therefore be filed in adult criminal court. In these cases, therefore, no distinction is drawn between adults and children for purposes of prosecution. This is normally reserved for serious felonies committed by older juveniles or juveniles who have prior adjudications for felonies in juvenile court (Griffin et al., 1998). Thus, statutory exclusion removes discretion from both the judge and the prosecutor, leaving only one place for the filing of certain charges for certain individuals—adult criminal court.

Intake and Detention

The *intake* process in the juvenile courts involves the immediate decision about what to do with the juvenile before a hearing with the judge occurs. An intake officer, usually a juvenile probation officer, screens the case based on the reported facts to determine whether the juvenile should simply be reprimanded and released, whether diversion of the juvenile to community resources should occur, or whether the juvenile should be held or released pending referral to the court and a hearing. Thus, the intake officer has considerable discretion about how to proceed and whether court involvement with the case is appropriate. Factors relevant to the decision about how to proceed are the age of the juvenile, the allegations of wrongdoing, the family and school situation of the juvenile, and prior contacts with the juvenile justice system.

A large number of cases involve releasing a juvenile to the custody of parents or guardians. This may occur when the police first intervene or may be done by the intake officer and is most appropriate for status offenders. Diversion refers to the removal of a juvenile from formal processing so that a court appearance is unnecessary. Often, mediation or other forms of dispute resolution are used to avoid a juvenile court adjudication and disposition. These usually allow the juvenile to meet with and witness the effects of their behavior on individuals and work to atone for their acts and learn from the experience. Consistent with the philosophy of the juvenile justice system, minor offenders who are likely to benefit from resources in the community are required to participate in resources such as organized youth programs, counseling services, or drug or alcohol treatment. In addition to the hoped-for benefits of such programs, diversion is characterized by informal supervision, either by the social service agency or the juvenile probation department, to provide accountability for the juvenile and awareness of his progress.

When the allegations against a juvenile are serious, detention occurs. Detention serves similar functions to that of pretrial incarceration of adult criminal—ensuring the return of the suspect for further processing and preventing further crime from occurring—but also is necessary because minors, unlike adults, are deemed unable to care for themselves and must remain in the "custody" of someone. Initially, detained juveniles can be held for no more than 24 to 48 hours before a detention hearing is held to determine whether the juvenile should be held longer or released. Detention typically occurs in a police station or juvenile facility, but juvenile suspects are held in a separate location apart from adult suspects.

Preventive Detention

The pretrial detention of juvenile suspects is an important troubling aspect of the juvenile justice process in which courts are faced with the task of determining what should be done with a juvenile alleged to be delinquent pending a hearing on that issue. *Preventive detention* is the term given to the detention of juveniles who are in custody because they are alleged to have committed a criminal offense and are perceived to be dangerous. Although adults charged with crime have the benefit of a bail hearing and the criteria and determination of whether bail is warranted is clear, no such mechanism exists in the juvenile court. The problem arises when a juvenile may pose a threat to the community, but this involves a prediction of future behavior, not present action. Because of the deprivation of liberty involved, the use of preventive detention raises the question of whether it violates the due process rights of juveniles.

In the case of *Schall v. Martin* (467 U.S. 253, 104 S. Ct. 2403, 81 L.Ed.2d 207 (1984), the issue of preventive detention of juveniles was addressed by the U.S. Supreme Court. *Schall* involved a New York statute that required juveniles whose cases were pending in juvenile court to be held if there was a serious risk that the juvenile would commit a crime before returning for the adjudicatory hearing. The case is found in **Case Decision 8.3**.

Case Decision 8.3 *Schall v. Martin*, 467 U.S. 253, 104 S. Ct. 2403, 81 L.Ed.2d 207 (1984)

Opinion of the Court by Justice Rehnquist:

Section 320.5(3)(b) of the New York Family Court Act authorizes pretrial detention of an accused juvenile delinquent based on a finding that there is a "serious risk" that the child "may before the return date commit an act which if committed by an adult would constitute a crime." Appellees brought suit on behalf of a class of all juveniles detained pursuant to that provision. The District Court struck down § 320.5(3)(b) as permitting detention without due process of law and ordered the immediate release of all class members. The Court of Appeals for the Second Circuit affirmed, holding the provision "unconstitutional as to all juveniles" because the statute is administered in such a way that "the detention period serves as punishment imposed without proof of guilt established according to the requisite constitutional standard." We noted probable jurisdiction, and now reverse. We conclude that preventive detention under the FCA serves a legitimate state objective, and that the procedural protections afforded pretrial detainees by the New York statute satisfy the requirements of the Due Process Clause of the Fourteenth Amendment to the United States Constitution.

I

Appellee Gregory Martin was arrested on December 13, 1977, and charged with first-degree robbery, second-degree assault, and criminal possession of a weapon based on an incident in which he, with two others, allegedly hit a youth on the head with a loaded gun and stole his jacket and sneakers. See petitioners' Exhibit 1b. Martin had possession of the gun when he was arrested. He was 14 years old at the time and, therefore, came within the jurisdiction of New York's Family Court. The incident occurred at 11:30 at night, and Martin lied to the police about where and with whom he lived. He was consequently detained overnight.

A petition of delinquency was filed, and Martin made his "initial appearance" in Family Court on December 14th, accompanied by his grandmother. The Family Court Judge, citing the possession of the loaded weapon, the false address given to the police, and the lateness of the hour, as evidencing a lack of supervision, ordered Martin detained under § 320.5(3)(b). A probable cause hearing was held five days later, on December 19th, and probable cause was found to exist for all the crimes charged. At the fact-finding hearing held December 27-29, Martin was found guilty on the robbery and criminal possession charges. He was adjudicated a delinquent and placed on two years' probation. He had been detained pursuant to § 320.5(3)(b), between the initial appearance and the completion of the fact-finding hearing, for a total of 15 days.

Appellees Luis Rosario and Kenneth Morgan, both age 14, were also ordered detained pending their fact-finding hearings. Rosario was charged with attempted first-degree robbery and second-degree assault for an incident in which he, with four others, allegedly tried to rob two men, putting a gun to the head of one of them and beating both about the head with sticks. See petitioners' Exhibit 2b. At the time of his initial appearance, on March 15, 1978, Rosario had another delinquency petition pending for knifing a student, and two prior petitions had been adjusted. Probable cause was found on March 21. On April 11, Rosario was released to his father, and the case was terminated without adjustment on September 25, 1978.

Kenneth Morgan was charged with attempted robbery and attempted grand larceny for an incident in which he and another boy allegedly tried to steal money from a 14-year-old girl and her brother by threatening to blow their heads off and grabbing them to search their pockets. See petitioners' Exhibit 3b. Morgan, like Rosario, was on release status on another petition (for robbery and criminal possession of stolen property) at the time of his initial appearance on March 27, 1978. He had been arrested four previous times, and his mother refused to come to court because he had been in trouble so often

---

188   Section II: Courts at Work

she did not want him home. A probable-cause hearing was set for March 30, but was continued until April 4, when it was combined with a fact-finding hearing. Morgan was found guilty of harassment and petit larceny and was ordered placed with the Department of Social Services for 18 months. He was detained a total of eight days between his initial appearance and the fact-finding hearing.

On December 21, 1977, while still in preventive detention pending his fact-finding hearing, Gregory Martin instituted a habeas corpus class action on behalf of "those persons who are, or during the pendency of this action will be, preventively detained pursuant to"§ 320.5(3)(b) of the FCA. Rosario and Morgan were subsequently added as additional named plaintiffs. These three class representatives sought a declaratory judgment that § 320.5(3)(b) violates the Due Process and Equal Protection Clauses of the Fourteenth Amendment.

At trial, appellees offered in evidence the case histories of 34 members of the class, including the three named petitioners. Both parties presented some general statistics on the relation between pretrial detention and ultimate disposition. In addition, there was testimony concerning juvenile proceedings from a number of witnesses, including a legal aid attorney specializing in juvenile cases, a probation supervisor, a child psychologist, and a Family Court Judge. On the basis of this evidence, the District Court rejected the equal protection challenge as "insubstantial," but agreed with appellees that pretrial detention under the FCA violates due process. The court ordered that "all class members in custody pursuant to Family Court Act Section [320.5(3)(b)] shall be released forthwith."

The Court of Appeals affirmed. After reviewing the trial record, the court opined that "the vast majority of juveniles detained under [[§ 320.5(3)(b)] either have their petitions dismissed before an adjudication of delinquency or are released after adjudication." The court concluded from that fact that § 320.5(3)(b) "is utilized principally, not for preventive purposes, but to impose punishment for unadjudicated criminal acts." The early release of so many of those detained contradicts any asserted need for pretrial confinement to protect the community. The court therefore concluded that § 320.5(3)(b) must be declared unconstitutional as to all juveniles. Individual litigation would be a practical impossibility because the periods of detention are so short that the litigation is mooted before the merits are determined.

II

There is no doubt that the Due Process Clause is applicable in juvenile proceedings. "The problem," we have stressed, "is to ascertain the precise impact of the due process requirement upon such proceedings." We have held that certain basic constitutional protections enjoyed by adults accused of crimes also apply to juveniles. But the Constitution does not mandate elimination of all differences in the treatment of juveniles. The State has "a parens patriae interest in preserving and promoting the welfare of the child," which makes a juvenile proceeding fundamentally different from an adult criminal trial. We have tried, therefore, to strike a balance—to respect the "informality" and "flexibility" that characterize juvenile proceedings, and yet to ensure that such proceedings comport with the "fundamental fairness" demanded by the Due Process Clause.

The statutory provision at issue in these cases permits a brief pretrial detention based on a finding of a "serious risk" that an arrested juvenile may commit a crime before his return date. The question before us is whether preventive detention of juveniles pursuant to § 320.5(3)(b) is compatible with the "fundamental fairness" required by due process. Two separate inquiries are necessary to answer this question. First, does preventive detention under the New York statute serve a legitimate state objective? And, second, are the procedural safeguards contained in the FCA adequate to authorize the pretrial detention of at least some juveniles charged with crimes?

A

Preventive detention under the FCA is purportedly designed to protect the child and society from the potential consequences of his criminal acts. When making any detention decision, the Family Court judge is specifically directed to consider the needs and best interests of the juvenile as well as the need for the protection of the community. As an initial matter, therefore, we must decide whether, in the context of the juvenile system, the combined interest in protecting both the community and the juvenile himself from the consequences of future criminal conduct is sufficient to justify such detention.

The "legitimate and compelling state interest" in protecting the community from crime cannot be doubted. We have stressed before that crime prevention is "a weighty social objective," and this interest

(Continues)

persists undiluted in the juvenile context. The harm suffered by the victim of a crime is not dependent upon the age of the perpetrator. And the harm to society generally may even be greater in this context given the high rate of recidivism among juveniles.

The juvenile's countervailing interest in freedom from institutional restraints, even for the brief time involved here, is undoubtedly substantial as well. But that interest must be qualified by the recognition that juveniles, unlike adults, are always in some form of custody. Children, by definition, are not assumed to have the capacity to take care of themselves. They are assumed to be subject to the control of their parents, and if parental control falters, the State must play its part as parens patriae. In this respect, the juvenile's liberty interest may, in appropriate circumstances, be subordinated to the State's "parens patriae interest in preserving and promoting the welfare of the child."

The New York Court of Appeals, in upholding the statute at issue here, stressed at some length "the desirability of protecting the juvenile from his own folly." Society has a legitimate interest in protecting a juvenile from the consequences of his criminal activity—both from potential physical injury which may be suffered when a victim fights back or a policeman attempts to make an arrest and from the downward spiral of criminal activity into which peer pressure may lead the child.

The substantiality and legitimacy of the state interests underlying this statute are confirmed by the widespread use and judicial acceptance of preventive detention for juveniles. Every State, as well as the United States in the District of Columbia, permits preventive detention of juveniles accused of crime. A number of model juvenile justice Acts also contain provisions permitting preventive detention. And the courts of eight States, including the New York Court of Appeals, have upheld their statutes with specific reference to protecting the juvenile and the community from harmful pretrial conduct, including pretrial crime. In light of the uniform legislative judgment that pretrial detention of juveniles properly promotes the interests both of society and the juvenile, we conclude that the practice serves a legitimate regulatory purpose compatible with the "fundamental fairness" demanded by the Due Process Clause in juvenile proceedings.

Of course, the mere invocation of a legitimate purpose will not justify particular restrictions and conditions of confinement amounting to punishment. It is axiomatic that "[d]ue process requires that a pretrial detainee not be punished." Even given, therefore, that pretrial detention may serve legitimate regulatory purposes, it is still necessary to determine whether the terms and conditions of confinement under § 320.5(3)(b) are in fact compatible with those purposes. Absent a showing of an express intent to punish on the part of the State, that determination generally will turn on "whether an alternative purpose to which [the restriction] may rationally be connected is assignable for it, and whether it appears excessive in relation to the alternative purpose assigned [to it]."

There is no indication in the statute itself that preventive detention is used or intended as a punishment. First of all, the detention is strictly limited in time. If a juvenile is detained at his initial appearance and has denied the charges against him, he is entitled to a probable-cause hearing to be held not more than three days after the conclusion of the initial appearance or four days after the filing of the petition, whichever is sooner. If the Family Court judge finds probable cause, he must also determine whether continued detention is necessary.

Detained juveniles are also entitled to an expedited fact-finding hearing. If the juvenile is charged with one of a limited number of designated felonies, the fact-finding hearing must be scheduled to commence not more than 14 days after the conclusion of the initial appearance. § 340.1. If the juvenile is charged with a lesser offense, then the fact-finding hearing must be held not more than three days after the initial appearance. In the latter case, since the times for the probable-cause hearing and the fact-finding hearing coincide, the two hearings are merged.

Thus, the maximum possible detention under § 320.5(3)(b) of a youth accused of a serious crime, assuming a 3-day extension of the fact-finding hearing for good cause shown, is 17 days. The maximum detention for less serious crimes, again assuming a 3-day extension for good cause shown, is six days. These time frames seem suited to the limited purpose of providing the youth with a controlled environment and separating him from improper influences pending the speedy disposition of his case.

The conditions of confinement also appear to reflect the regulatory purposes relied upon by the State. When a juvenile is remanded after his initial appearance, he cannot, absent exceptional circumstances, be sent to a prison or lockup where he would be exposed to adult criminals. Instead, the child is screened by an "assessment unit" of the Department of Juvenile Justice. The assessment unit places the child in either nonsecure or secure detention. Nonsecure detention involves an open facility in the community, a sort of "halfway house," without locks, bars, or security officers where the child receives schooling and counseling and has access to recreational facilities.

Secure detention is more restrictive, but it is still consistent with the regulatory and parens patriae objectives relied upon by the State. Children are assigned to separate dorms based on age, size, and behavior. They wear street clothes provided by the institution and partake in educational and recreational programs and counseling sessions run by trained social workers. Misbehavior is punished by confinement to one's room. We cannot conclude from this record that the controlled environment briefly imposed by the State on juveniles in secure pretrial detention "is imposed for the purpose of punishment" rather than as "an incident of some other legitimate governmental purpose."

The Court of Appeals, of course, did conclude that the underlying purpose of § 320.5(3)(b) is punitive rather than regulatory. But the court did not dispute that preventive detention might serve legitimate regulatory purposes or that the terms and conditions of pretrial confinement in New York are compatible with those purposes. Rather, the court invalidated a significant aspect of New York's juvenile justice system based solely on some case histories and a statistical study which appeared to show that "the vast majority of juveniles detained either have their petitions dismissed before an adjudication of delinquency or are released after adjudication." The court assumed that dismissal of a petition or failure to confine a juvenile at the dispositional hearing belied the need to detain him prior to fact-finding and that, therefore, the pretrial detention constituted punishment. Since punishment imposed without a prior adjudication of guilt is per se illegitimate, the Court of Appeals concluded that no juveniles could be held.

[W]e find that to be an insufficient ground for upsetting the widely shared legislative judgment that preventive detention serves an important and legitimate function in the juvenile justice system. We are unpersuaded by the Court of Appeals' rather cavalier equation of detentions that do not lead to continued confinement after an adjudication of guilt and "wrongful" or "punitive" pretrial detentions.

Pretrial detention need not be considered punitive merely because a juvenile is subsequently discharged subject to conditions or put on probation. In fact, such actions reinforce the original finding that close supervision of the juvenile is required. Lenient but supervised disposition is in keeping with the Act's purpose to promote the welfare and development of the child.

Even when a case is terminated prior to fact finding, it does not follow that the decision to detain the juvenile pursuant to § 320.5(3)(b) amounted to a due process violation. A delinquency petition may be dismissed for any number of reasons collateral to its merits, such as the failure of a witness to testify. The Family Court judge cannot be expected to anticipate such developments at the initial hearing. He makes his decision based on the information available to him at that time, and the propriety of the decision must be judged in that light. Consequently, the final disposition of a case is "largely irrelevant" to the legality of a pretrial detention.

It may be, of course, that in some circumstances detention of a juvenile would not pass constitutional muster. But the validity of those detentions must be determined on a case-by-case basis. We find no justification for the conclusion that, contrary to the express language of the statute and the judgment of the highest state court, § 320.5(3)(b) is a punitive rather than a regulatory measure. Preventive detention under the FCA serves the legitimate state objective, held in common with every State in the country, of protecting both the juvenile and society from the hazards of pretrial crime.

B

Given the legitimacy of the State's interest in preventive detention, and the nonpunitive nature of that detention, the remaining question is whether the procedures afforded juveniles detained prior to fact-finding provide sufficient protection against erroneous and unnecessary deprivations of liberty. In many respects, the FCA provides far more predetention protection for juveniles than we found to be constitutionally required for a probable-cause determination for adults. The initial appearance is informal, but the accused juvenile is given full notice of the charges against him and a complete stenographic record is kept of the hearing. The juvenile appears accompanied by his parent or guardian. He is first informed of his rights, including the right to remain silent and the right to be represented by counsel chosen by him or by a law guardian assigned by the court. The initial appearance may be adjourned for no longer than 72 hours or until the next court day, whichever is sooner, to enable an appointed law guardian or other counsel to appear before the court. When his counsel is present, the juvenile is informed of the charges against him and furnished with a copy of the delinquency petition. A representative from the presentment agency appears in support of the petition.

The nonhearsay allegations in the delinquency petition and supporting depositions must establish probable cause to believe the juvenile committed the offense. Although the Family Court judge is not

(Continues)

required to make a finding of probable cause at the initial appearance, the youth may challenge the sufficiency of the petition on that ground. Thus, the juvenile may oppose any recommended detention by arguing that there is not probable cause to believe he committed the offense or offenses with which he is charged. If the petition is not dismissed, the juvenile is given an opportunity to admit or deny the charges.

At the conclusion of the initial appearance, the presentment agency makes a recommendation regarding detention. A probation officer reports on the juvenile's record, including other prior and current Family Court and probation contacts, as well as relevant information concerning home life, school attendance, and any special medical or developmental problems. He concludes by offering his agency's recommendation on detention. Opposing counsel, the juvenile's parents, and the juvenile himself may all speak on his behalf and challenge any information or recommendation. If the judge does decide to detain the juvenile under § 320.5(3)(b), he must state on the record the facts and reasons for the detention.

As noted, a detained juvenile is entitled to a formal, adversarial probable-cause hearing within three days of his initial appearance, with one 3-day extension possible for good cause shown. The burden at this hearing is on the presentment agency to call witnesses and offer evidence in support of the charges. Testimony is under oath and subject to cross-examination. The accused juvenile may call witnesses and offer evidence in his own behalf. If the court finds probable cause, the court must again decide whether continued detention is necessary. Again, the facts and reasons for the detention must be stated on the record.

In sum, notice, a hearing, and a statement of facts and reasons are given prior to any detention under § 320.5(3)(b). A formal probable-cause hearing is then held within a short while thereafter, if the fact-finding hearing is not itself scheduled within three days. These flexible procedures have been found constitutionally adequate under the Fourth Amendment and under the Due Process Clause. Appellees have failed to note any additional procedures that would significantly improve the accuracy of the determination without unduly impinging on the achievement of legitimate state purposes.

Appellees argue, however, that the risk of erroneous and unnecessary detentions is too high despite these procedures because the standard for detention is fatally vague. Detention under § 320.5(3)(b) is based on a finding that there is a "serious risk" that the juvenile, if released, would commit a crime prior to his next court appearance. We have already seen that detention of juveniles on that ground serves legitimate regulatory purposes. But appellees claim, and the District Court agreed, that it is virtually impossible to predict future criminal conduct with any degree of accuracy. Moreover, they say, the statutory standard fails to channel the discretion of the Family Court judge by specifying the factors on which he should rely in making that prediction. The procedural protections noted above are thus, in their view, unavailing because the ultimate decision is intrinsically arbitrary and uncontrolled.

Our cases indicate, however, that from a legal point of view there is nothing inherently unattainable about a prediction of future criminal conduct. Such a judgment forms an important element in many decisions, and we have specifically rejected the contention, based on the same sort of sociological data relied upon by appellees and the District Court, "that it is impossible to predict future behavior and that the question is so vague as to be meaningless."

We have also recognized that a prediction of future criminal conduct is "an experienced prediction based on a host of variables" which cannot be readily codified. Judge Quinones of the Family Court testified at trial that he and his colleagues make a determination under § 320.5(3)(b) based on numerous factors including the nature and seriousness of the charges; whether the charges are likely to be proved at trial; the juvenile's prior record; the adequacy and effectiveness of his home supervision; his school situation, if known; the time of day of the alleged crime as evidence of its seriousness and a possible lack of parental control; and any special circumstances that might be brought to his attention by the probation officer, the child's attorney, or any parents, relatives, or other responsible persons accompanying the child. The decision is based on as much information as can reasonably be obtained at the initial appearance.

Given the right to a hearing, to counsel, and to a statement of reasons, there is no reason that the specific factors upon which the Family Court judge might rely must be specified in the statute. As the New York Court of Appeals concluded, "to a very real extent Family Court must exercise a substitute parental control for which there can be no particularized criteria." There is also no reason, we should add, for a federal court to assume that a state court judge will not strive to apply state law as conscientiously as possible.

The judgment of the Court of Appeals is reversed.

The Court in *Schall* upheld the preventive detention of juveniles, holding that dangerousness to the community is a compelling governmental justification for the detention. Although it found that a hearing and statement of the reasons supporting the detention are necessary, it concluded if it is deemed that a juvenile is likely to commit additional crimes if released, this is a sufficient reason for holding a juvenile until an adjudication hearing is held and an ultimate disposition determined. A central issue in the case, and an ongoing debate about the usefulness of preventive detention, is the ability of juvenile judges to predict the future dangerousness of a given juvenile. Although the Court in *Schall* found that judges are able to do this in a manner that warrants preventive detention, more recent studies have indicated that such predictions regarding youthful behavior may be inaccurate (Auerhahn, 2006).

Adjudication

An *adjudication hearing* is the equivalent of a trial in adult criminal court; however, usually the way in which the hearing is conducted is considerably different. First, as has been noted earlier, juries are not used in juvenile court. Thus, the hearing occurs before the judge who decides the facts, the requirements of the law, and what disposition is best for the juvenile. Although the hearing is less formal, some formalities must be maintained. For example, the judge speaks directly to the juvenile to make sure that he or she understands why the juvenile is in court and what is happening. The judge will also advise juveniles appearing without attorneys that they have the right to have an attorney present and ask whether they have waived that right. If a juvenile pleads guilty, the judge will make sure that the juvenile understands that this means that he or she will be found to be delinquent and a disposition ordered. If the juvenile pleads not guilty, the hearing will proceed with the presentation of evidence and the examination and cross-examination of witnesses. After hearing from the prosecutor and the juvenile, the judge will make findings of fact and a determination of whether the juvenile is delinquent. If a finding of delinquency is made, the case will proceed to the disposition phase, which typically involves a separate hearing in which the judge decides what rehabilitative efforts will best benefit the juvenile, usually taking into account the effects of the juvenile's behavior on victims and the protection of the community.

Disposition

A *disposition* in juvenile court parallels the sentencing phase in an adult criminal court. A disposition hearing is held to determine what course of action is best for the juvenile and the community after a finding of delinquency is made. A predisposition report will normally be prepared by a juvenile probation officer that summarizes the facts found by the judge, the juvenile's family and school situation, his or her prior contacts with the juvenile justice system, statements by witnesses or victims, reports from psychologists or social workers, and letters or recommendations from family members, teachers, clergy, or others. On the basis of the report and the availability of commu-

nity resources, the judge will determine what disposition best serves the needs of the juvenile and the community.

Generally, there are three types of dispositions that juvenile courts make: community-based sanctions, probation, and institutional commitment. Within each of these, there are numerous options from which a juvenile judge may choose to fashion a correctional plan for a juvenile.

Community-Based Sanctions

Community-based sanctions for juveniles may take many forms. They may include restitution of some form to those affected by the juvenile's behavior (e.g., washing walls and fences "tagged" with spray paint or financial restitution for theft), required participation in school or extracurricular activities, or volunteer service in shelters or other settings. Any of these would involve some form of supervision apart from court personnel. Community-based sanctions are rarely used after a finding of delinquency, largely because they are likely to have been tried previously with a juvenile as part of diversion.

Probation

Probation is the most common disposition in adjudicated cases (Snyder & Sickmund, 2006). Juvenile probation officers play a significant role in the juvenile justice system. In addition to serving as intake officers and assisting in the preparation of predisposition reports for the judge, juvenile probation officers provide oversight and supervision of the juvenile under court order after disposition. This involves maintaining contact, sometimes daily, with juveniles, making sure that all terms of the judge's disposition order are being complied with and providing informal counseling, advice, and other assistance to the juveniles under their charge.

Institutional Commitment

Institutional commitment means that a juvenile is sent to a residential facility. The facility may be one involving secure confinement or may involve lesser degrees of security. These include detention centers or training schools, group homes, and alternative programs such as boot camps and ranch or wilderness programs. All of these involve some degree of confinement during some part of the day, although it may be minimal (Livsey et al., 2009).

A detention center or "training school" is the most secure juvenile correctional facility. The most serious juvenile offenders are placed here. These secure facilities vary from those that look like and operate much as an adult prison, with locked doors, barbed wire fencing, and security officers, to more campus-like settings in which residents are housed in smaller "cottages" in an attempt to create a more family atmosphere. Regardless of the physical layout or the name, these facilities are marked by medium- to maximum-level security and a more punitive approach to maintaining discipline and order. Nonetheless, rehabilitation remains the goal, with programs designed to benefit juveniles during their time of being incarcerated and help prevent recidivism later. Typically, these facilities require attendance at school classes or vocational training and offer a variety of counseling and other treatment services.

Group homes are houses in the community that house a small number (usually 10 to 20) of juveniles together under the supervision of group home leaders who provide guidance and supervision of their charges. The group home is a nonsecure setting in which juveniles receive intense supervision, usually by both the group home leaders and juvenile probation officers. The purpose of the group home is to allow the juvenile to maintain some connection with the community while maintaining close supervision, without the high degree of security involved in a detention center. Residents of group homes typically will attend school or work in the community during the day but are required to return and remain in the group home in the evening.

Other residential disposition alternatives are boot camps and outdoor programs. Boot camps are military-style programs in which juveniles are taught discipline and respect for others and are expected to participate in physical work and exercise. Participants are usually given the option to volunteer for such programs as an alternative to a training school or detention center. Similarly, outdoor programs at ranches or wilderness settings are designed to teach participants the value of working with others and the consequences to the group of their actions. The combination of physical activity and the emotional bonds developed with others are expected to provide the juvenile with useful tools for living on his return to a societal setting.

Key Terms

House of Refuge	Petition
Child Savers	Preventive Detention
Parens Patriae	Waiver
Due Process	Diversion
Delinquent	Adjudication
Status Offender	Disposition
Rehabilitation	

Discussion Questions

1. How does the court system view children differently from adults?
2. What is the historical basis for the juvenile court?
3. What is *parens patriae*? Why is it important? In what ways does *parens patriae* affect the operation of the juvenile court?
4. What is the significance of the *Kent* case?
5. What is the goal of the juvenile court?
6. What types of cases do the juvenile courts handle?
7. What is preventative detention? What are some of the criticisms of this practice?
8. What are the disposition options of the juvenile court? In what ways do they differ?

Cases

Breed v. Jones, 421 U.S. 519, 95 S. Ct. 1779, 44 L.Ed.2d 346 (1975).
Ex Parte Crouse, 4 Whart. 9, 1839 WL 3700 (Pa. 1839).
In re Gault, 387 U.S. 1, 87 S. Ct. 1428, 18 L.Ed.2d 527 (1967).
In re Ronald S., 138 Cal. Rptr. 387, 69 Cal. App. 3rd. 866 (Cal. App. 1977).
In re Winship, 397 U.S. 358, 90 S. Ct. 1068, 25 L.Ed.2d 368 (1970).
Kent v. United States, 383 U.S. 541, 86 S. Ct. 1045, 16 L.Ed.2d 84 (1966).
McKeiver v. Pennsylvania, 403 U.S. 528, 91 S. Ct. 1976, 29 L.Ed.2d 647 (1971).
Schall v. Martin, 467 U.S. 253, 104 S. Ct. 2403, 81 L.Ed.2d 207 (1984).

Criminal Justice on the Web

 For an up-to-date list of Web links, go to *The American Courts: A Procedural Approach* online companion site at http://criminal justice.jbpub.com/AmericanCourts. The online companion site will introduce you to some of the most important sites for finding American courts information on the Internet.

References

Auerhahn, K. (2006). Conceptual and methodological issues in the prediction of dangerous behavior. *Crime and Public Policy*, 5, 771–778.
Bernard, T. J. (1992). *The Cycle of Juvenile Justice*. New York: Oxford University Press.
Griffin, P., Torbet, P., & Szymanski, L. (1998). *Trying Juveniles as Adults in Criminal Court: An Analysis of State Transfer Provisions*. Washington, DC: U.S. Department of Justice.
Livsey, S., Sickmund, M., & Sladky, A. (2009). *Juvenile Residential Facility Census, 2004: Selected Findings*. Washington, DC: Office of Juvenile Justice and Delinquency Prevention.
Platt, A. M. (1977). *The Child Savers: The Invention of Delinquency*. Chicago: University of Chicago Press.
Redding, R. E. (2008). Juvenile transfer laws: An effective deterrent to delinquency? *Juvenile Justice Bulletin*, August 2008, U.S. Department of Justice, Office of Juvenile Justice and Delinquency Prevention.
Snyder, H. N., & Sickmund, M. (2006). *Juvenile Offenders and Victims: 2006 National Report*. Washington, DC: Office of Juvenile Justice and Delinquency Prevention.

Civil Law and Procedure in the Courts

This section explores the ways in which courts interpret and apply the civil law in making decisions involving disputes alleging harm to individuals. The civil law seeks to protect the rights of individuals. These may be contract rights, property rights, personal rights, or constitutional and statutory civil rights. As a central part of a society based on the need for justice, American courts are designed to be the place to which citizens can turn in order to obtain recompense for their injuries. The substantive civil law governs the types of harm that are compensable, and civil procedure provides the rules that must be followed in order for a court to act.

Chapter 9 focuses on the topic of civil law. These include the common law areas of property law, contracts, and torts, which is the law of personal injuries. As the oldest branch of the law, property rights have always had a central place in American society. Recall that the due process clause of the Constitution's Fifth Amendment protects "life, liberty, and *property*." Rights in property may take a variety of forms, including real, personal property, and intellectual property, and such rights may be limited or extensive. The ownership, transfer, and invasion of property rights therefore continue to be topics requiring courts to interpret the law in the context of modern society.

The law of contracts, too, is a regular subject of court cases. Capitalism dictates that business transactions be governed by the benefits and responsibilities of the parties to a transaction, and contracts are used in a vast variety of circumstances to specify what these are. When uncertainty or disputes arise, courts rely on the law of contracts to resolve them.

People sometimes are injured as a result of the actions of others. These may be physical injuries or injuries to reputation, harm to one's livelihood or employment, or deprivation of rights guaranteed by law, such as free speech or the practice of religion. A large proportion of the work of the courts involves determining whether an individual is entitled to be compensated for the harm suffered.

A discussion of procedure in civil cases is also necessary for understanding how a court resolves civil disputes. This is the topic of Chapter 10. The rules that implement the civil law are as important as the law itself. By examining these rules that govern the process of litigating civil claims, the limitations on the actions of courts become clear.

Civil procedure is the law of process in civil cases. That is, it involves the legal principles that specify how a claim must be presented and pursued in the courts in order to obtain justice. It governs who may be a party to a civil case, what pleadings are necessary and what form they must take, how discovery may be conducted, and what procedures must be followed at trial. Civil law and procedure often make civil cases complex matters to pursue, but such complexity results from the desire of the courts (and society itself) to achieve just outcomes for the people that use the courts.

Substantive Civil Law 9

What Is This Chapter About?

This chapter discusses the substantive civil law and its importance in American society. We learn about the primary branches of the substantive civil law, including property law, contract law, and the law of torts. We will also consider family matters and cases involving governmental matters.

Perhaps the oldest substantive area of law, property law played an important role in the development of the United States and remains a growing area of law today. This chapter discusses the importance of property rights in our democracy. It also examines the nature of property rights and the types of disputes that arise regarding property.

Contract law involves the formation of contracts and remedies for breach of contract. Thus, we consider what it means to have a legally binding contract and what is required for the formation. We also examine what constitutes a breach and how damages may be assessed.

The law of torts is the law of personal injuries. This chapter discusses injuries to the person and what injuries the law recognizes as compensable. In addition, the requirements for establishing a *prima facie* case for various types of injuries, including negligence, strict liability, and intentional torts, are presented. Compensatory and punitive damages are also discussed.

Finally, this chapter discusses administrative and regulatory law and other areas of the substantive law regularly addressed by the courts involving government action, including claims involving violations of constitutional rights.

Learning Objectives

After reading this chapter, you should be able to

1. Recognize the primary areas of substantive civil law.
2. Understand the importance of property rights in American society.
3. Describe the ownership rights that may exist in property.
4. List the elements of contract formation.
5. Understand what may constitute a breach of contract.
6. Describe the types of damages available for breach of contract.
7. Describe the types of personal injuries that the law may compensate.
8. Explain how compensatory and punitive damages may be assessed.
9. Understand the basis for a civil rights claim.

Substantive civil law addresses "private" disputes between individuals and the government and the manner in which adjudication of such matters must occur. The term "individual" may refer to a person, a corporation or other business entity, or a group. Disputes may arise in nearly every facet of business and personal life, requiring intervention by court. The law has divided the most common of these areas into cases involving contracts, property, torts, and governmental claims based on statute. Many subcategories relating to these four areas exist, as well as some legal claims that do not fit neatly into any one. This chapter provides a broad overview of the most common civil claims and the requirements of the law when an aggrieved party relies on the courts to resolve a dispute in each of these areas.

Contracts

Contracts are a common part of life. Nearly every day some contractual arrangement exists that influences the life of each citizen. When a person goes to work, uses a credit card, installs software on a computer, drives a car, buys airplane tickets, uses a cell phone, and performs a myriad of other day-to-day activities, he or she is subject to some contract that governs the life activity. Without contracts, modern life would be more difficult in that the way in which people order their affairs would have less certainty.

Contracts create expectations. Contracts bring order to society by allowing people to rely on agreements that they make. Contracts, therefore, consist of promises that people and businesses make to each other—a promise to make monthly payments or to pay a bill when it comes due, a promise to provide good service, or a promise to provide serviceable goods. These agreements touch nearly every aspect of life, ranging from business relationships and commerce to employment, housing, transportation, and entertainment. For example, entering into a contract to buy a house allows the purchaser to rely on the fact that he or she will have exclusive access to it as long as payments are made or that the purchase of a vehicle will allow the buyer the keep and drive the vehicle and use it in whatever way he or she wishes. These expectations are warranted because of the enforceability of contracts. That is, the parties to a contract know that, should either fail to comply with the terms of the agreement, a court may force the breaching party to do so or otherwise provide a remedy for the problem. Thus, a contract is an enforceable agreement. More formally, a contract is "a promise . . . for the breach of which law gives a remedy, or the performance of which the law in some way recognizes a duty" (American Law Institute, 1981). This definition of a contract comes from the Restatement of Contracts, which is a compilation of recognized principles of contract law published by the American Law Institute, an organization consisting of legal scholars, lawyers, and judges that seeks to clarify and improve the law. There are restatements in various areas of the civil law that serve as model statements and principles of law, including property law, contracts, tort law, and many other legal topics. Although the restatements do not themselves have the authority of law, they are often relied upon by courts to resolve questions of law, and they have been adopted in part by state legislatures as statutory law in many states.

Regardless of the subject of a contract or what it is created to accomplish, all contracts consist of certain elements that must be addressed in order to give a contract legal validity. These are an offer, an acceptance, and consideration. In addition, contracts require that each of the parties has the legal capacity to enter into an agreement and that they do so freely. When these elements are present, the parties are said to have a "meeting of the minds" such that their agreement becomes binding on each.

Elements of a Contract

Legal Capacity

The parties to a contract must be capable of entering into one. This means that they must have the legal capacity to do so. Legal capacity in this context has two meanings. First, a person must have the authority to enter into an agreement. Adults are presumed to have authority to govern their own affairs, but not necessarily the affairs of others. For example, without specific authorization, an employee lacks the capacity to make a contract on behalf of his employer, but the owner of the company may probably do so. The second meaning of legal capacity refers to persons who are not minors, mentally ill, mentally disabled, intoxicated, or otherwise incapacitated. Contracts require that the parties be capable of understanding the terms to which they are binding themselves. When a person lacks legal capacity, a court will usually refuse to enforce contracts they make.

Offer

When a party makes an offer to enter into a contract, that party communicates to another party that he or she would like to make an agreement. Thus, an offer is an expression of willingness on the part of a person to bargain by specifying definite terms on which the parties might agree. An offer is a proposal that accomplishes something. It has a specific subject matter on which the parties may be able to agree. An offer cannot be a general intention to do something or buy or sell something. For example, a person who walks onto an automobile lot and states "I would like to buy one of your cars for $10,000" is not making an offer. The offer must be definite enough so that, if the person receiving the offer accepts it, it will lead to a contract whose terms will be known.

Offers need not be made in writing. Oral statements may be sufficient to create an offer. What is important is that the offer be made intentionally, communicated to another person, and specific enough to allow the other party to understand what the terms of the proposed deal are. Before an offer is accepted, it may be withdrawn, but after it is accepted, it becomes a completed contract.

Acceptance

There cannot be a "meeting of the minds" if there is not an acceptance of an offer. By accepting an offer, a person agrees with the terms stated in the offer. In order for an acceptance to create a binding contract, it must accept the offer as it was made. Any changes to the offer constitute rejection of the offer (although the changes may create a "counteroffer"). If an offer is once rejected, it no longer exists; it cannot later be accepted.

Acceptance can occur verbally, in writing, or by some act taken by the person accepting. For example, if a person receives an offer to buy a monthly magazine subscription by sending $1 a month, sending the first dollar will constitute acceptance. Anything that shows the person's intent to accept the offer is sufficient.

Consideration

Consideration is something of value that is exchanged by the parties to a contract in order to secure their respective promises. It is the thing that someone does in exchange for the promise of another party. For example, if Anne offers to sell Bob her car for $1,000 and if Bob accepts the offer, his payment of the money constitutes the consideration for the contract. Consideration may be either a benefit or a detriment to one or both parties, but without it, there is no contract. An offer and acceptance without consideration is a gift, not a contract.

Another way of thinking about the requirement of consideration is whether the parties stand to lose anything if the agreement is broken. If a person accepts an offer without consideration and the promise forming the offer is broken, the person accepting is in no worse of a situation than if the offer had not been made; therefore, no enforceable contract exists. For example, suppose that Tom offers to wash Mary's car and Mary accepts but Tom fails to wash the car. Mary has no legal recourse against Tom because she gave nothing for his agreement to wash her car; she is in the same condition she was before the offer was made.

The specific consideration contemplated by the parties need not be actually expressed in a contract, as long as the contract, whether oral or written, includes some indication that consideration supports it. There are times when the parties do not wish to explicitly state the consideration, either because it is of a personal nature or it is an amount of money that they wish to keep private. In such cases, the language "For valuable consideration" or "For value received" is often used.

Types of Contracts

Written Contracts

Most contracts used in everyday life are written. There are advantages to written contracts. When a contract is written, it provides a reference for what is required of each of the parties to the contract. This is important both for the parties themselves during the life of the contract and for a court should disputes arise that need court intervention. Although written contracts are not always clear, they are useful and sometimes necessary for documenting what was the intent of the parties in reaching an agreement.

Although not all contracts need to be written, the law requires that some must be in writing in order to be valid and legally enforceable. The most common of these is a contract governed by the Statute of Frauds, which was a 17th century English statute passed to prevent people from claiming an oral contract existed when one did not as well as other types of fraudulent behavior. The Statute of Frauds is now a common law principle in the United States, variations of which have been adopted in all states either by statute or court rulings or both. The most common contracts that must be in writing pursuant to the Statute of Frauds are contracts for the purchase and sale of land and contracts that are not capable of being performed within 1 year. Other contracts that also must generally be in writing are governed by the Uniform Commercial Code, which is a model set of statutes by the American Law Institute governing business affairs that has been adopted in nearly all states. The Uniform Commercial Code requires written contracts for the purchase or sale of certain goods, depending on their value, as well as contracts relating to some types of credit and other banking transactions. In most states, contracts for various types of insurance are highly regulated and also must be in writing.

Oral Contracts

As discussed previously here, many but not all contracts must be in writing; however, oral contracts may pose problems for parties that written contracts avoid. In order for an oral contract to be valid, it must satisfy the requirements necessary for all contracts, resulting from an offer, acceptance, and consideration, and be sufficiently definite in the terms of the agreement to show that a "meeting of the minds" occurred. The primary difficulty with oral contracts is one of proof—without a written document, evidence of the existence of the contract rests with the testimony and actions of the parties, and other documentary or testimonial evidence surrounding the alleged creation of the contract. This may lead to confusion or disputes between the parties because memories are fallible and the recollections of the parties about what they agreed to may vary with time.

Performance of Contracts

Parties to a contract "perform" the contract by doing what they are required to do under its terms; however, despite the best intentions of the parties, what constitutes performance is not always clear. For example, suppose a contract states that Acme Cleaning Company will clean Anne's house once each week for $100. Anne's duty under the contract is fairly clear (even if when she must pay is not), but what does "clean" mean? Acme's view of performance under the contract may differ in this respect from Anne's.

A failure of performance by either party may produce a "breach" of the contract. Lawsuits based on contract usually arise when there has been a breach. When this occurs, one or both of the parties asks a court to decide what the obligations of the parties are under the contract and what damages, if any, should be paid to the nonbreaching party. Some contracts provide that liquidated damages, usually a specific amount of money, will be paid to the nonbreaching party if a court finds a breach by another party. When a contract does not provide for liquidated damages, however, the court must determine what an appropriate measure of damages should be. In general, a court will seek to award a nonbreaching party with "the benefit of the bargain." This may be specific performance, in which the court orders the breaching party to fulfill its agreed-to duty under the contract, or the court may award an amount of money that puts the nonbreaching party in the same financial condition it would have been in had there been no breach.

Interpretation of Contracts

When courts are called on to resolve contract disputes, they are typically required to determine the meaning of the contract. Specifically, this involves determining the rights and obligations of each of the parties to the contract. In doing this, a court begins with the presumption that the parties intended to enter into a contract and that they intended to accomplish something by making the contract; therefore, the goal is to discover the intention of the parties and give effect to it. Furthermore, courts examine contracts with the assumption that everything included in a contract means something; otherwise, the parties would not have included it.

Courts may take different approaches to contract interpretation; however, the primary issue of contract interpretation is which sources of evidence should courts consider when deciding what a contract means? Specifically, should courts rely solely on the language found in the contract, or should they consider evidence of the parties' agreement that may be found outside the contract.

Contractual Language

Contractual disputes often relate to the meaning or terms of the contract. That is, to what did the parties agree? Where a written contract exists, the language used in the document is the first place to find what the contract means; however, it is the language that is often the source of the dispute, where one party believes the language means one thing and the other party finds a different meaning. For example, suppose a contract for the purchase of a home included "all appliances, fixtures, and furnishings." After the buyer moved in, she discovered that the seller removed a hot tub that was on the backyard patio. The buyer believed the hot tub was included in the contract, but the seller argued he never intended to sell it and it was not an appliance, fixture, or furnishing. Who owns it? A court first looks to see whether the contract's language is unclear or ambiguous. Contractual language is ambiguous if it is inconsistent or may lead to more than one interpretation as to its meaning. Whether such ambiguity exists will depend on the meaning of the words in dispute as well as their relationship to the remainder of the contract. A court will therefore consider the purpose and effect of the entire contract to create a context for determining whether the language it needs to interpret is ambiguous. If, after considering the contract as a whole, the language used is found not to be ambiguous, a court will give the words their normal meaning and determine the parties' intent from the language used. In the previous example, the terms "appliances, fixtures, and furnishings" are relatively clear in the context of a real estate purchase, and thus, the question for the court would be whether a hot tub falls into one of those categories. There is no need for the court to resort to other evidence of whether the parties intended to include the hot tub; the dispute could be resolved by looking at the contract language alone.

Consistent with the foregoing approach to interpreting language, courts often rely on the *parol evidence rule*. The term "parol evidence" generally refers to oral testimony, but in this context, parol evidence is any evidence that is extrinsic to, or outside of, a contract. The rule excludes consideration of any evidence other than the contract itself. It applies to problems of contract interpretation where the contract is susceptible to a reasonable interpretation based on the words used in the contract. Thus, jurisdictions that employ the parol evidence rule need not look beyond the contract itself in determining what it means.

Interpreting Context

When the language of a contract is ambiguous or unclear, a court must determine what the parties intended; that is, to what did they agree? The court does this by examining not only the contract language itself, but evidence relating to the parties' intent that may be found outside the contract. Such evidence may include the testimony of the parties about their understanding of the agreement, notes or other documents that may have been used by the parties, and negotiations that the parties conducted leading to the contract. Suppose that, in the previous house purchase example, the contract stated that the buyer was entitled to all "sports equipment on the premises." After closing, the buyer discovers a pool table was removed by the seller. Is a pool table "sports equipment?" If the court finds that the term "sports equipment" is ambiguous and subject to

different meanings, it may examine evidence of whether the parties contemplated that the pool table would be included in the deal.

Property

The law governing property interests is among the oldest branches of law. Many of the concepts of property law established in England in the Middle Ages remain in some form as part of the common law today, including American law. The law speaks of "property interests" because ownership of property refers to the interest one has in the property. What right or rights to the property does one own? For example, if a person leases an apartment, he or she "owns" the exclusive right to use the apartment for residential purposes, usually for a limited period of time. He or she does not own the right to conduct business from the apartment, raise chickens in the apartment, or sell the apartment. Similarly, if a person buys a piece of land, he or she may "own" the right to use the surface in whatever way he or she wishes, but may not own the right to minerals, oil, or water existing under the surface. If a person withdraws $1,000 from a bank account, drops the envelope containing the cash while walking home, and another finds it, who owns it? The law of property defines the nature of ownership rights in property, specifies how property may be validly transferred, and governs how disputes regarding property should be resolved.

The law distinguishes "real" property from "personal" property. Real property is land. Often included in this category of property are "fixtures," which are buildings and other structures that are permanently (in the sense that they cannot easily be moved) affixed to the land. Personal property comprises all other types of property.

Real Property

The American dream usually includes the ownership of real property. It most often becomes the "place" where a person lives or from which he or she earns a living. At its most basic, ownership of real property consists of some possessory interest in land—that is, some right to possess the land. Rules governing the right to possess real property and the manner of its transfer were complex at common law and remain so today. In every state, these rules, at least in part, have been codified in property statutes or probate laws relating to the distribution of property after death. This discussion is limited to the nature of the interest that one may hold in real property. Specifically, possession of real property may relate to a present interest or a future interest in land.

Present Interests

A present interest in real property is the present right to possess it. Present interests may be differentiated in terms of the nature of the interest, or right to the land, that one possesses. A "fee simple absolute" interest in land is one in which a person possesses all rights to the property, including the right to use it, lease it, give it away, sell it, or devise it to heirs. Fee simple ownership represents the greatest degree or extent of interests in real property that one may have.

Another present interest in real property is the "life estate." A life estate is just that—an interest in land that lasts as long as the person owning it is alive. After that, it reverts to the prior owner or some other person designated by the prior owner to receive a present interest in it. The owner of a life estate has a limited interest in the land, allowing him or her to use it, lease it, or even sell it, but only during his or her lifetime. In addition, the life estate owner may not act in a way that injures or otherwise diminishes the value of the real property, referred to as "waste."

One last common present interest in real property is the leasehold interest; essentially, a right to possess the property for a specified amount of time, where the conveying instrument (such as a lease agreement) indicates the date that possession begins and ends. Generally, the leasehold tenant has the right use the property for the purposes specified in the conveying instrument, such as residential or business. Other restrictions or specific rights may also be granted, such as limitations on noise or the number of occupants on the premises or the right to sublet the property.

Future Interests

A future interest, as the name implies, comes into effect at some time in the future. That is, it allows a person the right to possess real property at some time in the future. This usually occurs upon the happening of a specific event, such as the death of a person presently possessing the property. There are three types of future interests: remainders, reversions, and executory interests. A remainder interest is one that creates some right to possession of real property after a life estate has ended. There are various types of remainder interests, depending on the conditions that created the life estate that preceded the remainder. These differ according to whether the interest that "remains" is subject to being lost or otherwise limited. A reversion exists when a real property owner transfers less than the complete interest that he or she has. An executory interest comes into effect at some future time on the occurrence of a future event.

Methods of Ownership

The ownership of real property is normally evidenced by the existence of a "deed," which is a document that provides a legal description of the real property, including the nature or extent of the ownership interest, the person who previously owned it, and the person to whom it was transferred. Although a deed is not required to show ownership of property, it is usually the method of transfer for real estate transactions because it is recognized and governed by requirements specified in state statutes. One of these requirements is filing the deed (most often in the office of a County Clerk or other government agency), which records the existence of the deed in the public records in the state in which the property is located. Filing a deed is the way in which ownership rights in real property are preserved and notice of such rights is provided to the public. It also provides a "chain of title" to the property that allows one to trace its history of ownership.

Real property may be owned by an individual, a group of individuals, or a business entity. When real property is owned by two or more individuals, there are three common methods of joint ownership recognized by the law. These are "joint tenancy," "tenancy by the entirety," and "tenancy in common." A joint tenancy exists when two or more individuals own property together and has four requirements in order for this form of ownership to be valid: (1) the ownership interests are created together at the same time, (2) the interests are created in a single document, (3) all owners have an equal interest in the property, and (4) each owner has the right to full possession of the property. These are known as the "four unities" of joint tenancy, and although a deed or other instrument need not spell them out, if they are not satisfied, a joint tenancy will not exist. In most jurisdictions, the document creating the joint tenancy need contain only the names of the owners and the words "as joint tenants." Apart from these requirements for creating a joint tenancy, the most important characteristic of a joint tenancy is the right of survivorship. This means that if any of the owners dies, that owner's interest will automatically go to the surviving owners. For this reason, joint tenants are often referred to as "joint tenants with rights of survivorship," and some jurisdictions require the specific use of this language in creating a joint tenancy.

A tenancy by the entirety operates in the same fashion as a joint tenancy but has the additional requirement that the joint owners be married. As a result, a tenancy by the entirety has only two joint owners. This form of ownership developed under common law is a way in which married women could own property along with their husbands, and such property would be protected from the debts of the husband. Because women may now own property separately from their spouses, many states no longer allow or recognize this form of ownership.

Tenancy in common is a form of joint ownership characterized by the fact that the shares of the tenants in common do not pass on death to the surviving tenants. Rather, they remain as part of the estate of the deceased tenant in common and pass to that person's heirs. The ownership interests of tenants in common need not be equal, but each tenant has the right to possess the property completely. The interest owned is therefore referred to as "undivided." As a result, a tenancy in common, unlike a joint tenancy, has only one "unity," that of possession.

Personal Property

Personal property refers to property that is not real property. It may be either tangible or intangible. Tangible personal property is property that can be seen, touched, and capable of being moved from place to place. Things like vehicles, jewelry, computers, and cash are tangible personal property. Intangible personal property cannot be seen or touched but is property nonetheless. For example, a song is intangible personal property, although the medium through which it is heard is tangible. Shares of stock in a corporation are intangible, although a stock certificate is tangible.

Legal issues relating to personal property are those involving ownership and possession. Specifically, questions may arise as to what constitutes ownership of personal property. Some types of personal property have written evidence of ownership, such as the title to a car or the receipt for a computer, but other personal property has no such documentary evidence because personal property may be acquired by gift, inheritance, or loan. Who, for example, owns a diamond engagement ring—the future groom, who has the bill of sale, or the bride-to-be, who has the shiny ring? Thus, because personal property, whether tangible or intangible, is portable, the right to legal possession and its relationship to ownership become important and sometimes unclear. Possession of personal property occurs when it is on someone's person or within their knowledge and control. Legal possession exists when the possessor has permission from the owner to possess the property or acquires an ownership interest.

The right to possession of property interests may be violated in a variety of ways, including fraudulently obtaining property, larceny, and the infringement of patent or copyright. The latter category involves the right to possess, use, control, license, and otherwise exercise rights in creative property such as musical, written, or artistic works, as well as ideas such as inventions and software. For example, music companies and movie studios have pursued property claims against students and others for violation of copyright by downloading or otherwise sharing music via the Internet. In one such case, *Metro-Goldwyn-Mayer Studios Inc. v. Grokster, Ltd.* (545 U.S. 913, 125 S. Ct. 2764, 162 L.Ed.2d 781, 2005), the U.S. Supreme Court considered whether the distributor of free software that can be used for file sharing, Grokster, was liable for copyright infringement when the users of the software subsequently used it to download music and movie files without the copyright holders' permission. Finding that Grokster, even though it had no specific knowledge of the end users' actual use of the software, was liable for copyright infringement, the court explained that

The more artistic protection is favored, the more technological innovation may be discouraged; the administration of copyright law is an exercise in managing the tradeoff. The tension between the two values is the subject of this case, with its claim that digital distribution of copyrighted material threatens copyright holders as never before, because every copy is identical to the original, copying is easy, and many people (especially the young) use file-sharing software to download copyrighted works. This very breadth of the software's use may well draw the public directly into the debate over copyright policy, and the indications are that the ease of copying songs or movies using software like Grokster's and Napster's is fostering disdain for copyright protection. As the case has been presented to us, these fears are said to be offset by the different concern that imposing liability, not only on infringers but on distributors of software based on its potential for unlawful use, could limit further development of beneficial technologies.

[We hold that] one who distributes a device with the object of promoting its use to infringe copyright, as shown by clear expression or other affirmative steps taken to foster infringement, is liable for the resulting acts of infringement by third parties. We are, of course, mindful of the need to keep from trenching on regular commerce or discouraging the development of technologies with lawful and unlawful potential. Accordingly, mere knowledge of infringing potential or of actual infringing uses would not be enough here to subject a distributor to liability. Nor would ordinary acts incident to product distribution, such as offering customers technical support or product updates, support liability in themselves. The inducement rule, instead, premises liability on purposeful, culpable expression and conduct, and thus does nothing to compromise legitimate commerce or discourage innovation having a lawful promise. (545 U.S. at 928-29, 936-37, 125 S. Ct. at 2775, 2780, 162 L.Ed.2d at 793, 797)

Another interesting property rights case, *Dr. Seuss Enterprises, L.P. v. Penguin Books USA, Inc.* (109 F.3d 1394, 9th Cir., 1997), involved a clash between the beloved Dr. Seuss and the authors of a book about the notorious O.J. Simpson. Called *The Cat NOT in the Hat! A Parody by Dr. Juice*, Dr. Seuss's representatives claimed that the book violated the copyright and infringed on the trademark to the child favorite *Cat in the Hat* character and story. The case is found in **Case Decision 9.1**.

Case Decision 9.1 *Dr. Seuss Enterprises, L.P. v. Penguin Books USA, Inc.*, 109 F.3d 1394 (9th Cir. 1997)

Decision of the court by Circuit Judge O'Scannlain:

We must decide whether a poetic account of the O.J. Simpson double murder trial entitled *The Cat NOT in the Hat! A Parody by Dr. Juice*, presents a sufficient showing of copyright and trademark infringement of the well-known *The Cat in the Hat* by Dr. Seuss.

I

Penguin Books USA, Inc. ("Penguin") and Dove Audio, Inc. ("Dove") interlocutorily appeal the district court's preliminary injunction prohibiting the publication and distribution of *The Cat NOT in the*

Hat! A Parody by Dr. Juice, a rhyming summary of highlights from the O.J. Simpson double murder trial, as violating copyrights and trademarks owned by Dr. Seuss Enterprises, L.P. ("Seuss"), particularly from the book *The Cat in the Hat*.

Seuss, a California limited partnership, owns most of the copyrights and trademarks to the works of the late Theodor S. Geisel, the author and illustrator of the famous children's educational books written under the pseudonym "Dr. Seuss." Between 1931 and 1991, Geisel wrote, illustrated and published at least 47 books that resulted in approximately 35 million copies currently in print worldwide. He authored and illustrated the books in simple, rhyming, repetitive language, accompanied by characters that are recognizable by and appealing to children. The characters are often animals with human-like characteristics.

In *The Cat in the Hat*, first published in 1957, Geisel created a mischievous but well meaning character, the Cat, who continues to be among the most famous and well recognized of the Dr. Seuss creations. The Cat is almost always depicted with his distinctive scrunched and somewhat shabby red and white stove-pipe hat. Seuss owns the common law trademark rights to the words "Dr. Seuss" and "Cat in the Hat," as well as the character illustration of the Cat's stove-pipe hat. Seuss also owns the copyright registrations for the books *The Cat in the Hat*, *The Cat in the Hat Comes Back*, *The Cat in the Hat Beginner Book Dictionary*, *The Cat in the Hat Songbook*, and *The Cat's Quizzer*. In addition, Seuss has trademark registrations for the marks currently pending with the United States Trademark Office. Seuss has licensed the Dr. Seuss marks, including *The Cat in the Hat* character, for use on clothing, in interactive software, and in a theme park.

In 1995, Alan Katz and Chris Wrinn, respectively, wrote and illustrated *The Cat NOT in the Hat!* satirizing the O.J. Simpson double murder trial. Penguin and Dove, the publishers and distributors, were not licensed or authorized to use any of the works, characters or illustrations owned by Seuss. They also did not seek permission from Seuss to use these properties.

Seuss filed a complaint for copyright and trademark infringement, an application for a temporary restraining order and a preliminary injunction after seeing an advertisement promoting *The Cat NOT in the Hat!* prior to its publication. The advertisement declared:

> Wickedly clever author "Dr. Juice" gives the O.J. Simpson trial a very fresh new look. From Brentwood to the Los Angeles County Courthouse to Marcia Clark and the Dream Team. *The Cat Not in the Hat* tells the whole story in rhyming verse and sketches as witty as Theodore [sic] Geisel's best. This is one parody that really packs a punch!

Seuss alleged that *The Cat NOT in the Hat!* misappropriated substantial protected elements of its copyrighted works, used six unregistered and one registered Seuss trademarks, and diluted the distinctive quality of its famous marks. Katz subsequently filed a declaration stating that *The Cat in the Hat* was the "object for [his] parody" and portions of his book derive from *The Cat in the Hat* only as "necessary to conjure up the original."

II

We must first determine whether *The Cat NOT in the Hat!* infringes on Seuss' rights under the Copyright Act of 1976, 17 U.S.C. § 106. Seuss, as the owner of the Dr. Seuss copyrights, owns the exclusive rights (1) to reproduce the copyrighted work; (2) to prepare derivative works based on the copyrighted work; (3) to distribute copies or phonorecords of the copyrighted work to the public; (4) to perform the work publicly; and (5) to display the copyrighted work publicly. Seuss alleges that Penguin and Dove made an unauthorized derivative work of the copyrighted works *The Cat in the Hat*, *The Cat in the Hat Comes Back*, *The Cat's Quizzer*, *The Cat in the Hat Beginner Books Dictionary*, and *The Cat in the Hat's Song Book* in violation of [the Act].

To prove a case of copyright infringement, Seuss must prove both ownership of a valid copyright and infringement of that copyright by invasion of one of the five exclusive rights. First, Seuss is the owner of the Dr. Seuss copyrights and holds valid copyright registration certificates. Second, Katz admitted that the "style of the illustrations and lettering used in [*The Cat NOT in the Hat!*] were inspired by [*The Cat in the Hat*]. . . ." To satisfy the infringement test, Seuss must demonstrate "substantial similarity" between the copyrighted work and the allegedly infringing work. "Substantial similarity" refers to similarity of expression, not merely similarity of ideas or concepts.

(Continues)

Most courts have used some form of bifurcated test to demonstrate "substantial similarity," inquiring first if there is copying and second if an audience of reasonable persons will perceive substantial similarities between the accused work and protected expression of the copyrighted work. [T]he first question is labeled the "extrinsic" test and asks if there is similarity of ideas. "Analytic dissection" is allowed. "Analytic dissection" focuses on isolated elements of each work to the exclusion of the other elements, combination of elements, and expressions therein. The second question is labeled the "intrinsic" test and asks if an "ordinary reasonable person" would perceive a substantial taking of protected expression. At this stage, "analytical dissection" is not appropriate.

"The Cat in the Hat" is the central character in the original work, appearing in nearly every page of the Dr. Seuss work (26 times). Penguin and Dove appropriated the Cat's image, copying the Cat's Hat and using the image on the front and back covers and in the text (13 times). We conclude that substantial similarity exists on an objective and subjective level (see attachments # 1 and # 2). Penguin and Dove, however, maintain that they have not infringed on any one of Seuss' exclusive rights of copyright because *The Cat NOT in the Hat!* employed elements of the copyrighted work that are either uncopyrightable or that have fallen into the public domain.

Penguin and Dove's argument is based on an analytic dissection of the following elements: (1) infringement cannot be based on the title of the parody because it is "clear, as a matter of statutory construction by the courts (as well as Copyright Office regulations), that titles may not claim statutory copyright;" (2) the design of the lettering of the words used in the accused work cannot be found to infringe, because Congress decided not to award copyright protection to design elements of letters; (3) the poetic meter used in *Cat in the Hat* known as anapestic tetrameter is no more capable of exclusive ownership than its well-known counterpart, iambic pentameter; (4) no claim of ownership may be based on the whimsical poetic style that employs neologisms and onomatopoeia; and (5) the visual style of illustration using line drawing, coloring, and shading techniques similar to those used in *The Cat in the Hat* are not copyrightable. However, this kind of analytic dissection is not appropriate when conducting the subjective or "intrinsic test" (asking if an "ordinary reasonable person" would perceive a substantial taking of protected expression). Penguin and Dove's contentions on this issue are thus unavailing.

As for the objective analysis of expression, the district court's preliminary injunction was granted based on the back cover illustration and the Cat's Hat, *not* the typeface, poetic meter, whimsical style or visual style. For these reasons, we conclude that the court's findings that Penguin and Dove infringed on Seuss' copyrights are not clearly erroneous.

III

Even if Seuss establishes a strong showing of copyright infringement on these facts, Penguin and Dove maintain that the taking would be excused as a parody under the fair use doctrine. Fair use is an "equitable rule of reason," requiring careful balancing of multiple factors "in light of the purposes of copyright." The fair use defense "permits courts to avoid rigid application of the copyright statute when, on occasion, it would stifle the very creativity which that law is designed to foster."

In §107 of the 1976 Copyright Act, Congress laid down four factors to be considered and weighed by the courts in determining if a fair use defense exists in a given case: (1) the purpose and character of the accused use; (2) the nature of the copyrighted work; (3) the importance of the portion used in relation to the copyrighted work as a whole; and (4) the effect of the accused use on the potential market for or value of the copyrighted work. Congress viewed these four criteria as guidelines for "balancing the equities," not as "definitive or determinative" tests. Congress observed that "since the doctrine [of fair use] is an equitable rule of reason, no generally applicable definition is possible." The four fair use factors "are to be . . . weighed together, in light of the objectives of copyright 'to promote the progress of science and the useful arts.'" We now examine each factor.

A

The first factor in a fair use inquiry is "the purpose and character of the use, including whether such use is of a commercial nature or is for nonprofit educational purposes."§107(1). While this inquiry does not specify which purpose might render a given use "fair," the preamble to §107 provides an illustrative, though not limitative, listing which includes "criticism, comment, news reporting, teaching (including multiple copies for classroom use), scholarship, or research." Under this factor, the inquiry is whether *The Cat NOT in the Hat!* merely supersedes the Dr. Seuss creations, or whether and to what extent the new work is "transformative," i.e., altering *The Cat in the Hat* with new expression, meaning or message.

Parody is regarded as a form of social and literary criticism, having a socially significant value as free speech under the First Amendment. This court has adopted the "conjure up" test where the parodist is permitted a fair use of a copyrighted work if it takes no more than is necessary to "recall" or "conjure up" the object of his parody. Accordingly, the critical issue under this factor is whether *The Cat NOT in the Hat!* is a parody.

We first examine the definition of parody. Because debate still surrounds the proper definition of parody, we briefly explore the word itself for guidance. Parody is one of four types of satire: diatribe, narrative, parody and burlesque. The term has as its etymology the word "parodia" with the literal translation of "a song sung beside something." The parties disagree over the appropriate definition of parody under the fair use exception. The Supreme Court of the United States held that a rap group's version of Ray Orbison's song "Oh, Pretty Woman" was a candidate for a parody fair use defense. Justice Souter, the opinion's author, defined parody:

> For the purposes of copyright law, the nub of the definitions, and the heart of any parodist's claim to quote from existing material, is the use of some elements of a prior author's composition to create a new one that, at least in part, comments on that author's works. . . . . If, on the contrary, the commentary has no critical bearing on the substance or style of the original composition, which the alleged infringer merely uses to get attention or to avoid the drudgery in working up something fresh, the claim to fairness in borrowing from another's work diminishes accordingly (if it does not vanish), and other factors, like the extent of its commerciality, loom larger.

The Court pointed out the difference between parody (in which the copyrighted work is the target) and satire (in which the copyrighted work is merely a vehicle to poke fun at another target): "Parody needs to mimic an original to make its point, and so has some claim to use the creation of its victim's (or collective victims') imagination, whereas satire can stand on its own two feet and so requires justification for the very act of borrowing." Similarly, the American Heritage Dictionary defines "parody" as a "literary or artistic work that broadly mimics an author's characteristic style and holds it up to ridicule."

We now turn our attention to *The Cat NOT in the Hat!* itself. The first two pages present a view of Los Angeles, with particular emphasis on the connection with Brentwood, given the depiction of the news camera lights. The story begins as follows:

A happy town
Inside L.A.
Where rich folks play
The day away.
But under the moon
The 12th of June.
Two victims flail
Assault! Assail!
Somebody will go to jail!
Who will it be?
Oh my! Oh me!

The third page reads: "One Knife? / Two Knife? / Red Knife / Dead Wife." This stanza no doubt mimics the first poem in Dr. Seuss' *One Fish Two Fish Red Fish Blue Fish*: "One fish / two fish / red fish / blue fish. Black fish / blue fish / old fish / new fish." For the next eighteen pages, Katz writes about Simpson's trip to Chicago, the noise outside Kato Kaelin's room, the bloody glove found by Mark Fuhrman, the Bronco chase, the booking, the hiring of lawyers, the assignment of Judge Ito, the talk show interest, the comment on DNA, and the selection of a jury. On the hiring of lawyers for Simpson, Katz writes:

A plea went out to Rob Shapiro
Can you save the fallen hero?
And Marcia Clark, hooray, hooray
Was called in with a justice play.
A man this famous
Never hires

(Continues)

> Lawyers like
> Jacoby-Meyers.
> When you're accused of a killing scheme
> You need to build a real Dream Team.
> Cochran! Cochran!
> Doodle-doo
> Johnnie, won't you join the crew?
> Cochran! Cochran!
> Deedle-dee
> The Dream Team needs a victory.

These stanzas and the illustrations simply retell the Simpson tale. Although *The Cat NOT in the Hat!* does broadly mimic Dr. Seuss' characteristic style, it does not hold *his style* up to ridicule. The stanzas have "no critical bearing on the substance or style of" *The Cat in the Hat*. Katz and Wrinn merely use the Cat's stove-pipe hat, the narrator ("Dr. Juice"), and the title (*The Cat NOT in the Hat!*) "to get attention" or maybe even "to avoid the drudgery in working up something fresh." While Simpson is depicted 13 times in the Cat's distinctively scrunched and somewhat shabby red and white stove-pipe hat, the substance and content of *The Cat in the Hat* is not conjured up by the focus on the Brown-Goldman murders or the O.J. Simpson trial. Because there is no effort to create a transformative work with "new expression, meaning, or message," the infringing work's commercial use further cuts against the fair use defense.

B

The second statutory factor, "the nature of the copyrighted work," recognizes that creative works are "closer to the core of intended copyright protection" than informational and functional works, "with the consequence that fair use is more difficult to establish when the former works are copied." While this factor typically has not been terribly significant in the overall fair use balancing, the creativity, imagination and originality embodied in *The Cat in the Hat* and its central character tilts the scale against fair use.

C

The third factor asks whether "the amount and substantiality of the portion used in relation to the copyrighted work as a whole," are reasonable in relation to the purpose of the copying. This factor really raises the question of substantial similarity discussed in the preceding section, rather than whether the use is "fair." The district court concluded that "The Cat in the Hat" is the central character, appearing in nearly every image of *The Cat in the Hat*. Penguin and Dove appropriated the Cat's image, copying the Cat's Hat and using the image on the front and back covers and in the text (13 times). We have no doubt that the Cat's image is the highly expressive core of Dr. Seuss' work.

Under this factor, we also turn our attention "to the persuasiveness of a parodist's justification for the particular copying done, and the enquiry will harken back to the first of the statutory factors, for, as in prior cases, we recognize that the extent of permissible copying varies with the purpose and character of the use." Katz and Wrinn insist that they selected *The Cat in the Hat* as the vehicle for their parody because of the similarities between the two stories: Nicole Brown and Ronald Goldman were surprised by a "Cat" (O.J. Simpson) who committed acts contrary to moral and legal authority. The prosecution of Simpson created a horrible mess, in which the defense team seemed to impose "tricks" on an unwilling public, resulting in a verdict that a substantial segment of the public regarded as astonishing. Just as *The Cat in the Hat* ends with the moral dilemma of whether the children should tell their mother about their visitor that afternoon, Katz and Wrinn maintain that *The Cat NOT in the Hat!* ends with a similar moral dilemma:

> JUICE
> +ST
> JUSTICE
> Hmm . . . take the word JUICE.
> Then add ST.
> Between the U and I, you see.
> And then you have JUSTICE.

Or maybe you don't.
Maybe we will.
And maybe we won't.
'Cause if the Cat didn't do it?
Then who? Then who?
Was it him?
Was it her?
Was it me?
Was it you?
Oh me! Oh my!
Oh my! Oh me!
The murderer is running free.

In their Opening Brief, Penguin and Dove characterize *The Cat NOT in the Hat!* ("Parody") as follows:

The Parody is a commentary about the events surrounding the Brown/Goldman murders and the O.J. Simpson trial, in the form of a Dr. Seuss parody that transposes the childish style and moral content of the classic works of Dr. Seuss to the world of adult concerns. The Parody's author felt that, by evoking the world of *The Cat in the Hat*, he could: (1) comment on the mix of frivolousness and moral gravity that characterized the culture's reaction to the events surrounding the Brown/Goldman murders, (2) parody the mix of whimsy and moral dilemma created by Seuss works such as *The Cat in the Hat* in a way that implied that the work was too limited to conceive the possibility of a *real* trickster "cat" who creates mayhem along with his friends Thing 1 and Thing 2, and then magically cleans it up at the end, leaving a moral dilemma in his wake.

We completely agree with the district court that Penguin and Dove's fair use defense is "pure shtick" and that their post-hoc characterization of the work is "completely unconvincing."

D

The fourth fair use factor is "the effect of the use upon the potential market for or value of the copyrighted work." Under this factor, we consider both the extent of market harm caused by the publication and distribution of *The Cat NOT in the Hat!* and whether unrestricted and widespread dissemination would hurt the potential market for the original and derivatives of *The Cat in the Hat*. The good will and reputation associated with Dr. Seuss' work is substantial. Because, on the facts presented, Penguin and Dove's use of *The Cat in the Hat* original was nontransformative, and admittedly commercial, we conclude that market substitution is at least more certain, and market harm may be more readily inferred.

In light of the fair use analysis, we conclude that the district court's finding that Seuss showed a likelihood of success on the merits of the copyright claim was not clearly erroneous. After carefully reviewing the record and considering all of the arguments on appeal, we find no reason to disturb the district court's carefully crafted and well-reasoned injunction order. For the foregoing reasons, we affirm the district court's order granting a preliminary injunction prohibiting the publication and distribution of the infringing work.

The court in *Seuss* first considered whether Seuss had a protectable property interest, then examined whether it had been violated, and finally, examined whether the defendants could rely on a "fair use" defense. Finding that the Seuss copyright to the *Cat in the Hat* had been violated and the defendant's use of the work in their retelling of the O.J. Simpson murder trial was not entitled to a fair use defense, the court upheld the trial court's issuance of an injunction preventing distribution of the infringing work.

Another area involving the distinction between possession and ownership is the bailment of personal property.

Bailment refers to entrusting another with possession of personal property for a limited time and for a specific purpose. For example, when a hotel customer hands his or her car keys to a valet for parking, he or she has entrusted his or her vehicle to the valet for the specific purpose of parking it. The valet while having possession is not free to take a joy ride. When a restaurant patron leaves his or her winter coat with a coat check clerk, it is for the purpose of hanging it up until the meal has ended and he or she leaves for the evening. The clerk, by possessing the coat, does not gain the right to search through the pockets for loose change or to decide to wear the coat home. Thus, a bailment clearly distinguishes between ownership rights and possession of personal property.

Another common problem arising that relates to ownership and possession of personal property involves the finding of such property. Found property is property that has been lost or abandoned by the owner and discovered by another. The common law made a distinction between property that was lost, mislaid, or abandoned, but such categories have little or no application today because statutes generally govern procedures to be used when property is lost. For example, the Rhode Island statutes provide for the duties and rights of a finder of lost property:

§ 33-21.2-1. Report of lost money or goods by finder
Any person who finds money or goods of a value of fifty ($50.00) dollars or more, the owner of which is unknown, may, within two (2) days of the finding thereof report the finding to the officer in charge of the police station in the city or town where said property was found and deliver over the property to said officer.

§ 33-21.2-2. Restitution of lost money or goods
If within ninety (90) days of turning the lost money or goods over to the police the owner appears and pays all reasonable costs incurred by the finder and/or the police, he or she shall have restitution of the money or goods.

§ 33-21.2-3. Rights of finder if no owner appears
If the owner of lost money or goods does not appear and claim his or her property as provided in section 33-21.2-2, the property shall enure to the finder.

§ 33-21.2-4. Disposition of lost money or goods
If the finder fails to claim said money or goods within six (6) months of reporting and delivering the lost property to the police, the property shall be presumed abandoned and shall revert to the general fund of the state in accordance with the state's unclaimed intangible and tangible property program, pursuant to chapter 21.1 of this title.

Thus, the childhood saying "finder's keepers, loser's weepers" is not exactly the law, but may apply after statutory procedures have been followed.

Torts

Tort law is the branch of the civil law that allows injured people to seek a remedy in court. A tort, therefore, is a civil wrong committed by a person that injures another. It is some specific behavior that a person engages in, resulting in harm to another person or their property. Most tort law is judge made; therefore, the specific behaviors that are actionable under the law of torts vary over time as judges (and society itself) come to view harm resulting from certain behaviors as compensable.

The person who commits the tortuous act is often referred to as a tortfeasor, who becomes the defendant in a civil lawsuit based on tort law. The law of torts governs the elements of proof necessary to establish that a defendant is a tortfeasor, as well as the remedy for the resulting harm, usually money damages. The amount awarded to plaintiff in a tort case may be *compensatory damages*, which, as the name implies, are intended to compensate the plaintiff for the injuries suffered, or the damages awarded may be *punitive damages*, which are awarded to punish the defendant for the tortuous conduct. Compensatory damages must be related to the injuries suffered by the plaintiff and reasonably certain before an award may be made. The purpose of compensatory damages is to make the plaintiff "whole"—that is, as nearly as it is possible to do with money, to restore him or her to his or her status before the injury occurred. Punitive damages, when awarded, must be sufficient to "teach the defendant a lesson" and must not be excessive. They are therefore intended to have a deterrent effect. For most tort claims, punitive damages may not be awarded unless there has also been award of compensatory damages.

Tort law has some parallels to criminal law, which also involves wrongful behavior that results in harm. Like the criminal law, tort law seeks to prevent the commission of wrongful acts and to prevent the resulting harm to individuals or society itself. Tort law, however, accomplishes these deterrent effects through the award of money damages to the injured party, whereas the criminal law relies on punishment of offenders to achieve these outcomes. Unlike the criminal law, "wrongful" conduct that is compensable under tort law is unreasonable conduct. The law requires people to act as a reasonable person does; when a person's unreasonable actions result in harm to another, the law imposes civil liability on them, which usually involves payment of money damages to compensate for the harm.

Tort law can be compared and contrasted to criminal law in terms of three characteristics: (1) the nature of the interest, (2) the nature of the wrong, and (3) the nature of the remedy. These distinctions are summarized in **Table 9.1**. The nature of the interest is that which the law seeks to protect. Although the criminal law is concerned with public order and the protection of all individuals within society, tort law has as its primary focus the individual and thus provides a mechanism for individual persons to vindicate loss suffered. The nature of the wrong refers to the harm suffered and the requirements of law regarding its determination. The act, intent, and harm caused by the defendant are therefore the necessary focus of inquiry in both the criminal law and tort law. The harm suffered by tort victims may not differ from that of crime victims, but the differing standards of proof reflect the different goals that each seeks to accomplish. Finally, the nature of the remedy involves the outcomes to be achieved in each type of case. Criminal law relies on sentencing to accomplish the goals of punishment; tort law seeks to make the plaintiff "whole" while also seeking to deter harmful behavior.

Forms of Injury

The law of torts recognizes many forms of injury. Just as crimes may be committed against a person or property, torts may involve injury to a person, their property, or their relationships with others. Injuries to a person may occur in a variety of ways. These include physical (bodily) injury, psychological or emotional injuries, and loss of enjoyment

Table 9.1

Distinguishing Tort Law and Criminal Law

Aspect of Law	Criminal Law	Tort Law
Nature of Interest	Public	Private
Parties	State vs. individual	Individual vs. individual
Goals	Deterrence, rehabilitation retribution, incapacitation	Compensation, deterrence
Nature of Wrong	Societal	Individual
Act	Against public order, safety, morals	Against person
Intent	General, specific, purposeful, knowingly, recklessly, negligently	Negligent, intentional Strict liability
Standard of Proof	Beyond a reasonable doubt	Preponderance of evidence
Burden of harm	Society, individual	Individual
Nature of Remedy	Punishment	Compensation
Outcome	Sentencing options: loss of life, liberty, property	Monetary payment, equitable relief

of life. Injuries to property may involve either personal or real property. Injury involving personal property occurs when property is damaged (as in an automobile crash), destroyed (such as property lost in a house fire), or the owner is deprived of its use (as when money is fraudulently obtained or income is lost). Injury to real property may result from diminution in the value of the property (such as by creating a nuisance by operation of a pig farm in a residential neighborhood) or loss of the property itself (as when a neighbor erects a fence on part of a neighbor's property). Injury involving relationships may occur when a person is defamed or his or her reputation is otherwise harmed, when contractual relationships are interfered with, or when loss of consortium occurs. All of these forms of injury may be compensable when they result from conduct recognized as creating liability under the law of torts.

Negligence

The most common action in the law of torts is that of negligence. Negligence occurs when a defendant acts in an unreasonable manner, resulting in harm to the plaintiff. It is not necessary that the defendant intended to harm the plaintiff; indeed, in most cases, the harm was not intentional. It is when the defendant does not take reasonable care in his or her actions, and this lack of reasonable care results in harm that civil liability may be imposed.

The Standard of Care

Negligence is premised on the existence of a duty owed by the defendant to the plaintiff. When the defendant breaches this duty by some action that causes harm to the plaintiff, the defendant has acted negligently. When does a duty exist, however? The law presumes that a person has a general duty to avoid causing harm to another. Stated differently, the law imposes a duty of care on each person to act as a reasonable person would in similar circumstances, but it is not always clear how a reasonable person would act. The "reasonable person standard" is an objective one—one in which the actions of a person are judged

according to how a hypothetical person acting rationally would act. Therefore, a person's behavior is not examined according to their own thoughts or feelings about whether they acted reasonably; it is judged by a standard that is a collective one, based on the expectations of the community in which the act occurred. Thus, if a person throws a banana peel on the street and a person walking down the street steps on it, falls, and is injured, the act of discarding the banana peel in this manner may be negligent if such behavior is not in accordance with community standards, but if the community is one in which tossing banana peels on public streets is a common and accepted occurrence, the act of doing this may be seen as reasonable and not negligent. People within a community are assumed to possess knowledge of what constitutes acceptable behavior within the community; thus, an objective examination of a person's behavior considers what he or she should have known to be acceptable, not what he or she did know.

Whether a duty exists is often a question in cases of *premises liability*, one of the most common types of tort cases. Premises liability refers to a negligence-based action in which an *invitee*, a person visiting the premises of another, is injured while on those premises. For example, if a person is shopping at a local supermarket, he or she is a business invitee because the supermarket has "invited" him or her to come and shop. If, while in the produce section, the person is injured when he or she slips on a banana peel that was on the floor, the question in a subsequent negligence suit is this: What duty does the store owe to the shopper in those circumstances, and did the store's breach of that duty lead to the injuries? The existence of a duty will depend on the circumstances, such as the general cleanliness of the store, the store's policy in cleaning up spills, whether the shopper was running, and so forth. In one case of premises liability, *Hayden v. Notre Dame* (716 N.E.2d. 603, Ind. Ct. App. (1999)), the plaintiff was injured while attending a University of Notre Dame football game. The opinion is found in **Case Decision 9.2**.

Case Decision 9.2 *Hayden v. Notre Dame*, 716 N.E.2d 603 (Ind. Ct. App. 1999)

Opinion of the court by Judge Kirsch:

William and Letitia Hayden appeal from the trial court's grant of the University of Notre Dame's (Notre Dame) motion for summary judgment, presenting one issue for review: Whether the trial court erred in concluding that Notre Dame did not owe a duty to Letitia Hayden to protect her from the criminal acts of a third party.

We reverse.

Facts and Procedural History

On September 16, 1995, William and Letitia Hayden attended a football game on the Notre Dame campus. They were season ticket holders and sat in their assigned seats, which were in the south end-zone behind the goalpost. During the second quarter of the game, one of the teams kicked the football toward the goal. The net behind the goalposts did not catch the ball, and it landed in the stands close to Letitia Hayden's seat. Several people from the crowd lunged for the ball in an effort to retrieve it for a souvenir. One of them struck Letitia Hayden from behind, knocking her down and causing an injury to her shoulder.

The Haydens brought suit against Notre Dame for failing to exercise care to protect Letitia Hayden. Notre Dame moved for summary judgment, arguing that it did not have a legal duty to protect Letitia Hayden from the intentional criminal acts of an unknown third person. The trial court granted Notre Dame's motion. The Haydens now appeal.

Discussion and Decision

Summary judgment is appropriate when the designated evidence demonstrates that there is no genuine issue of material fact and that the moving party is entitled to judgment as a matter of law. The purpose of summary judgment is to terminate litigation about which there can be no material factual dispute and which can be resolved as a matter of law.

When reviewing a motion for summary judgment, this court applies the same standard utilized by the trial court, and we resolve any doubt as to a fact, or an inference to be drawn therefrom, in favor of the party opposing summary judgment. We will affirm a trial court's grant of summary judgment if it is sustainable on any theory found in the evidence designated to the trial court.

When the movant's affidavits and other evidence demonstrate the lack of a genuine issue, the burden shifts to the opposing party to demonstrate the existence of a genuine issue for trial. The non-moving party may not rest on the pleadings, but must set forth specific facts that show there is a genuine issue of material fact for trial. A defendant in a negligence action may obtain summary judgment by demonstrating that the undisputed material facts negate at least one element of the plaintiff's claim or that the claim is barred by an affirmative defense.

The Haydens claim that Notre Dame was negligent in failing to protect Letitia Hayden. In order to prevail on a claim of negligence, a plaintiff must prove: (1) a duty owed to the plaintiff by the defendant; (2) a breach of that duty by the defendant; and (3) injury to the plaintiff proximately caused by that breach. The only element at issue here is whether Notre Dame owed Letitia Hayden a duty under the circumstances. Whether a duty exists is generally a question of law for the court to determine.

The Haydens argue that this case is governed by premises liability principles and that the relevant standard of care is determined by Letitia Hayden's status as an invitee. The parties do not dispute that Letitia Hayden was a business invitee of Notre Dame. Nonetheless, Notre Dame argues that it owed no duty to protect Letitia Hayden from a third party's criminal act. For purposes of this appeal, we assume that the unknown third party's actions in lunging for the football and knocking Letitia Hayden down constitute a criminal act. It contends that the third party's action was unforeseeable, and that it therefore owed no duty to anticipate it and protect Letitia Hayden, a business invitee.

Our supreme court recently decided several cases which articulated the test for determining when a landowner's duty to its invitees extends to protecting them against the criminal actions of third parties that occur on its land. In *Delta Tau Delta v. Johnson*, 712 N.E.2d 968 (Ind. 1999), the court adopted a "totality of the circumstances" test for determining when such a duty arises. This test "requires landowners to take reasonable precautions to prevent foreseeable criminal actions against invitees." The court explained that, "[u]nder the totality of the circumstances test, a court considers all of the circumstances surrounding an event, including the nature, condition, and location of the land, as well as prior similar incidents, to determine whether a criminal act was foreseeable." "A substantial factor in the determination is the number, nature, and location of prior similar incidents, but the lack of prior similar incidents will not preclude a claim where the landowner knew or should have known that the criminal act was foreseeable."

Applying the totality of the circumstances test in the case before it, the court held that the defendant-fraternity owed a duty to the plaintiff, a young woman who attended a party at the fraternity house, to take reasonable precautions to protect her from sexual assault by third parties on its premises. The court looked at prior incidents of assault and forced alcohol consumption, as well as the fraternity's awareness of the prevalence of date rape (especially involving fraternity members) and of legal action taken against other fraternities for sexual assault, and concluded that under these circumstances such a duty existed.

In *Vernon v. Kroger Co.*, 712 N.E.2d 976 (Ind. 1999), the court applied the same test to the case of a plaintiff who was beaten on the defendant's store premises by a shoplifter attempting to flee. The plaintiff was attempting to exit the store's parking lot when he inadvertently blocked the vehicle of the fleeing shoplifter. The shoplifter pulled the plaintiff from his vehicle and beat him. The court noted that shoplifting at the store was not an unusual occurrence, that many shoplifters attempted to flee in waiting cars, that some shoplifters used force to escape, that criminal occurrences had happened in the parking lot, and that in the two years prior to this event, the police had made numerous runs to the store for crimes of violence and an increasing number of runs for battery and shoplifting. Based on the totality of the circumstances, the court held that the defendant owed the plaintiff a duty to protect him from the criminal acts of the third party-shoplifter.

Finally, in *L.W. v. Western Golf Ass'n*, 712 N.E.2d 983 (Ind. 1999), the court faced the issue of a landowner's duty for the criminal acts of a third party in the context of another sexual assault. In *L.W.*, a female student was raped by a male student in a co-educational residence hall owned by the defendant. Based on the totality of the circumstances, the court held that the defendant did not owe the plaintiff a duty. While the evidence showed a few pranks or childish behavior, there was no evidence of prior violent acts or sexual assaults at the residence hall. There was also no indication that the rapist would commit such a crime.

Applying this test to the case before us, we find that the totality of the circumstances establishes that Notre Dame should have foreseen that injury would likely result from the actions of a third party in lunging for the football after it landed in the seating area. As a result, it owed a duty to Letitia Hayden to protect her from such injury. The Haydens were seated in Notre Dame's stadium to watch a football game. Notre Dame well understands and benefits from the enthusiasm of the fans of its football team. It is just such enthusiasm that drives some spectators to attempt to retrieve a football to keep as a souvenir. There was evidence that there were many prior incidents of people being jostled or injured by efforts of fans to retrieve the ball. Letitia Hayden testified that she and her husband had attended Notre Dame football games for many years, and that she witnessed footballs land in the seating area around her many times. On numerous occasions, she saw people jump to get the ball. She testified that she witnessed another woman injured a number of years earlier when people in the crowd attempted to retrieve a football, and that she was knocked off her seat earlier in the game by crowd members attempting to retrieve the ball prior to the incident in which she was injured.

William Hayden testified that the net behind the goalpost caught the ball only about fifty percent of the time that it was kicked. The other half of the time, the ball would fall in the seating area around his seat, and people would try desperately to retrieve the ball. He stated that a few years prior to this incident, he had been knocked off his feet and thrown into the next row by fans eager to retrieve a football, and that he had been jostled a number of times. He stated that Notre Dame ushers witnessed fans being jostled in scrambles for the ball, but did not make aggressive attempts to recover the balls. He testified that in prior years, student managers, who were Notre Dame

(Continues)

employees, would aggressively attempt to retrieve balls from fans and were usually successful in returning the balls to the playing field. The managers, however, no longer tried to retrieve the balls and stayed on the playing field.

Based on the totality of the circumstances, we hold that Notre Dame owed Letitia Hayden a duty to take reasonable steps to protect her from injury due to the actions of other fans in attempting to retrieve footballs which land in the seating area. The trial court erred in finding that no duty existed and entering summary judgment in favor of Notre Dame.

Reversed.

In *Hayden*, the Indiana Court of Appeals succinctly summarized the three elements of a negligence case: (1) existence of a duty, (2) breach of the duty, and (3) injury resulting from the breach. In discussing whether Notre Dame owed the plaintiffs a duty, the court examined the "totality of the circumstances" to determine that it was foreseeable that excited football fans would be aggressive in trying to get a loose ball kicked into the stands and that injury could result. Thus, the existence of a duty is often determined by what the owner of premises can reasonably foresee; in the Hayden case, Notre Dame could have foreseen that fans would injure each other trying to get to a football kicked into the stands, and that resulting duty required them to take steps (such as placing more security in the end zone, or improving the netting to catch balls) to avoid that result.

Although the court in *Hayden* pointed out that determining whether a duty exists is a question of law to be decided by the court, deciding whether that duty has been breached, causing harm to the plaintiff is the function of the trier of fact, which is the jury. In making this judgment, the jury employs its knowledge of acceptable community standards and what a normally prudent person in the community would do. Reasonable behavior is not perfect behavior. Accidents do occur, and mistakes may be made by people who are not exhibiting negligent behavior. Nor does negligence involve morally wrong behavior, as is often the case in criminal law. The goal of tort law is to protect against and compensate for actions by people who do not act reasonably, regardless of whether their actions stem from any moral lapses or defects.

Causation

Negligence also requires a plaintiff to prove causation. That is, did the defendant's breach of its duty cause the harm? There are two aspects to causation in the law of torts: factual cause and legal, or proximate, cause. Factual cause exists when the defendant's actions were the actual cause of harm to the plaintiff. This is sometimes referred to as "but for" causation—"but for" the defendant's action, the harm would not have occurred. Legal cause refers to the question of foreseeability, which examines whether a reasonable person would have foreseen that his or her actions would have resulted in harm to the plaintiff. That

is, if a reasonable person would have foreseen that the actions would lead to harm, fairness dictates that the defendant, not the plaintiff, should "pay" for the harm. Thus, although foreseeability is an important determination in deciding whether a duty exists, it is also important in the analysis of causation.

Although the law of negligence requires proof of causation, in some situations, the plaintiff may not be able to establish a clear connection between the defendant's actions and the harm, despite its existence. In such cases, the concept of *res ipsa loquitur* (the thing speaks for itself) may apply. *Res ipsa loquitur* allows the judge or jury to infer from the defendant's actions that the plaintiff's harm resulted. Specifically, when no other cause of the plaintiff's harm exists and the harm would not ordinarily occur in the absence of the defendant's actions, the causation element in negligence cases is satisfied. For example, on July 11, 2006, Milena Del Valle was driving through a tunnel that had been rebuilt as part of the "Big Dig" in Boston, the most expensive road construction project in history. Ceiling tiles within the tunnel collapsed as she drove through, landing on the car and killing her. The case against numerous defendants was settled before trial for over $28 million (Slack & Estes, 2008). In such a case, one or more of the defendants' liability would have been established under the theory of *res ipsa loquitur*.

Intentional Torts

All intentional torts share the element of intent. These torts are distinguishable in terms of the action intended. Under the common law, there was one intentional tort, called trespass. This occurred when a person wrongfully and intentionally committed some act that injured another. This general tort sufficed for most intentional injuries, but more specific forms of pleading have developed where intentional torts are now recognized based on the harm involved and the elements that must be proven to establish the fault of the defendant. Many of these find their parallel in the criminal law, such as assault, battery, false imprisonment, and trespass on land, all of which require a showing of intent for civil liability as well as criminal liability. More recently recognized intentional torts, however, do not have counterparts in the criminal law. These include intentional infliction of emotional distress, tortious interference with contractual relations, and *prima facie* tort. Although not all jurisdictions recognize each of these, each requires proof of the defendant's intent to cause harm to the plaintiff.

Intent for purposes of tort law exists when a defendant "desires to cause the consequences of his act, or that he believes the consequences are substantially certain to result from it" (American Law Institute, 1965). Thus, intent in tort law is similar to "specific" intent in the criminal law, where the focus is on the intent to cause the result to occur, rather than the intent to commit the act, as with "general" intent in the criminal law. The intent requirement creates civil liability for volitional acts that result in harm; that is, the action is undertaken voluntarily in order to cause certain harmful consequences. For example, a business owner who sends letters to his competitor's customers or prospective customers that call into question the competitor's honesty without basis commits an intentional tort because he intends to cause harm to the competitor. Or, a person who intentionally harms another through the commission of a crime may be civilly liable for the consequences of his or her act. (see **Sidebar 9.1**).

Sidebar 9.1 *The Civil Cases of O.J. Simpson*

Few cases in recent history have garnered as much attention and public fascination as those in which former football great O.J. Simpson was a defendant. First found not guilty in the criminal trial in which he was accused of killing his former wife Nicole Brown and her companion Ronald Goldman, he was subsequently sued by the Brown and Goldman families, published a book about the events that was later recalled and republished, and was found guilty in a later criminal trial involving armed robbery of sports memorabilia, for which he was sentenced to a minimum of 9 years in a Nevada correctional facility. The criminal cases are highlighted in Sidebar 11.2. The focus of this discussion is the civil cases.

After the 1995 murder trial in which Simpson was acquitted, the families of Ronald Goldman and Nicole Brown sued Simpson for the wrongful death of the victims. Their tort claims asserted that Simpson assaulted and brutally murdered both victims. The families were outraged at what they believed to be the injustice of the verdict in the murder trial and sought to obtain alternative judgment of guilt by a civil jury and to strip Simpson of his assets. Because the standard of proof for plaintiffs in civil cases is the lower "preponderance of the evidence," instead of the "beyond a reasonable doubt" standard required in criminal cases, a civil judgment against Simpson could be more easily obtained. In addition, the defendant could be compelled to testify under cross-examination, an option unavailable in the murder trial because of a defendant's Fifth Amendment rights.

The outcome of the civil trial was different than that of the civil trial. On February 4, 1997, a Santa Monica, California, jury of 12 people unanimously decided that Simpson was liable for the wrongful death of Ron Goldman and Nicole Brown. Unlike the murder trial in which Simpson's freedom was at stake, the plaintiffs in this trial sought to deprive him of his assets and extravagant lifestyle. The jury deliberated for 6 days after the 4-month trial and awarded $8.5 million in compensatory damages to the Goldman family for the loss of their son's love, companionship, and moral support. In addition, the jury awarded punitive damages of $25 million to be shared between the Brown and Goldman families. Although some of the judgment was collected from Simpson's assets, including the sale of his Heisman trophy, under California law, Simpson's NFL pension of $25,000 per month could not be attached.

The plaintiffs, especially Ronald Goldman's father, Fred Goldman, however, continued their quest for justice by doggedly pursuing any means to seize Simpson's assets. When Simpson sought to release a book in 2007 entitled "If I Did It," which purportedly outlined the hypothetical steps Simpson would have taken had he participated in the murders, the Goldmans returned to court in California to prevent publication of the book and obtain any proceeds or advances from the publisher. He also sought to control any right to publicize the book. The Goldmans obtained an order from the court preventing Simpson from spending any money received from the publisher and to restrict his spending to ordinary living expenses, and the court subsequently ordered that the book rights be sold to satisfy the Goldmans' civil judgment. Before the sale, however, the company Simpson had formed to receive proceeds from the book declared bankruptcy in Florida. The Goldmans intervened as the largest creditor in the bankruptcy, claiming that they were entitled to any assets of the company. The bankruptcy court subsequently found the company to be a "sham" corporation and granted the Goldmans (with a portion to the estate of Nicole Brown) substantially all of the company's assets, primarily the book rights. The Goldman family subsequently published the book, with additional commentary, as "If I Did It: Confessions of the Killer."

Strict Liability in Tort

Just as some crimes are considered strict liability crimes because of the great potential for harm that certain actions entail, strict liability in tort exists to prevent the occurrence of harmful results from certain action. In strict liability cases, the plaintiff need show only that the defendant engaged in an activity that harmed the plaintiff; a "reasonableness" standard is not relevant. Not just any activity, however, is the subject of strict liability tort actions; only for those activities deemed to be dangerous does strict liability apply. For example, keeping wild animals, such as lions or venomous snakes, would constitute a dangerous activity. Similarly, conducting ultrahazardous activities such as using or storing explosives or manufacturing dangerous chemicals would make a defendant strictly liable when harm results.

The most commonly seen modern tort cause of action based on strict liability is for products liability. A tort claim for strict products liability allows a plaintiff who is injured by a product introduced into the "stream of commerce" to seek compensation from the product's manufacturer for the production of an unsafe and/or dangerous product. Despite the commonly used phrase *caveat emptor* ("let the buyer beware"), defective products sold to consumers that result in injury through their ordinary use will result in liability to the manufacturer and/or distributor. The purpose in allowing strict products liability claims is to minimize the risk to individuals and make society safer; however, the law does not require manufacturers to create absolutely safe conditions, even if it were possible to do so (see Owen, 1993). Indeed, from an economic perspective, the cost of making products as safe as possible could result in making their purchase cost-prohibitive or otherwise undesirable. For example, an automobile manufacturer could make a vehicle with a body of 1-inch plate steel, with 2-foot-thick air-cushioned bumpers, and electronic warning systems to indicate when another vehicle approaches too closely, but who would buy it?

For some products, however, the cost to increase safety for the consumer is minimal. In the seminal case on products liability, *Greenman v. Yuba Power Products* (59 Cal. 2d 57, 377 P.2d 897 (1963)), the plaintiff received as a Christmas present a power tool, called a Shopsmith, that could be used as a lathe. When he used it to turn and shape a piece of wood, the wood became unfastened from the lathe, flew from the tool, and struck him in the head, causing severe injuries. The court found that by replacing some screws or taking other low-cost measures, the injury could have been prevented. The author of the opinion, Justice Traynor, noted this:

> A manufacturer is strictly liable in tort when an article he places on the market, knowing that it is to be used without inspection for defects, proves to have a defect that causes injury to a human being. Recognized first in the case of unwholesome food products, such liability has now been extended to a variety of other products that create as great or greater hazards if defective.
>
> Although in these cases strict liability has usually been based on the theory of an express or implied warranty running from the manufacturer to the plaintiff, the abandonment of the requirement of a contract between them, the recognition that the liability is not assumed by agreement but imposed by law, and the refusal to permit the manufacturer to define the scope of its own responsibility for defective products, make clear that the liability is not one governed by the law of contract warranties but by the law of strict liability in tort.
>
> The purpose of such liability is to insure that the costs of injuries resulting from defective products are borne by the manufacturers that put such products on the market rather than by the injured persons who are powerless to protect themselves. Implicit in the machine's presence on the market, however, was a representation that it would safely do the jobs for which it was built. Under these circumstances, it should not be controlling whether plaintiff selected the machine because of the statements in the brochure, or because of the machine's own appearance of excellence that belied the defect lurking beneath the surface, or because he merely assumed that it would safely do the jobs it was built to do. To establish the manufacturer's liability it was sufficient that plaintiff proved that he was injured while using

the Shopsmith in a way it was intended to be used as a result of a defect in design and manufacture of which plaintiff was not aware that made the Shopsmith unsafe for its intended use. (59 Cal. 2d at 62–64, 377 P.2d at 900–901)

Thus, the cost of injuries should be borne by the manufacturer, rather than the unsuspecting consumer. This is the purpose of strict products liability.

Civil Rights Claims

Civil rights is a broad term that refers to rights and privileges granted to members of American society. The source of these rights may be constitutional or statutory. Examples of civil rights found in the federal constitution are those in the Bill of Rights, such as the First Amendment rights to free speech, press, and religious expression or the prohibition against unreasonable searches and seizures found in the Fourth Amendment. Civil rights granted by statute are found in such federal laws as the Civil Rights Act of 1964, the Age Discrimination in Employment Act, and the Americans with Disabilities Act, among many others. Although the U.S. Constitution creates civil rights enforceable against federal and state government action, Congress's creation of statutory civil rights has expanded those rights to prevent infringement by private actors, such as employers or others involved in interstate commerce. Civil rights law has therefore become a complex area of the law involving constitutional or statutory claims, state or federal, that apply against government actors and certain private individuals.

The primary mechanism for enforcement of Constitutional rights is found in 42 U.S.C. Section 1983, which provides:

* Every person who, under color of any statute, ordinance, regulation, custom, or usage, of any State or Territory or the District of Columbia, subjects, or causes to be subjected, any citizen of the United States or other person within the jurisdiction thereof to the deprivation of any rights, privileges, or immunities secured by the Constitution and laws, shall be liable to the party injured in an action at law, suit in equity, or other proper proceeding for redress, except that in any action brought against a judicial officer for an act or omission taken in such officer's judicial capacity, injunctive relief shall not be granted unless a declaratory decree was violated or declaratory relief was unavailable. For the purposes of this section, any Act of Congress applicable exclusively to the District of Columbia shall be considered to be a statute of the District of Columbia.

This section allows recourse to the courts by individuals who believe their civil rights have been violated by the government, including any governmental agency such as schools, police departments, and other government workers. An example of the use of Section 1983 is found in *Morse v. Frederick*, 551 U.S., 127 S. Ct. 2618, 168 L.Ed.2d 290 (2007), excerpted in **Case Decision 9.3**. In that case, the U.S. Supreme Court considered whether the First Amendment rights of a high school student were violated by their high school principal who confiscated a banner with the words "BONG HiTS 4 JESUS" and suspended the student who displayed it.

Decision of the Court by Chief Justice Roberts:

At a school-sanctioned and school-supervised event, a high school principal saw some of her students unfurl a large banner conveying a message she reasonably regarded as promoting illegal drug use. Consistent with established school policy prohibiting such messages at school events, the principal directed the students to take down the banner. One student—among those who had brought the banner to the event—refused to do so. The principal confiscated the banner and later suspended the student. The Ninth Circuit held that the principal's actions violated the First Amendment, and that the student could sue the principal for damages.

Our cases make clear that students do not "shed their constitutional rights to freedom of speech or expression at the schoolhouse gate." At the same time, we have held that "the constitutional rights of students in public school are not automatically coextensive with the rights of adults in other settings," and that the rights of students "must be 'applied in light of the special characteristics of the school environment.'" Consistent with these principles, we hold that schools may take steps to safeguard those entrusted to their care from speech that can reasonably be regarded as encouraging illegal drug use. We conclude that the school officials in this case did not violate the First Amendment by confiscating the pro-drug banner and suspending the student responsible for it.

I

On January 24, 2002, the Olympic Torch Relay passed through Juneau, Alaska, on its way to the winter games in Salt Lake City, Utah. The torchbearers were to proceed along a street in front of Juneau-Douglas High School (JDHS) while school was in session. Petitioner Deborah Morse, the school principal, decided to permit staff and students to participate in the Torch Relay as an approved social event or class trip. Students were allowed to leave class to observe the relay from either side of the street. Teachers and administrative officials monitored the students' actions.

Respondent Joseph Frederick, a JDHS senior, was late to school that day. When he arrived, he joined his friends (all but one of whom were JDHS students) across the street from the school to watch the event. Not all the students waited patiently. Some became rambunctious, throwing plastic cola bottles and snowballs and scuffling with their classmates. As the torchbearers and camera crews passed by, Frederick and his friends unfurled a 14-foot banner bearing the phrase: "BONG HiTS 4 JESUS." The large banner was easily readable by the students on the other side of the street.

Principal Morse immediately crossed the street and demanded that the banner be taken down. Everyone but Frederick complied. Morse confiscated the banner and told Frederick to report to her office, where she suspended him for 10 days. Morse later explained that she told Frederick to take the banner down because she thought it encouraged illegal drug use, in violation of established school policy. Juneau School Board Policy No. 5520 states: "The Board specifically prohibits any assembly or public expression that . . . advocates the use of substances that are illegal to minors. . . ." In addition, Juneau School Board Policy No. 5850 subjects "[p]upils who participate in approved social events and class trips" to the same student conduct rules that apply during the regular school program.

Frederick administratively appealed his suspension, but the Juneau School District Superintendent upheld it, limiting it to time served (8 days). In a memorandum setting forth his reasons, the superintendent determined that Frederick had displayed his banner "in the midst of his fellow students, during school hours, at a school-sanctioned activity." He further explained that Frederick "was not disciplined because the principal of the school 'disagreed' with his message, but because his speech appeared to advocate the use of illegal drugs."

The superintendent continued:

The common-sense understanding of the phrase 'bong hits' is that it is a reference to a means of smoking marijuana. Given [Frederick's] inability or unwillingness to express any other credible meaning for the phrase, I can only agree with the principal and countless others who saw the banner as advocating the use of illegal drugs. [Frederick's] speech was not political. He was not advocating the legalization of marijuana or promoting a religious belief. He was displaying a fairly silly message promoting illegal drug

(Continues)

(*Continued*)

usage in the midst of a school activity, for the benefit of television cameras covering the Torch Relay. [Frederick's] speech was potentially disruptive to the event and clearly disruptive of and inconsistent with the school's educational mission to educate students about the dangers of illegal drugs and to discourage their use.

[T]he superintendent concluded that the principal's actions were permissible because Frederick's banner was "speech or action that intrudes upon the work of the schools." The Juneau School District Board of Education upheld the suspension.

Frederick then filed suit under 42 U.S.C. § 1983, alleging that the school board and Morse had violated his First Amendment rights. He sought declaratory and injunctive relief, unspecified compensatory damages, punitive damages, and attorney's fees. The District Court granted summary judgment for the school board and Morse, ruling that they were entitled to qualified immunity and that they had not infringed Frederick's First Amendment rights. The court found that Morse reasonably interpreted the banner as promoting illegal drug use—a message that "directly contravened the Board's policies relating to drug abuse prevention." Under the circumstances, the court held that "Morse had the authority, if not the obligation, to stop such messages at a school-sanctioned activity."

The Ninth Circuit reversed. Deciding that Frederick acted during a "school-authorized activit[y]," and "proceed[ing] on the basis that the banner expressed a positive sentiment about marijuana use," the court nonetheless found a violation of Frederick's First Amendment rights because the school punished Frederick without demonstrating that his speech gave rise to a "risk of substantial disruption." The court further concluded that Frederick's right to display his banner was so "clearly established" that a reasonable principal in Morse's position would have understood that her actions were unconstitutional, and that Morse was therefore not entitled to qualified immunity.

We granted certiorari on two questions: whether Frederick had a First Amendment right to wield his banner, and, if so, whether that right was so clearly established that the principal may be held liable for damages. We resolve the first question against Frederick, and therefore have no occasion to reach the second.

II

At the outset, we reject Frederick's argument that this is not a school speech case—as has every other authority to address the question. The event occurred during normal school hours. It was sanctioned by Principal Morse "as an approved social event or class trip," and the school district's rules expressly provide that pupils in "approved social events and class trips are subject to district rules for student conduct." Teachers and administrators were interspersed among the students and charged with supervising them. The high school band and cheerleaders performed. Frederick, standing among other JDHS students across the street from the school, directed his banner toward the school, making it plainly visible to most students. Under these circumstances, we agree with the superintendent that Frederick cannot "stand in the midst of his fellow students, during school hours, at a school-sanctioned activity and claim he is not at school." There is some uncertainty at the outer boundaries as to when courts should apply school-speech precedents, but not on these facts.

III

The message on Frederick's banner is cryptic. It is no doubt offensive to some, perhaps amusing to others. To still others, it probably means nothing at all. Frederick himself claimed "that the words were just nonsense meant to attract television cameras." But Principal Morse thought the banner would be interpreted by those viewing it as promoting illegal drug use, and that interpretation is plainly a reasonable one.

As Morse later explained in a declaration, when she saw the sign, she thought that "the reference to a 'bong hit' would be widely understood by high school students and others as referring to smoking marijuana." She further believed that "display of the banner would be construed by students, District personnel, parents and others witnessing the display of the banner, as advocating or promoting illegal drug use"—in violation of school policy. ("I told Frederick and the other members of his group to put the banner down because I felt that it violated the [school] policy against displaying . . . material that advertises or promotes use of illegal drugs").

We agree with Morse. At least two interpretations of the words on the banner demonstrate that the sign advocated the use of illegal drugs. First, the phrase could be interpreted as an imperative: "[Take] bong hits . . ."—a message equivalent, as Morse explained in her declaration, to "smoke marijuana" or "use an illegal drug." Alternatively, the phrase could be viewed as celebrating drug use—"bong hits [are a good thing]," or "[we take] bong hits"—and we discern no meaningful distinction between celebrating illegal drug use in the midst of fellow students and outright advocacy or promotion.

The pro-drug interpretation of the banner gains further plausibility given the paucity of alternative meanings the banner might bear. The best Frederick can come up with is that the banner is "meaningless and funny." Gibberish is surely a possible interpretation of the words on the banner, but it is not the only one, and dismissing the banner as meaningless ignores its undeniable reference to illegal drugs.

IV

The question thus becomes whether a principal may, consistent with the First Amendment, restrict student speech at a school event, when that speech is reasonably viewed as promoting illegal drug use. We hold that she may.

[D]eterring drug use by schoolchildren is an "important—indeed, perhaps compelling" interest. Drug abuse can cause severe and permanent damage to the health and well-being of young people. Just five years ago, we wrote: "The drug abuse problem among our Nation's youth has hardly abated. In fact, evidence suggests that it has only grown worse."

Congress has declared that part of a school's job is educating students about the dangers of illegal drug use. It has provided billions of dollars to support state and local drug-prevention programs, and required that schools receiving federal funds under the Safe and Drug-Free Schools and Communities Act of 1994 certify that their drug prevention programs "convey a clear and consistent message that . . . the illegal use of drugs [is] wrong and harmful."

Thousands of school boards throughout the country—including JDHS—have adopted policies aimed at effectuating this message. Those school boards know that peer pressure is perhaps "the single most important factor leading schoolchildren to take drugs," and that students are more likely to use drugs when the norms in school appear to tolerate such behavior. Student speech celebrating illegal drug use at a school event, in the presence of school administrators and teachers, thus poses a particular challenge for school officials working to protect those entrusted to their care from the dangers of drug abuse.

Petitioners urge us to adopt the broader rule that Frederick's speech is proscribable because it is plainly "offensive." [M]uch political and religious speech might be perceived as offensive to some. The concern here is not that Frederick's speech was offensive, but that it was reasonably viewed as promoting illegal drug use.

School principals have a difficult job, and a vitally important one. When Frederick suddenly and unexpectedly unfurled his banner, Morse had to decide to act—or not act—on the spot. It was reasonable for her to conclude that the banner promoted illegal drug use—in violation of established school policy—and that failing to act would send a powerful message to the students in her charge, including Frederick, about how serious the school was about the dangers of illegal drug use. The First Amendment does not require schools to tolerate at school events student expression that contributes to those dangers.

The judgment of the United States Court of Appeals for the Ninth Circuit is reversed, and the case is remanded for further proceedings consistent with this opinion.

The Court found that the school principal had not deprived the student of his right to free speech found in the First Amendment because the message on the banner could reasonably be perceived as promoting drug use, in contrast to the mission of the school. Because the banner was unfurled during a school-sponsored activity, the school had a right to exercise reasonable control over student speech. Although the claimed right to free speech was not upheld in the case, 42 U.S.C. Section 1983 nonetheless allowed the student to seek a remedy in the federal courts, which ultimately included a hearing by the U.S. Supreme Court. Thus, the American courts frequently consider matters that begin as apparently minor incidents in out-of-way places, allowing people a forum for resolving alleged deprivations of their constitutional rights.

When civil rights are statutorily based, the statute itself provides the mechanism for enforcement. The Americans with Disabilities Act (ADA), which prevents discrimination against individuals with certain types of physical and mental disabilities, was the subject of *PGA Tour, Inc. v. Martin*, 532 U.S. 661, 121 S. Ct. 1879, 149 L.Ed.2d 904 (2001). The Martin case examined whether the PGA could prevent a physically disabled professional golfer from using a golf cart to compete in a qualifying tournament. The case is the subject of **Case Decision 9.4**.

Case Decision 9.4 *PGA Tour v. Martin*, 532 U.S. 661, 121 S. Ct. 1879, 149 L.Ed.2d 904 (2001)

Decision of the Court by Justice Stevens:

This case raises two questions concerning the application of the Americans with Disabilities Act of 1990, 104 Stat. 328, 42 U.S.C. § 12101 *et seq.*, to a gifted athlete: first, whether the Act protects access to professional golf tournaments by a qualified entrant with a disability; and second, whether a disabled contestant may be denied the use of a golf cart because it would "fundamentally alter the nature" of the tournaments, § 12182(b)(2)(A)(ii), to allow him to ride when all other contestants must walk.

I

Petitioner PGA TOUR, Inc., a nonprofit entity formed in 1968, sponsors and cosponsors professional golf tournaments conducted on three annual tours. About 200 golfers participate in the PGA TOUR; about 170 in the NIKE TOUR; and about 100 in the SENIOR PGA TOUR. PGA TOUR and NIKE TOUR tournaments typically are 4-day events, played on courses leased and operated by petitioner. The entire field usually competes in two 18-hole rounds played on Thursday and Friday; those who survive the "cut" play on Saturday and Sunday and receive prize money in amounts determined by their aggregate scores for all four rounds. The revenues generated by television, admissions, concessions, and contributions from cosponsors amount to about $300 million a year, much of which is distributed in prize money.

There are various ways of gaining entry into particular tours. For example, a player who wins three NIKE TOUR events in the same year, or is among the top-15 money winners on that tour, earns the right to play in the PGA TOUR. Additionally, a golfer may obtain a spot in an official tournament through successfully competing in "open" qualifying rounds, which are conducted the week before each tournament. Most participants, however, earn playing privileges in the PGA TOUR or NIKE TOUR by way of a three-stage qualifying tournament known as the "Q-School."

Any member of the public may enter the Q-School by paying a $3,000 entry fee and submitting two letters of reference from, among others, PGA TOUR or NIKE TOUR members. The $3,000 entry fee covers the players' greens fees and the cost of golf carts, which are permitted during the first two stages, but which have been prohibited during the third stage since 1997. Each year, over a thousand contestants compete in the first stage, which consists of four 18-hole rounds at different locations. Approximately half of them make it to the second stage, which also includes 72 holes. Around 168 players survive the second stage and advance to the final one, where they compete over 108 holes. Of those finalists, about a fourth qualify for membership in the PGA TOUR, and the rest gain membership in the NIKE TOUR. The significance of making it into either tour is illuminated by the fact that there are about 25 million golfers in the country.

Three sets of rules govern competition in tour events. First, the "Rules of Golf," jointly written by the United States Golf Association (USGA) and the Royal and Ancient Golf Club of Scotland, apply to the game as it is played, not only by millions of amateurs on public courses and in private country clubs throughout the United States and worldwide, but also by the professionals in the tournaments conducted by petitioner, the USGA, the Ladies' Professional Golf Association, and the Senior Women's Golf Association. Those rules do not prohibit the use of golf carts at any time. Instead, Appendix I to the Rules of Golf lists a number of "optional" conditions, among them one related to transportation: If it is desired to require players to walk in a competition, the following condition is suggested: "Players shall walk at all times during a stipulated round."

Second, the "Conditions of Competition and Local Rules," often described as the "hard card," apply specifically to petitioner's professional tours. The hard cards for the PGA TOUR and NIKE TOUR require players to walk the golf course during tournaments, but not during open qualifying rounds. The PGA TOUR hard card provides: "Players shall walk at all times during a stipulated round unless permitted to ride by the PGA TOUR Rules Committee." The NIKE TOUR hard card similarly requires walking unless otherwise permitted. Additionally, as noted, golf carts have not been permitted during the third stage of the Q-School since 1997. Petitioner added this recent prohibition in order to "approximat[e] a PGA TOUR event as closely as possible." On the SENIOR PGA TOUR, which is limited to golfers age 50 and older, the contestants may use golf carts. Most seniors, however, prefer to walk.

Third, "Notices to Competitors" are issued for particular tournaments and cover conditions for that specific event. Such a notice may, for example, explain how the Rules of Golf should be applied to a particular water hazard or manmade obstruction. It might also authorize the use of carts to speed up play when there is an unusual distance between one green and the next tee.

The basic Rules of Golf, the hard cards, and the weekly notices apply equally to all players in tour competitions. As one of petitioner's witnesses explained with reference to "the Masters Tournament, which is golf at its very highest level, . . . the key is to have everyone tee off on the first hole under exactly the same conditions and all of them be tested over that 72-hole event under the conditions that exist during those four days of the event."

II

Casey Martin is a talented golfer. As an amateur, he won 17 Oregon Golf Association junior events before he was 15, and won the state championship as a high school senior. He played on the Stanford University golf team that won the 1994 National Collegiate Athletic Association (NCAA) championship. As a professional, Martin qualified for the NIKE TOUR in 1998 and 1999, and based on his 1999 performance, qualified for the PGA TOUR in 2000. In the 1999 season, he entered 24 events, made the cut 13 times, and had 6 top-10 finishes, coming in second twice and third once.

Martin is also an individual with a disability as defined in the Americans with Disabilities Act of 1990 (ADA or Act). Title 42 U.S.C. § 12102 provides, in part: "The term 'disability' means, with respect to an individual (A) a physical or mental impairment that substantially limits one or more of the major life activities of such individual. . . ." Since birth he has been afflicted with Klippel-Trenaunay-Weber Syndrome, a degenerative circulatory disorder that obstructs the flow of blood from his right leg back to his heart. The disease is progressive; it causes severe pain and has atrophied his right leg. During the latter part of his college career, because of the progress of the disease, Martin could no longer walk an 18-hole golf course. Walking not only caused him pain, fatigue, and anxiety, but also created a significant risk of hemorrhaging, developing blood clots, and fracturing his tibia so badly that an amputation might be required. For these reasons, Stanford made written requests to the Pacific 10 Conference and the NCAA to waive for Martin their rules requiring players to walk and carry their own clubs. The requests were granted.

When Martin turned pro and entered petitioner's Q-School, the hard card permitted him to use a cart during his successful progress through the first two stages. He made a request, supported by detailed medical records, for permission to use a golf cart during the third stage. Petitioner refused to review those records or to waive its walking rule for the third stage. Martin therefore filed this action. A preliminary injunction entered by the District Court made it possible for him to use a cart in the final stage of the Q-School and as a competitor in the NIKE TOUR and PGA TOUR. Although not bound by the injunction, and despite its support for petitioner's position in this litigation, the USGA voluntarily granted Martin a similar waiver in events that it sponsors, including the U.S. Open.

III

In the District Court, petitioner moved for summary judgment on the ground that it is exempt from coverage under Title III of the ADA as a "private clu[b] or establishmen[t]," or alternatively, that the play areas of its tour competitions do not constitute places of "public accommodation" within the scope of that Title. The Magistrate Judge concluded that petitioner should be viewed as a commercial enterprise operating in the entertainment industry for the economic benefit of its members rather

(Continues)

(*Continued*)

than as a private club. Furthermore, after noting that the statutory definition of public accommodation included a "golf course," he rejected petitioner's argument that its competitions are only places of public accommodation in the areas open to spectators. The operator of a public accommodation could not, in his view, "create private enclaves within the facility . . . and thus relegate the ADA to hop-scotch areas." Accordingly, he denied petitioner's motion for summary judgment.

At trial, petitioner did not contest the conclusion that Martin has a disability covered by the ADA, or the fact "that his disability prevents him from walking the course during a round of golf." Rather, petitioner asserted that the condition of walking is a substantive rule of competition, and that waiving it as to any individual for any reason would fundamentally alter the nature of the competition. Petitioner's evidence included the testimony of a number of experts, among them some of the greatest golfers in history. Arnold Palmer, Jack Nicklaus, and Ken Venturi explained that fatigue can be a critical factor in a tournament, particularly on the last day when psychological pressure is at a maximum. Their testimony makes it clear that, in their view, permission to use a cart might well give some players a competitive advantage over other players who must walk. They did not, however, express any opinion on whether a cart would give Martin such an advantage.

Rejecting petitioner's argument that an individualized inquiry into the necessity of the walking rule in Martin's case would be inappropriate, the District Court stated that it had "the independent duty to inquire into the purpose of the rule at issue, and to ascertain whether there can be a reasonable modification made to accommodate plaintiff without frustrating the purpose of the rule" and thereby fundamentally altering the nature of petitioner's tournaments. The judge found that the purpose of the rule was to inject fatigue into the skill of shotmaking, but that the fatigue injected "by walking the course cannot be deemed significant under normal circumstances." Furthermore, Martin presented evidence, and the judge found, that even with the use of a cart, Martin must walk over a mile during an 18-hole round, and that the fatigue he suffers from coping with his disability is "undeniably greater" than the fatigue his able-bodied competitors endure from walking the course. As the judge observed: "[P]laintiff is in significant pain when he walks, and even when he is getting in and out of the cart. With each step, he is at risk of fracturing his tibia and hemorrhaging. The other golfers have to endure the psychological stress of competition as part of their fatigue; Martin has the same stress plus the added stress of pain and risk of serious injury. As he put it, he would gladly trade the cart for a good leg. To perceive that the cart puts him—with his condition—at a competitive advantage is a gross distortion of reality." As a result, the judge concluded that it would "not fundamentally alter the nature of the PGA Tour's game to accommodate him with a cart." The judge accordingly entered a permanent injunction requiring petitioner to permit Martin to use a cart in tour and qualifying events.

On appeal to the Ninth Circuit, petitioner did not challenge the District Court's rejection of its claim that it was exempt as a "private club," but it renewed the contention that during a tournament the portion of the golf course "'behind the ropes' is not a public accommodation because the public has no right to enter it." The Court of Appeals viewed that contention as resting on the incorrect assumption that the competition among participants was not itself public. The court first pointed out that, as with a private university, "the fact that users of a facility are highly selected does not mean that the facility cannot be a public accommodation." In its opinion, the competition to enter the select circle of PGA TOUR and NIKE TOUR golfers was comparable because "[a]ny member of the public who pays a $3000 entry fee and supplies two letters of recommendation may try out in the qualifying school." The court saw "no justification in reason or in the statute to draw a line beyond which the performance of athletes becomes so excellent that a competition restricted to their level deprives its situs of the character of a public accommodation." Nor did it find a basis for distinguishing between "use of a place of public accommodation for pleasure and use in the pursuit of a living." Consequently, the Court of Appeals concluded that golf courses remain places of public accommodation during PGA tournaments.

On the merits, because there was no serious dispute about the fact that permitting Martin to use a golf cart was both a reasonable and a necessary solution to the problem of providing him access to the tournaments, the Court of Appeals regarded the central dispute as whether such permission would "fundamentally alter" the nature of the PGA TOUR or NIKE TOUR. Like the District Court, the Court of Appeals viewed the issue not as "whether use of carts generally would fundamentally alter the competition, but whether the use of a cart by Martin would do so." That issue turned on "an intensively fact-based inquiry," and, the court concluded, had been correctly resolved by the trial judge. In its words, "[a]ll that the cart does is permit Martin access to a type of competition in which he otherwise could not engage because of his disability."

The day after the Ninth Circuit ruled in Martin's favor, the Seventh Circuit came to a contrary conclusion in a case brought against the USGA by a disabled golfer who failed to qualify for "America's greatest—and most democratic—golf tournament, the United States Open." The Seventh Circuit endorsed the conclusion of the District Court in that case that "the nature of the competition would be fundamentally altered if the walking rule were eliminated because it would remove stamina (at least a particular type of stamina) from the set of qualities designed to be tested in this competition." In the Seventh Circuit's opinion, the physical ordeals endured by Ken Venturi and Ben Hogan when they walked to their Open victories in 1964 and 1950 amply demonstrated the importance of stamina in such a tournament. As an alternative basis for its holding, the court also concluded that the ADA does not require the USGA to bear "the administrative burdens of evaluating requests to waive the walking rule and permit the use of a golf cart." Although the Seventh Circuit merely assumed that the ADA applies to professional golf tournaments, and therefore did not disagree with the Ninth on the threshold coverage issue, our grant of certiorari, encompasses that question as well as the conflict between those courts.

IV

Congress enacted the ADA in 1990 to remedy widespread discrimination against disabled individuals. In studying the need for such legislation, Congress found that "historically, society has tended to isolate and segregate individuals with disabilities, and, despite some improvements, such forms of discrimination against individuals with disabilities continue to be a serious and pervasive social problem." Congress noted that the many forms such discrimination takes include "outright intentional exclusion" as well as the "failure to make modifications to existing facilities and practices." After thoroughly investigating the problem, Congress concluded that there was a "compelling need" for a "clear and comprehensive national mandate" to eliminate discrimination against disabled individuals, and to integrate them "into the economic and social mainstream of American life."

In the ADA, Congress provided that broad mandate. In fact, one of the Act's "most impressive strengths" has been identified as its "comprehensive character," and accordingly the Act has been described as "a milestone on the path to a more decent, tolerant, progressive society." To effectuate its sweeping purpose, the ADA forbids discrimination against disabled individuals in major areas of public life, among them employment (Title I of the Act), public services (Title II), and public accommodations (Title III). At issue now, as a threshold matter, is the applicability of Title III to petitioner's golf tours and qualifying rounds, in particular to petitioner's treatment of a qualified disabled golfer wishing to compete in those events.

Title III of the ADA prescribes, as a "[g]eneral rule": "No individual shall be discriminated against on the basis of disability in the full and equal enjoyment of the goods, services, facilities, privileges, advantages, or accommodations of any place of public accommodation by any person who owns, leases (or leases to), or operates a place of public accommodation." The phrase "public accommodation" is defined in terms of 12 extensive categories, which the legislative history indicates "should be construed liberally" to afford people with disabilities "equal access" to the wide variety of establishments available to the nondisabled.

It seems apparent, from both the general rule and the comprehensive definition of "public accommodation," that petitioner's golf tours and their qualifying rounds fit comfortably within the coverage of Title III, and Martin within its protection. The events occur on "golf course[s]," a type of place specifically identified by the Act as a public accommodation. In addition, at all relevant times, petitioner "leases" and "operates" golf courses to conduct its Q-School and tours. As a lessor and operator of golf courses, then, petitioner must not discriminate against any "individual" in the "full and equal enjoyment of the goods, services, facilities, privileges, advantages, or accommodations" of those courses. Certainly, among the "privileges" offered by petitioner on the courses are those of competing in the Q-School and playing in the tours; indeed, the former is a privilege for which thousands of individuals from the general public pay, and the latter is one for which they vie. Martin, of course, is one of those individuals. It would therefore appear that Title III of the ADA, by its plain terms, prohibits petitioner from denying Martin equal access to its tours on the basis of his disability.

(Continues)

(Continued)

V

As we have noted, 42 U.S.C. § 12182(a) sets forth Title III's general rule prohibiting public accommodations from discriminating against individuals because of their disabilities. The question whether petitioner has violated that rule depends on a proper construction of the term "discrimination," which is defined by Title III to include "a failure to make reasonable modifications in policies, practices, or procedures, when such modifications are necessary to afford such goods, services, facilities, privileges, advantages, or accommodations to individuals with disabilities, *unless the entity can demonstrate that making such modifications would fundamentally alter the nature* of such goods, services, facilities, privileges, advantages, or accommodations" (emphasis added).

Petitioner does not contest that a golf cart is a reasonable modification that is necessary if Martin is to play in its tournaments. Martin's claim thus differs from one that might be asserted by players with less serious afflictions that make walking the course uncomfortable or difficult, but not beyond their capacity. In such cases, an accommodation might be reasonable but not necessary. In this case, however, the narrow dispute is whether allowing Martin to use a golf cart, despite the walking requirement that applies to the PGA TOUR, the NIKE TOUR, and the third stage of the Q-School, is a modification that would "fundamentally alter the nature" of those events.

In theory, a modification of petitioner's golf tournaments might constitute a fundamental alteration in two different ways. It might alter such an essential aspect of the game of golf that it would be unacceptable even if it affected all competitors equally; changing the diameter of the hole from three to six inches might be such a modification. Alternatively, a less significant change that has only a peripheral impact on the game itself might nevertheless give a disabled player, in addition to access to the competition as required by Title III, an advantage over others and, for that reason, fundamentally alter the character of the competition. We are not persuaded that a waiver of the walking rule for Martin would work a fundamental alteration in either sense. As we have noted, the statute contemplates three inquiries: whether the requested modification is "reasonable," whether it is "necessary" for the disabled individual, and whether it would "fundamentally alter the nature of" the competition. 42 U.S.C. § 12182(b)(2)(A)(ii). Whether one question should be decided before the others likely will vary from case to case, for in logic there seems to be no necessary priority among the three. In routine cases, the fundamental alteration inquiry may end with the question whether a rule is essential. Alternatively, the specifics of the claimed disability might be examined within the context of what is a reasonable or necessary modification. Given the concession by petitioner that the modification sought is reasonable and necessary, and given petitioner's reliance on the fundamental alteration provision, we have no occasion to consider the alternatives in this case.

As an initial matter, we observe that the use of carts is not itself inconsistent with the fundamental character of the game of golf. From early on, the essence of the game has been shotmaking—using clubs to cause a ball to progress from the teeing ground to a hole some distance away with as few strokes as possible. That essential aspect of the game is still reflected in the very first of the Rules of Golf, which declares: "The Game of Golf consists in playing a ball from the *teeing ground* into the hole by a *stroke* or successive strokes in accordance with the rules." Over the years, there have been many changes in the players' equipment, in golf course design, in the Rules of Golf, and in the method of transporting clubs from hole to hole. Originally, so few clubs were used that each player could carry them without a bag. Then came golf bags, caddies, carts that were pulled by hand, and eventually motorized carts that carried players as well as clubs. There is nothing in the Rules of Golf that either forbids the use of carts or penalizes a player for using a cart. That set of rules, as we have observed, is widely accepted in both the amateur and professional golf world as the rules of the game. The walking rule that is contained in petitioner's hard cards, based on an optional condition buried in an appendix to the Rules of Golf, is not an essential attribute of the game itself.

Indeed, the walking rule is not an indispensable feature of tournament golf either. As already mentioned, petitioner permits golf carts to be used in the SENIOR PGA TOUR, the open qualifying events for petitioner's tournaments, the first two stages of the Q-School, and, until 1997, the third stage of the Q-School as well. Petitioner, however, distinguishes the game of golf as it is generally played from the game that it sponsors in the PGA TOUR, NIKE TOUR, and (at least recently) the last stage of the Q-School—golf at the "highest level." According to petitioner, "[t]he goal of the highest-level competitive athletics is to assess and compare the performance of different competitors, a task that is meaningful only if the competitors are subject to identical substantive rules." The waiver of any possibly "outcome-affecting" rule for a contestant would violate this principle and therefore, in

222 Section III: Civil Law and Procedure in the Courts

petitioner's view, fundamentally alter the nature of the highest level athletic event. The walking rule is one such rule, petitioner submits, because its purpose is "to inject the element of fatigue into the skill of shot-making," and thus its effect may be the critical loss of a stroke. As a consequence, the reasonable modification Martin seeks would fundamentally alter the nature of petitioner's highest level tournaments even if he were the only person in the world who has both the talent to compete in those elite events and a disability sufficiently serious that he cannot do so without using a cart.

[T]he factual basis of petitioner's argument is undermined by the District Court's finding that the fatigue from walking during one of petitioner's 4-day tournaments cannot be deemed significant. The District Court credited the testimony of a professor in physiology and expert on fatigue, who calculated the calories expended in walking a golf course (about five miles) to be approximately 500 calories—"nutritionally . . . less than a Big Mac." What is more, that energy is expended over a 5-hour period, during which golfers have numerous intervals for rest and refreshment. In fact, the expert concluded, because golf is a low intensity activity, fatigue from the game is primarily a psychological phenomenon in which stress and motivation are the key ingredients. And even under conditions of severe heat and humidity, the critical factor in fatigue is fluid loss rather than exercise from walking.

Even if we accept the factual predicate for petitioner's argument—that the walking rule is "outcome affecting" because fatigue may adversely affect performance—its legal position is fatally flawed. Petitioner's refusal to consider Martin's personal circumstances in deciding whether to accommodate his disability runs counter to the clear language and purpose of the ADA. As previously stated, the ADA was enacted to eliminate discrimination against "individuals" with disabilities, and to that end Title III of the Act requires without exception that any "policies, practices, or procedures" of a public accommodation be reasonably modified for disabled "individuals" as necessary to afford access unless doing so would fundamentally alter what is offered. To comply with this command, an individualized inquiry must be made to determine whether a specific modification for a particular person's disability would be reasonable under the circumstances as well as necessary for that person, and yet at the same time not work a fundamental alteration.

Under the ADA's basic requirement that the need of a disabled person be evaluated on an individual basis, we have no doubt that allowing Martin to use a golf cart would not fundamentally alter the nature of petitioner's tournaments. As we have discussed, the purpose of the walking rule is to subject players to fatigue, which in turn may influence the outcome of tournaments. Even if the rule does serve that purpose, it is an uncontested finding of the District Court that Martin "easily endures greater fatigue even with a cart than his able-bodied competitors do by walking." The purpose of the walking rule is therefore not compromised in the slightest by allowing Martin to use a cart. A modification that provides an exception to a peripheral tournament rule without impairing its purpose cannot be said to "fundamentally alter" the tournament. What it can be said to do, on the other hand, is to allow Martin the chance to qualify for, and compete in, the athletic events petitioner offers to those members of the public who have the skill and desire to enter. That is exactly what the ADA requires. As a result, Martin's request for a waiver of the walking rule should have been granted.

The judgment of the Court of Appeals is affirmed.

Applying the ADA, the U.S. Supreme Court found that the professional golfer, Martin, was entitled to the right to use a golf cart in order to compete in golf tournaments because of his disability, a degenerative circulatory disorder that made it extremely painful and fatiguing for him to walk the golf course during a tournament. In addition, the Court found that the PGA Tour was an organization that was a place of "public accommodation" that fell within the requirements of the ADA and was required to not discriminate against members of the public who may seek to participate in the golf tournaments it offers. Use of a golf cart by Martin was found to satisfy the requirement.

In reaching its conclusion, the Court examined the nature of the right that Congress had granted and the goals it sought to achieve through the ADA: "to eliminate discrimination against disabled individuals, and to 'integrate them into the economic and social mainstream of American life.'" It was also necessary for the Court to discuss the requirements and rules of the game of golf in order to determine whether allowing Martin a golf cart would be a fundamental change in the central activity of the organization—sponsoring and operating golf tournaments. Because Martin was unable to participate in the activities of the PGA as a result of his disability under the rules of the organization, the ADA provided the mechanism for him to remedy the discrimination to which he was subjected.

Key Terms

Contracts	Damages
Offer	Property
Acceptance	Torts
Consideration	Negligence
Performance	Strict Liability
Parol Evidence Rule	Civil Rights

Discussion Questions

1. What are the primary areas of substantive civil law? What kinds of disputes do courts resolve in each of these areas?
2. What are the four elements of contract formation? Explain why each of these is necessary for the existence of a valid contract.
3. What is the parol evidence rule?
4. What is the difference between a present interest and a future interest in real property?
5. In what ways may property be owned?
6. How may tangible and intangible personal property be distinguished?
7. Tort law involves compensation for civil wrongs committed by another. In what ways is the law of torts similar and different from the criminal law?
8. What is the purpose of compensatory damages in tort cases? What purposes do punitive damages serve?
9. What is the basis for a civil rights claim?

Cases

Dr. Seuss Enterprises, L.P. v. Penguin Books USA, Inc., 109 F.3d 1394 (9th Cir. 1997).

Greenman v. Yuba Power Products, 59 Cal. 2d 57, 377 P.2d 897 (1963).

Hayden v. Notre Dame, 716 N.E.2d. 603 (Ind. Ct. App. 1999).

Metro-Goldwyn-Mayer Studios Inc. v. Grokster, Ltd., 545 U.S. 913, 125 S. Ct. 2764, 162 L.Ed.2d 781 (2005).

Morse v. Frederick, 551 U.S., 127 S. Ct. 2618, 168 L.Ed.2d 290 (2007).

PGA Tour, Inc. v. Martin, 532 U.S. 661, 121 S. Ct. 1879, 149 L.Ed.2d 904 (2001).

Criminal Justice on the Web

 For an up-to-date list of Web links, go to *The American Courts: A Procedural Approach* online companion site at http://criminal justice.jbpub.com/AmericanCourts. The online companion site will introduce you to some of the most important sites for finding American courts information on the Internet.

References

American Law Institute. (1981). *Restatement, Second, Contracts.* Philadelphia: American Law Institute.

American Law Institute. (1965). *Restatement, Second, Torts.* Philadelphia: American Law Institute.

Owen, D. G. (1993). The moral foundations of products liability law: Toward first principles. *Notre Dame Law Review, 68,* 427–464.

Slack, D., & Estes, A. (2008). Family to get $28m in Big Dig death. *The Boston Globe,* October 1.

Civil Procedure 10

What Is This Chapter About?

This chapter examines the rules of civil procedure and topics related to the process of pursuing a civil claim in the courts. Using the Federal Rules of Civil Procedure as a guide, we begin by considering the positions of plaintiffs and defendants as litigation is contemplated, who may be a party to a civil suit, and who may join the litigation.

In this chapter, we also discuss the forms and purposes of pleading. The chapter focuses on the contents of complaints, answers, and replies, as well as various motions that "test" the plaintiff's claims or the defendant's counterclaims.

The process of discovery is examined in some detail. This includes the use of interrogatories and requests for production of documents, as well as the use of requests for admissions. In addition, the purpose of depositions and the manner in which they are conducted are explored. The resolution of discovery disputes is also examined.

Rules governing the trial process are also a central focus of this chapter. The process of requesting and selecting a jury and creating a trial theme is discussed. The presentation of evidence and the use of subpoenas are considered, objections and trial motions examined, and jury instructions discussed. Posttrial matters, judgments, and appeals are also explored.

Learning Objectives

After reading this chapter, you should be able to

1. Understand how civil procedure relates to the substantive civil law.
2. Understand the purpose of pleading.
3. Explain the function and contents of a complaint and an answer.
4. Describe the types and purposes of pretrial motions.
5. Explain the methods and purposes of discovery.
6. Describe the functions of pretrial conferences.
7. Understand the types and purposes of trial motions.
8. Explain the relative roles of judge and jury.
9. Understand the basis for an appeal and the final judgment rule.

A large proportion of the caseload of the courts, state and federal, involves the resolution of civil disputes. The process through which such claims are resolved is governed by distinct rules that specify the way in which all aspects of the case are to proceed. *Civil procedure* refers to this process and the specific ways in which litigants must present their cases for resolution by a court. The methods available to litigants and their attorneys in accomplishing their goals by obtaining the relief they desire are therefore the subject of civil procedure.

Although the procedural civil law is distinct from the substantive civil law, it shares both statutory and case law sources. In addition, courts at each level develop rules that govern the flow of cases through the courts. Moreover, in some cases, the procedures themselves overshadow the original dispute and become the focus of the litigation or the subject of a subsequent appeal. As a result, the topic of civil procedure is not stagnant; rather, its application in a great variety of civil lawsuits results in the continuing development of the law of civil procedure and the effect of this form of law on court processes and the outcome of cases.

The goal of civil procedural rules is to provide a fair and just means of resolving disputes, while also creating an efficient method for processing cases. That is, when all parties to a dispute have a shared understanding of how the litigation will proceed and what the court will require in order to resolve it, the court proceeding will be fair to all parties in the sense that it does not create an advantage for one party over another. As stated in Rule 1 of the Federal Rules of Civil Procedure (FRCP), which have been adopted by the U.S. Supreme Court to govern civil procedure in the federal courts, the rules of civil procedure "should be construed and administered to secure the just, speedy, and inexpensive determination of every action and proceeding." This does not mean, however, that attorneys or their clients do not or should not use the procedural rules to their advantage. The American system of justice is an adversarial one. This means that the law, both substantive and procedural, may be used as both a sword and a shield because it governs the manner in which both sides of a case will proceed. The courts, the parties, and society itself therefore benefit from procedural rules by balancing fairness to the parties with the efficiencies that rules may create.

Generally, a civil lawsuit involves three categories of procedures: pleading, discovery, and trial processes. Each of these processes is necessary to resolve disputes that are brought before a court in a civil trial. The rules of civil procedures specify the requirements of each category as they develop in a civil lawsuit.

Pleading

The term "pleading" refers to documents that are filed with a court, but not just any document may be filed. Only those that comply with the local, state, or federal rules of civil procedure and that serve a particular purpose in accordance with those rules will be considered and acted on by the court. Thus, the form a pleading takes will have an effect on the progress of the litigation. Specifically, pleadings help to "frame" a lawsuit. That is, they specify what gave rise to the case and what the litigation will be about, the law that will help to resolve it, and the terms on which the parties believe it should be resolved.

A pleading may take one of many forms depending upon its purpose. The most basic and necessary pleadings are the civil Complaint and the Answer. These are prepared and filed by the plaintiff and the defendant, respectively, and allow each party to set forth initial positions with respect to the claims being made. This includes, to a limited extent in these initial pleadings, the facts and the law that comprise the case. Motions (and briefs in support of the motions) are pleadings that may be filed by either party in order to accomplish a specific goal. Because judges in civil lawsuits largely play a passive role in determining the legal claims presented, motions are used to ask the judge to take some action, based on the facts or the law or both.

The Complaint

A civil Complaint is a pleading that initiates a civil lawsuit. It states the legal basis for claims being made by the plaintiff and the facts to support those claims. FRCP Rule 8 states that a complaint need only contain "a short and plain statement of the claim showing that the pleader is entitled to relief." In order to be legally sufficient under FRCP Rule 8(a), the Complaint must accomplish three things: invoke the jurisdiction of the court by stating the basis for the court's jurisdiction, state the cause(s) of action or legal claims and how the elements of those claims are met on the basis of the facts, and request a remedy from the court. The Complaint usually sets forth its legal and factual allegations in separately numbered paragraphs; however, the federal courts and most state courts take a liberal approach to the manner in which a claim may be presented in a civil complaint, in accordance with the FRCP, or its parallel state rules. This means that a plaintiff need only indicate in some way the nature of claim and why that claim entitles him or her to some relief from the court. Tracing the history of this approach to pleading, Justice Stevens has explained the purpose of "notice" pleading:

> Rule 8 (a)(2) of the Federal Rules requires that a complaint contain "a short and plain statement of the claim

showing that the pleader is entitled to relief." The rule did not come about by happenstance and its language is not inadvertent. The English experience with Byzantine special pleading rules—illustrated by the hypertechnical Hilary rules of 1834—made obvious the appeal of a pleading standard that was easy for the common litigant to understand and sufficed to put the defendant on notice as to the nature of the claim against him and the relief sought. Stateside, David Dudley Field developed the highly influential New York Code of 1848, which required "[a] statement of the facts constituting the cause of action, in ordinary and concise language, without repetition, and in such a manner as to enable a person of common understanding to know what is intended." An Act to Simplify and Abridge the Practice, Pleadings and Proceedings of the Courts of this State, ch. 379, § 120(2), 1848 N.Y. Laws pp. 497, 521. Substantially similar language appeared in the Federal Equity Rules adopted in 1912. See Fed. Equity Rule 25 (requiring "a short and simple statement of the ultimate facts upon which the plaintiff asks relief, omitting any mere statement of evidence").

> A difficulty arose, however, in that the Field Code and its progeny required a plaintiff to plead "facts" rather than "conclusions," a distinction that proved far easier to say than to apply. As commentators have noted, it is virtually impossible logically to distinguish among 'ultimate facts,' 'evidence,' and 'conclusions.' Essentially any allegation in a pleading must be an assertion that certain occurrences took place. The pleading spectrum, passing from evidence through ultimate facts to conclusions, is largely a continuum varying only in the degree of particularity with which the occurrences are described. Weinstein & Distler, Comments on Procedural Reform: Drafting Pleading Rules, 57 Colum. L.Rev. 518, 520–521 (1957).

> Rule 8 was directly responsive to this difficulty. Its drafters intentionally avoided any reference to "facts" or "evidence" or "conclusions."

> Under the relaxed pleading standards of the Federal Rules, the idea was not to keep litigants out of court but rather to keep them in. The merits of a claim would be sorted out during a flexible pretrial process and, as appropriate, through the crucible of trial. Charles E. Clark, the "principal draftsman" of the Federal Rules, put it thus:

> Experience has shown . . . that we cannot expect the proof of the case to be made through the pleadings, and that such proof is really not their function. We can expect a general statement distinguishing the case from all others, so that the manner and form of trial and remedy expected are clear, and so that a permanent judgment will result. The New Federal Rules of Civil Procedure: The Last Phase-Underlying Philosophy Embodied in Some of the Basic Provisions of the New Procedure, 23 A.B.A.J. 976, 977 (1937).

Bell Atlantic v. Twombly, 550 U.S. 544, 127 S. Ct. 1955, 167 L.Ed.2d 929 (2007) (Stevens, J., dissenting).

The pleading requirements found in the federal rules were also discussed by the U.S. Supreme Court in *Swierkiewicz v. Sorema*, 534 U.S. 506, 122 S. Ct. 992, 152 L.Ed.2d 1 (2002). *Swierkiewicz* involved an employment discrimination claim made after a 53-year-old Polish worker was fired and his responsibilities were given to a 32-year-old Frenchman. The complaint was dismissed because the plaintiff had not "adequately alleged circumstances that support an inference of discrimination." The trial court and the court of appeals found that the complaint did not allege discrimination with enough specificity; that is, there were insufficient alleged facts in the complaint to show that the elements of a discrimination claim could be met. The Supreme Court, interpreting the liberal pleading requirements found in FRCP Rule 8, reversed the court of appeals, reinstating the complaint. The opinion is found in **Case Decision 10.1**.

As discussed in the *Swierkiewicz* case, the FRCP take a liberal approach to pleading referred to as *notice pleading*; the purpose of the Complaint is to place the defendant on notice of the claim against him, and the plaintiff need only provide some indication of the basis for the claim.

Jurisdiction and Venue

The importance and types of jurisdiction and the concept of venue were discussed in Chapter 2. Jurisdiction refers to the power of a court to hear and act on a matter, and venue refers to the place in which it should be heard. Thus, the complaint must state the basis for the court's authority in order for the court to proceed with the case. In addition, the Complaint will indicate why the case should be heard in the court in which the case was filed. For example, in a case involving injuries from a car accident, the plaintiff would state that the accident occurred in the state or county in which the court sits. Any actions taken by the court in a case in which it had no jurisdiction would not be valid, and thus, the Complaint at the outset shows why the case should be heard in that court.

Case Decision 10.1   *Swierkiewicz v. Sorema*, 534 U.S. 506, 122 S. Ct. 992, 152 L.Ed.2d 1 (2002)

Opinion of the Court by Justice Thomas:

This case presents the question whether a complaint in an employment discrimination lawsuit must contain specific facts establishing a prima facie case of discrimination under the framework set forth by this Court in *McDonnell Douglas Corp. v. Green*, 411 U.S. 792, 93 S. Ct. 1817, 36 L.Ed.2d 668 (1973). We hold that an employment discrimination complaint need not include such facts and instead must contain only "a short and plain statement of the claim showing that the pleader is entitled to relief." Fed. Rule Civ. Proc. 8(a)(2).

I

Petitioner Akos Swierkiewicz is a native of Hungary, who at the time of his complaint was 53 years old. In April 1989, petitioner began working for respondent Sorema N. A., a reinsurance company headquartered in New York and principally owned and controlled by a French parent corporation. Petitioner was initially employed in the position of senior vice president and chief underwriting officer (CUO). Nearly six years later, François M. Chavel, respondent's Chief Executive Officer, demoted petitioner to a marketing and services position and transferred the bulk of his underwriting responsibilities to Nicholas Papadopoulo, a 32-year-old who, like Mr. Chavel, is a French national. About a year later, Mr. Chavel stated that he wanted to "energize" the underwriting department and appointed Mr. Papadopoulo as CUO. Petitioner claims that Mr. Papadopoulo had only one year of underwriting experience at the time he was promoted, and therefore was less experienced and less qualified to be CUO than he, since at that point he had 26 years of experience in the insurance industry.

Following his demotion, petitioner contends that he "was isolated by Mr. Chavel . . . excluded from business decisions and meetings and denied the opportunity to reach his true potential at SOREMA." Petitioner unsuccessfully attempted to meet with Mr. Chavel to discuss his discontent. Finally, in April 1997, petitioner sent a memo to Mr. Chavel outlining his grievances and requesting a severance package. Two weeks later, respondent's general counsel presented petitioner with two options: He could either resign without a severance package or be dismissed. Mr. Chavel fired petitioner after he refused to resign.

Petitioner filed a lawsuit alleging that he had been terminated on account of his national origin in violation of Title VII of the Civil Rights Act of 1964, and on account of his age in violation of the Age Discrimination in Employment Act of 1967 (ADEA). The United States District Court for the Southern District of New York dismissed petitioner's complaint because it found that he "ha[d] not adequately alleged a prima facie case, in that he ha[d] not adequately alleged circumstances that support an inference of discrimination." The United States Court of Appeals for the Second Circuit affirmed the dismissal, relying on its settled precedent, which requires a plaintiff in an employment discrimination complaint to allege facts constituting a prima facie case of discrimination under the

(Continues)

---

framework set forth by this Court in *McDonnell Douglas*. The Court of Appeals held that petitioner had failed to meet his burden because his allegations were "insufficient as a matter of law to raise an inference of discrimination." We granted certiorari to resolve a split among the Courts of Appeals concerning the proper pleading standard for employment discrimination cases. The majority of Courts of Appeals have held that a plaintiff need not plead a prima facie case of discrimination under *McDonnell Douglas* in order to survive a motion to dismiss. Others, however, maintain that a complaint must contain factual allegations that support each element of a prima facie case. [We] now reverse.

II

Applying Circuit precedent, the Court of Appeals required petitioner to plead a prima facie case of discrimination in order to survive respondent's motion to dismiss. In the Court of Appeals' view, petitioner was thus required to allege in his complaint: (1) membership in a protected group; (2) qualification for the job in question; (3) an adverse employment action; and (4) circumstances that support an inference of discrimination.

The prima facie case under *McDonnell Douglas*, however, is an evidentiary standard, not a pleading requirement. In *McDonnell Douglas*, this Court made clear that "[t]he critical issue before us concern[ed] the order and allocation *of proof* in a private, non-class action challenging employment discrimination" (emphasis added). In subsequent cases, this Court has reiterated that the prima facie case relates to the employee's burden of presenting evidence that raises an inference of discrimination.

This Court has never indicated that the requirements for establishing a prima facie case under *McDonnell Douglas* also apply to the pleading standard that plaintiffs must satisfy in order to survive a motion to dismiss. For instance, we have rejected the argument that a Title VII complaint requires greater "particularity," because this would "too narrowly constric[t] the role of the pleadings." Consequently, the ordinary rules for assessing the sufficiency of a complaint apply. "When a federal court reviews the sufficiency of a complaint, before the reception of any evidence either by affidavit or admissions, its task is necessarily a limited one. The issue is not whether a plaintiff will ultimately prevail but whether the claimant is entitled to offer evidence to support the claims."

In addition, under a notice pleading system, it is not appropriate to require a plaintiff to plead facts establishing a prima facie case because the *McDonnell Douglas* framework does not apply in every employment discrimination case. For instance, if a plaintiff is able to produce direct evidence of discrimination, he may prevail without proving all the elements of a prima facie case. Under the Second Circuit's heightened pleading standard, a plaintiff without direct evidence of discrimination at the time of his complaint must plead a prima facie case of discrimination, even though discovery might uncover such direct evidence. It thus seems incongruous to require a plaintiff, in order to survive a motion to dismiss, to plead more facts than he may ultimately need to prove to succeed on the merits if direct evidence of discrimination is discovered.

Moreover, the precise requirements of a prima facie case can vary depending on the context and were "never intended to be rigid, mechanized, or ritualistic." Before discovery has unearthed relevant facts and evidence, it may be difficult to define the precise formulation of the required prima facie case in a particular case. Given that the prima facie case operates as a flexible evidentiary standard, it should not be transposed into a rigid pleading standard for discrimination cases.

Furthermore, imposing the Court of Appeals' heightened pleading standard in employment discrimination cases conflicts with Federal Rule of Civil Procedure 8(a)(2), which provides that a complaint must include only "a short and plain statement of the claim showing that the pleader is entitled to relief." Such a statement must simply "give the defendant fair notice of what the plaintiff's claim is and the grounds upon which it rests." This simplified notice pleading standard relies on liberal discovery rules and summary judgment motions to define disputed facts and issues and to dispose of unmeritorious claims. "The provisions for discovery are so flexible and the provisions for pretrial procedure and summary judgment so effective, that attempted surprise in federal practice is aborted very easily, synthetic issues detected, and the gravamen of the dispute brought frankly into the open for the inspection of the court." 5 C. Wright & A. Miller, Federal Practice and Procedure § 1202, p. 76 (2d ed. 1990).

Rule 8(a)'s simplified pleading standard applies to all civil actions, with limited exceptions. Rule 9(b), for example, provides for greater particularity in all averments of fraud or mistake. This Court, however, has declined to extend such exceptions to other contexts. Thus, complaints in these cases, as in most others, must satisfy only the simple requirements of Rule 8(a). These requirements are exemplified by the Federal Rules of Civil Procedure Forms, which "are sufficient under the rules and are intended to indicate the simplicity and brevity of statement which the rules contemplate." Fed. Rule Civ. Proc. 84. For example, Form 9 sets forth a complaint for negligence in which plaintiff simply states in relevant part: "On June 1, 1936, in a public highway called Boylston Street in Boston, Massachusetts, defendant negligently drove a motor vehicle against plaintiff who was then crossing said highway."

Other provisions of the Federal Rules of Civil Procedure are inextricably linked to Rule 8(a)'s simplified notice pleading standard. Rule 8(e)(1) states that "[n]o technical forms of pleading or motions are required," and Rule 8(f) provides that "[a]ll pleadings shall be so construed as to do substantial justice." Given the Federal Rules' simplified standard for pleading, "[a] court may dismiss a complaint only if it is clear that no relief could be granted under any set of facts that could be proved consistent with the allegations." If a pleading fails to specify the allegations in a manner that provides sufficient notice, a defendant can move for a more definite statement under Rule 12(e) before responding. Moreover, claims lacking merit may be dealt with through summary judgment under Rule 56. The liberal notice pleading of Rule 8(a) is the starting point of a simplified pleading system, which was adopted to focus litigation on the merits of a claim. "The Federal Rules reject the approach that pleading is a game of skill in which one misstep by counsel may be decisive to the outcome and accept the principle that the purpose of pleading is to facilitate a proper decision on the merits."

Applying the relevant standard, petitioner's complaint easily satisfies the requirements of Rule 8(a) because it gives respondent fair notice of the basis for petitioner's claims. Petitioner alleged that he had been terminated on account of his national origin in violation of Title VII and on account of his age in violation of the ADEA. His complaint detailed the events leading to his termination, provided relevant dates, and included the ages and nationalities of at least some of the relevant persons involved with his termination. These allegations give respondent fair notice of what petitioner's claims are and the grounds upon which they rest. In addition, they state claims upon which relief could be granted under Title VII and the ADEA.

Respondent argues that allowing lawsuits based on conclusory allegations of discrimination to go forward will burden the courts and encourage disgruntled employees to bring unsubstantiated suits. Whatever the practical merits of this argument, the Federal Rules do not contain a heightened pleading standard for employment discrimination suits. A requirement of greater specificity for particular claims is a result that "must be obtained by the process of amending the Federal Rules, and not by judicial interpretation." Furthermore, Rule 8(a) establishes a pleading standard without regard to whether a claim will succeed on the merits. "Indeed it may appear on the face of the pleadings that a recovery is very remote and unlikely but that is not the test."

For the foregoing reasons, we hold that an employment discrimination plaintiff need not plead a prima facie case of discrimination and that petitioner's complaint is sufficient to survive respondent's motion to dismiss. Accordingly, the judgment of the Court of Appeals is reversed, and the case is remanded for further proceedings consistent with this opinion.

Cause of Action

The purpose of the complaint is to allege a *cause of action* and give the defendant notice of it. A cause of action is the factual and legal basis for a plaintiff's claim. Nothing has been proven at the time the Complaint is filed; it merely makes allegations as to what the plaintiff believes to be true and will later set out to prove at trial. Thus, the cause of action states a legal claim based on a statute or the common law, summarizes the elements required to prove the claim, and alleges facts that, if proven, would support each claim. For example, in a Complaint for personal injury resulting from a driver's negligence, a plaintiff's cause of action might state that the driver had a duty to maintain control of his vehicle at all times, that he breached that duty by losing control of his vehicle and hitting the plaintiff's vehicle from behind, and that this breach of duty

caused injuries and property damage to the plaintiff. Although there is no specific language necessary under the liberal pleading rules as mentioned previously, the Complaint must prove a sufficiently clear statement of the cause of action for the defendant (and the court) to understand the basis for the Complaint.

Request for Relief

The Complaint must also make a *request for relief*. That is, what is the plaintiff asking the court to do? Historically, the remedy that a court could grant was dependent on whether it was a *court of law* or a *court of equity*. Cases in courts of law were heard by judges or juries and could award money damages. Cases in courts of equity were heard only by judges, who could fashion remedies as justice required, including injunctive relief, restitution, and the issuance of other orders that the judge deemed to be just. In America, the distinction between courts of law and courts of equity no longer exists, and judges may grant both legal and equitable remedies.

Most often, civil Complaints request monetary damages—either a specific amount or an "amount to be proven at trial." The judge is not bound to grant (or not grant) the relief requested, but may make whatever award is consistent with the evidence. As a result, the plaintiff also often includes a request for "such relief as the court deems just and proper."

The Answer

An *Answer* in a civil case refers to a pleading filed by the defendant. In it, the defendant responds to the allegations made by the plaintiff, in effect refuting the claims made in the Complaint. The defendant may respond in several ways to the allegations of the Complaint. The defendant may make a general denial of all allegations, may specifically deny each allegation, may claim an *affirmative defense*, or may admit an allegation. If a defendant has insufficient basis to either admit or deny an allegation, it may be denied on the basis of that insufficient knowledge. An affirmative defense is one that raises additional facts or legal arguments to refute allegations found in the Complaint. A common example of an affirmative defense is reliance on a *statute of limitations* by the defendant. A statute of limitations is a statutory provision that requires that a particular type of legal claim be raised within a certain amount of time in order to proceed in court. The defendant may raise as an affirmative defense the time limits shown in the statutory provision and facts showing that the plaintiff failed to file the Complaint within the allotted time. Affirmative defenses are important for at least two practical reasons (and many strategic reasons): They may result in dismissal of all or part of the claims made by the plaintiff, and if an affirmative defense is not raised in the Answer, it is usually waived, which means that it may not be raised at a later time.

The Answer is an important pleading for a number of reasons. First, if no Answer to a Complaint is filed, the allegations of the Complaint are taken by the court as true and a default judgment is entered. A default judgment is an order from the court in favor of the plaintiff, granting the relief requested by the plaintiff or whatever relief the judge believes to be just. Second, admissions and denials in the Answer help to limit and define the issues for trial. Only those facts denied by the defendant need be proven by the plaintiff at trial, and only the affirmative defenses will be issues to be proven by the defendant at trial. Third, the Answer provides a defendant with the opportunity to assert a *counterclaim*. A counterclaim is a defendant's request for relief from the court that is independent of that requested by the plaintiff, though related to the factual allegations of the Complaint. That is, a counterclaim is a response to the plaintiff's Complaint that it is the defendant who has been harmed by the plaintiff, not the other way around, and the court should award damages to the defendant. For example, if a plaintiff's Complaint asserts that a defendant has breached a contract by not making a

scheduled payment for a piece of equipment, the defendant may make a counterclaim alleging that the equipment was defective and inoperable.

Motions Attacking the Pleadings (Rule 12 Motions)

A *motion* is a request by a party for a ruling by the judge on a particular issue. In most jurisdictions, the motion must be accompanied by a brief explaining the basis for the motion and legal argument to support it. Motions may be made prior to trial, during trial, or after trial, but most are pretrial motions. Motions that attack the pleadings do just that: seek to obtain a ruling from the court that either the Complaint or the Answer are insufficient and that the pleading deficiency must be remedied. In the FRCP and its state counterparts, Rule 12 governs a variety of defensive motions on the pleadings. These include motions relating to improper jurisdiction and venue, the sufficiency of the form or manner in which a pleading is served, and a number of motions relating to specific substance of the allegations of a Complaint or defenses raised in an Answer. Most common among the Rule 12 motions are a Motion to Dismiss (Rule 12b), a Motion for a More Definite Statement (Rule 12e), and a Motion to Strike (Rule 12f).

A Motion to Dismiss, often referred to as a Rule 12b(6) motion, challenges the allegations made in the plaintiff's Complaint by arguing that, even if those allegations are true, the plaintiff is not entitled to relief. When considering a Motion to Dismiss, a court will accept all of the factual allegations of the complaint as true, and if the complaint's allegations do not allow recovery under the law, it must be dismissed. *Leatherman v. Tarrant County Narcotics Intelligence and Coordination Unit*, 507 U.S. 163, 113 S. Ct. 1160, 122 L.Ed.2d 517 (1993). That is, the law does not allow recovery to the plaintiff based on the facts alleged. In other words, the defendant argues that the plaintiff has failed to state a cause of action in the Complaint. A Motion to Dismiss may be directed at all of the allegations of the Complaint or may attempt to dismiss only certain claims.

A Motion for a More Definite Statement and a Motion to Strike are both addressed toward specific allegations of the Complaint or defenses raised in the Answer. The former asks the court to order the opposing party to clarify a portion of the pleading that is ambiguous or uncertain as to the claim or defense being raised. The latter seeks to have a portion of the questioned pleading removed because it is redundant, unnecessary, inflammatory, or otherwise inappropriate. Given that the purpose of the pleadings is to provide notice to the opposing party and to narrow the issues for trial, these motions allow the party raising them to more clearly understand the legal and factual issues being raised.

Discovery

Discovery is intended as a process of investigation and development of the evidence to be presented at trial. It allows the parties to "discover" in more detail the legal arguments and positions of the opposing party and the evidence that may be relevant to support those positions. In addition to revealing potential evidence to support the facts for trial, discovery allows the parties to preserve evidence that may no longer be available at the time of trial. Discovery also allows the parties to "capture" the testimony of witnesses so that it does not change at trial, either due to loss of memory or intentional fabrication or perjury.

In order to streamline the discovery process by saving time, cost, and reducing the potential for disputes about discovery, the federal courts and some state courts require mandatory disclosure of certain types of information in civil cases (Moskowitz, 2007). Except in certain types of cases specified by the rules, Rule 26 of the FRCP requires each party initially to provide the other with information that the disclosing party may use at trial, including (1) the names of individuals who "likely have discoverable information," (2) a copy or description of documents or tangible things in the party's possession, (3) a computation of the damages claimed by the disclosing party and documents relating to them, and (4) any insurance agreement that may apply to the payment of damages. In addition to these initial mandatory disclosures, each party must also subsequently provide the other with the names of expert witnesses and a report summarizing their opinions, as well as a list of witnesses and exhibits that will be introduced at trial. Although these mandatory disclosures should provide each party with considerable evidence that may be relevant at trial, there are many limitations on what constitutes "discoverable information," including *privileged* documents and materials such as notes from meetings with a party's attorney or documents prepared by an attorney in the case.

In addition to mandatory disclosures (or in jurisdictions that do not require disclosures), several discovery tools may be used to request and obtain information from an opposing party. Three such tools are most commonly used: interrogatories, requests for productions of documents, and depositions.

Interrogatories

Interrogatories are written questions that are formally served on a party who must respond within a time period specified in procedural rules, usually 30 days. Answers to the interrogatories must be given under oath. The questions may ask about any matter relevant to the case, but may not be served in order to burden or harass a party. Nonetheless, a party must respond to interrogatories that pertain to information it possesses, even if it requires review of documents, materials, or other sources of information. Many states place a restriction on the number of interrogatories that may be asked, and the federal rules limit the number to 25.

The purpose of interrogatories is to help educate the serving party about the facts in the case, at least facts in the possession of or from the perspective of the opposing party. For example, a hospital in a medical malpractice case might ask the plaintiff: "State the full and complete basis for your allegations in paragraph 12 of the Complaint that Dr. Smith's actions fell below the standard of care of other physicians within the community." The interrogatories thus serve the purpose of obtaining initial information from a party about his or her position in the case. They are discovery devices that allow a party to place the opposing party on record (as the answers are given under oath), and they provide an outline from which follow up information can later be obtained.

Requests for Production of Documents

Like interrogatories, *Requests for Production of Documents* are a discovery tool that seeks to obtain information in the possession of an opposing party, but a particular type of information: documents. These requests require the opposing party to provide to the requesting party relevant documents within the opposing party's possession. The "documents" requested may also include tangible things that may be relevant to determining the facts in a case. For example, in a car accident case, a request may be made to view the wrecked vehicle in order to determine how the accident occurred. The types of documents requested may be broad, but a party has no obligation to produce documents that are outside of its control.

The review of documents in civil cases can be very valuable. Although interrogatories may require a party to review its own documents in order to craft an answer, an opposing party's own review of those same documents may lead to different conclusions, or it may lead to other discoverable information. In complex litigation, document review may involve millions of documents, including electronically stored information and e-mails, and take considerable time and resources.

Depositions

A *deposition* is a proceeding in which a party or a witness is questioned in person under oath. A court reporter records and prepares a transcript of the testimony, which preserves in writing (and sometimes by video) the questions asked and the deponent's answers. A deposition is an important tool for ascertaining before trial the testimony that a witness will give at trial. A party may also be required to be deposed, although not required to testify at trial. As in a trial, a witness may be examined and cross-examined at a deposition, and the witnesses' testimony from the deposition transcript may later be used at trial for purposes of impeachment. Because deposition testimony is taken live under oath and is subject to cross-examination, it may also be introduced at trial when a witness is unavailable because of death or distance from the venue in which the trial is held.

Despite their usefulness in trial preparation, depositions may elicit more information before trial than may be useful. Specifically, when a witness has had opportunity to "rehearse" testimony at a deposition and review it before trial, the opportunity to later explain inconsistencies or inaccuracies at trial exists. In addition, the cost of depositions makes them the most expensive discovery tool. The costs stem from the fees for the time of all attorneys in the case, the cost of travel to and from depositions, and the cost of stenographic and transcription services.

Requests for Admissions

One way in which to limit issues for trial involves the use of *Requests for Admission*. This discovery method requests that the opposing party admit the truth of certain facts in a case. In addition to facts, Requests for Admission may relate to the applicability of the law or relate to the genuineness of documents or other evidence. Facts that are admitted need not be tried, which saves time and usually cost because evidence need not be presented at trial relating to those facts. Requests for Admission are governed by FRCP Rule 36 and its state counterparts.

A procedural and strategic reason for the use of Requests for Admissions involves sanctions provided by the rules for a party's failure to admit facts that are true. In particular, FRCP Rule 37(c)(2) states, "If a party fails to admit what is requested under Rule 36 and if the requesting party later proves a document to be genuine or the matter true, the requesting party may move that the party who failed to admit pay the reasonable expenses, including attorney's fees, incurred in making that proof." Although a party need not pay such expenses if the party has a reasonable belief that the matter may not be proven at trial, a party nonetheless has an incentive to admit facts it thinks might be true.

Discovery Disputes

Despite the liberal approach to the discovery of information taken by the federal and most state courts, given the adversarial nature of the justice system, parties do not always agree on the disclosure of information. Parties frequently object to all or part of a discovery request and may engage in informal negotiations regarding the objectionable nature of an interrogatory or document request. If the parties are unable to agree, they will request that the judge intervene and settle the dispute. This most often occurs when a *motion to compel discovery* is filed by one of the parties. This is a motion that explains why the informa-

tion is discoverable and should not be withheld and asks the judge to compel the nonmoving party to provide the information requested. The judge may then order the nonresponsive party to provide the information requested or may enter a *protective order*, which prevents disclosure of certain information or inquiry into certain topics during the course of discovery.

At times, parties or their attorneys delay responding to discovery requests, provide limited or incomplete information, or refuse to provide discoverable information at all. When this occurs, attorneys may be subjected to sanctions, usually fines or the costs of proceedings, for obstructing the discovery process. One such case, *Cunningham v. Hamilton County, Ohio*, 527 U.S. 198, 119 S. Ct. 1915, 144 L.Ed.2d 184 (1999), involved the failure of an attorney to participate in discovery despite a judge's order to do so. Moreover, she filed notices of deposition for witnesses she was ordered not to depose until she had fully complied with other discovery requests. She scheduled them on days other than those ordered by the court, and she filed a motion to compel the witnesses' attendance at the depositions. The opposing attorneys filed motions for sanctions for these discovery violations and refusal to obey a court order, which the judge granted, ordering the sanctioned attorney to pay $1,494 in costs and fees. The attorney was later removed from the case but filed an appeal of the order of sanctions. Although the issue in that case was whether an order for discovery sanctions is a final order that may be immediately appealed (the U.S. Supreme Court held that it was not), the case is also important because the Court found the determination of discovery sanctions to be "inextricably intertwined with the merits." Given the importance of discovery in addressing the merits of a case, the Court found that the sanctions order was not a "final order" entitled to an immediate appeal. Questions relating to appellate procedures discussed in this case are examined further later (**Case Decision 10.2**).

Case Decision 10.2 *Cunningham v. Hamilton County, Ohio*, 527 U.S. 198, 119 S. Ct. 1915, 144 L.Ed.2d 184 (1999)

Opinion of the Court by Justice Thomas:

Federal courts of appeals ordinarily have jurisdiction over appeals from "final decisions of the district courts." 28 U.S.C. § 1291. This case presents the question whether an order imposing sanctions on an attorney pursuant to Federal Rule of Civil Procedure 37(a)(4) is a final decision. We hold that it is not, even where, as here, the attorney no longer represents a party in the case.

I

Petitioner, an attorney, represented Darwin Lee Starcher in a federal civil rights suit filed against respondent and other defendants. Starcher brought the suit after his son, Casey, committed suicide while an inmate at the Hamilton County Justice Center. The theory of the original complaint was that the defendants willfully ignored their duty to care for Casey despite his known history of suicide attempts.

A Magistrate Judge oversaw discovery. On May 29, 1996, petitioner was served with a request for interrogatories and documents; responses were due within 30 days after service. See Fed. Rules Civ.

Proc. 33(b)(3), 34(b). This deadline, however, passed without compliance. The Magistrate Judge ordered the plaintiff "by 4:00 p.m. on July 12, 1996 to make full and complete responses" to defendants' requests for interrogatories and documents and further ordered that four witnesses—Rex Smith, Roxanne Dieffenbach, and two individual defendants—be deposed on July 25, 1996.

Petitioner failed to heed the Magistrate Judge's commands. She did not produce the requested documents, gave incomplete responses to several of the interrogatories, and objected to several others. Flouting the Magistrate Judge's order, she noticed the deposition of Rex Smith on July 22, 1996, not July 25, and then refused to withdraw this notice despite reminders from defendants' counsel. And even though the Magistrate Judge had specified that the individual defendants were to be deposed only if plaintiff had complied with his order to produce "full and complete" responses, she filed a motion to compel their appearance. Respondent and other defendants then filed motions for sanctions against petitioner.

At a July 19 hearing, the Magistrate Judge granted the defendants' motions for sanctions. In a subsequent order, he found that petitioner had violated the discovery order and described her conduct as "egregious." Relying on Federal Rule of Civil Procedure 37(a)(4), the Magistrate Judge ordered petitioner to pay the Hamilton County treasurer $1,494, representing costs and fees incurred by the Hamilton County prosecuting attorney as counsel for respondent and one individual defendant. He took care to specify, however, that he had not held a contempt hearing and that petitioner was never found to be in contempt of court.

The District Court affirmed the Magistrate Judge's sanctions order. The court noted that the matter "ha[d] already consumed an inordinate amount of the Court's time" and described the Magistrate's job of overseeing discovery as a "task assum[ing] the qualities of a full time occupation." It found that "[t]he Magistrate Judge did not err in concluding that sanctions were appropriate" and that "the amount of the Magistrate Judge's award was not contrary to law." The District Court also granted several defendants' motions to disqualify petitioner as counsel for plaintiff due to the fact that she was a material witness in the case.

Although proceedings in the District Court were ongoing, petitioner immediately appealed the District Court's order affirming the Magistrate Judge's sanctions award to the United States Court of Appeals for the Sixth Circuit. The Court of Appeals, over a dissent, dismissed the appeal for lack of jurisdiction. It considered whether the sanctions order was immediately appealable under the collateral order doctrine, which provides that certain orders may be appealed, notwithstanding the absence of final judgment, but only when they "are conclusive, . . . resolve important questions separate from the merits, and . . . are effectively unreviewable on appeal from the final judgment in the underlying action." In the Sixth Circuit's view, these conditions were not satisfied because the issues involved in petitioner's appeal were not "completely separate" from the merits. As for the fact that petitioner had been disqualified as counsel, the court held that "a non-participating attorney, like a participating attorney, ordinarily must wait until final disposition of the underlying case before filing an appeal." It avoided deciding whether the order was effectively unreviewable absent an immediate appeal but saw "no reason why, after final resolution of the underlying case . . . a sanctioned attorney should be unable to appeal the order imposing sanctions."

The Federal Courts of Appeals disagree over whether an order of Rule 37(a) sanctions against an attorney is immediately appealable under § 1291. We granted a writ of certiorari, limited to this question, and now affirm.

II

Section 1291 of the Judicial Code generally vests courts of appeals with jurisdiction over appeals from "final decisions" of the district courts. It descends from the Judiciary Act of 1789, where "the First Congress established the principle that only 'final judgments and decrees' of the federal district courts may be reviewed on appeal." In accord with this historical understanding, we have repeatedly interpreted § 1291 to mean that an appeal ordinarily will not lie until after final judgment has been entered in a case. As we explained in *Firestone Tire & Rubber Co. v. Risjord*, 449 U.S. 368, 101 S. Ct. 669, 66 L.Ed.2d 571 (1981), the final judgment rule serves several salutary purposes:

> It emphasizes the deference that appellate courts owe to the trial judge as the individual initially called upon to decide the many questions of law and fact that occur in the course of a trial. Permitting piecemeal appeals would undermine the independence of the district judge, as well as the special role that individual

(Continues)

(Continued)

plays in our judicial system. In addition, the rule is in accordance with the sensible policy of avoid[ing] the obstruction to just claims that would come from permitting the harassment and cost of a succession of separate appeals from the various rulings to which a litigation may give rise, from its initiation to entry of judgment. The rule also serves the important purpose of promoting efficient judicial administration.

Consistent with these purposes, we have held that a decision is not final, ordinarily, unless it "ends the litigation on the merits and leaves nothing for the court to do but execute the judgment."

The Rule 37 sanction imposed on petitioner neither ended the litigation nor left the court only to execute its judgment. Thus, it ordinarily would not be considered a final decision under § 1291. However, we have interpreted the term "final decision" in § 1291 to permit jurisdiction over appeals from a small category of orders that do not terminate the litigation. "That small category includes only decisions that are conclusive, that resolve important questions separate from the merits, and that are effectively unreviewable on appeal from the final judgment in the underlying action."

Respondent conceded that the sanctions order was conclusive, so at least one of the collateral order doctrine's conditions is presumed to have been satisfied. We do not think, however, that appellate review of a sanctions order can remain completely separate from the merits. [A] Rule 37(a) sanctions order often will be inextricably intertwined with the merits of the action. An evaluation of the appropriateness of sanctions may require the reviewing court to inquire into the importance of the information sought or the adequacy or truthfulness of a response. Some of the sanctions in this case were based on the fact that petitioner provided partial responses and objections to some of the defendants' discovery requests. To evaluate whether those sanctions were appropriate, an appellate court would have to assess the completeness of petitioner's responses. See Fed. Rule Civ. Proc. 37(a)(3) ("For purposes of this subdivision an evasive or incomplete disclosure, answer, or response is to be treated as a failure to disclose, answer, or respond"). Such an inquiry would differ only marginally from an inquiry into the merits and counsels against application of the collateral order doctrine. Perhaps not every discovery sanction will be inextricably intertwined with the merits, but we have consistently eschewed a case-by-case approach to deciding whether an order is sufficiently collateral.

Even if the merits were completely divorced from the sanctions issue, the collateral order doctrine requires that the order be effectively unreviewable on appeal from a final judgment. Petitioner claims that this is the case. In support, she relies on a line of decisions holding that one who is not a party to a judgment generally may not appeal from it. She also posits that contempt orders imposed on witnesses who disobey discovery orders are immediately appealable and argues that the sanctions order in this case should be treated no differently.

Petitioner's argument suffers from at least two flaws. It ignores the identity of interests between the attorney and client. Unlike witnesses, whose interests may differ substantially from the parties', attorneys assume an ethical obligation to serve their clients' interests. This obligation remains even where the attorney might have a personal interest in seeking vindication from the sanctions order. The effective congruence of interests between clients and attorneys counsels against treating attorneys like other nonparties for purposes of appeal.

Petitioner's argument also overlooks the significant differences between a finding of contempt and a Rule 37(a) sanctions order. "Civil contempt is designed to force the contemnor to comply with an order of the court." In contrast, a Rule 37(a) sanctions order lacks any prospective effect and is not designed to compel compliance. Judge Adams captured the essential distinction between the two types of orders when he noted that an order such as civil contempt

is not simply to deter harassment and delay, but to effect some discovery conduct. A non-party's interest in resisting a discovery order is immediate and usually separate from the parties' interests in delay. Before final judgment is reached, the non-party either will have surrendered the materials sought or will have suffered incarceration or steadily mounting fines imposed to compel the discovery. If the discovery is held unwarranted on appeal only after the case is resolved, the non-party's injury may not be possible to repair. Under Rule 37(a), no similar situation exists. The objective of the Rule is the prevention of delay and costs to other litigants caused by the filing of groundless motions. An attorney sanctioned for such conduct by and large suffers no inordinate injury from a deferral of appellate consideration of the sanction. He need not in the meantime surrender any rights or suffer undue coercion.

To permit an immediate appeal from such a sanctions order would undermine the very purposes of Rule 37(a), which was designed to protect courts and opposing parties from delaying or harassing tactics during the discovery process. Immediate appeals of such orders would undermine trial judges' discretion to structure a sanction in the most effective manner. They might choose not to sanction an attorney, despite abusive conduct, in order to avoid further delays in their proceedings. Not only would such an approach ignore the deference owed by appellate courts to trial judges charged with managing the discovery process, it also could forestall resolution of the case as each new sanction would give rise to a new appeal. The result might well be the very sorts of piecemeal appeals and concomitant delays that the final judgment rule was designed to prevent.

Petitioner finally argues that, even if an attorney ordinarily may not immediately appeal a sanction order, special considerations apply when the attorney no longer represents a party in the case. Like the Sixth Circuit, we do not think that the appealability of a Rule 37 sanction imposed on an attorney should turn on the attorney's continued participation. Such a rule could not be easily administered. For example, it may be unclear precisely when representation terminates, and questions likely would arise over when the 30-day period for appeal would begin to run. The rule also could be subject to abuse if attorneys and clients strategically terminated their representation in order to trigger a right to appeal with a view to delaying the proceedings in the underlying case. While we recognize that our application of the final judgment rule in this setting may require nonparticipating attorneys to monitor the progress of the litigation after their work has ended, the efficiency interests served by limiting immediate appeals far outweigh any nominal monitoring costs borne by attorneys. For these reasons, an attorney's continued participation in a case does not affect whether a sanctions order is "final" for purposes of § 1291.

We candidly recognize the hardship that a sanctions order may sometimes impose on an attorney. Should these hardships be deemed to outweigh the desirability of restricting appeals to "final decisions," solutions other than an expansive interpretation of § 1291's "final decision" requirement remain available. Congress may amend the Judicial Code to provide explicitly for immediate appellate review of such orders. Recent amendments to the Judicial Code also have authorized this Court to prescribe rules providing for the immediate appeal of certain orders, and "Congress' designation of the rulemaking process as the way to define or refine when a district court ruling is 'final' and when an interlocutory order is appealable warrants the Judiciary's full respect." Finally, in a particular case, a district court can reduce any hardship by reserving until the end of the trial decisions such as whether to impose the sanction, how great a sanction to impose, or when to order collection.

For the foregoing reasons, we conclude that a sanctions order imposed on an attorney is not a "final decision" under § 1291 and, therefore, affirm the judgment of the Court of Appeals.

Trial Processes

Summary Judgment

Although *summary judgment* is not technically part of the trial process, it is a pretrial procedure that is often used to resolve a case in favor of one party without trial. Summary judgment occurs, usually after discovery, when a party asks the court to rule in his or her favor because, applying the law to the facts disclosed and the evidence likely to be presented if a trial were to occur, the only conclusion is a ruling in that party's favor.

The standard for determining when summary judgment should be granted is found in FRCP Rule 56(c): "The judgment sought should be rendered if the pleadings, the discovery and disclosure materials on file, and any affidavits show that there is no genuine issue as to any material fact and that the movant is entitled to judgment as a matter of law." Thus, if there is evidence that contradicts the factual showing on some determinative issue in a case made by the moving party, an issue of fact exists, and summary judgment would not be proper. To be "entitled to judgment as a matter of law," the moving party must demonstrate that, given the undisputed facts, the law provides that judgment for the moving party is required.

Pretrial Conferences

The parties and their counsel, not the judge, are responsible for the progress of a civil lawsuit through the court system. The civil rules provide for orderliness and efficiency as this occurs. In this context, it is nonetheless necessary for counsel to work together with the judge so that the case can properly proceed. The judge can have considerable influence on the conduct of parties and the resolution of case before trial by encouraging settlement discussions, limiting the time for and nature of discovery, and encouraging agreement between the parties regarding issues in the case. Therefore, it is not unusual for attorneys in a case to meet with the judge several times before trial.

The judge has discretion to schedule any conferences with attorneys deemed necessary and, especially in complex litigation, may meet frequently with counsel for the parties, but there are specific times during the course of a civil case that the judge and counsel nearly always meet to set the course of the case. At the outset of a lawsuit, shortly after the complaint and answer have been filed, a *scheduling conference* is conducted. This is used to set deadlines for discovery, for filing motions, and for submitting lists of witnesses for trial and exchanging other information. Some jurisdictions also mandate one or more *settlement conferences* in order to resolve a case without trial. Even if not required by local procedural rules, a settlement conference may be particularly useful after discovery is complete and the positions of the parties are clear, as well as the evidence available to support their positions. A *status conference* is typically conducted at or near the close of the time for discovery, in which counsel for the parties meet with the judge to determine what factual issues remain in dispute for trial and evidentiary matters are resolved.

Jury Trials

After a trial date is established at a pretrial conference, the parties work toward preparing for trial on that date, unless the judge grants a continuance. The trial process in civil and criminal cases was discussed in Chapter 3. The focus of this discussion is the procedural rules governing jury trials in civil cases. In particular, the role of the jury as decision makers and the presentation of evidence to the jury in civil cases are examined.

Role of the Jury

A jury's role is to decide facts—indeed, the purpose of a trial is to resolve disputes about facts and how the law applies to those facts; therefore, the jury considers the evidence presented at trial and determines which facts are most likely to be true. It is the job of the judge to decide questions of law. Once instructed on the law by the judge, the jury can reach a conclusion about the proper outcome of the case based on the facts it determines to be true. For example, in a case involving personal injuries caused by alleged medical malpractice by a doctor, the judge instructs the jury on the elements of negligence—duty, breach of duty, causation, and harm—and the jury must decide what actions the doctor took and whether those actions constituted a breach of his or her duty to the patient that resulted in harm to the patient. Thus, the judge and jury must together consider and decide the two aspects of a legal proceeding, facts and law, to reach a just result.

When a civil case is presented to the jury for deliberation, the judge supplies a set of jury instructions that provide guidelines on the applicability of legal principles to the case and a verdict form on which the jury can indicate which party is entitled to a judgment and how damages should be assessed. Generally, there are two types of verdicts that the jury in a civil case may be asked to return. A *general verdict*, most commonly used, is one in which the jury indicates the "winning" party and the amount of damages. A general verdict form gives no indication of the basis for the jury's conclusions. A *special verdict* requires the jury to answer specific questions about the facts in the case. After the special verdict is returned, the judge applies the law to the facts found by the jury to reach a

conclusion. Some jurisdictions allow variations on the special verdict, which grants the jury the power to decide the party entitled to judgment, but also answer specific questions about the factual basis for its conclusion.

Presentation of Evidence

Trials are built around the presentation of evidence. Attorneys for the parties assemble physical, testimonial, documentary, and demonstrative evidence in order to "tell a story" about what happened in the case. The jury considers the evidence presented and, on the basis of the evidence that it believes to be credible, determines what occurred.

Although the rules of evidence for a jurisdiction govern the specific manner in which evidence may be admitted, generally, evidence must be relevant and trustworthy. Evidence is relevant if it is useful in making some fact more or less likely to be true. Thus, relevant evidence must have some bearing on one or more factual issues in a case. Evidence is trustworthy if it is presented in accordance with the rules of evidence and procedure. Thus, witnesses must be sworn and subjected to cross-examination and may not testify as to hearsay. Hearsay is an out-of-court statement offered for the truth of the matter asserted in the statement. Although there are exceptions to the hearsay rule, it is generally inadmissible because the person who made the statement is unavailable at trial to be examined about the statement. In addition, the trustworthiness of other types of evidence is supported by adherence to the rules. For example, a proper foundation must be laid before exhibits may be introduced. A foundation for physical or documentary evidence exists when its source may be established. The use of objections to the introduction of testimony or other evidence also assists the jury in determining which evidence may be relied on in deciding the facts.

Trial Motions

Several types of motions may be made at trial to narrow the issues in a case or resolve it altogether. Most common among these are a motion for a directed verdict, a motion for a new trial, and a motion for judgment notwithstanding the verdict.

A directed verdict (sometimes called judgment as a matter of law) is a decision in favor of one party based on the insufficiency of the evidence presented by the other party. The verdict is entered by the judge because the evidence presented cannot support a verdict for the party against whom the verdict is entered, and it is therefore unnecessary for the jury to deliberate about the facts. In deciding a motion for a directed verdict, the judge does not weigh the evidence of the opposing parties to decide which has more, or more credible, evidence. That is the province of the jury. Rather, the judge considers the evidence in a light favorable to the nonmoving party and resolving all questions about the weight of the evidence in favor of that party. Having done so, if the judge still concludes that no reasonable jury could decide in favor of the nonmoving party, the directed verdict will be entered.

A motion for a new trial may be made by a party for a variety of reasons. All of these involve some form of prejudice to one of the parties. That is, the reason for granting a new trial must stem from something occurring at the trial that was fundamentally unfair to the party requesting a new trial. Common grounds for a new trial include juror misconduct, errors of law, or extreme prejudice to a party, but a judge has discretion to consider whether a new trial is warranted. Juror misconduct can occur in various ways, such as failing to obey the judge's order to not discuss the case with other jurors before deliberation begins or reading newspapers or reference works on the law, despite a directive by the judge not to do so. An error of law can occur when, for example, the judge allows admission of prejudicial evidence that the moving party establishes was in violation of law, such as reference at trial to existence of an insurance policy covering a plaintiff's injuries. Other ways in which prejudice to a party requiring a new trial may occur involve inflammatory statements made by counsel during opening statements or closing arguments or objectionable derogatory statements about a party made by a witness during examination.

A judgment notwithstanding the verdict ("JNOV") is similar to a directed verdict but is granted after the jury has returned a verdict rather than at the close of the opposing party's evidence. The basis for a JNOV is that the jury's verdict was erroneous; that is, the jury erred in applying the law to facts in reaching its conclusion. In determining whether a motion for JNOV should be granted, the judge will not re-examine the facts but will consider whether the jury found sufficient facts to support the verdict given the applicable law in the case (**Sidebar 10.1**).

Sidebar 10.1   *Civil Court: Justice for the Wealthy?*

The criminal justice system, as is well known from the famous Miranda warnings, provides an attorney to criminal defendants who cannot afford one. The civil court system in the United States is different. There is no right to an attorney, and people who are sued or suing need to hire their own. Civil courts were intended as a means of allowing citizens seeking justice, including businesses, to have an independent decision maker resolve a private matter—one that did not affect the broader interests of society. Over time, the caseload of civil courts has increased dramatically, and cases usually take a long time from start to completion of a single case. Although small claims (less than $5,000 in many jurisdictions) may be handled more expeditiously, the civil justice system for cases involving higher amounts of money or equitable relief may take from 6 months to several years before a case can be resolved. Thus, although the civil justice system is designed to allow any person a forum in which he or she can receive a fair hearing to resolve disputes, who can afford it? Is the design consistent with reality? Can anyone, including those of modest means, really afford to access the courts? Or are they just places for the wealthy to sort things out?

Without question, the cost of bringing or defending a lawsuit and going to trial is high. Indeed, many groups seeking court reform cite the cost to businesses and individuals as a primary reason why the justice system doesn't work (see Sidebar 13.1). In large cities, hourly fees for attorneys typically range from $200 to $400, but may be as high as $1,000 for highly experienced lawyers in well-established law firms. Even with contingent fees, where attorneys collect a portion of any judgment or settlement amount, the percentage can exceed 50%. In addition, the costs associated with lawsuits, including the deposition, document review, economic or statistical analysis, expert witnesses, and even copying fees, can increase the cost of a lawsuit dramatically. Given the rising costs of litigation, many individuals and businesses seek protection against what could be devastating cost of defending a lawsuit. A significant component of many liability insurance policies is not the limits of liability that the company will pay but the terms and extent to which a policy will pay litigation costs in the event the policyholder is sued.

The question raised is this: Is a person or a business with a great deal of wealth better able to pursue cases in court that a person or company of lesser means cannot? Those who are able to afford a lengthy litigation process are often able to outlast those who are not; indeed, such wealth may be used as a litigation strategy by prolonging the proceedings using legitimate court processes. Is this justice? Has the civil justice system grown so costly that only the wealthy can afford to use it?

Generally, even large corporations involved in civil suits do not wish for lengthy legal proceedings, especially if the benefits do not outweigh the costs and risks to the company. Therefore, both small and large businesses alike advocate litigation reform; however, efforts at reform have brought about little in the way of suggested solutions for the problem, other than calls for limiting punitive or compensatory damages, exempting certain types of organizations (such as nonprofit corporations) from suit, or providing immunity from suit for certain products (such as some experimental drugs). Suggestions such as these may reduce the amount of litigation but would do nothing to reduce the costs or the potential advantage that those with wealth may hold.

Because the purpose of any court is to seek justice, bias experienced by one side in the form of financial effects of protracted litigation or the quality of representation is arguably in contrast to the goal of the courts. The cost of legal fees coupled with an overburdened legal system may prove to be the Achilles heel of the justice system. Perceptions of justice are important to the meaning of justice, and if the public perceives that the court system favors the wealthy or if a person believes he or she cannot afford justice, support for our justice system will erode. Above the steps of the U.S. Supreme Court is the inscription "Equal Justice Under Law." To the extent that the process of civil justice is affected by its cost, the quality of justice for those of lesser means may not be equal.

Appeals

A right to appeal civil judgments exists in every jurisdiction. The basis for the appeal and likelihood of prevailing on appeal varies considerably. Rules of appellate procedure govern the manner and deadlines within which an appeal may be brought, but two fundamental requirements are shared by appellate practice in all jurisdictions: the existence of a final judgment and one or more legal issues for appeal.

Final Judgment Rule

The final judgment rule states that the right to appeal exists only when a final judgment has been issued in a civil case. The question, of course, is this: What constitutes a "final judgment"? The U.S. Supreme Court has said that "a decision is not final, ordinarily, unless it 'ends the litigation on the merits and leaves nothing for the court to do but execute the judgment.' *Cunningham v. Hamilton County, Ohio*, 527 U.S. 198, 119 S. Ct. 1915, 144 L.Ed.2d 184 (1999). The *Cunningham* case held that an order for discovery sanction against an attorney was not a final appealable order because it was not an order that ended the litigation on the merits of the case. Thus, a final judgment is an order from the court that resolves all legal and factual issues in the case; nothing more is left to be decided.

The final judgment rule is intended to prevent multiple appeals from decisions that may be made by a court as litigation progresses. In *Firestone Tire & Rubber Co. v. Risjord*, 449 U.S. 368, 101 S. Ct. 669, 66 L.Ed.2d 571 (1981), the Court found that the final judgment rule has several purposes:

> It emphasizes the deference that appellate courts owe to the trial judge as the individual initially called upon to decide the many questions of law and fact that occur in the course of a trial. Permitting piecemeal appeals would undermine the independence of the district judge, as well as the special role that individual plays in our judicial system. In addition, the rule is in accordance with the sensible policy of avoid[ing] the obstruction to just claims that would come from permitting the harassment and cost of a succession of separate appeals from the various rulings to which a litigation may give rise, from its initiation to entry of judgment. The rule also serves the important purpose of promoting efficient judicial administration.

Thus, if appeals of each and every decision by the trial judge were allowed, the trial would likely be interrupted to obtain appellate court rulings and further extend an already time-consuming trial process. Furthermore, appellate courts would be forced to make decisions in piecemeal fashion that may or may not ultimately have a bearing on the outcome of a case. As the Court in *Firestone* indicated, the goal of the final judgment rule is efficiency in the operation of both the trial and appellate courts. By allowing the appellate court, in a single case, to decide the legality of all objections raised at trial, the trial and appellate courts can maintain independence in their functioning and the processes of justice can move forward orderly and efficiently for the courts and the parties that look to them for decisions.

Legal Issues for Appeal

Two general principles govern whether an appeal may be brought. First, only questions of law, not questions of fact, may form the basis for an appeal. It is the responsibility of the trial judge to decide issues of law. An issue of law requires interpretation of the law that applies in a case. When that interpretation is erroneous, it may be raised in the appellate court by the party against whom it was made. The appellate court will review the law, consider its proper interpretation in light of the facts found by the jury, and either sustain or reverse the decision regarding that issue made by the trial judge. Although the appellate court may overturn a verdict that is wholly without factual support, it must generally defer to the trial court in determinations of fact. *Metropolitan Stevedore Company v. Rambo*, 521 U.S. 121, 117 S. Ct. 1953, 138 L.Ed.2d 327 (1997). An appellate court will not disturb factual conclusions made at trial unless they are clearly erroneous. *Peterkin v. Jeffes*, 855 F.2d 1021 (1988).

Case Decision 10.3 *Salve Regina College v. Russell*, 499 U.S. 225, 111 S. Ct. 1217, 113 L.Ed.2d 190 (1991)

Opinion of the Court by Justice Blackmun:

The concept of a federal general common law, lurking (to use Justice Holmes' phrase) as a "brooding omnipresence in the sky," was questioned for some time before being firmly rejected in *Erie R. Co. v. Tompkins*, 304 U.S. 64, 58 S. Ct. 817, 82 L.Ed. 1188 (1938). *Erie* mandates that a federal court sitting in diversity apply the substantive law of the forum State, absent a federal statutory or constitutional directive to the contrary. In decisions after *Erie*, this Court made clear that state law is to be determined in the same manner as a federal court resolves an evolving issue of federal law: "with the aid of such light as [is] afforded by the materials for decision at hand, and in accordance with the applicable principles for determining state law. In this case, we must decide specifically whether a federal court of appeals may review a district court's determination of state law under a standard less probing than that applied to a determination of federal law."

I

The issue presented arises out of a contract dispute between a college and one of its students. Petitioner Salve Regina College is an institution of higher education located in Newport, R.I. Respondent Sharon L. Russell was admitted to the college and began her studies as a freshman in 1982. The following year, respondent sought admission to the college's nursing department in order to pursue a bachelor of science degree in nursing. She was accepted by the department and began her nursing studies in the fall of 1983.

Respondent, who was 5'6" tall, weighed in excess of 300 pounds when she was accepted in the nursing program. Immediately after the 1983 school year began, respondent's weight became a topic of commentary and concern by officials of the nursing program. Respondent's first year in the program was marked by a series of confrontations and negotiations concerning her obesity and its effect upon her ability to complete the clinical requirements safely and satisfactorily. During her junior year, respondent signed a document that was designated as a "contract" and conditioned her further participation in the nursing program upon weekly attendance at a weight-loss seminar and a realized average loss of two pounds per week. When respondent failed to meet these commitments, she was asked to withdraw from the program and did so. She transferred to a nursing program at another college, but had to repeat her junior year in order to satisfy the transferee institution's 2-year residency requirement. As a consequence, respondent's nursing education took five years rather than four. She also underwent surgery for her obesity. In 1987, respondent successfully completed her nursing education, and she is now a registered nurse.

Soon after leaving Salve Regina College, respondent filed this civil action in the United States District Court for the District of Rhode Island. She asserted, among others, claims based on (1) intentional infliction of emotional distress, (2) invasion of privacy, and (3) nonperformance by the college of its implied agreement to educate respondent. The amended complaint named the college and five faculty members as defendants and alleged discrimination in violation of the Rehabilitation Act of 1973, as amended, 29 U.S.C. § 701, *et seq.*; denial of due process and unconstitutional interference with her liberty and property interests; negligent and intentional infliction of emotional distress; invasion of privacy; wrongful dismissal; violation of express and implied covenants of good faith and fair dealing; and breach of contract. The District Court entered summary judgment for the defendants except as to the three state-law claims for intentional infliction of emotional distress, invasion of privacy, and breach of contract. The parties agree that the law of Rhode Island applies to all substantive aspects of the action.

At the close of plaintiff-respondent's case in chief, the District Court directed a verdict for the individual defendants on all three of the remaining claims, and for the college on the claims for intentional infliction of emotional distress and invasion of privacy. The court, however, denied the college's motion for a directed verdict on the breach-of-contract claim, reasoning that "a legitimate factual issue" remained concerning whether "there was substantial performance by the plaintiff in her overall contractual relationship at Salve Regina."

At the close of all the evidence, the college renewed its motion for a directed verdict. It argued that under Rhode Island law the strict commercial doctrine of substantial performance did not apply in the general academic context. Therefore, according to petitioner, because respondent admitted she had not fulfilled the terms of the contract, the college was entitled to judgment as a matter of law.

The District Court denied petitioner's motion. Acknowledging that the Supreme Court of Rhode Island, to that point, had limited the application of the substantial-performance doctrine to construction contracts, the District Court nonetheless concluded, as a matter of law, that the Supreme Court of Rhode Island would apply that doctrine to the facts of respondent's case. The Federal District Judge based this conclusion, in part, on his observation that "I was a state trial judge for 18 and ½ years, and I have a feel for what the Rhode Island Supreme Court will do or won't do." Accordingly, the District Court submitted the breach-of-contract claim to the jury. The court instructed the jury:

> The law provides that substantial and not exact performance accompanied by good faith is what is required in a case of a contract of this type. It is not necessary that the plaintiff have fully and completely performed every item specified in the contract between the parties. It is sufficient if there has been substantial performance, not necessarily full performance, so long as the substantial performance was in good faith and in compliance with the contract, except for some minor and relatively unimportant deviation or omission.

(Continues)

(Continued)

The jury returned a verdict for respondent, and determined that the damages were $30,513.40. Judgment was entered. Both respondent and petitioner appealed.

The United States Court of Appeals for the First Circuit affirmed. It first upheld the District Court's directed verdict dismissing respondent's claims for intentional infliction of emotional distress and invasion of privacy. It then turned to petitioner's argument that the District Court erred in submitting the breach-of-contract claim to the jury. Rejecting petitioner's argument that, under Rhode Island law, the doctrine of substantial performance does not apply in the college-student context, the court stated:

> In this case of first impression, the district court held that the Rhode Island Supreme Court would apply the substantial performance standard to the contract in question. In view of the customary appellate deference accorded to interpretations of state law made by federal judges of that state, we hold that the district court's determination that the Rhode Island Supreme Court would apply standard contract principles is not reversible error.

Petitioner college sought a writ of certiorari from this Court. It alleged that the Court of Appeals erred in deferring to the District Court's determination of state law. A majority of the Courts of Appeals, although varying in their phraseology, embrace a rule of deference similar to that articulated by the Court of Appeals in this case. Two Courts of Appeals, however, have broken ranks recently with their sister Circuits. They have concluded that a district-court determination of state law is subject to plenary review by the appellate court. We granted certiorari to resolve the conflict.

II

We conclude that a court of appeals should review *de novo* a district court's determination of state law. As a general matter, of course, the courts of appeals are vested with plenary appellate authority over final decisions of district courts. The obligation of responsible appellate jurisdiction implies the requisite authority to review independently a lower court's determinations.

Independent appellate review of legal issues best serves the dual goals of doctrinal coherence and economy of judicial administration. District judges preside alone over fast-paced trials: Of necessity they devote much of their energy and resources to hearing witnesses and reviewing evidence. Similarly, the logistical burdens of trial advocacy limit the extent to which trial counsel is able to supplement the district judge's legal research with memoranda and briefs. Thus, trial judges often must resolve complicated legal questions without benefit of "extended reflection [or] extensive information."

Courts of appeals, on the other hand, are structurally suited to the collaborative juridical process that promotes decisional accuracy. With the record having been constructed below and settled for purposes of the appeal, appellate judges are able to devote their primary attention to legal issues. As questions of law become the focus of appellate review, it can be expected that the parties' briefs will be refined to bring to bear on the legal issues more information and more comprehensive analysis than was provided for the district judge. Perhaps most important, courts of appeals employ multi-judge panels that permit reflective dialogue and collective judgment. Over 30 years ago, Justice Frankfurter accurately observed:

> Without adequate study there cannot be adequate reflection; without adequate reflection there cannot be adequate discussion; without adequate discussion there cannot be that fruitful interchange of minds which is indispensable to thoughtful, unhurried decision and its formulation in learned and impressive opinions.

Independent appellate review necessarily entails a careful consideration of the district court's legal analysis, and an efficient and sensitive appellate court at least will naturally consider this analysis in undertaking its review. Petitioner readily acknowledges the importance of a district court's reasoning to the appellate court's review. Any expertise possessed by the district court will inform the structure and content of its conclusions of law and thereby become evident to the reviewing court. If the court of appeals finds that the district court's analytical sophistication and research have exhausted the state-law inquiry, little more need be said in the appellate opinion. Independent review, however, does not admit of unreflective reliance on a lower court's inarticulable intuitions. Thus, an appropriately respectful application of *de novo* review should encourage a district court to explicate with care the basis for its legal conclusions.

Although some might say that this Court has not spoken with a uniformly clear voice on the issue of deference to a district judge's determination of state law, a careful consideration of our cases makes apparent the duty of appellate courts to provide meaningful review of such a determination. In a series of cases decided soon after *Erie* the Court noted that the appellate courts had applied general federal law instead of the law of the respective States, and remanded to the Courts of Appeals for consideration of the applicable principles of state law.

III

In urging this Court to adopt the deferential standard embraced by the majority of the Courts of Appeals, respondent offers two arguments. First, respondent suggests that the appellate courts professing adherence to the rule of deference actually are reviewing *de novo* the district-court determinations of state law. Second, respondent presses the familiar contention that district judges are better arbiters of unsettled state law because they have exposure to the judicial system of the State in which they sit. We reject each of these arguments.

A

Respondent primarily contends that the Courts of Appeals that claim to accord special consideration to the District Court's state-law expertise actually undertake plenary review of a determination of state law. According to respondent, this is simply *de novo* review "cloth[ed] in 'deferential' robes." In support of this contention, respondent refers to several decisions in which the appellate court has announced that it is bound to review deferentially a district court's determination of state law, yet nonetheless has found that determination to constitute reversible error. Respondent also relies on cases in which the Courts of Appeals, while articulating a rule of deference, acknowledge their obligation to scrutinize closely the District Court's legal conclusions.

We decline the invitation to assume that courts of appeals craft their opinions disingenuously. The fact that an appellate court overturns an erroneous determination of state law in no way indicates that the appellate court is not applying the rule of deference articulated in the opinion. Respondent would have us interpret this caveat as an acknowledgment of the appellate court's obligation to review the state-law question *de novo*.

In a case where the controlling question of state law remains unsettled, it is not unreasonable to assume that the considered judgment of the court of appeals frequently will coincide with the reasoned determination of the district court. Where the state-law determinations of the two courts diverge, the choice between these standards of review is of no significance if the appellate court concludes that the district court was clearly wrong.

Thus, the mandate of independent review will alter the appellate outcome only in those few cases where the appellate court would resolve an unsettled issue of state law differently from the district court's resolution, but cannot conclude that the district court's determination constitutes clear error. These few instances, however, make firm our conviction that the difference between a rule of deference and the duty to exercise independent review is "much more than a mere matter of degree." When *de novo* review is compelled, no form of appellate deference is acceptable.

B

Respondent and her *amicus* also argue that *de novo* review is inappropriate because, as a general matter, a district judge is better positioned to determine an issue of state law than are the judges on the court of appeals. This superior capacity derives, it is said, from the regularity with which a district judge tries a diversity case governed by the law of the forum State, and from the extensive experience that the district judge generally has had as practitioner or judge in the forum State.

We are unpersuaded. As an initial matter, this argument seems to us to be founded fatally on overbroad generalizations. Moreover, and more important, the proposition that a district judge is better able to "intuit" the answer to an unsettled question of state law is foreclosed by our holding in *Erie*. The very essence of the *Erie* doctrine is that the bases of state law are presumed to be communicable by the parties to a federal judge no less than to a state judge. Similarly, the bases of state law are as equally communicable to the appellate judges as they are to the district judge. To the extent that the available state law on a controlling issue is so unsettled as to admit of no reasoned divination, we can see no sense in which a district judge's prior exposure or nonexposure to the state judiciary can be said to facilitate the rule of reason.

IV

The obligation of responsible appellate review and the principles of a cooperative judicial federalism underlying *Erie* require that courts of appeals review the state-law determinations of district courts *de*

(Continues)

novo. The Court of Appeals in this case therefore erred in deferring to the local expertise of the District Court. The judgment of the Court of Appeals is reversed, and the case is remanded for further proceedings consistent with this opinion.

Dissent by Chief Justice Rehnquist, joined by Justices White and Stevens:

I do not believe we need to delve into such abstractions as "deferential" review, on the one hand, as opposed to what the Court's opinion calls, at various places, "plenary," "independent," and "*de novo*" review, on the other, in order to decide this case. The critical language used by the Court of Appeals, and quoted in this Court's opinion, is this: "In view of the customary appellate deference accorded to interpretations of state law made by federal judges of that state, we hold that the district court's determination that the Rhode Island Supreme Court would apply standard contract principles is not reversible error."

In order to determine the Court of Appeals' views as to "customary appellate deference," it seems only fair to refer to the page in *Dennis v. Rhode Island Hospital Trust Nat. Bank*, 744 F.2d 893 (1984), to which the court cites. There we find this language: "[I]n a diversity case such as this one, involving a technical subject matter primarily of state concern, we are 'reluctant to interfere with a reasonable construction of state law made by a district judge, sitting in the state, who is familiar with that state's law and practices.'"

The court does not say that it *always* defers to a district court's conclusions of law. Rather, it states that it is reluctant to substitute its own view of state law for that of a judge "who is familiar with that state's law and practices." In this case, the court concluded that the opinion of a District Judge with $18\frac{1}{2}$ years of experience as a trial judge was entitled to some appellate deference.

This seems to me a rather sensible observation. A district court's insights are particularly valuable to an appellate court in a case such as this where the state law is unsettled. In such cases, the courts' task is to try to *predict* how the highest court of that State would decide the question. A judge attempting to predict how a state court would rule must use not only his legal reasoning skills, but also his experiences and perceptions of judicial behavior in that State. It therefore makes perfect sense for an appellate court judge with no local experience to accord special weight to a local judge's assessment of state court trends.

If we must choose among Justice Holmes' aphorisms to help decide this case, I would opt for his observation that "[t]he life of the law has not been logic: it has been experience." O. Holmes, The Common Law 1 (1881). And it does no harm to recall that the Members of this Court have no monopoly on experience; judges of the courts of appeals and of the district courts surely possess it just as we do. That the experience of appellate judges should lead them to rely, in appropriate situations, on the experience of district judges who have practiced law in the State in which they sit before taking the bench seems quite natural.

For this very reason, this Court has traditionally given special consideration or "weight" to the district judge's perspective on local law. But the Court today decides that this intuitively sensible deference is available only to this Court, and not to the courts of appeals. It then proceeds to instruct the courts of appeals and the district courts on their respective functions in the federal judicial system, and how they should go about exercising them. Questions of law are questions of law, they are told, whether they be of state law or federal law, and must all be processed through an identical decisional mold.

I believe this analysis unduly compartmentalizes things which have up to now been left to common sense and good judgment. Federal courts of appeals perform a different role when they decide questions of state law than they do when they decide questions of federal law. In the former case, these courts are not sources of law but only reflections of the jurisprudence of the courts of a State. While in deciding novel federal questions, courts of appeals are likely to ponder the policy implications as well as the decisional law, only the latter need be considered in deciding questions of state law. To my mind, therefore, it not only violates no positive law but also is a sensible allocation of resources to recognize these differences by deferring to the views of the district court where such deference is felt warranted.

I think we run a serious risk that our reach will exceed our grasp when we attempt to impose a rigid logical framework on the courts of appeals in place of a less precise but tolerably well-functioning approach adopted by those courts. I agree with the Court that a court of appeals should not "abdicate" its obligation to decide questions of state law presented in a diversity case. But by according weight to the conclusion of a particular district judge on the basis of his experience and special knowledge of state law, an appellate court does not "suspend [its] own thought processes." I think the Court of Appeals did no more than that here, and I therefore dissent from the reversal of its judgment.

The question of deference to conclusions of law made by the trial judge was a central issue in *Salve Regina College v. Russell*, 499 U.S. 225, 111 S. Ct. 1217, 113 L.Ed.2d 190 (1991), found in **Case Decision 10.3**. That case involved an unusual contract between a student and the college she had attended, in which the student was required to attend weekly weight loss sessions and lose 2 pounds each week in order to stay enrolled in a nursing program. She sued the college on a variety of tort theories, as well as a state law breach of contract claim. The trial court granted motions for summary judgment or directed verdicts in favor of the college on all of the tort claims, but not on the breach of contract claim, which was submitted to the jury. The trial judge instructed the jury on the Rhode Island law of contracts in evaluating the facts of the case, in particular whether the student made a good faith effort and had "substantially performed" the contract. He interpreted the applicable requirements of contract law in Rhode Island based on what he believed the Rhode Island Supreme Court's interpretation of contract law would be, based on his many years of experience as a state and federal court judge in Rhode Island. On that claim, the jury awarded damages of about $30,000 to the student. On appeal, the Court of Appeals for the First Circuit upheld the award, giving deference to the interpretation of law made by the trial judge. The U.S. Supreme Court reversed the Court of Appeals, finding that it is the job of the appellate court to draw its own conclusions about questions of state law, not defer to the interpretations of law made by the trial judge. In dissent, three members of the Court believed that requiring appellate courts to decide for themselves what state law requires, independent of the trial judge who lives, works, and has considerable experience in the state, to be mistaken. It viewed the majority's decision to reflect a "rigid logical framework" that would make interpreting the meaning of state law less certain, not more. The holding of the case and the debate between the majority and dissenting views is instructive because it shows the difficulties that sometimes exist in deciding what the law is and how it should apply in a given case.

The second principle governing whether an appeal may be brought is that only those legal issues to which objections were made at trial ("preserved" for appeal) may be raised. Furthermore, the objection must have been made by the losing party who brings the appeal, and the objectionable issue of law must arguably have been related to the outcome of the case. The reason for requiring that objections have been made at trial is one of fairness. The appealing party may not wait until the time of appeal to object to a decision made by the trial when, if it were made at trial, the trial judge would have had the opportunity to "correct" the error. In other words, the appellant cannot wait to see whether the judge's evidentiary and other decisions during trial are beneficial or detrimental and, if ultimately the latter, raise it on appeal. The appeals court need only consider the matter properly brought before it, and in this context, "properly" means first raised at trial.

Key Terms

Civil Procedure	Discovery
Pleading	Summary Judgment
Cause of Action	Pretrial Conference
Affirmative Defense	Final Judgment Rule
Motions	

Discussion Questions

1. What is the relationship between civil procedure and substantive civil law?
2. What are the Federal Rules of Civil Procedure?
3. What is the purpose of pleading in a civil case? Why are pleadings necessary?
4. What is the function of a civil complaint and an answer? What information must they contain?
5. What are three types of pretrial motions? What is their purpose?
6. What does the use of discovery accomplish? What are four commonly used discovery tools?
7. Why is the use of pretrial conferences a necessary part of civil court procedures? What types of pretrial conferences are held?
8. What are the respective roles of the judge and jury in a civil case?
9. What is the final judgment rule? How does it apply to appeals?

Cases

Bell Atlantic v. Twombly, 550 U.S. 544, 127 S. Ct. 1955, 167 L.Ed.2d 929 (2007).
Cunningham v. Hamilton County, Ohio, 527 U.S. 198, 119 S. Ct. 1915, 144 L.Ed.2d 184 (1999).
Firestone Tire & Rubber Co. v. Risjord, 449 U.S. 368, 101 S. Ct. 669, 66 L.Ed.2d 571 (1981).
Leatherman v. Tarrant County Narcotics Intelligence and Coordination Unit, 507 U.S. 163, 113 S. Ct. 1160, 122 L.Ed.2d 517 (1993).
Metropolitan Stevedore Company v. Rambo, 521 U.S. 121, 117 S. Ct. 1953, 138 L.Ed.2d 327 (1997).
Peterkin v. Jeffes, 855 F.2d 1021 (1988).
Salve Regina College v. Russell, 499 U.S. 225, 111 S. Ct. 1217, 113 L.Ed.2d 190 (1991).
Swierkiewicz v. Sorema, 534 U.S. 506, 122 S. Ct. 992, 152 L.Ed.2d 1 (2002).

Criminal Justice on the Web

For an up-to-date list of Web links, go to *The American Courts: A Procedural Approach* online companion site at http://criminal justice.jbpub.com/AmericanCourts. The online companion site will introduce you to some of the most important sites for finding American courts information on the Internet.

References

Clark, C. E. (1937). The new federal rules of civil procedure: The last phase-underlying philosophy embodied in some of the basic provisions of the new procedure. *American Bar Association Journal, 23,* 976.
Moskowitz, S. (2007). Discovery in state civil procedure: The national perspective. *Western State University Law Review, 35,* 121–146.

Criminal Law and Procedure in the Courts

A significant amount of time and resources of courts are spent each year on the American criminal justice system and the adjudication of crime. Criminal law, both substantive and procedural, is the law that courts are called on to apply and interpret in vast numbers of cases each year.

This section explores criminal law and its applications. Chapter 11 focuses on substantive criminal law—that is, the "substance" of criminal behavior and its punishment. Recalling the introduction to the law in society from Chapter 2, Chapter 11 discusses in greater detail why criminal law is needed in the American democracy and the societal purposes it serves. In particular, the idea that society wishes to maintain order by prohibiting certain behaviors while also maintaining a free society in which individuals are free to act in all other ways is central to the goals of the criminal law. Providing citizens with expectations regarding how they must govern their behavior to be consistent with the common good is fundamentally a democratic idea. Furthermore, the requirements of proof of crime, the prosecutorial burden, and the "beyond a reasonable doubt" standard are all aspects of the criminal law that further its goals. Thus, considerable attention is paid to how crime is defined and the general elements that must be satisfied before a person accused of crime may be punished.

It becomes apparent that criminal law has a moral basis that helps determine what society believes is just. Criminal law does not punish thought. For the most part, it does not punish speech or writing. It punishes behavior. By focusing on and punishing only those behaviors deemed unacceptable to society, the criminal law reflects society's views about what is right and what is wrong. The divisions in criminal law—crimes against the person, crimes against property, and crimes against public order and morality—are each designed to mirror what society believes to be unacceptable and punishes behavior within each according to the "wrong-doer's" culpability.

Criminal law is not solely concerned with punishing wrongful behavior, however. Of equal concern is protecting the rights of the accused. Chapter 12 considers this topic. Criminal procedure involves the constitutional rights of criminal defendants and the ways in which courts are required and empowered to protect them. Without procedure, courts cannot effectively administer the law.

Chapter 12 examines the procedures employed by courts at each phase of the criminal justice process. Prearrest procedures involve steps that can and cannot be taken by law enforcement in the investigation of crime and uncovering evidence of crime. A great many rules have been developed by the courts that interpret the Fourth Amendment's prohibition against unreasonable search and seizures. Perhaps chief among these is the requirement of "probable cause," its meaning and application, and the use of the exclusionary rule that makes improperly obtained evidence inadmissible in court.

Arrest procedures are those through which a suspect becomes a defendant. Specifically, what constitutes an arrest is examined, and the use of a warrant to effect an arrest is discussed. The places in which an arrest may occur and the amount of force that may be used by police during an arrest are also explored.

Postarrest procedures are those governing the process of identifying and interrogating witnesses in custody. Central to this discussion is the use of Miranda warnings that notify suspects of their constitutional rights before questioning. Particular attention is paid to the right of a defendant to not incriminate himself under the Fifth Amendment and the role played by counsel in protecting this and other rights.

Chapter 12 also examines the process of sentencing employed by courts. The basis for punishment in our criminal justice system is considered, and the types and manner in which sentences may be imposed are discussed.

When the government decides to act against an individual believed to have engaged in criminal behavior, the machinery of justice is set in motion and not easily turned aside. Taken together, Chapters 11 and 12 encompass much of criminal law and present the ways in which courts have had to grapple with the societal goals of order and protection for people while also upholding the rights of individuals. Understanding the relationship between substantive criminal law and criminal procedure lends insight into how courts seek to achieve this balance.

Substantive Criminal Law 11

What Is This Chapter About?

This chapter discusses the need for criminal law, how crime is defined, the elements and types of crime, and the goals of punishment. Criminal law is necessary in our society to create order and give people expectations about their own conduct and that of others. Substantive criminal law addresses the behaviors that we as a society have decided to prohibit, the way in which those behaviors are defined, and what must be proven before a person may be punished. Thus, the "substance" of criminal law includes the formal rules that provide people with expectations as to what behavior is acceptable and what is not. This aspect of criminal law is the focus of this chapter.

We begin our study by considering the need for rules of prohibition that specify punishments. This requires that we revisit the meaning of justice, the moral basis for the law, and the distinction between right and wrong reflected in criminal law.

Our study then turns to the elements of crime, or what society requires the government to prove before punishment may be imposed. These elements, *actus reus*, *mens rea*, concurrence, causation, and harm, are examined in detail. We then explore defenses to these elements that may preclude criminal liability.

Substantive criminal law may be divided into crimes against the person, property crime, and crimes involving morals or public order. We consider each of these and the specific statutory and common law crimes that comprise each.

Learning Objectives

After reading this chapter, you should be able to

1. Understand the need for criminal law.
2. Describe the need for punishment in criminal law.
3. Describe each of the elements of crime.
4. Explain the purpose of a defense and primary defenses that defendants rely upon.
5. Distinguish crimes against the person, property crimes, and crimes involving public order and morality.
6. Give examples of each of the three categories of crime.

Crime and Behavior

Criminal law is the branch of law that addresses harm to the public, not disputes between private parties. Although an individual may be the victim of a crime, crimes are considered to be "public" offenses because of their effects on the larger society. If individuals were left to seek punishment of offenders for offenses against them, society would quickly deteriorate into one in which the weak are pitted against the strong, punishment for similar harmful behaviors would vary considerably depending on who was the perpetrator or the harmed, and most members of society would live in fear of their safety.

Like much of American law and the court system itself, criminal law stems from the law of England in the Middle Ages. In England, harmful actions by individuals were a breach of the peace and were punishable by the Crown. The King and his designated lords acted as prosecutors and judges when crimes such as theft, rape, and murder occurred. In colonial America, criminal law grew to include crimes and punishments found in the Bible, as well as punishment of lesser crimes in order to maintain public order. As government has grown and American society has changed, criminal law has developed into a large body of laws that identify an ever-growing number of prohibited behaviors. These behaviors and their punishments comprise the "substantive" criminal law.

The Need for Criminal Law

Criminal law, like all laws, has one central purpose: to create order in society. It accomplishes this through the protection of individual interests and the common good. Substantive criminal law involves the rules of responsibility that society imposes on individuals. These rules stem from the morals of a society; that is, substantive criminal law specifies those behaviors that society believes to be right and those it considers to be wrong. When an individual has been harmed either physically or by loss of property, the criminal law seeks to prevent the wrongdoer from repeating the harmful act, to deter others from acting that way, and to obtain some degree of compensation for the victim. This is accomplished by punishing the wrongdoer.

Few would disagree that those who violate the law should be punished; however, what punishment is most appropriate? Because harm to an individual is also harmful to society as a whole, the punishment must be such that it satisfies the need for societal order. Thus, to allow victims themselves to seek their own justice would lead to further disorder in society—when individuals "take the law into their own hands," there is no consistency in punishment and therefore no shared understanding as to which behaviors are acceptable and which are not. Criminal law, therefore, serves as the social mechanism through which society compels individuals to act appropriately, thereby creating an ordered society. Although imperfect, criminal law creates uniformity in the way in which individuals are held accountable for their antisocial behavior and creates uniformity in the punishment they receive. This idea and its implementation are central to the meaning of criminal justice. In addition, criminal law is more than just rules of behavior. It also incorporates the punishment that must accompany wrongful conduct. Without punishment, the law is both unenforceable and unjust.

What Is a Crime?

How do we determine what constitutes a crime? Most people have some moral rules that they use to guide their behavior and dealings with others. Most would condemn murder and theft on moral grounds, and these behaviors are also prohibited under the law. The moral perspective of people within a society thus plays a role in defining crime; however, some behavior that may be considered immoral is not criminal, and some criminal behavior is not immoral, based on personal or societal norms. For example, the practice of abortion, considered by many to be morally unacceptable, is no longer prohibited or punished under the law. Conversely, some financial crimes, such as insider trading, are not viewed by many as morally wrong, although the law has specified many types of financial transactions that are punishable because of their harmful effects on our system of capitalism.

Clearly, however, the majority of crimes for which a person may be punished are based on society's view of morality, or what is right and what is wrong. A crime is therefore an act that society prohibits by law. The acts that find their way into the law are those that society, through its legislative processes, deems to be harmful to individuals or society as a whole. By criminalizing certain behaviors, the government accomplishes its goals of maintaining order, providing safety to citizens, building confidence in our system of government, and encouraging compliance with its laws.

Through its elected representatives at the state or local level, society decides what behaviors should be punishable and what the punishment for the commission of those acts should be. Criminal law is therefore the body of law that protects the public against antisocial behavior by determining what those prohibited acts are and what must be done when they occur.

The English common law classified crimes as *mala in se* or *mala prohibita*. A mala in se crime is one involving behavior that is bad in and of itself, or inherently evil. From a moral standpoint, these are behaviors that are so bad that no civilized society could allow them. *Mala in se* crimes involve behaviors that are generally agreed to be wrong because of the nature of the act itself. For example, murder is an act universally recognized as *mala in se*. A *mala prohibita* crime is behavior prohibited because society has decided that it should be prohibited, not because the act itself is morally bad. For example, in most states, gambling is a crime that is *mala prohibita*.

The distinction between *mala in se* and *mala prohibita* helps to focus on the nature of the behavior that is criminalized and why. This has important implications for the seriousness of the offense and the punishment that should follow, but regardless of the nature of the prohibited behavior, all crimes have elements that need to be established before punishment can be imposed.

Elements of Crime

The substantive criminal law specifies which acts will be considered criminal in a precise manner. Whether found in a statute or in the common law, a crime is defined in terms of its *elements*, or the separate identifiable aspects of the crime that must be established in order for there to be criminal liability. These elements are *actus reus*, *mens rea*, *concurrence*, *causation*, and *harm*. Actus reus refers to the act for which punishment will be imposed. It addresses the question "What did the defendant do?" *Mens rea* requires proof of the mental state of the defendant. Specifically, the defendant must have intended to commit the prohibited act. Concurrence requires a showing that the defendant's intent and act co-occurred; that is, did they relate to each other? Causation examines whether the defendant's act resulted in harm. There is generally no criminal liability unless harm has resulted, and the harm must be attributable to the defendant's behavior. The harm must be a harm that the law, by criminalizing the behavior, intended to protect against. Each of these elements must be established by the prosecution by introducing evidence that satisfies the "beyond a reasonable doubt" standard. If one or more of the elements is not proven, there is no criminal liability.

In addition to these elements, some crimes require the existence of *attendant circumstances*. These are certain circumstances surrounding the commission of a crime at the time it occurs. For example, some sexual assault statutes specify the circumstance that there was no consent to the defendant's act on the part of the victim. For such crimes, the prosecution must prove this additional element.

There are some crimes for which the elements of crime, other than the criminal act, need not be proven by the prosecution. These are called strict liability crimes. Like the concept of strict liability in tort law, criminal liability for these crimes is imposed because the resulting harm from the act is so great that the mental state of the defendant does not matter. In these cases, the only element to be proven is the *actus reus*. If the prosecution proves that the defendant committed the act prohibited by statute, punishment should follow. Though limited, examples of crimes of this type include statutory rape and certain regulatory offenses.

Actus Reus

The Latin phrase *actus reus* means "wrongful (or guilty) act"; therefore, in order for there to be criminal liability for a person's behavior, there must an identifiable act committed by that person that the law prohibits. Shooting (or even pointing) a gun at another person, taking property belonging to another, or possessing certain drugs all may satisfy the element of *actus reus*. Persons may think whatever they wish, but it is their actions that may lead to punishment. It is intentional behavior that the law punishes. Furthermore, criminal law holds individuals responsible for their own actions, not the actions of others. Thus, even where more than one person engages in criminal behavior, the criminal defendants involved are prosecuted one at a time. Unless each defendant is found to have committed a criminal act, no criminal liability will attach. *Actus reus* therefore demands that the prosecution state and prove specifically what it is that a defendant has done and show that the behavior is prohibited by law.

There is a more precise definition of a criminal act, however. It is found in the Model Penal Code (MPC). Most of the states have drafted their criminal statutes in accordance with the MPC. The MPC is composed of sample criminal statutes in all areas of criminal law that was created to be used as a model by state legislatures. It was produced by a group of judges, lawyers, and other legal experts who make up the American Law Institute, an organization created in 1923 to bring uniformity and consistency to the language found in the statutory laws of the states. The MPC was first published by the American Law Institute in 1962, and substantial portions of it have been used since that time by state lawmakers in most states to revise their criminal statutes.

Section 2.01 of the MPC premises criminal liability on "conduct which includes a voluntary act or the omission to perform an act of which he is physically capable." Section 1.13(2) defines an "act" as "a bodily movement whether voluntary or involuntary." Thus, punishment for crime depends on some conduct involving a voluntary movement on the part of the defendant. It is that physical act that the law seeks to prevent. Notice, too, that the law requires that the act be voluntary, not involuntary. Voluntary acts are those over which a person has control. Involuntary ones are the result of spasms, seizures, or movements that a person cannot control. Voluntary acts may be punished as criminal behavior because they result from a free choice made by an individual. Justice is not served by punishing all those who, as a result of physical problems or diseases, or reflexive actions in unusual circumstances, make a movement that results in harm.

Omissions

As Section 2.01 of the MPC states, an "omission" may also satisfy the *actus reus* requirement. The MPC defines an omission as "a failure to act." Given that the criminal law generally punishes only volitional acts, how can nonaction result in criminal liability? Only in situations where a defendant has a legal duty to act, and fails to do so, may the law impose criminal liability; however, the circumstances in which this is true are limited. A legal duty may be created or exist in only three different circumstances. These are when a duty is created by statute, when a contract creates the duty to act, or when an individual has a special relationship with another such that the law imposes a duty because of that relationship. If one of these three circumstances exists and a duty to act is created, an "omission" may lead to criminal liability.

A state statute may create a duty to act by citizens because of public safety concerns. Normally, the government does not require citizens to put themselves in danger or render aid to another; however, some state legislatures have required people to summon aid in emergency situations, or when great harm is imminent. For example, the Rhode Island statutes state:

> § 11-37-3.1 Duty to report sexual assault.—Any person, other than the victim, who knows or has reason to know that a first degree sexual assault or attempted first degree sexual assault is taking place in his or her presence shall immediately notify the state police or the police department of the city or town in which the assault or attempted assault is taking place of the crime.
>
> § 11-37-3.3 Failure to report—Penalty.—Any person who knowingly fails to report a sexual assault or attempted sexual assault as required under § 11-37-3.1 shall be guilty of a misdemeanor and, upon conviction, shall be punished by imprisonment for not more than one year, or fined not more than five hundred dollars ($500), or both.

Thus, the Rhode Island legislature created a duty on the part of citizens to render aid by notifying the police when they are present and know a sexual assault is taking place.

A contract may also create a duty to act. Where an agreement between two parties exists requiring the parties to do certain things, the failure of one of the parties to act in accordance with the contract and that failure results in harm to another may be the basis for criminal liability in some circumstances. For example, doctors normally have a contractual arrangement with their patients before performing surgery. If a doctor agreed to perform life-saving surgery for a patient and then failed to do so and the patient died, the doctor's omission may lead to criminal liability.

A duty to act may also exist where a special relationship with another exists. Family and marriage relationships are such that one may owe a legal duty to another in certain circumstances. For example, parents have a duty to care for the normal needs of their children, and spouses generally have a duty to seek medical care should the other become ill and unable to seek medical assistance on his or her own.

It is important to remember that in each of the foregoing categories a moral or personal duty may also exist, such that a reasonable person may feel obligated to act, but failing to act when one has a moral duty to do so does not create criminal liability. Apart from compliance with its mandates, the law imposes few duties or responsibilities on citizens, and even when a duty in one of the categories above exists, the severity of the punishment for an omission is likely to be less than that for a volitional act.

Possession

Although a "passive" act, possession of contraband may satisfy actus reus. Contraband includes items that cannot legally be in one's possession, such as illegal drugs or weapons. A defendant may be criminally liable, whether possession is actual or constructive. Actual possession occurs when a defendant knowingly has contraband physically on his or her person. Constructive possession occurs when a person has knowledge and control of the contraband, even when it is not on his or her person. For example, illegal drugs found under the seat of a driver's car would be in the driver's constructive possession.

Mens Rea

Mens rea ("guilty mind") refers to the defendant's intent to commit a criminal act. The mental state of the defendant is important because it distinguishes accidental conduct resulting in harm from intentional conduct, which has as its purpose harm to another.

Under the common law, *mens rea* involved proof of one or more types of intent: general intent, specific intent, or transferred intent. General intent refers to the intent to commit the act, though not necessarily the intent to commit the resulting harm. For instance, a defendant who throws a stone at another in order to scare him off has the general intent to throw the stone, but if it strikes a victim in the head, killing him, the defendant may be found guilty for the death. Specific intent involves committing the act in order to produce the harm. If a defendant fires a gun at another intending to kill him and the victim dies, the defendant's specific intent will satisfy *mens rea*. Transferred intent exists when a defendant intends one harmful result but produces a different one. For example, if a defendant shoots a gun at one person intending to kill him but the bullet kills another person, the defendant's specific intent to kill is transferred to the resulting harm, satisfying *mens rea*. Some criminal statutes require general intent, and some require specific intent.

Another approach to defining *mens rea* is that found in the MPC.

The MPC classifies *mens rea* in one of four ways, each of which relates to the state of mind of the defendant. These involve whether the defendant acted *purposely*, *knowingly*, *recklessly*, or *negligently*. The definitions of these mental states are found in **Sidebar 11.1**, which shows that a defendant acts "purposely" when he or she has an intention to produce a specific result. If a defendant intends to kill a victim by shooting a gun at him and does so, the defendant has acted purposely, or he did it "on purpose."

Sidebar 11.1 *Levels of Culpability Under Section 2.02 of the Model Penal Code*

(1) Minimum Requirements of Culpability.

Except as provided in Section 2.05, a person is not guilty of an offense unless he acted purposely, knowingly, recklessly or negligently, as the law may require, with respect to each material element of an offense.

(2) Kinds of Culpability Defined.

(a) Purposely.

A person acts purposely with respect to a material element of an offense when:

(i) if the element involves the nature of his conduct or the result thereof, it is his conscious object to engage in conduct of that nature or to cause such a result; and

(ii) if the element involves the attendant circumstances, he is aware of the existence of such circumstances or he believes or hopes that they exist.

(b) Knowingly.

A person acts knowingly with respect to a material element of an offense when:

(i) if the element involves the nature of his conduct or the attendant circumstances, he is aware that his conduct is of that nature or that such circumstances exist; and

(ii) if the element involves a result of his conduct, he is aware that it is practically certain that his conduct will cause such a result.

(c) Recklessly.

A person acts recklessly with respect to a material element of an offense when he consciously disregards a substantial and unjustifiable risk that the material element exists or will result from his conduct. The risk must be of such a nature and degree that, considering the nature and purpose of the actor's conduct and the circumstances known to him, its disregard involves a gross deviation from the standard of conduct that a law-abiding person would observe in the actor's situation.

(d) Negligently.

A person acts negligently with respect to a material element of an offense when he should be aware of a substantial and unjustifiable risk that the material element exists or will result from his conduct. The risk must be of such a nature and degree that the actor's failure to perceive it, considering the nature and purpose of his conduct and the circumstances known to him, involves a gross deviation from the standard of care that a reasonable person would observe in the actor's situation.

Source: Model Penal Code, copyright 1985 by The American Law Institute. Reprinted with permission. All rights reserved.

A defendant acts "knowingly" by knowing that his conduct could result in harm, without intending that harm. Thus, if the defendant swings a baseball bat at his victim in the course of a fight, hits him in the head, and the victim dies, the defendant has acted knowingly.

A reckless state of mind exists when a defendant knows that there is a substantial and unjustifiable risk that his behavior may result in harm. A defendant who fires a gun into the air acts recklessly because he knows (or should know) that such an act creates a substantial and unjustified risk of injury to someone.

A "negligent" mental state is one in which the defendant acts in a way that creates a substantial risk of harm and is unaware that he or she is creating such a risk, but a reasonable person would have been aware of the risk.

Intent is not the same as motive. The reason that people sometimes act as they do (motive) does not necessarily reflect what they were thinking at the time they did it. Given that *mens rea* involves a defendant's mental state, proof of that mental state will nearly always be indirect, involving circumstantial evidence. For example, suppose that a man is accused of killing his wife, and during the investigation, it is found that the husband is a beneficiary of a 1 million dollar life insurance policy on his wife's life. The insurance policy may or may not be related to the man's *mens rea* at the time of the killing (assuming he committed the murder), but it does show a possible motive for killing his wife and circumstantially suggests what his mental state may have been. Thus, proof of motive may be useful to establish what a defendant may have been thinking at the time of the act, even if motive itself is not a necessary element of crime.

Concurrence

Concurrence is the connection between *actus reus* and *mens rea*. A person may do an act that is harmful, and a person may intend to harm another; however, unless the two happen together, the law does not impose liability. A person's wrongful act must be attributable to his or her "guilty" mental state. If the two do not coincide, there is no criminal liability. For example, if a man decides to kill his business associate in order to take over a business and later changes his mind, it may be that the requisite criminal intent exists at the same time as the occurrence of the act, but connection in time is not necessary. What is required to satisfy this element is that the defendant's mental state leads to or produces the act. Thus, the prosecution must establish a link between the defendant's act and the defendant's intent.

Causation

Causation connects the *actus reus* to the resulting harm. That is, the defendant's act must have led to harm to the victim. The prosecution must show that the intended act caused the harm. Either of two types of causation may be sufficient to satisfy the causation element. First, the defendant's act may be the *direct* cause of the harm. If a defendant fires a gun at a victim and the victim is hit and dies, the defendant's firing of the gun can be said to be the direct cause of the victim's death, but the law also recognizes *proximate cause*. Proximate cause exists when the resulting harm to a victim is reasonably foreseeable from the defendant's act. Thus, if a defendant drives his vehicle at an excessive rate of speed and strikes a pedestrian injuring her, the defendant will likely be criminally charged for the injuries to the pedestrian, but if the pedestrian goes to the hospital for surgery and dies as a result of the doctors' negligence, is the defendant who drove the car criminally

liable for her death? The answer turns on whether the defendant can be said to have caused her death. Proximate cause requires a determination of whether it is reasonably foreseeable that the defendant's actions could cause the resulting harm. In this example, it seems likely that the defendant would be charged with the pedestrian's death, even though the auto accident was not the direct cause.

From these examples, it can be seen that the legal cause of harm is not always straightforward and sometimes is the more difficult of the elements for the prosecution to prove; however, as is often the case in the law, there are exceptions to the rule. With respect to causation, there are some crimes that do not require proof of causation. These are known as "inchoate" crimes, which are incomplete crimes. Such crimes can be categorized as attempt, solicitation, and conspiracy. Attempt involves taking a substantial step toward the commission of a crime. Solicitation occurs when the defendant tries to get someone else to commit a crime, and conspiracy requires an agreement among two or more persons to commit a crime. For each of these, there is no need for the crime to have been actually committed in order for there to be criminal liability; therefore, because the harm has not yet occurred, it is not possible to establish a causal link to the defendant's act.

Harm

Typically, the harm resulting from the defendant's act is clear. Nonetheless, there must be evidence presented by the prosecution that harm resulted in accordance with the criminal offense charged. This evidence has been referred to as the *corpus delicti*, or "body of the crime." Specifically, *corpus delicti* requires the existence of some evidence other than the suspect's own statements that a crime was committed and evidence that the suspect's actions were criminal. In homicide cases, sometimes a *corpus delicti* problem arises when the body of the victim cannot be found, which would constitute evidence that a crime was committed. In most jurisdictions, however, a homicide prosecution may proceed without having found a dead victim, but connecting the defendant's actions to a nonexistent dead body may become a more difficult problem of proof, requiring significant circumstantial evidence such as motive or opportunity to commit the crime by the defendant or the victim's blood found on the defendant's clothing.

Defenses to Crime Allegations

At its most basic, a defense is nothing more than a response to allegations made by the prosecution. This may be a denial of the prosecution's factual allegations ("I didn't do it!"). It may affirmatively assert additional facts ("I wasn't in the city on the night he was murdered!"), or it may involve making legal claims ("Even if I did those things the prosecution claims, it's not a crime!"). When a criminal defendant is charged with a crime, he or she is not required to respond in any way, including the making of a plea (guilty, not guilty, *nolo contendere*), given that the burden of proof falls on the prosecution and the defendant is considered to be innocent until proven guilty. If the defendant chooses to make no response whatever, a plea of "not guilty" will be entered on his or her behalf, and the case will continue with the prosecution's burden of proof. Nonetheless, in most criminal cases, especially those involving serious charges, the defendant does "raise a defense" in response to the allegations made. One important reason for this is that after the prosecution has presented evidence relating to each of the elements of a crime, the defendant will likely be convicted unless some defense to the prosecution's case is made.

Various legal defenses may be raised, depending on the nature of the prosecutor's allegations and the facts of the case. These defenses are recognized in the common law, statutory law, or constitutional law. When a defense is raised, the defendant has the burden of proving it; however, unlike the prosecution's standard of proving the elements of crime beyond a reasonable doubt, the standard by which the defendant must prove a defense is a preponderance of the evidence. The differences among these standards of proof were discussed in Chapter 2.

There are two categories of recognized legal defenses to specific crimes: justifications and excuses. Justifications are those defenses in which the law makes the defendant's conduct acceptable given the circumstances in which the alleged criminal act occurred. Justifications can be classified as defenses of necessity and defenses of consent. Excuses are those defenses in which the defendant was unable to control his actions under the circumstances, and his or her failure to do so was excusable under the law.

Justification Defenses

Justification defenses are either those of necessity or those of consent. Defenses raising necessity as a justification are those that argue the defendant's actions were necessary in order to prevent harm to oneself or others. The most common of these is self-defense. Self-defense may be raised by a defendant when the defendant reasonably believes that the actions of another create a threat to result in serious bodily injury or death to the defendant; however, the threat must be imminent and the defendant must not have provoked the threat from another in order to rely on self-defense. In addition, the amount of force used by the defendant must be only as much as is reasonably necessary to prevent the harm posed by another, but this may include the use of deadly force. In some jurisdictions, however, the defendant must have attempted to retreat from the situation if that option was available before using deadly force. The laws of many jurisdictions incorporate the *castle doctrine*, which does not require a defendant to retreat and allows the use of deadly force against an intruder when the defendant is in his own home.

There are several variations of self-defense. Similar to self-defense is the defense of others, in which the defendant "steps into the shoes" of another in order to prevent harm to that person. As long as that other person could have used self-defense on his or her own behalf, the defense-of-others defense would be applicable. Also related to self-defense is the defense of property. This is a more restrictive defense than self-defense in that deadly force may never be used in defense of one's property. Finally, under the common law was a justification defense known as the choice-of-evils defense. This defense may apply when a defendant has caused harm or death to another in order to prevent some greater imminent harm from occurring. For example, if a passenger on a bus orders the driver, at gunpoint, to abandon the bus route and drive out of town and another passenger leaps forward and stabs the hijacker with a knife, the knife-wielding passenger would be able to rely on the choice-of-evils defense were he later to be charged with a crime as a result of the incident.

A second classification of justification defenses involves consent. Consent refers to whether the victim of a crime agreed to all or part of the defendant's criminal acts. In most criminal cases, the victim's consent may not be used as a defense; however, for crimes in which the victim's lack of consent is an element, the defendant may be able to show that the victim consented to the alleged criminal act. For example, larceny, which involves theft of property, requires the prosecution to show that the owner of the property did not allow the defendant to take it. Thus, if the owner of a car reports that it is stolen and the defendant is later arrested after being stopped while driving it, he may argue that the owner had consented to his use of the car.

Another common situation in which the consent defense is raised is in prosecutions for rape. If a defendant can show that the victim consented to sexual intercourse, the defense may preclude criminal liability; however, there are many factual situations involving sexual assaults in which the defense of consent is not allowed. These include when the victim is a minor ("statutory rape"), when the victim is under the influence of alcohol or drugs, and when the victim is under some form of duress. As with all defenses, the burden of proving that the victim consented falls on the defendant. Given that the sex act often occurs in private, evidence of consent is typically lacking, except for the contradictory statements of the parties. Most jurisdictions, however, have *rape shield laws*, which prevent testimony regarding the prior sexual behavior of the victim to be introduced. An example is Michigan's rape shield law, which provides:

(1) Evidence of specific instances of the victim's sexual conduct, opinion evidence of the victim's sexual conduct, and reputation evidence of the victim's sexual conduct shall not be admitted under sections 520b to 520g unless and only to the extent that the judge finds that the following proposed evidence is material to a fact at issue in the case and that its inflammatory or prejudicial nature does not outweigh its probative value:
    (a) Evidence of the victim's past sexual conduct with the actor.
    (b) Evidence of specific instances of sexual activity showing the source or origin of semen, pregnancy, or disease.
    (2) If the defendant proposes to offer evidence described in subsection (1)(a) or (b), the defendant within 10 days after the arraignment on the information shall file a written motion and offer of proof. The court may order an in camera hearing to determine whether the

proposed evidence is admissible under subsection (1). If new information is discovered during the course of the trial that may make the evidence described in subsection (1)(a) or (b) admissible, the judge may order an in camera hearing to determine whether the proposed evidence is admissible under subsection (1).

When a victim's prior sexual behavior with the defendant is raised to support a consent defense, an exception like that found in subsection (a) of the Michigan statute may exist. This subsection was the focus of *Michigan v. Lucas*, 500 U.S. 145, 111 S. Ct. 1743, 114 L.Ed.2d 205 (1991), in which the U.S. Supreme Court held that Michigan's exception, and the procedures that must be followed in order to allow evidence of the defendant's past sexual relationship with the victim, does not violate a defendant's Sixth Amendment right to confront the victim.

Excuse Defenses

A defendant who raises an excuse defense claims that something, recognized by law, prevented him from controlling his actions. Excuse defenses may be categorized by their focus: Some rely on the defendant's incapacity to act, whereas others present evidence that the situation in which the defendant found himself caused the act to occur. Regardless of these categories, however, it is important to realize that excuse defenses share the idea that the defendant acted in a way that he ordinarily would not, and that the law "excuses" the behavior because of its cause.

Perhaps most well known (though not most common) among the excuse defenses is the insanity defense. Insanity involves the defendant's mental incapacity to act in that he did not understand what he was doing at the time the act occurred. In cases where the insanity defense is raised, the defendant's attorney does not argue that the defendant did not commit the criminal act; rather, the attorney argues that the defendant lacked the mental capacity to understand what he was doing when he committed the act. If successful, the insanity defense allows the defendant to be found not guilty because of his insanity and to be committed to a mental institution for as long as he is deemed to be mentally incapacitated; however, not all states allow a defendant to assert a defense of insanity, and some states have passed statutes that allow juries to find a defendant "guilty but mentally ill." As the name indicates, this defense results in a verdict of guilt and commitment of the defendant to a mental institution for as long as he is mentally ill. If the defendant is later found by psychiatric professionals to be no longer insane, the defendant serves the remainder of his term in prison.

The courts of various jurisdictions have applied the insanity defense in four different ways. The primary and oldest test of insanity, known as the M'Naghten rule, was first successful in a British case in 1843. It was subsequently adopted in the United States and remains the test of insanity in many states today. The M'Naghten rule, sometimes known as the "right vs. wrong" test, results in a verdict of insanity if the defendant had "diseases of the mind" that caused him not to know the "nature and quality" of his act, or to know that it was wrong.

Some states found the M'Naghten rule to be unsatisfactory in serious cases because it requires proof of a "disease of the mind" along with the defendant's lack of knowledge about his actions. The rule would not allow an insanity defense when a "crime of passion" occurs where the defendant is "out of his mind" at the time of the act, but later recovers; therefore, an alternative was developed that allows a defendant to be found not guilty by reason of insanity if, as a result of a "mental defect" present when the crime was committed, he was unable to resist committing the criminal act. This is known as the "irresistible impulse" test.

A third test of insanity, the Durham test, was adopted in a case involving a defendant of that name in 1954. The Durham test attempted to simplify the analysis of the defendant's actions by asking whether the defendant committed the crime as a result of some mental disease. It is sometimes called the "product" test because it examines whether the criminal act was produced by the defendant's mental incapacity. Although in theory this test involves a straightforward link between the defendant's mental incapacity and his actions, in practice it is more difficult to establish such a causal connection.

Finally, the MPC adopts what is known as the substantial capacity test. This approach to the insanity defense requires proof that the defendant suffered from a mental disease and either lacked the capacity to understand that his or her criminal act was wrong or lacked the capacity to act in accordance with the law.

The insanity defense is unrelated to whether a defendant is competent to stand trial. Competency to stand trial focuses on the defendant's ability to understand the charges against him and her and whether he or she can assist in his own defense. Although it shares the issue of the defendant's mental status with the insanity defense, the issue of competency to stand trial differs in its focus by examining the defendant's mental status at the time of trial, not at the time of the criminal act. This distinction is an important one because of its consequences for the defendant, who can only be held for a "reasonable" amount of time if found to be not competent at the time of trial, or the charges against him must be dismissed. *Jackson v. Indiana*, 406 U.S. 715 (1972).

In addition to the insanity defense, other excuse defenses include duress, intoxication, and entrapment. Duress may apply when a defendant commits a criminal act because he or she is under a threat of death or serious bodily injury. For example, if an armed robber forces a store clerk to empty his or her cash register and then drive the getaway car at a high rate of speed to escape, the clerk could defend himself or herself by claiming that he or she acted under duress. Of course, many such situations would not be prosecuted at all, so the use of this defense is rare. The defense of intoxication refers to the involuntary ingestion of drugs or alcohol that renders the defendant at least partially incapacitated such that he or she was unable to form the requisite *mens rea* for the crime charged. Voluntary intoxication may not be used as a defense. The final excuse defense discussed here, entrapment, involves the use of deception by a government actor (commonly, an undercover police officer) to entice a person to commit a crime; however, for the defense to be successful, the defendant must not have been predisposed to commit the crime, and he must have been induced to commit the crime by the government. The purchase or sale of drugs by undercover officers is a common scenario in which entrapment may be raised, though in such situations, it is rarely successful because the defendant is unable to show that he was not predisposed to commit the crime.

Types of Crime

There are many ways of classifying crimes. One common way is to distinguish property crimes from crimes against a person. Property crimes are those in which the perpetrator seeks financial gain through the theft of property in some way. The category of crimes against a person involves those crimes that result (or could result) in physical harm to another. Because these are generally crimes involving some degree of violence to another, they tend to warrant greater punishments. In addition, some crimes target neither persons nor property, but are crimes involving public order or morality. Sometimes referred to as "victimless" crimes, these are actions typically aimed at the government or societal institutions, or actions that are *mala prohibita* because they are considered by society to be immoral.

Crimes Against the Person

Crimes against the person, as crimes with the potentially most serious consequences for the victim, play a protective role as part of the law in society. Whether the crime involves the death of another or a threat to another, society has keen interest in protecting its citizens and reducing the influence that fear of victimization would have in the way in which people conduct their lives. Thus, such crimes are generally prosecuted vigorously, and the punishments for crimes against people are the most severe.

Homicide

Under the common law, homicide was defined as the killing of another human being by the act, omission, or procurement of another. Given this definition, not all homicides resulted in criminal liability. The common law distinguished criminal homicide from noncriminal homicide. Noncriminal homicide may take two forms: justifiable and excusable. Justifiable homicide is killing that the law permits. Although the idea that law would permit some forms of killing sounds odd, examples include the use of the death penalty and the use of deadly force by police. Excusable homicide includes deaths that would result in criminal liability, but the circumstances were such that the defendant is "excused" from liability. The most common example of this is the killing of another in self-defense. Under the common law, therefore, criminal homicide included all homicide that was not justifiable or excusable. Some states continue these distinctions today, including common law definitions of the forms of homicide in their criminal statutes.

Most states today, however, define homicide in accordance with the approach taken by the MPC. Although common law definitions persist and are sometimes used in combination with the language found in the MPC, the MPC approach to criminal homicide was intended to simplify the legal analysis of culpable forms of killing. Under the MPC, criminal homicide is defined as "purposely, knowingly, recklessly or negligently taking the life of another human being" (MPC, Section 210.1). Thus, the types of criminal homicide coincide with the four mental states of the defendant, discussed earlier. There are three types: murder, manslaughter, and negligent homicide (MPC, Section 210.1). In addition, the MPC recognizes the purposeful causing of another to commit suicide as criminal homicide, if it is done through "force, duress, or deception" (MPC, Section 210.5).

Murder

Under the common law, murder was defined as the killing of a human being with malice aforethought. A person was considered to be a "human being" if born alive, thus excluding unborn fetuses and prohibiting criminal liability to those who harmed a pregnant woman resulting in death to the unborn child. Most states, however, have modified this rule to allow prosecution of defendants who harm fetuses. For example, in *People v. Pool*, 166 Cal. App. 4th 904, 83 Cal. Rptr. 3d 186 (Ct. App. 2008), the California Court of Appeal considered the effect of the defendant's knowledge about the victim's pregnancy on the charges he faced. *Pool* is found in **Case Decision 11.1**.

As the court in *Pool* discussed, malice aforethought refers to the *mens rea* of the killer. In particular, although killing with malice aforethought includes premeditation, it does not require premeditation. Murder with malice aforethought is death resulting from the defendant's wrongful action undertaken while he had a wanton or evil state of mind.

Whether malice aforethought exists is important in determining the degree of culpability for murder, which generally is codified as degrees of murder, first or second. For example, the Rhode Island murder statute states that "[t]he unlawful killing of a human being with malice aforethought is murder." Murders committed "by willful, deliberate, malicious, and premeditated killing," or murders committed in the course of committing various felonies, or while resisting arrest, are classified as first degree, whereas all others are considered to be second degree.

In Section 210.2 of the MPC, murder is defined as a homicide committed "purposely or knowingly; or . . . committed recklessly under circumstances manifesting extreme indifference to the value of human life." Although the facts and circumstances of a given case will determine when these mental states exist, any one of them is sufficient to satisfy the *mens rea* for murder when the defendant's actions result in the death of another. Different mental states, however, typically distinguish first degree from second-degree murders (**Sidebar 11.2**).

Case Decision 11.1   *People v. Pool*, 166 Cal. App. 4th 904, 83 Cal. Rptr. 3d 186 (Ct. App. 2008)

Opinion of the Court by Judge Robie:

A jury found defendant Timon Joel Pool guilty of the first degree murder of Lillian Best and the second degree murder of Best's unborn fetus and found true a multiple-murder special-circumstances allegation. Defendant was sentenced to state prison for life without possibility of parole. On appeal, defendant argues the trial court committed reversible error by misinstructing the jury on murder of a fetus. Finding no error, we will affirm.

Factual and Procedural Background

On July 23, 2006, defendant strangled his girlfriend, Lillian Best, to death. While performing an autopsy on July 24, the forensic pathologist noticed Best's uterus was noticeably larger than normal, and further investigation showed she had been pregnant. Because Best was in the early stages of pregnancy and was obese, her pregnancy was "not something obvious externally." The forensic pathologist, as well as a coroner's office pathologist who reviewed the forensic pathologist's report, both estimated the gestational age of the fetus to be about 12 weeks. Both pathologists also concluded that the fetus died as a result of the death of the mother.

Defendant claimed not to have known Best was pregnant until he was in the holding cell in court for his arraignment and received documents charging him with two murders. Defendant testified he was "[a]bsolutely devastated" to learn he had killed his unborn child.

Defendant was charged with two counts of willfully, unlawfully, and with malice aforethought murdering Lillian Best and her fetus, respectively, with a multiple-murder special-circumstances allegation.

Prior to trial, the court agreed with the prosecutor's contention that knowledge of the existence of the fetus was not a prerequisite for finding defendant guilty of fetal murder. Later, during closing arguments, the prosecutor stressed to the jury that defendant could be found guilty of murdering the fetus on an implied malice basis even if he did not know Best was pregnant.

The jury was instructed that in order to prove the crime of second degree murder as to the fetus, "the People must prove that: One, the defendant committed an act that caused the death of another person or a fetus; And, two, when the defendant acted, he had a state of mind called malice aforethought. There are two kinds of malice aforethought, express malice and implied malice. Proof of either is sufficient to establish the state of mind required for murder." The court did not include the optional "natural and probable consequences" paragraph from the standard instruction: "An act causes death if the death is the direct, natural, and probable consequence of the act and the death would not have happened without the act. A *natural and probable consequence* is one that a reasonable person would know is likely to happen if nothing unusual intervenes. In deciding whether a consequence is natural and probable, consider all of the circumstances established by the evidence."

However, the trial court gave the following special instruction for murder of a fetus: "Malice is a separate element that must be proved for each of the two murders charged. When a defendant commits an act, the natural consequences of which are dangerous to human life, with a conscious disregard for life in general, he acts with implied malice towards those he ends up killing. There is no requirement that the defendant specifically know of the existence of each victim [i.e., the fetus]."

Discussion

Defendant argues that the trial court committed reversible error by giving the prosecutor's special instruction that knowledge of the fetus's existence was not a prerequisite to a murder conviction and compounded that error by omitting from the jury instructions the "natural and probable consequences" paragraph. We find no error.

I

Knowledge of Existence of the Fetus Is Not a Prerequisite to Fetal Murder

Defendant first contends the special jury instruction "that knowledge of the existence of the fetus was not a prerequisite for finding [defendant] guilty of fetal murder" was erroneous. Defendant notes that

(Continues)

"[a]lthough neither the court nor the prosecutor expressly referred to *People v. Taylor* (2004) 32 Cal. 4th 863, 11 Cal. Rptr. 3d 510, 86 P.3d 881 (*Taylor*), that case was the unquestionable basis for the prosecutor's instruction." Defendant "submits, however, that the holding in *Taylor* should be narrowly construed and should not have applied to the circumstances in [defendant's] case" in which the victim was strangled rather than shot. We see no reason to distinguish *Taylor*.

The facts in *Taylor* are remarkably similar to the facts here. In *Taylor*, the defendant engaged in a physical struggle with his ex-girlfriend, eventually shooting her in the head and killing her. She died of a single gunshot wound to the head. The autopsy revealed she was pregnant, and the fetus was between 11 and 13 weeks old. The examining pathologist could not discern that the victim, who weighed approximately 200 pounds, was pregnant just by observing her on the examination table. The prosecution proceeded on a theory of second degree implied malice murder as to the fetus, and the defendant was convicted of two counts of second degree murder. Noting that the " '[defendant] did not know [the victim] was pregnant,' " Division Four of the First District Court of Appeal reversed the conviction for fetal murder. Specifically, the court asked, " '[w]here is the evidence that [defendant] acted with knowledge of the danger to, and conscious disregard for, fetal life?' " and answered " '[t]here is none. This is dispositive.' "

Our Supreme Court reversed the judgment of the Court of Appeal, holding that "[w]hen a defendant commits an act, the natural consequences of which are dangerous to human life, with a conscious disregard for life in general, he acts with implied malice towards those he ends up killing. There is no requirement that the defendant specifically know of the existence of each victim." "[B]y engaging in the conduct that he did, defendant demonstrated a conscious disregard for life, fetal or otherwise, and hence is liable for all deaths caused by his conduct."

Defendant asks us to distinguish the holding in *Taylor*, arguing that "the differences between *Taylor* . . . and [defendant's] case should be obvious." Defendant argues that in *Taylor* "the Supreme Court arrived at its holding by focusing on the defendant's act of firing two bullets at the victim during the assault, specifically concluding that in shooting [his victim] the defendant acted with conscious disregard for life in general." Defendant then argues that "[a] reasonable person should know that when he fires a gun at an intended target he runs the risk of killing another person with a stray bullet [and] [i]t is undisputable that firing a weapon is an inherently reckless act dangerous to all those around . . . irrespective of whether he is aware of their presence."

"By contrast," in defendant's view, "a reasonable person with no knowledge, or even suspicion, that his victim is pregnant, should not be expected to know that strangling the victim might result in the death of another victim. Unlike discharging a weapon, or driving a car while drunk both of which are potentially lethal to anyone who gets in the way, the act of strangling a person is not inherently dangerous to anyone other than the person being strangled. . . . [S]trangling an intended victim indicates only a conscious disregard for that life *in particular*."

We are unpersuaded by defendant's arguments. We find no basis in law or reason for distinguishing between murdering a pregnant woman by gunshot or by strangulation. Our Supreme Court in *Taylor* could hardly have been more clear: "In battering and shooting [the victim], defendant acted with knowledge of the danger to and conscious disregard for life in general. That is all that is required for implied malice murder. He did not need to be specifically aware how many potential victims his conscious disregard for life endangered." Here, in strangling Best, defendant likewise acted with knowledge of the danger to and conscious disregard for life.

Finally, in trying to distinguish *Taylor*, defendant asks us to consider an earlier California Supreme Court case, *People v. Roberts* (1992) 2 Cal. 4th 271, 6 Cal. Rptr. 2d 276, 826 P.2d 274, to further support his contentions. In *Roberts*, the defendant, a prison inmate, stabbed another inmate, Gardner, 11 times, after which Gardner grabbed the knife off the floor, staggered some distance up a flight of stairs, and stabbed a prison guard in the chest. Both Gardner and the guard eventually died from their wounds. The prosecution presented expert testimony that the sudden loss of blood to Gardner caused him to go into shock and unconsciously stab the guard. The defendant was convicted of the first degree murders of Gardner and the guard. In instructing the jury on the proximate cause of death, the trial court told the jury that it was "immaterial that the defendant could not reasonably have foreseen the harmful result" to the prison guard when he stabbed Gardner. In reversing the defendant's conviction, the Supreme Court noted that "implied malice may be found when a defendant, knowing that his or her conduct endangers life and acting with conscious disregard of the danger, commits an act the natural consequences of which are dangerous to life." The court then observed that "[a] result cannot be the natural and probable cause of an act if the act was unforeseeable." Defendant argues that because the death of a fetus whose existence is unknown is not the natural and probable consequence of a strangling, "[t]he effect of the prosecutor's special instruction in this case was analogous to the improper instruction given in *Roberts* because "the court effectively told the jury that, as in *Roberts*, it was 'immaterial that the defendant could not reasonably have foreseen the harmful result' to the fetus."

We think the facts here are readily distinguishable from those in *Roberts*. Here, there was expert testimony that the defendant directly caused the fetus's death when he killed Best. Defendant does not dispute this fact. In *Roberts*, however, the court noted there was an issue as to whether the defendant was an indirect, and likely unforeseeable, cause of the guard's death, which the jury never considered. The *Roberts* court found that "[a]n instruction that told the jury to disregard foreseeability would inevitably lead it to ignore the nature of Gardner's response to defendant's attack, and hence would substantially distract the jury from considering the causation element of the offense—an element that was very much at issue in the case." In other words, the *Roberts* court found that the trial court had incorrectly stated the law of proximate cause by expressly instructing the jury not to consider whether Gardner's unconscious response to being stabbed (i.e., stabbing the prison guard) was foreseeable. We are faced with no such "chain of causation" question here. On the facts before us, *Taylor*, decided 12 years after *Roberts* and with facts nearly identical to those here, is controlling. Accordingly, the trial court did not err in giving the special instruction. The judgment is affirmed.

Sidebar 11.2 *The Criminal Trials of O.J. Simpson*

No other murder trial in history has been as watched, analyzed, discussed, and disdained as that of former football and movie star O.J. Simpson. His ex-wife, Nicole Brown, lived in the wealthy Brentwood area of Los Angeles with her children, whose father was Simpson. In June of 1994, a man walked through the back entrance to Brown's home, cornered her near the front gate, and slashed her throat, nearly severing her head from her body. He then stabbed Ronald Goldman numerous times, killing him almost instantly. Brown's neighbor later found both victims after a small white dog came to their door with blood on its paws. Meanwhile, Simpson was aboard an airplane to Chicago that took off from Los Angeles at 11:45 p.m. the night of the murders. Police located Simpson and informed him of the deaths early the next morning, but he did not ask what happened. Police gathered enough evidence to obtain a warrant for his arrest. It was arranged that he would turn himself in on June 17, 1994, at 10 a.m. When he did not arrive at the police station by 1 p.m., officers began looking for him. Around 6:30 that evening, they received reports that Simpson had been seen riding in a white Ford Bronco. What followed was a televised low-speed chase of the vehicle that millions viewed. He finally returned to his own driveway and surrendered and was found with $8,750, a fake beard, and a loaded gun.

At his arraignment on June 21, 1994, Simpson pleaded not guilty to the two murders. The trial began on January 24, 1995, lasting 99 days. The trial became a spectacle, with a constant media presence both within and outside the courtroom, as well as television cameras broadcasting nearly all of the proceedings. A central piece of evidence was a bloody glove found outside of Simpson's home. Johnnie Cochran, Simpson's attorney, had him attempt to try on the glove. Before a nationwide audience he declared that the glove was "too tight"—it

"wouldn't fit." Later, in closing, Cochran reminded the jury that the glove wouldn't fit, famously arguing "if the glove won't fit, you must acquit!"

On October 13, 1995, 10 black people, 1 Hispanic person, and 1 white juror returned a verdict of not guilty. Most people in the country who watched the televised trial, however, believed that he was guilty. Some felt that the jury refused to convict on racial grounds; others believed that jury nullification (in which a jury disregards clear evidence to the contrary) was at work. Regardless, many people, especially the Goldman and Brown families, felt that justice was not served. Turning to the civil courts, they successfully sued Simpson for the wrongful deaths of Brown and Goldman and were awarded over $33 million (see Sidebar 9.1). They continue their crusade for justice by trying to collect the judgment, attaching Simpson's assets wherever possible.

Over a decade later, Simpson was again in trouble with the law. On September 13, 2007, Simpson, with four companions, entered a Las Vegas casino hotel room whose occupants had sports memorabilia to be sold. They confronted the dealers, accused them of stealing items belonging to Simpson, and held them at gunpoint while Simpson and his companions stole the memorabilia. When the dealers reported the incident and showed evidence of ownership of the stolen items, Simpson and his friends were arrested and charged with armed robbery, kidnapping, and conspiracy, among other crimes.

Although this trial received extensive media attention, it was more tightly controlled by the judge, and cameras were not allowed in the courtroom. After hearing 13 days of testimony, and taking 13 hours to deliberate, the jury found Simpson guilty on all counts. The Las Vegas decision came 13 years to the day after Simpson was acquitted of murder. Subsequently, the judge sentenced him to

(Continues)

33 years in prison, with eligibility for parole after 9 years. The judge made a point of stating that her sentence focused solely on the charges and evidence in the Las Vegas case and was not related to Simpson's earlier acquittal in the Brown and Goldman murders.

In May of 2009, O.J. Simpson appealed his conviction and sentence. The appeal is based on various rulings by the trial judge relating to evidence and jury instructions, as well as the judge's decision to allow references that were made about Simpson's 1994 trial. In addition, the judge allowed the prosecution to strike the only two black people in the venire from the jury. Simpson awaits his fate at Lovelock Correctional Center near Reno, Nevada.

Manslaughter

The common law considered all killings committed without malice aforethought to be manslaughter. Because the defendant did not have the mental state required for murder, it was (and remains) a less serious offense than murder. Common law manslaughter was always voluntary; that is, the defendant acted with the intent to kill or cause serious bodily harm. Generally, however, manslaughter resulted from some provocation to the defendant. The provocation had to be such that the defendant acted in the "heat of passion." This means that the situation in which the killing occurred was such that a reasonable person would lose his or her self-control in attacking another. Today, many states distinguish voluntary from involuntary manslaughter. Involuntary manslaughter is unintentional killing resulting from the reckless or grossly negligent behavior of the defendant. Generally, this occurs when a defendant does not consider the consequences of his actions, that is, the risk of death to the victim that such actions may cause. In many states, vehicular homicide is defined as a distinct form of involuntary manslaughter, where the defendant's reckless operation of a motor vehicle, or operation of the vehicle while under the influence of alcohol or drugs, results in the death of another.

Assault and Battery

At common law, assault and battery were two separately defined crimes. Today, in most jurisdictions, they are charged together, usually under the crime of "assault." Nonetheless, understanding the common law distinction between the two is useful in thinking about the elements of assault crimes. Battery is the unlawful touching of another. Touching involves any physical contact with another person that results in harm or is otherwise offensive to the victim. Assault is the threat to injure another that the other person reasonably perceives to be threatening or an attempt to commit a battery.

The crime of assault requires conduct that is threatening to the victim along with the intent to threaten the victim. Thus, although common law assault did not require any actual touching of the victim, today an attempt to hit or somehow batter the victim or place him or her in fear of being battered will constitute assault, as well as the actual battery; however, where no physical contact with the victim occurs, the threat must be specifically directed at the victim, as opposed to a generalized threat such as "someone is going to pay." In addition, in most instances, words alone are insufficient; some threatening action must accompany what the defendant says.

It is not always clear when the *actus reus* for assault is met. In *People v. Chance*, 44 Cal. 4th 1164, 189 P.3d 971, 81 Cal. Rptr. 3d 723 (2008), the California Supreme Court considered whether the threat constituting an assault must involve the actual ability by the defendant to carry it out. The court interpreted the California Penal Code's definition of assault, "an unlawful attempt, coupled with a present ability, to commit a violent injury on the person of another," finding that "present ability" does not require an ability to immediately cause harm (Case Decision 11.2).

To satisfy the *actus reus* for battery, the contact must actually result in harm to the victim or be such that a reasonable person would find the contact offensive. The crime of battery is usually classified in criminal statutes as either simple or aggravated. The distinction between these

Case Decision 11.2 *People v. Chance*, 44 Cal. 4th 1164, 189 P.3d 971, 81 Cal. Rptr. 3d 723 (2008)

Opinion of the Court by Justice Corrigan:

Here we consider the actus reus required for assault. Since 1872, the Penal Code [section 240] has defined assault as "an unlawful attempt, coupled with a present ability, to commit a violent injury on the person of another." This case involves only the "present ability" aspect of the crime. Nevertheless, we must consider the effect of statements in prior opinions analyzing the intent required for assault.

In *People v. Colantuono* (1994) 7 Cal. 4th 206, 216, 26 Cal. Rptr. 2d 908, 865 P.2d 704 (*Colantuono*), and *People v. Williams* (2001) 26 Cal. 4th 779, 784–785 (*Williams*), we reaffirmed the established rule that assault is a general intent crime. We noted that attempt crimes generally require specific intent, but that the "unlawful attempt" term of section 240 is different. Assault requires an act that is closer to the accomplishment of injury than is required for other attempts. Other criminal attempts, because they require proof of specific intent, may be more remotely connected to the attempted crime. When

258   Section IV: Criminal Law and Procedure in the Courts

discussing the intent requirement, we have characterized assault as "unlawful conduct immediately antecedent to battery."

Here, defendant relies on that characterization to argue that he lacked the present ability to commit assault because his conduct did not immediately precede a battery. The Court of Appeal, in a split decision, agreed. We reject this application of *Colantuono* and *Williams*. Neither case discussed the present ability element of assault. That element is satisfied when "a defendant has attained the means and location to strike immediately." In this context, however, "immediately" does not mean "instantaneously." It simply means that the defendant must have the ability to inflict injury on the present occasion. It has long been established that the "injury" element of the assault statute is satisfied by any attempt to apply physical force to the victim, and includes even injury to the victim's feelings. Numerous California cases establish that an assault may be committed even if the defendant is several steps away from actually inflicting injury, or if the victim is in a protected position so that injury would not be "immediate," in the strictest sense of that term. *Colantuono* and *Williams* did not discuss or disturb this settled authority.

Facts

The facts are undisputed. On the afternoon of November 29, 2003, sheriff's officers drove to a house in a rural area of El Dorado County to arrest defendant pursuant to felony warrants. The officers had information that defendant was there and armed with a handgun. Defendant, evidently alerted to their approach, ran from the house. Sergeant Tom Murdoch pursued him on foot. Murdoch wore a vest marked with a large yellow star and the word "SHERIFF" on the front and back. Defendant saw Murdoch and kept running.

After defendant turned up the driveway to another home, Murdoch twice shouted, "Sheriff's Department, stop." From a distance of 30 to 35 feet, Murdoch saw that defendant was carrying a handgun. Defendant ran around the front end of a trailer. Murdoch approached, looking and listening for any indication that defendant was still fleeing. Detecting none, and anticipating that defendant might be lying in wait for him, Murdoch advanced to his left, around the back of the trailer. Carefully peering around the corner, he saw defendant pressed against the trailer, facing the front end. He was holding the gun in his right hand, extended forward and supported by his left hand.

Defendant looked back over his right shoulder at Murdoch, who had his own gun trained on defendant. Murdoch repeatedly told defendant to drop the weapon. The officer testified, "I was in fear of my life. I was afraid . . . he was going to try to shoot me any second." After some hesitation, defendant brought the gun toward the center of his body, then flipped it behind him. He began to run again, but fell after only a few steps. Defendant was arrested and the gun recovered. It was fully loaded with 15 rounds in the magazine. There was no round in the firing chamber, but defendant could have chambered one by pulling back a slide mechanism. The safety was off.

A jury convicted defendant of assault with a firearm on a peace officer under section 245(d)(1), along with other offenses. Only the assault conviction is at issue on this appeal by the Attorney General.

Discussion

The Court of Appeal majority reversed the assault conviction, concluding that defendant did not have the "present ability [ ] to commit a violent injury" required for assault under section 240, because his act of pointing a gun at a place where he thought Sergeant Murdoch would appear was not immediately antecedent to a battery. For the proposition that an assault must immediately precede a battery, the majority relied on our decision in *Williams*. Its reliance was misplaced. *Williams* involved only the mental state required for assault, and did not construe the present ability requirement.

Williams clarified our holding in *Colantuono* that assault is a general intent crime, "established upon proof the defendant willfully committed an act that by its nature will probably and directly result in injury to another, i.e., a battery." To ensure that an assault conviction cannot be based on facts unknown to a defendant, the *Williams* court held that a defendant must "actually know [ ] those facts sufficient to establish that his act by its nature will probably and directly result in physical force being applied to another."

The language deemed controlling by the Court of Appeal majority here is found in *Williams*' review of the distinction between ordinary criminal attempt, which requires specific intent, and the "unlawful attempt . . . to commit a violent injury" required for assault under section 240. This statutory language

(Continues)

(Continued)

has remained unchanged since its enactment. *Williams* explained that when the Legislature employed the word "attempt" in section 240, it used the term in a particular sense. We quote the relevant paragraphs in their entirety, to provide the context:

> "In determining which meaning of 'attempt' the Legislature intended to use in section 240, we must look to the historical 'common law definition' of assault. Assault 'is not simply an adjunct of some underlying offense [like criminal attempt], but an independent crime statutorily delineated in terms of certain unlawful conduct immediately antecedent to battery.' Unlike criminal attempt where the 'act constituting an attempt to commit a felony may be more remote,' '[a]n assault is an act done toward the commission of a battery' and must 'immediately' precede the battery. (Perkins & Boyce, Criminal Law (3d ed. 1982) p. 164 (Perkins).) Indeed, our criminal code has long recognized this fundamental distinction between criminal attempt and assault by treating these offenses as *separate and independent* crimes.
>
> "Consequently, criminal attempt and assault require different mental states. Because the act constituting a criminal attempt 'need not be the last proximate or ultimate step toward commission of the substantive crime,' criminal attempt has always required 'a specific intent to commit the crime.' In contrast, the crime of assault has always focused on the nature of the act and not on the perpetrator's specific intent. An assault occurs whenever '[t]he next movement would, *at least to all appearance*, complete the battery.' (Perkins, p. 164, italics added.) Thus, assault 'lies on a definitional . . . *continuum of conduct* that describes its essential relation to battery: An assault is an incipient or inchoate battery; a battery is a consummated assault.' As a result, a specific intent to injure is not an element of assault because the assaultive act, by its nature, subsumes such an intent."

The Attorney General argues that these passages in *Williams* and *Colantuono* have inappropriately incorporated the concept of "apparent present ability" into section 240. We disagree. As explained below, the discussion of the proximity between assault and battery in *Williams* and *Colantuono* was confined to the intent requirement for assault, and did not mention or change the well-established understanding of the "present ability" element of section 240.

Here, defendant does not dispute that he had the general intent required for assault. Like the Court of Appeal majority, however, he relies on the statements in *Williams* and *Colantuono* that an assault must *immediately* precede the battery. Defendant also notes that *Williams* and *Colantuono* characterized assault as occurring whenever *the next movement* would complete the battery. Therefore, he argues, he did not have the "present ability" to inflict injury required by section 240, because he would have had to turn, point his gun at the officer, and chamber a round before he could shoot at Murdoch.

This application of *Williams* and *Colantuono* is mistaken. In those cases, we were concerned with distinguishing assault from the later developed criminal attempt doctrine. The holdings in *Williams* and *Colantuono* were not intended to and did not transform the traditional understanding of assault to insulate defendants from liability until the last instant before a battery is completed. Although temporal and spatial considerations are relevant to a defendant's "present ability" under section 240, it is the ability to inflict injury on the present occasion that is determinative, not whether injury will necessarily be the instantaneous result of the defendant's conduct.

Thus, it is a defendant's action enabling him to inflict a present injury that constitutes the actus reus of assault. There is no requirement that the injury would necessarily occur as the very next step in the sequence of events, or without any delay. [A]ssault does not require a direct attempt at violence. "There need not be even a direct attempt at violence; but any indirect preparation towards it, under the circumstances mentioned, such as drawing a sword or bayonet, or even laying one's hand upon his sword, would be sufficient."

"Nothing suggests this 'present ability' element was incorporated into the common law to excuse defendants from the crime of assault where they have acquired the means to inflict serious injury and positioned themselves within striking distance merely because, unknown to them, external circumstances doom their attack to failure. This proposition would make even less sense where a defendant has actually launched his attack—as in the present case—but failed only because of some unforeseen circumstance which made success impossible. Nor have we found any cases under the California law which compel this result. The decisions holding a defendant lacks 'present ability' when he tries to shoot someone with an unloaded gun or a toy pistol do not support any such proposition. In those situations, the defendant has simply failed to equip himself with the personal means to inflict serious injury even if he thought he had."

Here, defendant's loaded weapon and concealment behind the trailer gave him the means and the location to strike "immediately" at Sergeant Murdoch, as that term applies in the context of assault. Murdoch's evasive maneuver, which permitted him to approach defendant from behind, did not deprive defendant of the "present ability" required by section 240. Defendant insists that, unlike the defendants in the cases discussed above, he never pointed his weapon in Murdoch's direction. That degree of immediacy is not necessary. [D]efendant's mistake as to the officer's location was immaterial. He attained the present ability to inflict injury by positioning himself to strike on the present occasion with a loaded weapon. This conduct was sufficient to establish the actus reus required for assault.

is whether the actual or threatened contact has the potential of death or serious bodily injury.

Sex Offenses

Whereas the crime of rape was recognized in the common law, today there are a variety of sex offenses in states' criminal statutes. These typically include different degrees of sexual assault that vary according to the extent of force used by the defendant or the helplessness of the victim, as well as sexual contact with minors, and child molestation. Although prostitution may also be viewed as a sex crime, it is more aptly considered a crime against public order and morality, discussed later here.

Common law rape was defined as unlawful "carnal knowledge," or sexual intercourse of a female without her consent. It was not unlawful for a man to have forcible sexual intercourse with his wife regardless of her consent. Today, rape laws are not gender specific, and they do not exclude nonconsensual sexual intercourse with a spouse.

An important distinction in law relating to sexual assault involves the *actus reus*. Although first-degree sexual assault requires sexual intercourse involving penetration, lesser degrees of sexual assault may be established when sexual contact not amounting to penetration occurs. Sexual penetration differs from sexual contact in that it usually involves any intrusion into the genital or anal openings of a person, whereas sexual contact involves intentional touching of a victim's intimate parts for the sexual gratification or arousal of the defendant, whether the victim is clothed or unclothed. As a result, rape is no longer defined solely in terms of the act of sexual intercourse. Sexual assault can occur through sexual contact, as long as it is nonconsensual.

Cases of sexual assault, whether involving penetration or contact, often turn on whether the victim consented to the sex act. Commonly, a defendant will raise a defense claiming the victim consented to sexual intercourse or contact. Because the lack of consent by the victim is an element of the offense, the prosecution carries the burden of proving it; however, as discussed earlier, the defendant may attempt to introduce evidence of the victim's sexual activity in the past to show circumstantially that he or she was likely to have consented. As a result, many jurisdictions have rape shield laws preventing the introduction of evidence of the victim's sexual history, in whole or in part.

Thus, the modern approach to rape is considerably broader than that of the common law, and the conse-

quences are severe. In addition to lengthy jail terms, many jurisdictions require registration of sexual offenders and notification to the public of their locations within a community. This has been held not to violate a defendant's right to not be subjected to double jeopardy in the punishment of an offense.

Statutory rape is generally defined as sexual intercourse with a minor by an adult. The age of consent differs from state to state, and the age of the minor at the time of the rape also varies considerably. The Rhode Island statute defining statutory rape as third-degree sexual assault is typical: "A person is guilty of third degree sexual assault if he or she is over the age of eighteen (18) years and engaged in sexual penetration with another person over the age of fourteen (14) years and under the age of consent, sixteen (16) years of age." Statutory rape is a strict liability crime. The prosecution need not prove the defendant intended to have sex with the victim, nor may the defendant defend by claiming he or she thought the victim was an adult.

Robbery

The crime of robbery is sometimes referred to as a "hybrid" crime because its focus is obtaining money or other property, but it involves the threat of injury to persons as well. Robbery is taking or attempting to take anything of value from someone by the actual use or threat of using violence, intimidation, or other means of putting the victim in fear for his or her safety. As a result, robbery is a feared crime that remains ever present in the mind of the public because of the seeming randomness of its victims.

Kidnapping/False Imprisonment

Kidnapping and false imprisonment are similar, although separate offenses. False imprisonment involves restricting a person's freedom against his or her will. There is no requirement that this be done by the use of force or intimidation, although it usually accompanies the act preventing the victim from leaving. All that is required is that the defendant confined the victim in such a way that the victim is not free to go where she wishes. The confinement need not be for a lengthy period of time and may occur in buildings, vehicles, even outdoors. As long as the victim has no reasonable means of escape from the situation, the *actus reus* for false imprisonment exists. The defendant must specifically intend to confine or otherwise deprive a person of freedom to satisfy *mens rea*.

There are some exceptions to the crime of false imprisonment in which a person may detain or confine another without criminal liability. The most obvious and common of these is detention by the police. As long as the police lawfully detain a person, false imprisonment has not occurred. Lawful detention occurs, for example, when a police officer has reasonable suspicion for a traffic stop or has probable cause to support an arrest. Another situation in which a person may confine another without committing false imprisonment is in retail stores or restaurants. Known as the *shopkeeper's rule*, this exception allows the manager of a store to detain a person suspected of shoplifting or trying to leave without paying for goods or services. There is no criminal liability for doing this, even if the manager later finds he was mistaken, as long as he had a reasonable belief that the theft occurred and the amount of time involved was not excessive.

Kidnapping is defined in a similar way to false imprisonment but also includes the removal or movement of the victim from one place to another. Most kidnapping statutes also include the use of force or intimidation by the defendant as part of the *actus reus*. Thus, generally, the elements of kidnapping are satisfied when the defendant confines someone by some forceful means and moves the person from one location to another, with the intent to deprive them of freedom.

Kidnapping has become a growing problem as divorce rates have risen, and disputes about child custody arrangements have increased. Noncustodial parents who are displeased with the terms of court orders on child custody have kidnapped their children and taken them to hidden locations beyond the reach of the custodial parent or the courts. In response to this problem, Congress passed the Parental Kidnapping Prevention Act (PKPA) of 1980, 28 U.S.C. 1738. The PKPA requires states to enforce orders from courts in other states regarding child custody. It also prevents a court in a new state from exercising jurisdiction over a child once a court in another state already has jurisdiction. The intent of the law is to reduce the extent of parental kidnapping by preventing parents from seeking new court-approved custody arrangement in more states that may be more favorable to them.

Crimes Against Property

Crimes involving property are the largest category of crimes in the United States. Approximately seven times as many property crimes occur each year than do violent crimes. Property crimes are those that involve the theft or destruction of property. Property crimes depend on depriving the owner of his or her rights in the property. Property is categorized according to the nature of the property. Real property consists of land and its fixtures, which are buildings and other improvements made a permanent part of it. Personal property is anything that is not real property or affixed to real property. Personal property may be tangible or intangible. Tangible property is personal property that can be seen and touched, including chattel, which is items that may be moved. Intangible property has no physical existence, but exists nonetheless.

It is property that includes ideas, inventions, stocks or other financial instruments, music, or computer programs. Both tangible and intangible personal property may be subjected to criminal activity.

Most, although not all, property crimes involve some form of theft. The term theft means some form of stealing the property of another person, but the way in which it occurs differentiates various crimes. In addition, theft crimes are typically distinguished by the value of the property that is the subject of the theft. Thus, the term "grand" theft usually refers to theft of property whose value exceeds a minimum amount (such as $500) that makes the crime a felony, whereas "petty" theft is a misdemeanor involving theft property valued at less than this amount. The common methods by which theft is committed, as specified in the criminal law, as well as other crimes relating to personal property, are detailed later here.

Larceny

The most common way in which property crime occurs is by larceny, which was defined in the common law as the unlawful taking of property from the possession of another with the intent to steal. Thus, the *actus reus* for larceny involves a trespassory taking, that is, a taking of property that interferes with the rights of the owner. Under the common law, the *actus reus* also required *asportation*, which is a carrying away of property or movement of it from one place to another. Today, movement of the property is not required, provided that there has been some deprivation of ownership rights. The *mens rea* for larceny is simply the intent to steal or to deprive the owner of the property permanently; therefore, borrowing property will generally not rise to the level of property, nor will situations in which the defendant was under the mistaken belief that the owner consented to the defendant's possession of the property.

In most jurisdictions, larceny of a motor vehicle constitutes a separately defined crime. This is due in part to the relative ease with which motor vehicles may be stolen, their value, and their importance to American society. In addition, the theft of motor vehicles as part of the operation of "chop shops," where vehicles are stripped for the sale of their parts, is often part of larger criminal enterprises.

Along with larceny, the receipt or possession of stolen property is a crime; however, mere possession of something that has been stolen is insufficient. The person receiving the property must have actual knowledge or reason to believe that the property was stolen, along with the intent to deprive the owner of the property. In many jurisdictions, possession of stolen property is evidence of the fact that the possessor knew that it was stolen, unless it can be proven otherwise.

Embezzlement

Embezzlement is the theft of property that has been entrusted to a person. This distinguishes embezzlement from larceny in that possession of the property has been delivered to the defendant by the owner and the defendant then keeps the property for himself. Under the common law, embezzlement was not a crime, and it created a somewhat unique situation in that it was possible for those to whom property had been entrusted to escape liability for theft by claiming that the owner had authorized their possession of the property, defeating a larceny charge. Today, many states have criminalized embezzlement, and others have included it within the definition of larceny or theft. Embezzlement typically arises in the employment context, where an employee takes cash or other property (such as office supplies) from the employer with the intent to make it his or her own.

False Pretenses/Fraud

The crime of false pretenses, also referred to as fraud, is a form of theft in which the property is obtained from the owner through deceit. The crime of false pretenses occurs when the owner is tricked or otherwise deceived into voluntarily handing over the property. Because property that is voluntarily delivered to another by its owner cannot be the subject of larceny (which requires an unauthorized taking), the crime of false pretenses, found in state statutes today, allows prosecution of this form of theft that could not be prosecuted under the early common law. The crime of false pretenses is differentiated from larceny or other theft crimes by its elements. In particular, the *actus reus* involves obtaining the property by making a false representation of fact. A representation of fact may be distinguished from a statement of opinion, which is an insufficient basis for a conviction on false pretenses. If the defendant knows the statement to be false, intends the victim to act on it by handing over his property, and intends to deprive the victim of the property, the *mens rea* for the crime has been satisfied.

Burglary

Burglary is a common law crime that was defined as the breaking and entering into the dwelling of another at night with the intent to commit a felony. Many state statutes today refer to the crime of "breaking and entering," which broadens the common law definition of burglary by removing the requirement that burglary occur at nighttime or in a dwelling. More simply, breaking and entering into any building at any time with the intent to commit any criminal offense is a crime. Thus, today, most state statutes criminalizing breaking and entering require three elements: breaking, entering, and intent to commit a crime. Breaking into a building occurs when the security of the building is pierced, but this may occur with the slightest amount of force, such as pushing open an unlocked window. Entering occurs when any part of a burglar, such as reaching an arm through a window, enters the building. Finally, the defendant's entry into the building must be with the intent to commit a crime inside, which is usually larceny. Some jurisdictions, however, do not require this specific intent, only the general intent to break into the building.

Arson

Arson was a common law crime defined as the malicious burning of a dwelling in which another person lived. A person's dwelling also included other buildings that were considered to be inside the *curtilage*, or the area surrounding the main house, such as barns, sheds, and other outbuildings. Thus, the *actus reus* under the common law was setting a fire to a dwelling, and the *mens rea* was the intent to set fire to the dwelling; however, actual flame was not needed for arson, nor was destruction of the building. Any charring of the building was sufficient.

Arson is a crime that involves destruction of property, but unlike with other property crimes, the goal of the perpetrator typically involves more than just the destroying of property. Collecting insurance proceeds ranks high in motives for arson, and committing arson as an act of vandalism, for political reasons, or to destroy evidence have all been found. Thus, although it is possible to view arson as a form of theft from insurance companies, other reasons for its commission place it in a somewhat unique and particularly dangerous class of crimes. All states now include more than just "dwellings" in their arson statutes, such as any building, motor vehicles, aircraft, and some types of personal property. Given the seriousness of the crime and potential for loss of life that it poses, first-degree arson in some states may subject the defendant to capital punishment where a death results from the arson.

Crimes Against Public Order and Morality

Public safety is a central goal of the criminal law. Moreover, criminal law is prescriptive; it specifies what behavior is acceptable and what is not acceptable. Crimes involving public order are those that govern individual behavior that is harmful to the functioning of an orderly society. They include common law crimes such as disorderly conduct (breach of the peace), vagrancy, and loitering, as well as modern efforts to maintain public order by increasing punishment for crimes involving weapons and limiting possession through gun control.

Most crimes can be said to involve a moral perspective. That is, they distinguish between behavior that is "right and wrong" based on the harmfulness of the activity to society and to the individual; however, some crimes specifically involve a moral judgment by the legislature that certain behavior should be outlawed because it is immoral and therefore unacceptable, even where the behavior is not necessarily harmful to society. These include such crimes as prostitution, gambling, and obscenity, as well as those involving pornography.

Disorderly Conduct

Under the common law, "breach of the peace" was punishable when a person engaged in any behavior that disturbed the quiet, orderly conduct of people's lives and their affairs—in short, actions that were disruptive to life. The crime today, commonly known as disorderly conduct, is little changed from the common law, although more specific. Disorderly conduct may be charged for any one of a number of acts commonly found in state statutes, such as that of New Mexico:

NMSA 30-20-1. Disorderly Conduct
Disorderly conduct consists of:

A. engaging in violent, abusive, indecent, profane, boisterous, unreasonably loud or otherwise disorderly conduct which tends to disturb the peace; or

B. maliciously disturbing, threatening or, in an insolent manner, intentionally touching any house occupied by any person.

Vagrancy and Loitering

Under the common law, vagrancy was defined as wandering around without any means of support. Because of the fear that individuals who cannot support themselves and wander from place to place within a community are more likely to commit other crimes or to become a burden to society, such laws were intended to provide safety for the community and ensure that citizens remain productive. Loitering occurs when a person hangs around in a particular place without reason for doing so and is thus related to vagrancy in that its goal is to ensure that people have a productive reason for being where are found instead of being "up to no good." Today, of course, the problem of homelessness raises the issue of whether criminalizing, either loitering or vagrancy, targets a particular population for their status of being homeless (whether as a result of economic disadvantage, mental illness, or other reason beyond the control of the individual) and whether such laws are sufficiently clear in specifying the behavior prohibited. In *Kolendar v. Lawson*, 461 U.S. 352, 103 S. Ct. 1855, 75 L.Ed.2d 903 (1983), in which a California statute required individuals to provide "credible and reliable" identification and "to account for their presence when requested by a peace officer," the U.S. Supreme Court held that the law was void for vagueness, finding that it

contains no standard for determining what a suspect has to do in order to satisfy the requirement to provide a "credible and reliable" identification. As such, the statute vests virtually complete discretion in the hands of the police to determine whether the suspect has satisfied the statute and must be permitted to go on his way in the absence of probable cause to arrest. An individual, whom police may think is suspicious but do not have probable cause to believe has committed a crime, is entitled to continue to walk the public streets "only at the whim of any police officer" who happens to stop that individual. . . . The concern of our citizens with curbing criminal activity is certainly a matter requiring the attention of all branches of government. As weighty as this concern is, however, it cannot justify legislation that would otherwise fail to meet constitutional standards for definiteness and clarity. . . . We conclude [the statute] is unconstitutionally vague on its face because it encourages arbitrary enforcement by failing to describe with sufficient particularity what a suspect must do in order to satisfy the statute. 461 U.S. at 358-61, 103 S. Ct. at 1858-60, 75 L.Ed.2d at 906-908.

Weapons Charges

More directly related to concerns about public safety than vagrancy and loitering is the possession of guns by individuals. Every state more severely punishes individuals who use guns in the commission of crimes, and every state has also enacted various forms of gun control (some as a result of federal legislation), from registration and waiting periods before purchase to limits on who may possess a weapon to where it may be kept or used. Such restrictions are intended to protect society from the criminal use of weapons, improve investigation and prosecution of those who use them for such purposes, and generally maintain public order. In *District of Columbia v. Heller*, 128 S. Ct. 2783, 171 L.Ed.2d 637 (2008) (found in **Case Decision 11.3**), the U.S. Supreme Court addressed such law. The D.C. law effectively outlawed the possession of handguns by not allowing their registration and making it a crime to carry an unregistered handgun. When a police officer, Heller, wished to keep a handgun in his home, he was prevented from registering it and sued the District. The question presented was whether the D.C. law was contrary to the Second Amendment, which preserves "the right to keep and bear arms."

Prostitution

Sometimes characterized as the "world's oldest profession," prostitution is defined as exchanging sex for money. Both those who provide sexual "services" and those who pay for

---

Case Decision 11.3 *District of Columbia v. Heller*, 128 S. Ct. 2783, 171 L.Ed.2d 637 (2008)

Opinion of the Court by Justice Scalia:

We consider whether a District of Columbia prohibition on the possession of usable handguns in the home violates the Second Amendment to the Constitution.

I

The District of Columbia generally prohibits the possession of handguns. It is a crime to carry an unregistered firearm, and the registration of handguns is prohibited. Wholly apart from that prohibition, no person may carry a handgun without a license, but the chief of police may issue licenses for 1-year periods. District of Columbia law also requires residents to keep their lawfully owned firearms, such as registered long guns, "unloaded and dissembled or bound by a trigger lock or similar device" unless they are located in a place of business or are being used for lawful recreational activities.

Respondent Dick Heller is a D.C. special police officer authorized to carry a handgun while on duty at the Federal Judicial Center. He applied for a registration certificate for a handgun that he wished to keep at home, but the District refused. He thereafter filed a lawsuit in the Federal District Court for the District of Columbia seeking, on Second Amendment grounds, to enjoin the city from enforcing the bar on the registration of handguns, the licensing requirement insofar as it prohibits the carrying of a firearm in the home without a license, and the trigger-lock requirement insofar as it prohibits the use of "functional firearms within the home." The District Court dismissed respondent's complaint. The Court of Appeals for the District of Columbia Circuit, construing his complaint as seeking the right to render a firearm operable and carry it about his home in that condition only when necessary for self-defense, reversed. It held that the Second Amendment protects an individual's right to possess firearms and that the city's total ban on handguns, as well as its requirement that firearms in the home be kept nonfunctional even when necessary for self-defense, violated that right. The Court of Appeals directed the District Court to enter summary judgment for respondent. We granted certiorari.

II

We turn first to the meaning of the Second Amendment.

A

The Second Amendment provides: "A well regulated Militia, being necessary to the security of a free State, the right of the people to keep and bear Arms, shall not be infringed." In interpreting this text, we are guided by the principle that "[t]he Constitution was written to be understood by the voters; its words and phrases were used in their normal and ordinary as distinguished from technical meaning." Normal meaning may of course include an idiomatic meaning, but it excludes secret or technical meanings that would not have been known to ordinary citizens in the founding generation.

The two sides in this case have set out very different interpretations of the Amendment. Petitioners and today's dissenting Justices believe that it protects only the right to possess and carry a firearm in connection with militia service. Respondent argues that it protects an individual's right to possess a firearm unconnected with service in a militia, and to use that arm for traditionally lawful purposes, such as self-defense within the home.

The Second Amendment is naturally divided into two parts: its prefatory clause and its operative clause. The former does not limit the latter grammatically, but rather announces a purpose. The Amendment could be rephrased, "Because a well regulated Militia is necessary to the security of a free State, the right of the people to keep and bear Arms shall not be infringed." Although this structure of the Second Amendment is unique in our Constitution, other legal documents of the founding era, particularly individual-rights provisions of state constitutions, commonly included a prefatory statement of purpose. See generally Volokh, The Commonplace Second Amendment, 73 N.Y.U.L. Rev. 793, 814–821 (1998).

Logic demands that there be a link between the stated purpose and the command. The Second Amendment would be nonsensical if it read, "A well regulated Militia, being necessary to the security of a free State, the right of the people to petition for redress of grievances shall not be infringed." That requirement of logical connection may cause a prefatory clause to resolve an ambiguity in the operative clause ("The separation of church and state being an important objective, the teachings of canons shall have no place in our jurisprudence." The preface makes clear that the operative clause refers not to canons of interpretation but to clergymen.) But apart from that clarifying function, a prefatory clause does not limit or expand the scope of the operative clause. Therefore, while we will begin our textual analysis with the operative clause, we will return to the prefatory clause to ensure that our reading of the operative clause is consistent with the announced purpose.

1. Operative Clause.

a. "Right of the People." The first salient feature of the operative clause is that it codifies a "right of the people." The unamended Constitution and the Bill of Rights use the phrase "right of the people" two other times, in the First Amendment's Assembly-and-Petition Clause and in the Fourth Amendment's Search-and-Seizure Clause. The Ninth Amendment uses very similar terminology

(Continues)

(Continued)

("The enumeration in the Constitution, of certain rights, shall not be construed to deny or disparage others retained by the people"). All three of these instances unambiguously refer to individual rights, not "collective" rights, or rights that may be exercised only through participation in some corporate body.

Three provisions of the Constitution refer to "the people" in a context other than "rights"—the famous preamble ("We the people"), § 2 of Article I (providing that "the people" will choose members of the House), and the Tenth Amendment (providing that those powers not given the Federal Government remain with "the States" or "the people"). Those provisions arguably refer to "the people" acting collectively—but they deal with the exercise or reservation of powers, not rights. Nowhere else in the Constitution does a "right" attributed to "the people" refer to anything other than an individual right.

What is more, in all six other provisions of the Constitution that mention "the people," the term unambiguously refers to all members of the political community, not an unspecified subset. This contrasts markedly with the phrase "the militia" in the prefatory clause. As we will describe below, the "militia" in colonial America consisted of a subset of "the people"—those who were male, able bodied, and within a certain age range. Reading the Second Amendment as protecting only the right to "keep and bear Arms" in an organized militia therefore fits poorly with the operative clause's description of the holder of that right as "the people."

We start therefore with a strong presumption that the Second Amendment right is exercised individually and belongs to all Americans.

b. "Keep and bear Arms." We move now from the holder of the right—"the people"—to the substance of the right: "to keep and bear Arms."

Before addressing the verbs "keep" and "bear," we interpret their object: "Arms." The 18th-century meaning is no different from the meaning today. The 1773 edition of Samuel Johnson's dictionary defined "arms" as "weapons of offence, or armour of defence." 1 Dictionary of the English Language 107 (4th ed.) (hereinafter Johnson). Timothy Cunningham's important 1771 legal dictionary defined "arms" as "any thing that a man wears for his defence, or takes into his hands, or useth in wrath to cast at or strike another." 1 A New and Complete Law Dictionary (1771); see also N. Webster, American Dictionary of the English Language (1828) (reprinted 1989) (hereinafter Webster) (similar). The term was applied, then as now, to weapons that were not specifically designed for military use and were not employed in a military capacity.

Some have made the argument, bordering on the frivolous, that only those arms in existence in the 18th century are protected by the Second Amendment. We do not interpret constitutional rights that way. Just as the First Amendment protects modern forms of communications, and the Fourth Amendment applies to modern forms of search, the Second Amendment extends, prima facie, to all instruments that constitute bearable arms, even those that were not in existence at the time of the founding.

We turn to the phrases "keep arms" and "bear arms." Johnson defined "keep" as, most relevantly, "[t]o retain; not to lose," and "[t]o have in custody." Webster defined it as "[t]o hold; to retain in one's power or possession." No party has apprised us of an idiomatic meaning of "keep Arms." Thus, the most natural reading of "keep Arms" in the Second Amendment is to "have weapons."

The phrase "keep arms" was not prevalent in the written documents of the founding period that we have found, but there are a few examples, all of which favor viewing the right to "keep Arms" as an individual right unconnected with militia service. William Blackstone, for example, wrote that Catholics convicted of not attending service in the Church of England suffered certain penalties, one of which was that they were not permitted to "keep arms in their houses. Petitioners point to militia laws of the founding period that required militia members to "keep" arms in connection with militia service, and they conclude from this that the phrase "keep Arms" has a militia-related connotation. This is rather like saying that, since there are many statutes that authorize aggrieved employees to "file complaints" with federal agencies, the phrase "file complaints" has an employment-related connotation. "Keep arms" was simply a common way of referring to possessing arms, for militiamen *and everyone else*.

From our review of founding-era sources, we conclude that this natural meaning was also the meaning that "bear arms" had in the 18th century. In numerous instances, "bear arms" was unambiguously used to refer to the carrying of weapons outside of an organized militia. The most prominent examples are those most relevant to the Second Amendment: Nine state constitutional provisions written in the 18th century or the first two decades of the 19th, which enshrined a right of citizens to "bear arms in defense of themselves and the state" or "bear arms in defense of himself and the state." It is clear from those formulations that "bear arms" did not refer only to carrying a weapon in an organized military unit. These provisions demonstrate—again, in the most analogous linguistic context—that "bear arms" was not limited to the carrying of arms in a militia.

c. Meaning of the Operative Clause. Putting all of these textual elements together, we find that they guarantee the individual right to possess and carry weapons in case of confrontation. This meaning is strongly confirmed by the historical background of the Second Amendment. We look to this because it has always been widely understood that the Second Amendment, like the First and Fourth Amendments, codified a *pre-existing* right. The very text of the Second Amendment implicitly recognizes the pre-existence of the right and declares only that it "shall not be infringed."

Between the Restoration and the Glorious Revolution, the Stuart Kings Charles II and James II succeeded in using select militias loyal to them to suppress political dissidents, in part by disarming their opponents. These experiences caused Englishmen to be extremely wary of concentrated military forces run by the state and to be jealous of their arms. They accordingly obtained an assurance from William and Mary, in the Declaration of Right (which was codified as the English Bill of Rights), that Protestants would never be disarmed: "That the subjects which are Protestants may have arms for their defense suitable to their conditions and as allowed by law." This right has long been understood to be the predecessor to our Second Amendment. It was clearly an individual right, having nothing whatever to do with service in a militia. To be sure, it was an individual right not available to the whole population, given that it was restricted to Protestants, and like all written English rights it was held only against the Crown, not Parliament. But it was secured to them as individuals, according to "libertarian political principles," not as members of a fighting force.

And, of course, what the Stuarts had tried to do to their political enemies, George III had tried to do to the colonists. In the tumultuous decades of the 1760's and 1770's, the Crown began to disarm the inhabitants of the most rebellious areas. That provoked polemical reactions by Americans invoking their rights as Englishmen to keep arms. A New York article of April 1769 said that "[i]t is a natural right which the people have reserved to themselves, confirmed by the Bill of Rights, to keep arms for their own defence." They understood the right to enable individuals to defend themselves.

There seems to us no doubt, on the basis of both text and history, that the Second Amendment conferred an individual right to keep and bear arms. Of course the right was not unlimited, just as the First Amendment's right of free speech was not. Thus, we do not read the Second Amendment to protect the right of citizens to carry arms for *any sort* of confrontation, just as we do not read the First Amendment to protect the right of citizens to speak for *any purpose*. Before turning to limitations upon the individual's right, however, we must determine whether the prefatory clause of the Second Amendment comports with our interpretation of the operative clause.

2. Prefatory Clause.
The prefatory clause reads: "A well regulated Militia, being necessary to the security of a free State. . . ."

a. "Well-Regulated Militia." In *United States v. Miller*, 307 U.S. 174, 179, 59 S. Ct. 816, 83 L.Ed. 1206 (1939), we explained that "the Militia comprised all males physically capable of acting in concert for the common defense." That definition comports with founding-era sources. Petitioners take a seemingly narrower view of the militia, stating that "[m]ilitias are the state- and congressionally-regulated military forces described in the Militia Clauses (art. I, § 8, cls. 15-16)." Although we agree with petitioners' interpretive assumption that "militia" means the same thing in Article I and the Second Amendment, we believe that petitioners identify the wrong thing, namely, the organized militia. Unlike armies and navies, which Congress is given the power to create ("to raise . . . Armies"; "to provide . . . a Navy," Art. I, § 8, cls. 12–13), the militia is assumed by Article I already to be *in existence*. Congress is given the power to "provide for calling forth the militia," § 8, cl. 15; and the power not to create, but to "organiz[e]" it—and not to organize "a" militia, which is what one would expect if the militia were to be a federal creation, but to organize "the" militia, connoting a body already in existence, *ibid.*, cl. 16. This is fully consistent with the ordinary definition of the militia as all able-bodied men. From that pool, Congress has plenary power to organize the units that will make up an effective fighting force. That is what Congress did in the first militia Act, which specified that "each and every free able-bodied white male citizen of the respective states, resident therein, who is or shall be of the

(Continues)

(Continued)

age of eighteen years, and under the age of forty-five years (except as is herein after excepted) shall severally and respectively be enrolled in the militia." Act of May 8, 1792, 1 Stat. 271. To be sure, Congress need not conscript every able-bodied man into the militia, because nothing in Article I suggests that in exercising its power to organize, discipline, and arm the militia, Congress must focus upon the entire body. Although the militia consists of all able-bodied men, the federally organized militia may consist of a subset of them. Finally, the adjective "well-regulated" implies nothing more than the imposition of proper discipline and training.

b. "Security of a Free State." The phrase "security of a free state" meant "security of a free polity," not security of each of the several States. Joseph Story wrote in his treatise on the Constitution that "the word 'state' is used in various senses [and in] its most enlarged sense, it means the people composing a particular nation or community." It is true that the term "State" elsewhere in the Constitution refers to individual States, but the phrase "security of a free state" and close variations seem to have been terms of art in 18th-century political discourse, meaning a "'free country'" or free polity. See Volokh, Necessary to the Security of a Free State, 83 Notre Dame L. Rev. 1, 5 (2007). Moreover, the other instances of "state" in the Constitution are typically accompanied by modifiers making clear that the reference is to the several States—"each state," "several states," "any state," "that state," "particular states," "one state," "no state." And the presence of the term "foreign state" in Article I and Article III shows that the word "state" did not have a single meaning in the Constitution.

There are many reasons why the militia was thought to be "necessary to the security of a free state." First, of course, it is useful in repelling invasions and suppressing insurrections. Second, it renders large standing armies unnecessary—an argument that Alexander Hamilton made in favor of federal control over the militia. Third, when the able-bodied men of a nation are trained in arms and organized, they are better able to resist tyranny.

3. Relationship between Prefatory Clause and Operative Clause

We reach the question, then: Does the preface fit with an operative clause that creates an individual right to keep and bear arms? It fits perfectly, once one knows the history that the founding generation knew and that we have described above. That history showed that the way tyrants had eliminated a militia consisting of all the able-bodied men was not by banning the militia but simply by taking away the people's arms, enabling a select militia or standing army to suppress political opponents. This is what had occurred in England that prompted codification of the right to have arms in the English Bill of Rights.

The debate with respect to the right to keep and bear arms, as with other guarantees in the Bill of Rights, was not over whether it was desirable (all agreed that it was) but over whether it needed to be codified in the Constitution. During the 1788 ratification debates, the fear that the federal government would disarm the people in order to impose rule through a standing army or select militia was pervasive in Antifederalist rhetoric. John Smilie, for example, worried not only that Congress's "command of the militia" could be used to create a "select militia," or to have "no militia at all," but also, as a separate concern, that "[w]hen a select militia is formed; the people in general may be disarmed." Federalists responded that because Congress was given no power to abridge the ancient right of individuals to keep and bear arms, such a force could never oppress the people. It was understood across the political spectrum that the right helped to secure the ideal of a citizen militia, which might be necessary to oppose an oppressive military force if the constitutional order broke down.

It is therefore entirely sensible that the Second Amendment's prefatory clause announces the purpose for which the right was codified: to prevent elimination of the militia. The prefatory clause does not suggest that preserving the militia was the only reason Americans valued the ancient right; most undoubtedly thought it even more important for self-defense and hunting. But the threat that the new Federal Government would destroy the citizens' militia by taking away their arms was the reason that right—unlike some other English rights—was codified in a written Constitution.

Besides ignoring the historical reality that the Second Amendment was not intended to lay down a "novel principl[e]" but rather codified a right "inherited from our English ancestors," petitioners' interpretation does not even achieve the narrower purpose that prompted codification of the right. If, as they believe, the Second Amendment right is no more than the right to keep and use weapons as a member of an organized militia, that is, the *organized* militia is the sole institutional beneficiary of the Second Amendment's guarantee—it does not assure the existence of a "citizens' militia" as a safeguard against tyranny. For Congress retains plenary authority to organize the militia, which must include the authority to say who will belong to the organized force. That is why the first Militia Act's requirement that only whites enroll caused States to amend their militia laws to exclude free blacks. Thus, if petitioners are correct, the Second Amendment protects citizens' right to use a gun in an organization from which Congress has plenary authority to exclude them. It guarantees a select militia of the sort the Stuart kings found useful, but not the people's militia that was the concern of the founding generation.

B

Our interpretation is confirmed by analogous arms-bearing rights in state constitutions that preceded and immediately followed adoption of the Second Amendment. Four States adopted analogues to the Federal Second Amendment in the period between independence and the ratification of the Bill of Rights. Two of them—Pennsylvania and Vermont—clearly adopted individual rights unconnected to militia service. Pennsylvania's Declaration of Rights of 1776 said: "That the people have a right to bear arms *for the defence of themselves*, and the state. . . ." (emphasis added). In 1777, Vermont adopted the identical provision, except for inconsequential differences in punctuation and capitalization.

North Carolina also codified a right to bear arms in 1776: "That the people have a right to bear arms, for the defence of the State. . . ." This could plausibly be read to support only a right to bear arms in a militia—but that is a peculiar way to make the point in a constitution that elsewhere repeatedly mentions the militia explicitly. Many colonial statutes required individual arms-bearing for public-safety reasons—such as the 1770 Georgia law that "for the security and *defence of this province* from internal dangers and insurrections" required those men who qualified for militia duty individually "to carry fire arms" "to places of public worship." (emphasis added). That broad public-safety understanding was the connotation given to the North Carolina right by that State's Supreme Court in 1843.

The 1780 Massachusetts Constitution presented another variation on the theme: "The people have a right to keep and to bear arms for the common defence. . . ." Once again, if one gives narrow meaning to the phrase "common defence" this can be thought to limit the right to the bearing of arms in a state-organized military force. But once again the State's highest court thought otherwise. Writing for the court in an 1825 libel case, Chief Justice Parker wrote: "The liberty of the press was to be unrestrained, but he who used it was to be responsible in cases of its abuse; like the right to keep fire arms, which does not protect him who uses them for annoyance or destruction." The analogy makes no sense if firearms could not be used for any individual purpose at all.

We therefore believe that the most likely reading of all four of these pre-Second Amendment state constitutional provisions is that they secured an individual right to bear arms for defensive purposes. Other States did not include rights to bear arms in their pre-1789 constitutions—although in Virginia a Second Amendment analogue was proposed (unsuccessfully) by Thomas Jefferson. (It read: "No freeman shall ever be debarred the use of arms [within his own lands or tenements]."

Between 1789 and 1820, nine States adopted Second Amendment analogues. Four of them—Kentucky, Ohio, Indiana, and Missouri—referred to the right of the people to "bear arms in defence of themselves and the State." Another three States—Mississippi, Connecticut, and Alabama—used the even more individualistic phrasing that each citizen has the "right to bear arms in defence of himself and the State." Finally, two States—Tennessee and Maine—used the "common defence" language of Massachusetts. That of the nine state constitutional protections for the right to bear arms enacted immediately after 1789 at least seven unequivocally protected an individual citizen's right to self-defense is strong evidence that that is how the founding generation conceived of the right.

The historical narrative that petitioners must endorse would thus treat the Federal Second Amendment as an odd outlier, protecting a right unknown in state constitutions or at English common law, based on little more than an overreading of the prefatory clause.

We conclude that nothing in our precedents forecloses our adoption of the original understanding of the Second Amendment. It should be unsurprising that such a significant matter has been for so long judicially unresolved. For most of our history, the Bill of Rights was not thought applicable to the States, and the Federal Government did not significantly regulate the possession of firearms by law-abiding citizens. Other provisions of the Bill of Rights have similarly remained unilluminated for lengthy periods. This Court first held a law to violate the First Amendment's guarantee of freedom of speech in 1931, almost 150 years after the Amendment was ratified, and it was not until after World War II that we held a law invalid under the Establishment Clause. Even a question as basic as the scope of proscribable libel was not addressed by this Court until 1964,

(Continues)

nearly two centuries after the founding. It is demonstrably not true that, as Justice Stevens claims, "for most of our history, the invalidity of Second-Amendment-based objections to firearms regulations has been well settled and uncontroversial." For most of our history the question did not present itself.

III

Like most rights, the right secured by the Second Amendment is not unlimited. From Blackstone through the 19th-century cases, commentators and courts routinely explained that the right was not a right to keep and carry any weapon whatsoever in any manner whatsoever and for whatever purpose. For example, the majority of the 19th-century courts to consider the question held that prohibitions on carrying concealed weapons were lawful under the Second Amendment or state analogues. Although we do not undertake an exhaustive historical analysis today of the full scope of the Second Amendment, nothing in our opinion should be taken to cast doubt on longstanding prohibitions on the possession of firearms by felons and the mentally ill, or laws forbidding the carrying of firearms in sensitive places such as schools and government buildings, or laws imposing conditions and qualifications on the commercial sale of arms. We identify these presumptively lawful regulatory measures only as examples; our list does not purport to be exhaustive.

We also recognize another important limitation on the right to keep and carry arms. [A]s we have explained, that the sorts of weapons protected were those "in common use at the time." We think that limitation is fairly supported by the historical tradition of prohibiting the carrying of "dangerous and unusual weapons."

It may be objected that if weapons that are most useful in military service—M-16 rifles and the like—may be banned, then the Second Amendment right is completely detached from the prefatory clause. But as we have said, the conception of the militia at the time of the Second Amendment's ratification was the body of all citizens capable of military service, who would bring the sorts of lawful weapons that they possessed at home to militia duty. It may well be true today that a militia, to be as effective as militias in the 18th century, would require sophisticated arms that are highly unusual in society at large. Indeed, it may be true that no amount of small arms could be useful against modern-day bombers and tanks. But the fact that modern developments have limited the degree of fit between the prefatory clause and the protected right cannot change our interpretation of the right.

IV

We turn finally to the law at issue here. As we have said, the law totally bans handgun possession in the home. It also requires that any lawful firearm in the home be disassembled or bound by a trigger lock at all times, rendering it inoperable.

As the quotations earlier in this opinion demonstrate, the inherent right of self-defense has been central to the Second Amendment right. The handgun ban amounts to a prohibition of an entire class of "arms" that is overwhelmingly chosen by American society for that lawful purpose. The prohibition extends, moreover, to the home, where the need for defense of self, family, and property is most acute. Under any of the standards of scrutiny that we have applied to enumerated constitutional rights, banning from the home "the most preferred firearm in the nation to 'keep' and use for protection of one's home and family," would fail constitutional muster.

Few laws in the history of our Nation have come close to the severe restriction of the District's handgun ban. And some of those few have been struck down. [T]he Georgia Supreme Court struck down a prohibition on carrying pistols openly (even though it upheld a prohibition on carrying concealed weapons). [T]he Tennessee Supreme Court likewise held that a statute that forbade openly carrying a pistol "publicly or privately, without regard to time or place, or circumstances," violated the state constitutional provision (which the court equated with the Second Amendment). That was so even though the statute did not restrict the carrying of long guns.

It is no answer to say, as petitioners do, that it is permissible to ban the possession of handguns so long as the possession of other firearms (*i.e.*, long guns) is allowed. It is enough to note, as we have observed, that the American people have considered the handgun to be the quintessential self-defense weapon. There are many reasons that a citizen may prefer a handgun for home defense: It is easier to store in a location that is readily accessible in an emergency; it cannot easily be redirected or wrestled away by an attacker; it is easier to use for those without the upper-body strength to lift and aim a long gun; it can be pointed at a burglar with one hand while the other hand dials the police. Whatever the reason, handguns are the most popular weapon chosen by Americans for self-defense in the home, and a complete prohibition of their use is invalid.

We must also address the District's requirement (as applied to respondent's handgun) that firearms in the home be rendered and kept inoperable at all times. This makes it impossible for citizens to use them for the core lawful purpose of self-defense and is hence unconstitutional. The District argues that we should interpret this element of the statute to contain an exception for self-defense. But we think that is precluded by the unequivocal text, and by the presence of certain other enumerated exceptions: "Except for law enforcement personnel. . . , each registrant shall keep any firearm in his possession unloaded and disassembled or bound by a trigger lock or similar device unless such firearm is kept at his place of business, or while being used for lawful recreational purposes within the District of Columbia." D.C. Code § 7-2507.02.

Apart from his challenge to the handgun ban and the trigger-lock requirement respondent asked the District Court to enjoin petitioners from enforcing the separate licensing requirement "in such a manner as to forbid the carrying of a firearm within one's home or possessed land without a license." The Court of Appeals did not invalidate the licensing requirement, but held only that the District "may not prevent [a handgun] from being moved throughout one's house." It then ordered the District Court to enter summary judgment "consistent with [respondent's] prayer for relief." Before this Court petitioners have stated that "if the handgun ban is struck down and respondent registers a handgun, he could obtain a license, assuming he is not otherwise disqualified," by which they apparently mean if he is not a felon and is not insane. Respondent conceded at oral argument that he does not "have a problem with . . . licensing" and that the District's law is permissible so long as it is "not enforced in an arbitrary and capricious manner." We therefore assume that petitioners' issuance of a license will satisfy respondent's prayer for relief and do not address the licensing requirement.

In sum, we hold that the District's ban on handgun possession in the home violates the Second Amendment, as does its prohibition against rendering any lawful firearm in the home operable for the purpose of immediate self-defense. Assuming that Heller is not disqualified from the exercise of Second Amendment rights, the District must permit him to register his handgun and must issue him a license to carry it in the home.

We are aware of the problem of handgun violence in this country, and we take seriously the concerns raised by the many *amici* who believe that prohibition of handgun ownership is a solution. The Constitution leaves the District of Columbia a variety of tools for combating that problem, including some measures regulating handguns. But the enshrinement of constitutional rights necessarily takes certain policy choices off the table. These include the absolute prohibition of handguns held and used for self-defense in the home. Undoubtedly some think that the Second Amendment is outmoded in a society where our standing army is the pride of our Nation, where well-trained police forces provide personal security, and where gun violence is a serious problem. That is perhaps debatable, but what is not debatable is that it is not the role of this Court to pronounce the Second Amendment extinct.

We affirm the judgment of the Court of Appeals.

---

them may be subject to criminal liability. In addition, soliciting prostitution by asking or demanding that a person engage in prostitution is a crime. Prostitution is typically viewed as a *mala prohibita* crime that society in most states (all but Nevada) considers to be in contrast to public views of moral behavior and therefore should be punished in order to be prevented. Although specific harms resulting from such behavior may be identified (such as fear of disease and relationship to other crimes or immoral behavior such as drug use), it is nonetheless viewed as a "victimless" crime in which the parties to the behavior are consenting adults.

Obscenity and Pornography

Like prostitution, obscenity and pornography-related crimes reflect the moral viewpoint of the elected official in the legislature about what is best for society. Obscenity refers to any material describing or depicting sexual conduct that an average person, applying contemporary community standards, would find to be (1) appealing to a prurient interest in sex; (2) patently offensive; and (3) lacking in serious literary, artistic, political, or scientific value, *Miller v. California*, 413 U.S. 15, 93 S. Ct. 2607, 37 L.Ed.2d 419 (1973); however, when the material at issue involves children, the U.S. Supreme Court has allowed a broader definition of obscenity:

A trier of fact need not find that the material appeals to the prurient interest of the average person; it is not required that the sexual conduct portrayed be done so in a patently offensive manner; and the material at issue need not be considered as a whole. *New York v. Ferber*, 458 U.S. 747, 102 S. Ct. 3348, 73 L.Ed.2d 1113 (1982).

Pornography generally refers to any sexually explicit material. Thus, obscenity involves pornographic material, but not all pornography is obscene. Although the meanings of "pornography" and "obscenity" are not the same, the distinction is typically not important in the law or in individual cases because any pornographic material that is obscene is generally subject to governmental regulation.

All states and the federal government regulate the possession and distribution of various forms of obscene and pornographic material, including the imposition of criminal penalties. The voluminous case and statutory law that has developed in this area primarily addresses the central problem with governmental regulation of these types of materials: Do they violate the free speech provision of the First Amendment? In general, pornographic materials that satisfy the *Miller* definition of obscenity are not protected from government regulation by the First Amendment. Thus, although there has been a proliferation of pornographic material as a result of digital filming technologies and distribution over the Internet, states may still regulate such material when it rises to the level of obscenity. For example, California, the "adult" film capital of the world, nonetheless has adopted in its criminal code the following:

> Section 311.2. (a) Every person who knowingly sends or causes to be sent, or brings or causes to be brought, into this state for sale or distribution, or in this state possesses, prepares, publishes, produces, or prints, with intent to distribute or to exhibit to others, or who offers to distribute, distributes, or exhibits to others, any obscene matter is for a first offense, guilty of a misdemeanor. If the person has previously been convicted of any violation of this section, the court may, in addition to the punishment authorized in Section 311.9, impose a fine not exceeding fifty thousand dollars ($50,000).

Crimes Against the Government

The Framers of the Constitution were concerned about the survival of the newly formed American government. The relative weakness of the national government compared with the states, the presence of many English loyalists in the colonies, and the interests of foreign governments in expansion into territories to the west and north of the states raised the specter of attacks against the new country and its governmental order. As a result, Article III, Section 3 was adopted: "Treason against the United States, shall consist only in levying War against them, or in adhering to their Enemies, giving them Aid and Comfort." The Framers also recognized that public officials may be tempted to place their own self-interest above that of the people; when they do so, their actions are contrary to the workings of a representative government and citizens' confidence in it. Therefore, Article II, Section 4 states this: "The President, Vice President and all civil Officers of the United States, shall be removed from Office on Impeachment for, and Conviction of, Treason, Bribery, or other high Crimes and Misdemeanors." Criminalizing breaches of trust by government officials as well as actions by others hostile to the

workings of government thus has a long tradition in the United States.

Treason

Treason occurs when one attempts to overthrow the government or acts in such a way to betray the interests of the government to foreign powers. Elements of the crime of treason include an allegiance owed to government, which is usually satisfied through citizenship, commission of an act that violates a person's allegiance to the country, and the intent to overthrow the government or to provide information that will be used to harm the government. Espionage is a form of treason in which a person gathers information relating to the national defense with the intent to distribute it to others so that it can be used against the government. Sedition is also related to treason and is defined as a communication whose purpose is to stir up treason. Shortly after the adoption of the U.S. Constitution, Congress passed the Sedition Act in 1798. The Act was intended to punish those who publicly criticized the U.S. government in order to protect the government against foreign sympathizers but was used more broadly against U.S. citizens who expressed political views, particularly newspaper editors. It proved to be very unpopular, and because it was authorized for only a limited time, it expired before its provisions could have greater negative effect. It would be over 100 years before the more limited Sedition Act of 1918 was adopted to quell criticism of the government during World War I, but it, too, expired after the war.

Perjury

The justice system and the operation of the courts depend on veracity of witnesses who present evidence in order to uncover the truth. Those who lie or otherwise deceive a court are acting in a way that undercuts the goals of the system. When this occurs, punishment may be imposed in order to protect our system of justice. The crime of perjury refers not just to the act of lying, but to any false statement made under oath in any judicial proceeding with the intent to deceive. Former President Clinton was found by a federal court in Arkansas to have committed perjury when he falsely testified in a deposition about his sexual relationship with intern Monica Lewinsky. As a result, Clinton was held in civil contempt of court and was subsequently disbarred from the practice of law by the Arkansas Supreme Court.

Obstruction of Justice

As with the crime of perjury, obstruction of justice is a serious crime that is intended to preserve the integrity of the justice system. It may occur in a variety of ways, all of which involve some manner of interference with the orderly processes of the courts, such as interfering with a police investigation, destroying evidence, intimidating witnesses, tampering with a jury. The seriousness of the crime becomes evident through many cases in which an individual is investigated for the commission of another crime and, in the course of the investigation, the suspect attempts to cover up evidence that leads to an obstruction of justice charge. For example, in 2002, domestic television personality and corporate CEO Martha Stewart was investigated for insider trading of stock, a crime in which it is illegal to trade stock on the basis of information about a company that is not generally available to the public. Stewart sold nearly 4,000 shares of the biotech company ImClone, on learning that the company's application for a new drug was about to be rejected by the Food and Drug Administration the next day, which would result in the collapse of the price of its shares on the stock market. As part of the federal investigation, she was asked whether she had contact with anyone in the company or with her stockbroker regarding the imminent drop in the stock's price. Her denial resulted in a federal obstruction of justice conviction, for which she received a 10-month prison sentence, 5 of which was served in prison and 5 served in her Connecticut mansion under home detention.

Bribery

Bribery occurs when a person gives or receives something of value in order to influence the action of public officials. As with all of the crimes against the government, bribery constitutes an attack on the proper operation of government institutions, reducing public confidence in their functioning. It is a crime for either the official being bribed or the person doing the bribing. Both state and federal law criminalize various acts of bribery. The New Mexico statute exemplifies a general approach:

30-24-1 Bribery of public officer or public employee.
Bribery of public officer or public employee consists of any person giving or offering to give, directly or indirectly, anything of value to any public officer or public employee, with intent to induce or influence such public officer or public employee to:
    A. give or render any official opinion, judgment or decree;
    B. be more favorable to one party than to the other in any cause, action, suit, election, appointment, matter or thing pending or to be brought before such person;
    C. procure him to vote or withhold his vote on any question, matter or proceeding which is then or may thereafter be pending, and which may by law come or be brought before him in his public capacity;
    D. execute any of the powers in him vested;
    E. perform any public duty otherwise than as required by law, or to delay in or omit to perform any public duty required of him by law.
Whoever commits bribery of a public officer or public employee is guilty of a third degree felony.

Key Terms

Substantive Criminal Law	Excuses
Actus Reus	Crimes Against the Person
Mens Rea	Crimes Against Property
Concurrence	Crimes Against Public Order
Causation	Crimes Against Morality
Plea	Felony
Justifications	Misdemeanor

Discussion Questions

1. What is the function of criminal law? In what ways does it benefit or not benefit society?
2. What is the meaning and significance of the terms *mala in se* and *mala prohibita*? How do they relate to criminal law?
3. What are the elements of most crimes? Why are they necessary?
4. When is an omission sufficient to satisfy *actus reus*?
5. What are the four classifications of culpability under the Model Penal Code?
6. What is the purpose of a defense? What are two primary types of defenses?
7. In what ways do crimes against the person differ from property crimes?
8. What are crimes involving public order and morality? Why is this behavior criminalized?

Cases

District of Columbia v. Heller, 128 SCt. 2783, 171 L.Ed.2d 637 (2008).

Jackson v. Indiana, 406 U.S. 715 (1972).

Kolendar v. Lawson, 461 U.S. 352, 103 S. Ct. 1855, 75 L.Ed.2d 903 (1983).

Michigan v. Lucas, 500 U.S. 145, 111 S. Ct. 1743, 114 L.Ed.2d 205 (1991).

Miller v. California, 413 U.S. 15, 93 S. Ct. 2607, 37 L.Ed.2d 419 (1973).

New York v. Ferber, 458 U.S. 747, 102 S. Ct. 3348, 73 L.Ed.2d 1113 (1982).

People v. Chance, 44 Cal.4th 1164, 189 P.3d 971, 81 Cal. Rptr. 3d 723 (2008).

People v. Pool, 166 Cal. App. 4th 904, 83 Cal. Rptr. 3d 186 (Ct. App. 2008).

Criminal Justice on the Web

For an up-to-date list of Web links, go to *The American Courts: A Procedural Approach* online companion site at http://criminal justice.jbpub.com/AmericanCourts. The online companion site will introduce you to some of the most important sites for finding American courts information on the Internet.

Criminal Procedure 12

What Is This Chapter About?

This chapter discusses the constitutional rights of criminal defendants and procedures that must be followed before a court can determine that a defendant has violated the law and should be punished. This includes rules that have been developed by the courts affecting the process of implementing criminal law. Implementation of criminal law involves procedures that must be followed at various points before prosecution of a criminal defendant begins: prearrest procedures, arrest procedures, and postarrest procedures. These are the focus of this chapter.

The Fourth Amendment of the U.S. Constitution prevents the government (police, prosecutors) from unreasonably searching or seizing persons or property. This chapter examines what this means, the circumstances under which a search may take place, and when a person may be arrested and charged with a crime. Furthermore, the Fifth Amendment right against self-incrimination and the use of Miranda warnings will be explored, as well as the meaning of due process in the context of information gathering by the police after arrest.

Learning Objectives

After reading this chapter, you should be able to

1. Understand the significance of the relationship between criminal law and procedure.
2. Understand the search and seizure requirements of the Fourth Amendment.
3. List and describe the exceptions to search warrant requirements.
4. Define "probable cause" and understand when it is required.
5. Explain the importance of the Miranda decision and right against self-incrimination.
6. Understand the importance of the right to counsel before and during police interrogation.
7. Understand limitations on interrogation by police and the use of confessions.
8. Understand the purpose of criminal sentencing and the options available to judges.

Criminal procedure focuses on the constitutional rights of criminal suspects and defendants. In particular, the scope of these rights, the ways in which action by the government may constitute a deprivation of rights, and the ways in which they are protected are the subject matter of criminal procedure. An understanding of the role of law enforcement and the relationship of police activities to the investigation and prosecution of crime gives meaning to these rights.

The procedures in criminal cases designed to protect individual rights may be divided into four categories related to aspects of the criminal process. First are prearrest procedures, which are those that apply to government action during the investigative phase of a case. Prearrest procedures are rules governing searches of people and places by the police, including the requirements and uses of warrants, as well as exceptions to the constitutional requirement of search warrants. In addition, the Fourth Amendment requirement of the existence of probable cause is considered. Prearrest procedures also involve the use of the exclusionary rule, which prevents the introduction of evidence obtained through an illegal search.

Arrest procedures deal with the circumstances under which an arrest by law enforcement may occur and the way in which an arrest must be conducted. This includes the use of arrest warrants and situations in which warrants are not required. In addition, the places where arrests may lawfully take place such as rules governing dwellings and pursuit of suspects in automobiles raise questions regarding the jurisdictional authority of police and rights of residents in their homes. Furthermore, attempts at arrest are sometimes met with resistance by suspects, and the use of force may be required by police to effectuate the arrest. This may lead to charges of excessive governmental force that impinge on the rights of suspects.

Postarrest procedures focus on information gathering from a suspect in custody. Thus, the role of a Miranda warning and the circumstances in which it must be used are threshold issues in the information gathering process, along with the issue of whether information obtained from a suspect is voluntarily given. These questions are central to the application of the Fifth Amendment and when confession or admissions by a suspect may be admissible in court. In addition, interrogations by law enforcement may serve various purposes, and when interrogations are conducted in such a way that they rise to the level of coercion, a suspect's Fifth Amendment rights are implicated.

Finally, criminal procedure also relates to the punishments that may be imposed on a criminal defendant. The constitution prevents the government from depriving a person of "life, liberty, or property" without due process of law. It also prevents the government from imposing "cruel and unusual" punishments. Thus, the manner in which sentencing occurs and the types of sentences that judges may use implicate the constitutional rights of criminal defendants. This chapter ends with a discussion of some of these issues.

Prearrest Procedures

Searches and Seizures

A search or seizure by the government for evidence of illegal activity represents the most important and potentially most intrusive aspect of the criminal justice system, as well as a visible show of governmental power (Rubenfeld, 2008). An understanding of searches necessarily begins with the Fourth Amendment: "The right of the people to be secure in their persons, houses, papers and effects, against unreasonable searches and seizures, shall not be violated. . . ." It is noteworthy that the Fourth Amendment does not prevent the government from conducting searches or seizing property or people. It is only "unreasonable" searches and seizures that are restricted. Much of the case law that has developed pertaining to the Fourth Amendment involves determining when a search and seizure is reasonable.

The U.S. Supreme Court has defined searches and seizures as follows:

> A "search" occurs when an expectation of privacy that society is prepared to consider reasonable is infringed. A "seizure" of property occurs when there is some meaningful interference with an individual's possessory interests in that property.

U.S. v. Jacobsen, 466 U.S. 109, 113, 104 S. Ct. 1652, 1656, 80 L.Ed.2d 85, 94 (1984). Thus, a search represents a breach by a governmental actor of a person's reasonable expectation of privacy in his or her "persons, houses, papers, and effects." A seizure involves an even greater degree of intrusion into those privacy interests, where a person is deprived of his or her property.

Search Warrants

A search warrant is an order issued from a court directed to a law enforcement officer to search in a particular place for some particular items of personal property and bring the items found to the court. Warrants hold an important place in American history because they stem from the use of writs of assistance, which were used in colonial times by the British Parliament to enforce the Trade Acts, which severely taxed goods in American ports. The writs of assistance allowed British officers to search houses and vessels in port for goods on which taxes had not been paid and to seize them if found. The British abused the writs by using them to seize whatever property they wished from colonists. There was no judicial or other oversight as to when the writ could be used; the British officer himself had nearly sole discretion as to where to search and what property to seize, as well as what was to be done with the property. This abuse of power was a central factor in the colonists' decision to declare their independence. After the American Revolution, the Framers of the Constitution sought to ensure that citizens' property could not be searched or seized without oversight by a court, and the requirement of obtaining warrants was later incorporated into the Fourth Amendment, which provides, "No warrants shall issue, but upon probable cause, supported by Oath or affirmation, and particularly describing the place to be searched and the person or things to be seized." Thus, a search warrant must be obtained from a court, and the basis for its issuance must be sworn to by a law enforcement officer.

The Basis for Search Warrants

The Fourth Amendment itself sets out the three requirements on which a search warrant must be based: probable cause, a description of the place to be searched, and a description of the person or things to be seized. In order to obtain the warrant, a law enforcement officer must provide a judge with a statement that addresses each of these three requirements. This is usually done with an affidavit in which the officer sets out the facts supporting probable cause that criminal activity has occurred in a particular place and that evidence of the crime or a suspect may be found there. If the judge is satisfied that probable cause exists based on the assertions made by the officer in the affidavit, the warrant will be issued.

Probable Cause   Probable cause is the amount of proof necessary for searches or seizures under the Fourth Amendment. It is defined as facts and circumstances that would lead a reasonable person to believe a crime has been committed or is about to be committed. These facts and circumstances may be based on a police officer's own senses or may be based on information obtained from others. They must be such that there is a "fair probability that contraband or evidence of crime will be found in a particular place." *Illinois v. Gates*, 462 U.S. 213, 238, 103 S. Ct. 2317, 2332, 76 L.Ed.2d 527, 548 (1983). Thus, as support for a search warrant, probable cause focuses on reasons that indicate it is likely that evidence of crime will be found.

If an officer observes crime or potentially criminal activity, probable cause for a search will exist. Indeed, in such circumstances, a search warrant will be unnecessary, given that a search incident to an arrest would be justified; however, there are times when an officer will observe something other than crime that will lead to probable cause. Most commonly, an officer may possess or be aware that evidence exists, warranting a search. For example, if a residential burglar mistakenly dropped his wallet (containing his driver's license) at a home that had been burglarized, probable cause would exist to search the address found on the burglar's license. Furthermore, if answers to questions by a criminal suspect suggest evidence may be found at his property, probable cause for a search will exist.

In addition, information pertaining to evidence of crime may come to the police from others. Traditionally, probable cause based on information from informants was allowed if its reliability could be independently established. This approach evolved into a "two-pronged" test following the Court's decisions in *Aguilar v. Texas*, 378 U.S. 108, 84 S. Ct. 1509, 12 L.Ed.2d 723 (1964), and *Spinelli v. U.S.*, 393 U.S. 410, 89 S. Ct. 584, 21 L.Ed.2d 637 (1969). For nearly 2 decades, the "Aguilar-Spinelli test" for probable cause required (1) that the basis of the informant's knowledge could be determined from the information provided and (2) that either the veracity or reliability of the information obtained could be supported. *Gates* abandoned this test in favor in favor of an approach that allows a judge to determine whether all of the circumstances on which the alleged crime are based together produce probable cause. When this occurs, probable cause exists when the "totality of the circumstances" indicates that evidence of crime may be found. *Illinois v. Gates*, 462 U.S. 213, 103 S. Ct. 2317, 76 L.Ed.2d 527 (1983). The court's reasoning and facts of the *Gates* case are found in **Case Decision 12.1**.

Under this new test from *Gates*, before issuing a search warrant, a court may consider a variety of factors known to police. In particular, these include the nature and specificity of the information, the source of the information conveyed by the other person, and whether the police had an opportunity to observe and/or verify facts obtained from another. *Aguilar v. Texas*, 378 U.S. 108, 84 S. Ct. 1509, 12 L.Ed.2d 723 (1964). If an independent source provides corroboration of the information obtained from another, probable cause may be found, even if other factors alone are insufficient. *Spinelli v. U.S.*, 393 U.S. 410, 89 S. Ct. 584, 21 L.Ed.2d 637 (1969).

Of course, when a police officer seeks a search warrant, he or she already has a personal belief that probable cause exists; however, the officer must convince an unbiased, independent decision maker, a judge, that probable cause exists in order to obtain the warrant. Thus, as the "reasonable person" making this determination, the judge, usually relying solely on statements made by the officer, must consider the likelihood that the evidence of crime exists and that a search in the place designated by the officer will reveal it. Specifically, the officer's description of the facts and circumstances must convince the judge to "a fair probability that contraband or evidence of a crime will be found in a particular place." *Illinois v. Gates*, 462 U.S. 213, 238,

---

Case Decision 12.1 *Illinois v. Gates*, 462 U.S. 213, 103 S. Ct. 2317, 76 L.Ed.2d 527 (1983)

Decision of the Court by Justice Rehnquist:

Respondents Lance and Susan Gates were indicted for violation of state drug laws after police officers, executing a search warrant, discovered marijuana and other contraband in their automobile and home. Prior to trial the Gates' moved to suppress evidence seized during this search. The affirmed the decisions of lower state courts, granting the motion. It held that the affidavit submitted in support of the State's application for a warrant to search the Gates' property was inadequate under this Court's decisions in *Aguilar v. Texas*, 378 U.S. 108, 84 S. Ct. 1509, 12 L.Ed. 2d 723 (1964) and *Spinelli v. United States*, 393 U.S. 410, 89 S. Ct. 584, 21 L.Ed.2d 637 (1969).

I

We granted certiorari to consider the application of the Fourth Amendment to a magistrate's issuance of a search warrant on the basis of a partially corroborated anonymous informant's tip. [W]e consider the question originally presented in the petition for certiorari, and conclude that the Illinois Supreme Court read the requirements of our Fourth Amendment decisions too restrictively.

II

We now turn to the question presented in the State's original petition for certiorari, which requires us to decide whether respondents' rights under the Fourth and Fourteenth Amendments were violated by the search of their car and house. A chronological statement of events usefully introduces the issues at stake. Bloomingdale, Ill., is a suburb of Chicago located in DuPage County. On May 3, 1978, the Bloomingdale Police Department received by mail an anonymous handwritten letter which read as follows:

This letter is to inform you that you have a couple in your town who strictly make their living on selling drugs. They are Sue and Lance Gates, they live on Greenway, off Bloomingdale Rd. in the condominiums. Most of their buys are done in Florida. Sue his wife drives their car to Florida, where she leaves it to be

(Continues)

loaded up with drugs, then Lance flys down and drives it back. Sue flys back after she drops the car off in Florida. May 3 she is driving down there again and Lance will be flying down in a few days to drive it back. At the time Lance drives the car back he has the trunk loaded with over $100,000.00 in drugs. Presently they have over $100,000.00 worth of drugs in their basement.

They brag about the fact they never have to work, and make their entire living on pushers.

I guarantee if you watch them carefully you will make a big catch. They are friends with some big drugs dealers, who visit their house often.

Lance & Susan Gates
Greenway
in Condominiums

The letter was referred by the Chief of Police of the Bloomingdale Police Department to Detective Mader, who decided to pursue the tip. Mader learned, from the office of the Illinois Secretary of State, that an Illinois driver's license had been issued to one Lance Gates, residing at a stated address in Bloomingdale. He contacted a confidential informant, whose examination of certain financial records revealed a more recent address for the Gates, and he also learned from a police officer assigned to O'Hare Airport that "L. Gates" had made a reservation on Eastern Airlines flight 245 to West Palm Beach, Fla., scheduled to depart from Chicago on May 5 at 4:15 p.m.

Mader then made arrangements with an agent of the Drug Enforcement Administration for surveillance of the May 5 Eastern Airlines flight. The agent later reported to Mader that Gates had boarded the flight, and that federal agents in Florida had observed him arrive in West Palm Beach and take a taxi to the nearby Holiday Inn. They also reported that Gates went to a room registered to one Susan Gates and that, at 7:00 a.m. the next morning, Gates and an unidentified woman left the motel in a Mercury bearing Illinois license plates and drove northbound on an interstate frequently used by travelers to the Chicago area. In addition, the DEA agent informed Mader that the license plate number on the Mercury registered to a Hornet station wagon owned by Gates. The agent also advised Mader that the driving time between West Palm Beach and Bloomingdale was approximately 22 to 24 hours.

Mader signed an affidavit setting forth the foregoing facts, and submitted it to a judge of the Circuit Court of DuPage County, together with a copy of the anonymous letter. The judge of that court thereupon issued a search warrant for the Gates' residence and for their automobile. The judge, in deciding to issue the warrant, could have determined that the *modus operandi* of the Gates had been substantially corroborated. As the anonymous letter predicted, Lance Gates had flown from Chicago to West Palm Beach late in the afternoon of May 5th, had checked into a hotel room registered in the name of his wife, and, at 7:00 a.m. the following morning, had headed north, accompanied by an unidentified woman, out of West Palm Beach on an interstate highway used by travelers from South Florida to Chicago in an automobile bearing a license plate issued to him.

At 5:15 a.m. on March 7th, only 36 hours after he had flown out of Chicago, Lance Gates, and his wife, returned to their home in Bloomingdale, driving the car in which they had left West Palm Beach some 22 hours earlier. The Bloomingdale police were awaiting them, searched the trunk of the Mercury, and uncovered approximately 350 pounds of marijuana. A search of the Gates' home revealed marijuana, weapons, and other contraband. The Illinois Circuit Court ordered suppression of all these items, on the ground that the affidavit submitted to the Circuit Judge failed to support the necessary determination of probable cause to believe that the Gates' automobile and home contained the contraband in question. This decision was affirmed in turn by the Illinois Appellate Court and by a divided vote of the Supreme Court of Illinois.

The Illinois Supreme Court concluded—and we are inclined to agree—that, standing alone, the anonymous letter sent to the Bloomingdale Police Department would not provide the basis for a magistrate's determination that there was probable cause to believe contraband would be found in the Gates' car and home. The letter provides virtually nothing from which one might conclude that its author is either honest or his information reliable; likewise, the letter gives absolutely no indication of the basis for the writer's predictions regarding the Gates' criminal activities. Something more was required, then, before a magistrate could conclude that there was probable cause to believe that contraband would be found in the Gates' home and car.

The Illinois Supreme Court also properly recognized that Detective Mader's affidavit might be capable of supplementing the anonymous letter with information sufficient to permit a determination of probable cause. In holding that the affidavit in fact did not contain sufficient additional information to sustain a determination of probable cause, the Illinois court applied a "two-pronged test," derived from our decision in *Spinelli v. United States*, 393 U.S. 410, 89 S. Ct. 584, 21 L.Ed.2d 637 (1969). The Illinois Supreme Court, like some others, apparently understood *Spinelli* as requiring that the anonymous letter satisfy each of two independent requirements before it could be relied on. According to this view, the letter, as supplemented by Mader's affidavit, first had to adequately reveal the "basis of knowledge" of the letter writer—the particular means by which he came by the information given in his report. Second, it had to provide facts sufficiently establishing either the "veracity" of the affiant's informant, or, alternatively, the "reliability" of the informant's report in this particular case.

The Illinois court, alluding to an elaborate set of legal rules that have developed among various lower courts to enforce the "two-pronged test," found that the test had not been satisfied. First, the "veracity" prong was not satisfied because, "there was simply no basis [for] . . . conclud[ing] that the anonymous person [who wrote the letter to the Bloomingdale Police Department] was credible." The court indicated that corroboration by police of details contained in the letter might never satisfy the "veracity" prong, and in any event, could not do so if, as in the present case, only "innocent" details are corroborated. In addition, the letter gave no indication of the basis of its writer's knowledge of the Gates' activities. The Illinois court understood *Spinelli* as permitting the detail contained in a tip to be used to infer that the informant had a reliable basis for his statements, but it thought that the anonymous letter failed to provide sufficient detail to permit such an inference. Thus, it concluded that no showing of probable cause had been made.

We agree with the Illinois Supreme Court that an informant's "veracity," "reliability" and "basis of knowledge" are all highly relevant in determining the value of his report. We do not agree, however, that these elements should be understood as entirely separate and independent requirements to be rigidly exacted in every case, which the opinion of the Supreme Court of Illinois would imply. Rather, as detailed below, they should be understood simply as closely intertwined issues that may usefully illuminate the commonsense, practical question whether there is "probable cause" to believe that contraband or evidence is located in a particular place.

III

This totality-of-the-circumstances approach is far more consistent with our prior treatment of probable cause than is any rigid demand that specific "tests" be satisfied by every informant's tip. Perhaps the central teaching of our decisions bearing on the probable cause standard is that it is a "practical, nontechnical conception." "In dealing with probable cause, . . . as the very name implies, we deal with probabilities. These are not technical; they are the factual and practical considerations of everyday life on which reasonable and prudent men, not legal technicians, act." Our observation in *United States v. Cortez*, 449 U.S. 411, 418, 101 S. Ct. 690, 695, 66 L.Ed.2d 621 (1981), regarding "particularized suspicion," is also applicable to the probable cause standard:

> The process does not deal with hard certainties, but with probabilities. Long before the law of probabilities was articulated as such, practical people formulated certain common-sense conclusions about human behavior; jurors as factfinders are permitted to do the same—and so are law enforcement officers. Finally, the evidence thus collected must be seen and weighed not in terms of library analysis by scholars, but as understood by those versed in the field of law enforcement.

As these comments illustrate, probable cause is a fluid concept—turning on the assessment of probabilities in particular factual contexts—not readily, or even usefully, reduced to a neat set of legal rules. Informants' tips doubtless come in many shapes and sizes from many different types of persons. "Informants' tips, like all other clues and evidence coming to a policeman on the scene may vary greatly in their value and reliability." Rigid legal rules are ill-suited to an area of such diversity. "One simple rule will not cover every situation."

Moreover, the "two-pronged test" directs analysis into two largely independent channels—the informant's "veracity" or "reliability" and his "basis of knowledge." There are persuasive arguments against according these two elements such independent status. Instead, they are better understood as relevant considerations in the totality-of-the-circumstances analysis that traditionally has guided probable cause determinations: a deficiency in one may be compensated for, in determining the overall reliability of a tip, by a strong showing as to the other, or by some other indicia of reliability.

(Continues)

(*Continued*)

If, for example, a particular informant is known for the unusual reliability of his predictions of certain types of criminal activities in a locality, his failure, in a particular case, to thoroughly set forth the basis of his knowledge surely should not serve as an absolute bar to a finding of probable cause based on his tip. Likewise, if an unquestionably honest citizen comes forward with a report of criminal activity—which if fabricated would subject him to criminal liability—we have found rigorous scrutiny of the basis of his knowledge unnecessary. Conversely, even if we entertain some doubt as to an informant's motives, his explicit and detailed description of alleged wrongdoing, along with a statement that the event was observed first-hand, entitles his tip to greater weight than might otherwise be the case. Unlike a totality-of-the-circumstances analysis, which permits a balanced assessment of the relative weights of all the various indicia of reliability (and unreliability) attending an informant's tip, the "two-pronged test" has encouraged an excessively technical dissection of informants' tips, with undue attention being focused on isolated issues that cannot sensibly be divorced from the other facts presented to the magistrate.

As early as 1813, Chief Justice Marshall observed, in a closely related context, that "the term 'probable cause,' according to its usual acceptation, means less than evidence which would justify condemnation. . . . It imports a seizure made under circumstances which warrant suspicion." More recently, we said that "the *quanta* . . . of proof" appropriate in ordinary judicial proceedings are inapplicable to the decision to issue a warrant. Finely-tuned standards such as proof beyond a reasonable doubt or by a preponderance of the evidence, useful in formal trials, have no place in the magistrate's decision. While an effort to fix some general, numerically precise degree of certainty corresponding to "probable cause" may not be helpful, it is clear that "only the probability, and not a prima facie showing, of criminal activity is the standard of probable cause."

We also have recognized that affidavits "are normally drafted by nonlawyers in the midst and haste of a criminal investigation. Technical requirements of elaborate specificity once exacted under common law pleading have no proper place in this area." Likewise, search and arrest warrants long have been issued by persons who are neither lawyers nor judges, and who certainly do not remain abreast of each judicial refinement of the nature of "probable cause." The rigorous inquiry into the *Spinelli* prongs and the complex superstructure of evidentiary and analytical rules that some have seen implicit in our *Spinelli* decision, cannot be reconciled with the fact that many warrants are—quite properly—issued on the basis of nontechnical, common-sense judgments of laymen applying a standard less demanding than those used in more formal legal proceedings. Likewise, given the informal, often hurried context in which it must be applied, the "built-in subtleties," of the "two-pronged test" are particularly unlikely to assist magistrates in determining probable cause.

Similarly, we have repeatedly said that after-the-fact scrutiny by courts of the sufficiency of an affidavit should not take the form of *de novo* review. A magistrate's "determination of probable cause should be paid great deference by reviewing courts." "A grudging or negative attitude by reviewing courts toward warrants," is inconsistent with the Fourth Amendment's strong preference for searches conducted pursuant to a warrant "courts should not invalidate . . . warrant[s] by interpreting affidavit[s] in a hypertechnical, rather than a commonsense, manner."

If the affidavits submitted by police officers are subjected to the type of scrutiny some courts have deemed appropriate, police might well resort to warrantless searches, with the hope of relying on consent or some other exception to the warrant clause that might develop at the time of the search. In addition, the possession of a warrant by officers conducting an arrest or search greatly reduces the perception of unlawful or intrusive police conduct, by assuring "the individual whose property is searched or seized of the lawful authority of the executing officer, his need to search, and the limits of his power to search." Reflecting this preference for the warrant process, the traditional standard for review of an issuing magistrate's probable cause determination has been that so long as the magistrate had a "substantial basis for . . . conclud[ing]" that a search would uncover evidence of wrongdoing, the Fourth Amendment requires no more. We think reaffirmation of this standard better serves the purpose of encouraging recourse to the warrant procedure and is more consistent with our traditional deference to the probable cause determinations of magistrates than is the "two-pronged test."

Finally, the direction taken by decisions following *Spinelli* poorly serves "the most basic function of any government": "to provide for the security of the individual and of his property." The strictures that inevitably accompany the "two-pronged test" cannot avoid seriously impeding the task of law enforcement. If, as the Illinois Supreme Court apparently thought, that test must be rigorously applied in every case, anonymous tips seldom would be of greatly diminished value in police work. Ordinary citizens, like ordinary witnesses, generally do not provide extensive recitations of the basis of their everyday observations. Likewise, as the Illinois Supreme Court observed in this case, the veracity of persons supplying anonymous tips is by hypothesis largely unknown, and unknowable. As a result, anonymous tips seldom could survive a rigorous application of either of the *Spinelli* prongs. Yet, such tips, particularly when supplemented by independent police investigation, frequently contribute to the solution of otherwise "perfect crimes." While a conscientious assessment of the basis for crediting such tips is required by the Fourth Amendment, a standard that leaves virtually no place for anonymous citizen informants is not.

For all these reasons, we conclude that it is wiser to abandon the "two-pronged test" established by our decisions in *Aguilar* and *Spinelli*. In its place we reaffirm the totality-of-the-circumstances analysis that traditionally has informed probable cause determinations. The task of the issuing magistrate is simply to make a practical, common-sense decision whether, given all the circumstances set forth in the affidavit before him, including the "veracity" and "basis of knowledge" of persons supplying hearsay information, there is a fair probability that contraband or evidence of a crime will be found in a particular place. And the duty of a reviewing court is simply to ensure that the magistrate had a "substantial basis for . . . conclud[ing]" that probable cause existed. We are convinced that this flexible, easily applied standard will better achieve the accommodation of public and private interests that the Fourth Amendment requires than does the approach that has developed from *Aguilar* and *Spinelli*.

Our earlier cases illustrate the limits beyond which a magistrate may not venture in issuing a warrant. A sworn statement of an affiant that "he has cause to suspect and does believe that" liquor illegally brought into the United States is located on certain premises will not do. An officer's statement that "affiants have received reliable information from a credible person and believe" that heroin is stored in a home, is likewise inadequate. [T]his is a mere conclusory statement that gives the magistrate virtually no basis at all for making a judgment regarding probable cause. Sufficient information must be presented to the magistrate to allow that official to determine probable cause; his action cannot be a mere ratification of the bare conclusions of others. In order to ensure that such an abdication of the magistrate's duty does not occur, courts must continue to conscientiously review the sufficiency of affidavits on which warrants are issued. But when we move beyond the "bare bones" affidavits present in [some] cases, this area simply does not lend itself to a prescribed set of rules, like that which had developed from *Spinelli*. Instead, the flexible, common-sense standard articulated better serves the purposes of the Fourth Amendment's probable cause requirement.

IV

Our decisions applying the totality-of-the-circumstances analysis outlined above have consistently recognized the value of corroboration of details of an informant's tip by independent police work. Our decision in *Draper v. United States*, 358 U.S. 307, 79 S. Ct. 329, 3 L.Ed.2d 327 (1959), however, is the classic case on the value of corroborative efforts of police officials. There, an informant named Hereford reported that Draper would arrive in Denver on a train from Chicago on one of two days, and that he would be carrying a quantity of heroin. The informant also supplied a fairly detailed physical description of Draper, and predicted that he would be wearing a light colored raincoat, brown slacks and black shoes, and would be walking "real fast." Hereford gave no indication of the basis for his information. On one of the stated dates police officers observed a man matching this description exit a train arriving from Chicago; his attire and luggage matched Hereford's report and he was walking rapidly. We explained in *Draper* that, by this point in his investigation, the arresting officer "had personally verified every facet of the information given him by Hereford except whether petitioner had accomplished his mission and had the three ounces of heroin on his person or in his bag. And surely, with every other bit of Hereford's information being thus personally verified, [the officer] had 'reasonable grounds' to believe that the remaining unverified bit of Hereford's information—that Draper would have the heroin with him—was likewise true."

The showing of probable cause in the present case was fully as compelling as that in *Draper*. Even standing alone, the facts obtained through the independent investigation of Mader and the DEA at least suggested that the Gates were involved in drug trafficking. In addition to being a popular vacation site, Florida is well-known as a source of narcotics and other illegal drugs. Lance Gates' flight to

(Continues)

(Continued)

Palm Beach, his brief, overnight stay in a motel, and apparent immediate return north to Chicago in the family car, conveniently awaiting him in West Palm Beach, is as suggestive of a pre-arranged drug run, as it is of an ordinary vacation trip.

In addition, the magistrate could rely on the anonymous letter, which had been corroborated in major part by Mader's efforts—just as had occurred in *Draper*. The Supreme Court of Illinois reasoned that *Draper* involved an informant who had given reliable information on previous occasions, while the honesty and reliability of the anonymous informant in this case were unknown to the Bloomingdale police. While this distinction might be an apt one at the time the police department received the anonymous letter, it became far less significant after Mader's independent investigative work occurred. The corroboration of the letter's predictions that the Gates' car would be in Florida, that Lance Gates would fly to Florida in the next day or so, and that he would drive the car north toward Bloomingdale all indicated, albeit not with certainty, that the informant's other assertions also were true. "Because an informant is right about some things, he is more probably right about other facts,"—including the claim regarding the Gates' illegal activity. This may well not be the type of "reliability" or "veracity" necessary to satisfy some views of the "veracity prong" of *Spinelli*, but we think it suffices for the practical, common-sense judgment called for in making a probable cause determination. It is enough, for purposes of assessing probable cause, that "corroboration through other sources of information reduced the chances of a reckless or prevaricating tale," thus providing "a substantial basis for crediting the hearsay."

Finally, the anonymous letter contained a range of details relating not just to easily obtained facts and conditions existing at the time of the tip, but to future actions of third parties ordinarily not easily predicted. The letter writer's accurate information as to the travel plans of each of the Gates was of a character likely obtained only from the Gates themselves, or from someone familiar with their not entirely ordinary travel plans. If the informant had access to accurate information of this type a magistrate could properly conclude that it was not unlikely that he also had access to reliable information of the Gates' alleged illegal activities. Of course, the Gates' travel plans might have been learned from a talkative neighbor or travel agent; under the "two-pronged test" developed from *Spinelli*, the character of the details in the anonymous letter might well not permit a sufficiently clear inference regarding the letter writer's "basis of knowledge." But, as discussed previously, probable cause does not demand the certainty we associate with formal trials. It is enough that there was a fair probability that the writer of the anonymous letter had obtained his entire story either from the Gates or someone they trusted. And corroboration of major portions of the letter's predictions provides just this probability. It is apparent, therefore, that the judge issuing the warrant had a "substantial basis for . . . conclud[ing]" that probable cause to search the Gates' home and car existed. The judgment of the Supreme Court of Illinois therefore must be reversed.

103 S. Ct. 2317, 2332, 76 L.Ed.2d 527, 548 (1983). The judge, therefore, acts as an independent reviewer of the law enforcement determination that evidence of crime may be found and, if the judge believes it is likely that the evidence will be found, will issue the warrant (Cooley, 2006).

Places to Be Searched   The affidavit in support of the warrant application must specify the place where the search will be conducted. The term "place" is broadly construed and may include houses, apartments, barns, vehicles, a mailbox, and perhaps even a website. Although there may be exceptions to the warrant requirement for some of these locations in some circumstances (such as motor vehicles on public roadways), absent extenuating circumstances a warrant is required. When the location is a house, a street address is usually sufficient for identifying the place for the search, but what is important is that the description, whether an address or otherwise, must be specific enough that law enforcement is able to locate the

premises to be searched and be reasonably certain that a wrong location is not searched by mistake; therefore, a description of the house or other property, such as the color of the house, its style, whether it has a garage, and other distinct characteristics, is usually included to make sure the correct location is searched. This is particularly important when the place is an apartment; the street address is not sufficiently descriptive to identify where the search is to occur. Likewise, when the location is rural, a more specific description of the property (perhaps other buildings, roadway marker, vegetation, and surrounding buildings) will be necessary. Whether a description is sufficient will be judged in terms of the information available to law enforcement at the time the warrant was sought.

Not all premises are subject to search. Most importantly, locations that are not occupied by persons under suspicion of crime cannot justify a search warrant, unless a suspect is believed to be present at or frequents the premises.

Items to Be Seized   As with the places to be searched, the items that are the subject of the search must be stated with particularity. This does not mean that each and every item believed by law enforcement to constitute evidence need be listed or that only those items may be seized. Rather, the affidavit (and the warrant itself) must describe, with specificity, the types of items that will be the subject of the search and how they relate to the suspected crime. Nonetheless, a warrant does not allow a "fishing expedition" in which a law enforcement officer, once access to a place is gained through the warrant, may seize every item at the location. Only those items that fall within the description on the warrant are subject to seizure.

There are three categories of items that may be seized when a search warrant is obtained. These are found in the Federal Rules of Criminal Procedure, Rule 41(b), which states this:

> A warrant may be issued under this rule to search for and seize any (1) property that constitutes evidence of the commission of a criminal offense; or (2) contraband, the fruits of crime, or things otherwise criminally possessed; or (3) property designed or intended for use or which is or has been used as the means of committing a criminal offense. . . .

Although state rules may differ somewhat, most are based on these categories. Property that constitutes evidence of crime being or having been committed is a broad category that comprises nearly anything that could be admitted at trial; therefore, documents, photographs, clothing, weapons, money, and even blood and fingerprints can be the subject of a search warrant. The second category includes items that are illegal or that are the "fruits" of illegal activity. This would include drugs or drug paraphernalia, certain types of weapons, or some pornographic materials, photos, or videos. The third category allows law enforcement to search for items used by a suspect to commit a crime or that could have been used to commit a crime. This generally allows law enforcement to search for items at a home, in a vehicle, or at a business location after a suspect has been apprehended.

Execution of Warrants

Once obtained, a warrant is "executed" by an officer named in the warrant who brings it to the premises to conduct the search. Because the warrant is a court order, its execution involves carrying out the court's orders. The search therefore may be conducted without delay and without further authorization or permission, including that of the property owner. Depending on the facts of a case, particularly where premises are under surveillance and an arrest warrant has also been issued, delay in the execution of a search warrant may be permissible, as long as it is executed within a reasonable amount of time. After a search has begun, however, it cannot last longer than reasonably necessary to search fully for the items sought, and after the items sought have been found, the search must end. State statutes or local rules also sometimes specify time limits within which a warrant must be executed.

Officers executing a search warrant may use reasonable force, if necessary, to obtain access to the premises or items within that are described in the warrant. Generally, however, officers must attempt to gain access without the use of force. Breaking down doors, cutting off locks, even breaking through walls and floors may be allowed if the search requires it, particularly where a resident attempts to deny access. Nonetheless, officers may not be wantonly destructive and must do as little damage as possible while conducting a search, including not leaving furnishings in disarray or the contents of drawers strewn onto floors. "Excessive or unnecessary destruction of property in the course of a search may violate the Fourth Amendment. . . ." *U.S. v. Ramirez*, 523 U.S. 65, 71, 118 S. Ct. 992, 996, 140 L.Ed.2d 191, 198 (1998). Reasonable force may also be used against persons who attempt to obstruct or interfere with the search.

Scope of the Search   The scope of a search refers to the places that may be searched and the things that may be searched for. If a warrant does not accurately describe the premises to be searched, a search may exceed its scope if officers search the wrong property, adjoining properties, or parts of the property that could not conceal the items that are the subject of the search. Although a search warrant itself specifies the scope of a search, it is during its execution that the possibility is raised of a search going beyond its scope. Generally, all parts of a building that have been particularly described in a warrant, as well as the land on which it sits and the surrounding land, may be searched. In addition, sheds, garages, and vehicles on the property are subject to search.

Knock and Announce   The "knock and announce" rule requires officers to knock at entry doors and announce their presence and intention to execute a search warrant. As long as the officer has a warrant at the scene and affords the resident an opportunity to examine it, entry cannot be denied nor a search prevented. The knock and announce rule is intended to allow for an orderly and nonviolent search, as well as to protect the privacy interests of the residents of the property.

There are some circumstances in which the knock and announce rule does not apply. These include situations in which the occupants of the premises are already aware that the police are present, when the potential for destroying evidence exists, or when there is an imminent threat of harm to someone, including the officers executing the warrant. In all of these circumstances, a "no-knock" entry can occur only if the police "have reasonable suspicion that knocking and announcing their presence, under the particular circumstances, would be dangerous or futile, or that it would inhibit the effective investigation of the crime. . . ." *Richards v. Wisconsin*, 520 U.S. 385, 394, 117 S. Ct. 1416, 1421, 137 L.Ed.2d 615, 624 (1997). Despite the knock and announce requirement and its exceptions, the Supreme Court has held that the exclusionary rule (discussed later here) does not apply to violations of the knock and announce rule. *Hudson v. Michigan*, 547 U.S. 586, 126 S. Ct. 2159, 165 L.Ed.2d 56 (2006). This has led some to question whether the knock and announce rule is a requirement any longer in the execution of search warrants because it lacks an enforcement mechanism (Blair, 2007; Frakt, 2007).

Exceptions to Search Warrants

A search warrant is not always required in order for law enforcement to search and seize property. Several exceptions to the general rule requiring warrants exist.

Consent Searches

A consent search is one in which a person allows a search of his or her property. Sometimes a person consents because he or she is innocent and has nothing to hide. Sometimes he or she believes that the police will not find hidden contraband or evidence, and sometimes he or she believes it to be in his or her best interests (e.g., to avoid arrest) if he or she consents. When this occurs, the Fourth Amendment search and seizure requirements no longer apply because that person has waived them. Thus, when a person consents to a search, a warrant is not needed, and probable cause need not be established.

The primary issue relating to consent searches is whether the consent to search was voluntarily given. "Voluntary" means that a person freely gave his or her consent to search, and he or she understood what he or she was consenting to at the time it was given. The question of voluntariness is one that is based on the facts and circumstances at the time consent was given for the search.

Many factors may affect a person's ability to consent. These include characteristics of the person consenting and actions or statements made by the police. In addition, the situation or circumstances in which the consent is obtained may influence a court in determining whether consent was voluntary.

There are three primary characteristics of the person consenting that may affect his or her ability to voluntarily consent. These are whether the person has the mental capacity to consent, whether the person understands that he or she is giving consent, and whether he or she is in custody at the time consent is given. The mental capacity to consent may be affected by a variety of factors such as whether a person is mentally ill and his or her emotional state at the time of the search or whether he or she is under the influence of alcohol or drugs. Voluntariness also depends on whether the consent given is knowingly; that is, did the person understand what he or she was consenting to? The ability to know what a person consents to may be affected by his or her age, intelligence level, educational background, or his or her mistaken understanding of what the police were looking for. Furthermore, he or she may not understand that he or she is not required to give consent or that he or she can refuse a request for consent. In addition, if a person is in police custody when consent is given, the voluntariness of his or her consent is less clear than if he or she were free. This is because people who are detained may be more susceptible to police coercion or believe they must cooperate.

The conduct of police officers, including statements they make, may influence a suspect's ability to consent to a search. It is clear that the police may not use threats of bodily harm or destruction of property to obtain consent, but the "threat" of obtaining a search warrant is not sufficient to invalidate consent that is otherwise freely given. *U.S. v. Kaplan*, 895 F.2d 618 (9th Cir. 1990). Also, in general, deception may not be used by law enforcement to obtain consent to search, including a misrepresentation that police already have a search warrant. *Bumper v. North Carolina*, 391 U.S. 543, 88 S. Ct. 1788, 20 L.Ed.2d 797 (1968).

Plain View Doctrine

The "plain view" doctrine is an exception to the warrant requirement that allows police officers to seize as evidence items that an officer can see as long as he or she is lawfully in a position to see the items. Although there is no actual or thorough "search," it may be said that the officer "searches" with his or her eyes and, observing an item of contraband or potential evidence of crime in plain view, may seize it without a warrant; however, the application of the rule presumes that an officer makes the observation in a location that he or she is lawfully entitled to be, and the location affords a view of the item. In addition, the officer may not violate a person's reasonable expectation of privacy in viewing and seizing the item. Thus, the plain view doctrine is not an exception that allows law enforcement to conduct thorough searches; only an item in plain view that constitutes evidence of crime may be seized. Any further searching requires a warrant.

There are several situations in which an officer may lawfully be in a place where incriminating items may be in plain view. First, if officers are executing a valid search warrant and see contraband or evidence not described in the warrant, the items observed may be seized, provided they were in plain view. Second, police officers may seize items in plain view if they are conducting a search as part of the lawful arrest of a person; however, the search during arrest must be for weapons and is limited to searching the arrested suspect and the area immediately around him. Third, if police officers are actively pursuing a fleeing suspect, they may seize items in plain view that they may come on during the pursuit, including buildings. Similarly, where police are responding to an emergency, items of contraband or evidence of crime that are in plain view at the place of the emergency may be seized.

Vehicle Searches

Motor vehicles are unique in that contraband and evidence of crime may be hidden or transported in them, and they constitute a "moveable location" that increases the potential for loss of evidence. In addition, the vehicle is personal property that may be used in the commission of crime or itself be evidence that a crime has been committed. Motor vehicles are ubiquitous, and because most vehicles traveling public roads are not involved in criminal activity, ferreting out the few that are would hinder crime prevention if a warrant were required each time a vehicle is suspected of containing crime-related items.

Because vehicles may be moved great distances, are capable of being hidden, and subject to being destroyed, they present unique challenges for law enforcement.

For these reasons, exceptions to the warrant requirement for vehicles exist. The most common of these, the Carroll doctrine, allows warrantless searches of motor vehicles when law enforcement has probable cause. *Carroll v. U.S.*, 267 U.S. 132, 45 S. Ct. 280, 69 L.Ed. 543 (1925). The Carroll doctrine, however, is not a blanket exception for motor vehicles to the warrant requirement. When probable cause does not exist, search of a vehicle without a warrant is not justified. Furthermore, if a vehicle is not "readily mobile," it may not be searched without a warrant unless there are "exigent circumstances." *Pennsylvania v. Labron*, 518 U.S. 938, 940, 116 S. Ct. 2485, 2487, 135 L.Ed.2d 1031, 1036 (1996). A vehicle is not readily mobile if it is not in a condition to be driven away, such as when it is disabled. Exigent circumstances exist when police believe a vehicle contains contraband or evidence that may be removed or destroyed in the time it takes to get a warrant.

The rules governing searches conducted in impounded vehicles are slightly more restrictive. An impounded vehicle is one that has been taken into custody and secured. This usually occurs for safety reasons, such as when a car is damaged, left disabled on a roadway, or when a driver is impaired, but may also occur as part of an investigation such as when the driver has been arrested or the vehicle itself constitutes evidence. When a vehicle is impounded, a warrant is generally required to search for contraband or other evidence in the vehicle; however, as part of the impoundment, an inventory of items within the vehicle may be taken. This is a limited search to identify items belonging to the owner of the vehicle in order to protect the owner's property and protect the police against claims for subsequent loss of property from the vehicle. *Florida v. Wells*, 495 U.S. 1, 110 S. Ct. 1632, 109 L.Ed.2d 1 (1990). Essentially, what differentiates an "inventory" from a "search" is the scope of the inventory/search and whether the police conducting it have standard procedures in place for inventories. When an inventory occurs, illegal items found may be used as evidence against the operator or owner of the motor vehicle. When police have a procedure for the inventory (even if not written) or a form for cataloguing items found, the courts are more likely to interpret the inventory of an impounded vehicle as such, rather than a search. In addition, the scope of the "inventory" helps the courts to determine whether a violation of Fourth Amendment rights has occurred. The basic rule is that the inventory should be restricted to areas of the vehicle in which the owner's/operator's personal property may be kept. This usually includes unlocked areas, including the glove compartment or the trunk, on or under the seats, in door or console storage bins, behind visors, or in open areas of the vehicle.

Open Fields

The U.S. Supreme Court made reference to the term "open fields" as an exception to the warrant requirement in the case of *Hester v. U.S.*, 265 U.S. 57, 44 S. Ct. 445, 68 L.Ed. 898 (1924). In that case, the Court held that the warrant requirement does not extend to areas outside the curtilage, which it referred to as "the open fields." Moreover, it is not necessary to establish probable cause before searching if the area to be searched is part of the open fields. Thus, under the open fields doctrine, law enforcement may search on any open land, even if privately owned, as long as it is not a part of a house and immediately surrounding areas on a property. *Oliver v. U.S.*, 466 U.S. 170, 104 S. Ct. 1735, 80 L.Ed.2d 214 (1984). Whether the area to be searched is within the curtilage, therefore, becomes a central determination in deciding whether the open fields doctrine will apply.

The area of property that is within the curtilage and therefore entitled to Fourth Amendment protection is determined by four factors: (1) how close the area to be searched is to the home; (2) whether the area to be searched is within an enclosure around the home; (3) how the area to be searched is generally used, whether as a yard or other domestic use; and (4) whether the resident of the home has taken steps to protect the area from viewing by others. *U.S. v. Dunn*, 480 U.S. 294, 107 S. Ct. 1134, 94 L.Ed.2d 326 (1987). Each of these helps to determine whether a person occupying the home has a reasonable expectation of privacy in the area to be searched by considering and using it as part of the home. It is not necessary to satisfy all of these factors; any one may be sufficient to determine whether property is within the curtilage or part of the "open fields." What is important is whether the facts and circumstances show that the occupant of the property used the property as part of his or her home and thus had a reasonable expectation of privacy within it. If so, a warrantless search may not be conducted under the open fields exception.

The Exclusionary Rule

The exclusionary rule is perhaps the most important rule in criminal procedure. It states that no evidence illegally discovered or seized may subsequently be used in a criminal proceeding. At common law, relevant and reliable evidence could be used in court regardless of the manner in which it was gathered. It was not until the early 20th century that the U.S. Supreme Court created the rule to apply in federal cases and in 1961 required states to follow its mandate. *Weeks v. U.S.*, 232 U.S. 383, 34 S. Ct. 341, 58 L.Ed. 652 (1914); *Mapp v. Ohio*, 367 U.S. 643, 81 S. Ct. 1684, 6 L.Ed.2d 1081 (1961). The rule's importance stems from its effects, which are the dismissal of criminal cases as a result of lack of evidence and the care that must be taken by law enforcement in the process of gathering evidence.

The purpose of the exclusionary rule is to discourage misconduct by the police in the investigation of crime. In particular, the rule seeks to ensure that law enforcement does not trample on the Fourth Amendment rights of individuals by improperly conducting searches or improperly seizing property. Also, as a matter of fairness, the rule deprives the government of the benefit that it would receive at trial from its improper conduct. Thus, the exclusionary rule gives "teeth" to the Fourth Amendment; without it, the constitutional rights found in that amendment would have little meaning and no applicability to the lives of citizens. It is the procedural mechanism that enforces the Fourth Amendment.

Fruit of the Poisonous Tree

The *fruit of the poisonous tree* doctrine is an extension of the exclusionary rule that prevents the use in court of evidence obtained indirectly from a search conducted in violation of the Fourth Amendment, or resulting from the violation of any of a suspect's constitutional rights. Such indirectly obtained evidence is said to be tainted by its illegally obtained source. Thus, the fruit of the poisonous tree is a metaphor, where the poisonous tree is the unconstitutional action by the government; the fruit is all other evidence subsequently derived from it. For example, if the police searched the home of a suspected bank robber in violation of the constitution (e.g., by not obtaining a search warrant) and found a map that showed the money was buried on the outskirts of town, the map (and everything else found in the home) could not be used as evidence pursuant to the exclusionary rule, but the money itself also could not be used in court because it would constitute fruit of the poisonous tree. The doctrine therefore effectively prevents evidence obtained in an improper way from being used against a criminal defendant, even where the evidence did not directly result from the improper government action. It will apply only in situations where it is first determined that a violation of a suspect's constitutional rights occurred.

Despite the broad reach of the fruit of the poisonous tree doctrine, there are exceptions to its applicability. When one of these applies, the "fruit," or tainted evidence, may be used as evidence. The first of these is the *independent source doctrine*. This rule allows admission of tainted evidence in court if it was also discovered or obtained from a source independent of the constitutional violation. The independent source rule attempts to place police in the same position that they would have been in if evidence had not been improperly obtained. This balances society's interest in deterring the police from unlawful behavior against the interests of society in prosecuting crime. *Nix v. Williams*, 467 U.S. 431, 104 S. Ct. 2501, 81 L.Ed.2d 377 (1984).

Another exception is the *attenuation doctrine*, which allows the use of tainted evidence at trial if it was obtained in a manner that was sufficiently removed from the government's unconstitutional actions. That is, even if the evidence wouldn't have been discovered without the government's violation of constitutional rights, the evidence may be used if its discovery did not directly result from the violation. *Wong Sun v. U.S.*, 371 U.S. 471, 83 S. Ct. 407, 9 L.Ed.2d 441 (1963). For example, in Wong Sun, the police illegally searched the home of a man named Toy and arrested him for distribution of narcotics. Toy claimed to have gotten the drugs from Wong Sun, who the agents also illegally arrested and then released. Later, Wong Sun made incriminating statements that he sought to have excluded at trial. The Supreme Court found Wong Sun's statements to be admissible because, although they were related to the chain of events, they were not sufficiently connected to the original illegal search by the police.

Finally, an exception to the fruit of the poisonous tree doctrine is the *inevitable discovery doctrine*, which means just that if evidence would have been discovered anyway, even when a constitutional violation occurs, it is admissible at trial. This exception was created by the Supreme Court in *Nix v. Williams*, 467 U.S. 431, 104 S. Ct. 2501, 81 L.Ed.2d 377 (1984). In that case, a search for a missing girl was underway when police illegally questioned the defendant, who told them where the girl's body could be found. At trial, he sought to have evidence relating to the body excluded, claiming that the body was found as a result of the illegal interrogation. The Court held that the evidence could be admitted because it was found in an area where searchers would have eventually looked, and the discovery of the evidence was therefore inevitable. Thus, although it is based on a somewhat different rationale, the inevitable discovery doctrine may be seen as a variation of the independent source doctrine. *Murray v. U.S.*, 487 U.S. 533, 108 S. Ct. 2529, 101 L.Ed.2d 472 (1988).

Good Faith Exception to the Exclusionary Rule

Apart from the exception to the fruit of the poisonous tree doctrine, the primary exception to the exclusionary rule itself is the *good faith exception*. This exception allows evidence obtained pursuant to a search warrant to be admitted at trial even if the warrant is later found not to be valid. As long as the officer conducting the search sought the warrant in good faith and conducted the search within the scope of the warrant, the evidence discovered may be used. *U.S. v. Leon*, 468 U.S. 897, 104 S. Ct. 3405, 82 L.Ed.2d 677 (1984). The good faith exception also applies to the execution of arrest warrants. If a warrant is mistakenly issued and an officer acts on it in good faith, evidence obtained in a search incident to the arrest is admissible. *Arizona v. Evans*, 514 U.S. 1, 115 S. Ct. 1185, 131 L.Ed.2d 34 (1995).

Arrest Procedures

The Fourth Amendment governs the procedures that the government may and may not use when investigating crime and gathering evidence. As discussed previously, these "prearrest" procedures are necessary to protect the property of citizens from unwarranted government intrusion and seizure, and they protect the privacy interests of citizens in their homes from unjustified entry by the government. Just as the search and seizure provisions of the Fourth Amendment apply to "houses, papers, and effects," they apply to "persons" as well. When a person is arrested by the police, the "seizure" of that person by the government has occurred. Much of the previous discussion relating to searches and seizure of property applies to people as well, but the search and seizure of persons raises particular concerns about depriving a person of his or her freedom in a country that values freedom to the extent that America does. The constitution and rules that stem from it therefore also govern procedures used when an investigation results in the arrest of a suspect.

Arrests

At its simplest, the seizure of a person is an *arrest*. A person may be "detained," "held," "stopped," or "in custody" for a limited amount of time, for particular purposes, or in particular circumstances, but a formal arrest occurs when any of these is done for the purpose of charging them with a crime. Four elements must be present in order for an arrest that constitutes a seizure under the Fourth Amendment to have occurred. The first of these is an intention by an agent of the government to take someone into custody. Whether this intent is announced to the suspect is not determinative, but the officer must have decided to hold the person until he or she can be submitted to the processes of law. The second element is the authority to make the arrest by the governmental agent. The authority may exist in the duties entrusted to the officer or found in a warrant. The seizure of a person without authority to do so is not an arrest, but kidnapping. The third element is the restraint of a person by the government actor. This may occur through the use of physical force (e.g., holding one's arm or using handcuffs) or through a show of authority to which the suspect submits. Either physical force or submission by the suspect to a show of authority is necessary for there to be an arrest. *California v. Hodari D.*, 499 U.S. 621, 111 S. Ct. 1547, 113 L.Ed.2d 690 (1990). Finally, the person being arrested must understand that he or she is under arrest. This may occur by the officer telling the suspect he or she is under arrest, or it may occur by the circumstances that would cause a person to understand that he or she is being arrested, such as being told to lay on the ground or being placed in handcuffs. When these elements are present, a formal arrest has occurred, depriving a person of his or her freedom.

Arrest Warrants

An arrest warrant is an order from a court authorizing law enforcement to seize a person. As with search warrants, the Fourth Amendment does not prevent the arrest of a person suspected of crime, only an unreasonable arrest. When law enforcement seeks an arrest warrant from a court before an arrest is made, it is leaving the decision about reasonableness in the hands of a judge, and this decision must be based on a showing of probable cause. The showing of probable cause needed for an arrest warrant is similar to, but not the same as, the showing needed for a search warrant. Probable cause for an arrest warrant requires a more specific showing based on the facts and circumstances that the suspect is involved in criminal activity or has committed a crime. The facts supporting an arrest may therefore be different than the facts supporting a search warrant and will relate specifically to the actions of the person to be arrested and specify the crime that the person is accused of having committed, usually by citing the statute alleged to have been violated. In addition, the warrant must specifically name the person to be arrested, including any aliases the person may have used. If necessary to identify the correct person properly (particularly where the suspect's name is a common one), identifying characteristics may be included in the warrant (e.g., height, weight, scars, tattoos).

Generally, an arrest warrant is the favored mechanism for accomplishing an arrest. *Aguilar v. Texas*, 378 U.S. 108, 84 S. Ct. 1509, 12 L.Ed.2d 723 (1964). Particularly given the loss of freedom that arrests entail, a review of the decision to arrest and the basis for it is best left to the decision making of a judge who is detached from the crime-fighting circumstances in which the need for an arrest arises. When it is used, it provides the officer executing it with qualified immunity from liability. *Malley v. Briggs*, 475 U.S. 335, 106 S. Ct. 1092, 89 L.Ed.2d 271 (1986). This means that as long as the officer had a reasonable basis for believing that probable cause existed when obtaining the arrest warrant, he or she cannot be held civilly liable for the arrest, even if the arrest warrant is later found to be defective or the prosecution of defendant later fails.

An arrest warrant is also required when the arrest involves entry by law enforcement into the home of a suspect in order to find and apprehend the suspect, unless "exigent circumstances" exist. *Payton v. New York*, 445 U.S. 573, 100 S. Ct. 1371, 63 L.Ed.2d 639 (1980). Furthermore, even if an arrest warrant has been obtained, police may not enter the home of a third person to arrest the person identified in the warrant unless they first obtain a search warrant and unless there are exigent circumstances. *Steagald v. U.S.*, 451 U.S. 204, 101 S. Ct. 1642, 68 L.Ed.2d 38 (1981). This exigent circumstances exception to the warrant requirement will generally apply only when a serious crime has been committed. *Welsh v. Wisconsin*, 466 U.S. 740, 104 S. Ct. 2091, 80 L.Ed.2d 732 (1984). Exigent circumstances have been found to exist when one of the following is present: police are in hot pursuit of a fleeing felon; destruction of evidence is imminent; the suspect may escape; or there is a risk of danger to the police or others. *Minnesota v. Olson*, 495 U.S. 91, 110 S. Ct. 1684, 109 L.Ed.2d 85 (1990).

Warrantless Arrests

Despite the preference in the law for the use of arrest warrants, there are circumstances in which an arrest warrant cannot or need not first be obtained; however, an arrest, with or without a warrant, will always require the existence of probable cause. Whether an arrest warrant is required will depend on the seriousness of the crime and the involvement of the officer making the arrest in the circumstances giving rise to the allegations of crime. In general, the less serious the alleged crime, the more likely a warrant is to be necessary. Thus, the arrest of a person accused of committing a misdemeanor will usually require an arrest warrant, unless the arresting officer actually observed the misdemeanor being committed. Observation may occur through any of the officer's senses. Thus, smelling marijuana smoke emanating from a car would provide the basis for a warrantless arrest, as would hearing a woman inside a home scream, "Stop, you are hurting me!" When the misdemeanor occurs in the officer's presence, the arrest must be effectuated as soon as it is observed, not at some later time. In addition to the officer's observation of a misdemeanor, however, some state laws allow officers to arrest without a warrant for commission of certain misdemeanors, even if not committed in the officer's presence, as long as probable cause exists.

When a felony is committed, police officers in most states have more leeway in performing a warrantless arrest. As long as an officer has probable cause to believe that a crime has been committed, an arrest made without a warrant will be constitutional. It is also not necessary that the criminal act, chargeable as a felony, be directly observed by the officer. *U.S. v. Watson*, 423 U.S. 411, 96 S. Ct. 820, 46 L.Ed.2d 598 (1976).

Use of Force During Arrest

The amount of force that a police officer may use depends on the circumstances of the arrest in which it is deemed necessary. These circumstances vary according to the seriousness of the crime for which the suspect is being arrested, whether the suspect is armed, and whether the suspect resists arrest.

How Much Force?

The general rule is that officers may use as much force as is reasonably necessary to accomplish the arrest. If a suspect is wanted for commission of a misdemeanor, however, it is unreasonable for an officer to use deadly force for the suspect's apprehension unless the officer's life is at risk. Moreover, deadly force is never reasonable when a suspect poses no threat to the arresting officer or to others. *Tennessee v. Garner*, 471 U.S. 1, 105 S. Ct. 1694, 85 L.Ed.2d 1 (1985). The Garner case also teaches that it is a violation of a suspect's Fourth Amendment rights to shoot him or her when fleeing.

Resisting Arrest

When an arrest is performed, the suspect does not always "come quietly." It is to be expected that a suspect does not wish to lose his or her freedom; however, when a suspect actively uses force to prevent an officer from taking him or her into custody, the crime of resisting arrest may occur. In some jurisdictions, before a person may be convicted of resisting arrest, the arrest itself must be legal. In others, however, regardless of the legality of the arrest, a person may not resist an officer in the reasonable performance of his or her duties. Normally, this crime requires the direct use of force by the suspect against the arresting officer; running away or hiding are generally insufficient to constitute resisting arrest. Also, words are insufficient to constitute resistance by the suspect, even when shouted, unless they are of a threatening nature to the officer or others.

Excessive Force

In recent years, and as a result of the use of video cameras by the media and private citizens, allegations of excessive force used by the police when apprehending suspects have become more prominent. This is not to say that it has become more prevalent, however. For as long as police officers have been apprehending suspects, some degree of force has typically been necessary to restrain them. Excessive force may be defined as the use by law enforcement of more force than is reasonably necessary to take a suspect into custody (Blum & Ryan, 2008).

Postarrest Procedures

A considerable amount of police work usually precedes the arrest of an individual. The investigation of a case often does not stop with an arrest. When a suspect has been arrested, the police investigation has led to probable cause that the suspect has had some degree of involvement in a crime. After arrest, the constitutional rights of suspects are implicated by police procedures used to gather evidence relating to the alleged crime. The most important of these involve independent identification of the suspect and gathering information from the suspect by interrogation.

Pretrial Identification

The purpose of pretrial identification procedures is just that—to identify who is a proper defendant to be charged and tried for a crime. Most common are the use of "lineups" as a mechanism for identification of suspects by a witness (including a victim). Pretrial identification is a central tool for the government in prosecution of crime, and given its prevalence and consequences for suspects, the constitutional protections against self-incrimination and requiring due process, confrontation of witnesses, and representation by counsel cannot be violated in its implementation.

Lineups

A lineup is an identification method in which the police ask a witness to view several individuals along with the suspect at the same time and pick out the perpetrator of the crime under investigation. Generally, lineups are used soon after a suspect has been arrested in order to "confirm," through the use of witnesses, that the proper perpetrator of the crime has been apprehended. The suspect can therefore be compelled to stand in the lineup without violating the suspect's Fifth Amendment privilege against self-incrimination. See *Schmerber v. California*, 384 U.S. 757, 86 S. Ct. 1826, 16 L.Ed.2d 908 (1966); *U.S. v. Wade*, 388 U.S. 218, 87 S. Ct. 1926, 18 L.Ed.2d 1149 (1967).

The U.S. Supreme Court has noted that a lineup used for identification is a crucial stage of a criminal proceeding, and a defendant therefore has a right to counsel before being compelled to participate in a lineup. *U.S. v. Wade*, 388 U.S. 218, 87 S. Ct. 1926, 18 L.Ed.2d 1149 (1967); *Gilbert v. California*, 388 U.S. 263, 87 S. Ct 1951, 18 L.Ed.2d 1178 (1967). The Wade-Gilbert rule requires assistance of counsel in pretrial identification procedures because of the danger of conviction as a result of potential abuse, suggestion to the witness by the police, and resulting unreliability of the identification procedures.

In addition to lineups, other methods of pretrial identification are common. Related to lineups are *showups*, in which the suspect himself is shown alone to a witness to identify. This method is particularly susceptible to mistaken identification because the witness may conclude that the person shown would not be in custody and be shown unless he or she was the perpetrator. Nonetheless, showups may be used in limited circumstances, such as where there is a danger that evidence or testimony may be lost without an immediate identification. *Stovall v. Denno*, 388 U.S. 293, 87 S. Ct. 1967, 18 L.Ed.2d 1199 (1967).

As a substitute for identification of live persons either in a lineup or by showup, photographs are sometimes used where the witness is asked to identify a picture of the suspect out of several photographs of individuals presented; however, because there is no "confrontation" of the suspect when identification by photographs is used, the suspect has no right to the presence of counsel when this method is used. *U.S. v. Ash*, 413 U.S. 300, 93 S. Ct. 2568, 37 L.Ed.2d 619 (1973) (**Sidebar 12.1**).

Sidebar 12.1 *Eyewitness Identification and Wrongful Conviction*

It seems obvious that before a person may be charged with a crime, he or she must be identified as the perpetrator of that crime. Without some evidence connecting a suspect to a crime, there can be no prosecution. Often, the first (and sometimes only) source of evidence is the testimony of an eyewitness—someone who can identify the suspect as having committed the crime.

Testimony from an eyewitness may seem like ideal evidence, whether for identifying the suspect or to recount the criminal activities at trial; however, humans have limitations in their ability to perceive, sometimes do not understand what they are observing, and sometimes just make mistakes. This can create significant problems and miscarriages of justice because a defendant may be wrongfully convicted on the basis of eyewitness testimony that may not be accurate. According to the Innocence Project at the Benjamin Cardozo School of Law at Yeshiva University (www.innocenceproject.org), the incorrect identification of suspects by eyewitnesses has been the single leading source of wrongful convictions in the United States. The Innocence Project has found that "of the first 150 people who were exonerated on the basis of DNA found at the crime scene, approximately 70% had been identified incorrectly by seemingly honest, but mistaken eyewitnesses." Although it is not known in how many cases eyewitness identification is accurate, the problem of wrongful conviction and its relationship to improper identification of suspects is nonetheless a significant one.

The process of suspect identification and the use of lineups are central and problematic sources of misidentification. A lineup usually begins with instructions given to the eyewitness by a police officer working on the case. Although police procedures are often designed to make lineups fair and unbiased, the way in which the lineup is conducted can affect the accuracy of identification by the eyewitness. For example, an eyewitness may feel pressured to pick someone out of a lineup if he or she is not told that the suspect may not be in the lineup, and including only nonsuspects who look very similar to the suspect can reduce the accuracy of identification.

Two primary methods of conducting lineups have been used: simultaneous presentation and sequential presentation. In a simultaneous presentation, a number of individuals (often six to eight) are presented all at once to the eyewitness, who is asked to identify the suspect. Simultaneous lineups have been found to have a high rate of eyewitness misidentification because the eyewitness tends to believe the purpose is to pick someone from the lineup who most closely matches the person they saw, rather than choosing someone only if he or she saw the suspect at the crime scene.

An alternative method of lineup presentation in use today is the sequential lineup. A sequential lineup is usually presented as a photo lineup. The eyewitness is shown one photo at a time and asked to decide whether the person in the photo is the suspect he or she saw at the scene. If the eyewitness says "no," additional photos are presented; if the eyewitness says "yes," the lineup ends and no additional photos are shown. This process is intended to prevent the eyewitness from choosing an individual who looks most like the suspect by comparing his or her memory of the suspect to all others presented, rather than making an independent decision on each photo.

It is not known how often eyewitnesses make mistakes in identification because it is not currently possible to conduct DNA testing on every person convicted of crime, nor is DNA evidence available from most crime scenes. We may never know how many innocent people are wrongly convicted and sentenced to jail each year; however, with better practices to elicit accurate information and understanding regarding the potential inaccuracy of eyewitness testimony, the justice system can better protect the innocent and wrongfully accused, while also fulfilling it purpose of achieving justice by identifying and prosecuting only those who have committed crimes.

Interrogations

Although the questioning of suspects is central to the investigatory process of the police, the manner in which interrogations occur often raises questions about whether the information obtained from a suspect may later be used in court. Because confessions or incriminatory statements obtained from suspects are important and sometimes crucial in obtaining a conviction, the danger of the police obtaining such statements through the use of improper methods is frequently present. This is particularly true because the place of questioning most often is an interrogation room in the police station, away from public view.

No case has had more impact on the manner in which police interrogation is used than *Miranda v. Arizona*, 384 U.S. 436, 86 S. Ct. 1602, 16 L.Ed.2d 694 (1966). As is well known from the now-famous "Miranda warnings," the U.S. Supreme Court in Miranda held that the dangers of coercive interrogations and the confessions that follow must be guarded against, at a minimum, by advising suspects of their constitutional rights before questioning may occur. In particular, the *Miranda* case focused on the potential denial of the privilege against self-incrimination that custodial interrogations may create and the need for procedures to protect against such intrusions. The central problem, the Court noted, was a historical one:

> The maxim "Nemo tenetur seipsum accusare," ["No one is bound to accuse himself"] had its origin in a protest against the inquisitorial and manifestly unjust methods of interrogating accused persons, which (have) long obtained in the continental system, and, until the expulsion of the Stuarts from the British throne in 1688, and the erection of additional barriers for the protection of the people against the exercise of arbitrary power, (were) not uncommon even in England. While the admissions or confessions of the prisoner, when voluntarily and freely made, have always ranked high in the scale of incriminating evidence, if an accused person be asked to explain his apparent connection with a crime under investigation, the ease with which the questions put to him may assume an inquisitorial character, the temptation to press the witness unduly, to browbeat him if he be timid or reluctant, to push him into a corner, and to entrap him into fatal contradictions, which is so painfully evident in many of the earlier state trials, notably in those of Sir Nicholas Throckmorton, and Udal, the Puritan minister, made the system so odious as to give rise to a demand for its total abolition. The change in the English criminal procedure in that particular seems to be founded upon no statute and no judicial opinion, but upon a general and silent acquiescence of the courts in a popular demand. But, however adopted, it has become firmly embedded in English, as well as in American jurisprudence. So deeply did the iniquities of the ancient system impress themselves upon the minds of the American colonists that the States, with one accord, made a denial of the right to question an accused person a part of their fundamental law, so that a maxim, which in England was a mere rule of evidence, became clothed in this country with the impregnability of a constitutional enactment. Miranda, 384 U.S. at 442, 86 S. Ct. at 1611, 16 L.Ed.2d at 703 (quoting *Brown v. Walker*, 161 U.S. 591, 596-597, 16 S. Ct. 644, 646, 40 L.Ed. 819 (1896)).

The Court found that the dangers of forced incrimination that our Constitution's Framers were concerned with continued to be present, and that unless procedural safeguards were put into place, the Fifth Amendment right to not incriminate oneself would have no meaning:

> [T]he constitutional foundation underlying the privilege is the respect a government—state or federal—must accord to the dignity and integrity of its citizens. To maintain a "fair state–individual balance," to require the government "to shoulder the entire load," 8 Wigmore, Evidence 317 (McNaughton rev. 1961), to respect the inviolability of the human personality, our accusatory system of criminal justice demands that the government seeking to punish an individual produce the evidence against him by its own independent labors, rather than by the cruel, simple expedient of compelling it from his own mouth. In sum, the privilege is fulfilled only when the person is guaranteed the right "to remain silent unless he chooses to speak in the unfettered exercise of his own will." Miranda, 384 U.S. at 460, 86 S. Ct. at 1620, 16 L.Ed.2d at 712.

The Court therefore imposed seven procedural requirements that must be met when a person in police custody is interrogated:

> He must be warned prior to any questioning that [1] he has the right to remain silent, [2] that anything he says can be used against him in a court of law, [3] that he has the right to the presence of an attorney, and [4] that if he cannot afford an attorney one will be appointed for him prior to any questioning if he so desires. [5] Opportunity to exercise these rights must be afforded to him throughout the interrogation. [6] After such warnings have been given, and such opportunity afforded him, the individual may knowingly and intelligently waive these rights and agree to answer questions or make a statement. [7] But unless and until such warnings and waiver are demonstrated by the prosecution at trial, no evidence obtained as a result of interrogation can be used against him. Miranda, 384 U.S. at 479, 86 S. Ct. at 1630, 16 L.Ed.2d at 722 (numeration added).

These procedural rules constitute the Miranda "warnings" ubiquitously used by police today (Kamisar, 2007).

Voluntariness and Waiver

Despite the seeming clarity of the Court's pronouncement of the Fifth Amendment's requirements in Miranda, questions about its application continue to arise. Before Miranda, the test for whether an incriminating statement by a suspect could be obtained by police and used by the prosecution was whether it was offered voluntarily. This meant that, if the circumstances in which the statement was obtained indicated the suspect was not under undue pressure and gave the statement freely, it would later be admissible in court. Although this is no longer the test for compliance with the Fifth Amendment (because the Miranda procedure must be used), the voluntariness of statements continues to be an issue in criminal cases when the prosecution claims that, after a suspect was read the Miranda rights, he or she waived those warnings and agreed to questioning. In order for a suspect to waive his or her Miranda rights, the suspect must do so knowingly and voluntarily.

Whether one's Miranda rights are waived and a confession is voluntarily obtained were considered in *Missouri v. Seibert*, 542 U.S. 600, 124 S. Ct. 2601, 159 L.Ed.2d 643 (2004). The Seibert case involved a police procedure used to obtain confessions in which a suspect in custody is interrogated before Miranda warnings are given and a confession is obtained. Although this confession is not admissible, the police interrogator then reads the suspect his or her Miranda rights and proceeds to reinterrogate the suspect, who is likely to agree to continue talking, by confirming what the suspect already stated. The Court's analysis of this procedure is found in **Case Decision 12.2**.

It is clear from the *Seibert* opinion that *Miranda* maintains its vitality and continues to provide the standard for proper constitutional interrogation procedures. The Court in *Seibert* was disturbed by the two-stage interrogation procedure as an attempt to "get around" the requirements of *Miranda*. In addition, however, *Seibert* is important for

Case Decision 12.2   *Missouri v. Seibert*, 542 U.S. 600, 124 S. Ct. 2601, 159 L.Ed.2d 643 (2004)

Decision of the Court by Justice Souter:

This case tests a police protocol for custodial interrogation that calls for giving no warnings of the rights to silence and counsel until interrogation has produced a confession. Although such a statement is generally inadmissible, since taken in violation of *Miranda v. Arizona*, 384 U.S. 436, 86 S. Ct. 1602, 16 L.Ed.2d 694 (1966), the interrogating officer follows it with *Miranda* warnings and then leads the suspect to cover the same ground a second time. The question here is the admissibility of the repeated statement. Because this midstream recitation of warnings after interrogation and unwarned confession could not effectively comply with *Miranda's* constitutional requirement, we hold that a statement repeated after a warning in such circumstances is inadmissible.

I

Respondent Patrice Seibert's 12-year-old son Jonathan had cerebral palsy, and when he died in his sleep she feared charges of neglect because of bedsores on his body. In her presence, two of her teenage sons and two of their friends devised a plan to conceal the facts surrounding Jonathan's death by incinerating his body in the course of burning the family's mobile home, in which they planned to leave Donald Rector, a mentally ill teenager living with the family, to avoid any appearance that Jonathan had been unattended. Seibert's son Darian and a friend set the fire, and Donald died.

Five days later, the police awakened Seibert at 3 a.m. at a hospital where Darian was being treated for burns. In arresting her, Officer Kevin Clinton followed instructions from Rolla, Missouri, Officer Richard Hanrahan that he refrain from giving *Miranda* warnings. After Seibert had been taken to the police station and left alone in an interview room for 15 to 20 minutes, Officer Hanrahan questioned her without *Miranda* warnings for 30 to 40 minutes, squeezing her arm and repeating "Donald was also to die in his sleep." After Seibert finally admitted she knew Donald was meant to die in the fire, she was given a 20-minute coffee and cigarette break. Officer Hanrahan then turned on a tape recorder, gave Seibert the *Miranda* warnings, and obtained a signed waiver of rights from her. He resumed the questioning with "Ok, 'Trice, we've been talking for a little while about what happened on Wednesday the twelfth, haven't we?" and confronted her with her prewarning statements:

> Hanrahan: "Now, in discussion you told us, you told us that there was a[n] understanding about Donald."
> Seibert: "Yes."
> Hanrahan: "Did that take place earlier that morning?"
> Seibert: "Yes."
> Hanrahan: "And what was the understanding about Donald?"
> Seibert: "If they could get him out of the trailer, to take him out of the trailer."
> Hanrahan: "And if they couldn't?"
> Seibert: "I, I never even thought about it. I just figured they would."
> Hanrahan: " 'Trice, didn't you tell me that he was supposed to die in his sleep?"
> Seibert: "If that would happen, 'cause he was on that new medicine, you know. . . ."
> Hanrahan: "The Prozac? And it makes him sleepy. So he was supposed to die in his sleep?"
> Seibert: "Yes."

After being charged with first-degree murder for her role in Donald's death, Seibert sought to exclude both her prewarning and postwarning statements. At the suppression hearing, Officer Hanrahan testified that he made a "conscious decision" to withhold *Miranda* warnings, thus resorting to an interrogation technique he had been taught: question first, then give the warnings, and then repeat the question "until I get the answer that she's already provided once." He acknowledged that Seibert's ultimate statement was "largely a repeat of information . . . obtained" prior to the warning.

The trial court suppressed the prewarning statement but admitted the responses given after the *Miranda* recitation. A jury convicted Seibert of second-degree murder. On appeal, the Missouri Court of Appeals affirmed. The Supreme Court of Missouri reversed, holding that "[i]n the circumstances here, where the interrogation was nearly continuous, . . . the second statement, clearly the product of the invalid first statement, should have been suppressed." The court reasoned that "Officer

(Continues)

(Continued)

Hanrahan's intentional omission of a *Miranda* warning was intended to deprive Seibert of the opportunity knowingly and intelligently to waive her *Miranda* rights." Since there were "no circumstances that would seem to dispel the effect of the *Miranda* violation," the court held that the postwarning confession was involuntary and therefore inadmissible. To allow the police to achieve an "end run" around *Miranda* the court explained, would encourage *Miranda* violations and diminish *Miranda's* role in protecting the privilege against self-incrimination. Three judges dissented, taking the view that even though the police intentionally withheld *Miranda* warnings before the initial statement, and believing that "Seibert's unwarned responses to Officer Hanrahan's questioning did not prevent her from waiving her rights and confessing." (opinion of Benton, J.).

We granted certiorari to resolve a split in the Courts of Appeals. We now affirm.

II

"In criminal trials, in the courts of the United States, wherever a question arises whether a confession is incompetent because not voluntary, the issue is controlled by that portion of the Fifth Amendment . . . commanding that no person 'shall be compelled in any criminal case to be a witness against himself.'" A parallel rule governing the admissibility of confessions in state courts emerged from the Due Process Clause of the Fourteenth Amendment, which governed state cases until we concluded that "[t]he Fourteenth Amendment secures against state invasion the same privilege that the Fifth Amendment guarantees against federal infringement—the right of a person to remain silent unless he chooses to speak in the unfettered exercise of his own will, and to suffer no penalty . . . for such silence."

In *Miranda* we explained that the "voluntariness doctrine in the state cases . . . encompasses all interrogation practices which are likely to exert such pressure upon an individual as to disable him from making a free and rational choice." We appreciated the difficulty of judicial enquiry *post hoc* into the circumstances of a police interrogation, and recognized that "the coercion inherent in custodial interrogation blurs the line between voluntary and involuntary statements, and thus heightens the risk" that the privilege against self-incrimination will not be observed. Hence our concern that the "traditional totality-of-the-circumstances" test posed an "unacceptably great" risk that involuntary custodial confessions would escape detection.

Accordingly, "to reduce the risk of a coerced confession and to implement the Self-Incrimination Clause," this Court in *Miranda* concluded that "the accused must be adequately and effectively apprised of his rights and the exercise of those rights must be fully honored." *Miranda* conditioned the admissibility at trial of any custodial confession on warning a suspect of his rights: failure to give the prescribed warnings and obtain a waiver of rights before custodial questioning generally requires exclusion of any statements obtained. Conversely, giving the warnings and getting a waiver has generally produced a virtual ticket of admissibility; maintaining that a statement is involuntary even though given after warnings and voluntary waiver of rights requires unusual stamina, and litigation over voluntariness tends to end with the finding of a valid waiver. To point out the obvious, this common consequence would not be common at all were it not that *Miranda* warnings are customarily given under circumstances allowing for a real choice between talking and remaining silent.

III

The technique of interrogating in successive, unwarned and warned phases raises a new challenge to *Miranda*. Although we have no statistics on the frequency of this practice, it is not confined to Rolla, Missouri. An officer of that police department testified that the strategy of withholding *Miranda* warnings until after interrogating and drawing out a confession was promoted not only by his own department, but by a national police training organization and other departments in which he had worked. Consistently with the officer's testimony, the Police Law Institute, for example, instructs that "officers may conduct a two-stage interrogation. . . . At any point during the pre-*Miranda* interrogation, usually after arrestees have confessed, officers may then read the *Miranda* warnings and ask for a waiver. If the arrestees waive their *Miranda* rights, officers will be able to repeat any *subsequent* incriminating statements later in court." Police Law Institute, Illinois Police Law Manual 83 (Jan. 2001–Dec. 2003) (hereinafter Police Law Manual) (emphasis in original). The upshot of all this advice is a question-first practice of some popularity, as one can see from the reported cases describing its use, sometimes in obedience to departmental policy.

IV

When a confession so obtained is offered and challenged, attention must be paid to the conflicting objects of *Miranda* and question-first. *Miranda* addressed "interrogation practices . . . likely . . . to disable [an individual] from making a free and rational choice" about speaking, and held that a suspect must be "adequately and effectively" advised of the choice the Constitution guarantees. The object of question-first is to render *Miranda* warnings ineffective by waiting for a particularly opportune time to give them, after the suspect has already confessed.

Just as "no talismanic incantation [is] required to satisfy [*Miranda's*] strictures," it would be absurd to think that mere recitation of the litany suffices to satisfy *Miranda* in every conceivable circumstance. "The inquiry is simply whether the warnings reasonably 'conve[y] to [a suspect] his rights as required by *Miranda*.'" The threshold issue when interrogators question first and warn later is thus whether it would be reasonable to find that in these circumstances the warnings could function "effectively" as *Miranda* requires. Could the warnings effectively advise the suspect that he had a real choice about giving an admissible statement at that juncture? Could they reasonably convey that he could choose to stop talking even if he had talked earlier? For unless the warnings could place a suspect who has just been interrogated in a position to make such an informed choice, there is no practical justification for accepting the formal warnings as compliance with *Miranda* or for treating the second stage of interrogation as distinct from the first, unwarned and inadmissible segment.

There is no doubt about the answer that proponents of question-first give to this question about the effectiveness of warnings given only after successful interrogation, and we think their answer is correct. By any objective measure, applied to circumstances exemplified here, it is likely that if the interrogators employ the technique of withholding warnings until after interrogation succeeds in eliciting a confession, the warnings will be ineffective in preparing the suspect for successive interrogation, close in time and similar in content. After all, the reason that question-first is catching on is as obvious as its manifest purpose, which is to get a confession the suspect would not make if he understood his rights at the outset; the sensible underlying assumption is that with one confession in hand before the warnings, the interrogator can count on getting its duplicate, with trifling additional trouble. Upon hearing warnings only in the aftermath of interrogation and just after making a confession, a suspect would hardly think he had a genuine right to remain silent, let alone persist in so believing once the police began to lead him over the same ground again. A more likely reaction on a suspect's part would be perplexity about the reason for discussing rights at that point, bewilderment being an unpromising frame of mind for knowledgeable decision. What is worse, telling a suspect that "anything you say can and will be used against you," without expressly excepting the statement just given, could lead to an entirely reasonable inference that what he has just said will be used, with subsequent silence being of no avail. Thus, when *Miranda* warnings are inserted in the midst of coordinated and continuing interrogation, they are likely to mislead and "depriv[e] a defendant of knowledge essential to his ability to understand the nature of his rights and the consequences of abandoning them." By the same token, it would ordinarily be unrealistic to treat two spates of integrated and proximately conducted questioning as independent interrogations subject to independent evaluation simply because *Miranda* warnings formally punctuate them in the middle.

V

[T]he facts here, which by any objective measure[,] reveal a police strategy adapted to undermine the *Miranda* warnings. The unwarned interrogation was conducted in the station house, and the questioning was systematic, exhaustive, and managed with psychological skill. When the police were finished there was little, if anything, of incriminating potential left unsaid. The warned phase of questioning proceeded after a pause of only 15 to 20 minutes, in the same place as the unwarned segment. When the same officer who had conducted the first phase recited the *Miranda* warnings, he said nothing to counter the probable misimpression that the advice that anything Seibert said could be used against her also applied to the details of the inculpatory statement previously elicited. In particular, the police did not advise that her prior statement could not be used. Nothing was said or done to dispel the oddity of warning about legal rights to silence and counsel right after the police had led her through a systematic interrogation, and any uncertainty on her part about a right to stop talking about matters previously discussed would only have been aggravated by the way Officer Hanrahan set the scene by saying "we've been talking for a little while about what happened on Wednesday the twelfth, haven't we?" The impression that the further questioning was a mere continuation of the earlier questions and

(Continues)

(Continued)

responses was fostered by references back to the confession already given. It would have been reasonable to regard the two sessions as parts of a continuum, in which it would have been unnatural to refuse to repeat at the second stage what had been said before. These circumstances must be seen as challenging the comprehensibility and efficacy of the *Miranda* warnings to the point that a reasonable person in the suspect's shoes would not have understood them to convey a message that she retained a choice about continuing to talk.

VI

Strategists dedicated to draining the substance out of *Miranda* cannot accomplish by training instructions what Congress could not do by statute. Because the question-first tactic effectively threatens to thwart *Miranda* purpose of reducing the risk that a coerced confession would be admitted, and because the facts here do not reasonably support a conclusion that the warnings given could have served their purpose, Seibert's postwarning statements are inadmissible. The judgment of the Supreme Court of Missouri is affirmed.

Opinion by Justice Kennedy, concurring in the judgment:

The interrogation technique used in this case is designed to circumvent *Miranda*. It undermines the *Miranda* warning and obscures its meaning. The plurality opinion is correct to conclude that statements obtained through the use of this technique are inadmissible. Although I agree with much in the careful and convincing opinion for the plurality, my approach does differ in some respects, requiring this separate statement.

The *Miranda* rule has become an important and accepted element of the criminal justice system. At the same time, not every violation of the rule requires suppression of the evidence obtained. Evidence is admissible when the central concerns of *Miranda* are not likely to be implicated and when other objectives of the criminal justice system are best served by its introduction. Thus, we have held that statements obtained in violation of the rule can be used for impeachment, so that the truth-finding function of the trial is not distorted by the defense; that there is an exception to protect countervailing concerns of public safety; and that physical evidence obtained in reliance on statements taken in violation of the rule is admissible. These cases, in my view, are correct. They recognize that admission of evidence is proper when it would further important objectives without compromising *Miranda* central concerns. Under these precedents, the scope of the *Miranda* suppression remedy depends on a consideration of those legitimate interests and on whether admission of the evidence under the circumstances would frustrate *Miranda* central concerns and objectives.

An officer may not realize that a suspect is in custody and warnings are required. The officer may not plan to question the suspect or may be waiting for a more appropriate time. Skilled investigators often interview suspects multiple times, and good police work may involve referring to prior statements to test their veracity or to refresh recollection. In light of these realities it would be extravagant to treat the presence of one statement that cannot be admitted under *Miranda* as sufficient reason to prohibit subsequent statements preceded by a proper warning. That approach would serve "neither the general goal of deterring improper police conduct nor the Fifth Amendment goal of assuring trustworthy evidence would be served by suppression of the . . . testimony."

This case presents different considerations. The police used a two-step questioning technique based on a deliberate violation of *Miranda*. The *Miranda* warning was withheld to obscure both the practical and legal significance of the admonition when finally given. [T]he two-step technique permits the accused to conclude that the right not to respond did not exist when the earlier incriminating statements were made. The strategy is based on the assumption that *Miranda* warnings will tend to mean less when recited midinterrogation, after inculpatory statements have already been obtained. This tactic relies on an intentional misrepresentation of the protection that *Miranda* offers and does not serve any legitimate objectives that might otherwise justify its use.

Further, the interrogating officer here relied on the defendant's prewarning statement to obtain the postwarning statement used against her at trial. The postwarning interview resembled a cross-examination. The officer confronted the defendant with her inadmissible prewarning statements and pushed her to acknowledge them. ("Trice, didn't you tell me that he was supposed to die in his sleep?"). This shows the temptations for abuse inherent in the two-step technique. Reference to the prewarning statement was an implicit suggestion that the mere repetition of the earlier statement was not independently incriminating. The implicit suggestion was false.

The technique used in this case distorts the meaning of *Miranda* and furthers no legitimate countervailing interest. The *Miranda* rule would be frustrated were we to allow police to undermine its meaning and effect. The technique simply creates too high a risk that postwarning statements will be obtained when a suspect was deprived of "knowledge essential to his ability to understand the nature of his rights and the consequences of abandoning them." When an interrogator uses this deliberate, two-step strategy, predicated upon violating *Miranda* during an extended interview, postwarning statements that are related to the substance of prewarning statements must be excluded absent specific, curative steps.

The plurality concludes that whenever a two-stage interview occurs, admissibility of the postwarning statement should depend on "whether [the] *Miranda* warnings delivered midstream could have been effective enough to accomplish their object" given the specific facts of the case. This test envisions an objective inquiry from the perspective of the suspect, and applies in the case of both intentional and unintentional two-stage interrogations. In my view, this test cuts too broadly. *Miranda's* clarity is one of its strengths, and a multifactor test that applies to every two-stage interrogation may serve to undermine that clarity. I would apply a narrower test applicable only in the infrequent case, such as we have here, in which the two-step interrogation technique was used in a calculated way to undermine the *Miranda* warning.

If the deliberate two-step strategy has been used, postwarning statements that are related to the substance of prewarning statements must be excluded unless curative measures are taken before the postwarning statement is made. Curative measures should be designed to ensure that a reasonable person in the suspect's situation would understand the import and effect of the *Miranda* warning and of the *Miranda* waiver. For example, a substantial break in time and circumstances between the prewarning statement and the *Miranda* warning may suffice in most circumstances, as it allows the accused to distinguish the two contexts and appreciate that the interrogation has taken a new turn. Alternatively, an additional warning that explains the likely inadmissibility of the prewarning custodial statement may be sufficient. No curative steps were taken in this case, however, so the postwarning statements are inadmissible and the conviction cannot stand.

For these reasons, I concur in the judgment of the Court.

Opinion by Justice O'Connor, with whom the Chief Justice, Justice Scalia, and Justice Thomas join, dissenting:

I would analyze the two-step interrogation procedure under the voluntariness standards central to the Fifth Amendment. [I]f Seibert's first statement is shown to have been involuntary, the court must examine whether the taint dissipated through the passing of time or a change in circumstances: "When a prior statement is actually coerced, the time that passes between confessions, the change in place of interrogations, and the change in identity of the interrogators all bear on whether that coercion has carried over into the second confession." In addition, Seibert's second statement should be suppressed if she showed that it was involuntary despite the *Miranda* warnings. "The relevant inquiry is whether, in fact, the second statement was also voluntarily made. As in any such inquiry, the finder of fact must examine the surrounding circumstances and the entire course of police conduct with respect to the suspect in evaluating the voluntariness of his statements." Although I would leave this analysis for the Missouri courts to conduct on remand, I note that Officer Hanrahan referred to Seibert's unwarned statement during the second part of the interrogation when she made a statement at odds with her unwarned confession. ("'Trice, didn't you tell me that he was supposed to die in his sleep?"). Such a tactic may bear on the voluntariness inquiry.

I respectfully dissent.

its examination of whether an interrogation procedure such as the two-stage method in that case precludes the voluntariness of a statement made by a suspect and whether a waiver of *Miranda* rights can be knowingly made under such a procedure. Thus, waiver and voluntariness are closely related because voluntary statements are those given after a waiver of *Miranda* rights; conversely, where a court finds a waiver to be knowingly given, statements after the waiver are necessarily considered to be voluntary. The two-stage procedure in *Seibert* raised the question of whether the suspect, Seibert, under-

stood that she was waiving her Fifth Amendment right to not incriminate herself by speaking with Officer Hanrahan after he read her the *Miranda* warnings. As the Court pointed out, the procedure was one that was designed to get a suspect to confess, something she would not be likely to do if the *Miranda* warnings were effective. It was on this basis that the Court found the two-stage procedure to be unconstitutional.

Because of the danger of coerced statements from suspects, the right to counsel required by *Miranda* is particularly important. Under *Miranda*, a suspect has the right to an attorney both before and during any questioning by the police. As the Court in *Miranda* explained,

> Thus, the need for counsel to protect the Fifth Amendment privilege comprehends not merely a right to consult with counsel prior to questioning, but also to have counsel present during any questioning if the defendant so desires.
>
> The presence of counsel at the interrogation may serve several significant subsidiary functions, as well. If the accused decides to talk to his interrogators, the assistance of counsel can mitigate the dangers of untrustworthiness. With a lawyer present, the likelihood that the police will practice coercion is reduced, and, if coercion is nevertheless exercised, the lawyer can testify to it in court. The presence of a lawyer can also help to guarantee that the accused gives a fully accurate statement to the police, and that the statement is rightly reported by the prosecution at trial.
>
> An individual need not make a pre-interrogation request for a lawyer. While such request affirmatively secures his right to have one, his failure to ask for a lawyer does not constitute a waiver. No effective waiver of the right to counsel during interrogation can be recognized unless specifically made after the warnings we here delineate have been given. The accused who does not know his rights and therefore does not make a request may be the person who most needs counsel. *Miranda v. Arizona*, 384 U.S. 436, at 471–472.

Punishment and Sentencing Procedures

Criminal procedures also relate to the decisions that a court must make about what to do with those who violate the law. Thus, the sentencing phase of a criminal case is often nearly as important as the determination of guilt. Without punishment, criminal law is without meaning or effectiveness. Thus, the task of determining the proper punishment in a criminal case falls to the trial judge. The procedures used to accomplish this vary according to the geographic jurisdiction, the crime committed, the characteristics of the defendant, and the harm caused to a victim.

Goals of Punishment

Sometimes referred to as theories, rationales, or even philosophies of punishment, there are four dominant perspectives on what is to be achieved by punishing offenders. These goals, as well as variations and combinations of them, are used by lawmakers as they define crimes and how they are to be punished and are used by judges in deciding the appropriate sentence in a given case.

Retribution

Retribution refers to the view that offenders should be punished because they deserve it, given their behavior. This "just deserts" approach connects the severity of the offense with the severity of the punishment, forcing the offender to "pay" for his or her wrongdoing. Thus, the idea that an offender must "pay his debt to society" is grounded in a retributive approach. Retribution also encompasses the idea of revenge; one who violates society's rules must suffer society's vengeance. Rather than just making the offender pay, revenge is "payback" from society to the offender for the wrongful act. To a considerable extent, retribution guides sentencing decisions today.

Deterrence

Arguably, all punishments seek to deter crime, but if the goal is to prevent crime from occurring, the type, length, or severity of a sentence may vary from a retributive one. Deterrence focuses on the mental state or psychology of the offender. Specifically, it seeks to have a crime prevention effect by causing the offender or others to think about whether committing the crime will be worth the punishment if they are caught. There are two forms of deterrence, general and specific.

General deterrence refers to the goal of keeping other members of society from engaging in the behavior of the offender being punished. By seeing how the wrongdoer has been punished, others will want to avoid the same punishment by not committing the offender's crime. The purpose of the punishment therefore has little to do with the individual offender; rather, the focus is on others who may be inclined to act as the offender did.

Specific deterrence seeks to prevent the offender being punished from reoffending. It involves the view that the offender must be "taught a lesson." Thus, the punishment must be sufficiently severe that the offender would choose not to commit the offense again because the effect of suffering the punishment again (or a more severe punishment for reoffending) would be too great.

Incapacitation

Incarceration is the most common form of incapacitation, which has as its goal the removal of a wrongdoer from society. A person who is locked up will be unable to further offend against society, at least for the period the person is incarcerated. By not giving an offender the opportunity to commit another crime and by knowing where the offender is at all times, society can be assured of its safety. As noted previously here, deterrence represents psychological prevention of wrongdoing; incapacitation is physical prevention.

Rehabilitation

Rehabilitation adopts the view that an offender can be kept from reoffending if the reason for committing the crime is addressed. By examining why the offender commits crime, whether for psychological or social reasons, a plan can be developed to help the offender not engage in the prohibited behavior. Thus, a rehabilitative approach to punishment assumes that the causes of the offending can be identified and that the problems that caused the offender to commit the crime can be "fixed."

Types of Punishment

The types of punishment imposed by a court were anticipated in the due process clause of the Fifth and Fourteenth Amendments to the Constitution: "No person shall be . . . deprived of life, liberty, or property without due process of law." All punishments may be characterized as depriving a person of life, liberty, or property, and these three categories encompass the varying levels of severity that a criminal sentence may impose.

Capital Punishment

A death sentence is viewed by most as the severest of punishments. It continues to be a source of controversy, and lawmakers, religious groups, special interest organizations, and concerned citizens continue to debate its wisdom. Thirty-six states currently allow the death penalty for first-degree murder, and the federal government allows it for air piracy resulting in death. Except for a short period in the 1970s, the U.S. Supreme Court has repeatedly upheld the constitutionality of the death penalty as not violating the Eighth Amendment; however, in *Atkins v. Virginia*, 536 U.S. 304 (2002), the Court held that sentencing the mentally handicapped to death constitutes cruel and unusual punishment. The Court has also held that juveniles under the age of 18 years when their crime was committed may not be sentenced to death. *Roper v. Simmons*, 543 U.S. 551 (2005).

Incarceration

As odd as it may sound, the incarceration of offenders in jails and prison is a modern development that represents advances in society's view of punishment. For much of human civilized history, wrongdoers were put to death for wide range of offenses or were made to suffer physically or were banished from the community (see Sidebar 1.1). Today, instead of these forms of punishment, modern America has adopted the housing of criminals in a single location as the best approach to controlling the problem of serious crime.

Prison populations continue to increase as the population of the country increases and the decreasing tolerance of citizens, lawmakers, and judges for repeat offenders has led to a greater use of incarceration. It is clear that prisons are not pleasant places and that, rather than helping to reform offenders, they tend to produce ever more hardened criminals. The cost to society, both financial and sociological, of locking up large numbers of wrongdoers is ever increasing. Nonetheless, incarceration remains a central and necessary punishment for those who commit serious offenses in order to protect society.

Probation

Probation represents an alternative to incarceration that is frequently used by judges. It involves the release of an offender from custody with conditions such as meeting regularly with a probation officer, not being arrested for an additional crime, or not associating with certain individuals. If any condition is not met, the offender may be incarcerated.

Fines

Monetary fines involve the payment of money to the court and are frequently used for misdemeanor offenses or violations, but are also sometimes levied against white-collar criminals. For more serious offenses, they may be used in combination with probation or incarceration. Most state criminal statutes specify the maximum fines for various crimes, given judges' discretion to impose lesser fines in appropriate cases.

Community Service

Community service provides a mechanism for allowing the offender to "make amends" with society by performing some useful function, such as speaking in schools or to community groups, cleaning up graffiti, or participating in highway beautification. It is intended as a practical means of restorative justice that benefits both the offender and society. When used, it is often in conjunction with fines or probation. Although community service is theoretically beneficial, it typically requires some form of supervision of the offender while he or she is performing the service.

The Sentencing Process

How does a judge decide what sentence to impose? State statutes and guidelines usually offer a range of sentencing options that may be used for various crimes. The federal government and many states also require the preparation of presentencing reports that provide the judge with information about the educational, family, and criminal background of the offender, any aggravating or mitigating circumstances in the case, psychological evaluations, and victim impact statements. The judge also relies on his or her own experience with similar offenders committing the same offense in deciding the type and length of a sentence.

Several types of sentencing and alternatives for courts exist. Perhaps of most importance is the distinction between determinate and indeterminate sentences. Indeterminate sentencing gives judges the greatest latitude in sentencing an offender to incarceration for as much or as little time as the judge deems appropriate, up to a maximum. This approach has declined in use in this country because of the variation in sentences for the same offense it can produce. Public demand for harsher punishments has also caused legislatures to adopt other approaches to imposing sentences, such as determinate sentencing. This form of sentencing requires judges to impose a presumptive sentence within a specified range. It removes considerable discretion from a judge and minimizes the extent to which a judge may take into account individual factors relevant to a given offender.

Some states have also moved toward mandatory sentences for a wider range of crimes. These sentences specify that a minimum sentence of incarceration must be imposed on an offender who commits a certain crime. Along with the increasing use of such sentences, some states have also adopted "three-strikes" or habitual offender laws that increase the sentence that must be imposed on those who are repeat offenders.

Key Terms

Search	Lineups
Seizure	Interrogation
Warrant	Retribution
Probable Cause	Deterrence
Knock and Announce	Incapacitation
Plain View Doctrine	Rehabilitation
Exclusionary Rule	Determinate Sentencing
Arrest	Mandatory Sentencing
Use of Force	Habitual Offender Laws

Discussion Questions

1. What are the constitutional requirements for a lawful search or seizure by the government? Where are they found?
2. What are the exceptions to the requirement that a search warrant be obtained? What is the justification for each?
3. What is the exclusionary rule? What is its purpose? Are there other ways to accomplish the same goals?
4. How is "reasonable suspicion" distinguished from "probable cause?" When is each required? What purposes do they fulfill?
5. What are the four elements of an arrest?
6. What are Miranda rights? Why are they necessary?
7. How much force may be used by a police officer in order to arrest a person?
8. What limitations are placed on a government agent when conducting an interrogation?
9. Why is the due process clause significant to criminal law and procedure?
10. Why is the right to counsel important for a defendant in a criminal case?
11. What are four theories of punishment?
12. What factors do judges take into account when imposing a criminal sentence?

Cases

Aguilar v. Texas, 378 U.S. 108, 84 S. Ct. 1509, 12 L.Ed.2d 723 (1964).

Arizona v. Evans, 514 U.S. 1, 115 S. Ct. 1185, 131 L.Ed.2d 34 (1995).

Atkins v. Virginia, 536 U.S. 304 (2002).

Brown v. Walker, 161 U.S. 591, 16 S. Ct. 644, 40 L.Ed. 819 (1896).

Bumper v. North Carolina, 391 U.S. 543, 88 S. Ct. 1788, 20 L.Ed.2d 797 (1968).

California v. Hodari D., 499 U.S. 621, 111 S. Ct. 1547, 113 L.Ed.2d 690 (1990).

Carroll v. U.S., 267 U.S. 132, 45 S. Ct. 280, 69 L.Ed. 543 (1925).

Florida v. Wells, 495 U.S. 1, 110 S. Ct. 1632, 109 L.Ed.2d 1 (1990).

Gilbert v. California, 388 U.S. 263, 87 S. Ct. 1951, 18 L.Ed.2d 1178 (1967).

Hester v. U.S., 265 U.S. 57, 44 S. Ct. 445, 68 L.Ed. 898 (1924).

Hudson v. Michigan, 547 U.S. 586, 126 S. Ct. 2159, 165 L.Ed.2d 56 (2006).

Illinois v. Gates, 462 U.S. 213, 103 S. Ct. 2317, 76 L.Ed.2d 527, (1983).

Malley v. Briggs, 475 U.S. 335, 106 S. Ct. 1092, 89 L.Ed.2d 271 (1986).

Mapp v. Ohio, 367 U.S. 643, 81 S. Ct. 1684, 6 L.Ed.2d 1081 (1961).

Minnesota v. Olson, 495 U.S. 91, 110 S. Ct. 1684, 109 L.Ed.2d 85 (1990).

Miranda v. Arizona, 384 U.S. 436, 86 S. Ct. 1602, 16 L.Ed.2d 694 (1966).

Missouri v. Seibert, 542 U.S. 600, 124 S. Ct. 2601, 159 L.Ed.2d 643 (2004).

Murray v. U.S., 487 U.S. 533, 108 S. Ct. 2529, 101 L.Ed.2d 472 (1988).

Nix v. Williams, 467 U.S. 431, 104 S. Ct. 2501, 81 L.Ed.2d 377 (1984).

Oliver v. U.S., 466 U.S. 170, 104 S. Ct. 1735, 80 L.Ed.2d 214 (1984).

Payton v. New York, 445 U.S. 573, 100 S. Ct. 1371, 63 L.Ed.2d 639 (1980).

Pennsylvania v. Labron, 518 U.S. 938, 116 S. Ct. 2485, 135 L.Ed.2d 1031 (1996).

Richards v. Wisconsin, 520 U.S. 385, 117 S. Ct. 1416, 137 L.Ed.2d 615 (1997).

Roper v. Simmons, 543 U.S. 551 (2005).

Schmerber v. California, 384 U.S. 757, 86 S. Ct. 1826, 16 L.Ed.2d 908 (1966).

Spinelli v. U.S., 393 U.S. 410, 89 S. Ct. 584, 21 L.Ed.2d 637 (1969).

Steagald v. U.S., 451 U.S. 204, 101 S. Ct. 1642, 68 L.Ed.2d 38 (1981).

Stovall v. Denno, 388 U.S. 293, 87 S. Ct. 1967, 18 L.Ed.2d 1199 (1967).

Tennessee v. Garner, 471 U.S. 1, 105 S. Ct. 1694, 85 L.Ed.2d 1 (1985).

U.S. v. Ash, 413 U.S. 300, 93 S. Ct. 2568, 37 L.Ed.2d 619 (1973).

U.S. v. Dunn, 480 U.S. 294, 107 S. Ct. 1134, 94 L.Ed.2d 326 (1987).

U.S. v. Jacobsen, 466 U.S. 109, 104 S. Ct. 1652, 80 L.Ed.2d 85 (1984).

U.S. v. Kaplan, 895 F.2d 618 (9th Cir. 1990).

U.S. v. Leon, 468 U.S. 897, 104 S. Ct. 3405, 82 L.Ed.2d 677 (1984).

U.S. v. Ramirez, 523 U.S. 65, 118 S. Ct. 992, 140 L.Ed.2d 191 (1998).

U.S. v. Wade, 388 U.S. 218, 87 S. Ct. 1926, 18 L.Ed.2d 1149 (1967).

U.S. v. Watson, 423 U.S. 411, 96 S. Ct. 820, 46 L.Ed.2d 598 (1976).

Weeks v. U.S., 232 U.S. 383, 34 S. Ct. 341, 58 L.Ed. 652 (1914).

Welsh v. Wisconsin, 466 U.S. 740, 104 S. Ct. 2091, 80 L.Ed.2d 732 (1984).

Wong Sun v. U.S., 371 U.S. 471, 83 S. Ct. 407, 9 L.Ed.2d 441 (1963).

Criminal Justice on the Web

For an up-to-date list of Web links, go to *The American Courts: A Procedural Approach* online companion site at http://criminal justice.jbpub.com/AmericanCourts. The online companion site will introduce you to some of the most important sites for finding American courts information on the Internet.

References

Blair, C. (2007). *Hudson v. Michigan*: The Supreme Court knocks and announces the demise of the exclusionary rule. *Tulsa Law Review, 42,* 751–764.

Blum, K. A., & Ryan, J. J. (2008). Recent developments in the use of excessive force by law enforcement. *Touro Law Review, 24,* 569–591.

Cooley, D. (2006). Clearly erroneous review is clearly erroneous: Reinterpreting *Illinois v. Gates* and advocating de novo review for a magistrate's determination of probable cause in applications for search warrants. *Drake Law Review, 55,* 85–113.

Frakt, D. J. R. (2007). Fruitless poisonous trees in a parallel universe: *Hudson v. Michigan*, knock-and-announce, and the exclusionary rule. *Florida State University Law Review, 34,* 659–735.

Kamisar, Y. (2007). On the fortieth anniversary of the Miranda case: Why we needed it, how we got it—and what happened to it. *Ohio State Journal of Criminal Law, 5,* 163–206.

Rubenfeld, J. (2008). The end of privacy. *Stanford Law Review, 61,* 101–161.

The Changing American Courts

Although American courts as an institution of society have gone about their business of resolving disputes and interpreting the law since America's founding, they have been marked by change. The problems and issues they confront, the approaches they take to legal interpretation, and the resulting body of civil and criminal case law that has developed have been a reflection of a changing society. The increasing population and its demand for greater court intervention and services will likely drive changes in the future.

A dynamic institution such as the judiciary can hardly remain stagnant. Regardless of jurisprudential approach, judges respond to the needs and demands of society. The types of civil cases that are brought and the penalties that justice requires for a growing body of crimes recognized by the law will require judges to apply the law in new and unforeseen ways. Society's perception of the role and effectiveness of the courts influences its operations, and the decisions courts make influence societal behavior. It is the interaction of the two that makes our system of justice so dynamic.

Thus, the courts in America may be seen as instruments of social change. Their decisions influence the legislative and executive branches as they develop public policy whether through lawmaking or regulation. As Chapter 13 discusses, court decisions, although made to address the civil or criminal issues presented by the individual parties, often have broader implications that affect all of society, but the types of cases brought by individuals also affect the behavior and decisions of the courts, whether resulting from the crush of criminal cases prosecuted in the war on drugs or the litigation explosion and the realization of citizens that they can use the courts to resolve any problem, no matter how trivial. Which cases merit the courts' attention and which ones society is willing to pay for through its funding of the courts are continuing issues. Although it is not known what the future holds for the justice system of the United States, the courts are likely to continue to be responsive and forward thinking as they carry out their authority to make decisions, resolve disputes, and accomplish justice.

The American Courts Today and Tomorrow

13

What Is This Chapter About?

This chapter returns to some of the themes in this book regarding the work of the American courts and considers the issues facing the courts now and in the future. These issues fall broadly into three areas. First considered are the effects of the courts on American society. In particular, the courts may be viewed as instruments of social change, affecting public policy by the types of cases that come before them and their interpretation of state and federal law. This occurs in both the criminal and civil areas of law when the rights of individual litigants are restricted, and a court's order has the effect of changing the behavior of society as a whole.

Second, this chapter explores the present and potential future effects of societal changes on the courts. Political activity, whether initiated from the people or by elected officials, has a significant, and not necessarily negative, effect on the quality of justice provided through the courts. In addition, the "litigation explosion" of civil cases has placed demands on the court system that are unprecedented. Furthermore, these problems are exacerbated by the struggle for adequate public funding that, at times, does not keep pace with the problems facing the courts.

Third, this chapter considers future trends that impact courts, ranging from the use of juries to technological changes in the United States. In addition, the increasing use of alternative methods of achieving justice, whether through alternative dispute resolution or privatizing the courts, is discussed. Finally, the availability of legal services and access to justice by the poor are explored.

Learning Objectives

After reading this chapter, you should be able to

1. Understand some of the ways in which the American courts affect society.
2. Describe how interpretation of the law by courts affects public policy.
3. Understand how the courts' approaches to litigation affect the public.
4. Understand some of the ways in which changes in society affect the courts.

5. Describe the roles of politics in judicial decision making.
6. Explain the types of demands that increasing caseloads place on the court system.
7. Describe the ways in which inadequate funding of courts affects the quality of justice in America.
8. Describe alternative methods of dispute resolution and their importance in determining justice.
9. Understand the importance of availability of legal services and access to justice in America.

Courts are social institutions. This means that they are created by the society in which they function. They are affected by society's wishes, demands, and needs, and through their activities, they are active participants in changing society. Courts are both backward and forward looking. They rely on precedent and the established rule of law as the basis for their decision making, yet are sensitive to the context in which those decisions are made and the needs of a changing society.

Thus, the interplay between the courts and society is central to the effectiveness of the courts in their role as the third branch of government. Decisions by courts have anticipated consequences and sometimes unanticipated effects on society, even when the decisions address only the specific problem presented by the litigants that appear before the court, but courts are also affected by society, directly and indirectly. As society changes technologically, economically, morally, and in other ways, the types of cases and problems that courts must resolve call for new applications of legal principles. Public confidence in the courts also calls for the judicial branch to examine its operations to benefit from greater efficiencies and keep pace with changes in society (Flango et al., 2008). Although the future of the American courts and their operations is unknown, the ways in which they adapt to the society they serve will determine their continuing effectiveness.

The Effects of Courts on Society

Courts make decisions that affect the parties involved. In a criminal case, a defendant is taken into custody (or remains in custody, if not free on bail) immediately when

301

a guilty verdict is delivered. Likewise, if a criminal defendant is found not guilty, he or she is immediately set free. There is little debate about the immediate effect of a court ruling in a criminal case; its consequences for the criminal defendant are clear.

In most civil cases, too, the effects of court decisions are clear. One party "wins"; another loses. A plaintiff is entitled to money damages that the losing defendant pays voluntarily or after routine procedures to collect on the judgment; conversely, a plaintiff is not entitled to the relief requested, and the case is dismissed.

Decisions by the courts frequently have larger effects on society that reach beyond the individual litigants. This may be the intent of the parties in initiating the litigation. It may be the natural consequences of the ruling made, or it may be by design of the judge or judges involved in crafting the decision. It is decisions made in cases that affect larger groups of people or society as whole in which the power of the law becomes evident.

Instruments of Social Change

Courts sometime serve as the instruments through which social change occurs. Administrative policies from the executive branch of government may become legislative initiatives ultimately adopted as law, but the interpretation of statutory law by the courts has often resulted in societal change. For example, in the well-known U.S. Supreme Court case *Brown v. Board of Education*, 347 U.S. 483, 74 S. Ct. 686, 98 L.Ed. 873 (1954), the Court directed four school districts in Kansas, South Carolina, Virginia, and Delaware to stop segregating students in their schools on the basis of race. Although the ruling was limited to specific school districts in those specific states, the decision was far reaching, causing schools throughout the country to desegregate their schools, leading to years of social upheaval as states, cities, and towns began to address issues involving busing, school facilities, funding, and taxation.

Although litigants are usually compliant in carrying out the directives of a court, this is not always the case, particularly when the court order will result in unwanted changes in a locality. In the effort to desegregate schools after the *Brown* case, many school districts resisted. Perhaps the most famous example was the desegregation of the Little Rock, Arkansas public schools. Although school officials there were not opposed to and were planning to admit black students, citizens of the state, including the governor, Orval Faubus, were opposed. When a federal judge refused to enjoin racial integration in the schools, the governor used the Arkansas National Guard to surround Central High School in Little Rock to prevent nine black students from entering. The mayor of the city then asked President Eisenhower to send military troops to maintain order, which he did. The troops escorted the students into the school. The schools were subsequently peacefully integrated.

Five years later another famous example of defiance of court orders occurred, stemming also from the lack of societal acceptance of court decisions viewed as changing a way of life. In 1962, the University of Mississippi denied admission to James Meredith, a black applicant, who subsequently obtained a federal court order directing the university to admit him. The university had never admitted a black student before that time and refused to allow him to register. Furthermore, the governor of the state declared that no black student would ever be admitted, in open defiance of the court order. On the day that Meredith arrived to register for classes, he was met by mobs, and rioting ensued. Only when the President of the United States sent federal marshals and military troops to usher him into the school to register for and attend classes did the impact of the decision on Mississippi (and, in general, southern) society become felt, as black students in greater numbers began to enroll in southern colleges and universities, and the segregation policies of the south began to unravel.

Courts as Policy Makers

As these examples show, court decisions sometimes have the effect of changing public policy. The public policy of the state of Mississippi was that of segregating the races in most aspects of life. The court order in the Meredith case had the effect of changing that policy, at least with respect to higher education, but education and race are not the only areas in which court decisions have served to change or, in some cases, create public policy. *Roe v. Wade*, 410 U.S. 113, 93 S. Ct. 705, 35 L.Ed.2d 147 (1973), is a good example. The decision in that case, finding unconstitutional the statutes criminalizing most abortions in the state of Texas, had the effect of legalizing the practice of abortion throughout the United States. Although proponents of abortion rights hailed the decision, others believed that the Court was improperly engaging in social engineering and intruding into an area best left to the judgment of the local community.

More recently, the presidential election of 2000 was the subject of court intervention to determine its outcome. In *Bush v. Gore*, 531 U.S. 98, 121 S. Ct. 525, 148 L.Ed.2d 388 (2000), the state of Florida certified that George W. Bush had won its electoral votes, giving him sufficient votes to win the presidency. Al Gore contested the results in state court, arguing that the certification was improper because certain ballots had not been properly counted. The trial court denied the claims. On appeal, the Florida Supreme Court ordered recounts by hand of certain ballots cast on machines that had not correctly recorded a vote. This decision was appealed to the U.S. Supreme Court, which reversed, holding that the Florida Supreme Court had unconstitutionally imposed requirements on the recounting of ballots that were not authorized by state law. The decision effectively ended the recounting of ballots, and Bush therefore won the election.

In stating its conclusion, the Court noted the impact of its decision: "None are more conscious of the vital limits on judicial authority than are the Members of this Court, and none stand more in admiration of the Constitution's design to leave the selection of the President to the people, through their legislatures, and to the political sphere. When contending parties invoke the process of the courts, however, it becomes our unsought responsibility to resolve the federal and constitutional issues the judicial system has been forced to confront." Although the Court stated that it was "forced" to address the election of the President, Justice Breyer, joined by the three other dissenting Justices, was not so sure:

> I fear that in order to bring this agonizingly long election process to a definitive conclusion, we have not adequately attended to that necessary "check upon our own exercise of power," "our own sense of self-restraint." Justice Brandeis once said of the Court, "The most important thing we do is not doing." What it does today, the Court should have left undone. I would repair the damage done as best we now can, by permitting the Florida recount to continue under uniform standards.

Thus, both the majority and those in dissent recognized the consequences of the decision involving the national election of the president. While not implicating a particular public policy, the decision is notable for its reach in deciding the election, as well as the debate about when judges are required to decide cases and when they should refrain from judging. As the majority opinion showed, most often the former holds true.

Making Law Versus Interpreting Law

An ongoing debate not likely to be resolved soon involves the extent to which judges, by their interpretations of law, actually make law. Making the law, of course, is the job of the legislative branch, not the judicial, as constitutional provisions, both state and federal, assign that task to the legislative branch. Thus, the problem is really one of separation of powers. When does a judge's decision have the effect of imposing legal restrictions or requirements not intended by a legislature?

Sometimes called "activist" judges, these are judges whose decisions extend beyond the case before them. An example is that of the Massachusetts Supreme Judicial Court's ruling on gay marriage in *Goodridge v. Department of Public Health*, 440 Mass. 309, 798 N.E.2d 941 (2003), discussed in Chapter 7. Although marriage is a traditional religious and statutory right, the court found that the Massachusetts constitution required it to be extended to gay couples. In his State of the Union Address on January 20, 2004, President Bush responded by noting

> Congress has already taken a stand on this issue by passing the Defense of Marriage Act, signed by President Clinton. That statute protects marriage under federal law as a union of a man and a woman, and declares that one state may not redefine marriage for other states. Activist judges, however, have begun redefining marriage by court order, without regard for the will of the people and their elected representatives. On an issue of such great consequence, the people's voice must be heard. If judges insist on forcing their arbitrary will upon the people, the only alternative left to the people would be the constitutional process. Our nation must defend the sanctity of marriage.

Regardless of one's stand on this particular issue, the problem remains one of determining the proper role the courts should play when interpreting the law. As the President indicated, people may be forced to revise the constitution when their attempts at legislative enactments reflecting the will of the people fail. Is that, however, a proper mechanism for responding to judges who may overstep the bounds of their constitutional function?

Another case of judicial activism involved a lower court judge in New York. For example, in 2007, a Long Island, New York lower court judge found that a state statute preventing driving without a license was unconstitutionally discriminatory against illegal immigrants, who were unable to obtain licenses because of their nonresident (and illegal) status. The judge justified his decision on the grounds that he believed, as a matter of public safety, that illegal aliens should be given licenses so that they could obtain insurance, thereby protecting other drivers on the road (Sanderson, 2007). The decision came not long after Governor Eliot Spitzer's proposal to give licenses to illegal aliens was soundly rejected by lack of support in the legislature and public outcry (Spitzer himself was later forced to resign in a prostitution scandal). The national problem of illegal immigrants was of particular concern to the people of New York, where large numbers of illegal immigrants lived. Granting them drivers licenses was viewed as condoning their illegal status.

The judge's decision set off a firestorm of protests. An editorial in the New York Post titled "Judge Liotti Legislates" opined that the judge had engaged in "blatant judicial activism" (Editorial, 2007). The judge himself chronicled the events in another opinion in the same case, *People v. Quiroga-Puma*, 18 Misc.3d 1130(A), 859 N.Y.S.2d 897 (N.Y. Just. Ct. 2008), found in **Case Decision 13.1**.

Whether Judge Liotti's decision to find the licensing statute unconstitutional was judicial activism may be a matter for debate, but his written opinion, much of which amounts to a rant about the evils of racism in society, is certainly extrajudicial. By equating himself with civil rights leaders, referring to his own decision as requiring "courage" and asserting that the public, not he, was wrong in their overreaction, the judge seemed to misunderstand the role of the judiciary and mistook judicial independence for judicial fiat.

The problem is twofold. It involves both the matter of judicial restraint or the ability of judges to refrain from deciding some case or deciding more than is necessary to resolve it, and the matter of statutory or constitutional interpretation, in which conclusions drawn about a law may reach beyond legislative intent. With the former, courts have recognized that in certain matters they should refrain from making decisions because it would involve crafting new laws to be followed. With the latter, the issue is whether the judge is supplanting his or her views for those of the legislature. This was the problem with Judge Liotti's decision in the *Quiroga-Puma* case.

With respect to judicial restraint, Justice Stevens of the U.S. Supreme Court has said that it is a policy "that allows other decisional bodies to have the last word in

Case Decision 13.1 *People v. Quiroga-Puma*, 18 Misc.3d 1130(A), 859 N.Y.S.2d 897 (N.Y. Just. Ct. 2008)

Opinion of the court by Judge Liotti:

Perhaps due to the publicity generated in this case,[1] the Court has received a letter request from defense counsel for increased security for himself and his client. This Court is concerned about the safety of the defendant, defense counsel, others in the court, court personnel, and itself.[2] The Court is well aware of both positive and negative opinions concerning its decisions. It respects the rights of all to agree, disagree or take no position at all.

This Court would require a metal detector and Court Officers to be placed in the courtroom or just outside of it. The Legislature created the Justice Court Assistance Program ("JCAP") in 1999 to provide critical financial assistance to towns and villages having Justice Courts in their communities (see L.1999, c. 280). By that time, it had become clear that those Courts, funded locally, did not have the resources needed to meet increased reporting obligations, security demands and other responsibilities of a modern judiciary; and that, for those courts to remain viable institutions, some measure of supplementary State assistance was in order. Under JCAP, towns and villages were invited, on an annual basis, to apply to the Chief Administrative Judge for modest monetary grants to assist them in the purchase or procurement of computers, recording devices and other essential electronic equipment, small facilities' enhancements, training for their court personnel and legal materials for court use. The JCAP program covers up to $30,000 for a metal detector; however, JCAP procedure does not begin again until April, 2008 when the State Legislature passes the budget for the fiscal year. JCAP will not cover the cost of personnel additions, meaning that the Village of Westbury would have to foot the bill for Court Officers, as well as provide for training. As the security addition options are foreclosed to the Court at this time, the measures taken *infra* are justified for the security of the defendant, defense counsel, *et alia*.

Unfortunately, this Court has had some experience in dealing with individuals who have allegedly threatened or caused harm to lawyers, elected officials, or court personnel. Their comments and actions obviously go beyond the pale of fair comment and appropriate First Amendment protection. There are others though whose conduct is borderline; where they are obsessed with an issue or a person; whose obsession consumes them to the point where they are pushed over the edge beyond pandering to their electorate (if they are elected officials), and in some cases, into a delusional, episodic psychosis. In this case, the racist rhetoric by or cowardly expression of persons, anonymous or not, will be reported to the police. When it comes to irrational behavior, the fact that this Court is just a lower Village Court with relatively minor matters before it is of no moment. This Court will not be intimidated into a renunciation of its opinions and will never back down from them.

The hateful sentiments expressed by persons regarding non-citizens or undocumented Hispanic aliens, and that my previous decision on unlicensed operation of a motor vehicle somehow jeopardizes the foundations of civilization is an exaggeration beyond comparison and reinforces the Court's opinion that some of the views expressed are so out of proportion that they are racist and borderline delusional. One State Senator from Suffolk County, for example, called for my removal from the Bench without even having read my decision. My decision does not pose a threat to our way of life; it is meant to enhance it by promoting safety on our highways.

Judging from some of the anonymous internet postings and letters which this Court is aware of or has received, I find that defense counsel's concerns about security are warranted. Fortunately, this Court has never had an incident of violence or even contemptuous behavior occur before it. Our proceedings are largely uneventful, but when the Court makes a decision on legal issues before it as it did in this case, which some view as controversial, the frequency of communications and even anonymous threats directed at the Court or the parties increases.

This Court is mindful of the immortal words of Honorable Frank Santagata, the former Associate Justice of this Court for nearly thirty years, who often said that our judiciary must function "without fear or favor." This Court fondly remembers those words and strives to live by them.

---

[1] See Bill Sanderson, *Judge Gives Alien Pass On License*, *New York Post*, December 21, 2007 at 19; Laura Rivera, *LI Judge Enters The License Debate*, *Newsday*, December 22, 2007 at A8; Editorial, *Judge Liotti Legislates*, *New York Post*, December 26, 2007 at 30.

[2] See generally, Toobin, Jeffrey, "Death In Georgia." *The New Yorker*, February 4, 2008, p. 32, detailing the 2005 escape of Brian Nichols, a defendant being retried on rape charges, involving the shooting of the judge trying his case, the court reporter, and a deputy sheriff, before hijacking five cars, killing a federal agent, and taking a hostage, before surrendering to authorities.

When race and ethnic issues are involved, our country has shown its intolerance for minorities and its belligerence towards them. Abraham Lincoln was assassinated following the signing of the Emancipation Proclamation. John F. Kennedy, Medgar Evers, Robert F. Kennedy, James Meredith, and Martin Luther King, Jr. were all assassinated or assassination, in the case of Mr. Meredith, was attempted and each pioneered civil rights issues.

Justice Thurgood Marshall once wrote that "in recognizing the humanity of our fellow beings, we pay ourselves the highest tribute." However, Justice Marshall also warned, "Even if all parties approach the court's mandate with the best of conscious intentions, . . . that mandate requires them to confront and overcome their own racism on all levels, a challenge I doubt all of them can meet."

Fear is what enabled organizations like the Ku Klux Klan to flourish. Courage is what has essentially neutralized the effect of those groups. As Dr. Martin Luther King, Jr. once said, "The ultimate tragedy is not the oppression and cruelty by the bad people but the silence over that by the good people." The fight against bigotry was not won quickly. Facing a tyrannical and oppressive system, people fought for their rights. It was a collaborative effort between the oppressed and those who took a stand to help them. They faced many failures along the way, but always persevered.

There is no accounting for the extremes to which some will go when they believe that their way of life is being threatened by foreigners or so-called undocumented illegal aliens. While this Court recently declared V.T.L. § 509-1, unlicensed operation of motor vehicles, unconstitutional, this seemingly innocuous decision concerning safety on our highways, has fanned the fires of hatred and racism. This Court finds no difference in this extremism merely because it is occurring in the northeast rather than the *ante bellum* South. Mississippi is not the only place where churches burn or where civil rights workers are killed or where lynch mobs gather. The migrant workers or poor Hispanics who often appear in this Court are not terrorists and pose no threat whatsoever to our form of government or national security. They are for the most part hard working, good people who have come here for a better life. They may be here illegally, but if given the choice, this Court believes that most would strive to become citizens and pay their taxes. But, we choose not to legalize them. Instead, we put barriers in the way. Those who must work with their hands and backs, those with a darker skin tone or different features or who are shorter than us or do not speak our language may not fit neatly into our pristine, homogeneous communities, but why do they not deserve to be here? The feelings of nationalism and ethnocentricity keep them from being legalized. Instead of being three-fifths of a person as our Founders provided or as Justice Taney provided for in the abhorrent *Dred Scott* decision, they are afforded no rights at all. In addition, they must fear arrest, deportation, eviction, and now, for their safety in our courthouses. While these issues are being debated in the ivory towers of Presidential debates and Lou Dobbs' television show, everyday people and courts of law must live with the miscalculations and errors in judgment by a government in Washington whose sole solution to this vexing problem is to build electronic fences at our borders, rather than dealing with the estimated 15–20 million undocumented aliens in this country and an estimated one million in New York State. "We have a lot of systemic, built-in bias and prejudice not just against race, but against those others who are different than the majority of us in this country." It is the oath and responsibility of this Court to endeavor to counteract such forces when those matters are before it.

While this Court does not have resources for increased security, it will not operate in secret either. However, providing defense counsel furnishes the Court with an authorization to appear in his client's behalf and pay any fines that may be due thereon, all future appearances by this defendant will be excused unless defense counsel is otherwise notified. This Court is also ordering that the defendant's address shall be placed under seal and shall not be revealed to anyone without the Court's prior written order.

As for defense counsel, this Court will endeavor to provide for his security in a limited manner permitted by our budget. Those precautions are deliberately not set forth herein. The Court also again wishes to emphasize to our State government that Village and Town Courts have real security concerns that should be addressed forthwith and hopefully prior to any incidence of violence. The Village cannot afford to be saddled with additional costs for more security merely because its Court has decided a controversial legal issue. The State should act immediately to provide the necessary funds for equipment and personnel to ensure that safety in our court and all others is maintained.

legal interpretation until it is truly necessary for [a] Court to intervene." *Michigan v. Long*, 463 U.S. 1032, 1067, 103 S. Ct. 3469, 77 L.Ed.2d 1201 (1983) (Justice Stevens, dissenting). Thus, judicial restraint is the essence of separation of powers—to let the branch empowered to decide a matter of law do so and only when no other resolution can be reached should a court intervene. In this most extreme view, however, it seems likely that a court would have very little to say other than that which is absolutely necessary to decide a case on the facts before it.

Regarding statutory or constitutional interpretation, the general rule followed by courts is to first determine whether there is any ambiguity in the language of the document being interpreted. That is, is it susceptible to more than one meaning? If not, then only the language of the document should be examined to determine its plain meaning. It is when ambiguity exists that problems may arise leading to questions of "law making" by judges. One approach is to resolve ambiguity by referring to the history of the document being interpreted. What did the drafters intend when they wrote it? However, courts cannot resort to history to create ambiguity; under this approach, they may refer to it only to resolve ambiguity if found in the language. Another approach is to examine the language in the context of modern life. Under this approach, a statute is not static but changes with the times in that it must be applied in new and novel situations that the drafters may not have anticipated. This "dynamic" approach is used to justify ignoring (or at least minimizing) the intent of those who drafted the law in favor of a modern interpretation that takes into account the views of society (see Murphy et al., 2006).

What approach a given judge will take now or in the future depends on a number of factors and constraints. First among these are the facts and legal issues requiring decision. In somewhat settled areas of the law, a routine personal injury matter, or a contract dispute, there may be neither need nor opportunity to stray far from established precedent or clear statutory language. Second is the moral or ethical perspective of the judge that is informed by the judge's understanding of the role of judicial power. Although most judges do not think of themselves as omnipotent, the power of reasoning at times allows them to address more than necessary or to keep from employing expansive legal interpretations not necessary to a decision. Finally, there are political and public perception aspects to judicial decision making that restrain judges. Decisions are open to public view and public reaction. Although judges need not be subject to the whims of the public, their decisions need to stand up to public, not just judicial, scrutiny.

Societal Effects on the Courts

Although it is a truism to say that courts do not operate in a vacuum, the way in which society affects the operation of the courts is a subject of interest because of the varied and increasing ways in which this occurs. The current events and issues facing society are also topics affecting the courts, sometimes themselves becoming problems for the courts to resolve. This section explores two such

issues: the so-called explosion of new case filings and the political pressures that courts face.

Litigation Explosion

Much has been said about the "litigation explosion"—the rapid increase in the number of civil cases filed by lawyers (Johnson, 2007). These cases have primarily been personal injury cases, but also include cases alleging employment discrimination, professional liability, and products liability. Some suggest that these cases place a terrible burden on society in terms of increasing the cost of products and services, including insurance, and provide a disincentive for some professionals, such as healthcare providers, to enter or remain in their fields. The litigation explosion is associated with the view of lawyers as "ambulance chasers," filing frivolous lawsuits for no other reason than to make money. Others bemoan the litigious society that the United States has become, where citizens are no better than the lawyers they hire.

Whatever financial, personal, or social consequences the increase in litigation has caused, it has had significant effects on the courts across the country. In some parts of the country, it has produced backlogs of cases going back years, resulting in delays for hearings on pretrial motions or discovery disputes, as well as the scheduling of trials. It has stretched court resources thin in terms of the personnel who process the cases and the judges who handle them, as well as the courtroom facilities that must be scheduled to conduct hearings and hold trials.

Judges are not in a position to refuse to hear civil disputes. They may dismiss a nonmeritorious case or one that they lack jurisdiction to hear. They may resolve a matter early by summary judgment, but parties have a right to have their claims heard. Thus, the dilemma is this: How can the courts serve society, as they are constitutionally or statutorily required to do, when society continues to place increased demands on court operations? Although this will continue to be a problem in the future, courts do take action to resolve the problem now. For example, the growing use of technology has been embraced by courts to ease the burden of processing cases. Encouraging parties to settle cases through alternative dispute resolution has also been used effectively. Adequately staffing the courts with personnel and judges through increased compensation has also long been a plea from the courts. Each of these is discussed more fully later here, but each represents a response to the effects that society itself has on the court system (**Sidebar 13.1**).

Sidebar 13.1   *The American Courts: Open Access to All Claims?*

In 1994, 81-year-old Stella Liebeck sued McDonald's in state court in Albuquerque, New Mexico, for injuries she suffered when the coffee she purchased spilled on her lap, causing third-degree burns and requiring skin grafts. She was awarded $160,000 plus punitive damages of $2.7 million. The case became a lightning rod for all that was wrong with our system of civil justice, where courts would grant large damage awards to those who, many believed, had the most tenuous of claims.

In another case, a Washington, D.C., attorney sued the owners of a laundry on his own behalf for failing to live up to signs in their store window that said "Satisfaction Guaranteed" and "Same Day Service." The attorney claimed that the laundry had failed to return a pair of pants to him and that it tried to give him another pair of pants that were not his. He sued for $54 million. After a trial and appeal, the case was dismissed.

Are these cases "normal" claims of injured parties, or do they reflect an overly litigious society? Are the courts open to anyone who believes they have been injured, no matter how slight? Should they be?

According to an ABC News report on May 29, 2009, the famed *Guinness Book of World Records* named Jonathan Lee Riches, a federal prisoner, the most litigious man in the world, having sued defendants such as Plato, the Lincoln Memorial, Black History Month, and the product "I Can't Believe It's Not Butter." The Guinness Book claimed he had filed over 5,500 lawsuits. Riches disputed the number, asserting that he had filed only around 4,000, and promptly sued the *Guinness Book* for falsely naming him the "most litigious." Many of the federal courts in which he has filed lawsuits have barred him from making further claims. Regardless of the exact number, most people would agree that no individual should need recourse to the courts several thousand times in one lifetime, and with each court filing, time is taken from the real work of the courts, time funded by taxpayer dollars.

The perception that some lawsuits are frivolous often makes them the target of the media and special interest groups that have formed to eliminate lawsuits that abuse the court process. Such organizations as the Heartland Institute, the American Tort Reform Association, the American Legislative Exchange Council, HALT—An Organization of Americans for Legal Reform, the Center for Legal Policy at the Manhattan Institute, and the Washington Legal Foundation seek the reform of the justice system by bringing to public attention lawsuits whose merit is questionable and legislation that encourages legal claims. A sampling of cases reported by these organizations follows.

Cheerleading is among the most dangerous sports because of the intense jumping and landing on hard surfaces, tossing of teammates into the air, and risks of falls, but that did not stop a lawsuit by a cheerleader in Wisconsin whose "spotter" failed to catch her; she fell backward, hitting her head on the floor. She sued for the spotter's and the school district's negligence in failing to prevent the injury. The suit was ultimately dismissed by the Wisconsin Supreme Court, who determined that cheerleading was a contact sport, immune from suit under a state law.

When a Los Angeles traffic cop was changing into her Victoria's Secret thong to go home after her shift, a rhinestone on the minimal article of underclothing popped off, striking her in the eye. She recovered, but not before suing Victoria's Secret and appearing on morning talk shows with her lawyer to recount her ordeal.

In Merritt Island, Florida, a 20-year-old temporary worker constructing a dock was dared to run down the dock and dive off the end into the water. Sadly, there was only one foot of water, and he was paralyzed as a result of his dive. Although there was a rail on the end of the dock that he jumped over, he sued the construction company, a small business. The owner could not afford a lawyer to defend the company, and the jury awarded $76 million.

When an Arizona rancher came on 16 illegal immigrants from Mexico on his land, he held them at gunpoint while waiting for the U.S. Border Patrol to arrive. The Mexicans sued him in Tucson for assaulting them, violating their civil rights, and inflicting emotional distress, seeking damages of $32 million. The civil rights claims were dismissed, but the jury awarded almost $78,000.

A Nebraska man sued God. His claims were that God had allowed death and destruction of earth's inhabitants to occur. The plaintiff sought injunctive relief from the court ordering God to stop such behavior. The trial judge dismissed the case because there was no proof that God had been properly served. Several lawyers offered to represent God in court, although He apparently needed no legal assistance.

Is everyone entitled to have access to the courts for any dispute, real or imagined? Who decides which cases can go forward and which should not? The courts themselves must be the gatekeepers of justice, applying the law to trivial cases as well as significant ones.

Political Pressure

Politics plays a role in the operation of the courts. This may occur directly, as in those states that require judges to run periodically in partisan elections, or indirectly, as when special interest groups use the courts to further their agendas. Politicians in the executive and legislative branches often send less than subtle signals to the judiciary regarding their displeasure with rulings. President Bush's comment regarding activist judges redefining marriage after the *Goodridge* case was an example of this.

Some judges have lost their positions as a result of decisions made on the bench. In 1986, after three California Supreme Court Justices, Rose Bird, Cruz Reynoso, and Joseph Grodin, voted against the death penalty, they were driven from office by wide margins by voters who were angry with their decision. Even apart from the power of the vote, citizens are influential in speaking out against unpopular court rulings or approaches by judges to deciding cases.

The significance of political effects on judicial decision making involves the issue of judicial independence. Judicial independence refers to the view of the Framers of the Constitution that the judicial branch should be free to make decisions that may, at times, be unpopular without fear of reprisal. The provision for lifetime appointment of federal judges in Article III was included for this reason. As Alexander Hamilton noted in The Federalist No. 78,

> If then the courts of justice are to be considered as the bulwarks of a limited constitution against legislative encroachments, this consideration will afford a strong argument for the permanent tenure of judicial offices, since nothing will contribute so much as this to that independent spirit in the judges, which must be essential to the faithful performance of so arduous a duty. This independence of the judges is equally requisite to guard the constitution and the rights of individuals from the effects of those ill humours which the arts of designing men, or the influence of particular conjunctures, sometimes disseminate among the people themselves, and which, though they speedily give place to better information and more deliberate reflection, have a tendency in the meantime to occasion dangerous innovations in the government, and serious oppressions of the minor party in the community.

Political pressure may threaten judicial independence but is a reality in a democratic form of government.

In a New York drug case, *U.S. v. Bayless*, 201 F.3d 116 (2d Cir. 2000), which involved nearly 100 pounds of cocaine and heroin found in the trunk of the defendant's car, a federal District Court Judge suppressed the evidence based on an illegal search and dismissed the case. Despite the large quantity of drugs found and a videotaped confession by the defendant, the judge found the testimony of the police officer who stopped the vehicle to not be credible regarding his reasonable suspicion to stop the car, which involved seeing four men run away from the defendant's car after loading duffle bags in the trunk. Furthermore, he found the testimony of the defendant regarding the facts leading to the stop to be credible. If that were not enough to upset the citizens of New York, the judge noted in his suppression ruling:

> Police officers, even those travelling in unmarked vehicles, are easily recognized, particularly, in this area of Manhattan. In fact, the same United States Attorney's Office which brought this prosecution enjoyed more success in their prosecution of a corrupt police officer of an anti-crime unit operating in this very neighborhood. Even before this prosecution and the public hearing and final report of the Mollen Commission, residents in this neighborhood tended to regard police officers as corrupt, abusive and violent. After the attendant publicity surrounding the above events, had the men not run when the cops began to stare at them, it would have been unusual.

After considerable public furor, including veiled threats by the President that the judge's decision may have been improper, he reconsidered his earlier ruling suppressing the drugs, concluding that there was no reason to suppress the evidence. The defendant ultimately pled guilty.

On appeal, in addition to claiming that the evidence should have been suppressed, the defendant argued that the judge should have recused himself from the case because he was influenced by political and public pressure. The opinion of the U.S. Court of Appeals is found in **Case Decision 13.2**.

Case Decision 13.2   *U.S. v. Bayless*, 201 F.3d 116 (2d Cir. 2000)

Decision of the Court by Judge Calabresi:

In this appeal from a conviction of narcotics offenses, defendant-appellant Carol Bayless argues that the district judge (Harold Baer, Jr., J.) who presided over a pre-trial suppression hearing was obliged to recuse himself in the interest of the appearance of justice. Judge Baer's original decision to grant Bayless's motion to suppress drugs seized from her car was fiercely criticized by politicians and press alike, some of whom called for his impeachment. In the midst of the furor over his ruling, Judge Baer granted the government's motion for reconsideration of his decision, reopened the suppression hearing and heard significant new evidence, and then denied the motion to suppress. After the motion to suppress was denied, Bayless moved for Judge Baer's recusal.

We conclude that the most difficult issues potentially raised by this remarkable case need not be decided. Thus, we do not determine when, if ever, criticism of an unpopular decision becomes so severe as to constitute grounds for recusal of the judge who made that decision. Similarly, we do not establish the conditions under which a defendant who waits to move for a judge's disqualification until after that judge has ruled against her may totally waive her right to seek recusal. Finding, simply, that in the circumstances of this case, Judge Baer did not commit plain error in failing to recuse himself *sua sponte*, and further finding that Judge Baer did not err when, after hearing all the relevant evidence, he concluded that the drugs seized from Bayless's car were properly admissible against her, we affirm Bayless's conviction.

Background

A. Bayless's Arrest and the Search of Her Car

The story begins on April 21, 1995, the day of Bayless's arrest. The parties agree that the arresting police officers, Officer Carroll and Sergeant Bentley, were patrolling the Washington Heights area of

---

Manhattan in an unmarked police car when they observed Bayless, in a car with Michigan license plates, double-parked on 176th Street, near St. Nicholas Avenue. While Bayless was stopped, the officers saw four men load two heavy duffel bags into the trunk of her car. Almost immediately, the men stepped away from the car, and Bayless drove off alone. The officers followed Bayless for about two blocks, during which time she did not drive erratically or commit any traffic violations. They nevertheless pulled her over. After discovering that the car was a rental car and that Bayless was not an authorized driver, the officers asked her about the bags that had been placed in her trunk. When Bayless denied knowledge of the bags, they asked her for the keys, opened the trunk, and discovered that the bags contained a large quantity of cocaine, along with some heroin. (The exact amount of each was later determined to be thirty-four kilograms of cocaine and two kilograms of heroin.)

Bayless was arrested and taken to the 33rd Precinct, where the case was turned over to federal authorities. After being read her *Miranda* rights, Bayless was interviewed by federal agents and confessed to acting as a drug courier for her son, who sold drugs in the Detroit area. She then repeated her statement on videotape. On June 21, 1995, Bayless was indicted by a grand jury in the United States District Court for the Southern District of New York. She was charged with possession of cocaine and heroin with intent to distribute, in violation of 18 U.S.C. § 2 (1994) and 21 U.S.C. § 812, § 841(a)(1) and § 841(b)(1)(A) (1994), and with conspiracy to distribute cocaine and heroin and possess them with intent to distribute, in violation of 21 U.S.C. § 846 (1994). Her case was assigned to Judge Baer.

B. The January 1996 Suppression Hearing

On October 3, 1995, Bayless moved to suppress the drugs seized from her car and her post-arrest statements on the ground that the police did not have reasonable suspicion to stop her car. In early January, 1996, Judge Baer held a suppression hearing, at which the government introduced the testimony of one of the arresting officers, Officer Carroll, and the court viewed the videotaped statement Bayless gave after her arrest.

At the hearing, Officer Carroll testified that on the morning of April 21, he and his partner, Sergeant Bentley, both members of the Street Crime Unit, were in plain clothes, patrolling Washington Heights in an unmarked police car. At about 5 a.m., the officers entered 176th Street, and observed a 1995 Chevrolet with Michigan license plates moving slowly along the street. The officers saw the car pull over to the north side of the street, near the intersection with St. Nicholas Avenue, and double park. At that time, Officer Carroll could not tell who was driving the car, but could tell that there was no passenger. As soon as the car stopped, four men came from between parked cars on the south side of the street. Walking in single file, they crossed the street and approached the Chevrolet. Just before the men reached the car, the driver leaned over to the passenger side of the car, and the trunk opened a few inches. The first of the four men opened the trunk all the way, the second man put a large duffel bag into the trunk, the third man put a second large duffel bag into the trunk, and the last man closed the trunk. There was no conversation or other interaction between the four men and the driver, and the entire transaction was concluded in seconds.

After the trunk was shut, the driver immediately drove away, stopping at a red light at the intersection. The officers followed the car, stopping opposite the four men, who were standing on the sidewalk on the north side of 176th Street. Officer Carroll testified that at least two of the men noticed him and his partner and spoke briefly to each other (he could not hear what they said) and that the four men then moved rapidly in different directions. Officer Carroll watched one of the men, who walked to the corner and then began to run north on St. Nicholas Avenue.

The officers followed the Chevrolet and, after about two blocks, placed a red flashing light on their dashboard and pulled the car over. After stopping the car, Officer Carroll ordered Bayless to turn the motor off, which she did, and asked her for her license, registration, and insurance. Bayless told Carroll that it was a rented car, and he asked for the rental agreement and her license, which she gave him. When he asked her to whom the car was rented, she said she did not know. The rental agreement was not in Bayless's name, and it did not authorize any other drivers. Officer Carroll asked Bayless who the men who had put bags in her trunk were, and she denied that anyone had put bags in her trunk. He then asked Bayless to get out of the car and, handcuffing her, arrested her for unauthorized operation of a motor vehicle. After the arrest, Sergeant Bentley unlocked the trunk, opened the duffel bags, and found the drugs. The officers then took Bayless to the 33rd Precinct.

Upon questioning by the court, Officer Carroll gave several reasons why he and his partner were suspicious of Bayless. First, Officer Carroll claimed that the area around 176th Street, and the

(Continues)

Washington Heights/Inwood neighborhood in general, was "known as a hub . . . for the drug trade." Second, the "orchestrated" manner in which the four men loaded the trunk suggested to Carroll a rehearsed transaction, and he found it abnormal and suspicious that the four men had no conversation or interaction with the driver of the car. Third, the men dispersed upon spotting the officers, and one of them began to run. Fourth, the car had out-of-state license plates. Finally, Officer Carroll noted that he and his partner pulled Bayless over when they did because they wanted to prevent her from reaching the highway, which led to the George Washington Bridge and thence out of New York state.

At the hearing, the court also viewed Bayless's videotaped statement, which described the events surrounding her arrest in a somewhat different fashion. According to Bayless, she left Detroit on the afternoon of April 20 with five duffel bags full of cash (she estimated the total to be about $1 million), planning to purchase drugs in New York and to bring them back to Detroit. She was a passenger in the Chevrolet, which was driven by an associate, Terry, and they were accompanied by three other men driving a van (Robert, Chubb, and another man whose name she could not remember). When they reached 176th Street, where they were met as planned by the people selling them the drugs, Terry double-parked and got out of the car and went to move the van. The other men took the money out of the trunk of the Chevrolet and went into an apartment building to exchange the cash for drugs. Bayless waited in the car for about ten minutes, until the men returned. The men put two duffel bags containing drugs in the trunk of the car, and handed her the keys. Bayless then drove by herself down 176th Street, and saw Robert and Chubb walking in the same direction that she was driving. Bayless stopped for a red light at the corner of St. Nicholas Avenue, proceeded for a short distance until she saw the flashing red light in the police car and pulled over. She waited until the police officers got out of the car; they asked her for her license and registration, which she gave them. When they asked her what was in the trunk, she responded that she did not know. The officers asked for her keys and opened the trunk, and arrested her.

C. Judge Baer's Decision of January 22, 1996

After hearing Officer Carroll's testimony and viewing Bayless's videotaped statement at the hearing, Judge Baer on January 22 issued a ruling suppressing the cocaine and heroin seized from Bayless's car, along with her post-arrest statements. Judge Baer began by noting that Officer Carroll's testimony and Bayless's videotaped statement "differ[ed] dramatically," and that, given its inculpatory nature, he found Bayless's statement more credible. He pointed out that if Bayless was telling the truth, "Officer Carroll apparently missed or overlooked the fact that the car had come to a halt, never saw the man exit the [car], and missed the million dollars being taken out of the trunk," making his version "incredible." Judge Baer also asked rhetorically where the officer in charge, Sergeant Bentley, was during the suppression hearing: "[w]hile presumably available to corroborate [Officer Carroll's] gossamer," the judge commented, "he was never called to testify."

Judge Baer highlighted two major disparities between Officer Carroll's testimony and Bayless's statement: first, Carroll testified that one of the men ran from the scene, while Bayless stated that they all walked away; and, second, Carroll testified that the men had no conversation or other interaction with Bayless, while Bayless said that they gave her the car keys after loading the bags into the trunk. Judge Baer made it clear that he credited Bayless's version on both counts. He found that the remaining facts articulated by Carroll—the "high-crime" neighborhood, the early morning hour, the out-of-state license plates, the duffel bags, and the double parking—did not, without more, give rise to reasonable suspicion, and he therefore suppressed the seized drugs and Bayless's post-arrest statements.

Judge Baer's holding rested on the conclusion that Bayless's account was more credible than Officer Carroll's, and that the men loading the bags into her trunk had not run away upon seeing the officers. In dicta, however, he went on to say that even had one or more of the men run away, "it [would be] hard to characterize this as evasive conduct." In the passage of his opinion that subsequently drew the most fire from critics, he added:

> Police officers, even those travelling in unmarked vehicles, are easily recognized, particularly, in this area of Manhattan. In fact, the same United States Attorney's Office which brought this prosecution enjoyed more success in their prosecution of a corrupt police officer of an anti-crime unit operating in this very neighborhood. Even before this prosecution and the public hearing and final report of the Mollen Commission, residents in this neighborhood tended to regard police officers as corrupt, abusive and violent. After the attendant publicity surrounding the above events, had the men not run when the cops began to stare at them, it would have been unusual.

D. The Publicity Following Judge Baer's January 22, 1996 Ruling

Judge Baer's ruling immediately drew heavy criticism in the press and from local political figures, including New York's Mayor and Police Commissioner, as well as Governor George Pataki. The decision itself, and the language in the opinion, referring as it did to widespread police corruption, was perceived by many as an affront to the police and to victims of drug-related crime. An editorial in the *New York Times* called Judge Baer's decision "judicial malpractice," and accused him of "undermin[ing] respect for the legal system, encourag[ing] citizens to flee the police and deter[ring] honest cops in drug-infested neighborhoods from doing their job." *Judge Baer's Tortured Reasoning*, N.Y. Times, Jan. 31, 1996, at A16.

In February, the government filed a motion for reconsideration of the order granting the suppression motion. The decision, however, continued to attract attention and quickly became the focus of a nationwide controversy and a flashpoint for the 1996 Presidential campaign, as Democrats and Republicans competed to enhance their reputations as proponents of law and order by denouncing Judge Baer. In early March, more than two hundred members of Congress, led by Republican Representatives Bill McCollum, Fred Upton, and Michael Forbes, sent a letter to President Clinton calling Judge Baer's ruling "a shocking and egregious example of judicial activism." The letter claimed Judge Baer had "sid[ed] with drug traffickers and against hard-working police officers and the frightened residents of violence-ridden communities," and that he had "demonstrated a level of ideological blindness that render[ed] him unfit for the proper discharge of his judicial duties." The writers asked President Clinton to join them in calling for Judge Baer's resignation.

When asked about the letter at a White House press conference, President Clinton's spokesperson Mike McCurry said that the President would defer deciding whether to call for Judge Baer's resignation until the Judge ruled on the government's motion for reconsideration, adding that, while the President would evaluate Judge Baer's record "on the full breadth of his cases," the White House was "interested in seeing how he rules" in response to the motion. The press interpreted McCurry's comment as a veiled warning. Subsequently, in a written response to Rep. McCollum, the White House disavowed any intent to ask for Judge Baer's resignation, saying that the issues should be resolved in the courts. Then-Senate Majority Leader and Presidential candidate Bob Dole joined the fracas by saying that if Judge Baer did not resign, he should be impeached.

E. The Hearing of March 15, 1996

In February, and well before the furor had died down, Judge Baer presumably began to consider the government's motion asking him to revisit his ruling. On March 5, he granted the government's motion to reopen the hearing for the presentation of additional evidence—specifically testimony by Sergeant Bentley that would corroborate Officer Carroll's earlier testimony.

At the hearing on March 15, Sergeant Bentley testified to the events surrounding the arrest. He confirmed Officer Carroll's account that the loading of the trunk appeared "orchestrated" and that there was no communication between the men and the driver of the car. He also confirmed Officer Carroll's statement that he had seen one of the men who had loaded the trunk run away. In fact, Sergeant Bentley claimed to have seen *two* of the men run away: one, he said, ran east on 176th Street and then north on St. Nicholas Avenue, while the other ran west on 176th Street.

Carol Bayless again testified about the events surrounding her arrest. Her account now included some details not present in her videotaped statement; for example, on cross-examination, Bayless for the first time said that she had a cellular phone with her in the car, with which she could have contacted the men who had made the trip with her, who also had a cell phone. Bayless continued to claim that she had seen the men walk toward the corner after they loaded the bags into her car, and denied seeing them run. She conceded, however, that she would not have been able to see what they did after turning the corner. On cross-examination, Bayless insisted that she was alone in the car for ten minutes without the keys while her companions were getting the drugs, and that she did not open the trunk, but that the men had opened it with a key. She also claimed that while her confession was being videotaped, the police coached her on what to say, and stopped and started the videotape when her answers did not satisfy them.

F. Judge Baer's Decision of April 1, 1996

On April 1, Judge Baer vacated his earlier order suppressing the seized drugs and Bayless's post-arrest statements. He emphasized that he had not changed his evaluation of the evidence presented by the government at the earlier hearing, which he still found to be legally insufficient. The testimony

(Continues)

(Continued)

presented at the second hearing, however, had changed his mind as to the relative credibility of the police officers and Carol Bayless.

Taking into account the newly presented evidence, and crediting Sergeant Bentley and Officer Carroll's account over that of Bayless, Judge Baer determined that the government had now met its burden of articulating facts sufficient to give the police reasonable suspicion to stop Bayless's car. He closed by apologizing for the controversial dicta in his earlier opinion:

> [U]nfortunately the hyperbole (dicta) in my initial decision not only obscured the true focus of my analysis, but regretfully may have demeaned the law-abiding men and women who make Washington Heights their home and the vast majority of the dedicated men and women in blue who patrol the streets of our great City.

G. Bayless's Recusal Motions

On April 12, counsel for Bayless made an oral motion that Judge Baer recuse himself from further proceedings in the case, arguing that "because of the high profile or the type of publicity that this case has received, and . . . meddlers from the outside public concerning this matter, there seems to be . . . an appearance of impropriety in the way the decision was done." He pointed out that the calls for Judge Baer's resignation or impeachment created the appearance that the judge "may have been influenced by outside forces" in his April 1 decision to deny the motion to suppress. Judge Baer denied the motion for recusal from the bench, saying:

> [T]he time to have [moved for recusal] would have been between the date of the rehearing and the decision, or earlier. Regardless of the fact that you failed to raise the issue, I considered it carefully while the matter was pending. Indeed, several friends whom I respect and admire made just such unsolicited suggestions. . . . I concluded that the proper and intellectually honest approach was to continue, feeling that recusal would have certainly been easier for the court. Even where outside influence was never a part of my thinking, which is indeed the fact here, in my view not recusing myself was the far more appropriate path for a federal judge to follow for three different reasons:
>
> First, to be swayed by outside influence would run counter to the central theme of judicial independence. You or your client, may not understand—and you are not alone—this position of United States District Court judge comes with life tenure. And no one, not even the President of the United States, can take it away unless, as one great Southern District judge—I think Tom Murphy—said, "They find your hand in the cookie jar.". . . So, you may rest assured that while I was surprised at the fire storm that developed . . . to me the fallout constituted little more than political posturing—some of what I saw I cannot say I am proud of—but political posturing in an election year, nevertheless. And it was in that fashion that I regard it and continue to regard most of the rhetoric I read . . . in the paper.
>
> The second thought was that . . . it would simply be passing the buck to another jurist. That did not seem appropriate or fair.
>
> And, lastly, it seemed to me that it would be a significant waste of judicial time to have someone else have to go through any part of what I had done already.

On April 22, Bayless filed a written motion seeking Judge Baer's recusal, again arguing that the publicity accorded the case and the pressure put on the judge compromised the impartiality of his decision and created the appearance of impropriety. On May 16, Judge Baer issued a written opinion denying the motion as both untimely and without merit, but requesting that the case be transferred to another district judge.

Bayless's case was transferred to Judge Robert P. Patterson, Jr., of the Southern District. On June 21, Bayless pleaded guilty before Judge Patterson to the counts in the indictment, subject to a stipulation that she be allowed to appeal the outcome of her suppression motion, and on October 1, 1998, she was sentenced to fifty-four months in prison.

Discussion

On appeal, Bayless argues (1) that Judge Baer was required to recuse himself *sua sponte* before deciding the government's motion for reconsideration; (2) that the failure of her counsel below to file a motion for recusal prior to Judge Baer's ruling on that motion constituted ineffective assistance of counsel; (3) that Judge Baer erred when he reopened the suppression hearing at the government's request; and (4) that Judge Baer's final disposition of the merits of her suppression motion was erroneous, because the police officers had no reasonable suspicion to stop her car on the morning of the arrest.

Recusal

The statutory scheme.—Bayless's claim that Judge Baer should have recused himself rests on 28 U.S.C. § 455(a) (1994), which provides simply: "Any justice, judge, or magistrate of the United States shall disqualify himself in any proceeding in which his impartiality might reasonably be questioned." Notably, under § 455(a), recusal is not limited to cases of actual bias; rather, the statute requires that a judge recuse himself whenever an objective, informed observer could reasonably question the judge's impartiality, regardless of whether he is actually partial or biased.

We have stated the standard for recusal under § 455(a) as follows:

> [A] court of appeals must ask the following question: Would a reasonable person, knowing all the facts, conclude that the trial judge's impartiality could reasonably be questioned? Or phrased differently, would an objective, disinterested observer fully informed of the underlying facts, entertain significant doubt that justice would be done absent recusal?

The standard is "designed to promote public confidence in the impartiality of the judicial process." Nevertheless, the existence of the appearance of impropriety is to be determined "not by considering what a straw poll of the only partly informed man-in-the-street would show[,] but by examining the record facts and the law, and then deciding whether a reasonable person knowing and understanding all the relevant facts would recuse the judge." In the instant case, the parties do not dispute this legal standard, but differ as to whether, on the facts before us, recusal was mandated.

Because it is unnecessary to the resolution of this case, we do not now identify the situations in which a judge's failure to recuse himself *sua sponte* would constitute plain error. We hold merely that, on the facts before us, Judge Baer's decision not to recuse himself was not plain error, in part because Bayless made a strategic choice not to move for his recusal until he had ruled against her.

In this case, Judge Baer faced a difficult choice. Confronted with unrestrained criticism from both politicians and the press, including calls for his resignation and even his impeachment, he was forced to decide whether to disqualify himself when doing so could readily have been perceived as a capitulation to political pressure—a capitulation, moreover, that might well have encouraged such pressure on judges in the future. And he was aided in making his choice neither by clear legal principles nor by a timely motion from the defendant.

The circumstances under which criticism of a judge from political figures or from the media might be grounds for recusal under § 455(a) are anything but clear. Nevertheless, many cases that have considered whether media criticism constituted grounds for recusal have found that it was not. This circuit has expressly urged caution in allowing media accounts to become the focus of a recusal inquiry:

> [W]e cannot adopt a *per se* rule holding that when someone claims to see smoke, we must find that there is fire. That which is seen is sometimes merely a smokescreen. Judicial inquiry may not therefore be defined by what appears in the press. If such were the case, those litigants fortunate enough to have easy access to the media could make charges against a judge's impartiality that would effectively veto the assignment of judges. Judge-shopping would then become an additional and potent tactical weapon in the skilled practitioner's arsenal.

In doing so, our court emphasized one of the serious problems with ruling that media attacks on a judge can be readily made the basis for recusal: parties who are sophisticated in their dealings with the press might then be able to engineer a judge's recusal for their own strategic reasons.

Reasonable Suspicion

Because it was proper to grant the reconsideration motion, we review this case on the basis of the evidence before Judge Baer at the second hearing. Accordingly, we need not and do not consider whether Judge Baer's initial decision to grant Bayless's suppression motion, made on the basis of the evidence before him in the first hearing, was erroneous.

The governing legal standard.—*Terry v. Ohio*, 392 U.S. 1, 88 S. Ct. 1868, 20 L.Ed.2d 889 (1968), first delineated the contours of a limited investigative stop, now frequently called a *Terry* stop.

(Continues)

Terry held that a police officer can stop and briefly detain a person if the officer has a reasonable suspicion "that criminal activity may be afoot." In deciding whether a *Terry* stop is reasonable under the Fourth Amendment, a reviewing court must determine, first, "whether the officer's action was justified at its inception, and [second,] whether it was reasonably related in scope to the circumstances which justified the interference in the first place." It is the first prong of the *Terry* test that is at issue here.

This circuit has characterized the quantum of suspicion necessary under the first prong of *Terry* as "reasonable suspicion, based on specific and articulable facts, of unlawful conduct." As we have also said, "the concept of reasonable suspicion is not susceptible to precise definition." Nevertheless, it is clear that "some minimal level of objective justification" is required, and that "inchoate suspicion or mere hunch" will not suffice. Reasonable suspicion is an objective standard; hence, the subjective intentions or motives of the officer making the stop are irrelevant.

The evidence before Judge Baer at the second hearing.—At the second hearing, Judge Baer was able to hear the testimony of Sergeant Bentley, the officer in charge on the morning of Bayless's arrest. Sergeant Bentley and Officer Carroll testified that several factors combined to make them suspicious of Bayless: (1) she was out at an early hour (5 a.m.); (2) her car had out-of-state license plates; (3) she was spotted driving slowly and double-parking; (4) the neighborhood where she was observed, Washington Heights, was known for drug activity; (5) at least one of the men who loaded the trunk ran away from the scene upon observing the police officers; and (6) the men loading the car did so very quickly and in an "orchestrated" fashion, and had no conversation or interaction with Bayless. Judge Baer, at the second hearing, credited the testimony of Sergeant Bentley, which corroborated the earlier testimony of Officer Carroll. Accordingly, we must decide whether these factors, to which Sergeant Bentley testified, taken together, provided "a particularized and objective basis for suspecting" Bayless of a crime.

The factors invoked by the police to justify their stop of Bayless vary in their weightiness, that is, their salience to the question whether crime is afoot. Standing alone, some of these factors would be innocuous, and some perhaps even inappropriate. The final factor—the strange behavior of the men who loaded the duffel bags into the trunk of her car—however, is itself an appropriate and weighty factor. The speed with which the men loaded the bags into the trunk and dissociated themselves from the car, together with the absence of any communication between the driver and the men, provide a specific basis for the police officers' suspicion that they were witnessing an illicit transaction that the participants did not want to prolong.

This weighty factor makes the case before us easy. In its presence, the sometimes innocuous factors such as the time of day and Bayless's out-of-state license plates take on added significance. When joined to the furtive loading of the car, they strengthen the likelihood of a drug transaction. Similarly, the men's odd behavior while loading the car makes factors such as the high-crime neighborhood and flight more significant.

Taken all together, the facts and circumstances relied on by the police were sufficient to give rise to reasonable suspicion. The *Terry* stop of Bayless's car was therefore warranted, and Judge Baer was not in error when he decided, after hearing all the evidence, that no Fourth Amendment violation had occurred.

The judgment of the district court is affirmed.

Whether Judge Baer in the *Bayless* case succumbed to political pressure may not ever be known. On one hand, he did reconsider and change his original decision shortly after being faced with intense public and political outcry. On the other, as discussed by the Court of Appeals, he refused to recuse himself immediately after the outcry, when a recusal could have been seen as capitulating to political pressure and thereby weakening perceptions of an independent judiciary. As he himself noted, "To be swayed by outside influence would run counter to the central theme of judicial independence."

Future Trends

Although American courts are stable institutions, they are regularly reinventing themselves in order to respond more effectively to the society they serve. In looking at the present with an eye to the future, several key issues will likely need to be addressed for courts to remain effective. Although not an exhaustive list, some central ones are as follows: (1) the continued effectiveness of the jury system, (2) court financing, (3) the use of technology, (4) alternative dispute resolution, and (5) access to justice (Flango et al., 2008).

Juries

Since the U.S. Supreme Court's ruling in *Batson v. Kentucky*, 476 U.S. 79, 106 S. Ct. 1712 (1986), that race could not be used as a factor in the selection of juries, many courts have increased their focus on the makeup, role, and workings of the American jury. This includes efforts to make the jury process more efficient and "user friendly." Jury satisfaction with the experience of jury service was traditionally low. By using such methods as phone or online check-in for jurors, increasing juror compensation, and mounting public education campaigns about the importance of jury service, courts have been able to increase satisfaction and improve understanding of the need for jury service.

Courts have also tried to increase efforts to have the jury pool better reflect the local community by using nondiscriminatory means of assembling and selecting from juror lists. Shorter terms of service require an increase in the number of jurors summoned and allow greater numbers of people to serve, and to want to serve, because of the more limited time commitment. Also, by allowing jurors to defer service rather than requiring them to serve at a particular time that may be extremely disruptive to their lives, greater numbers of jurors from all walks of life have been able to serve. Moreover, limitations on the use of race- and gender-based peremptory challenges have led to greater numbers and diversity of individuals serving on juries. It is estimated that only 6% of the population had ever served on a jury in 1977; 29% had served by 2004 (Munsterman, 2008).

In addition, courts have been able to improve jury decision making by using educational methods to encourage retention and understanding by jurors of presentation of information at trial. A law review article addressing the topic and a statewide study of the jury system in Arizona led to changes in trial procedures that have since been adopted in many states (Munsterman, 2008). These include allowing juror note taking, written questions for witnesses, increased discussion among jurors before deliberation on a verdict, and the use of additional evidence or argument when a jury is deadlocked (Munsterman, 2008).

Financing the Courts

Like all government agencies, the courts, both state and federal, depend on public budgets funded largely by tax revenue; therefore, during periods of recession, when state or federal budgets suffer, so too do those of the courts. It may be that economy-proof financing of courts will never be possible, but it is difficult for courts to keep pace with society without adequate funding. The judicial branch is beholden to the legislative branch for its funding; other than asking for money through budget requests and otherwise informing the legislature, the judiciary has no power to fund itself.

Because the largest portion of judicial branch budgets goes toward personnel costs, these are the first that must be limited during economic downturns, through salary reductions, hiring freezes, layoffs, and delaying the implementation of new programs and services. The latter is particularly problematic because it has been the courts' ability to experiment with innovative programs, such as specialized problem-solving courts and court-annexed mediation services, that has helped courts to find more effective means of resolving problems. One solution to funding problems has been to require or increase user fees for court services; however, there is concern that this would create a system of courts that many would be unable to afford.

It is of interest that one of Judge Liotti's complaints in the *Quiroga-Puma* case was the inadequacy of funding for security measures, noting that a metal detector costs upward of $30,000. The costs of even well-established technologies are not low, and even reasonable measures to ensure courtroom security may pose a problem for publicly funded courts.

Compensation of Judges

For most judges, compensation is not a primary reason why they join the judiciary. Even the highest paid federal judge, the Chief Justice of the U.S. Supreme Court, earns less than the typical lawyer practicing in any of the large law firms in the country. Nonetheless, in order to attract and retain the best judges, particularly as judges retire and new ones must fill their seats, compensation must be reasonably set and at least keep pace with inflation. In 2007, the average salary for state court judges in courts of general jurisdiction was $130,533 (Kauder & Davis, 2008). Salaries for federal District Court judges in 2008 were $169,300. Although this may seem like significant compensation to the average person, it must be remembered that, in terms of training, experience, and the requirements of the job they perform, neither state nor federal judges can be considered average government workers.

Chief Justice John Roberts has called the problem of judicial compensation a "constitutional crisis that threatens to undermine the strength and independence of the federal judiciary," and various organizations, such as the Brookings Institution and the American College of Trial Lawyers have recognized the importance of fairly compensating judges (American College of Trial Lawyers, 2007; Roberts, 2007). The Chief Justice has pointed out that 60% of federal judges now come from public sector jobs, not the practicing bar. Fifty years ago that figure was 40% (Roberts, 2007). As desirable as being a judge may seem, it should not be the domain of only the wealthy, for whom compensation does not matter, or those for whom a judgeship represents a promotion with a higher salary (Roberts, 2007).

The problem of compensation is not limited to judges. Court personnel, too, have fallen behind in compensation, especially at the state level as budgets have shrunk. In particular, as courts come to rely to an increasing extent on technology and computer-based systems, the expertise to operate and maintain these systems increases, requiring higher pay in a competitive marketplace.

Changes in Technology

As in most areas of life, technology has changed the operation of court systems in significant ways. Not only has it made the paper-driven business of the courts more streamlined, but it has advanced the effectiveness of courts in important ways.

Technology in place in many courts has moved beyond case management systems and computer-based transcription services. Today, document imaging, electronic filing, and video systems in the courtroom are commonplace. In addition to greater ease in accomplishing everyday tasks, the effect of such technologies has been to rewrite rules of courtroom and practice procedure. Courts now have websites, with detailed information of the court, its judges and staff, and often the availability of forms in specific practice areas. They also provide access to court records online, including pleadings, case reports, statutes and other laws, and the ability to search these databases with relative ease. Online payment of traffic citations is widespread.

Courts have largely embraced new technologies, especially as caseloads have risen. The only real limitation has been funding. The newest computer and software technology is the most costly, and the expense of updating or replacing record-keeping and other systems as they become obsolete and are replaced with newer, more effective technologies is significant (Walker, 2008).

There are numerous recognized and realized benefits to technological improvements in the courts, some of which have been mentioned here previously. These include paper-on-demand traffic citation systems, electronic court records, the development of e-courts, and greater information sharing. Further technology has assisted courts in handling specific legal problems in ways unimaginable not long ago. For example, courts in Indiana have used computer-based systems to address domestic violence, drunk driving, police officer safety, and child support collection (Shepard, 2008). For example, in that state, police officers have 24/7 access to protective orders from their patrol cars to improve their onsite decision-making capabilities. Similarly, officers use hand-held bar code scanners to scan a driver's license and produce traffic citations in minutes. License suspensions for drunk drivers are now nearly immediate because of electronic delivery of arrest information to the bureau of motor vehicles from the officer at the scene. In addition, litigants in divorce cases are now able to calculate child support amounts online, saving time in court and promoting early settlement of cases. State court websites also offer webcasts of information of interest to the public, such as jury service and child custody, in order to increase public access to the courts and public awareness of its activities (Shepard, 2008). Courts are just beginning to understand the myriad ways in which new technology can expedite their work.

Alternative Dispute Resolution

Alternatives to court involvement in order to resolve disputes, until recently, have largely been handled outside of the court setting with little or no court involvement. With the growth in the number of court case filings and its strain on resources, courts now play a more active role in encouraging out-of-court settlements. The most common methods of alternative dispute resolutions are mediation and arbitration.

Mediation is a proceeding in which parties are brought together before a mediator, who is a person trained to help people find a middle ground in their disputes. The process usually involves the opportunity for each party to present his or her version of the dispute to the mediator in the presence of the other party. The parties may or may not be represented by counsel, depending on their preferences and that of the mediator. There is no evidence presented at the mediation, although the parties may submit documentation to the mediator along with written statements of their case before the mediation. The mediator then meets with each party individually to help each party understand the strengths and weaknesses of his or her position and to suggest ways in which an impasse might be avoided. The process is an informal one, in which the parties may confide in the mediator or in which the mediator may cajole or encourage a certain course of action by either or both parties in order to reach a conclusion acceptable to each. If successful, the mediation will result in a settlement agreement between the parties.

Arbitration is a more formal process, with some of the hallmarks of a trial, usually with opening and closing statements, the examination and cross-examination of witnesses, and the presentation of evidence; however, the arbitrator is a more active participant in the process, questioning witnesses and the parties. The arbitrator does not, however, discuss the case individually with the parties in an attempt to help them reach a settlement. Although settlement may always be a goal, it is not the purpose of arbitration. The purpose of arbitration is to obtain a final resolution from the arbitrator, which is why in most cases arbitration is binding on the parties.

As effective as mediation or arbitration may be, there are some cases in which they are not. For example, cases involving complex questions of law or cases involving divorce or child support issues cannot be mediated or arbitrated. Some states have explored using private hired judges to decide cases. Particularly in jurisdiction in which it may take years to bring a case to trial, the use of private judges has appeal to some litigants, especially in business matters, where a quick resolution is essential. For example, California has experimented with allowing the use of private judges to render a binding decision and allowing the decision to be appealed to the state appellate courts if necessary. Rhode Island passed the Retired Justice Trial Act, which allows judges who are retired from state service to be hired by parties wishing to have their case heard before the retired judge.

Access to Justice

In criminal cases, the government must provide a lawyer to defendants who are unable to afford one. The same is not true in civil cases. Access to justice refers to the inability to obtain legal services by those of limited means in civil matters, such as a collection case for defaulting on a loan, a landlord/tenant dispute, a divorce, or an employment problem. Although contingency fees collected by lawyers usually allow injured people who could not otherwise afford a lawyer to pursue a legal claim for damages, such fees are not normally used in other types of cases. Thus, for many people, not just those who are impoverished, the payment of legal fees is a hurdle that cannot be overcome, and those people are left to suffer the consequences of their inability to seek legal advice.

There are ongoing efforts spearheaded by the courts, lawyers associations, nonprofit organizations, and government agencies to remedy this growing problem. The first "legal aid society" was established in New York in 1876 to provide legal services to German immigrants. Since that time, every state has a legal aid society or referral service so that the poor have access to legal services. Legal aid societies are funded by state, federal, and private grants and donations and are staffed by attorneys who are paid minimal amounts or who donate their time *pro bono*, which means "for the public good." Many states have adopted rules of professional conduct suggesting that lawyers have an ethical responsibility to provide legal services to those who cannot afford them. In addition, as part of their legal training, many law students, with the encouragement of the judiciary, are able to work in legal clinics usually run by law schools under the supervision of law professors and members of the bar. Although these efforts help, they have by no means solved the problem of representation for the poor because the number of people in need of legal services outpaces the ability to provide them each year.

When individuals are unable to afford a lawyer and cannot obtain pro bono representation, they often resort to self-representation. Self-representation means just that an individual serves as his or her own lawyer. Neither the law nor the courts prevent self-representation, and by some estimates, over half of the litigants appearing in court represent themselves (Bladow & Johnson, 2008). This creates some problems for courts in a system that is based upon knowledge of the procedural rules and substantive law, neither of which most self-represented litigants possess. Because it is necessary for judges to remain impartial, it is difficult for them to provide too much assistance to a self-represented party whose pleadings are unclear or who misunderstands the proper introduction of evidence at trial.

Courts have begun to introduce more "user-friendly" features in their operations in order to make it easier for people to represent themselves fairly and properly while taking some of the burden from judges and court staff to remain neutral. Some states have taken a courthouse "booth" approach, in which attorneys or paralegals volunteer to staff the courthouse location where litigants can walk up to obtain on-the-spot advice or legal forms. In at least a dozen states, courts have made legal forms available online or introduced document-assembly software that allows an unsophisticated user to complete forms and pleadings step by step (Bladow & Johnson, 2008). This makes the process less of an exercise in frustration for either the litigant or the court.

Another initiative to assist self-represented individuals is through training of judges to understand better how to structure a court proceeding to make it understandable for self-represented litigants (Zorza, 2008). The goal is to facilitate communication during a proceeding so that the self-represented litigant feels that the court has been fair and the judge has some tools to better deal with such parties. Efforts like these serve to maintain court efficiencies and allow those who traditionally have not had access to the courts to have satisfaction that their claims have been heard and to build a greater degree of confidence in the American system of justice.

Key Terms

Social Change	Court Financing
Policy Making	Judicial Compensation
Statutory Ambiguity	Technology
Dynamic Interpretation	Alternative Dispute
Plain Meaning	Resolution
Litigation Explosion	Access to Justice
Political Pressure	Pro Bono
Jury Effectiveness	

Discussion Questions

1. How do courts sometimes become instruments of social change?
2. In what ways do decisions by courts affect public policy?
3. What is meant by "judicial activism?" What is the effect of activist judges on the courts?
4. What is the relationship between judicial restraint and the separation of powers?
5. What is statutory or constitutional ambiguity? What approaches do courts take to resolve ambiguity when interpreting the law?
6. In what ways have changes in American society had an effect on the courts?
7. What are five issues that will likely affect the operation of American courts in the future?

Cases

Batson v. Kentucky, 476 U.S. 79, 106 S. Ct. 1712 (1986).
Brown v. Board of Education, 347 U.S. 483, 74 S. Ct. 686, 98 L.Ed. 873 (1954).
Bush v. Gore, 531 U.S. 98, 121 S. Ct. 525, 148 L.Ed.2d 388 (2000).
Goodridge v. Department of Public Health, 440 Mass. 309, 798 N.E.2d 941 (2003).
Michigan v. Long, 463 U.S. 1032, 1067, 103 S. Ct. 3469, 77 L.Ed.2d 1201 (1983).
People v. Quiroga-Puma, 18 Misc.3d 1130(A), 859 N.Y.S.2d 897 (N.Y. Just. Ct. 2008).
Roe v. Wade, 410 U.S. 113, 93 S. Ct. 705, 35 L.Ed.2d 147 (1973).
U.S. v. Bayless, 201 F.3d 116 (2d Cir. 2000).

Criminal Justice on the Web

 For an up-to-date list of Web links, go to *The American Courts: A Procedural Approach* online companion site at http://criminal justice.jbpub.com/AmericanCourts. The online companion site will introduce you to some of the most important sites for finding American courts information on the Internet.

References

American College of Trial Lawyers. (2007). *Judicial Compensation: Our Federal Judges Must Be Fairly Paid (White Paper)*. Irvine, CA: American College of Trial Lawyers.

Bladow, K., & Johnson, C. (2008). Access to justice. In C. R. Flango, A. M. McDowell, C. F. Campbell, & N. B. Kauder (Eds.), *Future Trends in State Courts 2008*. Williamsburg, VA: National Center for State Courts.

Editorial. (2007). Judge Liotti legislates. *New York Post*, December 26, 2007, p. 30.

Flango, C. R., McDowell, A. M., Campbell, C. F., & Kauder, N. B. (Eds.). (2008). *Future Trends in State Courts 2008*. Williamsburg, VA: National Center for State Courts.

Johnson, M. D. (2007). The litigation explosion, proposed reforms, and their consequences. *Brigham Young University Journal of Public Law, 21,* 179–207.

Kauder, N. B., & Davis, P. K. (2008). Judicial compensation. In C. R. Flango, A. M. McDowell, C. F. Campbell, & N. B. Kauder (Eds.), *Future Trends in State Courts 2008*. Williamsburg, VA.: National Center for State Courts.

Munsterman, G. T. (2008). Jury systems. In C. R. Flango, A. M. McDowell, C. F. Campbell, & N. B. Kauder (Eds.), *Future Trends in State Courts 2008*. Williamsburg, VA: National Center for State Courts.

Murphy, W. F., Pritchett, C. H., Epstein, L., & Knight, J. (2006). *Courts, Judges, & Politics: An Introduction to the Judicial Process* (6th ed.). New York: McGraw-Hill.

Roberts, J. (2007). *2006 Year-End Report on the Federal Judiciary*. Washington, DC: U.S. Supreme Court.

Sanderson, B. (2007). Judge gives alien pass on license. *New York Post*, December 21, 2007, p. 19.

Shepard, R. T. (2008). Indiana court technology is about service, not bytes and bandwidth. In C. R. Flango, A. M. McDowell, C. F. Campbell, & N. B. Kauder (Eds.), *Future Trends in State Courts 2008*. Williamsburg, VA: National Center for State Courts.

Walker, L. (2008). Technology. In C. R. Flango, A. M. McDowell, C. F. Campbell, & N. B. Kauder (Eds.), *Future Trends in State Courts 2008*. Williamsburg, VA: National Center for State Courts.

Zorza, R. (2008). New curriculum helps improve access for the self-represented. In C. R. Flango, A. M. McDowell, C. F. Campbell, & N. B. Kauder (Eds.), *Future Trends in State Courts 2008*. Williamsburg, VA: National Center for State Courts.

Glossary

A

Abstention   The doctrine that requires federal courts to "abstain" or refuse to hear cases that primarily involve state matters.

Abuse of discretion   The most deferential standard of review by an appellate court, in which the appellate court will set aside a trial court's findings only if they are arbitrary, capricious, or have no reasonable justification.

Acceptance   An indication by a person to whom an offer is made that they agree to be bound by the offered terms, forming a "meeting of the minds."

Access to justice   The availability of legal services for the poor.

Activist judges   Judges whose decisions are intended to substitute for that of the legislature.

Actus Reus   From the Latin, "wrongful act," an element of crime that requires proof of a defendant's behavior.

Adequate and independent state grounds   The basis for a state court's decision that will prevent the U.S. Supreme Court from setting aside its decision because a state's court of last resort is the final arbiter of state law that does not involve a federal question.

Adjudication   A hearing in which a juvenile court makes a determination of whether a juvenile is delinquent.

Adoption   The acquisition of parental rights over a child not naturally born to a person.

Adversarial system   A system of justice in which the opposing interests of the parties allow an independent decision maker to determine the truth and, consequently, the correct outcome.

Adverse   Referring to the opposing positions of the parties in a civil or criminal case, and their legal and factual positions.

Advice and consent   The requirement found in Article II, Section 2 of the Constitution that the President's power to appoint judges and other officials is limited by Senate action.

Affidavit   A sworn statement.

Affirmative defenses   Defenses raised in response to a civil or criminal complaint that allege additional facts or legal positions.

Alternative dispute resolution   Ways in which disputes may be resolved with minimal or no need for court intervention, such as mediation, arbitration, and plea bargaining.

Amicus curiae   From the Latin, "friend of the court"; this refers to the filing of an appellate brief by a person or organization not a party to a case, in order to inform the court on some issue of law.

Ancillary jurisdiction   A form of jurisdiction that allows a court to make all decisions and assert all powers necessary to exercise its subject matter jurisdiction.

Answer   A civil defendant's response to a complaint.

Appellate jurisdiction   Authority of an appellate court to decide matters of law first raised in a trial court.

Arraignment   A pretrial hearing in which formal charges against the accused are read and a plea is entered.

Arrest   The seizure of a person by the government.

Arson   A common law crime involving the malicious burning of a dwelling in which another person lived.

Asportation   Carrying away of property or movement of it from one place to another.

Assault   A threat to injure another that the other person reasonably perceives to be threatening; commonly used interchangeably with battery.

Attendant circumstances   An element of some crimes that requires proof of certain circumstances existing at the time the prohibited behavior occurs.

Attenuation doctrine   The rule that allows use of tainted evidence at trial if its seizure was sufficiently removed from an illegally conducted search.

Attorney general   The chief legal officer of state government, who acts as representative to state agencies and enforces criminal and civil laws.

B

Bailment   Entrusting another with possession of personal property for a limited time for a specific purpose.

Battery   The unlawful touching of another.

Bench trial   A trial held before a judge, who decides issues of both fact and law.

Bill of Rights   The first 10 amendments to the United States Constitution, setting out the rights of individuals and the states with respect to the federal government.

Branches of government   The structure of the United States and each state government, consisting of separate functions for the legislative, executive, and judicial branches.

Bribery   Giving or receiving something of value in order to influence the actions of public officials.

Burden of proof   The party in a court case who is required to produce evidence sufficient to establish some fact.

Burglary   The common law crime of breaking and entering into the dwelling of another at night with the intent to commit a felony.

C

Capacity   The existence of legal authority and sufficient mental state to enter into a contract.

Capital punishment   The death penalty.

Caption   The heading of a case decision naming the parties, court, and date of the opinion.

Carnal knowledge   Sexual intercourse.

Case decision   A written opinion by a court that applies law to a set of facts in order to reach a binding conclusion.

Case law   The requirements of law found in the written decisions of judges.

Castle doctrine   The rule that a person, while in his or her own home, may use force (in some jurisdictions deadly force) in defense of persons or property.

Causation   A requirement in a negligence action to show that a breach of duty by a defendant resulted in harm to the plaintiff; an element of crime that requires proof that a defendant's act resulted in harm.

Cause of action   The factual and legal basis for a plaintiff's claim in a civil case.

Caveat emptor   From the Latin, "let the buyer beware"; the law imposes a duty on sellers, not buyers, to beware of defective products found in the stream of commerce.

Certification   An avenue of appeal to the U.S. Supreme Court in which a lower federal appellate court "certifies" a question of law it feels unable to decide; this procedure is never used. More generally, certification refers to the process in which a lower state court or a federal trial court asks a state supreme court to answer a question of first impression.

Certiorari   From the Latin "to make more certain"; this is the process by which the U.S. Supreme Court accepts cases to hear.

Character witness   A witness who testifies as to the character of a party or another witness.

Child savers   A progressive movement of the late 1800s that advocated the use of reformatories and governmental control of wayward and delinquent children, as well as court intervention in such cases.

Child support   Money paid, usually by court order following divorce, for the care and upbringing of children.

Civil law   The branch of law involving the protection of private, individual interests.

Civil procedure   Procedural law and rules governing manner in which civil cases may be brought to trial.

Civil rights   Rights protected by constitution or statute for which compensation may be obtained when violated by the government.

Civil union   A legal mechanism in a small number of states that allows same-sex couples to have their relationships recognized under law.

Commingling   The merging of a spouse's separate property with community property during marriage such that it can no longer be identified as separate and is considered to be marital property.

Common law   Decisions made by judges in past cases that comprise recognized principles of law to be applied in future cases.

Common law marriage   Marriage recognized in some states in which a man and woman live together and hold themselves out as husband and wife, despite not having satisfied the formalities of a marriage agreement under statutory law.

Community-based sanctions   A disposition option for juveniles involving restitution or community service.

Community property   Property acquired during a marriage by either spouse in which each spouse is considered to own 50% of the property.

Community service   A sentencing option in which an offender is required to engage in activities beneficial to the local community.

Complaint   A document filed with a court to begin formal criminal or civil proceedings.

Concurrence   An element of crime that requires proof of the co-occurrence of a defendant's wrongful act and intent to commit a crime.

Concurrent jurisdiction   The authority of more than one court to decide a particular type of case.

Concurring opinion   A separate opinion in a case written by an appellate judge who agrees with the court's decision but for different reasons.

Consideration   Something of value exchanged by the parties to a contract in order to secure their respective promises.

Constitutional courts   Federal courts created under the authority of Article III of the Constitution.

Constitutional law   The requirements of law found in federal or state constitutions.

Continuance   An order from a court extending the deadline for trial.

Contraband   Any item the possession of which is prohibited by law, such as unprescribed, scheduled drugs.

Contracts   Legal agreements between two or more parties consisting of an offer, acceptance, and consideration.

Corpus delicti   From the Latin, "body of the crime"; the existence of evidence that a crime was committed.

Corrective justice   A form of justice that relates to the manner in which individuals who violate the law should be punished.

Counterclaim   A claim made against a plaintiff by a defendant in the same lawsuit filed by the plaintiff and pertaining to matters alleged in that lawsuit.

Court   A tribunal or institution in which parties may submit their disputes for decision.

Court characteristics   Aspects of a court affecting its jurisdiction, operation, or decision making.

Court financing   An issue that affects the nature and extent of court operations and the future of the justice system.

Court of equity   Traditionally, a court in which cases were decided by a judge who could fashion a remedy other than monetary damages. Today, nearly all U.S. courts may grant both monetary and equitable relief.

Court of last resort   The last court to which an appeal may be taken, usually named a "supreme" court.

Court of law   Traditionally, a court in which cases were decided by judge or jury where the remedy was monetary damages. Today, nearly all U.S. courts may grant both monetary and equitable relief.

Court of record   A court in which all proceedings before the court are recorded and a transcript is produced.

Courtroom work group   The term given to the group of participants in criminal cases involved in the handling of a case, including the judge, prosecutor, defense attorney, and court staff.

Coverture   Traditionally, the condition of a woman during marriage in which she obtains protection from the world by her husband.

Crimes against morality   The category of criminal behavior that involves behavior considered by society to be immoral, such as prostitution.

Crimes against property   The category of criminal behavior that involves the theft or destruction of property.

Crimes against public order   The category of criminal behavior that involves behavior disruptive to an orderly society, such as disorderly conduct or fighting.

Crimes against the person   The category of criminal behavior that results in harm to a person.

Criminal law   The branch of law used to enforce compliance with social norms by specifying prohibited behaviors and the punishment for their occurrence, as well as the processes that must be followed before punishment may be imposed.

Critical legal theory   The theory of law that views the purpose of law as a mechanism for producing social change.

Cross-claim   A claim against a co-defendant by a defendant in the same lawsuit filed by the plaintiff and pertaining to matters alleged in that lawsuit.

Cross-examination   Questioning of an adverse witness after direct examination has occurred in order to impeach, discredit, limit, or elicit additional facts from a witness.

Curtilage   The area and buildings immediately surrounding a home.

Custody   Primary physical responsibility for the care and upbringing of children.

D

Damages   The measure of harm determined to be caused by a defendant in a civil case.

De novo review   Independent review by an appellate court of decisions about the law made by a trial judge, giving no deference to the conclusions of law the trial judge made.

Default judgment   A judgment entered on behalf of a party, usually as a result of the adverse party's failure to comply with procedural rules.

Defendant   The party alleged to have caused the plaintiff harm in a civil case or alleged to have violated criminal law in a criminal case.

Delinquent   A designation given to minors who are adjudicated to have violated the law.

Deposition   A discovery method in which a party or witness is questioned under oath and a transcript of the proceeding is produced for use at or before trial.

Determinate sentencing   A form of sentencing that requires judges to impose a presumptive sentence within a specified range.

Deterrence   The philosophy that punishment should be used to deter wrongdoers from re-offending and to deter others from offending.

Direct examination   Questioning of a witness favorable to a party, usually a witness who has been called by that party.

Direct file   A method of transfer from juvenile to adult court in which a prosecutor has discretion to file charges against a juvenile in adult court, provided that certain criteria are met.

Discovery   The process of developing facts and evidence that may be used at trial.

Disorderly conduct   Any behavior that disturbs the quiet, orderly conduct of people's lives and their affairs.

Disposition   The outcome of a case heard in juvenile court.

Dispute resolution   The process of resolving disputes between parties, whether by a court decision or agreement between the parties.

Dissenting opinion   A separate opinion in a case written by an appellate judge who disagrees with the decision of a majority of the court's members.

Distributive justice   A form of justice that involves the manner in which the benefits of membership in a society are allocated among its members.

District attorney   A state prosecutor with responsibility for prosecuting crime within a specified district usually defined by state statute, such as a county.

Diversion   Removal of a juvenile from formal processing in the juvenile justice system, thus preventing a juvenile court appearance.

Diversity jurisdiction   Federal court authority to decide matters involving parties from more than one state.

Divorce   The legal process for dissolution of a marriage.

Documentary evidence   Documents introduced at trial to prove a fact.

Dual system of government   The arrangement whereby both federal and state authority exists together; one result of this arrangement is the side-by-side operation of both federal and state courts.

Due process   Procedures that courts have determined are required by the U.S. Constitution before an accused may be tried or convicted of crime.

Dynamic interpretation   A method of statutory interpretation that views laws as changeable over time; thus, what a statute meant at the time it was written may differ from its current meaning.

E

Economic analysis of law   The theory of law that views legal rules as influencing individual behavior and how legal rules may be structured to affect behavior.

Economic justice   A form of justice that focuses on the access to and distribution of economic resources among people.

Embezzlement   The wrongful taking of property by one to whom it was entrusted.

En banc   A decision by all appellate judges sitting on a court, rather than a smaller panel.

Equitable distribution   The rule that property owned by spouses during marriage be divided fairly and equitably on divorce.

Evidence   The use of testimony, documents, or physical things at trial to prove facts.

Excessive force   The use of an unreasonable amount of force to effectuate an arrest.

Exclusionary rule   A rule of procedure preventing the introduction at trial of any evidence resulting from an illegal search or seizure.

Exclusive jurisdiction   The sole authority of a court to hear a particular type of case, to the exclusion of other courts.

Excuses   A category of defenses to crime in which a defendant was prevented from controlling his or her actions as a result of mental incapacity (such as insanity) or the circumstances in which the act occurred (such as duress).

Exigent circumstances   An exception to the requirement of a warrant, used in the investigation of a serious crime when there is danger of destruction of evidence or fleeing of a person sought.

Expert witness   A witness with specialized knowledge of some relevant matter who testifies in order to assist the trier of fact.

Extradition The process through which a criminal defendant may be brought to a court to stand trial when the defendant is found in an area outside of the court's geographic jurisdiction.

Eyewitness A witness who testifies as to what he or she saw or heard.

F

Fact witness A witness who testifies as to the occurrence of relevant facts.

Facts The circumstances and incidents involving the parties that are taken to be true and to which the law is applied by a court to reach a conclusion.

False imprisonment A crime in which a person's freedom is restricted against his or her will.

False pretenses A form of theft in which property is taken from its owner through deceit; fraud.

Federal courts Courts created pursuant to federal law whose jurisdiction involves federal matters.

Federal question A central requirement for federal court jurisdiction; a case must involve federal law before it may be heard by a federal court.

Federalism The concept of shared authority reflected in the dual system of government and courts in the United States, in which state authority is sovereign with respect to state matters.

Federalist Papers A series of newspaper articles written in the late 1700s to gain public support for the country's new Constitution and form of government.

Felony A serious crime resulting in incarceration for 1 year or more.

Final judgment rule A rule of procedure that creates a right to appeal only when a trial court issues a final decision that ends the litigation and the trial court has nothing more to do but execute the judgment.

Fine A monetary punishment for the commission of crime or violations of law.

First impression The consideration of an issue of law by a court for the first time.

Foreseeability A test for proximate cause by examining whether a reasonable person would have foreseen that his or her actions would result in harm.

Formality The requirement that the authority of law is based on its lack of vagueness (specificity), its ability to address fully the topics to which it applies (comprehensiveness), and the situations and processes through which it applies (applicability).

Fraud A form of theft in which property is taken from its owner through deceit; false pretenses.

Fruit of the poisonous tree An extension of the exclusionary rule that prevents the use in court of all evidence obtained indirectly from an illegally conducted search.

G

General deterrence A philosophy of punishment in which punishment should be used to deter others from committing the punished offense.

General jurisdiction Authority of trial courts to handle any case not specifically authorized for trial in a limited jurisdiction court.

General verdict A verdict issued by a jury in a civil case in which only the prevailing party and the amount of damages are given.

Geographic jurisdiction The boundaries within which a court may exercise authority (territorial jurisdiction).

Good faith exception An exception to the exclusionary rule that allows evidence obtained pursuant to a search warrant to be admitted at trial even if the warrant is later found to be invalid, as long as the officer conducting the search obtained the warrant in good faith and conducted the search within the scope of the warrant.

H

Habeas corpus From the Latin "produce the body," which is a procedure giving a prisoner the right to a hearing before a court in which the government must justify the prisoner's detention.

Habitual offender laws Statutes that allow for increased sentences for offenders who reoffend.

Harmless error A mistake made by the trial court that does not result in prejudice or harm to the party asserting its existence on appeal.

Holding The decision a court reaches regarding a legal issue presented in a case.

Homicide The killing of a human being by the act, omission, or procurement of another.

House of refuge An institution created in the early 1800s as part of a reform movement to improve the lives of delinquent children, which required hard work, maintained severe discipline, and taught minimal basic skills.

Hung jury The inability of a jury to reach a verdict.

I

In personam A form of jurisdiction in which a court has authority over some identifiable person.

In rem A form of personal jurisdiction that gives a court authority over some property, regardless of who may own it.

Incapacitation The philosophy in which punishment should be used to physically prevent wrongdoers from re-offending, such as by incarceration.

Incorrigible A minor who repeatedly commits delinquent acts.

Independent source doctrine The rule that allows admission of tainted evidence in court if it was also discovered or obtained from a source independent of an illegally conducted search.

Indeterminate sentencing A form of sentencing that gives judges the greatest discretion in sentencing an offender to incarceration for as much time as the judge deems appropriate, up to a maximum prescribed by statute.

Inevitable discovery doctrine An exception to the fruit of the poisonous tree doctrine that allows tainted evidence to be admitted at trial if the evidence would have been discovered if a constitutional violation had not occurred.

Initial appearance The first appearance by a criminal defendant before a judge in which an accused is given notice of the charges against him, counsel is appointed if the accused is not represented, and a determination of whether to release the accused pending trial or set bail is made.

Injunction A court order preventing a party from doing a particular thing.

Inquisitorial system A system of justice used in some countries in which a judge is actively involved in gathering evidence and determining the facts of a case in order to reach a decision.

Insanity   A legal term that allows a defense to criminal behavior as a result of mental incapacity.

Institutional commitment   The juvenile counterpart to incarceration, which may involve secure confinement or a lesser degree of security, depending on the seriousness of the offense.

Intake   The juvenile court process that involves the immediate decision by an intake officer about whether a juvenile should be released, diverted, or held for hearing before a juvenile judge.

Intermediate appellate court   Used in some states as the court to which an appeal of right may be taken.

Interrogation   The questioning of a suspect by a law enforcement officer.

Interrogatories   A discovery method in which written questions are formally served on one party by another.

Invitee   A person who has a legal right to be on the premises of another.

Issue   The question of law and its applicability a court is asked to decide.

J

Joint tenancy   A form of joint ownership of property in which the surviving tenant becomes the sole owner of the property on the death of the other joint owners.

Judge   An independent and objective decision maker who presides over hearings and trials.

Judgment notwithstanding the verdict   A judgment entered by a court in a civil case when a jury's verdict is so inconsistent with the evidence that injustice would result.

Judicial activism   A violation of the principle of separation of powers that occurs when judges' decisions have the effect of reinterpreting statutes or constitutions in ways unintended by the drafters.

Judicial appointment   The process by which a federal or state court judge is appointed to the bench, usually by the head of the Executive Branch of government.

Judicial compensation   The pay and benefits given to judges to compensate them for their work and encourage well-qualified lawyers to leave the practice of law for the bench.

Judicial discretion   The authority of judges to decide when, where, and how to apply the law.

Judicial review   The power of the judicial branch of government to examine and determine whether acts taken by the legislative and executive branches comply with the Constitution.

Judicial waiver   A method of transfer from juvenile to adult court in which a juvenile court judge makes the decision to waive jurisdiction over a case.

Jurisdiction   Authority of a court to make decisions and issue orders.

Jurisprudence   The study of law, its purpose, and application to society.

Jury   A 6- or 12-person group responsible for determining the facts of a case, finding in favor of one party based on the facts.

Jury effectiveness   The view that jury decision making is unpredictable and therefore possibly ineffective.

Justice   A concept that relates to ideas about morality and fairness. It encompasses the ideals of behavior toward others for which humans should strive, how people should treat each other, and how government should treat its citizens.

Justice of the peace   A lower-level judicial position in which members of a community can have simple legal matters heard and resolved.

Justice system   Institutions and procedures used to settle disputes between individuals or between the government and one or more of its citizens.

Justifications   A category of defenses to crime that make the defendant's conduct acceptable given the circumstances, such as self-defense.

Juvenile court   A court of limited jurisdiction which, in most states, has authority to hear cases relating to those under the age of 18 years.

K

Kidnapping   A crime in which a victim is confined by forceful means and moved from one location to another.

Knock and announce   The rule requiring police officers to knock at entry doors and announce their presence and intention to execute a search or arrest warrant.

Knowingly   A level of culpability under the Model Penal Code in which a defendant knows that his or her conduct could result in harm, even if the specific harm was not intended.

L

Larceny   Theft.

Law   Binding rules of action or conduct adopted by some controlling authority.

Law of the land   The U.S. Constitution and all federal laws and treaties established in accordance with it, as provided by Article VI of the U.S. Constitution.

Legal positivism   The theory of law that considers all law to be man-made, based on rules adopted by members of society that they believe to be necessary to govern themselves.

Legal realism   The theory of law that the function of law is case specific; applying clearly articulated legal rules to individual disputes or problems leads to clear and consistent results that are just.

Legislative courts   Federal courts created under the authority of Article I of the Constitution.

Legislative intent   The purpose of a legislature in passing a law, often used by courts to determine how a law should be interpreted when it is ambiguous.

Limited jurisdiction   Authority of some courts to handle specific types of cases, such as civil cases involving small claims and criminal cases involving lesser charges.

Lineups   Identification method in which a witness views several individuals along with a crime suspect at the same time in order to pick out the perpetrator of the crime.

Litigation explosion   The increase in the number and variety of cases courts are called on to resolve.

Loitering   Under the common law, remaining in a particular place without any reason for doing so.

Long-arm statute   A state statute that allows a civil defendant located in one state to be subject to the jurisdiction of another state court.

M

Magistrate judge   A federal judge appointed by the Chief Judge of a federal district who assists trial judges in handling hearings, discovery matters, conferences, and sometimes conducts trials.

Mala in se From the Latin, "evil in itself," a classification of behaviors criminalized because they are universally recognized as wrong.

Mala prohibita From the Latin, "evil because prohibited," a classification of behaviors criminalized because of a legislative determination that they are harmful to society.

Mandamus A court order directing a public official to perform some act that the official's public office requires the official to perform.

Mandatory sentencing A form of sentencing required by statute in which criminal defendants are required to serve a minimum number of years of incarceration when convicted of specified crimes.

Manslaughter Voluntary or involuntary homicide without malice aforethought.

Marital property Property acquired during a marriage owned by both spouses.

Marriage The legal mechanism reflecting an agreement by a man and woman to be together in a personal and social way. A small number of states have defined marriage as allowing such an agreement for same-sex couples.

Memorandum opinion A written opinion that sets out an appellate court's decision with little or no rationale.

Mens rea From the Latin, "guilty mind," an element of crime that requires proof of a defendant's intent to commit a crime.

Merit selection The process of selecting judicial candidates in which their qualifications are reviewed by a committee of judges, lawyers, and the public.

Minimum contacts The rule requiring sufficient contacts with a state before a civil defendant may be subject to its courts.

Misdemeanor A crime resulting in punishment of less than one year of incarceration.

Mistrial Termination of a trial due to its inability to be fairly conducted.

Motions Formal requests by a party that a court order some action to be taken by an adverse party.

N

Natural law The theory that law derives from nature or God, and that it therefore has a moral basis.

Negligence A breach of the standard of care of a reasonably prudent person, resulting in harm to another.

Negligently A level of culpability under the Model Penal Code in which a defendant acts in a way that creates a substantial risk of harm and is unaware that he or she is creating such a risk, even though a reasonable person would have been aware of the risk of harm.

Nonpartisan judicial elections Elections for a judge in which the candidates may not identify themselves with a political party.

Notice pleading A simplified manner of pleading that requires only that a plaintiff in a civil case gives a defendant fair notice of the factual and legal basis for his or her claims.

Nullification A jury verdict reached in a criminal case that appears to be in contrast to the evidence.

O

Objectivity Unbiased decision making based on facts, uninfluenced by the personal opinions or feelings of the decision maker.

Obscenity Any material showing sexual conduct that appeals to a prurient interest in sex, is patently offensive, and lacks literary, artistic, political, or scientific value.

Obstruction of justice Any act that interferes with the processes of criminal justice.

Offer A willingness to enter into an agreement expressed by a party to another in which the terms of the agreement are clear.

On the merits Consideration by a court of the full record of proceedings in order to reach a decision in a case.

Open fields doctrine The rule that allows law enforcement searches on any open land, even if privately owned, as long as it is not within the curtilage.

Opinion of the court A written decision by an appellate court in which a majority of the judges sitting on the court hearing the case agreed as to what the conclusion should be.

Orbiter dicta From the Latin "remark by the way," which refers to comments made by a judge in a written opinion that are not part of the rationale of the case or necessary to the holding.

Order A directive by a court.

Original jurisdiction The power of a court to hear a case in the first instance.

P

Parens patriae From the Latin, "parent of the country," the concept that the government has the power to intervene in the lives of children when natural parents are unable or unwilling to "control" their children.

Parol evidence rule A rule of contractual interpretation that allows a court to rely on evidence extrinsic to the contract in order to determine its meaning.

Per curiam opinion An anonymous decision by an appellate court that reflects the view of the court regarding the appropriate disposition of a case.

Peremptory challenge A rule that allows a party to excuse a limited number of prospective jurors from a case for any reason except the prospective juror's race or gender.

Performance Doing whatever a contract requires.

Perjury A false statement made under oath in a judicial proceeding with the intent to deceive.

Personal jurisdiction A form of jurisdiction in which a court has authority over a person. Generally, a court has personal jurisdiction over all persons in its geographic area.

Personal property Any property that is not real property.

Petition In the juvenile justice context, a formal document alleging that a juvenile is delinquent.

Physical evidence Physical objects introduced at trial to prove a fact (e.g., a bloody shirt).

Plain error A mistake made by the trial court, whether preserved for appeal or not, that results in reversal of the outcome because of the fundamental unfairness to one of the parties at trial.

Plain meaning A method of statutory interpretation in which the words of a statute must be given their common meaning in order to avoid ambiguity.

Plain view doctrine An exception to the warrant requirement that allows police officers to seize evidence that an officer can see as long as the officer is lawfully in a position to see the items.

Plaintiff The party who files a lawsuit in a civil case.

Plea A criminal defendant's response to a grand jury indictment. A defendant may plead guilty, not guilty, nolo contendere (no contest), or remain silent (resulting in a not guilty plea).

Plea bargain   An agreement between a prosecutor and a criminal defendant in which the defendant pleads guilty to some crime, in exchange for a lower sentence recommendation.

Pleading   Documents filed with a court that comply with rules of procedure and that serve a particular purpose that advances the litigation in accordance with those rules.

Plurality opinion   An opinion of an appellate court in which less than a majority of the court's members agree about the reasons for the court's decision.

Policy making   The effect of judicial decisions by activist judges.

Political pressure   The effects of the political process and political maneuvering on courts.

Pornography   Sexually explicit material.

Possession   The passive act of actually or constructively controlling contraband.

Precedent   The rule that requires judges to apply legal principles from prior cases to decide current cases.

Preliminary hearing   A pretrial hearing in which a judge determines whether probable cause exists to support the formal charges against the defendant.

Premarital agreement   An agreement between a couple prior to marriage that defines property and other rights during the marriage and in the event of divorce.

Premises liability   A negligence-based action that holds the owner of unsafe premises liable when an invitee is injured while on the premises.

Preserved for appeal   The requirement that an appellate court may address only legal issues that a party at trial has brought to the trial court's attention, by objection or otherwise.

Presumption of innocence   A central tenant of the criminal justice system in which no person is considered guilty of a crime unless and until the government produces evidence beyond a reasonable doubt to establish guilt.

Pretrial conference   Any conference between the parties, their attorneys, or the judge in a civil case in which matters pertaining to trial are resolved and documented by court order.

Preventive detention   Incarceration of a juvenile pending an adjudication hearing in order to prevent him or her from committing further delinquent acts.

Prima facie   From the Latin "on its face"; usually referring to the sufficiency of allegations made in a civil complaint.

Pro bono   Free legal services provided by volunteer lawyers.

Pro se   From the Latin "for oneself"; the term used when a person represents himself in court.

Probable cause   Facts and circumstances that would lead a reasonable person to believe that a crime has been committed or is about to be committed or that contraband may be found in a particular place.

Probate exception   The exception to federal jurisdiction that prevents federal courts from determining the distribution of assets upon death, traditionally an exclusive state matter.

Probation   A suspended sentence of incarceration in which a defendant is released with conditions, usually including regular meetings with a probation officer and no subsequent arrests.

Procedural justice   A form of justice that considers fairness in terms of whether a person views the procedures used to resolve a dispute are fair.

Procedural law   The law of procedure that specifies how the substantive law applies.

Procedure   The process through which a court considers evidence and arguments in order to reach a decision.

Property   Something tangible or intangible subject to an ownership interest.

Prosecutor   The lawyer representing the government in a criminal case.

Prostitution   The exchange of sexual relations for money.

Protective order   An order by a court to prevent disclosure of certain information, usually during the course of discovery.

Purposely   A level of culpability under the Model Penal Code in which a defendant specifically intends a harmful result.

R

Rape shield law   The law of many states that prohibits or limits the use of evidence of a victim's prior sexual behavior in sexual assault cases.

Ratio decidendi   The Latin term that means "reason for deciding" and refers to the reasoning used by a court to reach a decision.

Rationale   The reasoning upon which a court's decision is based.

Recklessly   A level of culpability under the Model Penal Code in which a defendant knows that there is a substantial and unjustifiable risk that his or her behavior may result in harm.

Regulatory law   Rules found in regulations adopted by agencies of the executive branch of government.

Rehabilitation   The philosophy that punishment should be designed to reform offenders so that they can become productive members of society.

Relevant evidence   Evidence that increases the likelihood of proving or disproving a material fact.

Religion and law   The view that law and justice share with religion a moral focus, where concern for the individual is central.

Request for admissions   A discovery method in which a party requests that an opposing party admit the truth of certain facts in a case.

Request for production of documents   A discovery method in which a party seeks to obtain documents or tangible things in the possession of another party.

Res ipsa loquitur   From the Latin, "the thing speaks for itself"; a test for causation in the law of torts in which the only possible cause of a plaintiff's harm is the defendant's action.

Restorative justice   A form of justice in which offenders are required to consider the effects of their criminal offenses on victims and seeks to restore the offender to society by addressing those effects.

Restraining order   A court order preventing a person from having contact with another.

Retribution   The punishment philosophy that offenders should be punished because they deserve it, and society is entitled to revenge against the wrongdoer.

Retributive justice   A form of justice that specifies that those who act in ways harmful to others deserve to be punished in accordance with the seriousness of their offense.

Reverse waiver   A process through which a juvenile whose case was subject to direct file in criminal court may seek to have the case transferred to juvenile court.

Reversible error   A mistake made by the trial court that results in reversal of the outcome because of the fundamental unfairness to one of the parties at trial.

Robbery   A hybrid crime in which a victim is threatened with harm for the purpose of obtaining money or property.

Rule of law The concept that all people and the institutions that govern them will abide by the laws determined by the majority to be best for society.

Rules of procedure Rules that courts and the parties that submit disputes to the courts must follow in order to apply the law to reach a fair decision.

Runaway A minor who leaves home to escape the supervision of parents or guardians.

S

Sanctions An order by a court penalizing a party or its attorney for violation of procedural rules.

Scheduling conference A pretrial conference between the judge and the parties in which deadlines are set for discovery, for filing motions, and for submitting lists of witnesses for trial and exchanging other information.

Search An infringement by the government of a person's reasonable expectation of privacy.

Seizure A meaningful interference by the government with a person's possessory interest in property, or the arrest of a person.

Separate property Property owned by only one spouse during marriage.

Separation Often the initial step toward divorce; the termination of cohabitation by spouses.

Sequester During jury deliberations, to remove a jury from contact with others, often in a secure location.

Service of process The process of giving a party notice of the filing of a pleading.

Settlement conference A pretrial conference in which the parties in a civil case meet to clarify their positions in an attempt to resolve the case without trial.

Shopkeeper's rule A defense to the crime of false imprisonment that allows a store manager to detain a person suspected of shoplifting or trying to leave without paying for goods or services.

Showups A method of identification in which a witness is shown a suspect standing alone and asked whether the witness can identify him as the perpetrator of a crime.

Signed opinion An opinion written by an identifiable appellate judge with which a majority of the court's judges have agreed.

Social change The effect of some court decisions on society.

Social justice A form of justice that encompasses the way in which equal and fair treatment applies to all individuals and groups within a society.

Social norms Standards applied to everyday living that create order in society.

Special verdict A verdict issued by a jury in a civil case in which specific questions pertaining to the facts are answered by the jury in order for the judge to determine the prevailing party.

Specialized court A court whose jurisdiction is limited to resolving cases involving particular problems, such as a drug court, a gun court, or a truancy court.

Specific deterrence A philosophy of punishment in which punishment serves to deter an offender from re-offending.

Spousal support Money paid by one former spouse to another for his or her living or other expenses, as a result of a court order.

Standard of care In the law of torts, the duty one owes to another, for the breach of which the law imposes liability.

Standard of proof The amount of proof necessary to establish some fact.

Standard of review The degree of deference an appellate court will give to a trial judge's decisions.

Standing The right of a party, based on a personal interest in some matter, to invoke the jurisdiction of a court.

Stare decisis From the Latin "let the decision stand"; this phrase refers to the rule of precedent, which requires judges to apply legal principles from prior cases to a current case being decided.

State court structure The types of courts given authority to decide various matters within a state, and the relationship among them.

State courts Courts authorized under state law and operating within the boundaries of a state.

Status conference A pretrial conference between the judge and the parties in which remaining factual issues for trial are identified and evidentiary matters are resolved.

Status offender A minor who commits an offense that would not be illegal if committed by an adult.

Status offense Any violation of law by a minor that would not violate the law if committed by an adult.

Statute of limitations Any statute that specifies a time limit within which a legal claim must be filed.

Statutory ambiguity Uncertainty as to the meaning of a law, requiring a judge to engage in statutory interpretation.

Statutory exclusion A method of transfer from juvenile to adult court in which state law specified that certain offenses committed by juveniles must be filed in adult criminal court.

Statutory law Laws passed through the legislative process.

Strict liability Liability for the commission of certain behaviors regardless of intent.

Subject matter jurisdiction The particular subjects over which a court has authority, specified by statute or constitution.

Substantial evidence The standard of review on appeal that examines whether a trial court's decisions are in contrast to what most of the evidence in a case reasonably shows.

Substantive criminal law The branch of law that specifies prohibited behaviors and punishments for their commission.

Substantive law The "substance" of the law that defines prohibited behavior and punishments (substantive criminal law) and governs private rights and relationships (substantive civil law).

Summary disposition An order issued by an appellate court that states the court's decision with no explanation of the basis for the decision.

Summary judgment A pretrial procedure used to resolve a case in favor of one party without trial when there is no dispute as to any material fact and judgment should be granted as a matter of law.

Supremacy clause Article VI, paragraph two of the U.S. Constitution provides that the Constitution and U.S. laws "shall be the supreme Law of the Land and the Judges in every State shall be bound thereby," requiring all state laws to be consistent with the federal Constitution.

T

Technology The use of computer information systems and their effect on court operations.

Tenancy by the entirety Traditionally, a form of joint ownership of property in which wives could own property with their husbands and obtain it as their sole property on the husband's death.

Tenancy in common A form of joint ownership of property in which a joint owner's interest passes to his or her heirs on death.

Tender years doctrine The traditional presumption, mostly rejected by family courts, that children's best interests are served if they remain in the custody of their mother.

Termination of parental rights A legal process of ending a natural parent's right to direct the upbringing of a child, usually occurring after a finding of abuse or neglect.

Territorial jurisdiction The boundaries within which a court may exercise authority (geographic jurisdiction).

Testimonial evidence Testimony given by a witness under oath.

Theory of law An explanation of the meaning and purpose of law that includes a justification for law and the need for its existence.

Three-tier court system The system of federal courts and that of many states that operates with a general trial court, an intermediate appellate court, and a court of last resort (supreme court).

Tortfeasor A person who commits a tort.

Torts The law of personal injuries.

Transmutation A change in the character of separate property to community property.

Treason Any attempt to overthrow the government or to betray the interests of the government to foreign powers.

Trespass Any interference with the property rights of the owner of property.

Trial by battle An ancient approach to dispute resolution in which disputing parties fought; the victorious party in the battle would be victorious in the dispute.

Trial by ordeal An ancient approach to dispute resolution in which one or both disputing parties submitted to an ordeal (such as walking over hot coals or submersion in water) in order to show the truth of his position in the dispute. The unharmed party (if any) won the dispute.

Tribunal A court or other institution for hearing and deciding disputes.

Trier of fact The person or persons (either judge or jury) responsible at trial for determining the truth of a party's assertions based on the evidence presented.

U

Unified court system A state system in which concurrent jurisdiction among courts does not exist and a single source of financial and administrative oversight of courts exists.

Unilateral divorce A contested divorce in which one party seeks to dissolve the marriage.

United States Attorney The chief federal prosecutor in a federal district, appointed by the President.

United States Supreme Court The court of last resort in the federal system consisting of a Chief Justice and eight Associate Justices, all of whom are appointed for life by the President with the advice and consent of the Senate.

Use of force The reasonable use of physical force by a police officer necessary to effect an arrest.

V

Vacate To set aside or rescind an order or decision.

Vagrancy A common law crime of wandering around for no apparent purpose without any means of support.

Venire A pool of potential jurors from which a trial jury is chosen.

Venue The place in which a case may be heard by a court.

Visitation A right typically awarded by a family court following divorce allowing a noncustodial parent to spend time with children of the marriage.

Void for vagueness A doctrine used to invalidate laws that provide insufficient notice of what is necessary to comply with them.

Voir dire The process of questioning prospective jurors by the judge and/or attorneys for the parties in order to seat a jury for trial.

W

Waiver The process of transferring a juvenile accused of a serious crime to adult court.

Warrant An order issued by a judge and directed to a law enforcement officer to search in a particular place for some particular items of personal property or a specific person and bring the items or person found to court.

Witnesses Persons whose testimony at trial constitutes evidence, including fact witnesses, eye witnesses, character witnesses, and expert witnesses.

Writ of appeal An avenue of appeal to the U.S. Supreme Court allowed by federal statute, though rarely used.

Writs of assistance Orders issued by the British Parliament to British soldiers, allowing them to enforce the Trade Acts by searching houses and vessels in port for goods on which taxes had not been paid, and to seize them.

Index

Figures and tables are indicated by *f* and *t* following the page number.

Photo Credits

Criminal Justice on the Web: © juliengrondin/ShutterStock, Inc.

Section Opener: © Ken Cole/Dreamstime LLC

Chapter Openers
Chapter 1 © AbleStock; **Chapter 2** © Keith Brofsky/Photodisc/Getty Images; **Chapter 3** Courtesy of Mark Wolfe/FEMA; **Chapter 4** © Michael G. Smith/ShutterStock, Inc.; **Chapter 5**, **Chapter 6** © Junial Enterprises/ShutterStock, Inc.; **Chapter 7** © AbleStock; **Chapter 8** © Banana Stock/age fotostock; **Chapter 9** © Snehit/ShutterStock, Inc.; **Chapter 10** © Linda Macpherson/ShutterStock, Inc.; **Chapter 11** © Christophe Testi/ShutterStock, Inc.; **Chapter 12** © Corbis; **Chapter 13** © Rob Marmion/ShutterStock, Inc.

Unless otherwise indicated, all photographs and illustrations are under copyright of Jones and Bartlett Publishers, LLC.